# THE NEW
# AMERICAN
# COMMENTARY

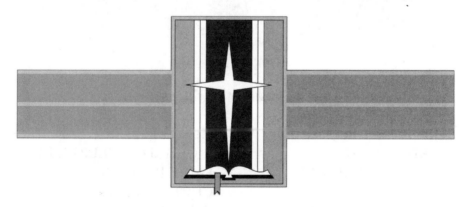

An Exegetical and Theological
Exposition of Holy Scripture

# THE NEW
# AMERICAN
# COMMENTARY

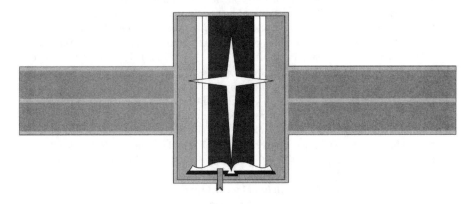

Volume
21A

## HAGGAI, MALACHI

Richard A. Taylor
E. Ray Clendenen

PUBLISHING GROUP
Nashville, Tennessee

© Copyright 2004 • Broadman & Holman Publishers
All rights reserved
ISBN 978-08054-0121-9
Dewey Decimal Classification: 224.9
Subject Heading: BIBLE. O.T. Haggai \ BIBLE. O.T. Malachi
Printed in the United States of America
14 13 12 11    8 7 6 5

*For*

Diane, Alison, Sophie, Bill, and Renee

"I thank my God every time I remember you"
(Phil 1:3)


*For*

My loving mother, Bertha Clendenen Pipes
with thanks and admiration for her strength of character,
her faith and faithfulness, her hard work on my behalf,
her kindness and wisdom.
For my mother-in-law, Mary Phipps,
whose constant communion with God has nurtured my faith
as it nurtured faith, wisdom, and love in my wife, Mimi,
my greatest earthly treasure.
And for my children, Ann and Jonathan.
My Lord has truly thrown open the floodgates of heaven
and flooded me with blessing.
(Mal 3:10)

# Editors' Preface

God's Word does not change. God's world, however, changes in every generation. These changes, in addition to new findings by scholars and a new variety of challenges to the gospel message, call for the church in each generation to interpret and apply God's Word for God's people. Thus, THE NEW AMERICAN COMMENTARY is introduced to bridge the twentieth and twenty-first centuries. This new series has been designed primarily to enable pastors, teachers, and students to read the Bible with clarity and proclaim it with power.

In one sense THE NEW AMERICAN COMMENTARY is not new, for it represents the continuation of a heritage rich in biblical and theological exposition. The title of this forty-volume set points to the continuity of this series with an important commentary project published at the end of the nineteenth century called AN AMERICAN COMMENTARY, edited by Alvah Hovey. The older series included, among other significant contributions, the outstanding volume on Matthew by John A. Broadus, from whom the publisher of the new series, Broadman Press, partly derives its name. The former series was authored and edited by scholars committed to the infallibility of Scripture, making it a solid foundation for the present project. In line with this heritage, all NAC authors affirm the divine inspiration, inerrancy, complete truthfulness, and full authority of the Bible. The perspective of the NAC is unapologetically confessional and rooted in the evangelical tradition.

Since a commentary is a fundamental tool for the expositor or teacher who seeks to interpret and apply Scripture in the church or classroom, the NAC focuses on communicating the theological structure and content of each biblical book. The writers seek to illuminate both the historical meaning and contemporary significance of Holy Scripture.

In its attempt to make a unique contribution to the Christian community, the NAC focuses on two concerns. First, the commentary emphasizes how each section of a book fits together so that the reader becomes aware of the theological unity of each book and of Scripture as a whole. The writers, however, remain aware of the Bible's inherently rich variety. Second, the NAC is produced with the conviction that the Bible primarily belongs to the church. We believe that scholarship and the academy provide an indispensable foundation for biblical understanding and the service of Christ, but the editors and authors of this series have attempted to communicate the findings of their research in a manner that will build up the whole body of Christ. Thus, the commentary concentrates on theological exegesis while providing practical, applicable exposition.

THE NEW AMERICAN COMMENTARY's theological focus enables

the reader to see the parts as well as the whole of Scripture. The biblical books vary in content, context, literary type, and style. In addition to this rich variety, the editors and authors recognize that the doctrinal emphasis and use of the biblical books differs in various places, contexts, and cultures among God's people. These factors, as well as other concerns, have led the editors to give freedom to the writers to wrestle with the issues raised by the scholarly community surrounding each book and to determine the appropriate shape and length of the introductory materials. Moreover, each writer has developed the structure of the commentary in a way best suited for expounding the basic structure and the meaning of the biblical books for our day. Generally, discussions relating to contemporary scholarship and technical points of grammar and syntax appear in the footnotes and not in the text of the commentary. This format allows pastors and interested laypersons, scholars and teachers, and serious college and seminary students to profit from the commentary at various levels. This approach has been employed because we believe that all Christians have the privilege and responsibility to read and seek to understand the Bible for themselves.

Consistent with the desire to produce a readable, up-to-date commentary, the editors selected the *New International Version* as the standard translation for the commentary series. The selection was made primarily because of the NIV's faithfulness to the original languages and its beautiful and readable style. The authors, however, have been given the liberty to differ at places from the NIV as they develop their own translations from the Greek and Hebrew texts.

The NAC reflects the vision and leadership of those who provide oversight for Broadman Press, who in 1987 called for a new commentary series that would evidence a commitment to the inerrancy of Scripture and a faithfulness to the classic Christian tradition. While the commentary adopts an "American" name, it should be noted some writers represent countries outside the United States, giving the commentary an international perspective. The diverse group of writers includes scholars, teachers, and administrators from almost twenty different colleges and seminaries, as well as pastors, missionaries, and a layperson.

The editors and writers hope that THE NEW AMERICAN COMMENTARY will be helpful and instructive for pastors and teachers, scholars and students, for men and women in the churches who study and teach God's Word in various settings. We trust that for editors, authors, and readers alike, the commentary will be used to build up the church, encourage obedience, and bring renewal to God's people. Above all, we pray that the NAC will bring glory and honor to our Lord who has graciously redeemed us and faithfully revealed himself to us in his Holy Word.

SOLI DEO GLORIA
The Editors

# Authors' Prefaces

### Haggai

In the spring of 1999 Dr. Ray Clendenen, general editor of The New American Commentary, honored me with an invitation to contribute a treatment of the Book of Haggai to The New American Commentary series. It is a pleasure for me to record here my appreciation to Dr. Clendenen for this invitation.

I am also appreciative of my family's sympathetic acceptance of the impact of this project on our shared times together. There were many occasions when Haggai demanded hours that I otherwise would have spent with them. There were other times when, though I was physically present at a family function, my mind was still pondering enigmas of the Book of Haggai. I doubt that these preoccupations always escaped the detection of those who were with me. Yet somehow through it all Haggai has remained a festal name in our household. I am especially grateful for my wife's patient acceptance of the time constraints created by my scholarly endeavors.

I also wish to record my appreciation for the excellent library resources that have been available to me during the preparation of this project. The fine biblical studies collection of Turpin and Mosher Libraries at Dallas Theological Seminary has been an immense help in my work. The resources of Bridwell Library at Southern Methodist University in Dallas have been very helpful to me as well. For published materials that were unavailable to me locally, the staff at Turpin Library were always eager to assist by contacting various libraries in other parts of the country. I also gratefully acknowledge the assistance of Mr. Chuck Van Hof, managing editor at Wm. B. Eerdmans Publishing Company, for making available to me an advance copy of Michael Floyd's important work on the form criticism of the Minor Prophets.

To comment on any portion of Scripture is both a welcome privilege and a daunting responsibility. Words of the Apostle Paul come to mind: "And who is equal to such a task?" (2 Cor 2:16). I am painfully aware of my own limitations in this regard. All I can claim to have done in what follows is to have set forth my present understanding of the Book of Haggai. I hope that this discussion will make a modest contribution to contemporary understanding of Haggai, especially on the part of theological students, preachers, and teachers of the Old Testament. I have tried to write with them in mind, stressing the historical and theological issues of Haggai and the literary and structural features of the book that are most essential for grasping its message, as opposed to minor linguistic or interpretive details that may turn out to be less helpful in the exposition of this book. For whatever shortcomings or mistakes that may yet remain in this discussion, I take full responsibility. For whatever may be worthwhile, *soli Deo gloria!*

—Richard A. Taylor

✳✳✳

May the bones of the twelve prophets
revive from where they lie,
for they comforted the people of Jacob
and delivered them with comfort and hope.
—*Sirach* 49:10, NRSV

✳✳✳

### Malachi

In 1968 a college sophomore stood in the religion section of the library at Rice University filled with insatiable curiosity, desperate to read all the books he saw before him. As he stumbled along ill-equipped to meet the challenges to his faith in a secular university, searching for answers as well as trying to find his place in the world, he reached into the toolkit of books by Merrill Unger given him by the girl who had led him to Christ two years before, and he reached out to books by Carl F. H. Henry, John W. Montgomery, C. S. Lewis, John Stott, and F. F. Bruce that were either recommended to him by his pastor or discovered in the library. But compared to the literature being pumped out of innumerable publishing houses attacking the Christian faith and the veracity of the Bible, the works defending the faith seemed exceedingly sparse. This young man's experience was representative of thousands at about the same time.

But since then God has raised up several generations of outstanding Christian scholars who in the face of ridicule and arguments to the contrary believed the Bible. They also believed that as the Word of God it deserved a lifetime devoted to its study, teaching, and exposition. Thirty-six years later personal and institutional libraries are full of works of academic scholarship at the highest level that not only defend but also advance the Christian faith. Dozens of commentary sets have been started (and a few even finished!), and hundreds of individual commentaries and monographs and thousands of articles have been written explaining books of the Bible, biblical texts, or biblical concepts from the standpoint of a firm commitment to the absolute truth of the Christian faith and the inerrancy of the Bible. Many outstanding evangelical reference works of lexicology, grammar, theology, etc. are now available as well as modern Bible translations, often in computer software that Bible students (including this one) have come to consider essential. (This commentary was written with the constant and blessed aid of Accordance software developed and maintained by Roy and Helen Brown, a brilliant and wonderful couple God has given to do his work.) Academic institutions in the United States and abroad are filled with highly trained administrators and professors with impeccable credentials who are committed to the complete truthfulness of the Bible as well as the urgency of making disciples of all the nations. We can only stand in awe of what God has done and will continue to do until Jesus comes and the task is complete. We must praise the One who promised to build his church, and we must be diligent to continue to meet the challenges of the day and to transmit our passion to each successive generation along with the skills and knowledge God has given us.

Writing a commentary on Holy Scripture is an immeasurably great privilege and awesome responsibility. I have had the opportunity and honor to edit twenty-seven volumes of The New American Commentary so far, but the assignment to write one myself, even on a book as small as Malachi, has given me a more profound respect for the authors of those volumes. We are all immensely grateful to God for the skills and knowledge he has given us for the task, and for the teachers and mentors who believed in us and more especially in God's faithfulness to make something worthwhile out of us that would glorify him. For my part, I am eternally in debt to the time and patience of men such as Dr. Edwin Blum, my college pastor and seminary professor and now my colleague in the work of Bible translation, George Mallone (now deceased), the InterVarsity staff worker who invested so much time in me and who wrote a commentary on Malachi himself, and Robert Longacre, my doctoral supervisor, who led me into the exciting world of textlinguistics. He is a model of courageous Christian scholarship and servanthood. I am especially awed by the discipline, determination, and mental labor (however enjoyable and rewarding) involved in producing a commentary on such mammoth and crucial books as Genesis, John, and so many others in our series. I am also awed by the kindness, sacrificial love, and encouragement shown by the families of those authors, not only allowing but supporting them in the enormous commitment of time and effort to make the task successful. I know from being the grateful recipient how many meals have been delivered to hungry but busy commentary writers, household chores done (quietly) by their wives and families so that "Daddy" could work.

I know I'm not the only writer whose family was even directly involved in the project. My wife, Mimi, has been creating the subject index for the last several volumes of the NAC and produced the one for this volume as well. No writer could have a more supportive and helpful "partner" (Mal 2:14) in ministry and a more effective sounding board for ideas than I. My daughter, Ann, a French major in college and now a student in seminary with her husband, helped with French translations and critiquing poorly written early drafts of portions of the commentary. Her husband, Will Cherry, read footnotes and (tactfully) pointed out some of his father-in-law's mistakes. Although my son, Jon, is only thirteen, his assistance retrieving books, copying articles, and sending and retrieving computer files, especially in the final stages of research, has been tremendous. I'd like to express here on behalf of all our writers how much we owe to our support teams who have made possible the work we have done. Not only family members but friends, librarians, and research assistants are often involved. I am grateful to friends like Ken Mathews and Peter Gentry and to students at Criswell College and several Southern Baptist seminaries who have listened patiently and critically to my thoughts on Malachi for several years. The assistance of the Dargan Library staff at Lifeway Christian Resources, especially Steve Gateley and Miriam Evans, was critical for my research. Also essential was the final month of work on the commentary at home and at Boyce Library of Southern Baptist Theological Seminary, for which I am grateful to the indulgence of my supervisor David Shepherd and the hospitality of the administrators of Southern Seminary, Dr. Albert R. Mohler, Jr., and Dr. Russell Moore. I also wish to thank Peter Gentry and the NAC editors, Ken Mathews, Paul House, Russ Bush, and Larry Walker, for plowing through the manuscript and making many useful suggestions. The typesetter and copy editor of the series, with whom I have worked for twelve years, Linda Scott, has again done a masterful job and is due shouts of praise for her skill, diligence, and sweet spirit.

Finally, I am grateful to Paige Patterson, Paul Pressler, and others whom God used to awaken the Southern Baptist Convention to the challenges facing us in the convention and in the world. It is because of the work they did that Broadman & Holman can assemble a group of writers, mostly from schools associated with the SBC, to write a series of commentaries on Scripture based on the firm conviction of its complete truthfulness. I do not take lightly the trust placed in me to shepherd this project, and I am grateful to those responsible for its launch, especially the founding editors and David S. Dockery, the editor of the first six volumes.

May God our Father and the Lord Jesus Christ, who always finishes what he starts (Phil 1:6), be praised.

—E. Ray Clendenen

# Abbreviations

## Bible Books

| | | |
|---|---|---|
| Gen | Isa | Luke |
| Exod | Jer | John |
| Lev | Lam | Acts |
| Num | Ezek | Rom |
| Deut | Dan | 1, 2 Cor |
| Josh | Hos | Gal |
| Judg | Joel | Eph |
| Ruth | Amos | Phil |
| 1, 2 Sam | Obad | Col |
| 1, 2 Kgs | Jonah | 1, 2 Thess |
| 1, 2 Chr | Mic | 1, 2 Tim |
| Ezra | Nah | Titus |
| Neh | Hab | Phlm |
| Esth | Zeph | Heb |
| Job | Hag | Jas |
| Ps (pl. Pss) | Zech | 1, 2 Pet |
| Prov | Mal | 1, 2, 3 John |
| Eccl | Matt | Jude |
| Song | Mark | Rev |

## Apocrypha

| | |
|---|---|
| *Add Esth* | *The Additions to the Book of Esther* |
| *Bar* | *Baruch* |
| *Bel* | *Bel and the Dragon* |
| *1,2 Esdr* | *1, 2 Esdras* |
| *4 Ezra* | *4 Ezra* |
| *Jdt* | *Judith* |
| *Ep Jer* | *Epistle of Jeremiah* |
| *1,2,3,4 Mac* | *1, 2, 3, 4 Maccabees* |
| *Pr Azar* | *Prayer of Azariah and the Song of the Three Jews* |
| *Pr Man* | *Prayer of Manasseh* |
| *Sir* | *Sirach, Ecclesiasticus* |
| *Sus* | *Susanna* |
| *Tob* | *Tobit* |
| *Wis* | *The Wisdom of Solomon* |

## Commonly Used Sources

| | |
|---|---|
| AASOR | Annual of the American Schools of Oriental Research |
| AB | Anchor Bible |
| ABD | *Anchor Bible Dictionary,* ed. D. N Freedman |
| ABR | *Australian Biblical Review* |
| ABRL | Anchor Bible Reference Library |
| ABW | *Archaeology and the Biblical World* |
| AC | An American Commentary, ed. A. Hovey |
| AcOr | *Acta orientalia* |
| AEL | M. Lichtheim, *Ancient Egyptian Literature* |
| Aev | *Aevum: Rassegna de scienze, storiche, linguistiche e filologiche* |
| AHW | W. von Soden, *Akkadisches Handwörterbuch* |
| AJA | *American Journal of Archaeology* |
| AJBA | *Australian Journal of Biblical Archaeology* |
| AJBI | *Annual of the Japanese Biblical Institute* |
| AJSL | *American Journal of Semitic Languages and Literature* |
| Akk. | Akkadian |
| AnBib | Analecta Biblica |
| ANET | *Ancient Near Eastern Texts,* ed. J. B. Pritchard |
| ANETS | *Ancient Near Eastern Texts and Studies* |
| ANEP | *Ancient Near Eastern Pictures,* ed. J. B. Pritchard |
| Ant. | *Antiquities* |
| Anuario | *Anuario de filología* |
| AOAT | Alter Orient und Altes Testament |
| AOS | American Oriental Society |
| AOTS | *Archaeology and Old Testament Study,* ed. D. W. Thomas |
| ARM | Archives royales de Mari |
| ArOr | Archiv orientální |
| AS | Assyriological Studies |
| ASOR | American Schools of Oriental Research |
| ATD | Das Alte Testament Deutsch |
| ATR | *Anglican Theological Review* |
| AusBR | *Australian Biblical Review* |
| AUSS | *Andrews University Seminary Studies* |
| AV | Authorized Version |
| BA | *Biblical Archaeologist* |
| BAGD | W. Bauer, W. F. Arndt, F. W. Gingrich, and F. W. Danker, *Greek-English Lexicon of the New Testament* |
| BALS | Bible and Literature Series |
| BARev | *Biblical Archaeology Review* |
| BASOR | *Bulletin of the American Schools of Oriental Research* |
| B. Bat | *Baba Batra* |
| BBR | *Bulletin for Biblical Research* |
| BDB | F. Brown, S. R. Driver, and C. A. Briggs, *Hebrew and English Lexicon of the Old Testament* |
| BEATAJ | Beiträge zur Erforschung des Alten Testaments und des antiken Judentum |

| | |
|---|---|
| BECNT | Baker Exegetical Commentary on the New Testament |
| BETL | Bibliotheca ephemeridum theologicarum lovaniensium |
| BFT | Biblical Foundations in Theology |
| *BHK* | *Biblia Hebraica,* ed. R. Kittel |
| *BHRG* | *A Biblical Hebrew Reference Grammar* |
| *BHS* | *Biblia Hebraica Stuttgartensia* |
| *Bib* | *Biblica* |
| BibOr | Biblica et orientalia |
| *BibRev* | *Bible Review* |
| *BJRL* | *Bulletin of the Johns Rylands University Library* |
| BJS | Brown Judaic Studies |
| BKAT | Biblischer Kommentar: Altes Testament |
| BMes | Bibliotheca mesopotamica |
| *BMik* | *Beth Mikra* |
| *BN* | *Biblische Notizen* |
| *BO* | *Bibliotheca orientalis* |
| *BR* | *Biblical Research* |
| *BSac* | *Bibliotheca Sacra* |
| BSC | Bible Student Commentary |
| BST | Bible Speaks Today |
| *BT* | *The Bible Translator* |
| *BTB* | *Biblical Theology Bulletin* |
| *BurH* | *Buried History* |
| BWA(N)T | Beiträge zur Wissenschaft vom Alten (und Neuen) Testament |
| *BZ* | *Biblische Zeitschrift* |
| BZAW | Beihefte zur ZAW |
| *CAD* | *The Assyrian Dictionary of the Oriental Institute of the University of Chicago* |
| *CAH* | *Cambridge Ancient History* |
| CAT | Commentaire de l'Ancien Testament |
| CB | Century Bible |
| CBC | Cambridge Bible Commentary |
| *CBQ* | *Catholic Biblical Quarterly* |
| CBQMS | Catholic Biblical Quarterly Monograph Series |
| CBSC | Cambridge Bible for Schools and Colleges |
| CC | The Communicator's Commentary |
| *CCK* | *Chronicles of Chaldean Kings,* D. J. Wiseman |
| *CCR* | *Coptic Church Review* |
| CCSL | Corpus christianorum: series latina |
| CD | Cairo *Damascus Document* |
| CGTC | Cambridge Greek Testament Commentaries |
| *CHAL* | *Concise Hebrew and Aramaic Lexicon,* ed. W. L. Holladay |
| *CHJ* | *Cambridge History of Judaism,* ed. W. D. Davies and Louis Finkelstein |
| Comm. | J. Calvin, *Commentary on the First Book of Moses Called Genesis,* trans., rev. J. King |
| ConB | Coniectanea biblica |
| ConBOT | Coniectanea biblica, Old Testament |

| | |
|---|---|
| *COT* | *Commentary on the Old Testament,* C. F. Keil and F. Delitzsch |
| *CR:BS* | *Currents in Research: Biblical Studies* |
| *CSR* | *Christian Scholar's Review* |
| *CT* | *Christianity Today* |
| *CTM* | *Concordia Theological Monthly* |
| *CTR* | *Criswell Theological Review* |
| *CurBS* | *Currents in Research: Biblical Studies* |
| *CurTM* | *Currents in Theology and Mission* |
| *DCH* | *Dictionary of Classical Hebrew,* ed. D. J. A. Clines |
| DG | J. C. L. Gibson, *Davidson's Introductory Hebrew Grammar—Syntax,* 4th ed. |
| *DISO* | C.-F. Jean and J. Hoftijzer, *Dictionnaire des inscriptions sémitiques de l'ouest* |
| DJD | Discoveries in the Judaean Desert |
| *DNWSI* | *Dictionary of Northwest Semitic Inscriptions* |
| *DOTT* | *Documents from Old Testament Times,* ed. D. W. Thomas |
| DSBS | Daily Study Bible Series |
| DSS | Dead Sea Scrolls |
| *EAEHL* | *Encyclopedia of Archaeological Excavations in the Holy Land,* ed. M. Avi-Yonah |
| EBC | Expositor's Bible Commentary |
| Ebib | Etudes bibliques |
| *EDBT* | *Evangelical Dictionary of Biblical Theology,* W. A. Elwell, ed. |
| *EE* | *Enuma Elish* |
| *EDNT* | *Exegetical Dictionary of the New Testament* |
| *EgT* | *The Expositor's Greek Testament* |
| *EM* | *Ensiqlopedia Miqra'it* |
| *EncJud* | *Encyclopaedia Judaica* (1971) |
| *ErIsr* | *Eretz Israel* |
| *ETL* | *Ephermerides theologicae lovanienses* |
| *ETR* | *Etudes théologiques et religieuses* |
| ETSMS | Evangelical Theological Society Monograph Series |
| EvBC | Everyman's Bible Commentary |
| EV(s) | English Version(s) |
| *EvQ* | *Evangelical Quarterly* |
| *ExpTim* | *Expository Times* |
| FB | Forschung zur Bibel |
| FOTL | Forms of Old Testament Literature |
| Gk. | Greek |
| *GBH* | P. Joüon, *A Grammar of Biblical Hebrew,* 2 vols., trans. and rev. T. Muraoka |
| GKC | Gesenius's Hebrew Grammar, ed. E. Kautzsch, trans. A. E. Cowley |
| *GTJ* | *Grace Theological Journal* |
| HALOT | L. Koehler and W. Baumgartner, *The Hebrew and Aramaic Lexicon of the Old Testament* |
| *HAR* | *Hebrew Annual Review* |

| | |
|---|---|
| HAT | Handbuch zum Alten Testament |
| *HBD* | *Harper's Bible Dictionary,* ed. P. Achtemeier |
| *HBT* | *Horizons in Biblical Theology* |
| HDR | Harvard Dissertations in Religion |
| Her | Hermeneia |
| HKAT | Handkommentar zum Alten Testament |
| *HS* | *Hebrew Studies* |
| HSM | Harvard Semitic Monographs |
| HT | Helps for Translators |
| *HTR* | *Harvard Theological Review* |
| *HUCA* | *Hebrew Union College Annual* |
| *IB* | *Interpreter's Bible* |
| IBC | International Bible Commentary, ed. F. F. Bruce |
| *IBD* | *Illustrated Bible Dictionary,* ed. J. D. Douglas and N. Hillyer |
| ICC | International Critical Commentary |
| *IBHS* | B. K. Waltke and M. O'Connor, *Introduction to Biblical Hebrew Syntax* |
| *IBS* | *Irish Biblical Studies* |
| *IDB* | *Interpreter's Dictionary of the Bible,* ed. G. A. Buttrick et al. |
| *IDBSup* | Supplementary volume to *IDB* |
| *IEJ* | *Israel Exploration Journal* |
| IES | Israel Exploration Society |
| *IJT* | *Indian Journal of Theology* |
| *Int* | *Interpretation* |
| INT | Interpretation: A Bible Commentary for Teaching and Preaching |
| *IOS* | *Israel Oriental Studies* |
| *ISBE* | *International Standard Bible Encyclopedia,* rev. ed., G. W. Bromiley |
| ITC | International Theological Commentary |
| *ITQ* | *Irish Theological Quarterly* |
| *JAAR* | *Journal of the American Academy of Religion* |
| *JAARSup* | *Journal of the American Academy of Religion,* Supplement |
| *JANES* | *Journal of Ancient Near Eastern Society* |
| *JAOS* | *Journal of the American Oriental Society* |
| Jastrow | *A Dictionary of the Targumim, the Talmud Babli and Yerushalmi, and the Midrashic Literature,* 2d ed., M. Jastrow |
| *JBL* | *Journal of Biblical Literature* |
| *JBR* | *Journal of Bible and Religion* |
| *JCS* | *Journal of Cuneiform Studies* |
| *JEA* | *Journal of Egyptian Archaeology* |
| *JETS* | *Journal of the Evangelical Theological Society* |
| *JJS* | *Journal of Jewish Studies* |
| *JNES* | *Journal of Near Eastern Studies* |
| *JNSL* | *Journal of Northwest Semitic Languages* |
| *JOTT* | *Journal of Translation and Textlinguistics* |
| *JPOS* | *Journal of Palestine Oriental Society* |
| JPS | Jewish Publication Society |

| | |
|---|---|
| JPSV | Jewish Publication Society Version |
| JPST | Jewish Publication Society Torah |
| *JRT* | *Journal of Religious Thought* |
| *JSJ* | *Journal for the Study of Judaism in the Persian, Hellenistic, and Roman Period* |
| *JSOR* | *Journal of the Society for Oriental Research* |
| *JSOT* | *Journal for the Study of the Old Testament* |
| JSOTSup | JSOT—Supplement Series |
| *JSS* | *Journal of Semitic Studies* |
| *JTS* | *Journal of Theological Studies* |
| *JTSNS* | *Journal of Theological Studies, New Series* |
| *JTT* | *Journal of Translation and Textlinguistics* |
| KAT | Kommentar zum Alten Testament |
| KB | L. Koehler and W. Baumgartner, *Lexicon in Veteris Testamenti libros* |
| *KD* | *Kerygma und Dogma* |
| LBBC | Layman's Bible Book Commentary |
| LBH | Late Biblical Hebrew |
| LBI | Library of Biblical Interpretation |
| LCC | Library of Christian Classics |
| *LLAVT* | E. Vogt, *Lexicon Linguae Aramaicae Veteris Testamenti* |
| LSJ | Liddell-Scott-Jones, *Greek-English Lexicon* |
| *LTQ* | *Lexington Theological Quarterly* |
| *LW* | *Luther's Works. Lecture's on Genesis,* ed. J. Pelikan and D. Poellot, trans. G. Schick |
| LXX | Septuagint |
| MT | Masoretic Text |
| MS(S) | Manuscript(s) |
| NAB | New American Bible |
| NASB | New American Standard Bible |
| NAC | New American Commentary, ed. R. Clendenen |
| *NB* | *Nebuchadrezzar and Babylon,* D. J. Wiseman |
| *NBD* | *New Bible Dictionary,* ed. J. D. Douglas |
| NCBC | New Century Bible Commentary |
| *NEAEHL* | *The New Encyclopedia of Archaeological Excavations in the Holy Land,* ed. E. Stern |
| NEB | New English Bible |
| NIB | The New Interpreter's Bible |
| NICNT | New International Commentary on the New Testament |
| NICOT | New International Commentary on the Old Testament |
| *NIDOTTE* | *The New International Dictionary of Old Testament Theology and Exegesis,* ed. W. A. VanGemeren |
| NJB | New Jerusalem Bible |
| *NJBC* | *The New Jerome Biblical Commentary,* ed. R. Brown et al. |
| NJPS | New Jewish Publication Society Version |
| *NKZ* | *Neue kirchliche Zeitschrift* |
| *NovT* | *Novum Testamentum* |
| NRSV | New Revised Standard Version |
| *NRT* | *La nouvelle revue the´ologique* |

| | |
|---|---|
| *NTS* | *New Testament Studies* |
| NTT | Norsk Teologisk Tidsskrift |
| OBO | Orbis biblicus et orientalis |
| OL | Old Latin |
| *Or* | *Orientalia* |
| OTL | Old Testament Library |
| *OTP* | *The Old Testament Pseudepigrapha,* ed. J. H. Charlesworth |
| *OTS* | *Oudtestamentische Studiën* |
| *OTWSA* | *Ou-Testamentiese Werkgemeenskap in Suid-Afrika* |
| *PCB* | *Peake's Commentary on the Bible,* ed. M. Black and H. H. Rowley |
| *PEQ* | *Palestine Exploration Quarterly* |
| *POTT* | *Peoples of Old Testament Times,* ed. D. J. Wiseman |
| POTW | Peoples of the Old Testament World, ed. A. E. Hoerth, G. L. Mattingly, and E. M. Yamauchi |
| PTMS | Pittsburgh Theological Monograph Series |
| *PTR* | *Princeton Theological Review* |
| *RA* | *Revue d'assyriologie et d'archéologie orientale* |
| *RB* | *Revue biblique* |
| REB | Revised English Bible |
| *ResQ* | *Restoration Quarterly* |
| *RevExp* | *Review and Expositor* |
| *RHPR* | *Revue d'histoire et de philosophie religieuses* |
| RSR | Recherches de science religieuse |
| *RTR* | *Reformed Theological Review* |
| SANE | Sources from the Ancient Near East |
| SB | Sources bibliques |
| SBH | Standard Biblical Hebrew |
| *SBJT* | *Southern Baptist Journal of Theology* |
| SBLDS | Society of Biblical Literature Dissertation Series |
| SBLMS | Society of Biblical Literature Monograph Series |
| SBLSP | Society of Biblical Literature Seminar Papers |
| SBT | Studies in Biblical Theology |
| SHCANE | Studies in the History and Culture of the Ancient Near East |
| *SJT* | *Scottish Journal of Theology* |
| *SJOT* | *Scandinavian Journal of the Old Testament* |
| SJLA | Studies in Judaism in Late Antiquity |
| *SLJA* | *Saint Luke's Journal of Theology* |
| *SOTI* | *A Survey of Old Testament Introduction,* G. L. Archer |
| SP | Samaritan Pentateuch |
| SR | Studies in Religion/Sciences religieuses |
| *SSI* | *Syrian Semitic Inscriptions* |
| *ST* | *Studia theologica* |
| STJD | Studies on the Texts of the Desert of Judah |
| Syr. | Syriac |
| *TBT* | *The Bible Today* |
| *TD* | *Theology Digest* |
| *TDNT* | *Theological Dictionary of the New Testament,* ed. G. Kittel and G. Friedrich |
| *TDOT* | *Theological Dictionary of the Old Testament,* ed. G. J. Botterweck and H. Ringgren |

| | |
|---|---|
| TEV | Today's English Version |
| Tg(s). | Targum(s) |
| TGUOS | Transactions of the Glasgow University Oriental Society |
| TJNS | Trinity Journal—New Series |
| TLOT | *Theological Lexicon of the Old Testament,* ed. E. Jenni and C. Westermann |
| TLZ | *Theologische Literaturzeitung* |
| TNTC | Tyndale New Testament Commentaries |
| TOTC | Tyndale Old Testament Commentaries |
| TrinJ | *Trinity Journal* |
| TS | *Theological Studies* |
| TToday | *Theology Today* |
| Tur | *Traditionsgeshichtliche Untersuchungen aum Richterbuch* |
| TWAT | *Theologisches Wörterbuch zum Alten Testament,* ed. G. J. Botterweck and H. Ringgren |
| TWOT | *Theological Wordbook of the Old Testament* |
| TynBul | *Tyndale Bulletin* |
| UF | *Ugarit-Forschungen* |
| Ug. | Ugaritic |
| UT | C. H. Gordon, *Ugaritic Textbook* |
| Vg. | Vulgate |
| VT | *Vetus Testamentum* |
| VTSup | Vetus Testamentum, Supplements |
| WBC | Word Biblical Commentaries |
| WEC | Wycliffe Exegetical Commentary |
| WHJP | *World History of the Jewish People,* ed. B. Mazer |
| WO | *Die Welt des Orients* |
| WTJ | *Westminster Theological Journal* |
| WMANT | Wissenschaftliche Monographien zum Alten und Neuen Testament |
| ZAW | *Zeitschrift für die alttestamentliche Wissenschaft* |
| ZDMG | *Zeitschrift der deutschen morgenländischen Gesellschaft* |
| ZDPV | *Zeitschrift des deutschen Palästina-Vereins* |
| ZPEB | *Zondervan Pictorial Encyclopedia of the Bible* |
| ZKT | *Zeitschrift für katholische Theologie* |

# Contents

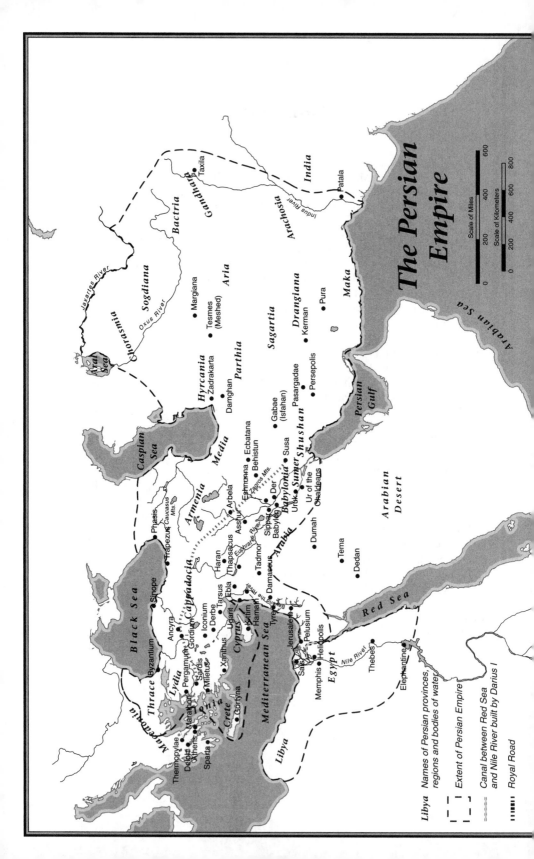

# The Persian Empire

Scale of Miles
0    200    400    600

Scale of Kilometers
0    200    400    600    800

*Libya*   Names of Persian provinces, regions and bodies of water

- - -   Extent of Persian Empire

·······   Canal between Red Sea and Nile River built by Darius I

▪▪▪▪   Royal Road

*India*
Taxila
*Gandhara*
*Bactria*
*Arachosia*
*Sogdiana*
*Chorasmia*
Jaxartes River
Oxus River
Aral Sea
• Margiana
Tesmes (Meshed)
*Aria*
*Maka*
*Drangiana*
• Pura
• Kerman
*Sagartia*
Pasargadae
• Persepolis
*Parthia*
*Hyrcania*
Zadrakarta
Damghan
• Gabae (Isfahan)
*Media*
Ecbatana
Behistun
Eshnuna
*Armenia*
Caucasus Mts.
Phasis
Trapezus
Sinope
*Cappadocia*
Ancyra
Gordium
Pergamum
Sardis
Miletus
*Lydia*
*Ionia*
*Thrace*
Byzantium
*Macedonia*
Thermopylae
Delphi
Marathon
Athens
Sparta
*Crete*
Gortyna
Xanthus
Iconium
Derbe
Tarsus
Ebla
Ugarit
*Cyprus*
Haran
Thapsacus
Damascus
Tadmor
Der
Assur
Arbela
Zagros Mts.
Euphrates River
Tigris River
*Babylonia*
Sippar
Babylon
*Sumer*
*Shushan*
Susa
Uruk
Ur of the Chaldeans
*Arabia*
Dumah
• Tema
• Dedan
Haman
Tyre
Jerusalem
Pelusium
Sais
Memphis
Heliopolis
*Egypt*
Nile River
Thebes
Elephantine
*Libya*
*Arabian Desert*
Red Sea
*Persian Gulf*
*Caspian Sea*
*Black Sea*
*Mediterranean Sea*
Arabian Sea

# INTRODUCTION

In addition to the actual interpretation of the text of the Book of Haggai, there are various introductory matters that in one way or another affect our understanding of this book. The decisions we make on such things as authorship, date, genre, literary structure, and unity—to mention just a few issues— will obviously have some influence on our discussions of other related matters. In order to avoid the need for lengthy digressions in the commentary, it seems best to deal separately with these matters at the outset. Following a discussion of these issues in the introduction, we will come to a systematic interpretation of the Book of Haggai in the commentary proper.

## 1. Contemporary Relevance of Haggai

"But seek first [God's] kingdom and his righteousness, and all these things will be given to you as well" (Matt 6:33). With these words Jesus summarized the acceptable priorities of life for those who would follow him. Such a view on life appears to have been for Jesus' disciples an entirely new and unexpected concept, one both liberating in its potential but no less intimidating in its demands. His disciples shared a natural inclination to worry about the basic necessities of life. A significant portion of their waking hours was spent providing for such basic family essentials as food, clothing, and shelter. But these concerns, if not balanced by a sense of urgency with regard to the service of God, can easily undermine a proper sense of what is actually most important in life, namely the advancement of the kingdom of God. In fact, preoccupation with such concerns can lead to a type of personal decision making that focuses first on meeting temporal human needs and offers God only what is left over after essential matters of personal security and comfort have first been decided.

This is not, however, the path of authentic discipleship. Jesus instead urged his followers to seek first the eternal priorities of the kingdom of God. In so doing, they could rest assured that their Heavenly Father was not only aware of their temporal needs, but that he would bountifully supply those needs for his people. In order to illustrate this truth, Jesus called attention to the natural order of creation. If God provides in abundance for defenseless birds and for vulnerable flowers (Matt 6:28–30), how can we expect that he will do less for mankind, who is the very pinnacle of his creation? And if God's common grace is such that provisions for life's necessities are generally available for all, does not logic suggest that these provisions will be no less available for those who seek to follow the will of God? Equipped with this confidence in divine provision, those who would serve God are free to focus their efforts and attention on what they can contribute to God's work in their midst. Their Heavenly Father is neither unconcerned over their condition in life nor careless about providing for their day-to-day needs.

It seems that every generation of believers, from ancient times to modern, must learn this lesson anew. It is a truth that was ignored, if in fact it was grasped at all, by the people of God to whom the prophet Haggai ministered in the sixth century B.C. Although they verbally might have articulated a belief to the contrary, their actions clearly disclosed their inverted priorities. In reality they sought first the kingdom of self and its comforts; they would get around to the work of God after those priorities had first been settled. But there was for them an unexpected irony. Due to the withdrawal of God's blessings upon their efforts, they painfully discovered that none of life's necessities was added to them to the degree that they would like—in spite of their determined efforts to the contrary. Their hard work was reduced to nothing. Their crops failed because of disease and disaster; their harvests yielded only meager results. Whatever financial profits they gained quickly disappeared, passing as it were through a shabby bag riddled with holes and

unable to retain what was deposited in it (Hag 1:6). In spite of their determined efforts, the prosperity that they craved eluded them. Their experience
calls to mind a paradox: "For whoever wants to save his life will lose it"
(Mark 8:35; Matt 16:25; Luke 9:24).

It fell to the prophet Haggai to show why the attitude of the postexilic Israelite community did not honor the God they professed to serve. Haggai's
ministry was one of calling his generation to a renewed commitment to the
task of the immediate restoration of Jerusalem's temple and normalization of
the religious life of Israel. In large measure this task that lay before them was
a test of whether they would put God first in their lives. It was a test whose
momentous significance the prophet drove home in a relentless and uncom-
promising fashion. The people would have to decide whose interests mat-
tered most to them—their own or the Lord's.

Haggai's message to the postexilic community of Israel is one that the
church of the twenty-first century needs to reflect on. To "seek first the kingdom
of God and his righteousness" is for us—as it was for them—a calling that runs
the risk of being eclipsed by self-serving interests. Far too often the affluence
of God's people, rather than encouraging a self-imposed measure of personal
sacrifice in order to advance the cause of God's work in this world, leads
instead to a hoarding of resources and to an ugly self-indulgence. The Book of
Haggai vividly points out this inconsistency and calls for the people of God to
move beyond such worldly ways of thinking. Haggai's sermons, though first
given two-and-a-half millennia ago, have a fresh and vital message for the
present generation of believers. In many ways the modern church mirrors the
spiritual lethargy and unresponsiveness of Haggai's original audience. But the
fact that his postexilic community eventually responded to the prophetic word
and committed themselves to a great task for God's glory holds out hope that
we too may lay aside every quest for personal advantage that detracts from the
greater cause of the kingdom of God in our midst.

## 2. Significance of the Book

The Book of Haggai is brief; it has only two chapters and a total of thirty-
eight verses. Of all the writings in the Hebrew Bible only Obadiah is shorter.
The brevity of this book has contributed to an unfortunate neglect of Haggai
within various communities of faith. Most parishioners probably would be hard
pressed to remember ever having heard a sermon or lesson based on Haggai.
Neither in Judaism nor in Christianity has the book attracted much of interest
among readers of Scripture. But the book has not escaped attention altogether.
The history of Christian interpretation of the book has its formal beginnings in
the patristic period. Origen, Theodore of Mopsuestia, Cyril of Alexandria, The-
odoret, and Jerome all wrote commentaries on the Twelve, although Origen's

work unfortunately has not been preserved.[1] Patristic exposition of Haggai tended to be typological, with Jehozadak and Zerubbabel being identified with Christ, the church, or John the Baptist.[2] Occasionally the Minor Prophets received attention during the medieval period, and at the time of the Reformation both Luther and Calvin commented on the Twelve. Recent biblical scholarship has shown enthusiastic interest in the period of postexilic restoration in general, including the contribution of Haggai. But it is fair to say that the Book of Haggai has been relatively overlooked by most readers of Scripture, in part because of its brevity.

Another factor in this neglect of Haggai has to do with the message of the book itself. Like Zechariah, Haggai is a book with a very different feel to it compared to the other prophetic writings of the Old Testament. In fact, Haggai and Zechariah have rightly been referred to as a "continental divide" in the development of the prophetic literature of the Old Testament.[3] The uniqueness of the message of these prophets of the restoration has sometimes led modern students to a rather low view of the content of their writings. Wolff, though he does not agree with the following sentiment, says that "Haggai is one of the most minor of the minor prophets, indeed one of the most despised."[4] The claim is not without warrant. Certainly the Book of Haggai has received its share of criticism, and the prophet himself has often been maligned by those who fail to see a theological depth to his message.[5]

---

[1] For a helpful survey of the history of Christian interpretation of Haggai through the patristic and medieval periods, see J. L. Vera, "Haggai," in *The International Bible Commentary: A Catholic and Ecumenical Commentary for the Twenty-First Century* (Collegeville, Minn.: Liturgical Press, 1998), 1181–85. On Origen's work in particular see I.-M. Duval, "Vers le commentaire sur Aggée d'Origène," in *Origeniana Quarta: Die Referate des 4. Internationalen Origeneskongresses (Innsbruck, 2.–6. September 1985)*, Innsbrucker theologische Studien (Innsbruck and Vienna: Tyrolia, 1987), 7–15.

[2] For selected examples see A. Ferreiro, ed., *The Twelve Prophets*, vol. 14 of *Ancient Christian Commentary on Scripture* (Downers Grove: InterVarsity, 2003), 219–29.

[3] This expression is C. Stuhlmueller's; see *Rebuilding with Hope: A Commentary on the Books of Haggai and Zechariah*, ITC (Grand Rapids: Eerdmans, 1988), 3.

[4] H. W. Wolff, *Haggai: A Commentary*, trans. M. Kohl (Minneapolis: Augsburg, 1988), 11. In a similar vein H. G. Mitchell remarks, "It has long been the fashion to disparage the Book of Haggai" (*A Critical and Exegetical Commentary on Haggai and Zechariah*, ICC [Edinburgh: T&T Clark, 1912], 36). P. R. Ackroyd's opinion of these later Hb. prophets is closer to the mark: "The commentator who chooses them as his field is not, in fact, to be pitied as having to deal with what is pedestrian; he is fortunate in having so rich a field to cultivate" (*Exile and Restoration: A Study of Hebrew Thought of the Sixth Century B.C.*, OTL [Philadelphia: Westminster, 1968], xiv).

[5] There is considerable merit to R. Mason's suggestion that some of this negative evaluation— not only of Haggai but of the other prophets of the restoration as well—may be due to the lingering influence of Wellhausen's low view of Jewish thought of the postexilic period in general as compared to that of the preexilic and exilic periods (see "The Prophets of the Restoration," in *Israel's Prophetic Tradition: Essays in Honour of Peter R. Ackroyd* [Cambridge: Cambridge University Press, 1982], 137).

Haggai is thought to be preoccupied with material things and devoid of the lofty concerns that characterized the writings of earlier biblical prophets.[6]

But how should a prophet's ministry be evaluated? Only in comparison to the rich ethical emphasis and elevated theology that is to be found in the classical prophets? It is true that by such a method Haggai will not fare very well. A better approach, however, might be to evaluate a prophet in terms of his faithfulness to the word that he claims came to him by divine revelation. After all, if we take seriously the idea that the prophet was a spokesman for God whose message had a divine origin that was ultimately separate from the human individual himself, our opinions will have to be adjusted accordingly. The calling of the Old Testament prophet was to deliver faithfully the message that he had received from God without addition, subtraction, or alteration of any kind. Judged in this way, Haggai—though his message was without question very different from that of an Isaiah, or Jeremiah, or Ezekiel—is to be viewed as a worthy servant of the Lord. He received from the Lord a prophetic word that was destined to be unpopular and at times even strident. Yet he relentlessly repeated this message, pressing his people to respond in an appropriate way.[7] He was in the end one of the most successful prophets described in Old Testament literature.

The fact that the Book of Haggai is brief, direct, and singular in its intent and purpose does not necessarily mean that a modern reader will find it easy to understand. In some ways the brevity of the book only contributes to the occasional elusiveness of its meaning. We may assume that some things in Haggai that seem unclear to us probably were obvious to the original audience. For example, the author or editor of the book assumed a great deal in terms of the history of this period and in terms of Old Testament content and teaching that are relevant to the message of the book. The writer takes for granted what some modern readers of his message fail to grasp: namely, that the Jewish temple was vested with unusual theological significance in the religious life of ancient Israel and that there could be no normalization of the religious and national

---

[6] E. Sellin, e.g., describes Haggai as "no more than an epigone of the prophets" (E. Sellin and G. Fohrer, *Introduction to the Old Testament* [Nashville: Abingdon, 1968], 460). Such claims, however, are exaggerated. C. L. Meyers and E. M. Meyers seem to be closer to an accurate appraisal when they find Haggai "to stand squarely in the tradition of his prophetic forebears in language, idiom, and point of view" (*Haggai, Zechariah 1–8: A New Translation with Introduction and Commentary*, AB, vol. 25B [New York: Doubleday, 1987], xli).

[7] For help on contextualizing Haggai's message to a modern setting see E. Achtemeier, "Preaching from the Book of Haggai," in *Preaching from the Minor Prophets* (Grand Rapids: Eerdmans, 1998), 104–11. M. E. Andrew also has some interesting thoughts on modern contextualization of the message of certain of the postexilic prophets, although he does not discuss Haggai directly; see "Post-Exilic Prophets and the Ministry of Creating Community," *ExpTim* 93 (1981): 42–46. Brief homiletical notes on Haggai may also be found in K. M. Yates, *Preaching from the Prophets* (Nashville: Broadman, 1942), 199–204.

experience of those Jews who returned from the exile apart from the rebuilding of the temple. Understanding Haggai's message therefore requires uncommon familiarity with the historical, religious, and theological roots that he takes for granted. Furthermore, in a number of places certain details of the book are elusive so far as their exact meaning is concerned. The result is that many interpreters disagree on how best to understand various specifics of Haggai's message. In addition, various questions of unity and integrity with regard to the original form of this book have also been raised by some interpreters. The decisions made on these issues will affect, sometimes significantly, our understanding of portions of the book.

In short, in spite of its brevity and its limited focus, the Book of Haggai is not without problems and difficulties sufficient to test the patience of modern readers. It is surprising therefore to read that "the exegesis of Haggai is in most respects relatively easy. Problems of text and translation are few."[8] Perhaps in a general sense this is true, at least when Haggai is compared to certain other books of the Old Testament that may rightly be said to be more difficult. But this should not be taken to mean that there is not work to do in recovering an accurate understanding of this portion of the prophetic writings of the Old Testament. As is true with any ancient text, Haggai has its share of interpretational difficulties. If there are fewer exegetical problems in this book than in certain other Old Testament writings, it is only due to the fact that the book is relatively brief. The reader who would grasp its historical and theological message will not lack for issues upon which to reflect and over which to labor.

## 3. Historical Background

The sixth-century B.C. holds great historical importance not only for biblical history in particular but for the history of influential ideas in general. It was, as is well known, the century that produced such philosophical and reli-

---

[8] J. Bright, "Haggai among the Prophets: Reflections on Preaching from the Old Testament," in *From Faith to Faith: Essays in Honor of Donald G. Miller on His Seventieth Birthday,* PTMS, vol. 31 (Pittsburgh: Pickwick Press, 1979), 221. Elsewhere Bright remarks, "Le message d'Aggée est en général clair, et exige peu d'explication" [The message of Haggai is generally clear and requires little explanation] ("Aggée: Un exercice en herméneutique," *ETR* 44 [1969]: 10). This view is expressed by other writers as well, among them M. Luther, who concluded that "Haggai is the easiest of all the prophets" ("Lectures on Haggai," in *Lectures on the Minor Prophets, I,* LW, vol. 18 [St. Louis: Concordia, 1975], 367). In a similar vein D. J. Clark says, "Most of the book is fairly straightforward: all the major problems come in the short section 2.15–19" ("Problems in Haggai 2.15–19," *BT* 34 [1983]: 432). While it is true that this section of Haggai is particularly difficult, that should not becloud the fact that other portions of the book also present certain interpretational problems as well. We may also note in passing that Clark followed up his helpful article on the structure of Haggai just alluded to with a similar discussion of structural elements found in the Book of Zechariah (see "Discourse Structure in Zechariah 7.1–8.23," *BT* 36 [1985]: 328–35).

gious thinkers as Confucius, Zoroaster, Buddha, and several of the ancient Greek philosophers as well.[9] It was the century that saw the rise of the influential Achaemenid Dynasty in Persia, with such illustrious rulers as Cyrus, Cambyses, and Darius. In terms of the history of Israel the sixth-century is especially remembered as the period of the exile to Babylon and the subsequent return and restoration to the ancient homeland.[10] It was the time of prophetic figures such as Haggai and Zechariah, of civil leaders such as Zerubbabel governor of Judah, and of religious leaders such as Joshua the high priest. It was also the time of the construction of the Second Temple, which was destined to serve the religious needs of the Jewish people for almost five centuries—from 515 B.C. until the extensive renovations of that temple that began in the eighteenth year of the reign of Herod the Great (ca. 20 B.C.).[11] The sixth-century in the ancient Near East was a time characterized by breathtaking historical events and despotic charismatic leaders. It was a time of tremendous innovation and change that drastically altered previously existing political landscapes, religious structures, and intellectual climates. It was for ancient Israel a period of incredible lows and unanticipated highs—rapid changes that amounted to the political and religious equivalent of a roller coaster ride of daring speeds and unprecedented heights.[12]

## (1) Babylon and the Destruction of the Temple

As the sixth-century begins, we find ourselves in the waning years of the Israelite monarchy. Tensions mounted between Israel and its distant overlord Babylon, leading eventually to military conflict. Nebuchadnezzar's forces began their siege of Jerusalem in 605 B.C., easily overcoming resistance and taking many of the Israelite nobility into captivity in Babylon. Among these were Daniel and his three friends. An additional deportation of even greater

---

[9] See, e.g., Ackroyd, *Exile and Restoration*, 7; D. W. Thomas, "The Sixth Century B.C.: A Creative Epoch in the History of Israel," *JSS* 6 (1991): 46; S. Cook, "Le VI$^e$ siècle, moment décisif dans l'histoire du judaïsme et dans l'évolution religieuse de l'Orient," *RHPR* 18 (1938): 323; W. A. L. Elmslie, "Prophetic Influences in the Sixth Century B.C.," in *Essays and Studies Presented to Stanley Arthur Cook in Celebration of His Seventy-Fifth Birthday*, Cambridge Oriental Series, no. 2 (London: Taylor's Foreign Press, 1950), 15.

[10] For a brief but helpful summary of the history of the period see P. R. Ackroyd, "The History of Israel in the Exilic and Post-Exilic Periods," in *Tradition and Interpretation* (Oxford: Clarendon, 1979), 320–50.

[11] Herod's renovated temple remained in use until A.D. 70, when it was destroyed by the Romans.

[12] According to Meyers and Meyers, "No period in the history of Israel so definitely shaped the destiny of the Jewish people as did the exilic age and its aftermath, the period of the return from Babylon to Yehud, once called Judah" (*Haggai, Zechariah 1–8*, xxix). Such a judgment does not lack historical corroboration.

magnitude occurred in 598 B.C. The final blow took place in 587–586 B.C., when Nebuchadnezzar's forces sacked the city of Jerusalem and destroyed the Solomonic temple, which had been the center of Israelite religious life for almost four centuries. The surrounding landscape of Judah was decimated and rendered inhospitable to both human and animal life (Jer 32:42–44). The protective walls of Jerusalem were demolished; its royal palace and common residences were destroyed by fire, as well as every building of any significance (2 Kgs 25:8–12; Jer 39:8). Nebuchadnezzar's army broke apart many of the bronze objects that had been utilized in the temple, taking the bronze back to Babylon along with other commodities of inestimable value (2 Kgs 25:13–15). The temple priests were taken into exile, and many of them were subsequently executed (2 Kgs 25:18–21).

The destruction of the temple was a defining moment for ancient Israel. As a result of the loss of the temple structure, it was no longer possible to worship the Lord according to the prescriptions of earlier Israelite practice.[13] A large portion of the community was either dead as a result of the conflict with the Babylonians or were in exile in Babylon with great restrictions imposed on their religious freedom. The destruction of the temple was for those who survived an unpleasant reminder of the spiritual failures of the nation; its absence was a painful metaphor of the religious and moral condition of the community itself. For this reason once the exile was over, the postexilic prophets Haggai and Zechariah entertained no hope for normalization of the life of the nation apart from the rebuilding of the temple. In the thinking of these prophets it was inconceivable that the temple should remain in its ignominious condition.

## (2) The Influence of Persia

The events of the Book of Haggai are situated in a period of time in ancient Near Eastern history dominated by the Achaemenid dynasty of Persian kings.[14] It is not possible fully to understand the Book of Haggai without some

---

[13] For a summary of the religious challenges posed by the historical realities of this period, see M. Smith, "Jewish Religious Life in the Persian Period," in *The Cambridge History of Judaism,* vol. 1, *Introduction: The Persian Period* (Cambridge: Cambridge University Press, 1984), 219–78.

[14] For a helpful survey of the attitudes of OT writers toward the Achaemenid kings, see P. R. Ackroyd, "The Biblical Portrayal of Achaemenid Rulers," in *The Roots of the European Tradition: Proceedings of the 1987 Groningen Achaemenid History Workshop,* Achaemenid History (Leiden: Nederlands Instituut voor het Nabije Oosten, 1990), 5:1–16. In a related essay Ackroyd evaluates the documentary evidence relating to Achaemenid affairs as they relate to the biblical material; see "The Written Evidence for Palestine," in *Centre and Periphery: Proceedings of the Groningen 1986 Achaemenid History Workshop,* Achaemenid History (Leiden: Nederlands Instituut voor het Nabije Oosten, 1990), 4:207–20.

awareness of this phase of extrabiblical history.[15] We will therefore summarize some of the more relevant details of the period, especially as they impact biblical history.[16] A convenient point of departure is to consider the primary contributions of the several Persian kings who ruled during this period.

*Cyrus.* The most celebrated of the Achaemenid leaders was Cyrus the Great, who ruled Persia from 559–530 B.C. Coming to the throne at about the age of forty, Cyrus ruled Persia for approximately three decades. He is remembered as an effective leader and innovative administrator of the vast Persian empire, a leader who for the most part succeeded in gaining the trust and goodwill of his subjects.[17] Persia's dominance in the ancient Near East was secured when Cyrus's forces captured Babylon in 539 B.C., marking the end of the once powerful Neo-Babylonian empire. This was for Cyrus, as Mallowan says, "the moment of his greatest triumph."[18] The Greek historian Herodotus recounts how the Persian army, having diverted the waters of the Euphrates that Babylon straddled, was able to enter the city with an element of complete surprise.[19] Actually welcomed by many of Babylon's inhabitants who were disgruntled by Nabonidus's inattention to the Babylonian deities, Cyrus took Babylon with little resistance.[20]

It was immediately clear that Cyrus's policies toward conquered peoples were cut from a different cloth when compared to the policies of those who

---

[15] For a discussion of themes and problems that receive attention from biblical prophets and psalmists who carried out their ministries during the Achaemenid period, see G. Wanke, "Prophecy and Psalms in the Persian Period," in *The Cambridge History of Judaism,* vol. 1, *Introduction: The Persian Period* (Cambridge: Cambridge University Press, 1984), 162–88.

[16] For a full accounting of the history of the Persian period, see especially P. Briant, *Histoire de l'empire Perse, de Cyrus à Alexandre* (Paris: Fayard, 1996); J. Wiesehöfer, *Ancient Persia from 550 BC to 650 AD* (London/New York: Taurus, 1996); J. L. Berquist, *Judaism in Persia's Shadow: A Social and Historical Approach* (Minneapolis: Fortress, 1995); M. A. Dandamaev, *A Political History of the Achaemenid Empire* (Leiden: Brill, 1989); J. M. Cook, *The Persian Empire* (New York: Schocken, 1983); A. T. Olmstead, *History of the Persian Empire* (Chicago: University of Chicago Press, 1948); J. M. Cook, "The Rise of the Achaemenids and Establishment of Their Empire," in *The Median and Achaemenian Periods, The Cambridge History of Iran,* vol. 2 (Cambridge: Cambridge University Press, 1985), 200–291. On Persian religion during this period and the influence of Zoroastrianism on Achaemenid rulers, see M. Boyce, "Persian Religion in the Achaemenid Age," in *The Cambridge History of Judaism,* vol. 1, *Introduction: The Persian Period* (Cambridge: Cambridge University Press, 1984), 279–307.

[17] Wiesehöfer's comments are apropos: "What a wealth of positive impressions we have of the first Persian king! Not only is he said to have led his people from small beginnings to great eminence, not only is he meant to have laid the foundations for the first universal empire of antiquity worthy of this name; but he is also considered to have shown discretion, modesty, tolerance and political sagacity in his day-to-day actions" (*Ancient Persia,* 42).

[18] M. Mallowan, "Cyrus the Great (558–529 B.C.)," in *The Median and Achaemenian Periods, The Cambridge History of Iran,* vol. 2 (Cambridge: Cambridge University Press, 1985), 408.

[19] See the account in Herodotus, 1.191.

[20] Cf. the description of the fall of Babylon found in Daniel 5.

preceded him. Unlike Assyrian and Babylonian despots before him, Cyrus sought to encourage and befriend his subjects by granting to them considerable religious freedom. He apparently wished to be perceived as a liberator of previously conquered peoples, and he saw to it that public documents and monuments would preserve that image of him. Those who had been dislocated from other areas were therefore permitted to return to their homelands, and religious shrines to non-Persian deities were not only tolerated but in some cases their construction was actually financed from government coffers. Cyrus's policies with regard to restoration of religious sanctuaries and resettlement of conquered peoples in their former homelands are summarized in the famous Cyrus Cylinder discovered in Babylon in 1879:

> I returned to (these) sacred cities on the other side of the Tigris, the sanctuaries of which have been ruins for a long time, the images which (used) to live therein and established for them permanent sanctuaries. I (also) gathered all their (former) inhabitants and returned (to them) their habitations. Furthermore, I resettled upon the command of Marduk, the great lord, all the gods of Sumer and Akkad whom Nabonidus has brought into Babylon . . . to the anger of the lord of the gods, unharmed, in their (former) chapels, the places which make them happy.[21]

Among others the Jews benefited from such policies that Cyrus initiated. In 538 B.C., just a year after his conquest of Babylon, Cyrus issued an edict permitting those Jews who wished to do so to return to their homeland and to rebuild the temple in Jerusalem that Nebuchadnezzar's forces had destroyed almost five decades earlier.[22] According to the Jewish historian Josephus,[23] Cyrus had been prompted to do this as a result of reading in the prophet Isaiah descriptions of a Cyrus who would be the Lord's "shepherd" *(rōʻî)* and his "anointed one" *(mĕšîḥô)*. In Isa 45:1 the prophet announces:

> This is what the LORD says to his anointed, to Cyrus, whose right hand I take hold of to subdue nations before him and to strip kings of their armor, to open doors before him so that gates will not be shut.[24]

---

[21] *ANET*, 316. For an insightful interpretation of the data of the Cyrus Cylinder as it relates to religious practices of the Achaemenid government and resettlement of conquered populations, see A. Kuhrt, "The Cyrus Cylinder and Achaemenid Imperial Policy," *JSOT* 25 (1983): 83–97.

[22] See Ezra 1:1–4 (in Hb.); 6:3–5 (in Aramaic); 2 Chr 36:22–23.

[23] Josephus, *Antiquities* 11.5–7. Josephus says: "These things Cyrus knew from reading the book of prophecy which Isaiah had left behind two hundred and ten years earlier. For this prophet had said that God told him in secret, 'It is my will that Cyrus, whom I shall have appointed king of many great nations, shall send my people to their own land and build my temple.' Isaiah prophesied these things one hundred and forty years before the temple was demolished. And so, when Cyrus read them, he wondered at the divine power and was seized by a strong desire and ambition to do what had been written."

[24] See also Isa 44:28; 45:13. Cf. Isa 41:2–3,25–26; 46:11.

As a result of Cyrus's policies many Jews returned to the land of their ancestors, and shortly thereafter some progress was made on restoring the temple in Jerusalem. Those efforts, however, could not be sustained, for the attention of the people gradually turned to other more pressing concerns. The opportunity afforded by Cyrus became a casualty of lesser pursuits on the part of the Jewish population. In the summer of 530 B.C., Cyrus died while executing a military campaign against the Massagetae in the northeastern frontier of his empire.[25] He would be followed by a less effective ruler.

*Cambyses.* Cyrus was succeeded by his son Cambyses, who ruled Persia from 530–522 B.C. Continuing the expansionistic policies of his father, Cambyses quickly focused his attention on gaining control of Egypt.[26] It is generally agreed that the most significant accomplishment of Cambyses was his conquest of Egypt in 525 B.C. and the annexation of that wealthy country to the Persian empire.[27] Although Cambyses presented himself as the new Pharaoh of Egypt,[28] his status in the land of the pharaohs was shaky; reports circulated that he was actually infirm and demented.[29] When his attempt to conquer Ethiopia failed, Cambyses returned to Egypt, where he had been before the Ethiopian expedition began. It was there that he learned in the spring of 522 B.C. of Gaumata's attempt back in Persia to wrest the kingdom from him. He immediately set out for Persia, but while passing through Syria he sustained a fatal injury. The historical records are not entirely clear about whether this injury was accidental or suicidal. According to Herodotus, as Cambyses was dismounting from his horse, he accidentally stabbed himself in the thigh with his own sword.[30] As a result of complications from the

---

[25] Herodotus, 1.214.

[26] For a helpful summary of the Persian presence in Egypt during this time see E. Bresciani, "The Persian Occupation of Egypt," in *The Median and Achaemenian Periods, The Cambridge History of Iran*, vol. 2 (Cambridge: Cambridge University Press, 1985), 502–28.

[27] So, e.g., E. Stern, "The Persian Empire and the Political and Social History of Palestine in the Persian Period," in *Introduction: The Persian Period*, vol. 1, *The Cambridge History of Judaism* (Cambridge: Cambridge University Press, 1984), 70–71; Mitchell, *Haggai and Zechariah*, 14; E. M. Yamauchi, *Persia and the Bible* (Grand Rapids: Baker, 1990), 93; Berquist, *Judaism in Persia's Shadow*, 45.

[28] The Persians were adept at exploiting royal titles and political offices for their own purposes when they conquered other countries. They tried to maintain as much of the previously existing political and religious order as possible, so as to confront the conquered population with no more noticeable change than was absolutely necessary. As J. M. Trotter points out, "The adaptation of local kingship traditions was an important mechanism utilized by the Achaemenids for the incorporation of conquered population groups into the empire. By participating in the traditional rites and adopting the traditional titles of the local kings, the Achaemenids were able to encourage the acceptance of their rule as a continuation of the native traditions rather than the imposition of a foreign administration" (*Reading Hosea in Achaemenid Yehud*, JSOTSup, vol. 328 (New York: Sheffield Academic Press, 2001), 107.

[29] Herodotus, 3.33,37–38.

[30] Ibid., 3.64–66.

injury, he died about three weeks later. In Darius's Behistun inscription, however, it is said that Cambyses "died his own death."[31] From this comment many scholars have concluded that Cambyses's death was actually a suicide, although according to some specialists the language employed in the inscription does not actually require this interpretation.[32]

Cambyses's rule was characterized by relative stability throughout the empire. His achievements, however, were far less dramatic than those of his father. From Josephus's perspective he was "naturally bad,"[33] a conclusion based in part on an unfavorable comparison with the achievements of his father. Cambyses's death set the stage for Darius, who had served in Cambyses's army as a spear-bearer, to return to Persia and claim the throne.

*Darius.*   Darius I Hystaspes came to power in 522 B.C. after first disposing of the impostor Gaumata. Darius was only twenty-eight years of age at the time.[34] Although the details are not entirely clear, apparently Gaumata had briefly seized the throne from Cambyses as a result of a coup by pretending to be Bardiya, Cambyses' brother.[35] Once Darius had squelched various revolts and unrest in the empire,[36] he settled into what would be a long and effective reign (522–486 B.C.). In addition to his military exploits Darius is remembered for his contributions to the organization of the empire, the development of roads and postal service within the empire, the organizational structure of the Persian military, the revision of legal and tax systems, the expansion of building infrastructure, and innovation with regard to coinage.[37] Some of his achievements were immortalized in his trilingual Behistun inscription, finally deciphered for the modern world in the nineteenth century by Henry Rawlinson and others.[38]

---

[31] See the discussion of this phrase in Yamauchi, *Persia and the Bible*, 125–26; see also E. Yamauchi, "Cambyses in Egypt," in *"Go to the Land I Will Show You": Studies in Honor of Dwight W. Young* (Winona Lake: Eisenbrauns, 1996), 389–90.

[32] For an English translation of the Behistun inscription, along with a transliteration of the inscription and critical notes, see R. G. Kent, *Old Persian: Grammar, Texts, Lexicon*, 2d ed., American Oriental Series 33 (New Haven: American Oriental Society, 1953), 116–35.

[33] Josephus, *Antiquities,* 11.26. Josephus's actual words are καὶ φύσει πονηρὸς ὤν ("and being evil by nature").

[34] Olmstead, *History of the Persian Empire*, 107.

[35] Herodotus, 3.66–70.

[36] The Behistun inscription mentions as provinces that rebelled against Darius: Persia, Elam, Media, Assyria, Egypt, Parthia, Margiana, Sattagydia, and Scythia. See Kent, *Old Persian,* 123. For a summary of the details of these revolts see Yamauchi, *Persia and the Bible,* 145–48.

[37] See the detailed discussion of these and other matters in Stern, "Persian Empire," 70–87.

[38] The Behistun (or Bisitun) inscription was written in Akkadian, Elamite, and Old Persian. Its decipherment played a key role in the modern understanding of ancient cuneiform languages. It is for good reason that J. Finegan calls the Behistun inscription "the Rosetta stone of cuneiform decipherment" (*Light from the Ancient Past: The Archeological Background of Judaism and Christianity*, 2d ed. [Princeton: Princeton University Press, 1959], 236).

Darius, like the other Achaemenid rulers, continued the enlightened policies that Cyrus had previously initiated with regard to religious tolerance and liberation. There were advantages to doing so, of course. On the surface it might appear that Cyrus had fostered a generous attitude toward the religious interests of his subjects. In reality his policies in this regard were merely an indication of "his political good sense, which passed for religious devotion."[39] Such policies adopted by Persian kings toward their non-Persian subjects were particularly evident in two areas. In matters pertaining to local law, considerable latitude was granted to the wishes of indigenous populations, and in matters pertaining to religious practice, government funding was made available for building temples of regional interest.[40] The Persians had much to gain by such policies.[41] A stable political situation in the distant frontiers of the Persian empire meant that the energies of the Achaemenid government could be directed toward a firm consolidation of the empire and the formulation of plans for further expansion in other regions. Furthermore, it would not have been politically expedient for Darius to put himself at odds with well-known policies of Cyrus, given the fact that Darius was not the expected heir to the throne but had gained power through rather unusual circumstances.[42] Continuance of the proven and successful policies of his predecessors was only prudent.

Darius figures prominently in the Book of Ezra in connection with Jewish attempts at rebuilding the temple in Jerusalem. Although some scholars have questioned the accuracy of the biblical accounts, there are good reasons for thinking that those portions of the Book of Ezra that describe Persian attitudes toward the rebuilding of the Jewish temple are reliable historical documents.[43] From this material we gain important insight into the attitudes of

---

[39] So R. de Vaux, "The Decrees of Cyrus and Darius on the Rebuilding of the Temple," in *The Bible and the Ancient Near East* (Garden City: Doubleday, 1971), 76.

[40] For a helpful discussion of the political dimensions of Persian support for local law and regional temples, see S. E. Balentine, "The Politics of Religion in the Persian Period," in *After the Exile: Essays in Honour of Rex Mason* (Macon, Ga.: Mercer University Press, 1996), especially pp. 137–43. Balentine rightly concludes that "the Persian Empire saw the temple as an important means for the social and political control of its colony" (p. 141). He identifies the following three ways in which the temple functioned as a means for social control: as an administrative center, as a religious center, and as a locus of regional power.

[41] As H. G. M. Williamson points out, the Persian administration of Palestine was "one of enlightened self-interest, exploiting with no little skill their varied ways of gaining favor with the local peoples for their own strategic and political ends" ("Palestine, Administration of [Persian]," *ABD* 5 [1992]: 86).

[42] For a summary of the historical details see Dandamaev, *Political History of the Achaemenid Empire*, 107–8.

[43] de Vaux, e.g., has provided an excellent survey of historical and linguistic issues relating to the decrees of Cyrus and Darius found in the Book of Ezra. The evidence he presents gives good reason for accepting the authenticity and essential accuracy of the biblical materials dealing with these decrees (see "The Decrees of Cyrus and Darius," 63–96).

the postexilic community toward rebuilding the temple. After the initial efforts under Cyrus to rebuild the temple following the return to Judah of the first exiles, progress had ground to a halt. As Ezra 4:24 records: "Thus the work on the house of God in Jerusalem came to a standstill until the second year of the reign of Darius king of Persia."

When work later resumed, it quickly met with resistance and opposition from neighboring groups. As a result official complaints were registered with the local authorities. When Tattenai the Persian governor of the Trans-Euphrates region was informed of what the Jews were doing, he reported the activity to Darius and inquired as to whether Cyrus had earlier endorsed such activity as the Jewish contingent claimed (Ezra 5:6–17).[44] An archival search confirmed that such was in fact the case (Ezra 6:1), and Darius sent word back authorizing continuation of the work and forbidding interference with it on penalty of death. He also authorized the use of royal funds for this purpose and instructed that the sacred vessels that Nebuchadnezzar had previously removed from the temple were to be returned to it (Ezra 6:3–12). Partly as a result of Darius's assistance, the temple was finally completed on March 12, 515 B.C. Ezra 6:14–15 reports:

> So the elders of the Jews continued to build and prosper under the preaching of Haggai the prophet and Zechariah, a descendant of Iddo. They finished building the temple according to the command of the God of Israel and the decrees of Cyrus, Darius and Artaxerxes, kings of Persia. The temple was completed on the third day of the month Adar, in the sixth year of the reign of King Darius.

Darius died in Persepolis in 486 B.C., having enjoyed a long and productive rule. He was succeeded by Xerxes (486–465 B.C.), who figures prominently in the Book of Esther. These early Persian kings shaped the course of ancient civilization, creating what was up to their time the greatest empire in the history of Near Eastern civilization. But their greatness was not without blemish. The opinion recited among the Persians themselves shows that, with the possible exception of Cyrus, the political and military exploits of their leaders were not so great as to erase entirely from memory their public and private faults. Herodotus says:

> The Persians called Darius the huckster, Cambyses the master, and Cyrus the father; for Darius made petty profit out of everything, Cambyses was harsh and arrogant, Cyrus was merciful and ever wrought for their well-being.[45]

---

[44] On the activities of Tattenai in this regard see J. Fleishman, "The Investigating Commission of Tattenai: The Purpose of the Investigation and Its Results," *HUCA* 66 (1995): 81–102.

[45] Herodotus, 3.89. The translation followed above is that of A. D. Godley in the Loeb critical edition. In the Greek text Herodotus's label for Darius is κάπηλος ("huckster"), for Cambyses δεσπότης ("master"), and for Cyrus πατήρ ("father").

Of these three rulers only Cyrus retained an unsullied reputation for genuine paternal oversight and guidance of his people.

## 4. Biography of Haggai

To ask the question Who was Haggai? is quickly to discover that there is a paucity of biblical information about this prophet. In reality very little is known concerning the biography of this leader of the postexilic Jewish community. The details of his family background and activity are not elaborated in the Old Testament or in other ancient literature. All we know about him must be pieced together from the contexts of the eleven times that his name is mentioned in the Old Testament. Nine of these references are found in the Book of Haggai itself (1:1,3,12,13; 2:1,10,13,14,20). The other two references are found in the Book of Ezra (5:1; 6:14). These latter two references have very little to contribute to our understanding of Haggai's personal life or prophetic career. Ezra 5:1 summarily reports the fact of the prophetic activity of both Haggai and Zechariah, while Ezra 6:14 includes a reference to the building activity that accompanied the ministries of these two prophets. The former nine references, all located in the Book of Haggai, link the prophet to the four sermons that are summarized in this book. But they do not provide much in the way of biographical information. Nor do the few references to Haggai found in the deuterocanonical writings (viz., *1 Esdr* 6:1; 7:3; *2 Esdr* 1:40) provide any additional information. These verses simply allude in a rather general way to Haggai's prophetic ministry, along with that of certain other Old Testament prophets.

In none of these references do we find any family information of the sort that is often provided for other biblical characters, such as the identity of his father or other next of kin. The opening verse of Haggai's book, where we might have expected to find some such allusion, identifies him only as "the prophet Haggai" *(ḥaggay hannābî')* This is the way in which he is most often referred to elsewhere in the book (1:1,3,12; 2:1,10; cf. Ezra 5:1; 6:14). Some scholars have concluded from Haggai's identification as a prophet that prophets may have been uncommon in his day,[46] but this is an unnecessary conclusion. Nor does the fact that he is repeatedly referred to in this book simply as "the prophet Haggai" apart from any patronymic identification necessarily mean that he was well known to his contemporaries,[47] although we may assume on other grounds that this probably was the case. Nor is it necessary to conclude from the lack of mention of a patronym that by the

---

[46] See, e.g., R. L. Smith, "Haggai," in *Micah–Malachi*, WBC (Waco: Word, 1984), 147.

[47] So R. B. Dillard and T. Longman III, *An Introduction to the Old Testament* (Grand Rapids: Zondervan, 1994), 421. Cf. P. A. Verhoef, *The Books of Haggai and Malachi*, NICOT (Grand Rapids: Eerdmans, 1987), 3.

time of writing his father had already been forgotten.[48] Such an argument from silence is hardly convincing. A few times we find this individual referred to simply as "Haggai" (1:13,14,20). Once, in 1:13, he is called "the LORD's messenger" *(mal'ak YHWH),* an expression intended to remind Haggai's readers that his at first unpopular message to them was one of divine origin and was not based merely on personal whim. But there is no elaboration on Haggai's family background to be found.

In this regard the biblical presentation of Haggai differs from that of most other Old Testament prophets, for whom references to personal genealogy or geographical origin or royal contemporaries are quite common.[49] In the absence of such information the Book of Haggai stands closest to the books of Obadiah, Habakkuk, and Malachi. It would seem that this absence of family connection for the prophet is intentional, serving the literary purpose of underscoring the prophet's divine commissioning as a representative of the Lord. What was most important to the author of this book was not Haggai's human connections or his line of family descent. Rather, it was the divine authority that provided the basis of his urgent word to Jews who had returned from exile in Babylon.

In none of these references do we find the sort of personal information about the prophet that our curiosity naturally leads us to seek. As one writer says, "The features on Haggai's face seem to blur before us."[50] As a result, attempts to draw a composite image of the prophet's personality have yielded conflicting results. Haggai has been viewed by some as a "political schemer" whose interest in rebuilding the temple was tied to hopes for political independence for Judah. Others have viewed Haggai as a "religious quietest" who saw Israel's hopes for the future to lie in confidence in the Lord rather than in political activism.[51] Although neither view tells the whole story, it is the latter understanding that lies closer to the truth.

Some early Christian writers describe Haggai as coming from a priestly ancestry. However, this may be little more than a guess deduced from Haggai's familiarity with priestly practice as described in his book (e.g., 2:11–13) and his commitment to the rebuilding of the temple. Hesychius, for example, claims that Haggai was a Levite, that he died in Jerusalem, and that "he was buried near the sepulcher of the priests with honor, like them,

---

[48] Such a suggestion is made by J. G. Baldwin (see *Haggai, Zechariah, Malachi: An Introduction and Commentary,* TOTC [Downers Grove: InterVarsity Press, 1972], 27).

[49] See, e.g., Isa 1:1; Jer 1:1-3; Ezek 1:1-3; Hos 1:1; Joel 1:1; Amos 1:1; Jonah 1:1; Mic 1:1; Nah 1:1; Zeph 1:1; Zech 1:1.

[50] Stuhlmueller, *Rebuilding with Hope,* 11.

[51] See P. R. Ackroyd, "Studies in the Book of Haggai," *JJS* 3 (1952): 10–11.

because he was of priestly stock."[52] But early Jewish tradition does not make the claim that Haggai was a priest. If Haggai in fact held a sacerdotal position, we might expect to find it first recorded in Jewish sources rather than in Christian writings. Instead, in the Jewish tradition, as in the biblical references found in Ezra 5:1; 6:14, Haggai is closely associated with the prophet Zechariah (and Malachi).[53] This is to be expected, since Haggai and Zechariah shared the common goal of encouraging the exiles who had returned from Babylon to finish the work of rebuilding the Jerusalem temple. According to Augustine, Haggai and Zechariah preached to the Israelite captives during the exile in Babylon,[54] although the basis for this assertion is not obvious. Unfortunately, such details do not take us very far in our attempt to understand this prophet.

Haggai is sometimes linked with the composition of other biblical material in addition to the book that bears his name. In the Greek, Syriac, and Latin textual traditions Haggai is identified as the author of certain psalms. In the Septuagint the superscriptions of Psalms 145–148 make mention of Haggai, along with Zechariah, as authors of this hymnic material. In the Latin Vulgate, Psalms 111 and 145–46 are associated with Haggai and Zechariah, and in the Syriac Peshitta the same is true of Psalms 125–126 and 145–148. But these ascriptions of authorship are absent from the MT, and the ancient versions are not entirely consistent about which psalms deserve this distinction of authorship by Haggai or Zechariah. These identifications lack adequate manuscript support and seem to be secondary additions to the text based on popular traditions. Their historical reliability cannot be taken for granted.

In a number of places Haggai employs agricultural language (e.g., 1:6,10–11; 2:16–17,19). Beuken takes this language to imply that Haggai was a farmer from somewhere in Judah.[55] But this conclusion does not necessarily follow from the mere mention of crops, drought, plant diseases, and the like that are found in the book. It does not require a farmer to describe such commonly observed features of agricultural production, especially in an agrarian economy in which such phenomena were part of the everyday experience of a majority of the population. Furthermore, the farming imagery found in Haggai is undoubtedly linked to the deuteronomic curses that form the backdrop for the employment of such language in this book. As such we need not assume that it necessarily derives from the experiences of a farmer. This lan-

---

[52] Hesychius, *In XII prophetas minores* (PG 93, 1361). Hesychius says, καὶ ἀποθανὼν ἐν Ιερουσαλήμ, ἐτάφη πλησίον τάφου τῶν ἱερέων ἐνδόξως, ὡς αὐτοί, ἐπειδὴ καὶ αὐτὸς ἦν ἐκ γένους ἱερατικοῦ.

[53] See, e.g., *Megillah* 3a.

[54] Augustine, *Enarrationes in Psalmos* 147.5 (CCSL 40, 2142).

[55] W. A. M. Beuken, *Haggai–Sacharja 1–8: Studien zur Überlieferungsgeschichte der frühnachexilischen Prophetie*, SSN 10 (Assen: Van Gorcum, 1967), 216–22.

guage may simply bear witness to the author's familiarity with the language and content of the Torah and his readiness to apply that material to the circumstances that prevailed in his own day.

Hanson, in setting forth his thesis of sixth-century opposition between the visionary party of Second Isaiah and the priestly party whose attentions were focused on the temple and its activities, attributes to Haggai a role of special importance. He describes Haggai as a leader of what he calls the hierocratic party who, along with Zechariah, succeeded in generating great public support for the program of the Zadokites. In fact, Hanson views Haggai as a hierocrat par excellence because of the prophet's strong emphasis on the temple.[56] Hanson says, "The most energetic champion of the temple party's cause known to us through the surviving literature was Haggai."[57] Hanson's attention to the role of Haggai and Zechariah in postexilic Judaism is a welcome emphasis, especially in light of the neglect that these prophets have sometimes endured in biblical scholarship. But his thesis overdraws the alleged bifurcation between these parties and attaches greater significance to these rival groups than can be clearly seen in the biblical texts. Furthermore, the historical reconstruction that Hanson presents does not seem to allow sufficiently for the variegated nature of Jewish thought during the period of the restoration.[58]

Some scholars have seen in Hag 2:3 a hint of the relative age of the prophet.[59] In that passage we find a reference to those of Haggai's day who may actually have seen the Solomonic temple prior to its destruction. The prophet asks, "Who of you is left who saw this house in its former glory?" The Babylonians had destroyed that temple and much of Jerusalem with it in the awful conflagration of 586 B.C. Now, more than six decades later, Haggai entertained the possibility that some of his audience yet retained childhood memories of that former structure in all of its magnificence. If Haggai should be understood to include himself among those who had actually seen the Solomonic temple, it would require that at the time of writing he was an old man, in his seventies if not older.[60] This could then be taken as a suffi-

---

[56] See P. D. Hanson, *The Dawn of Apocalyptic* (Philadelphia: Fortress, 1975), esp. pp. 209–79.

[57] Ibid., 173.

[58] For this latter point I am indebted to P. R. Ackroyd, "Archaeology, Politics and Religion: The Persian Period," *IR* 39 (1982): 22. Mason has also raised a question about whether Haggai's eschatological emphasis squares well with the sharp dichotomy between theocratic and eschatological groups that Hanson envisions (see *Prophets of the Restoration*, esp. p. 145).

[59] Presumably W. A. VanGemeren has this verse in mind when he says: "Haggai bridged the old and the new eras. He was born in the old Jerusalem, witnessed her desecration and destruction, and lived as an exile in Babylon" (*Interpreting the Prophetic Word* [Grand Rapids: Zondervan, 1990], 187).

[60] I. G. Matthews, e.g., deems the conclusion that Haggai was an old man at the time of the writing of his book—old enough to have actually seen the former temple—to be "a fair inference" based on Hag 2:3,9; see "Haggai," in *Minor Prophets*, vol. 2, An American Commentary (Philadelphia: The American Baptist Publication Society, 1935), vi, 10.

cient explanation for the brevity of Haggai's prophetic activity; due to his advanced age he may not have lived very long after the prophetic ministry described in his book.[61] But it is not clear that this is a deduction that should be drawn on the basis of Hag 2:3. If Haggai had been thinking of his own experience of having seen the Solomonic temple, we might expect him to ask "Who among us?" rather than "Who among you?"[62] More probably the prophet is simply eliciting memories from his audience rather than hinting at his own childhood recollections. Therefore this detail that some have taken to indicate the approximate age of the prophet is not really admissible for that purpose.[63] Some scholars speculate that Haggai was born while his parents were in captivity in Babylon.[64] If so, he may have been a relatively young man when he arrived in Jerusalem.

Nor is it clear that Haggai was himself actually among the returning exiles. His name does not appear in the list of the returnees found in Ezra 2, although this absence is not by itself sufficient grounds for concluding that he was not among those returnees. Likewise, the fact that he was a spiritual leader of the returnees who enthusiastically offered them his support and encouragement does not necessarily mean that he had returned with them from Babylon.[65] It may be, as Wolff seems to think, that Haggai was part of the rural population that had grown up in the homeland after the bulk of the people were deported to Babylon.[66] Curtis takes the absence of a patronym with Haggai's name to suggest that the prophet was from those Judeans who had remained in the land, since "such persons were perhaps less likely than the exiled Jews to use patronyms."[67] As with most details of the prophet's life, this aspect of Haggai's earlier history is unclear. And if the details of Haggai's birth and life are obscure, the same is also true concerning the end of his life. What happened to Haggai after the events described in his book? Did he live to see the completion of the temple in 515 B.C., only four years or so after he delivered his

---

[61] See, e.g., Mitchell, *Haggai and Zechariah*, 27.

[62] An observation also made by J. A. Motyer, "Haggai," in *The Minor Prophets: An Exegetical and Expository Commentary*, vol. 3 (Grand Rapids: Baker, 1998), 964.

[63] As W. Rudolph says, "Daß er ein alter Mann gewesen sei, ist ein falscher Schluß aus 2,3" [That he was an old man is a false conclusion from 2.3] (*Haggai–Sacharja 1–8–Sacharja 9–14–Maleachi, mit einer Zeittafel von Alfred Jepsen*, KAT, vol. 13/4 [Gütersloh: Gütersloher Verlagshaus Gerd Mohn, 1976], 21).

[64] See, e.g., R. K. Harrison, *Introduction to the Old Testament* (Grand Rapids: Eerdmans, 1969), 945; E. J. Young, *An Introduction to the Old Testament*, rev. ed. (Grand Rapids: Eerdmans, 1960), 276.

[65] Contrary to R. L. Smith, *Old Testament Theology: Its History, Method, and Message* (Nashville: Broadman & Holman, 1993), 291.

[66] Wolff, *Haggai*, 17, 38, 40.

[67] B. G. Curtis, "After the Exile: Haggai and History," in *Giving the Sense: Understanding and Using Old Testament Historical Texts* (Grand Rapids: Kregel, 2003), 308.

stirring sermons on that topic? Again we simply do not know. It is clear that his ministry was continued by his colleague the prophet Zechariah, and it may be that Haggai died not long after declaring his fourth message.[68] His recorded ministry was brief, lasting less than four months.

The effectiveness of Haggai's ministry, however, is without question. Just as Queen Esther was later in the sovereignty of God to "come to royal position for such a time as this" (Esth 4:14), so too Haggai was the right person for the right moment. As Smith remarks, "God calls some people for spot jobs."[69] Haggai understood his niche, and with God's help he made a very significant contribution to postexilic Judaism.[70] He was able to call a weary, discouraged, and self-indulgent community of his peers to a renewed commitment to things that were far more important than their own personal and mundane concerns. He was able to give to this community a vision of what they could accomplish for the glory of God. He was able to lead them to give generously of their resources and their energies in the fulfilling of what was for them nothing less than the will of God. In that sense Haggai's prophetic ministry is a model for modern servants of God who must also attempt to lead their congregations to a renewed understanding of their individual and corporate roles in the kingdom of God. Like Haggai, they too must convince their people that it is God's work that deserves our highest priorities, our most enthusiastic energies, and our absolutely unrestrained commitment. Those with such a calling may learn much from the single-mindedness and dogged determination of the prophet Haggai.

## 5. Meaning of the Prophet's Name

Although in the Old Testament only one individual is named Haggai, various forms of this appellative seem to have been fairly common throughout the ancient Near East. Onomastic parallels to this name appear not only in certain Hebrew contexts,[71] but also in various Aramaic,[72] Akkadian, Egyp-

---

[68] So, e.g., Verhoef, *Haggai and Malachi*, 6.

[69] R. L. Smith, "Haggai," 148.

[70] Stuhlmueller goes so far as to make the following assertion: "Judging from our documents, we can acclaim this prophet as *the* most responsible person for Israel's survival in the traumatic transition from exile to resettlement in its own land" (italics his; *Rebuilding with Hope*, 40). He may very well be right in this judgment.

[71] On the extrabiblical Hb. data see the following: *DCH* 3:159–60.

[72] On the Aramaic data see A. Cowley, *Aramaic Papyri of the Fifth Century B.C.* (Oxford: Clarendon, 1923), 286; M. Maraqten, *Die semitischen Personennamen in den alt- und reichsaramäischen Inschriften aus Vorderasien*, Texte und Studien zur Orientalistik, no. 5 (Heidesheim: Georg Olms, 1988), 162; E. G. Kraeling, *The Brooklyn Museum Aramaic Papyri: New Documents of the Fifth Century B.C. from the Jewish Colony at Elephantine* (New Haven: Yale University Press, 1953), 305; D. R. Hillers and E. Cussini, *Palmyrene Aramaic Texts* (Baltimore: Johns Hopkins University Press, 1996), 107, 434.

tian,[73] Phoenician,[74] old South Arabian,[75] and Eblaite[76] texts.[77] In the Elephantine papyri Bloomhardt counts about a dozen different individuals with this name.[78] As recently as 1970–71 the name was discovered in an Aramaic inscription on an ossuary dating to the final century of the Second Temple.[79] In an unrelated 1975 discovery a Hebrew bulla, or inscribed piece of clay pressed on a string and used for sealing a document, was found bearing the name of a certain Haggi son of Hoduyahu.[80] Taken together this evidence suggests that the name Haggai, in various permutations, was a fairly common one, particularly in postexilic times. It is no doubt the meaning of the name that helps to account for its popularity.

The name of the prophet Haggai is derived from the common Hebrew word *ḥag*, which means "procession" or "festival" or "feast."[81] Although a number of commentators assume the presence of a pronominal suffix here,[82] the /-ay/ ending on the name is probably adjectival, reflecting Aramaic influence.[83] In that case the prophet's name in Hebrew means "festal" or "per-

---

[73] On the Akkadian and Egyptian data see J. J. Stamm, *Beiträge zu hebräischen und altorientalischen Namenkunde*, OBO, vol. 27 (Freiburg: Universitätsverlag; Göttingen: Vandenhoeck & Ruprecht, 1980), 118–19.

[74] See F. L. Benz, *Personal Names in the Phoenician and Punic Inscriptions: A Catalog, Grammatical Study and Glossary of Elements*, Studia Pohl, no. 8 (Rome: Biblical Institute Press, 1972), 307.

[75] See W. W. Müller, "Altsüdarabische Beiträge zum hebräischen Lexikon," *ZAW* 75 (1963): 308.

[76] M. Dahood is able to point to a couple of parallels to the prophet's name in the cuneiform Eblaite materials from the third millennium B.C., one with the meaning "my feast is the Most High" and another with the meaning "my feast is Ya" ("The Minor Prophets and Ebla," in *The Word of the Lord Shall Go Forth: Essays in Honor of David Noel Freedman in Celebration of His Sixtieth Birthday*, ASOR Special Volume Series, vol. 1 [Winona Lake: Eisenbrauns, 1983], 62). For a general discussion of personal names in the Ebla texts see A. Archi, *Eblaite Personal Names and Semitic Name-Giving*, Archivi reali di Ebla studi, no. 1 (Rome: Missione archeologica italiana in Siria, 1988).

[77] For a helpful general survey of recent research on personal names in the Hb. Bible see R. S. Hess, "Issues in the Study of Personal Names in the Hebrew Bible," *CurBS* 6 (1998): 169–92.

[78] P. F. Bloomhardt, "The Poems of Haggai," *HUCA* 5 (1928): 176.

[79] See the following account of this discovery: L. T. Geraty, "A Thrice Repeated Ossuary Inscription from French Hill, Jerusalem," *BASOR* 219 (1975): 73–78.

[80] N. Avigad, *Hebrew Bullae from the Time of Jeremiah: Remnants of a Burnt Archive* (Jerusalem: Israel Exploration Society, 1986), 54–55. Avigad also draws attention to another occurrence of the name on the Hebrew seal of a certain official or wealthy landowner with this name; see "New Light on the Naʿar Seals," in *Magnalia Dei, The Mighty Acts of God: Essays on the Bible and Archaeology in Memory of G. Ernest Wright* (Garden City: Doubleday, 1976), 294–300.

[81] *Festus* is a Latin name with a similar derivation; in Greek there is the name *Hilary*.

[82] So, e.g., M. A. Sweeney, who understands the name to mean "my festival" ("Haggai," in *The Twelve Prophets*, vol. 2, Berit Olam: Studies in Hebrew Narrative and Poetry (Collegeville, Minn.: Liturgical Press, 2000), 529.

[83] On the probable Aramaic influence reflected in the suffix /-ay/, see *HALOT*, 290; H. Bauer and P. Leander, *Grammatik des Biblisch-Aramäischen* (1927; reprint, Hildesheim: Georg Olms, 1981), §51d.

taining to the feast."[84] We can only guess about why his parents gave him such a name. It is possible that the name was chosen without conscious awareness of its etymological connections, in which case the choice may have been due simply to euphonic preferences on the part of the parents or perhaps to their desire for honorific linkage to some other esteemed bearer of the same name. Perhaps, as VanGemeren suggests, the prophet's name expressed an anticipation that the major feasts of the nation would once again be restored.[85] But it is more probable that Haggai was so named because he was born during one of the great feasts of ancient Israel, such as Sukkot in the fall or Passover or Pentecost in the spring. If so, the time of his birth, and therefore the significance of his name as well, was associated with significant religious events such as those a major feast would call readily to mind. In that sense the parents may have wished for the name of their child permanently to recall the fact that Haggai was indeed their "festal" child. In that case his birth coincided with one of the feast days of the Israelite religious calendar.

In light of the fact that no information is provided in the Book of Haggai that expressly indicates the prophet's family linkage, such as the identity of his father or the place of his birth, some scholars have understandably wondered whether "Haggai" might be more of a descriptive label (i.e., "the festal one") than a proper name. If so, the label would serve to call attention to the festive occasion toward which this book points, namely the completion of the rebuilding of the Jerusalem temple. The word would thus be used as a metonym to refer to a person not otherwise identified in this book. A similar suggestion is sometimes made for the name Malachi. Many scholars have followed the Septuagint in understanding this word etymologically as a reference to an unnamed individual referred to simply as "my messenger" (Mal 3:1). But there is little, if anything, in the Book of Haggai to sustain such a view, and the fact that Haggai was such a common name lends no support to taking it merely as a descriptive label. There are in the book nine references to this individual by name. Three times he is simply referred to as "Haggai" (2:13,14,20); five times he is called "the prophet Haggai" (1:1,3,12; 2:1,10; cf. Ezra 5:1; 6:14); once he is designated as "Haggai, the LORD's messenger" (1:13). The most natural way to understand these references is as an individ-

---

[84] An alternative possibility entertained by J. Schwennen is that the name is a hypocoristic form of חגריה, "the LORD has gird." But this explanation of the name fails to account for the absence in the name of the letter ר from the supposed verbal root חגר, although one could perhaps compare Zakkai (for Zechariah). See Schwennen, *Biblische Eigennamen: Gottes-, Personen- und Ortsnamen im Alten Testament* (Hänssler: Neuhausen/Stuttgart, 1995), 190. See also A. S. van der Woude, *Haggai, Maleachi,* De Prediking van het Oude Testament (Nijkerk: Uitgeverij G. F. Callenbach, 1982), 9.

[85] VanGemeren, *Interpreting the Prophetic Word,* 476, n. 28.

ual bearing that name. This conclusion is supported by both biblical and
extrabiblical evidence, which make it clear that this name was not uncommon in the postexilic period during which this prophet ministered.

Haggai is not the only person in the Old Testament to have a name that
was possibly linked to holy days. There are various other individuals whose
names seem to carry similar associations. For example, in Gen 46:16 we read
of a descendent of Gad by the name of Haggi, and in Num 26:15 his descendants are called the Haggite clan. This name means "my feast day" or perhaps simply "festal." In 1 Chr 6:30 [ET 6:30] mention is made of a certain
Levite by the name of Haggiah the son of Shimea. The name Haggiah, in
addition to the part that refers to the feast, also has at its end the hypocoristic
theophoric element /-yah/ (shortened from "Yahweh," i.e., "the LORD").[86]
This name thus means "feast of the LORD" or "the LORD is my feast." Mitchell suggests that the name Haggai may be an altered form of the theophoric
name Haggiah,[87] but this view seems less likely than the view that understands Haggai to mean "festal." Furthermore, one of David's wives was
named Haggith; she was the mother of Adonijah (2 Sam 3:4; 1 Kgs 1:5,11;
2:13; 1 Chr 3:2). Her name, meaning "festal," is the feminine form of the
name Haggi, mentioned previously in this discussion.

All of these names have in common an etymological allusion to a feast
day. The names probably were intended to associate the birth of these individuals with the events of an unspecified religious holiday. It would seem
that such a practice was not unusual and that the name of the prophet who
figures prominently in the Book of Haggai reflects a common practice on the
part of ancient Israelite parents, namely that of linking the name of their new-
born child to significant events at the time of the child's birth.[88]

## 6. Position of Haggai among the Twelve

Ancient Judaism regarded the twelve Minor Prophets as a single unit,
referring to these writings collectively as the Book of the Twelve. This
expression has value for calling attention to the unity of the collection,
although some scholars have questioned the suitability of the term "book" in
describing this grouping. Petersen, for example, prefers to speak of this collection as a thematized anthology rather than a book as such.[89] Nevertheless,

---

[86] It seems to me best to understand the suffix in this way, although J. D. Fowler expresses some
hesitancy about this interpretation of the name's ending (see *Theophoric Personal Names in
Ancient Hebrew: A Comparative Study*, JSOTSup 49 [Sheffield: JSOT Press, 1988], 158, 343).

[87] See Mitchell, *Haggai and Zechariah*, 42.

[88] Cf. the name Shabbethai found in Ezra 10:15, Neh 8:7; 11:16. Apparently this name means
"born on the Sabbath" and commemorates the special day on which the child was born.

[89] D. L. Petersen, "A Book of the Twelve?" in *Reading and Hearing the Book of the Twelve*,
SBLSymS 15 (Atlanta: Society of Biblical Literature, 2000), 10.

the expression "Book of the Twelve" remains a useful designation so long as some elasticity is granted to the word. In the MT the statistical note of the *Masorah finalis* for the Twelve, which indicates that the total number of verses is 1,050 and the total number of sections is twenty-one, is found at the end of the entire collection. This singularity finds expression in ancient counts of the canonical books that make up the Hebrew Bible, where these twelve books were taken together and regarded as one.[90] As Jerome wrote to Paula and Eustochium, "The twelve prophets are one book."[91]

The specific order in which these writings appear in the Book of the Twelve, however, seems not to have been rigidly determined until relatively late in the transmission process. At Qumran, for example, we see evidence of an order that apparently included Jonah at the end of the collection rather than after Obadiah and before Micah.[92] Other variations in the order of these books are found in the ancient versions. Septuagint manuscripts, for example, place Micah and Joel together after Amos rather than following the order found in the MT that places Joel after Hosea and Micah after Jonah. This is also the order found in *2 Esdr* 1:39–40, apparently through Septuagintal influence. Ben Zvi calls attention to yet other orders for these books found in extrabiblical sources.[93] *Martyrdom and Ascension of Isaiah* 4:22, on the one hand, presents this order: Amos, Hosea, Micah, Joel, Nahum, Jonah, Obadiah, Habakkuk, Haggai, Zephaniah, Zechariah, and Malachi. *The Lives of the Prophets,* on the other hand, has this order: Hosea, Micah, Amos, Joel, Obadiah, Jonah, Nahum, Habakkuk, Zephaniah, Haggai, Zechariah, and Malachi.

It is clear that the order in which these writings appear in early canonical listings varies slightly. We should therefore be careful about assuming that our present order of these prophets is necessarily the one that was adopted when these books were first brought together. In all likelihood such is not the case. The order of these prophets in our modern versions probably is based to a large extent on two factors. First, it is influenced by certain ancient views concerning the relative age of the books, with the allegedly earlier books preceding the later ones. Second, it is influenced by certain

---

[90] For a discussion of a wide range of historical and theological issues regarding the OT canon see R. Beckwith, *The Old Testament Canon of the New Testament Church and Its Background in Early Judaism* (Grand Rapids: Eerdmans, 1985), and L. M. McDonald and J. A. Sanders, eds., *The Canon Debate* (Peabody, Mass.: Hendrickson, 2002).

[91] Jerome, "Prologus duodecim Prophetarum." Jerome says, "unum librum esse duodecim Prophetarum."

[92] So 4QXII[a].

[93] See E. Ben Zvi, "Twelve Prophetic Books or 'The Twelve': A Few Preliminary Considerations," in *Forming Prophetic Literature: Essays on Isaiah and the Twelve in Honor of John D. W. Watts* JSOTSup 235 (Sheffield: Sheffield Academic Press, 1996), 134, n. 24.

considerations pertaining to the relative length of the books. The internal evidence for the dates of these books, however, is not always supportive of such an arrangement. Some books that seem to date from a later period stand early in the collection. Obadiah and Joel, for example, are more likely to be dated in the sixth century or later, rather than in the ninth century as is often advocated, partly on the basis of their order in this collection. Furthermore, certain short books (e.g., Obadiah) stand early in the order, while certain long books (e.g., Zechariah) appear late in the order.

In the case of the final three books of this collection, however, there is no question about the relative dating of the books. Haggai, Zechariah, and Malachi are all late in relationship to the other parts of this collection. Haggai's placement toward the end of the Book of the Twelve is reflective, therefore, of the historical contents of the book. From a purely temporal standpoint Haggai is focused on events of Jewish history that took place near the conclusion of the period with which these prophets deal. Zechariah and Malachi deal with even later events. Haggai's emphasis on the rebuilding of the Jerusalem temple provides a fitting biblical transition to the Second Temple period.

In recent years considerable effort has been expended in an attempt to understand more fully the significance of the ordering of the Twelve in the collection of the Minor Prophets.[94] This development marks a distinct contrast with the way prior scholarship dealt with the Twelve. In the past scholars tended to focus on the separate compositions, with little or no attempt to read the individual writings as somehow contributing to a holistic message of the larger collection. One result of the new paradigm has been an increased awareness that there is an intentional unity to this collection and that each book of the Twelve can be viewed in its relationship to the other books. House has stressed the presence of common thematic elements in the Twelve such as sin, judgment, and restoration as a key to the structure

---

[94] See, e.g, the following representative contributions: R. E. Wolfe, "The Editing of the Book of the Twelve," *ZAW* 53 (1935): 90–129; D. A. Schneider, "The Unity of the Book of the Twelve" (Ph.D. diss., Yale University, 1979); A. Y. Lee, "The Canonical Unity of the Scroll of the Minor Prophets" (Ph.D. diss., Baylor University, 1985); P. R. House, *The Unity of the Twelve,* JSOTSup 97 (Sheffield: Almond Press, 1990); J. Nogalski, *Literary Precursors to the Book of the Twelve,* BZAW 217a (Berlin: Walter de Gruyter, 1993); id., *Redactional Processes in the Book of the Twelve,* BZAW 218 (Berlin: Walter de Gruyter, 1993); B. A. Jones, *The Formation of the Book of the Twelve: A Study in Text and Canon,* SBLDS 149 (Atlanta: Scholars Press, 1995); Ben Zvi, "Twelve Prophetic Books," 125–56; J. Barton, "The Canonical Meaning of the Book of the Twelve," in *After the Exile: Essays in Honour of Rex Mason* (Macon, Ga.: Mercer University Press, 1996), 59–73; R. Rendtorff, "How to Read the Book of the Twelve as a Theological Unity," in *Reading and Hearing the Book of the Twelve,* SBLSymS 15 (Atlanta: Society of Biblical Literature, 2000), 75–87.

of the collection.[95] He maintains that the Book of the Twelve has an organized plot and employs harmonious characterization and point of view. Likewise, Lee stresses the supplementary nature of the collection as a whole, concluding that by reading the Twelve as an interrelated group the message of each prophet is thereby enhanced beyond what it would be if taken by itself.[96] The editing of the Twelve as a single book thus reflects a holistic approach to the contents of these prophetic writings, although this scheme should not be overly pressed in an artificial manner. It must be kept in mind that this unity is the result of a subsequent editorial process that does not necessarily owe its origin to any of the actual authors of these books. While this structure bears witness to how later Judaism understood the interrelationships of the Twelve, that understanding is not automatically to be preferred.

One of the most thorough recent treatments of the unity of the Twelve as a single corpus is by Schneider. His analysis provides a coherent and feasible hypothesis, at least in its broad contours.[97] In his view there were four major stages in the process that brought the Twelve together. The first step involved the recognition of various relationships between Hosea, Amos, and Micah that resulted in their being brought together as a single small unit. This collection is thought to have served the purpose of supporting certain national policies implemented by king Hezekiah. Later, as a result of the revival that occurred during King Josiah's reign, there was a similar collection of the writings of the three prophets Zephaniah, Habakkuk, and Nahum. This collection probably retained independent status until sometime in the early exilic period, when it was joined to the prior collection of Hosea, Amos, and Micah. A third and more complex stage occurred with the books of Joel, Obadiah, and Jonah. Schneider thinks that Joel was composed to serve as a link between Hosea and Amos. Some decades later Obadiah was appended to Amos. Around the same time, or perhaps a bit later, Jonah was inserted before Micah because of its emphasis on Assyria. At about the same time Nahum, Habakkuk, and Zephaniah were added to the collection after Micah. Schneider thinks that this order for nine of the Minor Prophets was in place as early as halfway through the exilic period. The final stage of the collection of the Twelve, involving the addition of the books

---

[95] House, *Unity of the Twelve*. See also P. R. House, "The Character of God in the Book of the Twelve," in *Reading and Hearing the Book of the Twelve*, SBLSymS 15 (Atlanta: Society of Biblical Literature, 2000), 125–45. House's approach, however, has been questioned by some scholars. Nogalski, e.g., has criticized House's analysis for being too general in its categories and for lacking a clear indication of the specific phenomena to be used for discerning unity (*Literary Precursors*, 11–12). Further criticisms have come from Jones, who points to what he calls a reductionistic tendency in House's presentation (see *Formation of the Book of the Twelve*, 30–31).

[96] Lee, "Canonical Unity," 226.

[97] Schneider, "Unity of the Book of the Twelve," esp. pp. 235–42.

of Haggai, Zechariah, and Malachi to the collection, took place in the postexilic period, perhaps toward the end of the fifth century.

Much of Schneider's reconstruction seems to be plausible, and his view that the collection took place in stages rather than at a single moment in time seems very likely. His view, however, also encounters certain difficulties. First, it does not sufficiently explain contrary orders of the Twelve that are found in some of the ancient evidence, both with the ancient versions and with the Qumran evidence.[98] That the organization of these books into the order with which we are familiar took place as early as Schneider suggests is questionable. Second, his synthesis requires a date for certain biblical books, such as Joel and Jonah, that will not be equally convincing to all. A significantly earlier or later date of composition for any of these books would require a revision of Schneider's hypothesis. Some caution therefore seems in order here. The details of exactly how this organizational process occurred unfortunately remain a matter of speculation and uncertainty.[99]

Nonetheless, the position of Haggai in relationship to the rest of the Twelve is fairly clear. He, along with Zechariah, was a prophet of the period of restoration following the Babylonian exile. As such, he stands near the end of that period of history recounted by Old Testament literature. The placement of Haggai near the end of the collection of the Twelve is an appropriate reflection of the chronological and logical relationships of this book to those that precede and follow Haggai in the Book of the Twelve.

## 7. Authorship, Date, and Provenance of the Book

Although the Book of Haggai does not specifically claim that the Old Testament prophet by that name is the author of the book, this seems to be a reasonable conclusion to draw from the evidence of the text. It is the traditional Jewish and Christian interpretation concerning the authorship of this book.[100] Only in the last century or so has the authenticity of certain portions

---

[98] Jones, e.g., argues at length that the placement of Jonah after Malachi at the end of the collection of the Twelve, as indicated by 4QXII[a], probably is original (*Formation of the Book of the Twelve,* 129–69). But if he is right, this would require modification of Schneider's theory about the growth of the collection insofar as the role of Jonah is concerned. See also B. A. Jones, "The Book of the Twelve as a Witness to Ancient Biblical Interpretation," in *Reading and Hearing the Book of the Twelve,* SBLSymS 15 (Atlanta: Society of Biblical Literature, 2000), 68–70.

[99] For a brief history of recent research on issues related to the development of the Book of the Twelve, see P. L. Redditt, "The Formation of the Book of the Twelve: A Review of Research," in *Thematic Threads in the Book of the Twelve,* BZAW 325 (Berlin: Walter de Gruyter, 2003), 1–26.

[100] The question of Haggai's authorship and unity has been approached from a variety of perspectives, one of which is a statistical method. On the basis of computer-generated profiles of vocabulary frequency, Israeli scholars Radday and Pollatschek claim to have found in the Book of Haggai a level of homogeneity that is best accounted for on the basis of a single author for the book. They understand this single author to be the prophet Haggai himself. See Y. T. Radday and M. A. Pollatschek, "Vocabulary Richness in Post-Exilic Prophetic Books," *ZAW* 92 (1980): 333–46.

of the Book of Haggai been seriously questioned.[101]

Most scholars seem willing to grant the genuineness of much of the material found in the Book of Haggai.[102] But some have concluded that the issue of authorship for the book should be approached with a two-tier understanding. In this approach a core of genuine material from the prophet was later edited and expanded by an otherwise unknown individual who probably belonged to a circle of the prophet's disciples. Redditt maintains that on the one hand we find in this book an echo of the genuine voice of Haggai himself. But on the other hand, the book in its present shape is the work of a later editor or redactor who molded Haggai's message into the book as we now know it. Referring to this putative editor, Redditt says, "It is through his eyes that the reader sees Haggai."[103] According to this view, the redactor added the dates that preface each of the four messages in the book, as well as providing certain information with regard to people and events. Other scholars have attempted to identify the affinities of the supposed editor of Haggai. Beuken associates the editorial framework of Haggai and Zechariah 1–8 with the community of the Chronicler, suggesting that in their final form these books originated in what he calls a Chronisitic milieu,[104] whereas Mason sees influence from the deuteronomic writings, from Ezekiel, and from the P source of the Torah.[105]

But even if one were to grant that such views may have merit, it is difficult to see how the different contributions to the form of the book as we now have it could be objectively identified and disentangled from one another. Modern attempts to separate the editorial narrative in Haggai from the prophetic speeches found in the book must be regarded as a questionable enterprise, as Floyd has recently pointed out. It is, as he says, "a misconceived quest for an illusory goal."[106] Lack of an objective means by which the allegedly dis-

---

[101] G. A. Smith, writing in 1898, could say, "The authenticity of all these four sections [of Haggai] was doubted by no one, till ten years ago" (*The Book of the Twelve Prophets Commonly Called the Minor,* 2d ed., EBC (London: Hodder & Stoughton, 1898), 2:226.

[102] Archer's confidence requires some nuancing in order to be precise (G. L. Archer Jr., *A Survey of Old Testament Introduction,* rev. ed. [Chicago: Moody, 1994], 469). See also J. H. Raven, *Old Testament Introduction, General and Special* (London and Edinburgh: Revell, 1910), 239. That the date of the historical circumstances of the book is 520 B.C. is clear enough. But whether the book in its present form dates to 520 is a matter of dispute among many scholars.

[103] P. L. Redditt, *Haggai, Zechariah and Malachi,* NCB (Grand Rapids: Eerdmans; London: Marshall Pickering, 1995), 11.

[104] Beuken, *Haggai, Sacharja 1–8,* 27–48,80–83. Beuken's conclusion concerning a Chronistic milieu for the editor of Haggai is adopted by many other scholars, including, e.g., Nogalski (see *Literary Precursors,* 216–17, 236, n. 61).

[105] R. A. Mason, "The Purpose of the 'Editorial Framework' of the Book of Haggai," *VT* 27 (1977): 413–21.

[106] M. H. Floyd, "The Nature of the Narrative and the Evidence of Redaction in Haggai," *VT* 45 (1995): 479.

parate materials may be identified and sorted out poses a serious methodological problem.

There is nothing in the book that requires the conclusion that a later disciple collected the memoirs of a revered teacher or mentor, although one could point to the Book of Jeremiah as a biblical precedent of similar activity. Bentzen is among those who lean toward such a view of the composition of Haggai,[107] but his arguments in defense of it are few and unconvincing. Tollington makes a stronger case for thinking that the words of the prophet were brought together, perhaps before the building of the temple was finished, by the prophet Zechariah (or one of his disciples), who placed Haggai's sermons with a narrative framework.[108] She also allows for subsequent redactional activity that shaped the book in keeping with certain political or theological concerns. Kessler, who dates the book prior to the completion of the temple, concludes that it was produced either by an individual associate or by a circle of disciples who were close to the prophet.[109]

In the nineteenth-century the French commentator André put forth a novel suggestion concerning the name of the Book of Haggai. He thought that this book was originally anonymous and that the name Haggai, which means "festal," was given to it in light of the observation that its discourses are dated on Israelite feast days.[110] He concluded that the name referred not to a particular person but instead had only symbolic value for calling attention to the celebratory occasions on which the messages were first delivered. A complication for this view, however, is the fact that the reference in Hag 2:18 to the twenty-fourth day of the ninth month cannot be linked to an Israelite feast, as André himself acknowledged. Furthermore, the references in this book to Haggai as "the prophet" seem to suggest an individual whose identity the recipients of the book were expected to recognize. This view does not provide an adequate explanation for the name associated with this book.[111]

The possibility that the Book of Haggai was compiled by one or more of the prophet's disciples cannot be ruled out with certainty. On the other hand,

---

[107] A. Bentzen, *Introduction to the Old Testament*, 2 vols. (Copenhagen: Gads, 1949), 1:156.

[108] J. E. Tollington, *Tradition and Innovation in Haggai and Zechariah 1–8*, JSOTSup 150 (Sheffield: JSOT Press, 1993), 23, 180; also "Readings in Haggai: From the Prophet to the Completed Book, a Changing Message in Changing Times," in *The Crisis of Israelite Religion: Transformation of Religious Tradition in Exilic and Post-Exilic Times*, OtSt, vol. 42 (Leiden: Brill, 1999), 196.

[109] See J. Kessler, *The Book of Haggai: Prophecy and Society in Early Persian Yehud*, VTSup 91 (Leiden: Brill, 2002), 278.

[110] See T. André, *Le prophète Aggée: Introduction critique et commentaire* (Paris: Librairie Fischbacher, 1895), 8.

[111] The same negative conclusion is reached, e.g., by Tollington; see *Tradition and Innovation*, 48, n. 2.

it is not a necessary conclusion.[112] The easier explanation, and one that adequately accounts for the internal features of the book, is that it was the prophet Haggai himself who essentially authored the entirety of the book. The fact that the author speaks of Haggai only in the third person need not necessarily exclude Haggai as the author,[113] since this is a common literary technique in antiquity.[114] It may be, as Eissfeldt suggests, that the third person rather than the first was chosen by the prophet to emphasize the objectivity of the account.[115]

Views on redactional activity in this book often lead to positing a date for Haggai that is considerably later than the time of the prophet himself. Although most scholars see the alleged editorial process as taking place fairly early on,[116] some, like Ackroyd, think the book may actually date to a century or two after the time of Haggai.[117] Kaiser refuses to date the book before the early fourth century, and he even allows for the possibility that the Book of Haggai may not have reached its final form until the early third century.[118] But this conclusion seems to be very unlikely. One thing that should be kept in mind is that the book nowhere alludes to the completion of the temple rebuilding, which occurred in 515 B.C. If the book was finished sometime after the com-

---

[112] Motyer somewhat overstates the case for Haggai's authorship of the book when he suggests that "it seems almost perverse to deny Haggai such an obvious task as committing his oracles to writing" ("Haggai," 968).

[113] But this point is not conceded by all. B. S. Childs, e.g., says, "The reference to Haggai in the third person, as well as the structuring of his oracles, makes it obvious that the book has been edited by someone other than the prophet himself" (*Introduction to the Old Testament as Scripture* [Philadelphia: Fortress, 1979], 467). So also R. Mason: "We must attribute it [i.e., the third person of reported speech] to the circle of tradition in which the deeds and words of Haggai were remembered and passed on" (*The Books of Haggai, Zechariah and Malachi*, CBC [Cambridge: Cambridge University Press, 1977], 8). Likewise, E. Achtemeier says, "Because the prophet is referred to in the third person in the dated introductions, in the report (1:12), and in the abbreviated introduction (2:13,14), it is clear that the book was put together by an editorial hand" (*Nahum–Malachi*, IBC [Atlanta: John Knox, 1986], 94).

[114] Contrary to Baldwin, *Haggai, Zechariah, Malachi*, 29–30. Baldwin says, "The dated introductions (1:1; 2:1,10,20), the narrative (1:12), and the abbreviated introductions (2:13,14) all refer to Haggai in the third person, suggesting that someone other than the prophet was responsible for putting the book together."

[115] O. Eissfeldt, *The Old Testament: An Introduction* (New York: Harper & Row, 1965), 428. It must be admitted, however, that Eissfeldt's opinion on this matter has not found much acceptance on the part of other OT specialists. A possible exception is Soggin, who says, "But we cannot exclude the possibility that the prophet wrote in the third person to give the impression of greater objectivity" (*Introduction*, 325).

[116] Baldwin, e.g., thinks the editing took place early, perhaps before 500 B.C. (*Haggai, Zechariah, Malachi*, 30).

[117] P. R. Ackroyd, "Studies in the Book of Haggai," *JJS* 2 (1951): 163–76.

[118] O. Kaiser, *Introduction to the Old Testament: A Presentation of Its Results and Problems* (Minneapolis: Augsburg, 1975), 275.

pletion of the temple, it seems unlikely that this event would remain unmentioned in the book. After all, it is the completion of the temple that is the primary purpose of Haggai's preaching. That the very goal toward which the Book of Haggai points should not find any mention in the book suggests that this event had probably not yet occurred at the time of writing.[119] Many scholars have reached a similar conclusion on the date of Haggai.[120]

Admittedly the absence of any mention of completion of the temple is an argument from silence. But the only thing that seems adequately to account for such silence is the fact that the book was written, whether by Haggai or by a disciple, sometime shortly after the events that it recounts in the year 520 but before the year 515.[121] A further indication of an early date may be the absence in the book of any clarifying word about what happened to the governor Zerubbabel, since Hag 2:20–23 attaches to him such high expectations.[122] The best explanation is that at the time of writing he was still governor of Judah. Furthermore, that the Persian leader is referred to simply as Darius the king, and not as Darius king of Persia,[123] may also suggest a date roughly contemporaneous with the events described in the book. The author of Haggai seems to assume that his audience requires no clarification of the role of Darius, presumably because their status as political subjects of this Persian ruler rendered such clarification superfluous.[124] Further indi-

---

[119] Commenting on this striking feature of Haggai and Zechariah 1–8, Meyers and Meyers say: "Its absence can only be understood as a consequence of the fact that this prophetic work was completed *before* the rededication took place. That is, the ceremony of 515 is the *terminus a quo* of the Haggai-Zechariah 1–8 composite" (*Haggai, Zechariah 1–8*, xlv).

[120] Cf. J. Kessler's conclusion: "In my opinion there is no convincing reason for dating the final redaction of Haggai after 516 BCE but many persuasive arguments for placing it before that date." In addition to the absence of any mention in Haggai of completion of the temple, Kessler also appeals to the following factors: (1) "the presence, form, and variations in form of the date formulae"; (2) "the lack of redactional attenuation of the optimistic oracle to Zerubbabel in Hag 2.20–23"; (3) "the lack of any hesitation regarding diarchic communal leadership" ("Reconstructing Haggai's Jerusalem: Demographic and Sociological Considerations and the Search for an Adequate Methodological Point of Departure," in *'Every City Shall Be Forsaken': Urbanism and Prophecy in Ancient Israel and the Near East*, JSOTSup 330 [Sheffield: Sheffield Academic Press, 2001], 129, n. 53). See also Kessler, *The Book of Haggai*, 41–57.

[121] This point is emphasized in Schneider, "Unity of the Book of the Twelve," 124. Cf. Matthews, "Haggai," vii.

[122] J. A. Soggin says, "In any case, the book seems to have been drawn up a little after the events it describes, since . . . Zerubbabel soon disappeared mysteriously" (*Introduction to the Old Testament, from Its Origins to the Closing of the Alexandrian Canon*, rev. ed., OTL [Philadelphia: Westminster, 1980], 325).

[123] Cf. Ezra 1:1; Dan 1:20.

[124] Matthews, "Haggai," 9. On the other hand, the official roles of Zerubbabel and Joshua are repeatedly expressed in the Book of Haggai. But this repetition is a device of emphasis, underscoring the official governmental and religious backing that was an essential part of the prophet's call to rebuild the temple.

cation of an early date for the book may perhaps be seen in the dating formulae found in Haggai. Kessler and others have collected evidence that suggests that the order of year-month-day is consistent with preexilic biblical practice, whereas biblical books that are known to be late typically adopt the order day-month-year.[125] The order adopted in Haggai is not consistent, which may suggest that Haggai stands in a time of transition in this regard.[126] This would favor an early rather than a late date for the book.

Relevant to any discussion of dating of the Book of Haggai is the evidence of the dates cited in connection with Haggai's four sermons.[127] Each of the four sermons is dated. From these dates we can deduce that the sermons were all delivered within the space of about four months. The first of Haggai's sermons is dated "in the second year of king Darius, on the first day of the sixth month" (Hag 1:1). The modern equivalent of the date referred to in Hag 1:1 is August 29, 520 B.C.[128] The remaining three sermons were delivered in this same year. According to Hag 2:1, the second message was given "on the twenty-first day of the seventh month." The modern equivalent of this date is October 17, 520 B.C. The third and fourth messages were delivered "on the twenty-fourth day of the ninth month" (Hag 2:10,20). This date is December 18, 520 B.C.

Assuming then that the prophet Haggai is the essential author of the book and that any editorial activity that might have been involved took place early on, the book was written shortly after Haggai delivered its fourth and final message. This suggests for the book a date of 520 B.C. or shortly thereafter.

A likely provenance of the book may also be suggested with a degree of confidence. There is no reason to think that the book was written anywhere other than in Jerusalem, which is the scene of all of the activity that Haggai describes.

---

[125] See J. Kessler, "The Second Year of Darius and the Prophet Haggai," *Transeu* 5 (1992): 63–84; also *The Book of Haggai*, 44–48.

[126] Cf. Hag 1:1,15; 2:1,10,18,20.

[127] In counting four sermons in Haggai, I am assuming the unity of 2:10–19. Those who follow Rothstein in regarding 2:15–19 as a misplaced pericope belonging with 1:15a will see in Haggai five sermons rather than four. Motyer actually counts a total of six oracles in Haggai: 1:1–2, an oracle to Zerubbabel and Joshua; 1:3–11, an oracle to the people; 1:12–15a, an oracle to the workers; 1:15b–2:9, an oracle to the leaders and the people; 2:10–19, an oracle to the priests and the people; and 2:20–23, an oracle to Zerubbabel ("Haggai," 968–69).

[128] For the modern equivalents of the dates indicated in the Book of Haggai, I am relying on R. A. Parker and W. H. Dubberstein, *Babylonian Chronology, 626 B.C.–A.D. 75*, Brown University Studies 19 (Providence: Brown University Press, 1956). See also J. Finegan, *Handbook of Biblical Chronology: Principles of Time Reckoning in the Ancient World and Problems of Chronology in the Bible* (Princeton: Princeton University Press, 1964), §335. For issues of non-Babylonian accession year dating in the Persian period, see L. Depuydt, "Evidence for Accession Dating under the Achaemenids," *JAOS* 115 (1995): 193–204.

## 8. Genre, Message, and Purpose

Since "it is impossible to understand any text without at least an implicit recognition of the genre to which it belongs,"[129] it is necessary to describe the genre of the Book of Haggai as a basis for thinking in greater detail about its specific contents of this book. In general terms we may say that Haggai consists of a series of brief prophetic speeches that are cast in a narrative framework.[130] This narrative framework should be viewed as an essential part of the composition of the book and not as an artificial addition superimposed on the book.[131] Nonetheless, it is the speeches that account for most of the content of the book. Any description of genre for the Book of Haggai will therefore have to account for both the overall nature of the book as a whole as well as that of its constituent parts in particular.[132]

Since the Book of Haggai focuses on certain events during the Persian period that had relevance for the rebuilding of the Jerusalem temple, and since this book emphasizes a very precise chronology in connection with those events, we may surmise that Haggai is a historiographic text of

---

[129] J. Barton, *Reading the Old Testament: Method in Biblical Study*, rev. ed. (Louisville: Westminster John Knox, 1996), 16. Barton's definition of genre provides a helpful starting point: "A *Gattung* or genre is *a conventional pattern, recognizable by certain formal criteria* (style, shape, tone, particular syntactic or even grammatical structures, recurring formulaic patterns), which is *used in a particular society in social contexts which are governed by certain formal conventions*" (see p. 32, italics his). In establishing genre we must of course avoid an overly rigid approach that seeks for uniformity at the expense of what is actually a well-attested variety in the biblical forms. Some form-critics have not always been sufficiently sensitive to such variation in form, with the result that uniformities were sometimes emphasized while distinctive elements were minimized. But in fact particular genres of OT literature often exhibit both a remarkable uniformity in their patterns and a diversity that refuses to be bound to conventions. Furthermore, particular OT texts sometimes reflect multiple forms, and that mixture must be taken into account in any attempt toward classification. See also D. F. Murray, "The Rhetoric of Disputation: Re-Examination of a Prophetic Genre," *JSOT* 38 (1987): 95.

[130] On the forms of prophetic speeches in general see the following influential works: C. Westermann, *Basic Forms of Prophetic Speech* (1967; reprint, Philadelphia: Westminster; Cambridge: Lutterworth Press; Louisville: Westminster/John Knox, 1991); id., *Prophetic Oracles of Salvation in the Old Testament* (Louisville: Westminster/John Knox, 1991).

[131] I agree with the following assessment by M. H. Floyd: "Form-critical analysis must therefore take as its starting point the fact that we have here a narrative in which a prophetic speech plays the central role, and not a prophetic speech that has been incidentally framed by narration" ("Haggai," in *Minor Prophets,* part 2, FOTL (Grand Rapids: Eerdmans, 2000), 22:272.

[132] D. J. Clark thinks that overall Haggai can be labeled as a discourse containing four oracles. But his use of the term *discourse* in the singular does not mean Haggai's oracles were delivered all at the same time but that the book has a unified message, purpose, and structure ("Discourse Structure in Haggai," *JOTT* 5 [1992]: 14).

sorts.[133] But the book is also strongly theological, underscoring the divine will and presence as key to the proper interpretation of the historical events that it describes. The mix of discourse and historical material such as we find in Haggai is not without parallel elsewhere in the Old Testament. Lohfink has identified a genre found elsewhere in biblical literature that he calls the historical brief account.[134] The Book of Haggai has certain things in common with these historical accounts. Building upon Lohfink's category, Petersen finds seven similarities between such accounts and Haggai: (1) they are relatively short prose narratives; (2) they focus on one or more important persons; (3) they purport to be history; (4) they contain several different scenes; (5) the boundaries between the scenes are marked off by dates; (6) the scenes are of unequal length; (7) they have an apologetic purpose.[135] Stressing the last of these features, Petersen suggests that Haggai is an example of what he calls the brief apologetic historical narrative, similar in genre to Jeremiah 26; 36; 37–41 and 2 Kings 22–23. In other words, Haggai is a prophetic history that intends to interpret the religious and theological significance of the historical events that it recounts. The purpose of this collection of speeches is to motivate both the Israelite leadership (civil and religious) and the local lay population to finish the task of rebuilding the Jerusalem temple.[136]

The speeches themselves exhibit several specific subgenres. These genres are both similar to those displayed elsewhere in the Hebrew Bible in that their main features remain intact and recognizable, and they are dissimilar to earlier examples in that they are freely adapted to new situations. It is this lack of rigidity in form and content that justifies the claim that Haggai has to some degree transformed earlier genres.[137] The basic features of Haggai's adaptation of these genres may now be summarized.

Haggai's first message (1:2–11) is a disputation speech in which the prophet contests the people's claims to have legitimate reasons for not pro-

---

[133] So, e.g., Floyd. In defining the overall genre of Haggai, Floyd prefers the designation "prophetic history," by which he means a historical account with a plot requiring movement through a number of episodes related to one another ("Haggai," 260–62). Taking a slightly different approach to the classification question, Kessler labels Haggai as "dramatized prophetic compilation," with an apologetic focus (*The Book of Haggai*, 246).

[134] See N. Lohfink, "Die Gattung der »historischen Kurzgeschichte« in den letzten Jahren von Juda und in der Zeit des babylonischen Exils," *ZAW* 90 (1978): 319–47.

[135] D. L. Petersen, *Haggai and Zechariah 1–8: A Commentary*, OTL (Philadelphia: Westminster, 1984), 34–35.

[136] For a helpful evaluation of Petersen's approach to Haggai, see W. J. Wessels, "Haggai from a Historian's Point of View," *OTE* 1 (1988), esp. pp. 54–56.

[137] See, e.g., Wolff, *Haggai*, 21.

gressing with the important work that was set before them.[138] Common to disputation is the presence of a thesis, followed by a counterthesis, and then a dispute of the legitimacy of the counterthesis.[139] In general terms the thesis in Haggai's first sermon is that it is time for the temple to be rebuilt. The antithesis is the people's claim that the time for doing so is not yet right. The dispute maintains that while neglecting the Lord's interests, the people seem to have time to provide for their own interests.

The development of the disputation itself has several sections. The first part, found in v. 4, presents a pointed rhetorical question designed to call attention to the people's negligence in doing the Lord's will. The prophet asks, "Is it a time for you yourselves to be living in your paneled houses, while this house remains a ruin?" The question drips with stinging rebuke. It intends to deny legitimacy to the rationalizations that have characterized the prior inactivity of the people. The second part of the disputation, found in vv. 5–8, constitutes an effective rejection of the insipid and shallow replies of the people. They feel that life has simply been too hard for them to take on such a task. Haggai invites them to consider the futility that economic depression has brought upon them, implying that its reversal can come only through renewed obedience to the Lord. Haggai's language here has certain similarities to that of futility curses that were commonly used among the peoples of the ancient Near East.[140] The final part of the disputation speech, found in vv. 9–11, interprets the difficulties of the people as due to the Lord's judgment upon them for their failure to do what he expected of them.[141] Its tone is direct and unflinching, leaving the people with no alternative but to acknowledge their failure and to turn to the Lord for forgiveness. The concluding section of Haggai 1, found in vv. 12–15a, describes the people's

---

[138] On the use of the disputation speech in OT prophetic literature in general, see A. Graffy, *A Prophet Confronts His People: The Disputation Speech in the Prophets*, AnBib 104 (Rome: Biblical Institute Press, 1984).

[139] For a helpful discussion see Murray, "Rhetoric of Disputation," esp. pp. 98–99, 114–15.

[140] On futility curses in general see D. R. Hillers, *Treaty-Curses and the Old Testament Prophets*, BibOr (Rome: Pontifical Biblical Institute, 1964), esp. pp. 28–29; S. Gevirtz, "Curse Motifs in the Old Testament and in the Ancient Near East" (Ph.D. diss., University of Chicago, 1959). On the significance of ancient Semitic curses to questions relating to the origins of biblical law see S. Gevirtz, "West-Semitic Curses and the Problem of the Origins of Hebrew Law," *VT* 11 (1961): 137–58. On the use of this form in the OT in particular see K. M. Queen Sutherland, "The Futility Curse in the Old Testament" (Ph.D. diss., The Southern Baptist Theological Seminary, 1982); H. C. Brichto, *The Problem of "Curse" in the Hebrew Bible*, JBLMS 13 (1963; reprint, Philadelphia: Society of Biblical Literature, 1968).

[141] O. H. Steck views Hag 1:2–11 as originally containing two sayings of the prophet that a redactor has linked together. The first saying, found in vv. 4–8, was addressed to that part of the population that had remained in the land during the exile. The second saying, found in vv. 9–11, was addressed to those who had recently returned from the exile (see "Zu Haggai 1 2–11," *ZAW* 83 [1971]: 355–79).

favorable response to this first message of Haggai.[142]

Haggai's second speech (1:15b–2:9) is an oracle of encouragement.[143] It acknowledges the people's discouragement over what they viewed as an unfavorable comparison between the temple that they had begun to rebuild and the surpassing splendor of the earlier Solomonic temple. In the face of this discouragement the prophet urges the people to continue their work in the awareness that God is with them and that he will bestow even greater glory upon the new temple once it is completed. Into that temple, Haggai promises, will flow the wealth of surrounding nations, and its grandeur will exceed even their loftiest hopes for it. The final part of this unit, found in vv. 6–9, is a proclamation of salvation.[144] Here the Lord promises to intervene in human history, to bestow unprecedented glory upon the rebuilt temple, and to provide conditions of peace for his people.

The third speech (2:10–19) is a didactic speech that intends to demonstrate the corrupting nature of ritual defilement and the absolute need for purity in worship.[145] This speech has two parts. First, vv. 10–14 contain an oracle of warning. In this message a question is posed for the priests concerning how holiness and impurity can be transferred. Haggai then applies the priests' decision to the religious condition of the people. Their defilement, he maintains, has made their worship unacceptable to God. Second, vv. 15–19 contain an oracle of blessing. Here the Lord promises to bestow unparalleled blessing upon the people if they will but repent and turn to him. But their future is dependent upon their response to the didactic message that the Lord revealed to them through his servant, the prophet Haggai.

The fourth and final speech (2:20–23) is in the form of an oracle of salvation.[146] It is addressed to Judah's governor Zerubbabel, and it announces the Lord's grand plan to restore a Davidide to the throne of Israel. The Lord's seal of approval and his authentication will rest upon this royal heir who will be like a signet ring upon the Lord's hand. Through him will come Israel's deliverance. The Book of Haggai thus concludes with an eschatological

---

[142] It seems best to regard vv. 12–15a as a separate pericope, although admittedly the distinction is not a rigid one. But the adequacy of this division has been recently questioned by Floyd, who points out that v. 13 is reporting further aspects of Haggai's speech and cannot therefore be thought of as part of the people's response ("Haggai," 269). He prefers to see v. 12 and vv. 13–15a as two separate units. Although there is some merit to this division, it seems to me to be overly atomistic. If rigidity not be insisted on, we can regard vv. 12–15a as a unit.

[143] Floyd prefers the designation "prophetic exhortation" ("Haggai," 285).

[144] So, e.g., Westermann, *Prophetic Oracles of Salvation,* 104.

[145] Floyd prefers the designation "report of a prophetic symbolic action," with the speech in vv. 15–19 constituting a "prophetic exhortation" ("Haggai," 294–95).

[146] Some scholars prefer to refer to this pericope as a designation oracle. See, e.g., J. Becker, *Messianic Expectation in the Old Testament* (Philadelphia: Fortress, 1980), 64. Floyd prefers to label this section as a traditional "prophetic promise" ("Haggai," 300).

promise that reaches well beyond the historical parameters of Haggai's day in terms of its fulfillment.

The overall purpose of the Book of Haggai is thus quite clear. Its four messages seek to stir the people of Judah to turn from their self-centered ways and to undertake, with God's help, the restoration of the Jerusalem temple so that the Lord may once again uniquely manifest himself in this sacred place. If they will present themselves to him as a pure people, the Lord promises divine enablement for their task, unsurpassed glory for the new temple, and elevation of a Davidic heir to lead the people in triumph over their enemies.[147]

## 9. Literary Structure and Unity

A reader of the Book of Haggai is at least initially apt to think that the structure of this book is fairly obvious in that the book is largely a synopsis of four sermons Haggai delivered to urge completion of the temple. In each case the sermons recorded are very brief, although it may be assumed the original oral content of these sermons was considerably longer than their present written form. The formulaic introductions to the sermons, providing information regarding date and recipients, can be thought of as the prominent structural elements for the book.[148] In each of the sermons we have a brief account of the main ideas along with enough historical information to provide an adequate framework for understanding their occasion and purpose. To summarize these messages will be to summarize the content of the book itself.

There are five major sections in the book. (1) Following a chronological introduction (1:1), the first sermon is presented in 1:2–11. It upbraids the people for their selfishness and informs them that their economic and financial woes are not merely fortuitous circumstances but are instead the result of divine judgment for their disobedience to the Lord's will. (2) This first sermon is followed in 1:12–15a by a description of the favorable reception of this message on the part of the civil and religious leadership of the Jews as well as the people themselves. (3) The second sermon is found in 2:2–9; it is preceded by a brief historical introduction (2:1). In this message the prophet encourages the people to continue with the important task of building in anticipation of the eschatological blessing that the Lord promises will be displayed in the temple. (4) The third sermon, like the others, is given a

---

[147] As Kessler observes, "In the course of the book we move from failure (1:4–11; 2:15–18) to blessing (2:18–19), from humiliation (1:4–11; 2:15–17) to exaltation (2:6–9,20–23), and from alienation and rejection (1:2) to acceptance and restoration (1:13–14; 2:5, 18, 23)" (*The Book of Haggai*, 251).

[148] So, e.g., Nogalski, *Literary Precursors*, 221.

historical introduction (2:10), after which Haggai warns the people of the danger of ceremonial defilement (2:11–19). (5) The fourth and final sermon is actually the shortest of the four, consisting of only a few verses. Following a historical introduction (2:20), Haggai describes Zerubbabel in eschatological language that is reminiscent of the glories of Davidic kingship, promising that the Lord will vindicate him and cause him to prosper over his enemies.

This brief synopsis shows that the Book of Haggai is much more than a compendium of the prophet's oracles. It is a record of the contribution that his prophetic ministry made to the postexilic renewal of Israelite faith and worship that found expression in the centralized location of the temple. But not all scholars have been satisfied with such a straightforward reading of this book. Although the brevity of the book makes dubious those views that argue against its unity,[149] some scholars have found what they believe to be hints of broken structure within the book as we have it.[150]

A fundamental issue regarding the structure of Haggai concerns its literary relationship to Zechariah, which immediately follows it in the traditional canonical order. Clearly there is a connection between the two books. Both prophets preached to those who had returned to Jerusalem after the exile; both were concerned with the process of restoration; both ministered at about the same time and in the same historical circumstances. But is there a literary connection between the two works? Many scholars think so, maintaining that Haggai and Zechariah 1–8 should be viewed as a single composite book rather than as two separate prophetic writings. Meyers and Meyers are among those who argue in support of such a conclusion, pointing out various similarities in theme, date, cast of characters, program, worldview, stylistic features, genre, and literary structure. Their conclusion is that "Haggai–Zechariah 1–8 is a single compendious work, published in anticipation of the auspicious event of the temple's rededication."[151] They view the numerous

---

[149] Mitchell rightly observes, "The book is so brief that it seems almost ridiculous to suspect its unity" (*Haggai and Zechariah*, 28).

[150] For a presentation of the structure of Haggai determined by the division markers of the MT but also taking into account some of the versional evidence as well, see M. van Amerongen, "Structuring Division Markers in Haggai," in *Delimitation Criticism: A New Tool in Biblical Scholarship*, Pericope: Scripture as Written and Read in Antiquity, vol. 1 (Assen: Van Gorcum, 2000), 64–79.

[151] Meyers and Meyers, *Haggai, Zechariah 1–8*, xlvii. See also P. R. Ackroyd, "The Book of Haggai and Zechariah I–VIII," *JJS* 3 (1952): 151–56. More recently S. Sykes has also concluded that Haggai and Zechariah 1–8 are a unit. But Sykes takes the additional step of concluding that this unit is what he calls a prophetic parody of the Chronicles, one that critiques its worldview and subverts its authority. His analysis has a suspiciously modern flair to it ("Time and Space in Haggai–Zechariah 1–8: A Bakhtinian Analysis of a Prophetic Chronicle," *JSOT* 76 [1997]: 97–124). See also S. Sykes, *Time and Space in Haggai–Zechariah 1–8: A Bakhtinian Analysis of a Prophetic Chronicle*, Studies in Biblical Literature 24 (Frankfurt am Main: Peter Lang, 2002).

chronological notices found in Haggai and Zechariah 1–8 as creating a structure for this literary unit, and they suggest that it probably was the author of Zechariah 1–8 who assumed the task of organizing the material.

There is some merit to this view since, as Pierce says, "The story is incomplete without (at least) Zechariah 1–8."[152] Without question Haggai has thematic connections to Zechariah that make it advantageous to consider the two books together, even if the unity may be less tight than the aforementioned view envisions it to be. Such an understanding of the relationship of Haggai to Zechariah 1–8 would not necessarily require a separate origin for Zechariah 9–14, although most advocates of this view would dispute the unity of the Book of Zechariah on the basis of other considerations.

Craig has recently sought to reinforce the argument for seeing a literary connection between Haggai and the first eight chapters of Zechariah by calling attention to the similar use of interrogatives found in these two units of material.[153] He maintains that the interrogatives function as literary threads, serving to heighten the sense of unity between the two blocks of material. His isolation of this material in Haggai and Zechariah and his analysis of its four categories (viz., rhetorical questions, sequential questions, plot-advancing questions, and character-increasing questions) are very helpful. But that the question material functions as a literary connector for joining material from these compositions is less clear. It may simply be an indication of rhetorical techniques shared by the two writers due to their common world.

The most serious issue of unity yet to have been raised for Haggai concerns the placement of 2:15–19 and, in connection with that, the identity of "this people" and "this nation" *(hā'ām hazzeh, haggôy hazzeh)* referred to in 2:14. Rothstein maintained that 2:15–19 is wrongly placed after 2:14, belonging rather after 1:15a.[154] Rothstein's view on the structure of Haggai, first set forth in 1908, has been very influential throughout most of the twentieth century.[155] The problem essentially concerns the suitability of 2:15–19

---

[152] R. W. Pierce, "Literary Connectors and a Haggai/Zechariah/Malachi Corpus," *JETS* 27 (1984): 280; id., "A Thematic Development of the Haggai/Zechariah/Malachi Corpus," *JETS* 27 (1984): 401–11.

[153] K. M. Craig Jr., "Interrogatives in Haggai-Zechariah: A Literary Thread?" in *Forming Prophetic Literature: Essays on Isaiah and the Twelve in Honor of John D. W. Watts,* JSOTSup 235 (Sheffield: Sheffield Academic Press, 1996), 224–44.

[154] J. W. Rothstein, *Juden und Samaritaner: die grundlegende Scheidung von Judentum und Heidentum: eine kritische Studie zum Buche Haggai und zur jüdischen Geschichte im ersten nachexilischen Jahrhundert,* BWA(N)T 3 (Leipzig: Hinrichs, 1908).

[155] R. Pfeil, who has traced in some detail the influence of Rothstein's views on subsequent Haggai scholarship, thinks that the decisive endorsement came from E. Sellin's commentary on the Minor Prophets. Due to its popularity, that commentary became a significant conduit for transmitting Rothstein's approach to Haggai, particularly in European OT scholarship. As a result, Rothstein's views exercised considerable influence on the way subsequent scholars thought about the Book of Haggai. For further discussion see R. Pfeil, "When Is a *Gôy* a 'Goy'? The Interpretation of Haggai 2:10–19," in *A Tribute to Gleason Archer* (Chicago: Moody, 1986), esp. pp. 266–72.

to its surrounding context in Haggai 2. The present location of 2:10–14, according to Rothstein, causes awkwardness in style and inconsistency in content. Likewise in 1:15 we find a date formula that does not seem to fit its context, coming as it does at the conclusion of the section rather than, as we would expect, at its beginning. Rothstein resolved both of these problems by moving 2:15–19 after 1:15a. He maintained that 1:15a is actually the introduction to 2:15–19, which somehow became misplaced in the course of textual transmission. In this case there would be summaries of not four but five sermons in Haggai. Rothstein further argued that the reference to "this people and this nation" in 2:14 is not directed toward the prophet's own community, as appears to be the case if 2:15–19 is allowed to stand in its traditional position, but is rather a reference to the Samaritans, whose attempts at detraction from and hindrance to Jewish rebuilding of the temple is described in some detail in Ezra 4:1–5.

But such a relocation of 2:15–19 as Rothstein proposed would create conflict with the chronological references provided in the two passages. Haggai 1:15a is set in the *sixth* month of Darius's second year, whereas 2:18 is set in the *ninth* month. Advocates of this view normally follow one of two courses in order to resolve the obvious conflict. Either the chronological reference in 2:18 must be deleted altogether as a secondary gloss,[156] or the reference to the ninth month must be arbitrarily altered to the sixth month in order to agree with 1:15a.[157] Neither of these proposals has sufficient evidence to justify such action.

Rothstein's thesis yields a very different understanding of this section of Haggai, since apart from such a dislocation of text as he maintains there is no censure of the Samaritans to be found in this book. If the text of Haggai is read as it is, there is no fault attached to the Samaritans for the delay in rebuilding the temple. Haggai places the blame squarely on the self-centeredness of the postexilic Jewish community itself.

Rothstein's thesis cannot be easily sustained.[158] It falters for one very convincing reason. There is no external evidence in the form of manuscripts or ancient versions that indicates that 2:15–19 was ever in any position other than the traditional one. Furthermore, a form-critical analysis of Haggai's third sermon and its use of the expression "unclean people" argues in favor

---

[156] See the suggestion to this effect in the apparatus of *BHS*.

[157] So, e.g., J. S. Wright, "Haggai, Book of," in *NBD* (Grand Rapids: Eerdmans, 1962), 499.

[158] See, e.g., the discussions of Rothstein's conclusions in K. Koch, "Haggais unreines Volk," *ZAW* 79 (1967): 52–66; D. R. Hildebrand, "Temple Ritual: A Paradigm for Moral Holiness in Haggai II 10–19," *VT* 39 (1989): 154–68; H. G. May, "'This People' and 'This Nation' in Haggai," *VT* 18 (1968): 190–97. Koch, in particular, makes a strong case for the unity of 2:10–19 on form-critical grounds, a case so strong in fact that Hildebrand regards it as "fatal to Rothstein's displacement hypothesis" ("Temple Ritual," 159).

of the unity of 2:10–19 and against the relocation of 2:10–14 to a position after 1:15a, as Koch has effectively pointed out.[159] It seems best to reject Rothstein's attempt to relocate this pericope and with it his understanding of a negative Samaritan presence in Haggai. Even less satisfactory is the suggestion to move all of 2:15–23 after 1:15a and to understand the book to end at 2:14, as some scholars have suggested.[160] There is no adequate reason for such a radical conclusion.

Haggai 1:15, however, remains a problem in the MT. The second half of the verse has the formula "in the second year of King Darius," whereas the chronological note in 2:1 lacks such a phrase. One would expect it in 2:1, since such a note appears in the introduction to the first and third sermons (1:1; 2:10). It is not surprising that a chronological note is absent in the introduction to the fourth sermon (2:20), since that message was given on the same day as the third message and there is no need to repeat the date (cf. 2:10,19). It seems most likely that the date formula found in v. 15b actually belongs with 2:1. Its placement there provides symmetry with the other expressions of date that introduce Haggai's other sermons. In that case 1:15a belongs with what precedes in Haggai 1, providing an explanation of how long the preparations for the building project took after Haggai's first message was favorably received, namely, about three weeks. The LXX, Vulgate, and Syriac Peshitta are thus partially correct and partially incorrect in their placement of v. 15, in that they position the entire verse at the beginning of Haggai 2. For the reasons mentioned it seems best to take only v. 15b with Hag 2:1 and to understand v. 15a as the concluding observation of the preceding pericope.[161]

Reservations concerning the integrity of other portions of the Book of Haggai have also been entertained by certain scholars. As early as the nineteenth century André had raised questions about the origin of Hag 2:10–19.[162] In his view this section is an interpolation of unknown authorship dating to the first year of Darius rather than, as the text indicates, his second year. But most of his arguments in support of this conclusion are unconvinc-

---

[159] Koch, "Haggais unreines Volk," 52–66. See also R. Unger, "Noch einmal: Haggais unreines Volk," *ZAW* 103 (1991): 210–25. Although many scholars continue to assume the accuracy of Rothstein's conclusions on Haggai, Childs is one who has expressed his agreement with Koch's rebuttal of Rothstein (*Introduction*, 467). Another is Floyd, who speaks approvingly of "the emerging consensus that 2:10–14 and 2:15–19 belong together" ("Haggai," 289, 293).

[160] So, e.g., I. H. Eybers, "The Rebuilding of the Temple according to Haggai and Zechariah," in *Studies in Old Testament Prophecy* (Potchefstroom: Pro Rege, 1975), 19.

[161] Contrary to Nogalski, who says: "Nevertheless, the arguments for the relocation are more convincing than the arguments that 1:15a refers backward. The formula in 1:15a is too similar to the remaining *introductory* formulas to presume that it functioned as the conclusion to 1:12–14." See Nogalski, *Literary Precursors,* 223 (italics his).

[162] André, *Le prophète Aggée,* 24–39.

ing, and few subsequent scholars have followed André on this matter. Böhme has maintained that Hag 1:13 and Hag 2:20–23 are not authentic parts of the book,[163] but his views also lack evidence sufficient to sustain them.

Many scholars view the present form of the Book of Haggai as the result of a complex editorial process. Wolff identifies several growth rings in the transmission of this book.[164] The first of these is what he calls the prophetic proclamation, as found in Haggai's supposed five sermons (i.e., 1:4–11; 2:15–19; 2:3–9; 2:14; 2:21b–23). Wolff traces the origin of these prophetic proclamations not to Haggai himself but to a disciple of Haggai who preserved the details of Haggai's messages, including in what Wolff calls "scene sketches" such historical details as the effect of the sermons on the listeners. Wolff's identification of five sermons (rather than four) presupposes a dislocation of text in Hag 2:15–19, a section that is understood to belong earlier in the book as a sermon separate and distinct from Hag 2:3–9. As pointed out earlier, this relocation of text is unnecessary. Wolff discerns a second, or outer, growth ring consisting of the introductions to Haggai's sermons. These introductions provide details of date, origin, and addressees. According to Wolff this material is the work of a final editor of the text; Wolff describes him as the Haggai chronicler. Among other things this chronicler was responsible for the placement of 2:15–19 after 2:10–14. Wolff thinks this pericope originally appeared after Hag 1:15a, a view that should be rejected if for no other reason due to its lack of manuscript support. Wolff's third growth ring consists of various interpolations to the book, some of which appear in the Hebrew text (e.g., 2:5aa,17; the final two words of 2:18; the first four words in 2:19ab) and others of which appear in the Septuagint (e.g., 2:9,14, 21,22ba).

It is not at all clear that the evidence requires such a view of the composition of this book. It is possible, perhaps even preferable, to collapse Wolff's first two growth rings into the work of a single writer, if not Haggai himself then a disciple who executed his work very close to the time of the events he is describing. As for Wolff's third growth ring, that of various later additions to the book, we should understand this problem to be related to the textual history of the book. Certain ancient scribes and translators have expanded the book by incorporating various nonoriginal readings. But for the most part these can be rather easily identified and expunged from the text on the basis of normal text-critical procedures.

Other scholars have advocated various other views that are disruptive to the unity of the Book of Haggai. North, for example, has set forth a radical approach to Haggai in which the original basic narrative consists of only a

---

[163] W. Böhme, "Zu Maleachi und Haggai," *ZAW* 7 (1887): 210–17.

[164] Wolff, *Haggai*, 17–20.

small core of material that has been enlarged by the addition of secondary material sufficient to expand the book to five or six times its original size.[165] Though in its canonical form the Book of Haggai is short, in its original form it was actually much shorter, according to North. He finds as many as five different glosses in a single verse of Haggai (e.g., 1:12).[166] In spite of this sizable expansion, North remains confident that the nucleus of original material can still be identified and that the many later glosses and insertions can be recognized as such, mainly on the basis of infelicities of style and textual variations exhibited in the Hebrew manuscripts and the ancient versions. But North's conclusions are very suspect, in large measure because of his employment of subjective methods of analysis that lack rigorous controls. His abbreviated version of Haggai, which he thinks was later supplemented by numerous secondary glosses often rather awkwardly inserted into the account, leaves this book in a greatly impoverished condition. Haggai displays more of a coherent literary structure than North has allowed.

Holbrook has disagreed with those who attempt to resolve the alleged awkwardness of Haggai by reordering the text.[167] Using techniques of discourse analysis, he maintains that the book reflects a structural pattern whereby its information is ordered as an inverse pyramid with development from larger to smaller and from general to particular categories. In each of the three major themes in Haggai (viz., God, eschatology, and temple) there is evidence of these patterns. Furthermore, discourse markers found in the book (such as date formulae, the opening portions of oracles, Haggai's quoted speeches, and quotation formulae) also utilize the inverse pyramid pattern, according to Holbrook. In his view these patterns are integral to the organization of the book, and therefore any attempt to reorder the material would be disruptive to these patterns and in fact destructive of its internal structure.

Holbrook's analysis is interesting, but not all parts of it are equally persuasive. His suggestions of general-to-specific concerning the God theme (viz., mention first of creation, then all nations, then Israel, then the Davidic kingship) and the eschatology theme (viz., mention first of the nations, then Israel, then Zerubbabel) work reasonably well. But in the case of the temple theme he is forced to look not for movement from broad categories to more narrow ones but instead for quantitative decrease in the number of references to the temple found in the successive pericopes. This seems to be a bit contrived. Although not all of Holbrook's examples are equally convincing, much of the evidence he presents is suggestive of an intentional pattern of organization that in turn argues for the unity and coherence of the book overall.

---

[165] F. S. North, "Critical Analysis of the Book of Haggai," *ZAW* 68 (1956): 25–46.

[166] North, "Critical Analysis," 37.

[167] D. J. Holbrook, "Narrowing Down Haggai: Examining Style in Light of Discourse and Content," *JOTT* 7 (1995): 1–12.

In spite of various attempts to discover a more primitive structure to the Book of Haggai than that reflected in our extant evidence, there is no compelling reason to think that the original form of this book was significantly different from that found in our modern Hebrew text.

## 10. Language and Style

The Book of Haggai was originally written in Hebrew. Although many of the exiles who returned from Babylon no doubt knew Aramaic, since it was the *lingua franca* of the Achaemenid Persian empire, the rank and file of those who had remained in the land of Israel probably continued to use Hebrew as their primary language.[168] It is likely that only their well-educated upper class minority would have known Aramaic in any adequate sense. Haggai therefore wrote in Hebrew, a language that would have been known and utilized by both elements of his audience.

The Hebrew text of Haggai is written in what many scholars have described as a rather awkward or clumsy style.[169] According to some it is for the most part an unimaginative style that is symptomatic of Hebrew literature produced in the waning years of biblical prophecy.[170] The language of the book, however, is usually fairly clear and direct,[171] so much so that Haggai has been called "the most matter-of-fact of all the prophets."[172] His language is relatively unadorned and straightforward; it is not ornate from a literary standpoint.[173] Haggai's style

---

[168] On this matter see the helpful essay by J. Schaper, "Hebrew and Its Study in the Persian Period," in *Hebrew Study from Ezra to Ben-Yehuda* (Edinburgh: T&T Clark, 1999), 15–26.

[169] See, e.g., Soggin, *Introduction*, 326; Harrison, *Introduction*, 947.

[170] A. Causse, "From an Ethnic Group to a Religious Community: The Sociological Problem of Judaism," in *Community, Identity, and Ideology: Social Science Approaches to the Hebrew Bible*, Sources for Biblical and Theological Study, vol. 6 (Winona Lake: Eisenbrauns, 1996), 109.

[171] Compared to the other Minor Prophets there is a minimum of uncommon vocabulary in Haggai. See A. S. Carrier, "The Ἅπαξ Λεγόμενα of the Minor Prophets," *Heb* 5 (1889): 209–14.

[172] A. C. Jennings, "Haggai," in *Haggai, Zechariah and Malachi*, Layman's Handy Commentary Series (Grand Rapids: Zondervan, 1961), 11.

[173] To describe Haggai's style I have borrowed the word "unadorned" from previous scholars such as Pfeiffer, Stuhlmueller, and Kirkpatrick, since this seems to be a particularly appropriate way to summarize the style of the book. Driver uses the word "unornate" in summarizing Haggai's style, which also is an accurate label for this purpose. Stuhlmueller goes a bit further, speaking of what he calls Haggai's "meagre and starved style," and according to Kirkpatrick, Haggai's style is "thin and meagre." Other scholars use even more pointed language. E.g., Smith refers to Haggai's "crabbed style." De Wette says, "The style is devoid of all spirit and energy"; the language, according to him, is "somewhat Chaldaic, and poor." But such terms as these seem to be needlessly pejorative and perhaps even a bit biased in their lack of appreciation for Haggai's language and style. See further R. H. Pfeiffer, *Introduction to the Old Testament* (London: Adam & Charles Black, 1948), 603; Stuhlmueller, *Rebuilding with Hope*, 18,15; S. R. Driver, *An Introduction to the Literature of the Old Testament*, 5th ed., International Theological Library (Edinburgh: T&T Clark, 1894), 321; A. F. Kirkpatrick, *The Doctrine of the Prophets: The Warburtonian Lectures for 1886–1890*, 3d ed. (London: Macmillan, 1901), 430–31; G. A. Smith, *Twelve Prophets*, 252; W. M. L. de Wette, *A Critical and Historical Introduction to the Canonical Scriptures of the Old Testament*, vol. 2, 2d ed. (Boston: Little, Brown & Co., 1850), 471, 472.

does not rise to the rhetorical heights of the major prophets, although it is not completely lacking in certain rhetorical and stylistic devices.

Even though his style is not altogether unlike that of certain Old Testament prophets, Haggai need not be viewed as dependent on other prophets for his style of writing. Haggai exhibits certain parallels to Jeremiah's style, but claims of imitation are exaggerated.[174] The occasional clumsiness of the book seems to be due in part to the emotive nature of the speeches whose oral form has been partly retained in the written form of these addresses. Ackroyd suggests that Haggai incorporated certain didactic and homiletic elements into the oracular style that characterizes the writing of earlier prophets.[175] Haggai's mission was to enlist and motivate by every legitimate means at his disposal and at times even to embarrass, humiliate, and cajole those who had returned from the exile to complete the important task that lay before them.[176] The urgency of his mission has left its impact on the style of the book.

Some scholars have attempted to improve upon the style of Haggai by suggesting various emendations that are lacking in adequate manuscript support. Textual criticism undertaken for this purpose will seldom lead to sound conclusions. The text-critical canon of *lectio difficilior* teaches us that given a choice between a difficult reading and an easy one, the more difficult reading usually has greater claim to originality. The reason for this is obvious: scribes tended to smooth texts out, and not (at least consciously) to make them more difficult. Biblical writers sometimes wrote in styles that were not models of literary excellence. The task of an interpreter is not to improve upon the style of an ancient author but rather to listen carefully to what that author has said and to seek to understand the precise meaning of his text.[177] The occasional awkwardness of the language of this book is not something for modern scholars to attempt to eliminate by emendation. Rather, it may be a genuine reflection of the author's style.

Certain evidences of literary artistry are also present. Such elements bear

---

[174] Peckham considers the parallels to constitute imitation (*History and Prophecy: The Development of Late Judean Literary Traditions*, ABRL [New York: Doubleday, 1993], 741). But the evidence he cites is not entirely persuasive (pp. 748–50).

[175] P. R. Ackroyd, "Haggai," in *Harper's Bible Commentary* (New York: Harper & Row, 1988), 745.

[176] B. W. Anderson remarks, "Haggai preached with the fire of nationalism in his words" (*Understanding the Old Testament*, 4th ed. [Englewood Cliffs: Prentice-Hall, 1986], 518). Although there is a sense in which this is a correct assessment, the notion of nationalism should be balanced with Haggai's emphasis on religious priorities and obedience to the divine will.

[177] On the presence of anomalies of language in the biblical text and a caution against too readily assuming that such things are due to textual disturbance, see F. I. Andersen, "Linguistic Coherence in Prophetic Discourse," in *Fortunate the Eyes That See: Essays in Honor of David Noel Freedman in Celebration of His Seventieth Birthday* (Grand Rapids: Eerdmans, 1995), 137–56.

witness to the literary skill of the author. These rhetorical features found in the book may now be briefly summarized.

*Wordplay.* In several places in Haggai we find wordplays or puns that are obvious in the Hebrew text but are very difficult to preserve in translation. For example, 1:4,9,11 is linked by a lexical thread that hints at the reciprocal connection between the condition of the temple and the condition of the land. In vv. 4 and 9 the temple is said to be a "ruin" *(ḥārēb),* and in v. 11 the land is said to suffer from "drought" *(ḥōreb).*[178] The relationship is one of cause and effect; because the temple had been left in ruins, the Lord had punished the people by sending drought to their land. The choice of words serves to call attention to the connection between these two things. Another example of wordplay is found in 1:6,8–9, where several forms of the verb *bô'* ("to come") are used. In v. 6 the people have "harvested" *(hābē')* little in spite of their efforts at sowing. In v. 8 they are admonished to "bring" *(hăbē'tem)* timber to be used in construction. And in v. 9 the Lord scatters the wages that they "bring" *(hăbē'tem)* home. The same verb is used with various nuances, providing a lexical link between the selfishness that is the spiritual cause of the people's problems and the preparation for construction efforts that will lead to its solution.

*Repetition.* Haggai frequently makes use of repetition as a structural and rhetorical device. For example, stereotypical formulae attaching divine authority to the prophetic message appear surprisingly often in Haggai for this to be such a short book. The following phrases occur a total of twenty-six times within the space of a mere thirty-eight verses: "the word of the LORD came through" (or "to") the prophet Haggai (1:1,3; 2:1,10,20); "this is what the LORD Almighty says" (1:2,5,7; 2:6,11); "declares the LORD Almighty" (1:9; 2:4,7,8,9[2x],23[2x]); "says the LORD" (1:8; 2:4[2x], 14,17,23); "the voice of the LORD their God" (1:12); "this message of the LORD" (1:13). Clearly the prophet is anxious to emphasize the divine origin of his message. The imperative "give careful thought" or "give careful thought to your ways" is also a favorite of Haggai, occurring five times (1:5,7; 2:15,18[2x]). The words "I am with you," an assurance of divine presence, appear in 1:13 and 2:4. The word "spirit" occurs three times in 1:14. "Be strong" is found three times in 2:4, following a pattern probably taken from Josh 1:6–9. The warning "I will shake," referring either to "the heavens and the earth" or to "all nations," appears in 2:6–7,21. The phrase "is mine," referring to the wealth of the nations, is repeated in 2:8, and "I will overturn" (or "overthrow") is repeated in 2:22. In these cases the repetition has the effect of underscoring divine sovereignty. Details of family connection and

---

[178] The Hb. words in question here are חָרֵב ("ruin") and חֹרֶב ("drought"). Cf. הֶחָרְבָה ("the dry ground") in Hag 2:6.

official position for Zerubbabel and Joshua, though provided initially in 1:1, are repeated in 1:12,14; 2:2,4,21,23. The use of repetition is the most common rhetorical device found in the Book of Haggai.

*Rhetorical questions.* Haggai is fond of asking questions that are intended to bring his audience to certain conclusions. These questions are rhetorical in the sense that they are not asked in order to provide information to the asker. Rather, they are intended to awaken in the hearer or reader an awareness of conditions the asker knows all too well.[179]

The main examples of this technique in the Book of Haggai are as follows. In 1:4, in response to the people's claim that the time has not yet arrived for the rebuilding of the temple, the prophet presents the Lord as asking whether it is time for them to provide comfortable dwellings for themselves. The question effectively calls attention to the inverted priorities of the people. In 1:9 the prophet asks why they have so little in spite of all their hard work. He then provides an answer to the question, one that calls attention to divine displeasure over the desolate condition of the temple. The question framed in 1:9 is a particular form of the rhetorical question in which the prophet goes on to answer the question he has raised. This sort of question/answer schema is a common form that appears elsewhere both in prophetic and in extrabiblical literature.[180] Whedbee has discussed in some detail this feature of Haggai as found in 1:9–11, concluding that it is an important structural key for understanding Haggai's didactic strategies. It is, as he says, the glue by which the various parts of that pericope are held together.[181]

Other examples of this device occur as well. In 2:3 Haggai asks who among the people had seen the former temple in its glory. The question implies, first, that there are few among them of sufficient age to have done so and, second, that those few of whom this is true will without hesitation affirm the superiority of the former structure. In 2:12–13 the prophet sets forth certain questions that the people are to ask of the priest. The prophet knows the answers to the questions, but they are intended to bring his audience to the same conclusions. In 2:19 he asks whether there is any residue left from the harvest. Given the fact that it was winter and the seed had been planted earlier in the fall, the question apparently calls for a negative answer.

---

[179] As C. F. Keil says, Haggai "seeks to give liveliness to the discourse by frequently making use of interrogation" (*Introduction to the Old Testament* (1869; reprint, Peabody: Hendrickson, 1988), 1:420.

[180] See, e.g., the helpful discussion in B. O. Long, "Two Question and Answer Schemata in the Prophets," *JBL* 90 (1971): 129–39. Long identifies two separate question/answer schemata found in the prophets, distinguished in part by the presence or absence of direct quotation in the question and answer.

[181] J. W. Whedbee, "A Question-Answer Schema in Haggai 1: The Form and Function of Haggai 1:9–11," in *Biblical and Near Eastern Studies: Essays in Honor of William Sanford LaSor* (Grand Rapids: Eerdmans, 1978), 189.

*Linguistic features.* The Book of Haggai shows a preference for certain grammatical forms that characterize the style of this book.[182] Haggai is characterized by a fairly large number of imperative verbs for such a short book. The imperative is used fifteen times in Haggai's thirty-eight verses (1:5,7, 8[3x]; 2:2,4[4x],11,15,18[2x],21). These fifteen imperatives underscore both the urgency of Haggai's message and the necessity of an appropriate response on the part of the people. If they were to be obedient to the revealed will of the Lord, Haggai's audience had no choice in the matter of the temple. They must demonstrate a spirit of sacrificial obedience and commitment to proper priorities. Frequent use of the imperative in Haggai underscores this need for action on the part of the people.

Another grammatical form that finds frequent use in Haggai is the infinitive. Besides the stock infinitive construct *lēʾmōr* ("saying") used to introduce direct discourse in the book (1:1,2,3,13; 2:1,2,10,11,20,21), other infinitive construct forms appear an additional ten times in the book (1:2[2x],4,6[3x]; 2:5,15,16[2x]). In another seven instances the infinitive absolute is employed in this book (1:6[5x],9[2x]). Haggai 1:6 is particularly heavy with the infinitive absolute; it is used five times in that verse alone. Such usage may be indicative of a particularly lively style of Hebrew discourse.[183] The participle is used some eleven times in Haggai, with a variety of syntactical functions (1:4,6[3x]; 2:3[2x],5,6,21,22[2x]).

The Hebrew style of the Book of Haggai is thus characterized on the one hand by a certain awkwardness at times and on the other hand by an effective use of certain rhetorical devices. The book retains some of the oral flavor of its sermons, while also giving evidence of more complex features that befit a literary composition. There is ample reason for concluding that Haggai was one of the most effective rhetoricians to be found among the biblical prophets of the postexilic period.[184]

---

[182] On certain aspects of the grammatical structure of Haggai see L. Bauer, *Zeit des zweiten Tempels–Zeit der Gerechtigkeit: Zur sozio-ökonomischen Konzeption im Haggai–Sacharja–Maleachi–Korpus*, BEATAJ 31 (Frankfurt am Main: Peter Lang, 1992), 64–76.

[183] André, e.g., comments: "Dans le discours animé l'infinitif absolu s'emploie au lieu des autres temps ou modes pour mieux mettre en saillie l'idée du verbe. S'il est employé à la suite d'une autre forme verbale, c'est le temps ou le mode de cette dernière qu'il exprime" [In animated discourse the infinitive absolute is used in place of another tense or mode to set forth better the verbal idea. When it is used after another verbal form, it is the tense or mode of this latter form that it expresses] (*Le prophète Aggée*, 202–3).

[184] For a helpful development of this point see M. J. Boda, "Haggai: Master Rhetorician," *TynBul* 51 (2000): 295–304.

## 11. Haggai as Poetry

Scholars are not agreed about whether the Book of Haggai contains material that can properly be described as poetry.[185] Some see virtually no evidence of poetic structure in Haggai.[186] Others think that almost the entire book is poetry.[187] There are also those who find in Haggai a good deal of poetry that is embedded within a nonpoetic narrative framework.[188]

As Petersen has pointed out, these different viewpoints have influenced the layout of the Hebrew text of Haggai in editions of the Hebrew Bible and, we might add, that of modern translations as well.[189] Procksch, who edited Haggai for *BHK,* presented the book in prose form, allowing for no poetry at all. Likewise in the NIV and the NRSV the entire book is presented as prose.[190] On the other hand, Elliger, who edited the book for *BHS,* presented as poetry thirty-one verses out of a total of only thirty-eight verses in the book (1:4–11; 1:15 [taken with 2:15–19]; 2:3–9,14–19,20–23). Whether this much can properly be regarded as poetry rather than prose is doubtful. That certain portions of this book are more poetic than prose, however, seems clear. Both the metrical structure and the preponderance of rhetorical elements in various portions of the book support this conclusion.

In a study devoted to the musical background of the Book of Haggai, Christensen has attempted to demonstrate a rhythmic structure for the entire book.[191] He maintains that Haggai consists of three cantos (1:1–14; 1:15–2:9; 2:10–23), each of which is characterized by rhythmic structure and care-

---

[185] See, e.g., H. G. Reventlow's comments on Haggai's language in *Die Propheten Haggai, Sacharja und Maleachi,* ATD (Göttingen: Vandenhoeck & Ruprecht, 1993), 6–7. In fact, some scholars regard the distinction between poetry and prose as not really native to biblical texts and therefore irrelevant to their analysis. See, e.g., J. L. Kugel, *The Idea of Biblical Poetry: Parallelism and Its History* (New Haven: Yale University Press, 1981), esp. pp. 59–95.

[186] Soggin, *Introduction,* 325. D. J. Wiseman also describes Haggai's style as consisting more of prose than poetry. He says of Haggai, "He employs a rhythmic prose style rather than the common poetic form often characteristic of the prophets (but cf. 2:4,5,14)" ("Haggai," in *The New Bible Commentary, Revised* [Grand Rapids: Eerdmans, 1970], 782). Peckham has also concluded that Haggai is written in prose (*History and Prophecy,* 741,756). Matthews says, "The book is very ordinary prose. It is abrupt, often awkward and repetitious" ("Haggai," vi).

[187] Sellin, e.g., makes the following comment: "Haggai's sayings are not in prose; they are preserved in the metrical form of short verses" (*Introduction,* 238).

[188] See, e.g., R. L. Alden, "Haggai," in EBC, vol. 7 (Grand Rapids: Zondervan, 1985), 573–74. Alden says, "The Book of Haggai is a mixture of prose and poetry" (p. 573). VanGemeren describes the book as what he calls poetic prose (*Interpreting the Prophetic Word,* 188).

[189] Petersen, *Haggai and Zechariah 1–8,* 32.

[190] By way of comparison the NAB treats about half of the book (eighteen verses) as prose and the other half (twenty verses) as poetry.

[191] D. L. Christensen, "Poetry and Prose in the Composition and Performance of the Book of Haggai," in *Verse in Ancient Near Eastern Prose,* AOAT 42 (Neukirchen-Vluyn: Neukirchener Verlag, 1993), 17–30. Essentially the same essay appeared in id., "Impulse and Design in the Book of Haggai," *JETS* 35 (1992): 445–56.

ful symmetry.[192] Christensen suggests that the imperative verb found in 2:4 (*waʿăśû*, "and do"), which stands at the center of the book when viewed this way, may actually be a well-placed summary of the book's essential message. He takes the implied object of the verb to be sacrifice and celebration in connection with the work on the temple. Whether or not one accepts all of the details of Christensen's presentation, he seems to have succeeded in underscoring the literary art and unity of the Book of Haggai.

Some scholars link discussion of poetry in Haggai to certain conclusions concerning the redactional history of the book. Bloomhardt, for example, sees in Haggai four separate poems that in their original form lacked certain secondary accretions that are present in the canonical form of the book.[193] The four poems in his view are as follows: the first consists of 1:2,4,7, 9,10,11,8,13; the second consists of 2:21–23; the third consists of 2:3–9; and the fourth consists of 2:12–16,18–19. Bloomhardt maintains that at various points a later hand has injected into these poems the narrative passages. His reconstruction of these poetic passages requires stripping out a good deal of narrative material, especially in the first poem. This leaves his analysis with an impression of artificiality and special pleading. If Bloomhardt's reconstruction is correct, it would appear that the editor who introduced the narrative material did so without an appreciation of the poetic form he was disturbing.

The lack of consensus on whether Haggai is poetry or prose highlights the need for an objective method by which to distinguish between Hebrew prose and poetry. Observing the relative frequency of certain common particles such as the relative pronoun *(ʾăšer)*, the accusative marker *(ʾet)*, and the definite article *(ha-)* may be helpful in this regard. Freedman has shown that in classical Hebrew prose texts these particles are used approximately eight times as often as they are in classical Hebrew poetry.[194] In the case of Haggai (which Freedman does not discuss) the first two of these particles are used significantly more often than they are in such texts as Psalms, Job, and Proverbs but significantly less often than they are in such texts as Genesis, Deuteronomy, and Joshua. In this regard Haggai seems to stand somewhere between Old Testament texts that are clearly prose and those that are clearly

---

[192] Elliger also provides a metrical analysis of those parts of the book he regards as poetry (*Die Propheten Nahum, Habakuk, Zephanja, Haggai, Zacharja, Maleachi*, in *Das Buch der zwölf kleinen Propheten*, ATD 25 [Göttingen: Vandenhoeck & Ruprecht, 1982], esp. pp. 85, 89, 91, 93, 96–97).

[193] Bloomhardt, "Poems of Haggai," 153–95.

[194] D. N. Freedman, "Prose Particles in the Poetry of the Primary History," in *Biblical and Related Studies Presented to Samuel Iwry* (Winona Lake: Eisenbrauns, 1985). See also F. I. Andersen and A. D. Forbes, " 'Prose Particle' Counts of the Hebrew Bible," in *The Word of the Lord Shall Go Forth: Essays in Honor of David Noel Freedman in Celebration of His Sixtieth Birthday*, ASOR Special Volume Series, no. 1 (Winona Lake: Eisenbrauns, 1983), 165–83.

poetry.[195] This tends to confirm the impression gained from certain rhythmical and rhetorical features that Haggai may be an example of *Kuntsprosa,* or elevated prose,[196] frequently leaning in the direction of poetry while at the same time retaining many elements of prose literature.

## 12. Theology of Haggai

To judge from many modern treatments, the Book of Haggai has not exercised a significant role in Old Testament theological thought. Haggai's contribution to Old Testament theology is often dismissed in a few brief sentences or less.[197] This is somewhat understandable, given the brevity of Haggai's work and its preoccupation with such seemingly mundane things as the rebuilding of the Jerusalem temple. But it is fair to say that earlier biblical scholarship tended to overdraw the lines of distinction between theology of the preexilic prophets and that of their postexilic successors, with the result that postexilic prophetic literature came to be viewed in an unfavorable light.[198] Pfeiffer goes so far as to say that "Haggai and the prophets following him had little in common with the great Hebrew prophets of the preceding centuries."[199]

It is not that Haggai's theology contradicts or opposes that of the earlier prophets. Rather, his theological emphasis should be seen as complementing theirs.[200] Haggai's intention was not to explore in detail a theological pro-

---

[195] Verhoef speaks of Haggai's "rhythmic prose style," a designation that seems to allow for poetic features within a generally prosaic style (*Haggai and Malachi,* 17).

[196] Meyers and Meyers prefer the designation "oracular prose," a category utilized by Andersen and Freedman in their discussion of statistical analysis of certain prose particles in Hebrew (*Haggai–Zechariah 1–8,* lxiii–lxvii).

[197] E.g., in W. Brueggemann's recent and thorough OT theology, we find in 750 pages only three brief mentions of the Book of Haggai (*Theology of the Old Testament: Testimony, Dispute, Advocacy* [Minneapolis: Fortress, 1997], 192, 288, 618).

[198] The flurry of recent interest in the postexilic period on the part of both historians and OT scholars has led to a reevaluation of certain negative judgments drawn by earlier scholars. H. G. M. Williamson, e.g., can speak of the former sharp dichotomy made between the ethical emphasis of the preexilic prophets and the legalism of the postexilic prophets as "a relic of nineteenth-century scholarship" ("Exile and After: Historical Study," in *The Face of Old Testament Studies: A Survey of Contemporary Approaches* [Grand Rapids: Baker, 1999], 236).

[199] Pfeiffer, *Introduction,* 603.

[200] I agree with the following assessment of R. Mason: "In a broader, canonical aspect, Haggai and the preexilic prophets may be said to offer between them a more complete attitude to the institutions and structures of their religion than either does alone. The earlier prophets show how easily external things can become substitutes for the real response that God is seeking. Haggai reminds us, however, that, properly used, these institutions and structures can be a means of fostering and expressing a sense of God's presence and a proper response to him. It was important, if postexilic Judaism was to survive, that it had its central institution to give form to its life and faith. All religion needs structures. These may be 'means of grace,' but they need to be kept constantly under the reforming judgment of God if they are not to become autonomous" ("Haggai: Theology of," *NIDOTTE* 4 [1997]: 692).

gram as such. To some extent he was, as Childs remarks, a political activist.[201] But there is a noticeable lack of emphasis in the Book of Haggai on moral or social issues. In this regard Haggai does not fit the familiar profile of the classical Hebrew prophet.[202] A reader of this book may be led to ask certain questions in this regard. Why was Haggai not more concerned with issues of ethical behavior and less concerned with building programs? Why did he not take up issues of social justice in preference to his emphasis on construction efforts? To some modern students of this book Haggai's devotion to the temple seems rather materialistic and perhaps even misguided. Achtemeier probably speaks for many when she complains:

> We do not know what to do with Haggai in the canon. He crops up in the midst of the goodly fellowship of the prophets like a misguided stranger from the wrong part of town. No cry for social justice escapes his lips, no assurance that God dwells with the humble and contrite. Instead, he reeks of something that smells very much like the external and superficial religion of which we would all like to be rid.[203]

One reason for the absence of ethical admonition in both Haggai and Zechariah may have to do with the particular times in which these prophets ministered. Theirs was a period of rugged difficulty and harsh deprivation so far as the majority of those who had returned to Judah from the exile were concerned. As Tollington says, "Ethical norms and behaviour tend to deteriorate when societies have become settled and complacent, when life for large numbers in the community has become comfortable and when the problems caused by war or disaster have gone out of recent memory."[204] In a later generation ethical issues would again prove to be an urgent concern for the people of Judah. But for Haggai the defining issue in 520 B.C. was the temple. Everything else paled in significance before the task of restoring this house of worship.

Nonetheless, Haggai's contribution to Old Testament theology should not be minimized. His message to those who returned from the exile was in fact a theological message. What drove his relentless urging of the rebuilding of the temple was his theology of the temple, and not some sort of fanatical preoccupation with architectural grandeur. It was his theology of who the Lord is that framed his call for appropriate submission to the will of the sovereign Lord for postexilic Israel. It was his theology of holiness that mandated the warning that an impure people were incapable of pure worship but instead

---

[201] Childs, *Introduction*, 470.

[202] On elements of continuity and discontinuity between preexilic and postexilic prophets see D. L. Petersen, "Rethinking the End of Prophecy," in *»Wünschet Jerusalem Frieden«: Collected Communications to the XIIth Congress of the International Organization for the Study of the Old Testament*, BEATAJ 13 (Frankfurt am Main: Peter Lang, 1988), 65–71.

[203] Achtemeier, *Nahum–Malachi*, 95.

[204] Tollington, *Tradition and Innovation*, 77.

defiled everything with which they came into contact. It was his theology of the revelatory prophetic word that stimulated his demands for an appropriate response on the part of a lethargic and self-centered people who in spite of their disobedience remained a divinely chosen nation. It was his theology of human responsibility that formed the basis of his urgent call to the people for appropriate action. It was his theology of the prior promises to the royal line of David that caused him to attach special significance to Zerubbabel's governorship. To read Haggai without adequate reflection on his theology is therefore to fail to understand the message of this prophet.

In short there is an assumed theology that provides the underpinning for this brief book.[205] If that theology is not systematic or spelled out in detail, it is nonetheless a valuable prophetic contribution to the theology of post-exilic Judaism. It is a theology that caught the attention of at least one New Testament author who used Haggai's writings as a springboard for under-scoring certain eschatological elements of his own theology. The following discussion will summarize some of these theological themes.

*The Temple.*    It would be difficult to overestimate the importance of the Jerusalem temple to Old Testament literature and history of the first millennium B.C.[206] The temple plays a prominent theological role in much of the Old Testament in general and certainly in the Book of Haggai in particular. The single most important theological theme in the Book of Haggai concerns the centrality of the Jerusalem temple to the religious life of Jews of the post–exilic period.[207] This fierce prophet of the restoration was single-minded in his commitment to bring to rapid completion the task of rebuilding the house of the Lord. For Haggai the temple derived its great importance from the fact that it was nothing less than "the LORD's house" (*bêt YHWH,* 1:2) or "the LORD's temple" (*hêkal YHWH,* 2:15,18). Even more emphatically, the temple could be called "the house of the LORD Almighty" (*bêt YHWH ṣĕbāʾôt,* 1:14); that is to say, it was the one building that was particularly associated with the presence of the sovereign Lord. Because it was such, the Lord himself did not shrink back from calling the temple "my house" (*bêtî,* 1:9). It was in the rebuilding of this structure that the Lord "takes pleasure," and it is the one place where he would be uniquely "honored" (1:8). The Lord

---

[205] For a helpful summary of the theology not only of Haggai but of all the Minor Prophets, see R. B. Chisholm Jr., "A Theology of the Minor Prophets," in *A Biblical Theology of the Old Testament* (Chicago: Moody, 1991), 397–433.

[206] It is therefore not surprising that the Jerusalem temple has so captured the attention of people over the centuries. As Meyers points out, "No other building of the ancient world, either while it stood in Jerusalem or in the millennia since its final destruction, has been the focus of so much attention throughout the ages" ("Temple, Jerusalem," *ABD* 6 [1992]: 350).

[207] In the Hb. Bible there is considerable theological significance attached not only to the temple but to the city of Jerusalem as well. On the theological significance of the city of Jerusalem in the Hb. Scriptures, see S. Talmon, "The Biblical Concept of Jerusalem," *JES* 8 (1971): 300–316.

promised in the future to fill the temple with his glory in such a way that its splendor would surpass even that of the justly famous Solomonic temple (2:7,9; cf. 2:3). For Haggai the temple held tremendous theological significance as a structure with which the Lord had chosen to associate himself in a most unique way. A corollary to this belief was the conclusion that the temple should be afforded appropriate respect and commitment on the part of the followers of the Lord. Due to its central importance for the religious life of the Jewish people in Old Testament times, it is not too much to say that for centuries the temple actually helped define what it meant to be Jewish.[208]

Criticism of Haggai's restricted theological focus perhaps fails to grasp the theological importance of the temple to normative Jewish life in Old Testament times.[209] Without the temple it was impossible to fulfill certain basic aspects of Jewish religious life, such as various requirements of sacrifice and corporate worship. Furthermore, the temple was the special place where the Lord resided (1 Kgs 8:12; Ezek 43:7); it was his unique "resting place" (Ps 132:14). This is not to say that faithful Jews in the Old Testament period had a notion that somehow God could be entirely and exclusively contained in the temple. This was clearly not the case. Even Solomon, who initiated the building of the first temple, reasoned as follows:

> But will God really dwell on earth with men? The heavens, even the highest heavens, cannot contain you. How much less this temple I have built! (1 Kgs 8:27; cf. Isa 66:1)

Haggai himself, before the work of rebuilding the temple commenced, was able to announce to the people on the Lord's behalf, "'I am with you,' declares the LORD" (Hag 1:13). From such references it is clear that the realization of the divine presence did not absolutely require the existence of the temple.

Nevertheless, the temple was the defining center for much of Old Testament Judaism, both from a religious standpoint and from a national standpoint as well. For that reason the Babylonian destruction of the temple in 586 B.C. no doubt produced a level of religious despair and emotional confusion on the part of those who experienced it that is difficult for modern readers fully to comprehend. When in 538 B.C. the exile officially ended with Cyrus's decree permitting the Jews to leave Babylon and to return to their ancient homeland, the reconstruction of the demolished Solomonic temple should have been a major priority for all those who dreamed of a restored nation and a normalized religious life that could once again fulfill the

---

[208] For a discussion of how Jewish ethnicity was defined during the Persian period, see M. W. Hamilton, "Who Was a Jew? Jewish Ethnicity during the Achaemenid Period," *ResQ* 37 (1995): 102–17.

[209] As May points out, "When one appreciates the positive contribution of the temple to the religion of Israel in the pre-exilic period and what it meant in the development of post-exilic Judaism, Haggai's role is seen in better perspective" ("'This People' and 'This Nation,'" 195).

demands of the Torah. Since in the past the Lord had chosen to identify himself in such a unique way with Mount Zion and the temple (cf. Ps 78:68–69), the continuing state of degradation experienced by that structure was for the faithful Jewish remnant nothing less than an embarrassing reminder of the seeming absence of their God from their midst. Furthermore, those who were unsympathetic to the Jewish plight would no doubt have seen the ruined temple as a symbol of the utter helplessness of Israel's God, who appeared powerless to act on behalf of his people by preventing this national tragedy.

In such a context, what gave special significance to the temple was not the belief that God's presence could somehow be restricted to a building of this sort. Rather, its importance derived from its association with the Lord's name and person (cf. 2 Chr 6:5–9,20,26,33–34,38). The logical corollary of this association was this: to dishonor the temple was also to dishonor the Lord.[210] To allow the temple to continue in ruins, Haggai maintained, really amounted to a failure on the part of the people to honor appropriately the God of Israel.[211] It is as though they were unconcerned that the Lord should be left

---

[210] For helpful discussion of the significance of temples in ancient Israel and other cultures of the ANE see G. E. Wright, "The Significance of the Temple in the Ancient Near East. Part 3. The Temple in Palestine-Syria," *BA* 7 (1944): 65–77; V. Hurowitz, *I Have Built You an Exalted House: Temple Building in the Bible in Light of Mesopotamian and Northwest Semitic Writings,* JSOTSup 115 (Sheffield: Sheffield Academic Press, 1992). On religious and philosophical points of correspondence between heavenly and earthly temples in ANE thought, see A. S. Kapelrud, "Temple Building: A Task for Gods and Kings," *Or* 32 (1963): 56–62. On temples during the Achaemenid period, see J. Blenkinsopp, "Temple and Society in Achaemenid Judah," in *Second Temple Studies: Persian Period,* JSOTSup 117 (Sheffield: JSOT Press, 1991), 22–53; P. R. Bedford, *Temple Restoration in Early Achaemenid Judah,* JSJSup 65 (Leiden: Brill, 2001). On temple taxation and the economy of Achaemenid Yehud, see J. Schaper, "The Jerusalem Temple as an Instrument of the Achaemenid Fiscal Administration," *VT* 45 (1995): 528–39. For a summary of understanding of the temple in biblical and postbiblical Jewish literature, see L. Schaya, "The Meaning of the Temple," *SCR* 5 (1971): 241–46. On the temple in late biblical literature see D. L. Petersen, "The Temple in Persian Period Prophetic Texts," in *Second Temple Studies: Persian Period,* JSOTSup 117 (Sheffield: JSOT Press, 1991), 125–44. On the significance of the Jerusalem temple see Meyers, "Temple," 350–69. On the role of the temple in the postexilic period see S. Japhet, "The Temple in the Restoration Period: Reality and Ideology," *USQR* 44 (1991): 195–291. On the importance of the temple and the significance of its demise to Jewish apocalyptic literature, see J. J. Collins, *Jerusalem and the Temple in Jewish Apocalyptic Literature of the Second Temple Period,* International Rennert Guest Lecture Series 1 (Remat-Gan: Bar-Ilan University, 1998).

[211] D. J. A. Clines' argument that for Haggai the temple was nothing more than a treasury for storing and displaying valuables comes close to being a *reductio ad absurdum*. He disallows that Haggai can properly be viewed as understanding the temple to be a place of sacrifice, a place of prayer, a location of the presence of God, etc. As a result he attributes to Haggai a severely truncated view of the function of the temple, claiming that many commentators are guilty of illegitimate totality transfer with regard to the word "temple." But to situate Haggai's understanding of the temple within the broader context of the theology of the period, as most commentators seek to do, does not require illegitimate totality transfer to Haggai of nuances that the word "temple" carries only elsewhere, in the way that Clines avers (p. 57). Although the methodological fallacy of such totality transfer admittedly is a danger that is present in lexical research, it should not inhibit legitimate attempts to situate the biblical writers in their historical and cultural milieu, nor should it lead to an excessive isolation of the biblical writers from their proper contexts. In his attempts to deconstruct the Book of Haggai, Clines has rather surprisingly dismissed a good deal of competent scholarship on Haggai ("Haggai's Temple, Constructed, Deconstructed and Reconstructed," *SJOT* 7 [1993]: 51–77).

homeless among his own people, "a Jerusalemite vagabond" as it were.[212] To honor God by the restoration of the temple, however, would bring renewed evidence of God's presence with his covenant people, a theme by no means overlooked by Haggai (cf. 1:13; 2:4). In this matter it appears that "Haggai was following the ideals of Ezekiel with regard to the development of a priestly commonwealth, as indicated by the way he related the prophetic eschatology of salvation to the building of the Temple."[213]

But times were hard for the returnees, and the challenges of eking out a meager existence for themselves and their families must have been physically and emotionally draining during those early years. Religious enthusiasm for the temple was quickly eclipsed by the backbreaking rigors of simply making a living in a land that was not particularly hospitable to their return. To many the time did not seem right for such an expensive and demanding enterprise as the construction of a temple worthy of the name would require. It would take a strong prophetic voice to awaken the returnees' slumbering conscience and to enthuse in them a committed spirit to the task at hand. It fell to Haggai to translate a theology of the temple into a course of individual and corporate action that would be consistent with that theology.[214]

*Holiness as a Prerequisite for Worship.* Haggai's emphasis on the temple is of course related to his theology of worship. It seems clear from this book that the prophet did not entertain the notion that worship in the rebuilt temple could be merely a perfunctory matter of going through certain external rituals. Haggai stressed that worship must be accompanied by appropriate holiness and purity of motives on the part of those who would approach the Lord. He makes clear that it is possible for worship itself to become defiled to the point of being rejected by God. To drive this point home the prophet sent representatives of his audience to the priests to inquire about laws of ritual contamination (2:10–14). The priests clarified the questions posed to them by pointing out two quite different possibilities. On the one hand, holiness cannot be transmitted by contact from one thing to another; on the other hand, defilement can be so transmitted. So it was with the Jewish remnant. Those who were in a holy condition could be made unholy by involvement with unholy things. But those who were in an unholy condition could not be made holy by involvement with holy things. The words of 2:14 are blunt in their condemnation: "'So it is with this people and this nation in my sight,' declares the LORD. 'Whatever they do and whatever they offer there is defiled.'"

---

[212] The expression is M. C. Love's (*The Evasive Text: Zechariah 1–8 and the Frustrated Reader*, JSOTSup 296 [Sheffield: Sheffield Academic Press, 1999], 174).

[213] Harrison, *Introduction*, 947.

[214] For a helpful summary of the theology of the temple, particularly from the standpoint of certain of the psalms, see R. E. Clements, "Temple and Land: A Significant Aspect of Israel's Worship," *TGUOS* 19 (1963): 16–28.

This emphasis on purity and holiness is a significant element in Haggai's theology. It underscores the necessity that there be more than perfunctory ritualism in the worship of the Lord. Even so noble a task as the restoration of the temple would not by itself render an impure people holy before their God. By being impure, they in turn defiled everything with which they came into contact.[215] In light of this emphasis on holiness in the Book of Haggai, Kirkpatrick is quite correct to say: "It is the strangest misconception of the teaching of these prophets to charge them with a heartless and unspiritual formalism. It is abundantly clear that they looked for holiness as the true goal of Israel's training."[216]

*The Prophetic Word as Divine Revelation.* The Old Testament prophets viewed themselves as representatives of the Lord who were called to deliver a message that had been given to them by none other than the Lord himself. The specific message they preached varies widely from prophet to prophet and from occasion to occasion. Sometimes they pronounced fierce judgment upon the people because of their sin and spiritual failure. At other times they brought great hope and consolation for the future. They confronted kings and lesser figures alike, announcing the divine will for all sorts of situations. The content of their prophetic messages shifted according to need. But the Old Testament prophets have in common one consistent characteristic: they understood their message to be one that had come to them by divine revelation.

Haggai stands in this prophetic tradition. We repeatedly read in this book that "the word of the LORD came through" (or "to") the prophet Haggai (1:1,3; 2:1,10,20). Such formulaic expressions underscore Haggai's perception of the divine origin of his message. Furthermore, he tells the people that "this is what the LORD Almighty says" (1:2,5,7; 2:6,11), indicating his conviction that he functions as a spokesman for the Lord. He introduces his messages with such unflinchingly bold assertions as the following: "declares the LORD Almighty" (1:9; 2:4,7,8,9[2x],23[2x]); "declares the LORD" (1:13; 2:4[2x],14,17,23); "says the LORD" (1:8); "the voice of the LORD their God" (1:12); "this message of the LORD" (1:13).

The frequent occurrence of such language is significant.[217] Clearly this

---

[215] Stressing Haggai's emphasis on restoration of the temple, F. James says that "Haggai was apparently little troubled by the sin of the people" ("Thoughts on Haggai and Zechariah," *JBL* 53 [1934]: 231). But this is something of a caricature of Haggai's emphasis. The same prophet who was so emphatic about the importance of rebuilding the temple was also insistent on the need for holiness on the part of the people. To view Haggai as tolerant toward sin, or mechanical in his understanding of it, fails to take seriously his stress on holiness as a prerequisite for worship.

[216] Kirkpatrick, *Doctrine of the Prophets*, 433.

[217] For an analysis of these and other formulae used in OT literature in connection with prophetic speech and activity, see S. Bretón, *Vocación y misión: formulario profético*, AnBib 111 (Rome: Editrice Pontificio Istituto Biblico, 1987).

prophet viewed his message as originating not with himself but with the heavenly Lord who had commissioned him to speak boldly in this way. The oft-repeated assertion that his message was given by revelation from the Lord is perhaps "the most striking feature in Haggai's message."[218] The implication that all of this held for Haggai's audience was that his message should be afforded no less attention and obedience than what was due a message coming directly from the Lord.[219]

Haggai, along with Zechariah and Malachi, stands at the end of this succession of prophets who were the Lord's conveyors of divine revelation. When Malachi passed from the scene, revelatory activity of that sort ceased, not to be renewed for some four hundred years. In the later Jewish community the absence of the true prophetic voice was described in terms of a departure of God's Spirit from their midst, even though allowance was made for ongoing divine communication with the people through the so-called *Bat-Qol* (i.e., "daughter of the voice").[220]

*Divine Sovereignty.* Throughout the Book of Haggai, the Lord is pictured as an absolute sovereign who, rather than finding his intentions to be influenced adversely by persons or events outside of himself, is the one who moves in nature and in human history to bring about the accomplishment of his own purposes. He is very much in control of nature, as may be seen in the following references in Haggai. The Lord is capable of manipulating the weather, withholding precipitation if he chooses to do so (1:10–11). He can determine the success or failure of the harvest and the economic conditions that are the result thereof (1:5–6,10–11). He can, if he wishes, cause drought (1:11) and various plant diseases that destroy crops (2:17,19). He can send devastating hail and the sirocco, or east wind, that blows off the Arabian desert and mercilessly "blasts" the crops of Judah (2:17). The Lord has the power to disrupt the world order, bringing about cosmic shaking of unprecedented proportions (2:6,21). He can also bring renewed prosperity to failed agricultural productions if his people will but respond appropriately to his warnings (2:19).

Not only is the Lord viewed as being sovereign over nature, he is also sovereign over human activity. It is the Lord who awakens and stirs the spirit of Jewish leaders and laypeople alike, leading them to resume work on the temple (1:14). It is the Lord who can bring to nothing the misplaced efforts of

---

[218] So G. L. Robinson, "Haggai," *ISBE* 2 (1939): 1318.

[219] As I. H. Eybers remarks, "If Haggai's frequent claims that he was the mouthpiece of the Lord are true, then it is theologically unwarranted [sic] to neglect his words" ("Haggai, the Mouthpiece of the Lord," *TE* 1 [1968]: 62).

[220] *Sanh.* 11a records the following observation: "Our Rabbis taught: Since the death of the last prophets, Haggai, Zechariah and Malachi, the Holy Spirit [of prophetic inspiration] departed from Israel; yet they were still able to avail themselves of the *Bath-Kol*."

his people to ensure their own advantage while the work of God suffers due to their inattention to it (1:9). He can even move the leaders of pagan nations to fulfill his will by contributing their wealth for the building of his temple (2:7). After all, their silver and gold is not really theirs; it actually belongs to him (2:8). Those who arrogantly think otherwise will painfully discover that he can overturn their rule, shatter their power, and destroy their armies (2:22). But those who serve him will witness the peace, or wellness, that he promises to provide for his work (2:9). Clearly, in Haggai's thought Yahweh is a sovereign Lord. Related to this emphasis on divine sovereignty is the implied notion that by comparison human beings are powerless to thwart whatever God chooses to do.

Yahweh's sovereignty is also hinted at in the phrase "the LORD of hosts." Fourteen times in this book the Lord is referred to in this way (1:2,5,7,9,14; 2:4,6,7,8,9[2x],11,23[2x]). The same expression in earlier biblical books often carries military overtones, with the nuance that Yahweh is "Lord over (heavenly) armies." But in the postexilic literature this phrase seems to have become simply a way of referring to the sovereign Lord.[221] As such it emphasizes his ability, indeed his right, to rule over all creation and to govern the outcome of history.[222] "The LORD of hosts" is in Haggai a favorite designation for the deity, providing a fitting complement to this prophet's thoroughgoing emphasis on the Lord's sovereignty.

*Human Responsibility.* Haggai's emphasis on the sovereignty of God does not mean for him that human beings have no responsibility in the fulfillment of the divine will. It is assumed throughout Haggai that God's pur-

---

[221] The word צְבָאוֹת appears in divine titles some 285 times in the Hb. Bible, more often in later writings than in earlier ones. It does not occur at all in Genesis–Judges. The most frequent users of the expression are Isaiah (62 times), Jeremiah (82 times), Zechariah (53 times), Malachi (24 times), and Haggai (14 times). The expression יהוה צְבָאוֹת ("the LORD of hosts") occurs 265 times; the expression יהוה אֱלֹהֵי צְבָאוֹת ("the LORD God of hosts") occurs 18 times. *HALOT* summarizes the following views that have been advocated for interpreting the phrase. (1) It portrays Yahweh as the God of armies; as such he is in charge of his troops. (2) It portrays Yahweh as creator of the stars. (3) It portrays Yahweh as one who has stripped Canaanite mythological powers of their strength. (4) It portrays Yahweh as in charge of a heavenly household. (5) It portrays Yahweh as in control of both earthly and heavenly beings. (6) It portrays Yahweh in a general way as almighty; in this case צְבָאוֹת functions as an intensive abstract plural. It is this latter usage that seems especially to describe the postexilic usage of the phrase יהוה צְבָאוֹת in Haggai and elsewhere. See further *HALOT,* 996–97. The most exhaustive treatment to date of the expression יהוה צְבָאוֹת is that of B. N. Wambacq, *L'épithète divine Jahvé Seba'ôt: Étude philologique, historique et éxégétique* (Desclée: De Brouwer, 1947). See also T. N. D. Mettinger, *The Dethronement of Sabaoth: Studies in the Shem and Kabod Theologies,* ConBOT 18 (Lund: CWK Gleerup, 1982).

[222] This seems clearly to be the understanding of the word assumed by the ancient Greek translators. The LXX usually renders יהוה צְבָאוֹת ("the LORD of hosts") by κύριος παντοκράτωρ ("the Lord Almighty"). But Kessler emphasizes the cultic associations of this term as especially appropriate to Haggai's focus on the temple as a divine dwelling (*The Book of Haggai,* 122).

poses will be accomplished through dedicated human effort and endeavor. The fact that the Lord takes initiative by stirring up the spirit of individuals to do his will does not mean that they thereby become automated machines. Neither part of the synergism between divine sovereignty and human responsibility does Haggai take to exclude the other.[223] For this reason the prophet urges the people to consider their part in the advancement of the kingdom of God, and he warns of the consequences that will follow if they choose to shirk their divinely appointed role. Repeatedly he tells them, "Consider your ways" (1:5,7). The Lord will continue to be displeased with them so long as his house remains a ruin, while they busy themselves with their own houses (1:9). They are urged to "be strong," to "work," and to remind themselves that their covenant-keeping God has promised to be ever with them (2:4–5). God will sovereignly accomplish his purposes in their midst, but he will do so through the intermediate agency of his people. They must accept that covenantal responsibility and respond in an appropriate way. The prophet by divine appointment played an essential role in awakening the people to their responsibility.

*A Future for the Davidic Dynasty.* Haggai's final sermon shifts attention from the rebuilding of the temple to future prospects for a renewed Davidic rule. Haggai 2:20–23 in effect reverses the curse pronounced upon Jehoiachin in Jer 22:24 and promises that Zerubbabel will be as it were a signet ring on the Lord's hand. The imagery used in Hag 2:20–23 to describe Zerubbabel is suggestive of his being a divinely appointed representative who is thereby invested with royal authority. The scene is described in language that is ultimately eschatological in intent,[224] though at the same time the language is reminiscent of similar language used in the Torah to describe the Lord's mighty acts at the time of the exodus. It appears that Zerubbabel is here a representative figure, much as David is elsewhere in the Hebrew Bible.

---

[223] On the relationship between these two concepts within the framework of OT covenants, see D. N. Freedman, "Divine Commitment and Human Obligation: The Covenant Theme," *Int* 18 (1964): 419–31.

[224] I cannot agree with S. Mowinckel's assessment that "the message of Haggai and Zechariah has nothing to do with eschatology. What they are waiting for is a complete historical revolution in the Near East, attributed, of course, to the guidance of Yahweh and to the intervention of His miraculous power, but developing within the course of empirical history and working through normal human means. 'By His spirit' Yahweh will guide events so that the world powers destroy each other in the chaos which has arisen all over the east as a result of the death of Cambyses; and Israel alone will remain unscathed and will reap the benefit. This may be described as a fantastic and unrealistic expectation, but that does not make it eschatology" (*He That Cometh* [New York: Abingdon, n.d.], 121). To restrict Haggai's message entirely to its sixth-century context and to disallow any anticipation of more distant messianic hope does not do justice to certain portions of the book. For an approach that stresses the eschatological elements found in Haggai, see H. F. van Rooy, "Eschatology and Audience: The Eschatology of Haggai," *OTE* 1 (1988): 49–63; J. A. Kessler, "The Shaking of the Nations: An Eschatological View," *JETS* 30 (1987): 159–66.

The passage thus promises that a Davidide will at some future point again rule as the Lord's chosen agent. That this promise did not find fulfillment in Zerubbabel himself was not taken by the early readers of the book to mean that the promise had completely failed, as some modern readers have concluded. The ancient Jewish community entertained the hope for a full but future realization of the promise.[225] Although Davidic rule had been forfeited throughout the period of the exile as a consequence of national sin, the prophet held out prospects for a glorious reversal of fortunes. The Book of Haggai thus ends with an expression of divine faithfulness to earlier promises made with regard to the continuation of Davidic rule through a future heir to the throne.[226]

## 13. Intertextuality in Haggai

Old Testament writers neither thought nor wrote in a way that was detached from or inattentive to those sacred writings that the Lord had previously given to Israel. From a literary standpoint they were not islands to themselves. The natural reflex of their familiarity with earlier sacred writings was that they tended to call to mind images and/or phraseology from that literature in order to punctuate their own messages. In that sense they were somewhat like the modern preacher whose vocabulary and rhetoric may at times, even without conscious intention, reflect a deep familiarity with the Bible.[227]

Like other prophetic authors Haggai too makes use of earlier sacred writings, indicating both his familiarity with that material and his readiness to

---

[225] In more recent Jewish thought there has occasionally been an attempt to explain almost all of Haggai, and Zechariah as well, in a futuristic way. See A. Gross, "R. Abraham Saba's Abbreviated Messianic Commentary on Haggai and Zechariah," in *Studies in Medieval Jewish History and Literature,* Harvard Judaic Monographs 2 (Cambridge: Harvard University Press, 1984), 389–401.

[226] J. E. Tollington has argued, to the contrary, that the prologue and epilogue of the Book of Judges give evidence for thinking that that book was edited in the postexilic period in a way intended to lend support to Haggai's prophecies of a dynastic monarchy ("The Book of Judges: The Result of Post-Exilic Exegesis?" in *Intertextuality in Ugarit and Israel: Papers Read at the Tenth Joint Meeting of the Society for Old Testament Study and Het Oudestamentisch Werkgezelschap in Nederland en Belgie, Held at Oxford, 1997,* Oudtestamentische Studiën 40 [Leiden: Brill, 1998], 186–96).

[227] For a helpful discussion of many of the methodological issues involved in locating and evaluating instances of quotation in the prophetic literature of the Hb. Bible, see the following recent work: R. L. Schultz, *The Search for Quotation: Verbal Parallels in the Prophets,* JSOTSup 180 (Sheffield: Sheffield Academic Press, 1999). See also the following helpful collection of essays dealing with various aspects of intertextuality: J. C. de Moor, ed., *Intertextuality in Ugarit and Israel: Papers Read at the Tenth Joint Meeting of the Society for Old Testament Study and Het Oudtestamentisch Werkgezelschap in Nederland en Belgie, Held at Oxford, 1997,* Oudtestamentische Studiën 40 (Leiden: Brill, 1998).

use it to enhance his own writing and to advance his own argument.[228] In Haggai's case this use of prior sacred writings may be thought of in several categories. First, there are places where Haggai seems to be echoing earlier traditions in a somewhat general way, without actually quoting any particular biblical passage. Mason, for example, calls attention to Haggai's adaptation of the following thematic elements found in earlier biblical writers: the Zion traditions found in certain of the psalms, hopes expressed in the enthronement psalms, traces of Second Isaiah, and the motif of the Lord's glory as found in Ezekiel.[229] Although Haggai does not specifically quote passages from these themes, he does utilize this earlier material in the development of his own message. Tuell has also stressed Ezekiel's influence on Haggai and Zechariah 1–8, especially in matters of form.[230] Second, in some cases there is enough similarity between Haggai's words and those of another biblical writer as to make clear that an earlier specific passage was in the mind of Haggai, even though the reference does not include direct quotation and the correspondence may be somewhat faint. Third, in other cases the degree of verbal similarity that is present makes it clear that a specific passage is being more directly quoted or alluded to in Haggai. In such cases it is assumed that the reader of Haggai will be familiar not only with the citation itself, but also with its context in the original setting. That assumed context will be important for understanding the use Haggai is making of the earlier biblical text. Of these three categories mentioned, the latter two will be the focus of the following discussion.[231]

---

[228] For a helpful discussion of intertextuality in the Minor Prophets see J. D. Nogalski, "Intertextuality and the Twelve," in *Forming Prophetic Literature: Essays on Isaiah and the Twelve in Honor of John D. W. Watts*, JSOTSup 235 (Sheffield: Sheffield Academic Press, 1996), 102–24.

[229] See R. Mason, "The Messiah in the Postexilic Old Testament Literature," in *King and Messiah in Israel and the Ancient Near East: Proceedings of the Oxford Old Testament Seminar*, JSOTSup 270 (Sheffield: Sheffield Academic Press, 1998), 340. Mason has also discussed in some detail a number of correspondences between the Book of Haggai and the addresses found in the Books of Chronicles. The similarities he finds involve various details of theme and subject matter as well as certain items of style and form; see *Preaching the Tradition: Homily and Hermeneutics after the Exile* (Cambridge: Cambridge University Press, 1990), 185–95.

[230] Treating Haggai and Zechariah 1–8 as having been edited together, S. S. Tuell argues that this block of material shows influence from the Book of Ezekiel. He considers the following areas of possible contact: the centrality of temple and cult, the proper use of precise dating formulae, the vision reports of Zechariah, and the use of the first person in Zechariah ("Haggai–Zechariah: Prophecy after the Manner of Ezekiel," in *Thematic Threads in the Book of the Twelve*, BZAW 325 [Berlin: Walter de Gruyter, 2003], 273–91).

[231] Discussions of biblical intertextuality vary significantly with regard to what literary features should be included under the rubric of intertextuality. R. L. Schultz has pointed out some of the confusion that has resulted from this terminological imprecision and has appealed for stricter controls for determining what should pass for intertextuality ("The Ties That Bind: Intertextuality, the Identification of Verbal Parallels, and Reading Strategies in the Book of the Twelve," in *Thematic Threads in the Book of the Twelve*, BZAW 325 [Berlin: Walter de Gruyter, 2003], 27–45).

*Haggai 1:6,10–11 and Deut 28:18,22–23,38–40,51.*   When Haggai described the devastation of recent crop failure and the resultant economic depression that followed on its heels, he did so in language that is reminiscent of deuteronomic texts. Haggai did not regard these disasters as due merely to fortuitous events of nature. He interpreted the problems of the returnees as being grounded in theological patterns of blessing and cursing as articulated in Deuteronomy 28. It is this language that Haggai invoked as he described the plight of his people (cf. also Mic 6:14–15). They were a covenantal people who could not avoid the responsibilities that were an essential part of their unique relationship to the Lord. The implications of Haggai's appeal to Deuteronomy 28 are both positive and negative. On the one hand, the fact that this language is invoked has a positive side in that it implicitly acknowledges that this people stands in a covenant relationship with the Lord. Otherwise the language would have no appropriate place here. On the other hand, the language has a negative effect in that it calls attention to the status of the people as cursed for their failure to obey the Lord of the covenant. These verses thus carry with them deuteronomic associations that would not have escaped the attention of Haggai's audience. This deuteronomic connection forms a major element in the theological underpinning of Haggai's message.

*Haggai 1:10 and Zech 8:12.*   This example is different from the others in that it is not a case of Haggai using earlier biblical material but a case of a later biblical writer making use of Haggai. In Hag 1:10 the prophet informs the people that because of their failure to fulfill the Lord's will "the heavens have withheld their dew and the earth its crops." The lack of adequate rainfall, and with that the failed agricultural productivity they had experienced, according to Haggai were due to God's judgment upon them. Very similar language appears in Zech 8:12b. There Zechariah says, "The ground will produce its crops, and the heavens will drop their dew." Two differences between the Haggai text and the Zechariah text stand out. First, the order of the two statements is reversed in Zechariah, where mention of the heavens follows mention of the ground. Second, the negative effects of Haggai's statement are transformed into positive effects in Zechariah. It is possible that the order of the two statements has been reversed in Zechariah so as to call attention to the reversal of conditions that the Lord had brought about for his people by the time of Zechariah's message. Or perhaps this is just one more example of a general tendency in Zechariah to establish verbal linkage with Haggai, in this case with the added effect of "heavens" in Hag 1:10 and Zech 8:12 creating a chiastic structure that links the two sections together literarily.[232] This is not the only example of such an inverted quotation in Old Testament

---

[232] See Meyers and Meyers, *Haggai, Zechariah 1–8,* 423.

literature; it is a device that crops up a number of times elsewhere.[233]

*Haggai 2:4–5 and Josh 1:6–9.*   With the death of Moses the imposing task of leadership for the people who had experienced the exodus from Egypt fell to his successor Joshua. In need of encouragement for his task, Joshua no doubt drew great strength from the Lord's promise recorded in Josh 1:5: "No one will be able to stand up against you all the days of your life. As I was with Moses, so I will be with you; I will never leave you nor forsake you." In Josh 1:6–9 the imperatives "be strong" *(ḥăzaq)* and "be courageous" *('ĕmāṣ)* are repeated three times, along with promises to Joshua of divine presence and protection as blessings that the Lord would bestow on Moses' successor as he was faithful to the Lord's expectations of him. The language of Josh 1:6–9 (cf. v. 18) must have left an indelible impression upon the community in subsequent genera- tions who drew renewed encouragement from the example of God's faithful- ness to Moses and Joshua. It is this language that Haggai adopts in Hag 2:4–5 (cf. Deut 31:6,7,23). The imperative verb "be strong" *(ḥăzaq)* is repeated in Joshua-like fashion three times, along with the promise of divine presence to energize the work of the people. Haggai 2:5 even alludes to the exodus event as providing a reassuring precedent for the Lord's faithfulness to his postexilic people. It is clear that Haggai's language echoes the passage in Joshua and adapts it to the very different circumstances confronting Haggai and his people.

*Haggai 2:6,7,21 and Joel 4:16 [ET 3:16].*   In the eschatological con- clusion to the Book of Joel, the prophet promises: "The LORD will roar from Zion and thunder from Jerusalem; the earth and the sky will tremble. But the LORD will be a refuge for his people, a stronghold for the people of Israel." The language of Hag 2:6,7,21 may be reminiscent of Joel's lan- guage, although the actual verbal similarities are not decisive for this con- clusion. Both passages speak of an eschatological shaking of the heavens and earth, using identical (though admittedly common) vocabulary. There are minor differences in the verb forms that are used and in the definiteness of the object phrases. It is possible, perhaps even likely, that Haggai is adapting Joel's phraseology to his later, postexilic context. But some allow- ance must be made here for the possibility of a more coincidental agree- ment of wording.

*Haggai 2:17 and Amos 4:9.*   In his indictment against Israel for not hav- ing returned to her God, the prophet Amos, speaking in behalf of the Lord, says: "'Many times I struck your gardens and vineyards, I struck them with blight and mildew. Locusts devoured your fig and olive trees, yet you have not returned to me,' declares the LORD" (Amos 4:9). This language is echoed in Hag 2:17, where the prophet says, "I struck all the work of your hands

---

[233] The expression "inverted quotation" is P. C. Beentjes'. His discussion of this phenomenon in the Hb. Bible is helpful; see "Discovering a New Path of Intertextuality: Inverted Quotations and Their Dynamics," in *Literary Structure and Rhetorical Strategies in the Hebrew Bible* (Assen: Van Gorcum, 1996), 31–50.

with blight, mildew and hail, yet you did not turn to me,' declares the LORD."
The verbal correspondences between the two passages are obvious, even in
the English text.[234] In the Hebrew text the first four words of Hag 2:17
exactly match the first four words of Amos 4:9. The precise correspondence
in wording has led Elliger to suggest that the words in Haggai may be a later
addition,[235] but this is an unnecessary conjecture. It is not only later editors
of biblical material who quoted earlier biblical writers; biblical writers themselves also engaged in this practice. Although elsewhere it is often difficult
to determine priority in cases like these, here there can be no question of who
is quoting whom. Amos wrote in the eighth century, whereas Haggai wrote
in the late sixth century. It is therefore Haggai who borrows the language of
Amos. Furthermore, the language found in both prophets is ultimately drawn
from the curses of Deut 28:22, where blight and mildew are listed among the
judgments that the Lord will send upon his people Israel if they choose to
disobey the covenant stipulations that he gave to them.

*Haggai 2:22 and Exod 15:1.* In the song of Moses found in Exod 15:1–
21 we find a celebration of the Lord's salvific acts in behalf of Israel as evidenced in the defeat of the Egyptians and the successful exodus of the Israelites from Egypt under the leadership of Moses. Exodus 15:1 says, "Then
Moses and the Israelites sang this song to the LORD: 'I will sing to the
LORD, for he is highly exalted. The horse and its rider he has hurled into the
sea.'" In its Pentateuchal setting this language has a backward orientation; it
is focused on what the Lord did previously for his people through the exodus
event. But in Haggai's adaptation of this language it has a forward orientation; the focus is an eschatological scene of messianic proportions. Haggai
2:21 says: "I will overturn royal thrones and shatter the power of the foreign
kingdoms. I will overthrow chariots and their drivers; horses and their riders
will fall, each by the sword of his brother." The implication is that the messianic age will usher in a deliverance of the Lord's people that can be likened
to the exodus event in terms of its magnitude and significance.

Haggai's use of the Exodus passage in this way is a striking illustration of
the continuing vitality of the ancient sacred texts of Israel. Not only did such
texts have value for reminding later generations of the *magnalia Dei*, or mighty
acts of God, that he had previously performed in behalf of his people. Such
texts also took on new life as later prophets like Haggai invoked their images
and cadences to describe in vivid terms scenes of the coming eschaton.

*Haggai 2:23 and Jer 22:24.* With the exile fast approaching, Jeremiah
prophesied against the Judean king Jehoiachin (also known as Coniah),

---

[234] The NIV's rendering "yet you did not turn to me" in Hag 2:17 is problematic from a text-
critical perspective. For that matter the MT is very problematic here as well. For a brief treatment
of the text-critical issues see the discussion of that verse in the commentary.

[235] See note /ᵃ/ for Hag 2:17 in the critical apparatus of *BHS*.

warning of God's rejection of him. The Babylonians would soon take him into captivity, and he would live out the remainder of his life in a foreign land. The words of Jer 22:24–30 are bleak indeed:

"As surely as I live," declares the LORD, "even if you, Jehoiachin son of Jehoiakim king of Judah, were a signet ring on my right hand, I would still pull you off. I will hand you over to those who seek your life, those you fear—to Nebuchadnezzar king of Babylon and to the Babylonians. I will hurl you and the mother who gave you birth into another country, where neither of you was born, and there you both will die. You will never come back to the land you long to return to."

Is this man Jehoiachin a despised, broken pot,
    an object no one wants?
Why will he and his children be hurled out,
    cast into a land they do not know?
O land, land, land,
    hear the word of the LORD!
This is what the LORD says:
"Record this man as if childless,
    a man who will not prosper in his lifetime,
for none of his offspring will prosper,
    none will sit on the throne of David
    or rule anymore in Judah."

Jeremiah's imagery is striking, particularly the reference to the Lord's removal of a signet ring from his own finger as a metaphor for describing the divine rejection of this unfaithful Israelite king. Since the signet ring carried the royal seal signifying ownership and authority, its removal from the finger signified rejection and disapproval. As pictured by Jeremiah, the Lord has had enough of Jehoiachin's refusal to be a faithful and righteous co-regent over the Lord's people. Jehoiachin must be judged for his failures and set aside. Furthermore, this inexorable judgment upon King Jehoiachin was not limited to him personally. According to Jer 22:30, because of Jehoiachin's disobedience none of his descendants would be eligible for positions of royal authority in Judah.

Haggai's use of this text is remarkable for both its continuities and its discontinuities with the passage from Jeremiah. The metaphor of the signet ring on the Lord's hand to symbolize an Israelite leader is present in Haggai as it is in Jeremiah. In fact, Haggai's words are addressed to none other than the grandson of Jehoiachin, namely Zerubbabel. But rather than repeating the Lord's curse upon this line, Haggai signifies instead divine pleasure in Zerubbabel, promising in emphatic terms that "'On that day,' declares the LORD Almighty, 'I will take you, my servant Zerubbabel son of Shealtiel,' declares the LORD, 'and I will make you like my signet ring, for I have chosen you,' declares the LORD Almighty." Thus in Haggai we find reversal of the curse expressed by Jeremiah. It is inconceivable that Haggai recorded this promise to Zerubbabel without intending the connection to Jer 22:24 to be obvious to all who were familiar with earlier prophetic texts. Haggai 2:23 must be read in light of Jer 22:24.[236]

These instances of intertextuality suggest that Haggai saw himself as heir to the deuteronomistic traditions concerning blessing and cursing in connection with Israel's covenant faithfulness (or lack thereof). He also saw himself as heir to the prophetic traditions that described the Lord's relationship to Israel.[237] These deuteronomic and prophetic traditions provided an essential framework for casting new prophetic revelation from the Lord. Indeed, these earlier biblical writings formed one of the literary wells from which later prophets like Haggai drew much of the phraseology, imagery, and even content of their messages.

### 14. Haggai in the New Testament

The Book of Haggai is quoted only once in the New Testament, although certain language utilized in a few other New Testament passages may perhaps also be reminiscent of phraseology found in Haggai.

*New Testament Citation of Haggai.* In Heb 12:26 the unknown author of the epistle appeals to Haggai's prophecy that the Lord was about to shake both the heavens and the earth. Since this announcement appears twice in the Book of Haggai (Hag 2:6; 2:21), it is not entirely clear whether the New Testament writer has in mind one of these verses more than the other or whether

---

[236] Contrary to Y. Hoffman, I see no good reason to question the textual validity of Jer 22:24. Hoffman says: "It is inconceivable that Haggai, meaning to encourage Zerubbabel, would use the metaphor of a signet which had already lost its meaning by Jeremiah's prophecy. I therefore assume that Haggai was the first to use the metaphor. A counter-prophecy was then ascribed to Jeremiah and inserted into the prophetic anthology bearing his name, in order to nullify Haggai's theopolitical message. Both these prophecies, then, reflect a political polemic in Jerusalem in about 520 BCE. If this interpretation is correct, then Jer 22.24 is another example of the retrospective character of some of the apparent theopolitical sayings in the Bible" ("Reflections on the Relationship between Theopolitics, Prophecy and Historiography," in *Politics and Theopolitics in the Bible and Postbiblical Literature,* JSOTSup 171 [Sheffield: JSOT Press, 1994], 99).

[237] In light of the evidence discussed above, Alden's comment is somewhat surprising: "There is no clear evidence that Haggai borrowed from another prophet" ("Haggai," 574). The following comments by S. V. Wyrick also need some nuancing in that they overstate their case: "Haggai's authoritative appeal was to tradition, not to a received canon of sacred scripture; and, the traditions were how he imagined them to exist. . . . No authoritative writing is utilized by the prophet. The only authority is tradition" ("Haggai's Appeal to Tradition: Imagination Used as Authority," in *Religious Writings and Religious Systems: Systemic Analysis of Holy Books in Christianity, Islam, Buddhism, Greco-Roman Religions, Ancient Israel, and Judaism,* Brown Studies in Religion 1 (Atlanta: Scholars Press, 1989), 125.

he is merely summarizing the gist of both verses. The citation in Heb 12:26 is introduced by a quotation formula (i.e., *legōn,* "saying"), which seems to suggest that the writer has a specific text in mind. Certain verbal correspondences make it likely that the citation is based on the LXX rather than the Hebrew text and that it is primarily Hag 2:6 that is in view.

A textual problem in the LXX of Haggai, however, complicates the issue. In the MT, Hag 2:6 and 21 differ in that the Hebrew text of v. 6 has four objects of the shaking (i.e., heaven, earth, sea, and dry land), whereas in v. 21 only two objects are mentioned (i.e., heaven and earth). But in the LXX of v. 21 all four items appear, as in v. 6. It seems likely that the variation is due to a harmonistic expansion of v. 21 that was done (probably deliberately) by ancient scribes in order to bring the verse into conformity with the reading in v. 6. Apparently this adjustment to the text of v. 21 took place early on in the Greek textual tradition of Haggai, since most of the Greek manuscript evidence for Haggai has been affected in this way.[238]

Hebrews 12:26 does not cite the verse from Haggai in a precise fashion. Two variations call for comment. First, the New Testament writer reverses the word order in the reference to the heavens and earth (i.e., Heb 12:26 has [lit.] "the earth and the heaven").[239] Second, he injects the words "not only" (*ou monon*) before "the earth" (*tēn gēn*), a change apparently due to a desire to adapt the quotation to his argument in this epistle. The writer makes the point that God's shaking of the earth at Sinai (Exod 19:18; cf. Judg 5:4–5; Pss 68:8–9; 77:18; 114:7) was the harbinger of an even greater shaking of the heavens to take place in the eschaton. In that sense God will shake "not only" the earth, but he will shake the heavens as well. Furthermore, the presence of the words (lit.) "yet once" (*eti hapax*) in Heb 12:26 suggests that it is v. 6 (and not v. 21) of Haggai 2 that is mainly in view, since that phrase appears in the LXX of v. 6 but not of v. 21. On the other hand, Heb 12:26 cites a short form of the Old Testament reference, one that contains only two objects, not four. This agrees more closely with the Hebrew text of v. 21 than with the expanded LXX text. It thus appears that the New Testament writer may actually be splicing the two verses together to summarize their content without intending to replicate precisely their wording. He seems to be essentially following the LXX form of Hag 2:6, while at the same time taking

---

[238] In the Syrohexapla the additional words are set off by diacritical marks in order to call attention to their questionable status. See F. Field, *Origenis Hexaplorum quae supersunt; sive veterum interpretum graecorum in totum Vetus Testamentum fragmenta,* vol. 2 (Oxford: Clarendon, 1875), 1017. Of the many LXX manuscripts that exist, apparently only the eighth-century Codex V agrees with the MT in lacking the reference to sea and dry land in v. 21.

[239] R. T. McLay suggests that the NT writer reverses the word order of Hag 2:7 in order to link the citation to Exod 19:12–21; 20:18–19, where the mountain and earth are said to shake (see *The Use of the Septuagint in New Testament Research* [Grand Rapids: Eerdmans, 2003], 155).

some liberty in the way he presents this Old Testament text.

In Heb 12:27–29, in the explanation that follows the Haggai citation found there, the writer interprets the phrase "yet once" to imply a distinction between the fading away of the present world order and the permanence of the unshakable kingdom that has been inaugurated by the coming of the messianic age. Such superiority of the new order as compared to all that preceded it in the old dispensation, he argues, should inspire gratitude and unflagging service on the part of the believing community (Heb 12:27–28). It should also lead to appropriate reverence and awe toward the divine Shaker in the awareness that, as the author warns, "our God is a consuming fire" (Heb 12:29; cf. Deut 4:24).

*Possible New Testament Allusions to Haggai.* In addition to the citation of Hag 2:6,21 in Heb 12:26, various scholars have suggested that Haggai's language may also be detected in certain other New Testament references.[240] Some of these suggestions turn out to be more viable than others. For example, Jesus' words in Luke 21:26 ("the heavenly bodies [lit. "powers of heaven"] will be shaken") invite comparison both with Hag 2:6,21 and with Joel 2:10. It seems more likely, however, that Isa 34:4 is the main Old Testament text in view in the Lukan citation rather than the similar passages in Haggai or Joel. Some have suggested that Matt 12:18 ("Behold my servant whom I have chosen") may allude to God's choice of Zerubbabel described in Hag 2:23. However, Matt 12:17 specifically attributes the source of this prophecy to Isaiah rather than to Haggai (cf. Isa 42:1). The similarity in language found in these two instances (Luke 21:26; Matt 12:18) may be due to Haggai's use of phraseology borrowed from the earlier prophet Isaiah, in which case it is more likely that the New Testament writer primarily has in mind Isaiah as the source of the citation.

In other cases the language parallels to Haggai are even more remote. For example, does Matt 28:20 ("Surely, I am with you") consciously allude to Hag 1:13 ("'I am with you,' declares the LORD")? It does not seem likely that this is the case. Or does John 14:27 ("peace I give") faintly echo the words of Hag 2:9 ("'And in this place I will grant peace,' declares the LORD Almighty")? Probably not. The similarities in phraseology between these Old and New Testament verses are more probably coincidental.

In summary we may say that compared to other Old Testament writings the little Book of Haggai does not exercise an extensive influence on New Testament theology or argumentation. Haggai's direct contribution to the New Testament utilization of Old Testament themes is rather modest. In the

---

[240] See, e.g., the list entitled "Loci citati vel allegati" in the Nestle-Aland Greek New Testament (*Novum Testamentum Graece*, 27th ed. [Stuttgart: Deutsche Bibelstiftung, 1993], 770–806), esp. p. 799.

case of one citation, however, that of Heb 12:26, the message of Haggai is used to very good effect in a demonstration of the abiding permanence of God's new order that finds its fulfillment in the person of Jesus. The prophet Haggai could not have anticipated exactly how God would bring to fruition the promises revealed to him.[241] But the author of Hebrews saw a Christological dimension in the fulfillment of Haggai's words.

## 15. Hebrew Text and Ancient Versions

This commentary is based on a study of the Hebrew text of the Book of Haggai as presented in *Biblia Hebraica Stuttgartensia,*[242] along with certain other Hebrew sources and the primary ancient versions of the Hebrew text. An examination of the early manuscript evidence for the Minor Prophets leads to the conclusion that in antiquity there were at least three different forms of the Hebrew text of these prophets.[243] One of these text-forms is the forerunner of our MT; another is that attested by the Qumran manuscripts; the third is the Hebrew text underlying the Old Greek translation. Perhaps in time new manuscript discoveries will reveal additional dimensions to this picture. What is clear is that already in the pre-Christian period the text of these prophets had taken on certain distinguishing features that are reflected in our extant manuscript evidence.[244]

### (1) The Masoretic Text

The Hebrew text found in *BHS* is a diplomatic (i.e., not eclectic) edition that follows in almost all particulars the early eleventh-century Masoretic manuscript B19A. This codex is our earliest dated Hebrew manuscript containing all of the Old Testament.[245] Like its cousin the Aleppo Codex (which

---

[241] Bright, perhaps overstating the discontinuity between Haggai's prophecy and its NT realization, says, "The fulfillment that the New Testament gave to Haggai's expectations is something totally different from what the prophet envisioned" ("Haggai Among the Prophets," 229).

[242] K. Elliger and W. Rudolph, eds., *BHS* (Stuttgart: Deutsche Bibelgesellschaft, 1967–1977).

[243] For a penetrating discussion of the ramifications of this evidence for both textual and canonical studies, see Jones, *Formation of the Book of the Twelve.*

[244] Each strand of this evidence should be treated with appropriate respect. The interpreter should resist the inclination to show prejudicial favor to one text-form over another with regard to the resolution of specific textual difficulties. No single part of the MS witness should be given such a privileged status that it is allowed to drown out or automatically negate the other witnesses.

[245] In a colophon at its end this MS is dated by its scribe with a complex reference to various Jewish, Greek, and Islamic dating systems. The result is that the colophon presents several dates that conflict with one another; the discrepancy amounts to about two years (i.e., A.D. 1008, 1009, or 1010). The correct date is most likely A.D. 1008. For an Eng. translation of the colophon see E. Würthwein, *The Text of the Old Testament: An Introduction to the Biblia Hebraica,* 2d ed. (Grand Rapids: Eerdmans, 1995), plate 24, pp. 180–81. For V. V. Lebedev's suggestion to the effect that the copyist may have begun his work in 1008 and finished it in A.D. 1010; see D. N. Freedman et al., eds., *The Leningrad Codex: A Facsimile Edition* (Grand Rapids: Eerdmans, 1998), xxii.

dates to ca. A.D. 930), manuscript B19A is an outstanding representative of the Ben Asher family of Masoretic manuscripts.

Manuscript B19A, however, is removed from the original composition of Haggai by more than a millennium and a half. Even granting that Masoretic manuscripts were transmitted with unusual scribal care, it would be unrealistically optimistic to think that occasional copyist errors have not intruded into the text. In a limited number of places in the present work a decision was made to emend the MT based on other textual evidence.[246]

## (2) Early Hebrew Evidence

Discoveries in the 1940s and 1950s in the vicinity of the Dead Sea have dramatically improved our evidence for the biblical text in the period just before and just after the beginning of the Christian era.

*The Qumran Manuscripts of the Minor Prophets.* In 1952 fragments of seven Hebrew manuscripts containing portions of the Minor Prophets were discovered in cave four at Qumran, along with many other biblical and extrabiblical manuscripts. These fragments of the Minor Prophets are now designated as 4QXII[a,b,c,d,e,f,g].[247] The oldest of them (i.e., 4QXII[a] and 4QXII[b]) date to the second half of the second century B.C. (ca. 150–125 B.C.), and the youngest of them (i.e., 4QXII[g]) dates to the second half of the first century B.C. (ca. 50–25 B.C.). This means that the earliest of these manuscript fragments are among the oldest of the Dead Sea Scrolls.[248] In their original form these manuscripts apparently contained the text of all twelve of the Minor Prophets, although the manuscripts are in a poor state of preservation. Judging from the number of manuscripts involved, it appears that the Minor Prophets were an especially valued part of the ancient library at Qumran. This conclusion is borne out by the existence at Qumran of commentaries on certain of these prophets, the best known of which is the Habakkuk commentary.[249]

---

[246] Helpful discussions of the text-critical difficulties of Haggai may be found in D. Barthélemy, *Ézéchiel, Daniel et les 12 Prophètes*, vol. 3, *Critique textuelle de l'Ancien Testament*, OBO 50/3 (Fribourg: Éditions Universitaires Fribourg; Göttingen: Vandenhoeck & Ruprecht, 1992), 923–34; K. Budde, "Zum Text der drei letzten kleinen Propheten," *ZAW* 26 (1906), esp. pp. 7–17; S. P. Carbone and G. Rizzi, *Aggeo, Gioele, Giona, Malachia, secondo il testo ebraico masoretico, secondo la versione greca della LXX, secondo la parafrasi aramaica targumica* (Bologna: Edizioni Dehoniane, 2001), 33–120.

[247] R. E. Fuller has published the *editio princeps* of these MSS in *Qumran Cave 4*, vol. 10, *The Prophets*, DJD 15 (Oxford: Clarendon, 1997), 221–318. See also id., "The Minor Prophets Manuscripts from Qumrân, Cave IV" (Ph.D. diss., Harvard University, 1988).

[248] See F. M. Cross, *The Ancient Library of Qumran*, 3d ed. (Minneapolis: Fortress, 1995), 44, 121, n. 2. See also id., "The Oldest Manuscripts from Qumran," *JBL* 74 (1955): 147–72; R. Fuller, "The Text of the Twelve Minor Prophets," *CurBS* 7 (1999): 83.

[249] Portions of *pesharim* from Qumran have been identified for the following Minor Prophets: Hosea, Amos, Micah, Nahum, Habakkuk, Zephaniah, and possibly Malachi. These commentaries, only partially preserved, were found in Qumran caves one, four, and five.

Small portions of the Book of Haggai are found in two of these fragments; 4QXII$^b$ (= 4Q77) has portions of Hag 1:1–2; 2:2b–4, and 4QXII$^e$ (= 4Q80) has a few words from Hag 2:18–19 and a few words from 2:20–21. According to Fuller, the text of 4QXII$^b$ is generally closer to the MT, whereas the text of 4QXII$^e$ is closer to the LXX.[250] These small portions, however, are too limited in scope to be of much help for the text-criticism of Haggai. They provide no textual variations from the MT of Haggai other than orthographic variants.[251]

Although their overall contribution to the textual study of Haggai is not great, the Qumran manuscripts of the Minor Prophets are valuable in another way. These seven manuscripts provide important insight into certain issues pertaining to the canonical order of these books in the period prior to the stabilization of the Hebrew text toward the end of the first century A.D. The fact that Jonah apparently followed Malachi in the sequence of books adopted by 4QXII$^a$ seems to reflect a somewhat fluid state with regard to the order of the Twelve. Fuller has drawn some interesting conclusions with regard to the status of these prophets among the Qumran community, concluding that in the process of interpretation the text of the Twelve did not undergo the same sort of alteration as did the Mosaic law during the period in question.[252]

*The Wadi Murabbaʿat Scroll of the Minor Prophets (Mur 88).* In 1955 fragments of a scroll originally containing the entire Hebrew text of the twelve Minor Prophets were discovered in Cave 5 at Wadi Murabbaʿat,[253] which is located in the general vicinity of where the now-famous Dead Sea Scrolls were discovered.[254] A good part of the Book of Haggai is contained in this scroll, although the condition of the scroll is such that many portions of Haggai, especially in chap. 2, are lacking from the scroll due to the ravages of time. Since the Wadi Murabbaʿat scroll, now designated as Mur 88, probably dates to the first half of the second century A.D.,[255] it is an impor-

---

[250] See Fuller, "Text of the Twelve Minor Prophets," 86.

[251] E.g., in 4QXII$^b$ the name Darius in Hag 1:1 is spelled with *hēʾ* rather than *wāw* as the next to the last letter. Fuller suspects that this "probably reflects an alternate spelling to דריהוש as found in the Wâdi ed-Dâliyeh papyri" (*The Prophets,* 235).

[252] See R. Fuller, "The Form and Formation of the Book of the Twelve: The Evidence from the Judean Desert," in *Forming Prophetic Literature: Essays on Isaiah and the Twelve in Honor of John D. W. Watts,* JSOTSup 235 (Sheffield: Sheffield Academic Press, 1996), esp. pp. 96–98.

[253] For a description of this MS and a presentation of its Hb. text see the following *editio princeps:* P. Benoit, J. T. Milik, and R. de Vaux, *Les grottes de Murabbaʿât: Texte,* DJD 2 (Oxford: Clarendon, 1961), 50, 181–205.

[254] Wadi Murabbaʿat is located near the west side of the Dead Sea, about eleven miles south of Qumran and about fifteen miles southeast of Jerusalem.

[255] Mur 88 may actually be slightly older. Fuller suggests a date in the second half of the first century A.D. See Fuller, "Form and Formation of the Book of the Twelve," 87, 88; id., "Text of the Twelve," 86; id., "Minor Prophets," in *Encyclopedia of the Dead Sea Scrolls,* vol. 1 (Oxford: Oxford University Press, 2000), 556.

tant early witness to the Hebrew text of the Minor Prophets, antedating manuscript B19A and the Aleppo Codex by eight or nine centuries. In its extant portions Mur 88 provides support for the MT, differing in only a few details from the much later Masoretic manuscripts of Haggai.[256] In other words, Mur 88 has what might be called a proto-Masoretic Text.[257] So far as Haggai is concerned, textual differences between Mur 88 and the MT are minor, affecting only three words.[258] Overall this early manuscript inspires confidence in the accuracy of the Masoretic Text of the Book of Haggai.

### (3) The Ancient Versions

For text-critical work the most important and useful of the ancient translations of the Hebrew Bible, in the approximate order of their value, are the Greek Septuagint, the Syriac Peshitta, and the Latin Vulgate. Also of interest is *Targum Jonathan,* which provides an Aramaic paraphrase of the Hebrew text. For the purposes of the present study, each of these versions was carefully compared to the Hebrew Masoretic Text of the Book of Haggai. Although in most instances these versions provide support for (rather than against) the MT, there are also a number of significant departures from the MT that must be taken into account in any attempt to establish the best Hebrew text of the Book of Haggai. Allusions to these witnesses will be made where appropriate in the commentary proper, but a summary of their evidence is in order here.

*Naḥal Ḥever Greek Scroll of the Minor Prophets (8ḤevXIIgr).* In 1952 and 1961 fragments of a Greek scroll originally containing the twelve Minor Prophets were discovered at Naḥal Ḥever, in the vicinity of the Dead Sea.[259] These fragments include portions of Jonah, Micah, Nahum, Habakkuk, Zephaniah, and Zechariah.[260] Unfortunately, no portion of Haggai has sur-

---

[256] On the matter of paragraphing of material in Mur 88 (and 8ḤevXIIgr as well) see J. M. Oesch, *Petucha und Setuma: Untersuchungen zu einer überlieferten Gliederung im hebräischen Text des Alten Testaments,* OBO 27 (Freiburg: Universitätsverlag; Göttingen: Vandenhoeck & Ruprecht, 1979), 284–89, 303–9.

[257] For a discussion of suitable terminology for pre-Masoretic MSS see E. Tov, *Textual Criticism of the Hebrew Bible,* 2d rev. ed. (Minneapolis: Fortress, 2001), 22–24, 114–17.

[258] The words in question are as follows. First, in Hag 2:1 where MT has בְּיַד ("by the hand of") the scroll has אֶל ("to"); second, in Hag 2:3 the word אֹתוֹ ("it") is written as an interlinear addition, apparently having been at first overlooked by the scribe; third, in Haggai 2:4 the scroll apparently has the definite article before the word עַם ("people").

[259] The *editio princeps* of this MS is E. Tov, with the collaboration of R. A. Kraft and a contribution by P. J. Parsons, *The Greek Minor Prophets Scroll from Naḥal Ḥever (8ḤevXIIgr) (the Seiyal Collection I),* DJD, vol. 8 (Oxford: Clarendon, 1990). In this connection mention should also be made of Barthélemy's seminal work. Though now rather dated, it nonetheless continues to be an important discussion of both the textual implications of this MS and related textual issues as well. See D. Barthélemy, *Les devanciers d'Aquila,* VTSup 10 (Leiden: Brill, 1963).

[260] B. Lifshitz assigned nine other small fragments to Hosea, Amos, Joel, Jonah, Nahum, and Zechariah, but some of these identifications have been disputed by other scholars; see "The Greek Documents from the Cave of Horror," *IEJ* 12 (1962): 201–7.

vived. The scroll probably dates to the middle of the first century B.C. Its importance derives partly from the fact that it antedates Origen's text-critical activity in the third century A.D. Based on space considerations the editors are "relatively confident" that the Book of Haggai originally appeared in the Naḥal Ḥever scroll between Zephaniah and Zechariah, as it does in traditional arrangements of the Minor Prophets.[261] This scroll thus provides an important early witness to the condition of the text for those biblical passages for which it is extant. That the Haggai portion of 8HevXIIgr has not been preserved is a great loss to the textual study of the Book of Haggai.

*The Freer Greek Manuscript of the Minor Prophets.* In 1916 an agent working in behalf of Charles L. Freer and the J. Pierpont Morgan Library purchased in Cairo a number of ancient manuscripts, most of them written in Coptic. Among these were fragments of a Greek papyrus originally containing the text of the Minor Prophets.[262] Following a short stay at the library of the University of Michigan, this manuscript found a new home at the Freer Gallery in Washington, D.C. According to the editors these fragments date to the middle or end of the third century A.D. and provide a Greek text that shows no influence from Origen's textual activity, although some accommodations to the Hebrew text are at variance with similar activity on the part of Origen.[263] All of the Book of Haggai has been preserved from this manuscript. Its variations from the Greek text found in the Göttingen edition of the LXX are relatively minor, in most cases being due to instances of scribal error that have produced small pluses or minuses. The manuscript is important in that it provides an early witness to the Greek text of these prophets.

*Septuagint.* Partly due to its early date and partly due to the quality of many of its differences from the MT, the Septuagint is the single most important versional witness to the Old Testament text. The Greek translation of the Minor Prophets probably was completed in the second half of the second century B.C.[264] It presents for the most part an adequate Greek translation of the Book of Haggai, although in places the translator was reluctant to depart very far from the wording of his Hebrew *Vorlage*. The Greek wording of the Septuagint at times has a Hebraistic flavor to it, though occasionally the translator of the Book of Haggai resorts to a more natural Greek style. The *Vorlage* of the Septuagint in Haggai was close to our MT. Yet there are differences. Jones thinks that in proportion to its size the LXX of Haggai has more pluses than do any of the other Minor Proph-

---

[261] Tov, *The Greek Minor Prophets Scroll from Naḥal Ḥever*, 8.

[262] The *editio princeps* of this MS is H. A. Sanders and C. Schmidt, *The Minor Prophets in the Freer Collection and the Berlin Fragment of Genesis* (London: Macmillan, 1927).

[263] Sanders and Schmidt, *Minor Prophets in the Freer Collection*, 25.

[264] I have used the following edition of the LXX: J. Ziegler, ed., *Duodecim prophetae*, 3d ed., *Septuaginta, Vetus Testamentum graecum auctoritate academiae scientiarum gottingensis*, vol. 13 (Göttingen: Vandenhoeck & Ruprecht, 1984).

ets.[265] Most differences between the two can be explained as due to various issues of translation technique, especially in places where the nature of the Greek language creates different expectations with regard to such things as word order or subordination of clauses. There are places where the Greek translator of Haggai seems to have used a Hebrew *Vorlage* that was different from our Hebrew text. The more important of these instances will be discussed at appropriate points in the commentary.[266]

The LXX also formed the basis for certain other ancient translations of the Old Testament, such as the Coptic versions.[267] These daughter versions are characterized by a dependence upon a Greek rather than a Hebrew *Vorlage*. In most cases these translations are too far removed from the Hebrew text to be of special interest for the purposes of this commentary. They are, however, especially helpful in analyzing textual variants in the Greek tradition.

*Syriac Peshitta.* The Syriac Peshitta is second only to the LXX in terms of its age and authority as a version of the Old Testament.[268] It is a transla-

---

[265] Jones, *Formation of the Book of the Twelve*, 98.

[266] Examples include the following. In some places LXX has a text shorter than that of MT. E.g., in 1:2 the LXX lacks the first occurrence of the word "time" in the MT. In 1:10 the LXX lacks the MT "because of you." And in 2:5 the LXX lacks the MT "the word that I established with you when you came out of Egypt." But in other places the LXX has a longer text. In 2:9 the LXX has the following plus: "even peace of soul as a possession for every one who builds, to raise up this temple" (καὶ εἰρήνην ψυχῆς εἰς περιποίησιν παντὶ τῷ κτίζοντι τοῦ ἀναστῆσαι τὸν ναὸν τοῦτον). In 2:14 the LXX has the following plus: "because of their early material gains, they will suffer pain from their toils; and you were hating those who reprove in the gates" (i.e., in a public place) (ἕνεκεν τῶν λημμάτων αὐτῶν τῶν ὀρθρινῶν ὀδυνηθήσονται ἀπὸ προσώπου πόνων αὐτῶν καὶ ἐμισεῖτε ἐν πύλαις ἐλέγχοντας). And in 2:21 the LXX has the following plus: "and the sea and the dry land" (καὶ τὴν θάλασσαν καὶ τὴν ξηράν). In a few places the LXX adds such expressions as "governor of Judah" (1:12) or "son of Shealtiel" (2:21) or "prophet" (2:20) where these words are absent from the MT. These readings are probably expansionistic harmonizations due to the scribe of the Hebrew *Vorlage* rather than being due to such activity on the part of the Greek translator. In yet other places the LXX differs from the MT with regard to particular details. E.g., in 1:12 for the MT "their God" the LXX has "to them" (πρὸς αὐτούς). In 2:17 for the MT "there is not with you" the LXX has "you did not turn" (οὐκ ἐπεστρέψατε). In 1:15 the LXX takes the verse with what follows rather than with what precedes. And in 2:7 for the MT "the desire" in the singular the LXX has "the chosen things" in the plural (τὰ ἐκλεκτά). But in spite of such variants the text of the LXX is quite close to the MT text of Haggai.

[267] For a specialized study treating the second chapter of Haggai as found in the Bohairic dialect of Coptic see R. Kasser, H. Quecke, and N. Bosson, "Le second chapitre d'Aggée en bohaïrique *B74*," *Or* 61 (1992): 169–204.

[268] I have used the following edition of the Peshitta: A. Gelston, ed., *Dodekapropheten—Daniel-Bel-Draco*, part 3, fascicle 4, *Vetus Testamentum Syriace iuxta simplicem syrorum versionem*, or *The Old Testament in Syriac according to the Peshitta Version* (Leiden: Brill, 1980). In a separate work Gelston has provided a helpful analysis of the Syriac version of the Minor Prophets (*The Peshitta of the Twelve Prophets* [Oxford: Clarendon, 1987]). In a more recent work Gelston evaluates the relationship between the Syriac version and the Tg. of the Minor Prophets. See id., "The Twelve Prophets: Peshitta and Targum," in *Targum and Peshitta*, Targum Studies 2, South Florida Studies in the History of Judaism 165 (Atlanta: Scholars Press, 1998), 119–39.

tion of a Hebrew text, rendered into a dialect of the Aramaic language. Whether the Syriac translation was originally made for a Jewish or for a Christian community is not entirely clear.[269] This version was produced probably in the second century A.D., at least so far as the Old Testament is concerned. In the case of the Book of Haggai, the Peshitta is quite close to our MT, even to the point of sometimes reproducing the Hebrew wording at the expense of Syriac style. Several important textual variants also appear. These variants will be taken into account throughout the commentary.[270]

*Latin Vulgate.* Though not as important for text-critical purposes as the LXX or the Peshitta, the Latin Vulgate is nonetheless significant.[271] It was produced by Jerome during the late fourth and early fifth centuries A.D. In Haggai the Vulgate generally supports the MT.[272]

*Targum Jonathan.* The Aramaic paraphrases of the Hebrew Scriptures were designed to meet the needs of those Jews who from the intertestamental period onward tended to use Aramaic more than Hebrew. In the case of the Former and Latter Prophets, the most widely accepted Targum was that of

---

[269] M. P. Weitzman has recently advocated something of a compromise. In his estimation the Peshitta originated as a translation for a small circle of Syriac-speaking Jews who had separated from rabbinic Judaism. When this group eventually converted to Christianity, they continued to use the Peshitta in their Christian context. As a result the Peshitta, which was originally a translation made both by Jews and for Jews, gained acceptance in Christian circles. Such a thesis of course has parallels in the history of the LXX, where a translation that was originally made for Greek-speaking Jews eventually became the OT used instead by early Christians, a fact that led the Jewish community to discontinue using it. See id., *The Syriac Version of the Old Testament: An Introduction*, University of Cambridge Oriental Publications 56 (Cambridge: Cambridge University Press, 1999), 258–62.

[270] Examples include the following. In some places the Peshitta has a text shorter than that of the MT. E.g., in 1:2 the Peshitta lacks the first occurrence of the MT "time." In 1:9 and 2:11 the Peshitta lacks the MT "of hosts." And in 2:16 the Peshitta lacks the MT "winepress." But in other places the Peshitta has a longer text. E.g., in 1:13 the Peshitta has the equivalent of "of hosts" (*ḥyltn'*) where the MT lacks it. In 2:3 the Peshitta has "was reckoned" (*ḥšyb*) where the MT lacks it. And in 2:19 the Peshitta has "the Lord said to them" (*lhwn 'mr mrya*) where the MT lacks it.

[271] I have used the following edition of the Vg.: R. Weber, ed., *Biblia sacra, iuxta vulgatam versionem* (Stuttgart: Deutsche Bibelgesellschaft, 1969, 1983).

[272] Noteworthy readings in the Vg. of Haggai include the following. In a couple of places the Vg. has a text shorter than that of the MT. E.g., in 1:2 the Vg. lacks the first occurrence of the MT "time." And in 1:12 the Vg. lacks the MT "the Lord." But in other places the Vg. has a longer text. E.g., in 1:12 for the MT "their God" the Vg. has "their God to them (*Deus eorum ad ipsos*)," which is the result of dittography. In 2:4 the Vg. has "of hosts" (*exercituum*) after the first occurrence of "the Lord," harmonizing the expression to familiar usage elsewhere in Haggai. And in 2:17 the Vg. has "who will return" (*qui reverteretur*) before the words "to me." In yet other places the Vg. differs from the MT with regard to particular details. E.g., in 1:4 for the MT "your houses" the Vg. has simply "houses" (*domibus*), apparently lacking in its *Vorlage* the letter *kaph* of this Hb. word as it appears in the MT. The Vg. takes 1:15 with what follows rather than with what precedes. And in 2:7 the Vg. gives to the Hb. expression "desire of all the nations" a distinctly Messianic interpretation: "the one desired by all nations" (*desideratus cunctis gentibus*).

Jonathan.[273] Although its translation technique is too paraphrastic to be of great value for text-critical purposes, *Targum Jonathan* is occasionally of interest from an interpretive or exegetical standpoint.[274] Some of its readings shed light on how the early Jewish community understood the biblical text.[275] From time to time attention will be directed to readings of the Targum on the Book of Haggai that may be of special interest.[276] For the most part *Targum Jonathan* provides a fairly literal translation of the Hebrew text of Haggai.[277]

The textual evidence summarized here provides a wealth of data for evaluating the Hebrew text of the Book of Haggai. In the case of the Qumran

---

[273] I have used the following edition of the Tg.: A. Sperber, ed., *The Latter Prophets according to Targum Jonathan*, vol. 3, *The Bible in Aramaic, Based on Old Manuscripts and Printed Texts* (Leiden: Brill, 1962). See also K. J. Cathcart and R. P. Gordon, *The Targum of the Minor Prophets: Translated, with a Critical Introduction, Apparatus, and Notes*, vol. 14, *The Aramaic Bible* (Wilmington: Michael Glazier, 1989). For a helpful discussion of the significance of the Tg. to the Minor Prophets, see R. P. Gordon, *Studies in the Targum to the Twelve Prophets from Nahum to Malachi*, VTSup 51 (Leiden: Brill, 1994). See also the following volume that combines two collections of targumic studies: *Studies in Targum Jonathan to the Prophets by Leivy Smolar and Moses Aberbach and Targum Jonathan to the Prophets by Pinkhos Churgin*, Library of Biblical Studies (New York: Ktav; Baltimore: Baltimore Hebrew College, 1983).

[274] The Talmud claims that in composing the Tg., Jonathan had the guidance of Haggai, Zechariah, and Malachi (*Megillah* 3a). But given their respective dates, this can only mean that Jonathan was thought to have utilized materials that had been passed on from these prophets of the restoration. Jonathan was not their contemporary, nor could these prophets have been involved personally in Jonathan's work.

[275] For a helpful summary of lexical features and translation techniques utilized in the Haggai targum, see J. Ribera Florit, "La versión aramaica del profeta Ageo," *Anuario* 4 (1978), esp. pp. 285–88. In this article Ribera Florit also provides a critical edition of the targum to Haggai (based primarily on B. M. Or. Ms. 1474), along with a Spanish translation of the targum and philological annotations to the text.

[276] Some of the more interesting of these readings are the following. In 1:6 the MT "a bag with holes" (into which the worker put his wages only to watch them quickly disappear) is paraphrased as "for the curse (of poverty)." In 1:8 for the MT "I will be glorified" the Tg. further explains with the promise "I will cause my Shekinah to dwell in it in honor." In 1:9 for the MT "I will blow on it" the Tg. has "I will send a curse upon it," thereby avoiding the anthropomorphism of the Hb. text. In 1:10 for the MT "because of you" the Tg. has "because of your sins," thus making more specific the reason for God's displeasure with the people. In 1:12 for the MT "voice of the Lord" the Tg. has "the Memra of the Lord." In 1:13 for the MT "messenger of the Lord" the Tg. has "prophet of the Lord," since in the Tgs. מלאך ("messenger") is normally used of celestial rather than human messengers. In 1:13 and 2:4 for the MT "I am with you" the Tg. has "my Memra is your support," which is a common targumic circumlocution for this OT expression. In 2:5 for the MT "my spirit is remaining" the Tg. has "my prophets are teaching," which makes the reference to the divine presence less direct. In 2:22 for the MT "will go down" the Tg. has "will be killed," which is a more specific but correct understanding of the sense of the Hb. verb used here. In 2:23 the Tg. expands the reference to Zerubbabel as a "signet ring" to "the engraving (or setting) of a signet ring upon the hand," again making the idea more specific than it is in the MT.

[277] A fuller discussion of rabbinic materials dealing with the Book of Haggai is available in the following monograph: L. Tetzner, *Die rabbinischen Kommentare zum Buche Haggai* (Munich: Dissertationsdruck, 1969). Tetzner includes in his discussion Targum Jonathan, Rashi, Ibn Ezra, and David Kimchi.

material, meager though it is in terms of quantity of text that is actually preserved, we are within about four centuries of the autograph of this biblical book. The other textual materials, though later in date, help to provide a more complete witness to the textual transmission of Haggai. All of these materials will play an appropriate role in the commentary on Haggai that follows.

## OUTLINE OF HAGGAI

I. Haggai's First Message: It Is Time to Rebuild the Temple! (1:1–11)
   1. Introduction to the Message (1:1)
   2. The Lord Rejects the People's Excuse for Their Delay in Rebuilding the Temple (1:2)
   3. The Lord Responds to the People through Haggai the Prophet (1:3–11)

II. The People Respond to the Word of the Lord Given Through Haggai (1:12–15a)
   1. The People Respond Favorably to Haggai's Message (1:12)
   2. Haggai Reassures the People of the Lord's Presence with Them (1:13)
   3. The Leaders and the People Alike Commit Themselves to the Task of Rebuilding the Temple (1:14–15a)

III. Haggai's Second Message: The Glory of the Rebuilt Temple Will Surpass That of Solomon's Temple! (1:15b–2:9)
   1. Introduction to the Message (1:15b–2:2)
   2. The Present Condition of the Temple Is Deplorable (2:3–5)
   3. The Future Condition of the Temple Will Be Glorious (2:6–9)

IV. Haggai's Third Message: Disobedience Produces Defilement, but Blessing Will Attend Those Who Obey the Lord's Commands! (2:10–19)
   1. Introduction to the Message (2:10)
   2. The Lord Regards the People as Defiled (2:11–14)
   3. Only Obedience Can Lead to Removal of Divine Discipline (2:15–19)

V. Haggai's Fourth Message: The Lord Is Raising Up a New Leader! (2:20–23)
   1. Introduction to the Message (2:20)
   2. The Lord Will Interrupt Human Events by Judgmental Action (2:21–22)
   3. The Lord Will Sovereignly Establish Zerubbabel on the Davidic Throne (2:23)

I. HAGGAI'S FIRST MESSAGE: *IT IS TIME TO REBUILD THE TEMPLE!* (1:1–11)
  1. Introduction to the Message (1:1)
    (1) Date of the Message (1:1a)
    (2) Origin of the Message (1:1b)
    (3) Recipients of the Message (1:1c)
  2. The People's Excuse for Delay (1:2)
  3. The Lord's Response (1:3–11)
    (1) The Origin of the Prophet's Message (1:3)
    (2) The Cause and Consequence of Hard Times (1:4–11)
       Inverted Priorities of the People (1:4)
       Unsuccessful Efforts of the People (1:5–6)
       The Necessity of Obedience (1:7–11)
         The Lord's Requirement (1:7–8)
         The Lord's Discipline (1:9–11)

## I. HAGGAI'S FIRST MESSAGE (1:1–11)

The first of Haggai's four messages is in the form of a disputation speech that is intended to call into question the reasons advanced by the prophet's community for not completing the work of rebuilding the temple. That work had started shortly after the first returnees from Babylon made their way back to Jerusalem in the days of Cyrus. Although some progress had been made in the years following the initial return from Babylon, enthusiasm for the project had long since waned as the people increasingly focused on their own needs to the neglect of religious priorities. Now, almost two decades after the initial attempts, through a series of spoken messages Haggai sought to rekindle the flame of commitment.

The theme of Haggai's first sermon may be simply stated: *It is time to rebuild the temple!* In this message Haggai makes it clear that the Lord was unimpressed with the excuses the people had fabricated in order to justify their own selfish interests. Through the prophet the Lord disputes all attempts to justify putting personal interests ahead of spiritual priorities. Haggai argues that the economic and financial difficulties the people were experiencing—far from being an adequate excuse for their lack of substantive progress in the work that was set before them—were in reality a divine judgment directed against them because of their failures in this regard. He appeals to the people to recognize that this is the case, and he promises the energizing presence of God's Spirit in their midst if they will but commit themselves to the Lord's desires and move ahead in this vital matter.

Some scholars have challenged the unity of Hag 1:1–11, concluding that this section is actually a composite speech.[1] This conclusion is based in part on the fact that in Hag 1:2 after the messenger formula there is a quotation of what the people say rather than, as might be expected, a citation of the words of either the prophet or the Lord. Nogalski follows Steck in suggesting that in light of the contrasting conditions of the houses described in these verses (e.g., vv. 4,9), Hag 1:2,4–8 has in view that part of the population that had stayed in Judah rather than going into exile in Babylon, while Hag 1:9–11 has in view the returnees from the exile.[2] But such a bifurcation of the unit is not persuasive, and it seems best to regard this section as a single pericope. To some degree the abrupt and unexpected features of this section are related to the development of the disputation that is presented here.

## 1. Introduction to the Message (1:1)

The opening verse of Haggai provides three important pieces of information with regard to the prophet's initial sermon. First, there is a date that enables us to situate the message within the political history of the period. Second, the prophet is identified as the bearer of a message from the Lord. And third, the primary recipients of the message are identified by name, family descent, and official position.

### (1) Date of the Message (1:1a)

**[1]In the second year of King Darius, on the first day of the sixth month,**

**1:1** The Book of Haggai begins with a chronological note that situates its events in the reign of the Persian King Darius. This Darius is not to be confused with the later figure Darius II Nothus (423–408 B.C.) of Neh 12:12, who is referred to there as "Darius the Persian." Nor is he to be con-

---

[1] See, e.g., J. Nogalski, *Literary Precursors to the Book of the Twelve,* BZAW 217a (Berlin: Walter de Gruyter, 1993), 217–19. Nogalski regards it as "impossible to consider the entire unit as one continuous speech" (p. 217). Such language seems to overstate the difficulties involved.

[2] See O. H. Steck, "Zu Haggai 1 2–11," *ZAW* 83 (1971): 355–79.

fused with Darius the Mede of the Book of Daniel,[3] a figure associated with Cyrus the Persian in the overthrow of the Neo-Babylonian empire in 539 B.C.[4] The Darius of Hag 1:1 is Darius I Hystaspes, who ruled over Persia from 522 to 486 B.C. He ascended the throne of Persia after the death of Cambyses and was still relatively new to royal power when Haggai commenced the prophetic ministry described in this book. At that time Darius had been in power for only a couple of years, just long enough to have begun to settle in to what would be for him a lengthy rule over the mighty and far-flung Persian empire.

No empire in the ancient Near East exceeded the size of this superpower. Persia controlled an area reaching from northern Africa to southern Russia and from Asia Minor all the way to India.[5] In the period immediately preceding Darius, the Persian empire was governed first by Cyrus the Great (559–530 B.C.) and then by his son Cambyses (530–522 B.C.). In 522 B.C. Darius seized the reins of power after overthrowing Gaumata, an impostor who had briefly laid claim to the throne. The new king had to deal with rebellions in various parts of the empire in order to consolidate his rule. But by the time of Haggai's public ministry the initial unrest had been settled, even though some lingering signs of instability may have yet remained.[6] Increasingly Darius was able to solidify his control of the empire and focus on what would become his unique and lasting contributions to Persia's national life.

According to Hag 1:1 the prophet's first message dates to the second year of Darius, which is best understood to be 520 B.C.[7] The 520 date is

---

[3] Some scholars suppose that the author of the Book of Daniel, due to his inaccurate understanding of the history of the period, confused Cyrus's associate with a Darius who actually lived later than the time of the Persian conquest of Babylon. But this is a gratuitous conclusion. On the identity of Darius the Mede, in addition to the commentary literature, see J. M. Bulman, "The Identification of Darius the Mede," *WTJ* 35 (1973): 247–67; B. E. Colless, "Cyrus the Persian as Darius the Mede in the Book of Daniel," *JSOT* 56 (1992): 113–26; L. L. Grabbe, "Another Look at the *Gestalt* of 'Darius the Mede,'" *CBQ* 50 (1988): 198–213; W. H. Shea, "Darius the Mede: An Update," *AUSS* 20 (1982): 229–47; id., "Darius the Mede in His Persian-Babylonian Setting," *AUSS* 29 (1991): 235–57; S. D. Waterhouse, "Why Was Darius the Mede Expunged from History?" in *To Understand the Scriptures: Essays in Honor of William H. Shea* (Berrien Springs, Mich.: Institute of Archaeology/Siegfried H. Horn Archaeological Museum, 1997), 173–89; J. C. Whitcomb Jr., *Darius the Mede: A Study in Historical Identification*, International Library of Philosophy and Theology, Biblical and Theological Series (Philadelphia: Presbyterian & Reformed, 1963).

[4] Dan 5:31; 6:1,6,9,25,28; 9:1; 11:1. Cf. Ezra 4:24; 5:5–7; 6:1,12–15.

[5] See E. Stern, "The Archeology of Persian Palestine," in *Introduction: The Persian Period*, *CHJ* (Cambridge: Cambridge University Press, 1984), 1:88.

[6] For an account of various issues related to the commencement of Darius's reign see A. Poebel, "Chronology of Darius' First Year of Reign," *AJSL* 55 (1938): 285–314.

[7] For a discussion of the main issues see J. Kessler, "The Second Year of Darius and the Prophet Haggai," *Transeu* 5 (1992): 63–84; id., *The Book of Haggai: Prophecy and Society in Early Persian Yehud*, VTSup 91 (Leiden: Brill, 2002), 80–85; also S. Japhet, "'History' and 'Literature' in the Persian Period: The Restoration of the Temple," in *"Ah, Assyria . . .": Studies in Assyrian History and Ancient Near Eastern Historiography Presented to Hayim Tadmor*, ScrHier 33 (Jerusalem: Magnes, 1991), 176, n. 17.

based on the understanding that the Persians adopted the Babylonian accession year system of calculation, whereby the initial partial year of a new king was regarded not as the first year of his rule but as an accession year. With this understanding, the first year of the king's rule was the first full year following the accession year.[8]

The dates that we repeatedly encounter in Haggai provide clear indicators of the literary structure of this book. Of the various discourse markers used in Haggai it is the date indicators that have greatest significance, due to their frequent occurrence in this book.[9] There is, however, a striking difference in the way this book begins as compared with many earlier prophetic writings. Old Testament prophets typically related their historical circumstances to a particular king of Israel or, in some cases, to multiple Israelite kings. The Book of Isaiah, for example, is situated in the reigns of Uzziah, Jotham, Ahaz, and Hezekiah (Isa 1:1). The Book of Jeremiah links its events to the days of the Judean king Josiah and his son Jehoiakim (Jer 1:2–3). The Book of Ezekiel begins with a reference to the exile of Judah's king Jehoiachin (Ezek 1:2). The Book of Daniel refers to the reign of Jehoiakim king of Judah (Dan 1:1). Several of the Minor Prophets also have similar chronological notices at their beginning (e.g., Hos 1:1; Amos 1:1; Mic 1:1; Zeph 1:1).

Contrary to this convention, neither Haggai nor Zechariah relates their events to a king of Judah. The reason for this departure from the earlier norm is very simple. The Babylonian captivity had effectively brought an end to the Israelite monarchy. By the time of the events described in Haggai and Zechariah, the people of Israel had been without a king of their own for six decades and more. It was therefore necessary for these postexilic prophets to relate the events they describe to the only king Israel knew at that moment in history—a Persian king. This dating scheme implicitly calls

---

[8] E. J. Bickerman adopts a nonaccession year method for calculating Darius's second year, arriving at the date 521 ("La seconde année de Darius," *RB* 88 [1981]: 23–28). See also L. Waterman, "The Camouflaged Purge of Three Messianic Conspirators," *JNES* 13 (1954): 73–78. Bickerman prefers the earlier date in part because of an interpretation of 2:20–23 that understands Haggai to be predicting the soon demise of the Persian empire. Such a prediction would fit better the unsettled political conditions of 521 than it would the political climate of the following year, by which time Darius had consolidated his rule. This interpretation of 2:20–23, however, is tenuous, and it seems unlikely that Haggai should be seen as engaging in such risky political maneuvers. H. W. Wolff concludes that the evidence favors the 520 date (*Haggai: A Commentary* [Minneapolis: Augsburg, 1988], 74–76). W. H. Rose concludes that Darius's second year was most likely from April 3, 520 to March 22, 519 (*Zemah and Zerubbabel: Messianic Expectations in the Early Postexilic Period*, JSOTSup 304 [Sheffield: Sheffield Academic Press, 2000], 27–30). See also L. Depuydt, "Evidence for Accession Dating under the Achaemenids," *JAOS* 115 (1995): 193–204.

[9] D. J. Clark has isolated some seventeen major discourse markers used in Haggai, which he ranks in terms of relative significance; see "Discourse Structure in Haggai," *JOTT* 5 (1992): 23.

attention to the fact that since Israel was without a king of her own, her national life must sadly be defined in terms of subservience to a foreign, and in fact a pagan, king. The degree to which the population of Judah was able to chart its own course for the future had significant restrictions imposed from the outside.

Haggai's chronological notice in v. 1 continues with a further, more specific reference to "the first day of the sixth month" *(baḥōdeš haššiššî bĕyôm ʾeḥād)*. This reference to month is complicated by the fact that at different times ancient Israel used different calendrical systems. Before the exile the Israelites had used a calendar marking the beginning of the new year in the fall. But during and after the exile Israel adopted the Babylonian calendar, with the new year beginning in the spring. It is this latter system that is reflected in Haggai's usage. The sixth month (i.e., Elul) was therefore toward the end of summer.[10] In terms of modern reckoning the date in v. 1 corresponds to August 29, 520 B.C.[11]

The order in which the dating information is presented is significant. In chronological notices that provide full information on dates, as is the case in v. 1, the normal order utilized in preexilic biblical Hebrew is to cite first the year, followed by the month, and then the day. Notices that provide less detailed information show greater variation in the order in which the information is presented. In postexilic biblical Hebrew there was a preference for the order day-month-year.[12]

That the first day of the month was the occasion of Haggai's message is of interest in that according to Torah the first of every month was a time for special offerings to the Lord (cf. Num 28:11–15). As such it was to be a time of celebration and rejoicing (Num 10:10). But with the temple lying in ruins, there was no way properly to observe these festive occasions as had been done less than a century before. It may be that by delivering his message on this first day of the month Haggai intended the very timing of his message to call attention to the spiritual dilemma that confronted his people.

The other three messages found in the Book of Haggai also have very

---

[10] See the discussion in J. Finegan, *Handbook of Biblical Chronology: Principles of Time Reckoning in the Ancient World and Problems of Chronology in the Bible* (Princeton: Princeton University Press, 1964), §§65–81.

[11] As pointed out earlier in the introduction, for the conversion of ancient dates to their modern equivalents I am indebted to R. A. Parker and W. H. Dubberstein, *Babylonian Chronology, 626 B.C.–A.D. 75*, Brown University Studies 19 (Providence: Brown University Press, 1956).

[12] For a summary of biblical and extrabiblical evidence, both Hebrew and Aramaic, see Kessler, "The Second Year of Darius," 67–69; id., *The Book of Haggai*, 44–48. The description of dating formulae provided by Waltke and O'Connor may need to be nuanced so as to take into account the diachronic issues; see *IBHS* §15.3.2.

specific dates, as the following chart indicates.

| Verse | Year of Darius | Month | Day | Modern Equivalent |
|---|---|---|---|---|
| 1:1 | second | sixth | first | August 29, 520 B.C. |
| 1:15b–2:1 | second | seventh | twenty-first | October 17, 520 B.C. |
| 2:10 | second | ninth | twenty-fourth | December 18, 520 B.C. |
| 2:20 | [second] | [ninth] | twenty-fourth | December 18, 520 B.C. |

To these dates we may add that of Hag 1:15a, which marks the actual beginning of the work on the temple shortly after Haggai's first sermon. That date is "the twenty-fourth day of the sixth month" *(běyôm ʿeśrîm wěʾarbāʿâ laḥōdeš baššiššî)*, which corresponds to September 21, 520 B.C.

The use of exact dates at the beginning of prophetic oracles is not unusual in biblical literature from this general period (cf., e.g., Ezek 1:1–2; 8:1; Zech 1:1,7; 7:1). But the repeated occurrence of precise dates in a book as brief as Haggai is striking.[13] No other prophetic book exceeds Haggai in terms of its density of dated material.[14] The specificity with which these dates are given in Haggai serves two purposes. First, it underscores the factuality of the events that are described, situating them within a verifiable historical context. Second, it lends credibility to the predictive portions of the prophet's message, since his accuracy on past allusions can be readily established.[15]

The dates cited in Haggai reveal that the prophet's recorded ministry spanned only a very brief time. The events of this book are confined to a period of about three and a half months. In that brief time Haggai was able to move his community from stark apathy to vigorous action. That a single individual was able to accomplish so much in so short a time speaks impressively of the prophet's effectiveness.

### (2) Origin of the Message (1:1b)

**the word of the LORD came through the prophet Haggai to Zerubbabel son of Shealtiel, governor of Judah, and to Joshua son of Jehozadak, the high priest:**

---

[13] E. H. Merrill likens Haggai's interest in chronology (and Zechariah's as well) to that found in extrabiblical texts of roughly the same period, pointing out that such attention "is characteristic of the annalistic style of history writing employed in Neo-Babylonian and Persian times" (*An Exegetical Commentary: Haggai, Zechariah, Malachi* [Chicago: Moody, 1994], 4).

[14] So R. B. Dillard and T. Longman III, *An Introduction to the Old Testament* (Grand Rapids: Zondervan, 1994), 423; S. Amsler, "Aggée, Zacharie 1–8," in *Aggée, Zacharie 1–8, Zacharie 9–14, Malachie,* 2d ed., CAT 11c (Geneva: Labor et Fides, 1988), 9.

[15] See further P. A. Verhoef, "Notes on the Dates in the Book of Haggai," in *Text and Context: Old Testament and Semitic Studies for F. C. Fensham* (Sheffield: JSOT Press, 1988), 263–64.

This statement calls attention to two equally important features of Haggai's message.[16] First, it underscores the divine origin of his message, claiming for it revelatory status. Though conveyed by a human spokesman, the message did not originate with that messenger. It is a message whose importance derived from its suprahuman and divine nature. It is "the word of the LORD" (*dĕbar* YHWH). Thus from the start of this book the prophet stresses the notion that through his message it is ultimately the Lord who speaks. This is a theme to which Haggai will repeatedly return in the remainder of this book. The prophetic word as divine revelation is an essential part of the theology of this book; it is a component of Haggai's thought that is emphasized over and over.[17] Second, the expression in v. 1 links this divine word to the human messenger who delivered it to the Lord's people. It is a message that came "through" (*bĕyad*, lit. "by the hand of") Haggai.[18] The more familiar expression for describing prophetic reception of a divine message speaks of the word of the Lord coming "to" (*ʾel*) the prophet rather than "through" (*bĕyad*) him.[19] This expression appears in Hag 2:10,20, for example. There is a slight distinction of meaning in the two phrases. The expression *hāyâ bĕyad* ("it was by the hand of") directs attention to the transmission of the message to the audience for whom it was intended, while *hāyâ ʾel* ("it was to") focuses on the prophet's reception of the divine oracle. In the former instance the emphasis is on the prophet's role as intermediate agent through whom the divine message was communicated to a third party, whereas in the latter instance the emphasis is on the prophet's role as chosen recipient of the divine message.[20] In v. 1 it is the former construction that appears.

---

[16] In 1:1 the LXX includes the words λέγων Εἰπόν ("saying, Say"), thus treating the following portion of v. 1 as part of the direct discourse rather than, as in the MT, a narrative identification of the intended recipients of the divine word that was mediated by Haggai. This addition in the Gk. text probably is due to harmonization with Hag 2:1–2, where we find in the MT the words לֵאמֹר אֱמָר־נָא ("saying, Say"). The reading of the MT is preferable here.

[17] See further on this point the discussion of Haggai's theology found in the Introduction.

[18] Cf. Hag 1:3; 2:1; Mal 1:1. The phrase is also employed frequently throughout the OT in expressions other than those that describe reception of divine revelation. R. L. Smith's comment is therefore not accurate as it stands: "This construction 'by the hand of . . .' is rare in the prophets. It is found only in Hag 1:1,3; 2:1; and Mal 1:1" ("Haggai," in *Micah–Malachi*, WBC [Waco: Word, 1984], 152). On the contrary, the expression appears often in Isaiah, Jeremiah, and Ezekiel; it occurs occasionally in certain other prophetic writings as well.

[19] See, e.g., Hos 1:1; Joel 1:1; Jonah 1:1; Mic 1:1; Zeph 1:1; Zech 1:1.

[20] This distinction, however, should not be rigidly pressed. Hag 2:1 has בְּיַד where we might have expected אֶל instead. Kessler attributes the exception to the work of a redactor who was inconsistent with the practice followed elsewhere in Haggai. M. McEntire insists on a distinction between the expressions here and understands the author to be signaling disruption in the narrative. But whether the variation is a reflection of intentional narrative strategy, as McEntire suggests, or whether the distinction between the expressions has simply blurred is not easy to say. The latter seems more likely (see McEntire, "Haggai—Bringing God into the Picture," *RevExp* 97 [2000]: 70, 72; Kessler, *The Book of Haggai*, 117.

The several uses of the expression "through Haggai" suggest that in a sense the prophet is merely a conduit through which the message must pass. He will deliver the message, and it will be his personality and persona that will provide its human characteristics. But it is really the Lord's message more so than it is Haggai's. The implication that lies just below the surface of such language is that failure to receive this message and to act upon its counsel is tantamount to rejecting not just the prophet but the Lord himself. Haggai's message is predicated upon a solemn description of its divine origin, hinting at the imperative need for submission and obedience that must accompany its reception if the people are to avoid the Lord's judgment.

### (3) Recipients of the Message (1:1c)

Two individuals are singled out as recipients of Haggai's initial message. The first is Zerubbabel, who represented political power as the Persian-appointed governor over Judah, and the second is Joshua, who represented religious authority as the duly appointed high priest. Five times these two names appear together in Haggai (1:1,12,14; 2:2,4), always in the same order. This suggests a diarchic form of rule in which civil and religious leadership were merged in the governing body. The consistent listing of Zerubbabel first hints at his primacy in this arrangement.

The larger constituency of the people is not directly mentioned in v. 1 as part of Haggai's intended audience, although their inclusion is presupposed in the accusations that follow later in this message (e.g., vv. 2–3).[21] That they are an assumed part of Haggai's audience is also clear from v. 12, where their response to this message is described. Since nothing of significance could take place with regard to rebuilding the temple apart from the approval and encouragement of the political and the religious leadership of the people, it is the leaders—Zerubbabel and Joshua—who are the main target of Haggai's first message. This reflects the assumption that if their involvement can first be secured, the enlistment of the people will be that much easier. Haggai's message is thus directed primarily, though not exclusively, to these civil and religious leaders.

It is Zerubbabel who is first singled out. Not all of the biblical details concerning the family relationships of Zerubbabel are equally clear. The probable meaning of his name (i.e., "seed of Babylon")[22] suggests that he was born in

---

[21] I agree with J. E. Tollington, who describes the words "this people" (NIV "these people") in v. 2 as "a phrase that has no meaning unless a wider section of the community, not solely the two leaders, was listening to his words" (*Tradition and Innovation in Haggai and Zechariah 1–8*, JSOTSup 150 [Sheffield: JSOT Press, 1993], 20).

[22] See BDB, 279; *HALOT,* 279. The name Zerubbabel is probably a Hb. adaptation of the Akk. *zēr bābili.*

the captivity. The name may also hint at the extent to which the Jewish community of the exile had accepted its Babylonian environment.[23] Zerubbabel is described here as the "son of Shealtiel."[24] Unlike the name Zerubbabel, Shealtiel reflects a northwest Semitic environment. In Hebrew the name means "I have asked God." It is presumably an allusion to parental prayer for the birth of a child. The name may be an indication that Zerubbabel's father had been born before the exile, since during the exile west Semitic influences in names probably gave way to Babylonian influences.[25]

Shealtiel was an older son of the Judean king Jehoiachin, according to 1 Chr 3:17. The Chronicler presents Zerubbabel's genealogy in terms slightly different from those found in Haggai. According to 1 Chr 3:19, Zerubbabel's father was not Shealtiel but Pedaiah, who was a younger son of Jehoiachin (1 Chr 3:17). This would seem to imply that Shealtiel was actually Zerubbabel's uncle, not his father. How is this discrepancy to be accounted for? We can only conjecture. Suggestions that the problem is due to textual error in the MT are not convincing.[26] It may be that in keeping with the law of Levirite marriage (Deut 25:5–6) Pedaiah had married Shealtiel's widow, in which case a male child born to that relationship could properly be called the son of the presumably deceased Shealtiel. This proposal would seem to be an adequate explanation for the problem,[27] although it must be stressed that it goes beyond the silence of the biblical passages in the matter.

Another problem concerns the relationship of Zerubbabel to Sheshbazzar, who is mentioned in the Book of Ezra as among the Jews who returned from Babylon to Judah and who was appointed governor by Cyrus (Ezra 1:8,11; 5:14,16).[28] The details of the biblical material in this regard are dif-

---

[23] So, e.g., J. A. Soggin, *Introduction to the Old Testament, from Its Origins to the Closing of the Alexandrian Canon*, rev. ed., OTL (Philadelphia: Westminster, 1980), 325.

[24] Cf. Hag 1:12,14; 2:2,23; Ezra 3:2,8; Neh 12:1; Matt 1:12; Luke 3:27.

[25] So C. L. Meyers and E. M. Meyers, *Haggai, Zechariah 1–8: A New Translation with Introduction and Commentary*, AB (New York: Doubleday, 1987), 10.

[26] The LXX of 1 Chr 3:19 has Shealtiel rather than Pedaiah as the father of Zerubbabel. But this is the easier reading text-critically and is likely due to scribal harmonization.

[27] For a fuller discussion of this view see C. F. Keil, *Minor Prophets*, Commentary on the Old Testament, vol. 10 (Grand Rapids: Eerdmans, 1982), 175–76. It is an interpretation that has been adopted by a number of modern commentators, although Meyers and Meyers regard it as an unconvincing attempt at harmonization (see *Haggai, Zechariah 1–8*, 10).

[28] A further complication is Sheshbazzar's relationship to Shenazzar of 1 Chr 3:18. Is this one individual referred to by two different names, or are these two separate individuals? Most probably, they are separate individuals. See, e.g., S. Japhet, "Sheshbazzar and Zerubbabel—Against the Background of the Historical and Religious Tendencies of Ezra-Nehemiah," *ZAW* 94 (1982): 95–96; L. L. Grabbe, *Judaism from Cyrus to Hadrian* (Minneapolis: Fortress, 1992), 76. But some scholars equate the two. See, e.g., E. Stern, "The Persian Empire and the Political and Social History of Palestine in the Persian Period," in *Introduction: The Persian Period, CHJ* (Cambridge: Cambridge University Press, 1984), 70; J. Bright, *A History of Israel*, 3d ed. (Philadelphia: Westminster, 1981), 362.

ficult to sort out. The traditional view, which is at least as old as Josephus,[29] is that Zerubbabel and Shesbazzar are different names for the same individual. The view held by most modern scholars, however, is that they are two different individuals.[30] In that case Sheshbazzar was responsible for starting the work on the foundations of the temple, while Zerubbabel at a later time was responsible for bringing the work to completion (cf. Ezra 3:8–10; 5:16).

As governor of Judah, Zerubbabel was in charge of a very small district of the enormous Persian empire. This tiny region was commonly known by its Aramaic name Yehud; it was a part of the much larger region the Persians referred to as the Trans-Euphrates.[31] Persian governance of Yehud (Judah) followed precedents established by earlier overlords of the region. It appears that to a large degree the Persians merely adopted and developed the administrative structures for this region that had been put in place earlier by the Assyrians and Babylonians.[32] Although it is sometimes claimed that in the early Achaemenid period Judah was governed as a part of Samaria, it seems more likely that the Persians dealt with Judah as a separate region.[33] At this time Judah had no autonomous identity apart from the rights and privileges extended to it by Persia. Its size and potential threat to its distant overseer were totally insignificant in comparison to other political entities of the period. So limited was its geographical area that Soggin estimates that in a single day one could easily have walked from one extremity of the province to the other.[34] The population of Judah at this time was no doubt also quite small, although it is difficult to guess

---

[29] See Josephus, *Ant.* 11.13.

[30] For a summary of the issues see J. Lust, "The Identification of Zerubbabel with Sheshbassar," *ETL* 63 (1987): 90–95; J. S. Wright, *The Building of the Second Temple* (London: Tyndale, n.d.), esp. pp. 10–12; Japhet, "Sheshbezzar and Zerubbabel," 90–94. Lust concludes that Zerubbabel is to be identified with Sheshbazzar, while Wright maintains that Sheshbazzar (to be equated with Shenazzar of 1 Chr 3:18) was the uncle of Zerubbabel. Japhet sees the two as separate individuals. T. André also discusses the issue at some length, concluding that Zerubbabel and Sheshbazzar should be viewed as separate individuals (*Le prophète Aggée: Introduction critique et commentaire* [Paris: Librairie Fischbacher, 1895], 48–63).

[31] Lit., "Beyond-the-River" (Aram., עֲבַר־נַהֲרָא). For a helpful summary of the history of this region see A. F. Rainey, "The Satrapy 'Beyond the River,'" *AJBA* 1 (1969): 51–78.

[32] See E. Stern, "New Evidence on the Administrative Division of Palestine in the Persian Period," in *Centre and Periphery: Proceedings of the Groningen 1986 Achaemenid History Workshop*, Achaemenid History 4 (Leiden: Nederlands Instituut voor het Nabije Oosten, 1990), 221–26.

[33] See the discussion of this point in H. Williamson, "Judah and the Jews," in *Studies in Persian History: Essays in Memory of David M. Lewis,* Achaemenid History 11 (Leiden: Nederlands Instituut voor het Nabije Oosten, 1998), 152–54.

[34] Soggin, *Introduction*, 323.

what the actual population might have been.[35]

Persia granted to the province of Yehud a certain amount of autonomy to govern itself. The gesture was not entirely magnanimous. It was in Persia's best interests to acquiesce to the desire of the inhabitants of Judah to have a Davidic ruler and a properly constituted priesthood. Yehud lay at a geographical crossroads for the eastern Mediterranean world, and it was therefore of strategic importance for Persia to maintain control, foster stability, and encourage goodwill to the fullest extent possible.[36]

Zerubbabel's title is "governor of Judah" (*paḥat yĕhûdâ*), according to v. 1.[37] The word for governor *(peḥâ)* is a loanword that derives from the Akkadian word *pāḥāti*, which is a shortened form of *bēl paḥāti,* meaning "lord of a district."[38] In Haggai this word occurs four times, all in reference

---

[35] Population estimates for Judah during the Persian period vary a good deal depending in part on how much weight is placed on the relevant biblical material. Ezra 2:64 and Neh 7:66 indicate there were 42,360 returnees from Babylon, not counting 7,337 servants and more than 200 singers. In addition to these who returned from Babylon was an unknown number of Jews who had remained in the land during the exile. The numbers provided by these texts seem compatible with C. Stuhlmueller's suggestion that of Jerusalem's former 100,000 inhabitants, no more than 30,000 were in the city at the time of Haggai's ministry (*Rebuilding with Hope: A Commentary on the Books of Haggai and Zechariah*, ITC [Grand Rapids: Eerdmans, 1988], 13). But modern scholarship tends to be quite skeptical about the accuracy of the figures found in Ezra and Nehemiah. Using a variety of analytical techniques a number of scholars have suggested the population of Judah in the early Persian period probably was fewer than 20,000. See, e.g., L. H. Schiffman, *From Text to Tradition: A History of Second Temple and Rabbinic Judaism* (Hoboken: Ktav, 1991), 36; E. M. Meyers, "Second Temple Studies in the Light of Recent Archaeology: Part I: The Persian and Hellenistic Periods," *CurBS* 2 (1994): 30; Bright, *History of Israel*, 365. In an important socioeconomic analysis of Yehud during the postexilic period, C. E. Carter has estimated the population to be considerably lower than most other estimates. Taking a rather minimalist approach, he suggests that in the Persian I period (538–450 B.C.) Yehud had a population of about 13,350 and in the Persian II period (450–332 B.C.) about 20,650, while Jerusalem had at most about 1,500 inhabitants. But such estimates clash with the biblical record and can only be correct if there is distortion in the figures provided in Ezra and Nehemiah or in their interpretation. But see Carter, *The Emergence of Yehud in the Persian Period: A Social and Demographic Study,* JSOTSup 294 (Sheffield: Sheffield Academic Press, 1999), esp. p. 201. See also id., "The Province of Yehud in the Post-exilic Period: Soundings in Site Distribution and Demography," in *Second Temple Studies, 2, Temple Community in the Persian Period,* JSOTSup 175 (Sheffield: JSOT Press, 1994), 106–45; J. Kessler, "Reconstructing Haggai's Jerusalem: Demographic and Sociological Considerations and the Search for an Adequate Methodological Point of Departure," in *'Every City Shall Be Forsaken': Urbanism and Prophecy in Ancient Israel and the Near East,* JSOTSup 330 (Sheffield: Sheffield Academic Press, 2001), 137–58.

[36] On various aspects of Persian administration of the province of Judah see H. G. M. Williamson, "The Governors of Judah under the Persians," *TynBul* 39 (1988): 59–82.

[37] In Hag 1:1 for the MT פַּחַת יְהוּדָה ("governor of Judah") the LXX has ἐκ φυλῆς Ιουδα ("of the tribe of Judah") here and in 1:14; 2:2,21. But this translation confuses the word פֶּחָה ("governor") with the word מִשְׁפָּחָה ("clan"). As a result, in the LXX this phrase describes Zerubbabel's genealogy as a member of the tribe of Judah, whereas in the Hb. text it describes his political domain over the geographical region known as Judah.

[38] See BDB, 808, and *HALOT*, 923.

to Zerubbabel (1:1,14; 2:2,21). The word is also common in Ezra and
Nehemiah to describe Persian governors assigned to territories in the Trans-
Euphrates region. It is used elsewhere to refer to Assyrian (e.g., 2 Kgs
18:24) or Babylonian (e.g., Dan 3:2) governors. What exactly it meant to be
a "governor" in the Persian empire probably varied from place to place,
since the word was used to refer to appointed officials of differing governmental status and responsibilities.[39] That Zerubbabel could legitimately
claim the title governor reflects to some degree the confidence of Persian
authorities in his ability to lead his people in a way that would not undermine expected allegiance to Persia.[40] Zerubbabel was considered capable of
effective leadership of his people. He could also be trusted with the imple-
mentation of imperial policy in a way consistent with Persian requirements.

An important issue related to v. 1 concerns the genealogical connections
of the governor Zerubbabel and the high priest Joshua. Both Zerubbabel
and Joshua had significant predecessors in their family backgrounds.
According to 1 Chr 3:17, Zerubbabel was the grandson of Jehoiachin, who
was one of the final kings of Judah at the time of the beginnings of the
exile. Thus Zerubbabel was linked in ancestry to the Davidic kings of
Judah. Though only a governor and not a king, and though accountable to
Persia for what transpired in the Judean province that he governed, Zerubbabel was nonetheless a Davidide who stood in a long line of Israelite royal
figures. This fact will be an important consideration for understanding the
prophecy about Zerubbabel found at the end of the Book of Haggai (2:20–
23), where he is described in elevated language.

As for Joshua,[41] he is repeatedly designated "the high priest" *(hakkōhēn
haggādôl),* indicating his position as the highest ranking priest (Hag
1:1,12,14; 2:2,4). Beginning with Aaron and then following with his
descendants, one priest was acknowledged as head of the sanctuary service
with special privileges and responsibilities. The expression "high priest,"
however, occurs for the first time in Lev 21:10, where this individual is
described as "the high priest who is exalted above his fellows, on whose
head the anointing oil has been poured and who has been consecrated to

---

[39] See the discussion in J. Elayi and J. Sapin, *Beyond the River: New Perspectives on Transeu-
phratene,* JSOTSup 250 (Sheffield: Sheffield Academic Press, 1998), 151–52.

[40] S. E. McEvenue maintains that Zerubbabel was not really a governor as such but only a lesser
official who was authorized to take charge of the postexilic return of the Jews to their land. But the
Book of Haggai seems to envision a more formal role for Zerubbabel than McEvenue allows ("The
Political Structure in Judah from Cyrus to Nehemiah," *CBQ* 43 [1981], esp. pp. 356–57).

[41] Elsewhere the names Joshua and Jehozadak appear as Jeshua and Jozadak. See Ezra 2:2;
3:2,8; 4:3; 5:2; 10:18; Neh 7:7; 12:1,7,10,26.

wear the vestments" (NRSV).[42] The position underwent various changes as Israel's circumstances changed.[43] The time of the exile and restoration would have been a major transitional phase in the history of the priesthood. Its exact nature in Haggai's time is unclear, but the term was clearly a technical one, even when allowance is made for Tollington's conclusion that in Joshua's case the expression "does not carry with it the connotation of the later post-exilic title."[44] In her view Joshua may simply have been a senior priest who assumed special duties in connection with the financing and building of the temple. The repeated use of the expression in Haggai, however, along with the patronymic designation of Joshua seems to suggest more of a technical sense for the phrase than Tollington allows. The Book of Haggai provides little information concerning Joshua's priestly responsibilities or the length of his tenure in office.[45] What few clues that exist regarding Joshua's priestly duties and official garments are to be found in the Book of Zechariah. But even there the information is meager.[46] We simply do not know a great deal about how the high priest functioned in the early postexilic period.

Joshua is said to be the "son of Jehozadak." This Jehozadak was of priestly lineage, and in 1 Chr 6:14–15 his ancestry is traced all the way back to Aaron. That same passage indicates that Jehozadak was among the exiles whom Nebuchadnezzar took to Babylon. Thus Joshua represented to the postexilic community a return to the priestly office that was in place at the beginning of the exile. Just as Zerubbabel called to mind precaptivity Israelite royalty, so Joshua called to mind the Levitical priesthood prior to the exile. These leaders thus represented for the restoration community an important link to the past.

In the disputation speech found in Hag 1:2–11 the prophet essentially does three things. First, he quotes a statement that summarizes the popular

---

[42] See also Num 35:25,28; Josh 20:6; 2 Kgs 12:11[Eng. 10]; 22:4,8; 23:4; 2 Chr 34:9; Neh 3:1,20; 13:28. Some ancient witnesses (e.g., SP, LXX, P) also support reading the phrase in Num 35:32.

[43] For a summary of the biblical evidence, with attention to the Books of Ezra and Chronicles, see K. Koch, "Ezra and Meremoth: Remarks on the History of the High Priesthood," in *"Sha'arei Talmon": Studies in the Bible, Qumran, and the Ancient Near East Presented to Shemaryahu Talmon* (Winona Lake: Eisenbrauns, 1992), esp. pp. 106–8.

[44] Tollington, *Tradition and Innovation*, 131.

[45] J. C. VanderKam thinks Joshua may have continued as high priest until the early part of the fifth century B.C.; see "Jewish High Priests of the Persian Period: Is the List Complete?" in *From Revelation to Canon: Studies in the Hebrew Bible and Second Temple Literature*, Supplements to the Journal for the Study of Judaism 62 (Leiden: Brill, 2000), 198.

[46] See the discussion in VanderKam, "Joshua the High Priest and the Interpretation of Zechariah 3," ibid., 157–76. Joshua's role in the postexilic period is also discussed by M. Barker, "The Two Figures in Zechariah," *HeyJ* 18 (1977): 38–46.

point of view he intends to dispute (v. 2). That point of view, summed up by
an oft-recited slogan used by the community, includes what is a false
premise that in turn has led to a wrong conclusion. The prophet lays bare
for critical examination the theoretical basis the people have given to justify
their inertia in making the restoration of the temple a priority for their personal and collective endeavors. Second, the prophet challenges the legitimacy of this popular conclusion. In the process of doing so he draws a
counterconclusion that points out the unacknowledged impropriety that is
involved in their thinking (vv. 3–4). Third, the prophet provides specific
argumentation for this disputation, calling attention to the tangible consequences of divine retribution that this community has already experienced
as a result of behavior that was unacceptable to the Lord (vv. 5–11). The
speech is carefully crafted, it is direct in its accusation, and it leads to a
theological conclusion that the prophet's audience would find difficult to
avoid or to counter.

## 2. The People's Excuse for Delay (1:2)

²**This is what the LORD Almighty says: "These people say, 'The time has not
yet come for the LORD's house to be built.'"**

**1:2**  Haggai's message strikes right to the heart of the matter. No time is
wasted with nonessential asides or lengthy introduction. Nor is the message
presented simply as an expression of the prophet's opinion or advice.
Instead, Haggai boldly announces, "This is what the LORD Almighty says."
This is the first of fourteen occurrences in Haggai of the phrase *YHWH
ṣĕbāʾôt* (lit. "YHWH of hosts").[47] It is the most frequent designation for
God in this book. The expression is used some 265 times in the Hebrew
Bible; another eighteen times the longer expression *YHWH ʾĕlōhê
(haṣ)ṣĕbāʾôt* (lit. "YHWH God of [the] hosts") appears.[48] The Hebrew
word for "host" *(ṣābāʾ)* in the Old Testament often means "army," either in
reference to human armies prepared for conflict (e.g., Judg 8:6; 9:29; Isa

---

[47] The genitive construction in the phrase יְהוָה צְבָאוֹת is difficult from a grammatical standpoint, since we would not expect a proper name in Hb. to take a genitive in this way. Many scholars
assume the expression is elliptical, with the appellative idea of the proper name having been sup-
pressed. So, e.g., GKC §125h; cf. *GBH* §131o. In that case the fuller expression, regarded by Gesenius as actually a secondary expansion, is יְהוָה אֱלֹהֵי צְבָאוֹת, "Yahweh (the God) of hosts."
Less likely is Joüon's suggestion that the construction is appositional, meaning "Yahweh (the)
hosts" (see *GBH* §131o). Another possibility, also suggested by Joüon, is that צְבָאוֹת in this
expression came to be regarded as itself part of the proper name, although this does not seem fully
to account for the earliest usage of the phrase when the word "hosts" presumably retained its ordinary meaning.

[48] See *HALOT,* 996.

34:2; Jer 51:3; 2 Chr 28:9, etc.) or in reference to heavenly gatherings of angels (e.g., 1 Kgs 22:19, Neh 9:6; Pss 103:21; 148:2; Dan 8:10, etc.). The word can also be used to refer to the sun, moon, and stars as "the host of heaven" (e.g., Deut 4:19; 17:3; 2 Kgs 17:16; 21:3,5, etc.). The expression "Yahweh of hosts" occurs in early biblical literature to describe God as a warrior in charge of heavenly armies. But in postexilic literature the expression seems to be used mainly to emphasize the sovereignty of God, having lost some of its earlier specificity. In the Book of Haggai the expression serves to remind the prophet's audience of God's transcendence and control over all human affairs. The NIV translation "the LORD Almighty," though not very literal, adequately captures this nuance and is consistent with the LXX rendering, *kurios pantokratōr* ("almighty Lord").

Following the introduction to the Lord's words in v. 2, we expect to find his initial instructions through Haggai to the people. Instead, v. 2 abruptly continues with a citation of what the people were saying in defense of their actions.[49] The Lord's remarks begin with the expression "these people" *(hā'ām hazzeh)*.[50] There is a notion of contempt and disparagement in the words. The Lord does not refer to them as "my people," although in light of earlier covenantal promises extended to their ancestors he might have done so. Instead he calls them "this people." The personal pronoun "my," which might have brought a measure of reassurance to the people in the midst of their hardships, is replaced by the cold and detached demonstrative pronoun "this" (cf. Isa 6:9,10). The word signals at the outset of this message that something was wrong in the relationship between the Lord and the inhabitants of Judah.

The problem is more specifically identified in the people's confident words, quoted here by the Lord.[51] Their explanation for failure to rebuild the temple is that the time was not yet right for such an undertaking. The verb *('āmĕrû, "say")* that introduces their claim suggests that this is an assertion that had been set forth repeatedly in defense of their inactivity. It indicates not a claim that was given on a single occasion but one that was rehearsed repeatedly.[52] In the view of the people it was not apathy or self-

---

[49] More than a century ago this problem was noticed by A. P. Sym, who concluded that a dislocation of part of Haggai's message had occurred ("A Textual Study in Zechariah and Haggai," *ExpTim* 7 [1895–1896]: 257–60, 317–21). According to Sym most of Zech 4:6–10 actually belongs after Hag 1:2, since it fits here better than it does in Zechariah. The reasons advanced for this view, however, are not compelling, and there is no external evidence that supports such a conclusion. That there is an awkwardness to this pericope in Haggai is clear; that the solution to the problem lies in shifting Zech 4:6–10 to a position following Hag 1:2 seems unlikely.

[50] The Hb. expression is singular, "this people," but English translators often prefer to render this collective singular as a plural, "these people" (so NIV, ESV, NRSV, Tanak, NET Bible).

[51] As Kessler points out, the key words of 1:1–15 are found in the citation of v. 2: אָמַר ("to say"), עֵת ("time"), בּוֹא ("to come"), בָּנָה ("to build"), בֵּית יהוה ("the house of Yahweh") (*The Book of Haggai*, 109).

[52] The verb אָמְרוּ ("say") is best understood as a customary use of the perfect. On this use of the perfect in Hb. see GKC §106k.

ishness that had caused delay in this important project. They would eventually get around to restoring the temple. It was a question of timing. According to them the time was not yet right for the rebuilding of the temple. The temple would indeed be rebuilt, but not now.

In this section Haggai repeatedly pictures the temple as a house *(bêt)* in which the Lord resides. The choice of terms is significant. In biblical language the description of the temple as God's house suggests a roofed building equipped with furniture suitable to its function as a dwelling place for the deity. The temple perceived as a house differs in Old Testament thought from an altar, which could stand in the open by itself and which functioned not as a dwelling for the deity but as a place of sacrifice.[53] This notion of the temple as the house of God is thus important for understanding the urgency Haggai attaches to this structure. To leave the Lord's dwelling in a state of disrepair was to show disrespect to its occupant.

Furthermore, the word used in v. 2 to refer to the temple is a general word for "house" *(bêt),* the specific meaning of which can only be determined by context (cf. 2 Samuel 7). Its flexibility enables Haggai to use the same word in two very different senses, highlighting the contrast between the people's personal interests and their religious concerns. Sometimes in this chapter the word refers to the temple as the place of the Lord's residence (e.g., 1:2,4,8,9,14). Other times it refers to private houses as the place of the people's residence (e.g., 1:4,9[2x]). The fundamental problem to which Haggai points is that the people were concerned about the wrong house—they were looking after their own homes while neglecting the temple. The versatility of the word thus underscores a contrast to which Haggai repeatedly points in this chapter. It is a contrast between indulgent concern over matters of personal comfort on the one hand and callused disregard for spiritual responsibilities on the other hand.

In v. 2 the Lord quotes from the people their reason for not moving ahead with the temple reconstruction. The problem, in their view, was that the time for rebuilding was not yet right. The stress on appropriate timing for initiation of the temple project plays a prominent role in chap. 1. Timing, albeit in a different sense, is also an emphasis in Zephaniah 3,[54] which immediately precedes Haggai in the familiar canonical order of the book of the Twelve. This theme of timing may have played a role in the decision to place these two books side by side.[55]

In the Hebrew text the statement "The time has not yet come" is in the form

---

[53] On this distinction see further M. Haran, "Temples and Cultic Open Areas as Reflected in the Bible," in *Temples and High Places in Biblical Times: Proceedings of the Colloquium in Honor of the Centennial of Hebrew Union College–Jewish Institute of Religion, Jerusalem, 14–16 March 1977* (Jerusalem: Nelson Glueck School of Biblical Archaeology of Hebrew Union College–Jewish Institute of Religion, 1981), 31–37.

[54] Note the repeated use of the phrases "in that day" and "in that time" in Zeph 3:11,16,19,20.

[55] So P. L. Redditt, "The Production and Reading of the Book of the Twelve," in *Reading and Hearing the Book of the Twelve*, SBLSymS 15 (Atlanta: Society of Biblical Literature, 2000), 23.

of a negated noun clause. The word of negation employed is *lō'* ("not") rather than *'ên* ("there is not"). The negation is to be understood as going especially with the noun (*'et*, "time"). It is an emphatic structure that calls attention to the word "time" as representing the issue at hand.[56] Furthermore, the word for "time" is repeated in the Hebrew text, calling attention to the precise issue that is being disputed.[57] The dispute was not over whether the temple should be rebuilt but whether the appropriate time for doing so had yet arrived.

The phraseology of v. 2 is awkward.[58] It is not immediately clear how much of v. 2 constitutes a quotation of the people and how much, if any of it, is an explanation of the people's claim. The problem is due to the fact that ancient biblical manuscripts utilized no punctuation to mark the end of a quotation; there was nothing that functioned as the equivalent of our close-quotation mark. The NIV reflects the common understanding of v. 2: 'These people say, 'The time has not yet come for the LORD's house to be built.'" This rendering, which is shared with most translations of the verse, understands all of the latter part of v. 2 to be a quotation of the people's comment. But this understanding finds it difficult to explain the repetition of the word *'et* in the Hebrew text.

Neither of the two most common explanations for the twofold occurrence of *'et* provides an adequate explanation of the verse. One sees the repetition as due to emphasis on the idea of time. The latter part of the verse, however, has more of an explanatory than an emphatic function. The repetition does not emphasize the concept of time so much as it explains what is meant by the first of the two references to time. It is a time suitable for beginning the rebuilding project. A second approach to the problem suspects textual disturbance in the MT to be the cause of the awkwardness in phraseology. Both the LXX and P have a single occurrence of the word "time" here,[59] and some scholars have proposed emending the MT in light

---

[56] See GKC §152d.

[57] On this point see Amsler, "Aggée, Zacharie 1–8," 22.

[58] K. Marti, e.g., describes the phrase as "sehr verschrobene," or "very eccentric" (*Das Dodekapropheton*, KHC 13 [Tübingen: Mohr, 1904], 382).

[59] The LXX (οὐκ ἥκει ὁ καιρός) and P (*l' mty zbn'*) have a more straightforward reading in v. 2: "The time . . . has not come." *Targum Jonathan* has עַד כֵּן לָא מְטָא עִידָן בֵּית מַקְדְּשָׁא דַּיְיָ לְאִתְבְּנָאָה ("the time has not yet arrived for the Lord's sanctuary to be built"). But it is not necessary to conclude that these versions reflect a Hebrew *Vorlage* that lacked the first עֵת of the MT. It is more likely that the translators have simplified a Hebrew text whose reading was actually identical to that of the MT. Furthermore, the fact that the reading of the LXX and P is easier than that of the MT is not really an argument in its favor, since it cannot adequately explain the origin of the other reading. The same criticism applies to Elliger's suggestion in the apparatus of *BHS* to change the vocalization to read עַתָּה בָא ("now has come") in place of the MT עֵת־בֹּא ("time to come"). This too is an easier, but not a preferable, reading. It is better to retain the *lectio difficilior* ("more difficult reading") of the MT here. See further the discussion of this variant in D. Barthélemy, *Ézéchiel, Daniel et les 12 Prophètes*, vol. 3, *Critique textuelle de l'Ancien Testament*, OBO 50/3 (Fribourg: Éditions Universitaires Fribourg; Göttingen: Vandenhoeck & Ruprecht, 1992), 923–24. On the targum rendering of this verse see Y. Komlosh, "The Etymological Basis of Certain Translations in the Targum Jonathan to the Twelve Prophets" [in Hb.], in *Studies in Hebrew and Semitic Languages Dedicated to the Memory of Prof. Eduard Yechezkel Kutscher* (Ramat-Gan: Bar-Ilan University Press, 1980): 163.

of this evidence.[60] But this reading is most likely due to translation technique employed in these versions rather than being due to textual variation in their *Vorlage*.[61] For this reason it seems best to accept the MT as the original reading here and look to exegesis for an answer to the problem.

Tadmor has proposed an attractive solution to this problem.[62] According to him the quoted portion consists of only three words in the Hebrew text: "The time has not come" *(lō' 'et bō')*. The rest of the verse is not part of the quotation but is the Lord's explanation of what the people meant by this use of the word "time." The quoted words probably formed a populist slogan that epitomized why the temple should not yet be rebuilt. Tadmor likens it to the modern slogan "No more war."[63] It is a brief and effective summary of the position of those who used it, and it is expressed in a short, staccato fashion that enhanced its effectiveness. What follows this slogan in v. 2 is the Lord's (or the prophet's) explanation of the use of the word "time" in the quoted slogan "that is, the time for the LORD's house to be rebuilt." This understanding accounts for the repetition of the word "time" *('et)* in v. 2 in that the second occurrence of the word proffers an exposition of the meaning of the word in the quotation that precedes. It also yields a vivid and effective slogan that summarizes the people's point of view with regard

---

[60] M. Sebök, e.g., concludes that the first עֵת is due to dittography and should be deleted and that the infinitive בֹא should be repointed as a perfect (בָּא). This makes for an easier reading, but in terms of text criticism that is not necessarily an argument in its favor. But see Sebök [Schönberger], *Die syrische Uebersetzung der zwölf kleinen Propheten und ihr Verhältniss zu dem massoretischen Text und zu den ältern Uebersetzungen, namentlich den LXX. und dem Targum* (Breslau: Preuss und Jünger, 1887), 67.

[61] In this regard Eng. translations of v. 2 provide an instructive analogy. The presence of a single occurrence of the word "time" in the NIV rendering of this verse is likely due not to a text-critical decision to eliminate one of the two occurrences of the word, but rather to a concern over readability in the target language. The wording of the Hb. text has apparently been leveled in the Eng. as a translation technique intended to assist the reader. In such cases one must be careful about drawing conclusions as to the form of the Hb. *Vorlage* on the basis of translations that may simply reflect functional rather than formal correspondence.

[62] H. Tadmor, "'The Appointed Time Has Not Yet Arrived': The Historical Background of Haggai 1:2," in *Ki Baruch Hu: Ancient Near Eastern, Biblical, and Judaic Studies in Honor of Baruch A. Levine* (Winona Lake: Eisenbrauns, 1999), 402–3.

[63] From American presidential politics we might call to mind the slogan "I like Ike!" (used by supporters of Dwight D. Eisenhower in the 1952 presidential campaign) or more recently the slogan "No more Gore!" (used by opponents of Albert Gore in the 2000 presidential campaign). A slogan that epitomized opposition to American involvement in the Vietnam War on the part of those whose age made them candidates for the military draft was "Hell no, we won't go!" What made such slogans popular was their pithy content and their effective use of rhythmic cadences to capture widely held public sentiments of either support or opposition to a particular cause.

to the temple project: *lōʾ ʿet bōʾ* ("The time has not come!").[64] The slogan was short, rhythmic, memorable, and no doubt very effective.

The people of Haggai's community did not question whether the temple should at some point in the future be rebuilt; on that there was a general consensus. What they did challenge was that that time to do so had already arrived. The reason for their claim is not stated. What exactly were they thinking? Surely not that the labor requirements of harvest left no further time for this work; it was then the sixth month, and the harvest was over. Nor could they claim Samaritan interference as a hindrance to the work; that issue had been addressed many years earlier (cf. Ezra 4:1–5). The political events of the day may have contributed to a sense of uncertainty on the part of the Jewish population, perhaps leading to skepticism about the temple project. The recent Persian conflict with Egypt, the unexpected death of Cambyses, Darius's rapid consolidation of power—such events had perhaps left many of Haggai's people wondering whether the time was right for new and expensive initiatives. Furthermore, times were difficult, and they were unable to provide even the bare necessities of life required by their families. Perhaps they reasoned that the time was not right because they lacked the necessary resources to accomplish such an expensive task. In that case the endeavor would have to wait until better economic and financial times arrived, providing a more propitious time for undertaking such a project.[65] It is also possible that some of the people may have resented the notion that a pagan king should be the means by which restoration of the temple would come, believing that such initiatives should instead come entirely from Jewish quarters.[66]

There may even have been theological reasons for the hesitancy of the people. Ezekiel had described a glorious temple that would come as the result of divine initiative (Ezek 40–48). But to attempt to bring about such a temple apart from a clear word from the Lord indicating that this was something that in fact should be done could be viewed as presumptuous or ill-advised, perhaps even as "a betrayal of the eschatological hope."[67] Ancient Near Eastern peoples typically sought to determine the will of the particular deity involved before pre-

---

[64] The rhythmic quality of the vocalization of the words in the MT *(lōʾ ʿet bōʾ),* if they are in fact to be understood as a slogan, argues in favor of accepting that vocalization as correct, as opposed to various suggestions to emend the words in question in order to achieve a smoother text. R. L. Smith's comment, e.g., becomes unnecessary: "If retained the inf. בֹא must be read as a perf. בָּא" *(Micah–Malachi,* 151, n. 2.a). Such a proposal overlooks the sound pattern that is involved in the slogan. Grammar has given way here to cadence and rhyme.

[65] See J. Kessler, "ʿt (le temps) en Aggée I 2–4: Conflit théologique ou 'sagesse mondaine'?" *VT* 48 (1998): 555–59.

[66] See, e.g., E. J. Bickerman, "The Edict of Cyrus in Ezra 1," *JBL* 65 (1946): 266–67.

[67] The expression is R. G. Hamerton-Kelly's; see "The Temple and the Origins of Jewish Apocalyptic," *VT* 20 (1976), esp. p. 12.

suming to build a shrine or temple in his honor. The perceived absence of an indication from the Lord that the task should be undertaken could lead to reluctance in attempting such a project, even on the part of those who otherwise did not doubt that it was a worthwhile undertaking.

An even more pointed theological question may underlie the people's claim that the time was not right. There was common acknowledgment that the Babylonian captivity was a divinely imposed punishment that only the Lord could bring to conclusion. Jeremiah had predicted that the exile was to last for seventy years (Jer 25:11–12; 29:10). If Jeremiah was correct, in order to determine the end of the exile one only needed to know the precise point at which it began and add to that seventy years. If the seventy years started at the destruction of the temple in 586 B.C., then those years had not yet run their full course at the time of the delivery of Haggai's message. Several years yet remained for that scheme to be fulfilled. In that case to embark on a rebuilding project prematurely could be viewed as a failure to submit to the Lord's appointed discipline for its stipulated time of duration. It could be argued that such an undertaking was wrong in its timing and therefore lacked the Lord's approval and blessing. The experiences of the destruction of Jerusalem and the temple and the captivity of the exiles in Babylon were understood to be due to God's displeasure with their ancestors.[68] The claim that "the time has not yet come" may be based on uncertainty about whether the Lord's anger had relented to the point that restoration of the temple could be safely initiated.[69] In that case the word *ʿet* in v. 2 may carry a somewhat technical sense, specifically connoting the time at which the Lord was no longer angry at the people for their prior failures.

Whether or not any of these notions are exactly what lie behind the people's reluctance to begin work on the temple is unclear. Such reasonings may well have been a part of their thinking in this matter. In the following verses of chap. 1 the prophet focuses on the economic issues that were involved, which suggests that this is the issue that carried the greater weight in their thinking, although the other possibilities should not be ruled out altogether.

## 3. The Lord's Response (1:3–11)

Whatever might have been the specific basis of the reasoning for delaying the temple project, it is clear that neither the Lord nor Haggai was impressed by it. In the remainder of this message (vv. 3–11) the prophet

---

[68] See, e.g., 2 Kgs 21:10–15; 23:26–27; 24:20; Ps 79:1–4; Lam 1:12; 2:1,3,21–22; 3:1,43; 4:11; Ezek 5:13; 7:8,13; 8:17–18; 2 Chr 36:16.

[69] See, e.g., P. R. Bedford, "Discerning the Time: Haggai, Zechariah and the 'Delay' in the Rebuilding of the Jerusalem Temple," in *The Pitcher Is Broken: Memorial Essays for Gösta W. Ahlström*, JSOTSup 190 (Sheffield: Sheffield Academic Press, 1995), 75.

spells out the Lord's unsympathetic response to their delays in doing his work and underscores what they must do to regain his favor.

### (1) The Origin of the Prophet's Message (1:3)

**³Then the word of the LORD came through the prophet Haggai:**

**1:3** The claim of divine authority made in v. 1 is now repeated in v. 3 in essentially the same terms. By repeating this formula the prophet stresses the belief that his message did not originate by his initiative, nor was its harsh analysis the result of his personal reflections. The prophet's audience is exhorted to hear the voice of the Lord in his words to them.

### (2) The Cause and Consequence of Hard Times (1:4–11)

**⁴"Is it a time for you yourselves to be living in your paneled houses, while this house remains a ruin?"**

**⁵Now this is what the LORD Almighty says: "Give careful thought to your ways. ⁶You have planted much, but have harvested little. You eat, but never have enough. You drink, but never have your fill. You put on clothes, but are not warm. You earn wages, only to put them in a purse with holes in it."**

**⁷This is what the LORD Almighty says: "Give careful thought to your ways. ⁸Go up into the mountains and bring down timber and build the house, so that I may take pleasure in it and be honored," says the LORD. ⁹"You expected much, but see, it turned out to be little. What you brought home, I blew away. Why?" declares the LORD Almighty. "Because of my house, which remains a ruin, while each of you is busy with his own house. ¹⁰Therefore, because of you the heavens have withheld their dew and the earth its crops. ¹¹I called for a drought on the fields and the mountains, on the grain, the new wine, the oil and whatever the ground produces, on men and cattle, and on the labor of your hands."**

In the remainder of this pericope Haggai shows that the difficulties the people experienced were not simply coincidental. Their problems were the result of the Lord's discipline directed against them due to their misplaced priorities. Because of their religious failures they were undergoing physical suffering and deprivation. These problems would not disappear until their underlying causes were corrected, the prophet warns. Although scholars have raised questions about the unity of vv. 4–11, the passage provides good internal evidence of being a sound unit.[70]

INVERTED PRIORITIES OF THE PEOPLE (1:4). **1:4** In response to the

---

[70] For a succinct and helpful presentation of arguments for the unity of 1:4–11, as well as interaction with opposing points of view, see W. S. Prinsloo, "The Cohesion of Haggai 1:4–11," in *"Wünschet Jerusalem Frieden": Collected Communications to the XIIth Congress of the International Organization for the Study of the Old Testament, Jerusalem 1986*, BEATAJ 13 (Frankfurt am Main: Peter Lang, 1988), 337–43.

claim that the time was not right for rebuilding the temple, Haggai asks in the Lord's behalf how it could be that the time was right for building their private dwellings. The prophet's use of the word "time" (*'et*) at the beginning of v. 4 resumes the people's reference to time in v. 2. The question is rhetorical.[71] It is not intended to elicit information unknown to the asker, as though the prophet had a measure of mental uncertainty about the contrasting situations that form the content of his question in v. 4. Rather, by means of an interrogative the prophet hints at the indignation he feels toward the callused display of selfish interests on the part of the people. The question may also have the effect of expostulation, inviting the listeners or readers to draw a conclusion similar to that of the prophet on this matter. His point is that it is repulsive to suggest, as some of them have done, that it is not yet time to rebuild the temple while at the same time suggesting that it is time to undertake building projects that contribute to their personal security and comfort.

The question invites reflection on priorities. Whose interests were most important to them—their own or those of their God? It is a question with which believing communities have often had to struggle. To answer the question properly requires breaking with the familiar and comfortable patterns of the past and turning to God with urgent sincerity.[72] The New Testament counterpart to this lamentable attitude is expressed by the apostle Paul: "For everyone looks out for his own interests, not those of Jesus Christ" (Phil 2:21).

Haggai's question presents a set of concerns that ironically are a reversal of those concerns assumed in David's comment to the prophet Nathan at the time just before the building of the Solomonic temple. David muses, "Here I am, living in a palace of cedar, while the ark of God remains in a tent" (2 Sam 7:2). David was concerned over the disparity between his lavish palace and the meager surroundings for the ark, and he resolved to correct that disparity. Haggai's people were unconcerned over the disparity between their lavish homes and the ruined condition of the temple, and they devised ways to defend their lethargy. The irony is striking.

The Hebrew wording used in v. 4 is emphatic in its reference to the people (*lākem 'attem*, "for you yourselves"); it calls attention to the one-sided

---

[71] More specifically the figure of speech used here is erotesis, either of indignation or perhaps expostulation. On erotesis in general see E. W. Bullinger, *Figures of Speech Used in the Bible, Explained and Illustrated* (1898; reprint, Grand Rapids: Baker, 1968), 943–56. Although Bullinger's discussion of figurative language is obviously dated and at times needlessly polemical, its abiding value lies in its somewhat encyclopedic treatment of the topic. In the case of erotesis, e.g., he describes nineteen different types of this figure as used by biblical writers.

[72] J. G. Baldwin aptly speaks of "the dangerous state of moral paralysis which accepts as normal conditions that demand drastic changes" (*Haggai, Zechariah, Malachi: An Introduction and Commentary*, TOTC [Downers Grove: InterVarsity Press, 1972], 27).

nature of their interests.[73] By using the independent personal pronoun (*'attem*), Haggai heightens the contrast between what they do for themselves versus what they leave undone for the Lord. In referring to dwellings the same word (*bayit*, "house") is used both for the private houses of the people and for the temple as God's house. The more specific word for temple (*hêkal*) used later in Hag 2:15,18 is not used here. Generally speaking, in the prophetic literature as the temple receives greater emphasis the use of the word *hêkal* tends to give way to the more common term *bayit* to refer to the temple.[74] By using the same word to refer both to individual homes and to the temple, Haggai stresses the inappropriate priorities of the people. If a choice is to be made with regard to which of the two "houses" should be built first, does it not stand to reason that the Lord's wishes should take precedence over their own? Such is the logical basis of the prophet's complaint.

In v. 4 Haggai speaks of the "covered" houses in which the people live.[75] The specific nuance of *sĕpûnîm* in this description is not entirely clear.[76] Is the prophet referring to lavish expenditures for houses with interior paneling made of costly material (so apparently NIV), and if so, how does this relate to the economic hard times in which they were living? Given the mess the economy was in, as described in vv. 5–11, one wonders where money for such elaborate spending would have come from. Or does Haggai merely mean houses that are

---

[73] The independent personal pronoun (אַתֶּם, "you") is used here in apposition to the object of the preposition in the phrase "for you" (לָכֶם). See GKC §135g; *IBHS* §16.3.4; T. Muraoka, *Emphatic Words and Structures in Biblical Hebrew* (Jerusalem: Magnes; Leiden: Brill, 1985), 62.

[74] On this point see the discussion in Th. Chary, "Le culte chez les prophètes Aggée et Zacharie," in *Les prophètes et le culte à partir de l'exil*, vol. 3, Bibliothèque de théologie, series 3, Théologie biblique (Paris: Desclée, 1955), 127.

[75] That the Hb. infinitive used here (שֶׁבֶת, "to sit," "dwell") forms a merism with the participle in v. 9 (רָץ, "running"), as suggested by Meyers and Meyers (*Haggai, Zechariah 1–8*, 23,30), is not entirely clear to me. If the words are in fact to be taken as a merism, the sense would be that in all of their activities (whether sitting or running) it is self-advantage the people are seeking.

[76] In 1:4 the MT סְפוּנִים ("covered") lacks the definite article, although the preceding expression (בְּבָתֵּיכֶם, "in your houses") is definite by virtue of having a pronominal suffix. We would expect agreement in definiteness between the noun and the adjective that modifies it. The construction in the MT is somewhat awkward but not impossible from a grammatical standpoint. The adjectival participle can be explained as an accusative of state that may then be translated as "in your houses (which are at present) paneled"; see *GBH* §127a. This understanding seems preferable to the suggestion of Waltke and O'Connor that the word is an accusative of specification ("in your houses with paneling"), although the difference in emphasis is slight; see *IBHS* §14.3.3c. On the other hand, the possibility of textual error in the MT cannot be completely ruled out. Some MSS of the LXX (e.g., A, Q, and a corrected hand of S) lack the possessive pronoun (ἡμῶν, "you") in v. 4, as is also true of *Tg. Jonathan* and the Vg. In order to gain the expected agreement between the participle and the noun, some scholars have therefore proposed emending the definite בְּבָתֵּיכֶם to the indefinite בְּבָתִּים. In that case the letter *kaph* of the pronominal suffix in the MT may be due to dittography.

"roofed," in contrast to the demolished temple structure that had no such cover? The Hebrew word *sĕpûnîm* in v. 4 has been understood both ways.

The root *spn* basically means "to cover"; the precise nuance can only be determined by context. Related nouns include *sippun*, "ceiling" (1 Kgs 6:15), referring to the overhead covering of a building, and *sĕpînâ*, "ship" (Jonah 1:5), referring to a seagoing vessel with covered decks and space for storing cargo below. In its six Old Testament occurrences the verbal root *spn* refers to the closing in of Solomon's temple with beams for roofing (1 Kgs 6:9),[77] or to the paneling of Solomon's palace with such expensive items as cedar (1 Kgs 7:3,7; Jer 22:14). In these passages the emphasis is on the extravagance and wealth represented by such expensive coverings. On one occasion (Deut 33:21) the word has the derived sense of "reserved" or "laid up," referring to the allocation of the best portion of land for the leader. In Deut 33:19 the word has the sense of "hidden" or "concealed" (though here the root is spelled *śpn*).

The word *sĕpûnîm* in Hag 1:4 likely refers to the covering of interior walls with paneling, having in mind primarily the practice of the well-to-do few rather than that of the financially hard-pressed majority.[78] It may be significant in this regard that it is the governor and the high priest who are specifically singled out in this first sermon (1:1). Haggai's point is that while some of the people live in comfortable, convenient, and even lavishly appointed dwellings,[79] the temple of God by contrast lies in rubble and is the object of disinterest and neglect on the part of the people.[80]

In contrast to the nicely decorated houses of at least some of the people, the Lord's house "remains a ruin." The Hebrew word for "ruin" is *ḥārēb* (cf. v. 9, where the idea is repeated). This adjective is used sometimes in the Hebrew Bible with the sense of "dry" in reference to a grain offering (Lev 7:10) or a morsel of food (Prov 17:1). Other times it is used with the sense of "devas-

---

[77] The precise meaning of בֻ ("beams"?) in 1 Kgs 6:9 is uncertain; the word is a *hapax legomenon*. It probably refers to a beam or rafter (so BDB, 155), but some scholars have taken it to refer to a coffer or recess in a paneled ceiling (so *DCH* 2:297).

[78] D. R. Slavitt, e.g., translates the phrase as "your wainscoted houses" (*The Book of the Twelve Prophets* [Oxford: Oxford University Press, 2000], 103).

[79] R. Mason takes a more restrictive interpretation of סְפוּנִים than the one suggested here, concluding that the word "probably suggests something a good deal more makeshift than the 'paneled' of most Eng. versions" ("Haggai: Theology of," *NIDOTTE* 4 [1997]: 691). In a similar way Meyers and Meyers understand the word not to imply richness but to denote "the final stage of construction work when the wooden finishing, whether laid across stone or wooden walls, has been completed" (*Haggai, Zechariah 1–8*, 23).

[80] This ancient problem is not without its modern counterpart. Excessive discretionary spending on personal interests, accompanied by paltry giving to the work of God, continues to the present. As Baldwin reminds us, "The conflict between expenditure on luxury homes and worthy support of God's work is still with us" (*Haggai, Zechariah, Malachi*, 40).

tated," "desolate," or "in ruins" in reference to a city (Ezek 36:35; 36:38) or a place (Jer 33:12). The specific nuance of the word when used of the temple is disputed. There are two main views. Some scholars take the word to describe the temple as a deserted or abandoned facility that at this time saw no use. In this view the word *ḥārēb* in v. 4 does not point to the physical condition of the temple, as though it were lying in ruins.[81] Rather, it refers to the isolated and uninhabited condition of this structure. Other scholars have taken this occurrence of the word to describe a condition of physical destruction and ruin,[82] not merely a condition of desertion and absence of human occupation.[83] This need not imply that the structure in Haggai's day was completely obliterated or devoid of any recognizable feature whatsoever, since it seems clear from Ezra 3:2–3 that sacrifices were being offered on a rebuilt altar. But in light of Haggai's insistence of rebuilding, it is likely that in v. 4 *ḥārēb* assumes some degree of physical destruction and disrepair.

The use of the word *ḥārēb* in v. 4 sets up a wordplay, forming a semantic link to v. 11, where the word for "drought" is the cognate noun *ḥōreb*. Haggai thus connects the "ruin" of the temple to the "ruin" of the land. The relationship, as will be made even more clear in the verses that follow, is one of cause and effect. It is precisely *because* of the people's inactivity with regard to the temple that the Lord sent hard times to the land.[84] From the prophet's point of view the Lord had demonstrated his covenantal faithfulness by bringing the Jews into favor with Cyrus, who permitted them to return to their homeland. Now the time had come for the people to demonstrate their covenantal faithfulness to the Lord by seeing to it that his temple was rebuilt in Jerusalem. Yet this is precisely where they had failed. In Haggai's theology acceptance of human responsibility is an essential part of the outworking of divine purposes within the believing community. Conversely, recalcitrant rejection of that responsibility invites divine judgment.[85]

---

[81] See Amsler, "Aggée, Zacharie 1–8," 22; Meyers and Meyers, *Haggai, Zechariah 1–8*, 24, Kessler, *The Book of Haggai*, 128–30.

[82] See *DCH* 3:306; *HALOT,* 349.

[83] F. I. Andersen's comment does not seem to me to capture adequately the nuance of this word in Haggai: "Haggai's complaint is not that the house of God is not in existence, but that it is deserted. It is not that the people are building their own homes and not building the temple, it is that they sit in their homes when they should be working in the temple, and they run off home when they should be in church" ("Who Built the Second Temple?" *ABR* 6 [1958]: 25).

[84] J. A. Bewer has called attention to ANE parallels to Haggai's linkage of famine and temple building. He points to certain similarities between Haggai and the Gudea inscriptions with regard to the concepts of temple and the ushering in of a golden age; see "Ancient Babylonian Parallels to the Prophecies of Haggai," *AJSL* 35 (1919): 128–33.

[85] In terms of biblical theology God usually accomplishes his purposes through the committed efforts of a redeemed community. When that community fails in its responsibility, the work of God suffers as a consequence. As W. A. VanGemeren puts it, "The canonical function of Haggai clearly points the way in which God's people must participate to bring in the kingdom of God" (*Interpreting the Prophetic Word* [Grand Rapids: Zondervan, 1990], 192).

UNSUCCESSFUL EFFORTS OF THE PEOPLE (1:5–6). **1:5** Once again the prophet stresses the divine origin of the prophetic word: "Now this is what the LORD Almighty says." He urges the people to "give careful thought to [their] ways,"[86] suggesting that it is their religious failures that have triggered their economic misfortunes.[87] The expression is a negative one, suggesting that their ways or paths have deviated from behavior characterized by integrity and obedience. The figure surfaces the concern that things were not as they should be. There were prior failures that had not yet been sufficiently addressed.

**1:6** As described here, the people were caught in a web of diminishing return for their dogged efforts to provide life's necessities. Five areas of economic failure are singled out in v. 6. First, abundant planting has produced only a meager harvest; second, the food supply has been of insufficient quantity to satisfy hunger; third, drink is in such limited supply as to fail to quench thirst;[88] fourth, clothing is of inadequate quality and quantity to keep the wearer sufficiently protected from the elements; fifth, wages have such meager purchase power that it is as though they are placed into purses riddled with holes, quickly falling through and disappearing from sight.[89] The language is lively but a bit choppy. Five infinitives, rather than

---

[86] The Hb. expression used here is שִׂימוּ לְבַבְכֶם עַל־דַּרְכֵיכֶם ("set your heart upon your ways"). Cf. Hag 1:7; 2:15,18; Deut 32:46; Isa 41:22; Ezek 40:4; 44:5. "Heart" in this sense refers not to the seat of the emotions but to the rational faculties of the mind. See *HALOT*, 513–15; BDB, 524–25; *DCH* 4:498. J. Calvin, commenting on v. 5, says, "It is commonly said, that experience is the teacher of fools; and the Prophet has this in view in these words, *apply your hearts to your ways;* that is, 'If the authority of God or a regard for him is of no importance among you, at least consider how God deals with you" (*Habakkuk, Zephaniah, Haggai, Commentaries on the Twelve Minor Prophets* [Grand Rapids: Eerdmans, 1950], 328).

[87] The TEV adopts here a translation technique that converts the imperative of the Hb. text to a question in the Eng. text, "Don't you see what is happening to you?" But this translation seems to direct attention more to the present predicament of the people and less toward the moral root of their problem. An imperative rendering rather than an interrogative one would seem preferable here as an accurate translation. But for a defense of the interrogative as an effective translation of the Hb. imperative in this verse see L. J. de Regt, "Discourse Implications of Rhetorical Questions in Job, Deuteronomy and the Minor Prophets," in *Literary Structure and Rhetorical Strategies in the Hebrew Bible* (Assen: Van Gorcum, 1996), 74.

[88] In biblical Hb. the verb שָׁכַר normally means to be or become drunk, whether in the literal sense of inebriation or in the figurative sense of morally or religiously staggering out of control. In Hag 1:6, however, this verb seems to be used not in reference to drunkenness but rather to having enough to drink so as to be able to quench one's thirst. See F. Luciani, "Il verbo *šākar* in *Aggeo* 1,6," *Aev* 46 (1972): 498–501.

[89] In 1:6 the MT צְרוֹר נָקוּב ("a bag with holes") is paraphrased in *Tg. Jonathan* as לִמְאִירְתָּא ("for the curse [of poverty]"). For other examples in Jewish literature of מְאִירְתָא ("curse") referring to poverty see Jastrow, 2:724.

finite verbs, are used to advance the prophet's line of thought.[90]

Haggai's reference to wages being placed in a pierced bag probably pre-supposes the use of coins for remuneration. The prophet's passing comment sheds unexpected light on the use of currency in Palestine in the sixth century B.C. Not until the Persian period do we find evidence of coined money in Palestine to any significant degree,[91] although the Greeks made use of coins for currency at least by the seventh century B.C.[92] It may in fact have been Darius Hystaspes who introduced coinage into Persia,[93] borrowing the practice from the Lydians.[94] The allusion in Hag 1:6 to putting money into a purse may be the earliest reference in biblical literature to coined money.[95] The pierced purse mentioned by Haggai envisions, according to

---

[90] The first verb in this sequence (זְרַעְתֶּם, "you have planted") is followed by four infinitives absolute (הָבֵא, "harvested"; אָכוֹל, "eat"; שָׁתוֹ, "drink"; לָבוֹשׁ, "put on clothes"), which continue the chain initiated by the finite verb. A fifth infinitive absolute (הִתְבָּרֵ) is used adverbially with the initial verb. The use of the infinitive absolute as a substitute for a finite verb is common in classical Hb., particularly in later books of the Hb. Bible. See *GBH* §123x; GKC §113z.

[91] According to E. Stern, the two earliest coins discovered so far in Palestine date to the second half of the sixth century B.C. One of these is an Attic coin discovered in Jerusalem, and the other is a coin from Thasos found at Shechem. It is likely, however, that widespread circulation of coins in Palestine did not occur until toward the end of the fifth century (*Material Culture of the Land of the Bible in the Persian Period 538–332 B.C.* [Warminster, England: Aris & Phillips, 1982], 215, 236). More recently Stern refers to a Greek coin minted on the island of Kos and dating to ca. 570 B.C. as the earliest Greek coin found in Palestine. It was discovered at the site of Ketef Hinnom in Jerusalem ("Coins," in *The Assyrian, Babylonian, and Persian Periods: 732–332 BCE, Archaeology of the Land of the Bible*, ABRL [New York: Doubleday, 2001], 2:558–59.

[92] See D. Kagan, "The Dates of the Earliest Coins," *AJA* 86 (1982): 343–60. On evidence for coinage in ancient Persia see A. D. H. Bivar, "Achaemenid Coins, Weights and Measures," in *The Median and Achaemenian Periods, The Cambridge History of Iran* (Cambridge: Cambridge University Press, 1985), 2:610–39; P. Vargyas, "Silver and Money in Achaemenid and Hellenistic Babylonia," in *Assyriologica et Semitica* [Fs J. Oelsner], AOAT 252 (Münster: Ugarit, 2000), 513–21.

[93] Some scholars date the introduction of coinage to Persia a bit earlier than this. M. Mallowan, e.g., entertains the possibility that Cyrus rather than Darius was responsible for this significant innovation ("Cyrus the Great [558–529 B.C.]" in *The Median and Achaemenian Periods, The Cambridge History of Iran* [Cambridge: Cambridge University Press, 1985], 2:415). Stern suggests that coins were first introduced to Palestine as early as the Babylonian period, sometime in the first half of the sixth century B.C. ("Coins," 555). Notice should also be taken of the fact that E. S. G. Robinson has discussed certain issues of Achaemenid chronology and monetary manufacturing techniques of ancient Persia in light of two hoards of Persian sigloi discovered at old Smyrna in 1951. These coins date to ca. 500 B.C. and are therefore of some interest to consideration of Haggai's allusion to coined money, although Robinson does not actually discuss the reference in Hag 1:6; see "The Beginnings of Achaemenid Coinage," *NumC*, 6th series, 18 (1958): 187–93.

[94] D. J. Wiseman, "Money. I. In the Old Testament," in *NBD*, 3d ed. (Downers Grove: Inter-Varsity, 1996), 780. Wiseman says, "It would seem that after the Persian wars against Lydia, coinage was introduced into Persia by Darius I (521–486 BC), whose name was used to denote the thick gold coin, or daric, which portrays the king, half-length or kneeling, with bow and arrow; with the die-punch mark in reverse (see Herodotus iv. 166)." See also *Grabbe, Judaism from Cyrus to Hadrian,* 70, 125.

[95] So R. Loewe, "The Earliest Biblical Allusion to Coined Money?" *PEQ* 87 (1955): 147–50.

Loewe, a situation where workers were paid such an inadequate wage that the small coins fell through little holes in the workers' purses.

The impact of such dismal conditions as Haggai describes had clearly taken a huge toll on the outlook and perspective of the people.[96] Not being able to provide for even the basic necessities of life,[97] how could they be expected to underwrite the significant financial costs and labor demands of an expensive project such as the temple?

THE NECESSITY OF OBEDIENCE (1:7–11).   The paragraph found in vv. 7–11 develops along two lines. First, Haggai calls on the people to acknowledge their need to obey the Lord's instructions about the temple given to them through the word that he had received from the Lord. Second, they must also acknowledge that they are experiencing the Lord's discipline because of their own failure. The only thing that could lead to removal of the severe chastisement that had befallen them is genuine repentance and sincere obedience to the Lord's instructions.

*The Lord's Requirement (1:7–8).*   **1:7**   Once again the prophet calls attention to the fact that it is the Lord who is speaking through the prophetic message (cf. vv. 1,2,3,5). And once again he urges the people to consider their ways (cf. v. 5). The implication is that proper reflection on their past course of action should lead to a change of behavior for the future.

**1:8**   Now the people are urged to go up to the mountains to secure the necessary timber for construction.[98] Although the Hebrew word for "mountain" *(hāhār)* is singular, that need not mean that it is the temple mount specifically to which reference is made.[99] The Hebrew word *hār* is often used broadly to

---

[96] J. A. Motyer seems to minimize the economic difficulties described here, suggesting that the main problem the people experienced was not the lack of life's necessities but rather an absence of satisfaction with the advantages they possessed. He says, "What the prophet exposes here is not hardship but nonfulfillment" ("Haggai," in *The Minor Prophets: An Exegetical and Expository Commentary* [Grand Rapids: Baker, 1998], 3:976–77). But it is doubtful that Haggai's description of the effects of famine in vv. 9–11 can be entirely accounted for in this way. It appears instead that many of Haggai's people were in dire straits from a physical and tangible perspective.

[97] The issue may not have been low wages as such but the economic pressures created by runaway inflation. As Meyers and Meyers point out, "The image does not suggest an inadequate income so much as an extraordinary drain on existing income" (*Haggai, Zechariah 1–8*, 27). This difference, however, is a subtle one. Clearly, the result of excessive inflation is to render incomes inadequate unless they keep pace with increasing prices.

[98] The structure of the main portion of v. 8 (excluding the formula "says the LORD") consists of five verbs, at the center of which is the command to "build the house." This marks the conceptual center of Haggai's message and its main emphasis. See Kessler, *The Book of Haggai*, 111.

[99] Contrary to M. A. Sweeney, who says, "The Hebrew word *hāhār* is singular and refers to 'the hill' or 'the mountain' on which the Temple is located" ("Haggai," in *The Twelve Prophets,* Berit Olam: Studies in Hebrew Narrative and Poetry [Collegeville, Minn.: Liturgical Press, 2000], 2:538). Likewise, Kessler suggests that a particular mountain is intended, perhaps one that was in sight of Haggai's audience and to which the prophet gestured as he spoke (*The Book of Haggai*, 133, n. 212).

refer to the hill country in general, as opposed to a particular hill.[100]

The Lord's instructions as recounted here call for taking the necessary initiatives for gathering the timber needed for reconstructing the temple. It is timber that is emphasized, since the stone also needed for the project was readily available in the immediate environs of Jerusalem.[101] Timber would have to be acquired elsewhere for such things as roofing the structure and the necessary carpentry work both inside and outside the edifice. That the necessary large items of timber would have been available in the then-forested areas nearby to Jerusalem seems unlikely. In the construction of the earlier Solomonic temple many building materials were imported from distant places such as Lebanon (1 Kgs 5:6,8–10,13–14; cf. Ezra 3:7), and that may be what is intended here.[102] On the other hand, it may be that the main reference in v. 8 is to timber that would be used for such things as scaffolding and ladders,[103] in which case what may be intended is an inferior form of lumber available locally as opposed to the better woods secured from more distant places.

As a result of their efforts, the Lord assures them, he will take pleasure in the rebuilt structure and will be glorified in it.[104] The final two verbs in the citation of v. 8 are best understood as conveying purpose or result for the prior three imperative verbs pertaining to the work of rebuilding.[105] The verb "take pleasure in" *(rāṣâ)* is part of the theological vocabulary of the Hebrew Bible; it is often used to signify the Lord's acceptance of persons or sacrificial offerings.[106] Haggai uses the word to refer to the Lord's acceptance of the temple reconstruction. Although the verb *kābēd,* rendered

---

[100] See BDB, 249–51; *HALOT*, 254–55; *DCH* 2:582–88.

[101] That the reference to wood in v. 8 is a synecdoche of part for whole and includes all kinds of work to be performed seems to me less likely than the conclusion that it is a specific reference to construction timber. But for a contrary opinion see Kessler, *The Book of Haggai*, 124.

[102] So, e.g., B. Peckham, *History and Prophecy: The Development of Late Judean Literary Traditions*, ABRL (New York: Doubleday, 1993), 743.

[103] See Meyers and Meyers, *Haggai, Zechariah 1–8*, 27–28.

[104] The Hb. cohortative verb אֶכָּבְד is spelled defectively here, lacking the final letter *hē'*. The marginal *qere* restores the *hē'* missing in the *kethib*. Since the letter *hē'* can have the numerical value of five, some ancient rabbis fancifully interpreted the missing *hē'* in this word to indicate that in the Second Temple five things were missing. *Yoma* 21b of the Talmud offers the following explanation: "To indicate that in five things the first Sanctuary differed from the second: in the ark, the ark-cover, the Cherubim, the fire, the *Shechinah*, the Holy Spirit [of Prophecy], and the *Urim-we-Thummim* [the Oracle Plate]." (The first three items in the list are apparently regarded as a single unit, thereby yielding a total of five items.)

[105] Since these two verbs are best understood as indirect volitives, the *wāw* should be rendered as "so that" (so NIV, NRSV; cf. ESV, NAB, NASB, NKJV) rather than as "and" (so KJV, ASV, NJB). On this construction see GKC §108d; *GBH* §169b.

[106] See G. Gerleman's discussion in *TLOT* 3:1259–61.

here by the NIV as "be honored," can have this sense,[107] it probably is better to understand it here to mean "appear in one's glory," a sense well-attested elsewhere for this verb.[108] The context suggests that the sense of the word is that the Lord will be pleased once again to manifest himself within the temple, or to appear in his glory, once the construction has been completed.[109]

*The Lord's Discipline (1:9–11).* In 1:9–11 (and elsewhere) Haggai employs a question-and-answer device that is a familiar part of prophetic rhetorical speech. The use of this device in the Old Testament prophets, particularly in Jeremiah and Ezekiel, has been carefully analyzed from a form-critical perspective by B. O. Long, who detects in that literature two slightly different types of question-and-answer schema.[110] Although the question-and-answer schema found in Hag 1:9–11 does not exactly fit either of Long's two types, it does have certain features in common with each of them.[111] From these features it appears that Haggai is using a slightly modified form of a literary device found elsewhere not only in certain biblical prophets but in ancient extrabiblical Semitic literature as well. This part of his message is conveyed in common structural forms that were probably quite familiar to his audience.

---

[107] It is possible that the *niphal* of this verb is used here in a tolerative sense: "I will permit myself to be glorified." On this use of the *niphal* see GKC §51c; *IBHS* §23.4f–g.

[108] See *HALOT*, 455.

[109] In 1:8 for the MT וְאֶכָּבֵד ("I will be glorified") *Tg. Jonathan* further explains with the promise בִּיקָר לְאַשְׁרָאָה שְׁכִינְתִּי בֵיהּ ("I will cause my Shekinah to dwell in it in honor"). Here "Shekinah" is used to express the Lord's beneficent presence. For a helpful discussion of the Tg. reading see J. Ribera Florit, "La versión aramaica del profeta Ageo," *Anuario* 4 (1978): 285.

[110] In the first type, which Long calls type *A*, three elements are found: a setting, which identifies those asking the question; the question itself, which is presented as a direct quotation; and the answer to the question, which is also presented as a direct quotation. In type *B* there are also three elements: a setting, which is cast in future terms; the formulation of an anticipated question; and a prescribed answer to that question. A primary identifying feature of this type is that it is presented as a divine speech given directly to the particular prophet. Use of this type of schema was not limited to biblical literature; it probably has its origins in ancient Assyrian literature. Long is able to cite several parallels from the records of Ashurbanipal's ninth military campaign, and he seems justified in concluding that this question-and-answer schema is an element of typical Assyrian historiography ("Two Question and Answer Schemata in the Prophets," *JBL* 90 [1971]: 133).

[111] As J. W. Whedbee has observed: "Like type A, Haggai's question-answer schema has a 'why–because' sequence, though in contrast to type A it has *ya'an me*[h] and *ya'an* for 'why–because' and the whole speech is in the form of a first-person Yahweh speech. Like type B, Haggai's schema is divine speech: Yahweh asks 'why?' and then answers his own question with a 'because . . .'" ("A Question-Answer Schema in Haggai 1: The Form and Function of Haggai 1:9–11," in *Biblical and Near Eastern Studies: Essays in Honor of William Sanford LaSor* [Grand Rapids: Eerdmans, 1978], 191).

**1:9** In v. 9 the prophet focuses on two things: first, there is the painful reminder of unrealized expectations on the part of the people. They had expected much in return for their hard labor and sustained efforts, but their anticipations had not come to fruition.[112] Instead, the return for their work had been poor agricultural conditions resulting in failed crops, spiraling inflation accompanied by miserably low incomes, and a standard of living that plunged many of them into despair and depression. No doubt some of them were led to ask, as people of faith have often asked with regard to disappointing circumstances, "Why has the Lord not prevented all of this?" Many of the returnees would have found it difficult to understand the absence of prosperity in the land and the incredibly difficult times that the residents of the country were experiencing. After all, the return to the land had been undertaken in the belief that the Lord was finally bringing to an end the disciplinary hardships of the exile and was at long last renewing his magnanimous blessing upon a restored covenantal people. But those optimistic expectations were not being realized in any tangible sort of way. Instead of prosperity there was economic depression; instead of abundance there was deprivation; instead of joy there was frustration over present difficulties and anxiety with regard to the future. A heavy cloud of discouragement cast its darkening shadows over the people.

Haggai's reply was not that the Lord had somehow been passively removed from their plight or had carelessly failed to notice what was going on. Rather, according to Haggai, it was the Lord who had actually caused their misfortunes! In a vivid anthropomorphism Haggai says that what little advantage the people were able to collect from their labors the Lord himself "blew away" *(nāpaḥtî).*[113] And why had he done so? It was because of their decision to leave the temple in ruins while they expended tremendous efforts on their own dwellings. According to v. 9 what little they could gain they brought to the wrong "house"—their own house rather than the house

---

[112] In 1:9 for the MT וְהִנֵּה ("and behold") the LXX (καὶ ἐγένετο), P (*whwʾ*), and *Tg. Jonathan* (וַהֲוָה) possibly understood the verb וְהָיָה ("it was"). Some scholars have therefore suggested emending the MT וְהִנֵּה either to the perfect וְהָיָה or to the infinitive וְהָיֹה, both of which may be rendered "and it was." But the MT is acceptable as it stands here. In fact, the different reading in the versions may be due not to textual variation at all but instead to translation technique. As K. J. Cathcart and R. P. Gordon point out, "The idiomatic requirements in the respective versions are sufficient to account for the changes" (*The Targum of the Minor Prophets: Translated, with a Critical Introduction, Apparatus, and Notes,* The Aramaic Bible 14 [Wilmington: Michael Glazier, 1989], 178, n. 9).

[113] In 1:9 for the MT וְנָפַחְתִּי בוֹ ("and I will blow on it") *Tg. Jonathan* has וְאַנָא שְׁלַח בֵּיהּ מְאֵירְתָא ("and I will send a curse upon it"), thereby avoiding the anthropomorphism of the Hb. text.

of the Lord.[114] The Lord had therefore scattered to the wind the meager results of their hard labors. Behind this imagery may lie the notion of a threshing floor where winds blow away chaff as the harvested grain is winnowed, since temples were sometimes erected on such sites (2 Sam 24:18–25; 1 Chr 21:18–22:1).[115]

The word translated in the NIV as "blew away" *(nāpaḥ)* is not especially common in the Hebrew Bible. It occurs a total of a dozen times.[116] Sometimes the word is used in a purely descriptive sense, as in the following instances. In Isa 54:16 it describes the blacksmith who *fans* coals until they produce a flame; in Ezek 22:20 it refers to the process of *melting* ore with intense heat; in Jer 1:13 and Job 41:12[Eng. 20] it describes a *boiling* pot. Other times the word is used in a life-giving sense. For example, in Gen 2:7 it refers to God's action of *breathing* into man's nostrils the breath of life; similarly, in Ezek 37:9 the prophet prays that God will *breathe* into the lifeless bodies of those slain, enabling them to live. The opposite of this is to breathe one's last or to expire in death (so, e.g., Jer 15:9). Apparently this is also the sense of the word in Job 31:39: "If I have eaten its yield without payment and *caused the death* of its owners" (NRSV).[117] Occasionally the word is used figuratively of God's judgment. Ezekiel 22:21, for example, speaks of the Lord *blowing* on the wicked with his fiery wrath, and Jer 20:26 speaks of an unfanned fire that will consume the wicked. In Mal 1:13

---

[114] According to v. 9 what the people "brought to the house" (הֲבֵאתֶם הַבַּיִת) the Lord "blew upon" (נָפַחְתִּי). The phrase הֲבֵאתֶם הַבַּיִת is capable of different interpretations. If הַבַּיִת refers here to the temple rather than to a private dwelling, as it clearly does on certain other occasions, the preceding verb הֲבֵאתֶם can be understood as referring to the offering of sacrifices. The verb would then be speaking of large offerings made at the temple site that were not efficacious because the Lord had rejected them. So F. Peter, "Zu Haggai 1,9," *TZ* 7 (1951): 150–51. But it seems better to understand הַבַּיִת here to refer to the people's homes, since the temple was as yet not restored. As such the word stands in contrast to the use of the same word later in v. 9 to refer to the temple (בֵּיתִי, "my house"). Understood in this way, the verse pictures the people taking home the results of their work but all to no avail because of the Lord's judgment upon them for their inattention to his house.

[115] So Sweeney, "Haggai," 539.

[116] This verb appears mainly in the *qal* stem but twice each in the *pual* and *hiphil*. There is one other possible occurrence of the word, but it requires textual emendation. In Num 21:30 some scholars have suggested that in place of the name Nophah we should read a *pual* form of the verb נָפַח (i.e., עַד־נֹפַח אֶשׁ; cf. LXX, προσεξέκαυσαν πῦρ). BDB, e.g., tentatively suggests the translation "until fire was blown (hot) as far as Medeba." But this seems to be an unnecessary suggestion, since the MT is acceptable here as it stands.

[117] This rendering of Job 31:39 enjoys considerable support from modern scholars and probably is correct. The NIV understands the meaning of נָפַח in this verse differently, rendering "or broken the spirit of its tenants," an understanding that finds some support in the ancient versions. *HALOT*, 709, suggests for this occurrence of the word the meaning "cause to groan or sigh." *DCH*, 5:714 entertains the possibility that we may have here a homonym, נָפַח II, meaning "beat or afflict."

the word describes an irreverent attitude on the part of the people toward the Lord's altar: "And you *sniff* at it contemptuously." Haggai 1:9 describes the Lord's judgmental action of scattering the attempts of a disobedient people to gain for themselves economic prosperity: "What you brought home, I blew away," the Lord asserts. The language is figurative;[118] it vividly pictures the Lord's disciplinary interference with the vain attempts of his people at personal gain while the work of God suffered decline due to their inattention. The opposite image in biblical literature is that of smelling with satisfaction and approval the pleasant aroma of sacrifice (cf., e.g., Gen 8:21).

As v. 9 makes abundantly clear, the damage inflicted by prior adverse climactic conditions and failed agricultural efforts was not coincidental, nor was it unrelated to the choices made by the people. Rather, these problems were due to the Lord's intentional judgment upon his people because of their mistaken priorities. The logical connection between their religious choices and the difficulties that had befallen them is made apparent in Haggai's argument by the *ya'an* ("because") clauses found in v. 9. There was a cause-and-effect relationship between the actions of the people and the crushing events that had transpired.

The word *ya'an* occurs more than ninety times in the Hebrew Bible. It is regularly used in oracular speech that reports the intentions of God and sets forth the reasons for those intentions. It is a frequent feature of what has sometimes been referred to as reason-announcement speeches. Sometimes the word is directly attributed to God, but most often it is linked to a prophet who functions as the Lord's messenger.[119] In 1:9–11 *ya'an* appears twice in connection with Haggai, who functions as the Lord's messenger and reports his speech. The *ya'an*-clause thus introduces the reasons for the actions of the Lord to which Haggai refers. Because the Lord's house had been left in ruins (*ḥārēb*, vv. 4,9), the land experienced drought (*ḥōreb*, v. 11).

For the first time in v. 9 we encounter what is a frequent expression in Haggai. The formulaic statement "utterance of Yahweh of hosts" (*nĕ'um YHWH ṣĕbā'ôt,* NIV "declares the LORD Almighty"), or its shorter counterpart "utterance of Yahweh" (*nĕ'um YHWH,* NIV "declares the LORD") occurs often in Haggai. For a book that is so brief, it is surprising that the former expression appears six times (1:9; 2:4,8,9,23[2x]), and the latter expression appears six times as well (1:13; 2:4[2x],14,17,23), for a total of twelve occurrences of this phrase in its two permutations. The reason for its repetition is fairly obvious: the writer of this book is anxious to underscore

---

[118] The figure of speech is hypocatastasis.

[119] As D. E. Gowan points out, "The *ya'an*-sentence is divine speech, spoken either by God himself or by an inspired messenger" ("The Use of *ya'an* in Biblical Hebrew," *VT* 21 [1971]: 177).

the divine origin of his message to the people. If the task to which the prophet is calling the fledgling nation is to be realized at all, it will only be due to a sincere response to a divine calling and not to fleeting enthusiasm generated by a mere human figure, no matter how charismatic that figure might be. The people must understand that Haggai's message is in fact an "utterance of Yahweh."

The final part of v. 9 once again sets the neglect of the temple in the context of selfish pursuits on the part of the people. The NIV's "while each of you is busy with his own house" translates the clause *wĕʾattem rāṣîm ʾîš lĕbêtô* (lit. "and you run a man to [or for] his house"). "Running" as a figurative expression can have a positive nuance in the Hebrew Bible. Runners, for example, are dispatched to carry important messages (e.g., Esth 3:13,15; 8:10), and runners serve as the escort or guards for a king or other important person (e.g., 1 Sam 22:17; 2 Sam 15:1; 1 Kgs 1:5; 14:27). The word also is used sometimes to describe the activity of those who engage in service for God (e.g., Ps 147:15). But sometimes the nuance of the word seems to be decidedly negative. In Jer 23:21, for example, the word is used to describe the activity of false prophets who "run with their message" even though the Lord has not sent them. So also in Hag 1:9 the Lord registers the complaint that the people are busy running after their own needs when they should instead be busy attending to the Lord's desires. When it came to their own interests, they exerted a flurry of activity; but when it came to the Lord's interests, they would not lift a finger. Furthermore, their selfish pursuits are pictured not as a single instance of failure but as a continual, ongoing habit or way of life.[120] Surely the Lord would not tolerate such contradiction indefinitely.

**1:10–11**   The final two verses of Haggai's first sermon trace the origins of the people's difficulties to the Lord's sovereign actions. The language of this section is reminiscent of the covenant curses found in Deuteronomy 28–30. There the Lord promised great blessings in return for obedience to the covenant obligations that he spelled out; but he also warned of the serious consequences that would overtake his people if they did not remain faithful to their covenantal obligations. Those curses included such things as the withholding of moisture from the planted crops (Deut 28:24); failed harvests (Deut 28:30,38–42); and hunger, thirst, lack of clothing, and poverty (Deut 28:48). By invoking this language Haggai implied that the disasters being currently experienced were due to nothing less than the failure of the people to live up to their covenantal obligations. Because of their actions "the heavens have withheld their dew and the earth its crops,"

---

[120] The use of the participle רָצִים rather than a finite verb suggests a linear, progressive, or durative action as opposed to a single occurrence of the verbal action.

according to v. 10.[121] The implied contrast between people and nature is striking. The elements of nature modeled obedience to the divine will, while Haggai's community modeled inattention to divine priorities.[122]

The mention of dew in v. 10 is significant.[123] Palestine receives almost all its rainfall during just one-half of the year. Once the rainy season ends in the spring, the dew brought by the westerly winds that blow in off the Mediterranean becomes extremely important. When those moist winds are absent, intolerably dry conditions are the result. All forms of life, as v. 11 points out, are then adversely affected.

The drought referred to in v. 11 presumably had been under way for quite some time.[124] Haggai's message was given in late August, toward the end of the summer season. Dry conditions prevail throughout the summer months in Palestine, and such conditions would not have been a surprise to the people at this time of year. But if drought had gone for a considerable time prior to Haggai's message, it would only have been exacerbated by the dry summer months. All the major crops of Palestine are summarized in v. 11: the grain, new wine, and oil (cf. Deut 7:13; 11:14; Jer 31:12; Hos 2:8). Following the reference to these crops Haggai adds a summarizing reference to "whatever the ground produces" *(wĕ'al 'ăšer tôṣî' hā'ădāmâ)*, as if not to overlook the forms of crop production that were of lesser significance than those specifically named.[125] The

---

[121] Although the NIV has the definite article before both "heavens" and "earth," the MT lacks the article before "heavens" (שָׁמַיִם) but has it before "earth" (הָאָרֶץ). The reason for the anomaly is unclear. Meyers and Meyers make the interesting suggestion that the absence of the article with "heavens" may partly serve to distinguish this entity (as the cause) from the other entities in the context (which are the affected objects). They also suggest that the final word in v. 11 lacks the article perhaps to emphasize its function as a summarizing item ("product of [your] hands"); see *Haggai, Zechariah 1–8*, 31.

[122] Baldwin calls attention to the paradox: "The heavens and the earth obeyed their Creator's word but His people did not" (*Haggai, Zechariah, Malachi*, 42).

[123] In Hag 1:10 the MT מִטַּל ("from dew") should probably be emended to טַלָּם (NIV "their dew"), taking the word as the direct object of the verb כָּלְאוּ ("withheld") rather than as a prepositional phrase. This is more in keeping with the normal usage of this verb. Cf. the immediately following colon in v. 10, where יְבוּלָהּ ("its produce") is the object of כָּלְאָה ("withheld"). See further, *HALOT*, 374–75. *Tg. Jonathan* has מִטְרָא ("rain") rather than מִטַּל ("from dew"), leading some scholars to suggest emendation of the MT to מָטָר ("rain"). See Mitchell, *Haggai and Zechariah*, 49, 53. Contrariwise, if the reading of the MT is retained, the function of the preposition מִן would be partitive, suggesting that some (but not all) dew had been withheld. Overall, emendation to טַלָּם ("their dew") seems to be the best option.

[124] As noted earlier, the word חֹרֶב ("drought") in v. 11 forms a wordplay with חָרֵב ("desolate") in v. 4.

[125] The absence in the MT of כֹּל ("all") in v. 11 before אֲשֶׁר תּוֹצִיא הָאֲדָמָה ("that the ground produces") has been noticed by many commentators, leading to the suggestion that the text be emended to include it. Many medieval Hb. MSS, as well as the ancient versions, do in fact have "all" here. The suggestion found in the apparatus of *BHS* that כֹּל be inserted in v. 11 probably should be accepted.

point is that nothing of significance had been left untouched by the recent drought to which Haggai alludes.

Furthermore, it was the Lord himself who had called for this drought, according to v. 11.[126] All this had happened, Haggai informs them in v. 10, "because of you"[127] (*'ălêkem*). In such an oracle as we have here, we would normally expect an announcement of judgment-to-come. Instead, Haggai's pronouncement is that the judgment has already occurred. Not only could it not be avoided; the people were in fact already experiencing its dire consequences. This is a distinctive element in Haggai's use of this form.[128]

Haggai's first message ends abruptly in v. 11 with no stated conclusion or direct call for action. But the implications are obvious. There could be no return to prosperity or normalization of relationship with the Lord until first there was a genuine repentance and a change of heart on the part of these people. They must acknowledge their prior sinful choices. They must accept the notion that their difficulties were a due recompense from the Lord for their failure to keep the stipulations of their covenant with him. And they must determine to correct their course of action immediately. Specifically, they must give to the task of rebuilding the temple in Jerusalem the priority that the Lord through his prophet Haggai attached to it. Only in this way would God again look with favor upon them and bless them with renewed prosperity. To their credit, the people did respond to Haggai's message in a favorable way, as vv. 12–15a make clear.

---

[126] In 1:11 for the MT וָאֶקְרָא חֹרֶב ("and I called for a drought") the LXX has καὶ ἐπάξω ῥομφαίαν ("and I will bring a sword"), apparently mistaking the word חֹרֶב ("ruin," "drought") for the word חֶרֶב ("sword"). The MT is to be preferred here.

[127] The NIV's causal translation of the preposition עַל used here (עֲלֵיכֶם, "because of you") seems preferable to the local sense of the preposition as suggested by the KJV ("over you"). Clearly it is the culpability of the people that forms a major strand in Haggai's argument in this section. But for a brief defense of the translation "over you" see R. Wolff, *The Book of Haggai: A Study Manual*, Shield Bible Study Outlines (Grand Rapids: Baker, 1967), 35. The phrase עֲלֵיכֶם is absent in the LXX, but this may be due to haplography with the preceding עַל־כֵּן ("therefore"). The similarity between the two expressions easily accounts for the omission in the LXX. This explanation seems preferable to Elliger's suggestion in the apparatus of *BHS* that the MT's עֲלֵיכֶם should be deleted as a dittography. The prepositional phrase actually provides an important factor in Haggai's accusation, namely, the reason for the agricultural drought. It was "because of you," he tells the people. That is to say, the problems they were experiencing could be traced back to their lack of obedience as a covenant people. *Tg. Jonathan* has בדיל חוביכון ("because of your sins"), thus making even more specific the reason for the Lord's displeasure with the people.

[128] See, e.g., A. Cody, "Haggai, Zechariah, Malachi," in *NJBC* (Englewood Cliffs, N.J.: Prentice Hall, 1990), 350.

## I. THE PEOPLE'S RESPONSE (1:12–15a)

Haggai's first message met with amazing success. It had the effect of immediately lifting the people from their lethargy and self-indulgence and stimulating them to energetic involvement in the temple project. This was true not only of the political and religious leaders Zerubbabel and Joshua, who were the named recipients of Haggai's sermon, but it was true of Haggai's broader audience as well. The frustration caused by the economic difficulties of the day no doubt played a preparatory role in the responsiveness of the people. When times are prosperous, it may be easier to dismiss a word of prophetic rebuke; but hard times often expose raw nerves of the spiritual life that has grown insensitive to God's spirit. Frequently it is in the midst of exceptional human difficulty that God's word finds its greatest success.[1]

No time was wasted. Together leaders and lay population alike committed themselves to the great task at hand. Though their initial enthusiasm would soon be challenged by seemingly insuperable difficulties that lay just ahead, and though discouragement would quickly set in as they compared their fledgling project with memories of the more impressive Solomonic temple, nonetheless they had finally begun to chart a right course. Within the space of just a few weeks the necessary preparations had taken place, and before the conclusion of the very month in which Haggai first preached to them the people began the task of restoring the Jerusalem temple. Lethargy and reluctance had finally given way to obedience, at least for the moment!

---

[1] C. S. Lewis's thought-provoking comment on the theological purpose of pain comes to mind: "God whispers to us in our pleasures, speaks in our conscience, but shouts in our pains: it is His megaphone to rouse a deaf world" (*The Problem of Pain* [New York: Macmillan, 1947], 81).

## 1. A Favorable Response (1:12)

[12]**Then Zerubbabel son of Shealtiel, Joshua son of Jehozadak, the high priest, and the whole remnant of the people obeyed the voice of the LORD their God and the message of the prophet Haggai, because the LORD their God had sent him. And the people feared the LORD.**

**1:12** The response to Haggai's message was immediate and decisive. The people acknowledged the prophet as a bona fide spokesman for the Lord, accepted his message to them, demonstrated appropriate reverence for the Lord and his word, and committed themselves to the work to which Haggai called them. Not all biblical prophets were so fortunate. In many cases prophets found that their messages were favorably received by only a small number of listeners; in other cases their messages went unheeded altogether. But not so with Haggai. The governor, the high priest, and all the people acknowledged that the Lord had sent Haggai to them. Through Haggai they had heard not just the impassioned political or religious reasonings of a compatriot. They had heard "the voice of the LORD their God" (v. 12).[2] Their receptivity to the prophet's message was grounded in an understanding that the Lord had sent him to them, as the causal construction of v. 12 indicates.[3] The notion of divine sending of the prophetic messenger underscores Haggai's role as an authorized courier of the Lord's message for this community.

The words "their God" (*ʾĕlōhêhem*), which appear twice in v. 12 and again in v. 14, are significant.[4] In the preceding disputation the Lord spoke contemptuously of those who because of their disobedience to covenantal responsibilities he termed "this people" (*hāʿām hazzeh*) rather than "my people." They were behaving as though Yahweh were not in reality their

---

[2] The Hb. text has a compound direct object after the verb: the leaders and people "obeyed the voice of the LORD their God and the message of the prophet Haggai." The *wāw,* however, may be *wāw explicativum,* in which case the second unit explains the first one: "the voice of the LORD their God, namely, the message of the prophet Haggai." The two things, Yahweh's voice and Haggai's message, are inseparably linked together. See GKC §154, n. 1(b); *IBHS* 39.2.4.

[3] In biblical Hb. the construction כַּאֲשֶׁר can indicate time ("when"), comparison ("as"), supposition ("as though"), or cause ("because"). In Hag 1:12 Meyers and Meyers (*Haggai, Zechariah 1–8,* 4) understand כַּאֲשֶׁר to have temporal significance, rendering it as "when" (so also Tanak). It seems more likely that in v. 12 the word carries a causal nuance (so NIV, NAB), indicating the rationale for the people's reception of Haggai's message rather than the timing of their acceptance. See further BDB, 455; *HALOT,* 455; *IBHS* §38.4,5,7.

[4] In 1:12 in place of the MT אֱלֹהֵיהֶם ("their God") many MSS of the LXX have πρὸς αὐτούς, the Hb. counterpart to which is אֲלֵיהֶם. In a consonantal Hb. text the difference amounts only to the absence of the letter *hēʾ* in the latter reading. A number of other witnesses have not one but both readings: "their God to them." E.g., the Vg has *Deus eorum ad ipsos* ("their God to them"), and P has *ʾlhhwn lwthwn* ("their God to them"). But this reading is almost certainly the result of dittography, making the shorter reading of MT the preferred reading here.

God. But in v. 12 we find affirmation of their obedience to the Lord's voice as mediated through Haggai's prophetic ministry. Now at long last they had begun to display the obedience that befitted their identity as a people of God, and with that obedience came renewed confidence that Yahweh was in fact "their God." They obeyed the instructions he gave through Haggai, demonstrating by their actions the reverential awe that, at least in some measure, they had toward him.

The inclusion of the people along with Zerubbabel and Joshua in the response described in v. 12 is significant. Although v. 1 mentioned only the leaders as recipients of Haggai's message, it is clear from the people's response that the message was not directed to the leaders exclusively. The people were implicitly included as part of Haggai's audience. They are called in v. 12 "the remnant of the people" (*šěʾērît hāʿām;* cf. 1:14; 2:2). The concept of remnant is used in various ways in the prophetic literature of the Old Testament.[5] It sometimes refers to a faithful segment of a larger group that included less committed Israelites (e.g., Amos 5:15; Isa 10:20–22; cf. 1 Kgs 19:18). Other times the word is more inclusive, serving as a general designation for all Israelites who had escaped a particular disaster (e.g., Jer 8:3; Ezek 5:10; 9:18; 11:13). Although the Jewish population of Haggai's day consisted of two distinct groups, namely, those who had returned from the exile and those who had remained behind in the land during that same period, Haggai's use of "remnant" probably is not limited to one or the other of these two groups.[6] The prophet seems to use the term in a broad theological sense, referring to those who were truly part of the covenant community, whether they had returned from the exile or had been present in the land all along.[7]

It is significant that the word "remnant" does not occur in Haggai until v. 12, which describes the people's obedient response to Haggai's message. It is this obedience to the Lord's message that qualifies them to be thought of as a remnant, a designation that invokes the remnant theology of earlier Old Testament prophets such as Isaiah and Jeremiah. The collocation "heard" (*wayyišmaʿ*; NIV "obeyed") and "feared" (*wayyirʾû*) in v. 12 is a common one in the Hebrew Bible. It calls attention to the appropriate human reaction to a display of divine grace. The only proper

---

[5] See H. Wildberger, "שאר *šʾr* to remain," *TLOT* 3, esp. pp. 1286–91.

[6] H. Wolf understands the term to refer only to those who had returned from Babylon (*Haggai and Malachi* [Chicago: Moody, 1976]). I. G. Matthews, on the other hand, understands it to refer to those who had remained in Judah during the exile ("Haggai," in *Minor Prophets,* An American Commentary [Philadelphia: The American Baptist Publication Society, 1935], 12:12). Both of these views seem to be overly restrictive in the way that they identify Haggai's audience.

[7] So, e.g., P. A. Verhoef, *The Books of Haggai and Malachi,* NICOT (Grand Rapids: Eerdmans, 1987), 81.

response to hearing the word of the Lord that the prophets entertained was one of reverential awe and prompt obedience.[8]

## 2. Reassurance from the Prophet (1:13)

**[13]Then Haggai, the LORD's messenger, gave this message of the LORD to the people: "I am with you," declares the LORD.**

**1:13** Many scholars have questioned whether v. 13 is an original part of the Book of Haggai. Among the reasons advanced for concluding that the verse is a secondary addition to the book are the following: it interrupts the flow between vv. 12 and 14; it repeats the "I am with you" promise of 2:4; it needlessly duplicates the language of v. 12; and the expression "messenger of the LORD" is a unique designation for Haggai.[9] Although each of these claims warrants attention, none of them demonstrates inauthenticity. Repetition is in fact a characteristic of the Book of Haggai. There seems to be no sufficient reason for concluding that v. 13 is not an original part of the text.

Haggai, who elsewhere is designated as "the prophet," is here given the additional title "the LORD's messenger" *(mal'ak YHWH)* . The word "messenger" is not often used in reference to the Old Testament prophet, leading some commentators to conclude that this verse is a later interpolation.[10] But the expression is appropriate here. The biblical concept of prophet includes the notion that one called to that office was sent forth as an envoy or representative of God (cf. Isa 6:8; Jer 1:7; Ezek 2:3,4; 3:5,6). As such the prophet was to represent not himself or his own interests but the interests of the divine sovereign who commissioned him. In this sense Haggai is the Lord's *mal'ak* ("messenger").[11] In this book the term *mal'ak* is used more or less as a synonym for *nābî'*,[12] which is the more common term for

---

[8] Verhoef's comment in my opinion is not likely to be correct: "This 'fear' is not a reverential attitude toward the Lord, which manifests itself in obedience to and trust in the God of the covenant . . . but it is an expression of their holy awe, their terror because of the wrath of the Lord" (*Haggai and Malachi,* 83).

[9] See the discussion of these points in Verhoef, *Haggai and Malachi,* 15, 83–84.

[10] So, e.g., H. G. Mitchell, *A Critical and Exegetical Commentary on Haggai and Zechariah,* ICC (Edinburgh: T&T Clark, 1912), 55.

[11] In 1:13 for the MT מַלְאַךְ יְהוָה ("messenger of the LORD") *Tg. Jonathan* has נְבִיא דַיוי ("the prophet of the Lord"), since in the Tgs. מַלְאַךְ is normally used of celestial rather than human messengers. In 1:13 and 2:4 for the MT אֲנִי אִתְּכֶם ("I am with you") *Tg. Jonathan* has מֵימְרִי בְסַעֲדְכוֹן ("my Memra is your support"), which in the Tg. is a common circumlocution for this OT expression.

[12] I say "more or less" because, while these words may in some contexts be used interchangeably, there remains a technical difference between them. The term "messenger" can be used more broadly than the term "prophet." As M. H. Floyd says, "All prophets might be called 'messengers of Yahweh' in some sense . . but all 'messengers of Yahweh' cannot be called prophets" ("Haggai," in *Minor Prophets,* part 2, FOTL 22 [Grand Rapids: Eerdmans, 2000], 275–76).

referring to a prophet.[13]

Like the Greek word *angelos,*[14] the Hebrew word *mal'āk* may refer either to a heavenly messenger (i.e., "angel") or, as here, to an earthly one.[15] Only the context can make clear which meaning is intended. In Haggai *mal'āk* was misunderstood by some ancient interpreters. Jerome was aware of some in his day who on the basis of this word concluded that Haggai was actually an angelic appearance rather than a human being.[16] Such a conclusion transfers to this occurrence of the word a nuance that, however appropriate in other contexts, does not fit here. Haggai was a human messenger, not a celestial one. By foisting upon the word a sense foreign to its context in Haggai, Jerome's protagonists were guilty of a basic lexical error.[17]

The reason for the use of the word "messenger" in v. 13 in this distinc-

---

[13] N. G. Cohen has maintained that in the exilic and postexilic prophetic literature the term מַלְאָךְ was at first used interchangeably with the term נָבִיא to refer to a prophet, and then at a later time מַלְאָךְ completely replaced נָבִיא as a designation for the prophetic figure ("From *Nabi* to *Mal'ak* to 'Ancient Figure,'" *JJS* 36 [1985]: esp. pp. 16–17). E. W. Conrad, building on Cohen's work, makes an interesting case for thinking that in the Book of the Twelve the distinction between human and divine messengers is blurred, as is the distinction between the heavenly and the earthly in the portrayal of the temple in this same literature. He says, "In the Book of the Twelve Haggai, as both מלאך and נבי, represents a transition point in the literature between the end of the LORD being with his people by means of his prophets (Hosea through Zephaniah) and a period of time when there will be מלאכים present in the rebuilt temple (Haggai through Malachi), a time when prophecy will come to an end" ("The End of Prophecy and the Appearance of Angels/Messengers in the Book of the Twelve," *JSOT* 73 [1997]: 78). See also id., "Messengers in Isaiah and the Twelve: Implications for Reading Prophetic Books," *JSOT* 91 (2000): 83–97. On the OT use of the messenger motif in connection with Israel's prophets see J. F. Ross, "The Prophet as Yahweh's Messenger," in *Israel's Prophetic Heritage: Essays in Honor of James Muilenburg* (London: SCM Press, 1962), 98–107; W. Böhme, "Zu Maleachi und Haggai," *ZAW* 7 (1887): 215–17.

[14] The LXX has in Hag 1:13 ὁ ἄγγελος κυρίου ("the messenger of the Lord"), which permits the same lexical ambiguity found in the Hb. text.

[15] Cf. Isa 42:19; 44:26; 63:9; 2 Chr 36:16; Mal 2:7; 3:1.

[16] Jerome, *Commentary on Haggai 1.13* (CCSL 76A, 726). Apparently J. Calvin has the same group in mind when he makes the following comment: "The word מַלְאָךְ, *malak,* means a messenger; and as angels are called מַלְאָכִים, *malakim,* some foolish men have thought that Haggai was one of the celestial angels, clothed with the form of man; but this is a most frivolous conjecture" (*Habakkuk, Zephaniah, Haggai,* vol. 4, *Commentaries on the Twelve Minor Prophets* [Grand Rapids: Eerdmans, 1950], 4:344).

[17] Nor is it helpful when A. Rofé concludes that "the classical prophets saw themselves as the inheritors of the angels and overtook the functions these had in folk-religion. At a later stage the prophets were indeed termed 'angels' (Isa. 44.26; Hag. 1.13; Mal. 1.1; 2 Chron. 36.15–16)" (*Introduction to the Prophetic Literature* [Sheffield: Sheffield Academic Press, 1997], 61). This reads too much into the word and uses the term "angels" in a potentially misleading way. It seems to imply that the Eng. word "angel" has the same semantic range as the Hb. word מַלְאָךְ. For the same reason W. E. Barnes's translation also is misleading: "And Haggai said, The Angel of JEHOVAH is here with a message of JEHOVAH for the people" (*Haggai and Zechariah, with Notes and Introduction,* CBSC (Cambridge: Cambridge University Press, 1917], 9–10).

tive way may lie in the surrounding context. The phrase "messenger of the LORD" *(mal'ak YHWH)* is immediately followed by the somewhat redundant phrase "by the message of the LORD" *(běmal'ăkût YHWH)* .[18] A little later, in v. 14, the prophet refers to the "work" *(mělā'kâ)* the people engaged in. Haggai may be anticipating these words and forming a subtle semantic link between them. The wordplay underscores the prophet's role. He is the Lord's messenger *(mal'ak)* who is proclaiming the Lord's message *(mal'ăkût)* and is calling people to the Lord's work *(mělā'kâ)*.[19] These lexical choices form a literary thread that connects the several statements by the use of sound patterns.

In light of their favorable response to his message Haggai conveyed to the people the reassuring promise that the Lord's presence would be with them in their endeavors.[20] The encouragement Haggai offered the people would play a determinative role in their response. For that reason v. 13 plays an important role in the change of attitude displayed by the people. The comforting words "I am with you" *('ănî 'ittekem)* call to mind similar promises found elsewhere in biblical literature. Jacob received such a promise at Bethel as he began his journey to Haran (Gen 28:15). Joseph's amazing success in Egypt was attributed to the fact that "the LORD was with him" in all he undertook (Gen 39:2,21,23). Moses heard similar words at the burning bush (Exod 3:12). So too did Joshua, Moses' successor, as he assumed the mantel of leadership upon the death of Moses (Josh 1:5), as did Gideon when he faced the Midianites (Judg 6:16). So also did David when the Lord entered into a covenant with him (2 Sam 7:9) and Jeremiah when he began his prophetic ministry (Jer 1:8). When faced with the Assyrian threat, the Israelites took comfort in such words (Isa 8:10; cf. Ps

---

[18] The word מַלְאָכוּת ("message") is found only here in the Hb. Bible. In 1:13 the MT "by the message of the LORD" (בְּמַלְאָכוּת יְהוָה) is lacking in the LXX, probably because of parablepsis. A scribe's eye apparently jumped from the first occurrence of יְהוָה to the second occurrence, thereby skipping the intervening phrase. Since in the MT these words are immediately preceded by the phrase מַלְאַךְ יְהוָה ("the messenger of the LORD"), which modifies the word "Haggai" in v. 13, some scholars have wondered whether this second phrase in v. 13 may not be an embedded textual variant to the first phrase inserted by an early scribe. If so, it should be removed from the text. But the evidence for removing the word seems to be inadequate, and the phrase should probably be allowed to stand in v. 13. On the possible presence of such variants elsewhere in the text of the Hb. Bible see S. Talmon, "Double Readings in the Massoretic Text," *Text* 1 (1960): 144–84.

[19] I presume that something similar to this is what W. E. March means when he describes the latter word as recalling the former; see "The Book of Haggai: Introduction, Commentary, and Reflections," *IB* (Nashville: Abingdon, 1996), 7:720.

[20] The Hb. text has אֲנִי אִתְּכֶם ("I am with you") in v. 13 (cf. Jer 42:11; Hag 2:4). More often in the OT the promise of divine presence is expressed with the preposition עִם, but the difference is insignificant. H. W. Wolff suggests that "אֵת may perhaps point rather to spatial nearness, עִם rather to accompaniment and fellowship," but this distinction should not be pressed (*Haggai: A Commentary* [Minneapolis: Augsburg, 1988], 50).

46:7,11). And in the New Testament messianic expectations and hopes were fulfilled in one who was called "Emanuel, God with us" (Matt 1:23).

Though their task must have seemed daunting in light of their meager resources, the postexilic community could take great comfort from the promise that God was with them, enabling their work and helping them to overcome all obstacles just as he consistently had done in the past for his people. As he had been with earlier generations of his people, so too he would be with them. They need not face the task that lay before them in their own strength alone.

## 3. A Renewed Commitment (1:14–15a)

**[14]So the LORD stirred up the spirit of Zerubbabel son of Shealtiel, governor of Judah, and the spirit of Joshua son of Jehozadak, the high priest, and the spirit of the whole remnant of the people. They came and began to work on the house of the LORD Almighty, their God, [15]on the twenty-fourth day of the sixth month**

**1:14** Haggai now makes clear that the enthusiasm experienced by the people for the rebuilding project was not merely the result of hype that had been artificially induced, whether by themselves or by their leaders. It was the Lord who "stirred up" *(wayyā'ar)* the spirits of all those concerned with the work.[21] The verb *'ûr,* "to stir up," draws on the imagery of sleepiness. Like those roused from slumber to participate in activity from which they otherwise would have been absent, so these people had been roused from their spiritual inattentiveness to participate in the urgent task before them.

The focus of the Lord's ministry to them is centered on their spirits. "Spirit" *(rûaḥ)* in the Hebrew Bible can mean many different things (e.g., breath, breeze, wind, the human spirit, God's spirit).[22] Here the word is used of God's arousing the human frame of mind to important activity, namely, the work on the temple. As Eichrodt points out, in the language of the Hebrew Bible, God may choose to awaken the spirit to decisive action, as here in Haggai, or he may choose to harden the spirit, leading to punitive action.[23] It is to God's stirring of the minds of the people that Haggai attributes the decision to move ahead with the work.

Whether the verbal construction "they came and began to work" is sim-

---

[21] Calvin's sermonic comment on Haggai's reference to the Lord's "rousing" of the people is apropos: "Let us at the same time learn, that princes and those to whom God has committed the care of governing his Church, never so faithfully perform their office, nor discharge their duties so courageously and strenuously, but that they stand in need of being roused, and, as it were, stimulated by many goads" ("Haggai," 322).

[22] See, e.g., *HALOT,* 1197–1201.

[23] See W. Eichrodt, *Theology of the Old Testament,* OTL (Philadelphia: Westminster, 1961), 2:133.

ply a verbal hendiadys referring to what those already in Jerusalem started to do, or whether the verb "came" has in view those living away from the city who temporarily relocated their place of residence so as to join the local residents in the work (cf. Ezra 3:1) is not completely clear. The former idea is probably what is in view.

**1:15a** The first part of v. 15 specifies the day on which the temple work began. It was "the twenty-fourth day of the sixth month." The modern equivalent is September 21, 520 B.C. According to Hag 1:1 the prophet delivered this initial message on the first day of that same month, that is, August 29, 520 B.C. This means that just a little more than three weeks had elapsed between the delivery of that sermon and the actual beginning of the work on the temple. Assuming the people's response to Haggai's message was more or less immediate, these several weeks probably were spent in getting things ready for the work.[24] The preparations of gathering construction material, organizing the labor force, and securing the initial outlay of funds all would have taken some time. But now they were ready to move ahead. Haggai's initial message had been eminently successful in motivating the people for the important task before them. Although the path before them would prove to be discouraging at times, finally the people were moving in the right direction. Three more messages from the prophet would soon follow, each one providing at pivotal points the encouragement or prodding needed for the people to continue the work.

Haggai 1:15 poses a major problem for understanding the structure of the book. At least three different approaches have been advocated for this verse. First, many modern works on Haggai follow Rothstein in advocating a dislocation in the text of Haggai at this point.[25] The suspicion that v. 15a does not provide a fitting conclusion to the preceding pericope but seems rather to be an introduction to something no longer found in this location has led to a search for a section elsewhere in Haggai that might in fact be displaced from its original location. The best candidate for textual dislocation is 2:15–19, which Rothstein argued should be moved to a position following 1:15a.[26] In spite of its popularity this view, as we discussed earlier,

---

[24] D. J. Wiseman, on the other hand, views these twenty-three days as the length of time it took the people to respond to Haggai's call ("Haggai," in *The New Bible Commentary, Revised* [Grand Rapids: Eerdmans, 1970], 783).

[25] J. W. Rothstein, *Juden und Samaritaner: die grundlegende Scheidung von Judentum und Heidentum: eine kritische Studie zum Buche Haggai und zur jüdischen Geschichte im ersten nachexilischen Jahrhundert,* BWA(N)T 3 (Leipzig: Hinrichs, 1908).

[26] The influence of this view may be seen in the apparatus of *BHS,* where the editor advocates inserting 2:15–19 after 1:15a. But there is no manuscript evidence supporting this conclusion. It is based in part on a tenuous interpretation of 2:10–19 concerning alleged conflict between the returnees and the Samaritans, as discussed earlier in the introduction.

should be rejected for lack of adequate evidence in its favor.[27] Second, some scholars have maintained that 1:15a is a secondary gloss that should be removed from the passage on text-critical grounds.[28] This view also falters for lack of external evidence. Essentially all our textual evidence has the verse in this location. There seems to be no adequate reason to question the authenticity of 1:15a. Third, it is possible to understand 1:15a as the concluding observation of this section (1:12–15a). As such its purpose is to disclose how much time elapsed between the reception of Haggai's first message and the commencement of work of the temple. The location of v. 15a at the end of this section thus forms an inclusio with the date found at the beginning of this chapter (1:1).[29] Together the two dates call attention to the requirements laid out in Haggai's message to the people and the favorable response to that message. This third view offers the best understanding of the first half of v. 15 because it functions rhetorically in context and is consistent with the textual evidence.

The date that is indicated in v. 15b is problematic in terms of deciding whether the phrase "in the second year of King Darius" belongs with what precedes in v. 15 or with what follows in 2:1. The traditional verse division takes it with what precedes (e.g., NIV). But on the basis of the full date given in 1:1, which specifies year-month-day in Darius's reign, we probably should expect a similar pattern in 2:1 (e.g., NRSV). A full date is given in 2:10, for example, marking the beginning of Haggai's third message, although the order of the phrases is not the same in the two instances. The date given in 2:20, marking the beginning of Haggai's fourth and final message, has only month and day with no mention of year. But that is probably because the third and fourth messages were delivered on the same day (cf. 2:10,20). There is no need in that case to supply the year for the fourth message. We would expect, however, the information provided in 2:1 to correspond to what we have in 1:1 and 2:10.

Some scholars have maintained that the phrase "in the second year of King Darius" actually serves double duty, functioning both to conclude the previous section (vv. 11–14) and at the same time to open the following section (2:1–9).[30] But given the stereotypical and formulaic nature of such chronological language, this interpretation is not convincing. It seems likely that 1:15 is wrongly divided in the MT. Scribes mistakenly assumed that the information pertaining to the year belonged with the statement in v. 15a, which concerns commencement of work on the temple. The first half of

---

[27] Rothstein's views are discussed in greater detail in the introduction.

[28] See the discussion in P. R. Ackroyd, "Studies in the Book of Haggai," *JJS* 2 (1951): 170–71.

[29] See D. J. Clark, "Discourse Structure in Haggai," *JOTT* 5 (1992): 17.

[30] So, e.g., P. A. Verhoef, "Notes on the Dates in the Book of Haggai," in *Text and Context: Old Testament and Semitic Studies for F. C. Fensham* (Sheffield: JSOT Press, 1988), 262.

v. 15 should instead be viewed as the conclusion to the unit begun in v. 12, and the phrase "in the second year of King Darius" should be understood to mark the beginning of 2:1 (contrary to NIV).[31] It is with that understanding that we take the final pericope of chap. 1 to consist of vv. 12–15a, leaving v. 15b to go with 2:1.[32]

---

[31] In the LXX and Vg all of v. 15 is taken with chap. 2.

[32] Against this conclusion C. L. Meyers and E. M. Meyers argue that all of 1:15 should instead be taken as the conclusion to the preceding pericope. In their view it "is perfectly and properly positioned at the end of the first chapter" (*Haggai, Zechariah 1–8: A New Translation with Introduction and Commentary,* AB [New York: Doubleday, 1987], 36–37, 49). As to the problem this leaves 2:1 with no mention of Darius's second year, they suggest that either the phrase "in the second year of Darius" of 1:15b serves the twofold purpose of both concluding chap. 1 and beginning chap. 2 or a repetition of the phrase has been lost in 2:1 due to scribal haplography. It seems preferable to allow that the traditional verse division is mistaken.

III. HAGGAI'S SECOND MESSAGE: *THE GLORY OF THE REBUILT TEMPLE WILL SURPASS THAT OF SOLOMON'S TEMPLE!* (1:15b–2:9)
1. Introduction to the Message (1:15b–2:2)
    (1) Date of the Message (1:15b–2:1a)
    (2) Origin of the Message (2:1b)
    (3) Recipients of the Message (2:2)
2. The Present Condition of the Temple (2:3–5)
    (1) An Unfavorable Comparison with the Former Temple (2:3)
    (2) The Promise of Divine Presence and Strength (2:4–5)
3. The Future Condition of the Temple (2:6–9)
    (1) Divine Intervention in the Cosmos (2:6)
    (2) Financial Assistance from the Nations (2:7–8)
    (3) The Splendor of the Rebuilt Temple (2:9)

## III. HAGGAI'S SECOND MESSAGE (1:15b–2:9)

Less than two months had elapsed from the time of Haggai's first message when work on the temple stalled due to discouragement on the part of the participants. The reason for their growing disinterest in the project was simple. In spite of all their effort the appearance of the temple under construction gave little evidence of being a worthy successor to the Solomonic temple. The few people who were old enough actually to have seen the former temple could feel only a sense of embarrassment and discouragement as they compared the meager structure on which they were working to that magnificent earlier structure. As a result severe discouragement beset the people, and with that lack of enthusiasm came inevitable delays in the work.

Haggai's second message was an oracle of encouragement to the people to press on. This message has for its theme the notion that the glory of the rebuilt temple would surpass that of Solomon's famous temple. Haggai admonished the people to be strong and draw encouragement from the reality of the Lord's presence with them as they continued to fulfill his will. Speaking through the prophet, the Lord promised to supply the needed material resources for this project. He assured the people that this temple would not only compare favorably with Solomon's great temple, but it would exceed that earlier temple in its magnificence. Haggai's discouraged audience would have had great difficulty understanding how this could possibly be the case in light of the humble beginnings that were before them. Nonetheless, the prophet's words brought hope and anticipation to those whose faith could see beyond the rubble of their present circumstances.

## 1. Introduction to the Message (1:15b–2:2)

As is the case with Haggai's first sermon, his second message begins by providing specific information with regard to the date, origin, and recipients of the message.

### (1) Date of the Message (1:15b–2:1a)

**in the second year of King Darius.**

**¹On the twenty-first day of the seventh month,**

**1:15b–2:1a**   Like Haggai's first message, this sermon was given in the second year of King Darius, or 520 B.C. More specifically, it was delivered on October 17, 520 B.C. In the Jewish calendar the twenty-first day of the seventh month (i.e., Tishri) was the seventh day of the Feast of Sukkot, at which time work was customarily suspended in order to celebrate the time of the harvest (cf. Lev 23:33–36,39–43; Num 29:12–40; Ezek 45:25). The timing of Haggai's message was therefore opportune in that his audience had reason to be in Jerusalem and available for communal gatherings.

In addition to commemorating the experiences of the Israelite wilderness wandering, Sukkot was also a time for celebrating God's provision through the harvest. But on this occasion a dark cloud hung over what should have been a time of joyous remembrance. Conditions of drought had reduced agricultural production to a fraction of what it should have been. Because of these recent failures with the crops, the people probably were less inclined to be in a celebratory mood than they might have been had times been good.

Since the presentation of Haggai's first sermon on August 29, less than two months had passed. In that small amount of time, however, a significant change had occurred in the people's outlook. Discouragement over the enormity of their task now threatened the success of the mission. The challenge confronting Haggai was to address these issues and instill in the people a vision of what the future held for the temple structure and for the nation.

### (2) Origin of the Message (2:1b)

**the word of the LORD came through the prophet Haggai:**

**2:1b**   As in the first sermon, there is stress on the divine origin of Haggai's prophetic word. His message is presented as "the word of the LORD" *(děbar YHWH),* even though it was given "through" *(běyad,* "by the hand of") Haggai.[1] Although Haggai was the conduit through which the message would flow, the message was ultimately sourced in God himself.

### (3) Recipients of the Message (2:2)

[2]"Speak to Zerubbabel son of Shealtiel, governor of Judah, to Joshua son of Jehozadak, the high priest, and to the remnant of the people. Ask them,

**2:2** As in the first sermon, the political and religious leadership of the Judean community are singled out as recipients of the message. Haggai is instructed by the Lord to speak once again to Zerubbabel the governor of Judah and to Joshua the high priest. It was their leadership that would be crucial for effective solicitation of involvement and participation on the part of the people. A third audience, however, is mentioned here whose presence was implied but not directly stated in the first sermon. That audience is the people in general. Haggai refers to them here as "the remnant of the people" *(šě'ērît hā'ām).*[2] As noted in connection with the use of this expression in 1:12, the term for remnant is apparently intended as a general designation for the entire Judean population, consisting of both those who had returned from Babylon and those who had remained in the land.

## 2. The Present Condition of the Temple (2:3–5)

Haggai begins this message by tackling the source of the people's discouragement, namely, the unimpressive condition of the present temple as compared to the wonder of Solomon's temple. The section makes two main points. First, in what has been described as "a tactically brilliant maneuver"[3] on the part of a skilled politician, the prophet acknowledges that the present temple is in an unenviable condition. Concerning this there was no basis for dispute. This structure was but a faded and dim shadow of that former one that been the pride of a nation. Second, the prophet indicates that the antidote to discouragement lies in reflection on the Lord's continued presence, as evidenced in his prior salvific deeds in behalf of his peo-

---

[1] In 2:1 for the MT בְּיַד ("by the hand of") Mur 88 has אֶל ("to"). The reading of the MT is to be preferred. Mur 88 has likely conformed the expression to that of 2:10,20, as H. W. Wolff suggests *(Haggai: A Commentary* [Minneapolis: Augsburg, 1988], 70).

[2] In 2:2 the LXX (πάντας) and P *(-klh)* have "all" before "remnant." Since this reading probably is due to scribal harmonization with the similar expression in 1:12,14, the MT should be accepted here. That the MT has lost כֹל due to haplography caused by homoeoteleuton, as C. L. Meyers and E. M. Meyers suggest, does not seem likely *(Haggai, Zechariah 1–8: A New Translation with Introduction and Commentary,* AB [New York: Doubleday, 1987], 47, n. /a/, 49).

[3] The phrase is D. L. Petersen's; see *Haggai and Zechariah 1–8: A Commentary,* OTL (Philadelphia: Westminster, 1984), 63–64.

ple. As Zechariah would later say, they should not despise the day of small things (Zech 4:10). Persistent obedience to God's calling for them would be accompanied by the enabling blessing of his presence for the accomplishment of things greater than they could imagine. They should forge ahead with their work, drawing strength from the Lord's invigorating presence with them.

### *(1) An Unfavorable Comparison with the Former Temple (2:3)*

[3]"Who of you is left who saw this house in its former glory? How does it look to you now? Does it not seem to you like nothing?"

**2:3** Invoking a comparison with the Solomonic temple was perhaps partly related to calendrical considerations. The dedication of Solomon's temple took place in connection with the Feast of Sukkot more than four centuries earlier (2 Chr 7:8–10; 1 Kgs 8:2). Now, at about the same time of year, Haggai's community was involved in restoration of that temple. The solidarity of the latter structure with the former one is reflected in the use of the singular word "house" *(bayit)* to refer both to the prior and to the future buildings.[4] In Haggai's theology the two buildings were but different manifestations of one and the same temple.

The Lord instructs Haggai to inquire concerning who among the population had seen the former temple prior to its destruction in 586 B.C. The Hebrew interrogative pronoun *mî* is used with the prepositional phrase that follows in a partitive sense: "Who among you?"[5] There were probably not many of those still living who fell into this category, since destruction of the Solomonic temple occurred some sixty-six years earlier. There is no reason to think that Haggai includes himself in this group of individuals who in their childhood had seen that earlier temple. The fact that he asks "Who among you?" rather than "Who among us?" hints at the prophet's exclusion of himself from the pool of potential candidates.[6] But there were at least some of whom this was true, or the question loses its relevance. Whether the accuracy of childhood memories of the temple could be relied on or whether idealism and hyperbole influenced such recollections is hard to say. Often what adults remember from their childhood is embellished and larger than life. But even when allowance is made for the possibility of unintentional exaggeration on the part of Haggai's audience, any such comparison could only leave the present structure in an uncomplimentary light. It was far from equaling the grandeur of Solomon's temple. No one, includ-

---

[4] The Hb. is הַזֶּה הַבַּיִת. Cf. vv. 3,7,9.

[5] See DG §7 (a).

[6] See J. A. Motyer, "Haggai," in *The Minor Prophets: An Exegetical and Expository Commentary* (Grand Rapids: Baker, 1998), 3:964.

ing Haggai, was going to contest that.

The rhetorical question, "Does it not seem to you like nothing?" drew no dissent—neither from the prophet nor from his audience. The language of dissimilarity used here is emphatic. The Hebrew text literally has "is it not the case that like it, like nothing, in your eyes?" Although forms of the preposition *kĕ* ("like") are used in both parts of the comparison, the point of the idiom is not so much to say that the one thing is like the other, as if to indicate a certain resemblance that could be found between the two. The expression instead emphatically calls attention to the fact that this building and nothingness amounted to the same thing! In other words, the disappointment the people felt could only be formulated in terms of nothingness. Haggai pointedly asks, "It and nothing, are they not identical in your sight?"[7] There was no comparison between the two buildings, and the people were loathe to pretend there was. The high hopes they had entertained at the beginning of their work had now turned to disappointment. The description calls to mind a scene that occurred at the laying of the foundation stone for the temple in 537 B.C., some seventeen years earlier. Ezra 3:12–13 provides this account:

> But many of the older priests and Levites and family heads, who had seen the former temple, wept aloud when they saw the foundation of this temple being laid, while many others shouted for joy. No one could distinguish the sound of the shouts of joy from the sound of weeping because the people made so much noise. And the sound was heard far away.

### (2) The Promise of Divine Presence and Strength (2:4–5)

**[4]But now be strong, O Zerubbabel,' declares the LORD. 'Be strong, O Joshua son of Jehozadak, the high priest. Be strong, all you people of the land,' declares the LORD, 'and work. For I am with you,' declares the LORD Almighty. [5]'This is what I covenanted with you when you came out of Egypt. And my Spirit remains among you. Do not fear.'**

**2:4** The tone of the message now shifts, as indicated by the adverb "now" *(wĕ'attâ)* that begins v. 4.[8] This word calls attention to the crisis of that moment. Decisions made at a crucial juncture in time often determine the outcome of the future.[9] Haggai counters the people's discouragement with a thrice-repeated imperative: "Be strong" *(ḥāzaq).* Each element of his

---

[7] On this construction see *GBH* §174i.

[8] In 2:4 the NIV renders וְעַתָּה as "but now." The contrastive sense the word carries here could also be rendered "nevertheless." So *HALOT,* 902. On the uses of וְעַתָּה in the Hb. Bible see H. A. Brongers, "Bemerkungen zum Gebrauch des Adverbialen *wᵉ'attāh* im Alten Testament (ein lexikologischer Beitrag)," *VT* 15 (1965), esp. p. 295.

[9] As J. H. Miller remarks, *"Now* is the critical moment, the fulcrum on which is balanced a plethora of future blessings on the one hand, and a recital of past failures on the other" ("Haggai—Zechariah: Prophets of the Now and Future," *CurTM* 6 [1979]: 100).

tripartite audience (Zerubbabel, Joshua, and the people) is the recipient of the admonishment "be strong." Each of them is called upon to allow God's Spirit to renew their determination and moral courage for the task ahead. The language is reminiscent of Josh 1:6–9, where the imperatives "be strong" and "be courageous" are repeated three times to an audience that faced similar discouragement due to the recent death of Moses and their understandable concerns for the future.[10] It is that scene of discouragement in Joshua that Haggai invokes as holding lessons adequate to answer the discouragement of his audience as well. The use of this earlier sacred text with contemporary application for the issue at hand is striking. The ancient prophet and the modern preacher alike share a conviction that God's Word to past generations speaks with equal force to present believers who stand in need of hearing God's message for their situation. The sacred text speaks afresh to each generation.

The way in which Zerubbabel and Joshua are described in v. 4 differs. Although Zerubbabel is mentioned by name only and without patronymic or title, the reference to Joshua includes both items. This may be due to nothing more than stylistic variation. That it suggests a higher level of leadership for Joshua as opposed to Zerubbabel is not a necessary conclusion, although some scholars have been drawn in that direction.[11] The repetition of details concerning the recipients of the message, since those details have already been provided in v. 2, has been viewed by some scholars as unnecessary and perhaps due to scribal gloss.[12] But in spite of seeming clumsiness, there is insufficient manuscript evidence for deleting the words. Nor should the repetition of the phrase "declares the LORD" (*nĕʾum YHWH* ) be viewed as excessive. The repetition may be indicative of the prophet's perception of himself as the intermediate agent through whom the Lord's message reached this audience.[13]

Haggai's larger audience is designated in v. 4 as "the people of the land" (*ʿam hāʾāreṣ*). The significance of this expression in the Hebrew Bible has

---

[10] D. J. McCarthy suggests the language of 2:4 may be related to what he calls an installation genre, similar to what is found in Deut 31:23 ("An Installation Genre?" *JBL* 90 [1971], esp. pp. 33–34). The general characteristics of this genre are (1) encouragement, (2) description of the task, and (3) assurance of divine aid. It is true that these elements are present in Hag 2:4. However, the function of the pericope in Haggai does not correspond to the motif of the installation of a successor as we find in the Deuteronomy text, and this parallel should not be unduly pressed.

[11] Meyers and Meyers ask the question, "Can this be a sign of the ascendancy of the high priest over the governor from the perspective of the internal organization of the postexilic community?" They seem to think so (*Haggai, Zechariah 1–8*, 50).

[12] See, e.g., the textual suggestions for v. 4 in the apparatus of *BHS*. See also J. E. Tollington, *Tradition and Innovation in Haggai and Zechariah 1–8*, JSOTSup 150 (Sheffield: JSOT Press, 1993), 22.

[13] See C. Meyers and E. M. Meyers, "Haggai, Book of," *ABD* 3 (1992): 22.

been interpreted in various ways.[14] The expression has a varied usage in the Hebrew Bible; its specific nuance can only be determined from context. In earlier literature it is used to refer to the general population of the country (e.g., 2 Kgs 11:14,18; 21:24; 23:20). But in later literature the expression sometimes has negative connotations, being used to refer to those from whom the faithful should disassociate (e.g., Ezra 10:11). In Hag 2:4 the expression is used in a rather general and neutral way as referring to all of Haggai's otherwise unnamed audience, whether they were returnees from the exile or had remained in the land all along. "The people of the land" are thus the general population of the land, as distinct from the civil and religious leaders who are identified separately in v. 4. It is the same audience that earlier was referred to as "the remnant of the people" (1:12,14; cf. 2:2).

The words "I am with you" renew the promise expressed earlier in 1:13. Their repetition here calls attention to a need for such reassurance on the part of Haggai's audience and also underscores the certainty of the Lord's presence with them. In 1 Chr 28:20 David encouraged his son Solomon with similar words:

> Be strong and courageous, and do the work. Do not be afraid or discouraged, for the LORD God, my God, is with you. He will not fail you or forsake you until all the work for the service of the temple of the LORD is finished.

Just as the Lord's presence with his people made possible the completion of

---

[14] In postbiblical rabbinic literature the expression עַם הָאָרֶץ eventually became a pejorative expression used to describe those who were less zealous for their religion than they should have been, at least in the opinion of the rabbis. But the precise meaning of this expression in the OT is disputed. As E. W. Nicholson explains, the expression עַם הָאָרֶץ in the Hb. Bible has been interpreted as referring to (1) a rural population as opposed to an urban one; (2) what was the equivalent of an ancient two-tier Hb. parliament; (3) the lay population as distinguished from the ruling elite; (4) the landed aristocracy of the population; (5) the poorest commoners of the society; or (6) property owning citizens who led the country politically, economically, or militarily ("The Meaning of the Expression עַם הָאָרֶץ in the Old Testament," *JSS* 10 [1965]: 59–66). According to Nicholson the latter view is the one most widely accepted. These views all share the belief that עַם הָאָרֶץ is a technical term for designating a particular societal group that was a subset of the general population. But Nicholson has questioned this assumption, maintaining that "the term has no fixed and rigid meaning but is used rather in a purely general and fluid manner and varies in meaning from context to context" (p. 66). See also S. Daiches, "The Meaning of עַם הָאָרֶץ in the Old Testament," *JTS* 30 (1929): 245–49; M. Sulzberger, *The Am Ha-Aretz, The Ancient Hebrew Parliament: A Chapter in the Constitutional History of Ancient Israel* (Philadelphia: Julius H. Greenstone, 1909); id., "The Polity of the Ancient Hebrews," *JQR* 3 (1912–1913): 1–81; E. Würthwein, *Der 'amm ha'arez im Alten Testament,* BWA(N)T 69 (Stuttgart: Kohlhammer, 1936); R. de Vaux, "Le sens de l'expression «peuple du pays» dans l'Ancien Testament et le rôle politique du people en Israël," *RA* 58 (1964): 167–72; J. Weinberg, "The *'Am Hā'āreṣ* of the Sixth to Fourth Centuries BCE," in *The Citizen–Temple Community,* JSOTSup 151 (Sheffield: Sheffield Academic Press, 1992), 62–74. De Vaux's article has an especially helpful bibliography of prior research dealing with this expression.

Solomon's temple, so it would be his presence that would make possible the completion of Haggai's temple. Haggai's audience could draw strength from the realization that they were not alone in their work. The Lord was indeed with them.

**2:5** According to v. 5 Haggai's audience is to draw encouragement for their task from the implications of the Lord's prior blessings upon them throughout their history. The Lord's presence had been in evidence with his people since the time of their exodus from Egypt. Haggai does not seem to have in mind a single specific text that embodies this promise. The idea of God's presence at the time of the exodus and subsequent events can be found in several passages (cf. Exod 33:14; Num 11:16–17,25; Isa 63:11). Haggai's comment summarizes this teaching. In a way consistent with and corresponding to Israel's prior experience throughout her history, the Lord promises that "my spirit remains among you" *(wĕrûḥî 'ōmedet bĕtôkĕkem)*.[15] Use of the participle *'ōmedet* ("is standing") rather than a finite verb suggests that the promise is viewed in terms of permanence rather than as a momentary event. The notion of the Spirit standing in their midst may hint at the exodus event, where a pillar of cloud stood over the people in a similar way.[16] As a consequence of this reassurance concerning the divine presence, there was no need for them to face their present task with undue anxiety.

The syntax of v. 5 in the Hebrew text is difficult. The verse begins with the particle *'et,* which is normally the marker for a definite direct object. Since what follows this particle is not easily linked as an object to anything in the immediately preceding or following context, it is difficult to follow the thought of vv. 4–6. In the NIV the words "this is" at the beginning of v. 5, which have the effect of smoothing out the syntax, have been supplied; they have no counterpart in the Hebrew text. A number of options for dealing with the difficult syntax of vv. 4–6 have been suggested by scholars.[17] For convenience' sake these views may be grouped into four general categories, depending on how they treat the *'et* of v. 5.

1. *'et* as introducing an accusative.—Some interpreters take the *'et* of v. 5 in its common function of marking a definite direct object. One must

---

[15] In v. 5 for the MT עֹמֶדֶת וְרוּחִי ("and my spirit is remaining") the Tg. has וּנְבִיֵּי מַלְפִין ("and my prophets are teaching"), which makes the reference to the divine presence less direct. According to the Tg. it is through the prophetic ministry that Yahweh's Spirit is present among the people.

[16] So Kessler, *The Book of Haggai*, 172.

[17] In a lengthy note devoted to this problem T. André divides the various views into those that understand אֵת here to mark the accusative case, those that understand אֵת to be a preposition meaning "with," and those that understand אֵת to mark the nominative case (*Le prophète Aggée: Introduction critique et commentaire* [Paris: Librairie Fischbacher, 1895], 249–54).

then identify the verb for which this accusative is the direct object. Two possibilities may be mentioned. First, the clause at the beginning of v. 5 could perhaps go with the imperative verb wa‘ăśû ("and do") found back in v. 4.[18] The sense would be "and fulfill . . . the thing that I covenanted." This suggestion seems artificial here, since at the time of the exodus there was no promise of divine presence as found in v. 5. Furthermore, as Fishbane points out, on the basis of this understanding it is difficult to account for the intervening words " 'for I am with you,' says the LORD of hosts." They would separate the verb from its object in an unnatural way. Furthermore, this view requires the uncommon sense of "fulfill" for the verb ‘āśâ.[19] In a variation of this view Clark suggests that a second occurrence of the imperative verb ‘ăśû may have dropped out of the text due to haplography or ellipsis.[20] But there is no textual evidence to support this possibility. This approach to v. 5 is beset with difficulty.

Second, it is possible that ’et should be understood as introducing the direct object of an implied verb such as "remember."[21] But the difficulty that such an ellipsis creates in v. 5 is not an argument in its favor. Ellipsis of words is understandable as a stylistic technique in cases where the words to be supplied are fairly obvious. But ellipsis that trips the reader is undesirable to any writer who aims to communicate with his readers. Neither of these possibilities is convincing.

2. ’et as textually corrupt.—Many scholars conclude that the difficulty in v. 5 is due to textual disturbance in the MT, either with regard to the entire phrase or with regard to some part of it. Specific suggestions for emendation vary considerably. Some interpreters maintain that ’et occasionally serves to mark a secondary gloss, which in v. 5 is a promise that the Lord will be with the postexilic community in the same way that he was with their ancestors at the time of the exodus.[22] According to this view the gloss is not an original part of the composition but was clumsily

---

[18] T. Muraoka, e.g., allows for the possibility that כִּי־אֲנִי אִתְּכֶם נְאֻם יְהוָה צְבָאוֹת may be parenthetical, in which case אֶת־הַדָּבָר would go with וַעֲשׂוּ in v. 4 (*Emphatic Words and Structures in Biblical Hebrew* [Jerusalem: Magnes; Leiden: Brill, 1985], 155, n. 135). Meyers and Meyers interpret v. 5 in the same way, suggesting that the separation of verb and object may be "an intentional displacement of the object to heighten the authority of the command and to include citation of Yahweh's involvement" (*Haggai, Zechariah 1–8*, 51).

[19] M. Fishbane, *Biblical Interpretation in Ancient Israel* (Oxford: Clarendon, 1985), 49. On pp. 48–51 Fishbane discusses at some length what he calls "formulaic uses of אֵת."

[20] See D. J. Clark, "Discourse Structure in Haggai," *JOTT* 5 (1992): 19.

[21] BDB (85), citing Hag 2:5 and 1 Sam 30:23, adopt this conclusion.

[22] See, e.g., P. R. Ackroyd, "Some Interpretative Glosses in the Book of Haggai," *JJS* 7 (1956): 163–67. See also id., "Studies in the Book of Haggai," *JJS* 2 (1951): 169, n. 2.

inserted by a later editor of Haggai's work.[23]

Certain other proposals for emendation are more limited in scope. K. Elliger, who edited the Minor Prophets for *BHS*, thought that in place of *'et haddābār*("the word") in the MT we should probably read *zō't habbĕrît* ("this is the covenant"). This implies that *'et* is due to scribal corruption of an original *zō't* ("this"), a difference of only one consonant in Hebrew, and that *haddābār*("the word") is due to scribal corruption of an original *habbĕrît* ("the covenant"), since to "cut a covenant" (not a "word") is the normal biblical expression. In the apparatus of *BHS* Elliger calls attention to another suggestion, namely, that *'et* may be due to partial dittography of the immediately preceding word (*ṣĕbā'ôt,* "hosts") in v. 5. According to this view, a scribe mistakenly repeated letters from that word, creating the problematic reading *'et* at the beginning of v. 5. This possibility lacks any confirming evidence in the manuscript tradition for the Book of Haggai. Rather than emending *'et* or deleting it without adequate external evidence, it seems better to accept it as part of the text of v. 5 and look instead for a syntactical explanation.

3. *'et* as introducing a *casus pendens.*—Some interpreters conclude that the construction introduced by *'et* is an independent construction devoid of syntactical connections to what precedes. This is the view of Hoftijzer. He maintains that in Hag 2:5 *'et* introduces a suspended case, which provides a general background for what is said without providing formal connections to the prior sentence in v. 4. Hoftijzer translates the clause of v. 5 as follows: "as to the covenant that I made with you when you left Egypt, my spirit remains amongst you; i.e., in agreement with the covenant . . ."[24] This yields an acceptable understanding of the construction, though a certain awkwardness still remains in the syntax.

4. *'et* as introducing a nominative. Other interpreters take the *'et* in v. 5 to introduce a nominative (not accusative) construction that has syntactical connections to the context. Two forms of this approach may be mentioned.

---

[23] All of the MT אֶת־הַדָּבָר אֲשֶׁר־כָּרַתִּי אִתְּכֶם בְּצֵאתְכֶם מִמִּצְרַיִם is absent in the LXX, leading many scholars to suspect that the presence of these words in the MT is due to an early scribal gloss. W. Eichrodt, e.g., says that this reading "is certainly a corruption of the text, introduced as a gloss on *rūḥī*" (*Theology of the Old Testament,* OTL [Philadelphia: Westminster, 1961], 2:62, n. 1). But it is possible to account for the omission in the LXX as being due to scribal error rather than as reflecting the original reading of the Hb. text here. Cf. D. R. Jones, *Haggai, Zechariah and Malachi: Introduction and Commentary,* TBC (London: SCM Press, 1962), 46, and Tollington, *Tradition and Innovation,* 20.

[24] J. Hoftijzer, "Remarks Concerning the Use of the Particle *'t* in Classical Hebrew," *OtSt* 14 (1965): 76. Hoftijzer's lengthy essay (of almost a hundred pages) is an important contribution to this aspect of Hb. syntax. There is also a considerable amount of other research on the usage of אֵת in biblical Hb. to be found in the secondary literature. Much of that research is referenced in Hoftijzer, "Remarks," 1, n. 1; and *IBHS* §10.3c, nn. 31, 32.

First, some commentators regard *'et* in v. 5 as introducing a subject. Keil attempts to explain *haddābār* ("the word") as parallel with *rûḥî* ("my spirit"), forming with it the subject of the participle *'ōmedet* ("standing"). He suggests that *'et* is used as a connector linking this statement with the one that goes before.[25] The resultant meaning is, "The word that I concluded with you at your coming out of Egypt, and my Spirit, stand in the midst of you." But that the first member of a compound subject would be marked with *'et* and not the other seems very unlikely. This view is not persuasive.

A second view, which also regards *'et* as introducing a nominative, provides the most viable solution. The particle *'et* sometimes carries a deictic force, introducing a nominative (rather than accusative) case construction.[26] Saydon, who understands *'et* in v. 5 in this way, translates the words with an emphatic sense: "This indeed is the word."[27] In a similar way Joüon takes *'et* to function as the practical equivalent of a pronoun, with the resultant meaning "this is the word."[28] This is the view reflected in the NIV (i.e., "This is what I covenanted with you"), and it seems to provide a satisfactory solution to the difficulty.

Haggai's point is that just as the Lord covenanted to be with Israel as far back as the exodus event, and just as his presence had been evident throughout their prior history, so now the community should confidently face their difficulties in the enabling power of the Spirit and free from the paralysis of fear about the future. Haggai's exhortation not to fear has its biblical roots in military language. Warriors were often admonished in this way prior to engaging in battle.[29] Given the similarity in wording between the admonition in Hag 2:5 and the one in 1 Chr 28:20, Haggai may be drawing on the instructions David gave to his people prior to the building of the Solomonic temple.

---

[25] C. F. Keil, *Minor Prophets*, Commentary on the Old Testament (reprint; Grand Rapids: Eerdmans, 1982), 187–88. Cf. E. Henderson, *The Book of the Twelve Minor Prophets, Translated from the Original Hebrew, with a Commentary, Critical, Philological, and Exegetical*, 2d ed. (London: Hamilton, Adams, 1858), 354.

[26] For numerous examples of אֵת used as a so-called *nota nominativi*, emphasizing the subject, see P. P. Saydon, "Meanings and Uses of the Particle אֵת," *VT* 14 (1964): 192–210; N. Walker, "Concerning the Function of *'ēth*," *VT* 5 (1955): 314–15.

[27] Saydon, "Meanings and Uses of the Particle אֵת," 202. J. Macdonald has reinforced Saydon's analysis with further examples taken from a Samaritan chronicle written in classical Hb. ("The Particle אֵת in Classical Hebrew: Some New Data on Its Use with the Nominative," *VT* 14 [1964]: 264–75).

[28] See *GBH* §125j. Cf. DG §94, rem. 6; *DCH* 1:446.

[29] For a discussion of this formula in OT literature see E. W. Conrad, *Fear Not Warrior: A Study of* 'al tîrā' *Pericopes in the Hebrew Scripture*, BJS 75 (Chico, Calif.: Scholars Press, 1985).

### 3. The Future Condition of the Temple (2:6–9)

In this final section of Haggai's second sermon the Lord promises to work in unusual ways to insure the supply of needed resources for the temple. As a result of the Lord's initiatives, wealth from non-Israelite nations will become available for this purpose. The result will be that the rebuilt temple will not only compare favorably to the former Solomonic temple; it will actually surpass that temple in terms of the glory that the Lord will bestow upon it.

### *(1) Divine Intervention in the Cosmos (2:6)*

**⁶"This is what the LORD Almighty says: 'In a little while I will once more shake the heavens and the earth, the sea and the dry land.**

**2:6**  This section begins with another reminder of the divine origin of Haggai's message. Only a conviction that the Lord is speaking to them through his prophet is likely to provide adequate motivation for the daunting task before the people. The prophet therefore never lets them lose sight of the theological basis of his message. Repeatedly he invokes the Lord's self-disclosure of his will as the proper underpinning for all that he has to say to this people. If they choose to accept his message, it will be the Lord's word they thereby accept. On the other hand, if they reject his message, it will be nothing less than the Lord's word they reject.

In v. 6 Haggai announces a cosmic shaking of the heavens and earth. Its effects will be felt in both sea and dry land. The double merism used here ("heavens and earth," "sea and dry land") underscores the scope of the Lord's actions; nothing will be left unaffected. The portrayal of the Lord as Shaker underscores his divine omnipotence; nothing evades his might and power. The shaking of the heavens and earth is described in terms of imminence: "I am about to . . ."[30] The adverb "once more" likens these events to the theophany and shaking of Mount Sinai that occurred in connection with the giving of the law (Exod 19:18). On the other hand, the accompanying temporal phrase "in a little while" suggests a near rather than a distant ful-

---

[30] The *hiphil* participle מַרְעִישׁ is best understood as *futurum instans,* pointing to the imminent future: "I am about to shake . . ." Cf. 2:21. This seems preferable to M. A. Sweeney's view that the participle here describes the action as presently taking place. As Sweeney notes, in v. 7 the verbs are perfects with *wāw* consecutive, clearly referring to future time ("Haggai," in *The Twelve Prophets,* Berit Olam: Studies in Hebrew Narrative and Poetry (Collegeville, Minn.: Liturgical Press, 2000), 2:548.

fillment for these events.[31] However, that this language means that "Haggai was anticipating the imminent collapse of the Persian empire," as Kuntz supposes, is not a necessary conclusion.[32]

Haggai envisioned a situation in which God would so move among the non-Israelite nations that they would supply the needed revenues for the project of temple rebuilding. The prophet Isaiah also spoke of the wealth of the nations one day being diverted to Zion in acknowledgment of God's sovereign blessings to be bestowed upon Jerusalem. Isa 60:5 says:

> Then you will look and be radiant, your heart will throb and swell with joy; the wealth on the seas will be brought to you, to you the riches of the nations will come.

In Haggai's day this enrichment took place as a result of the decision on the part of the Persian rulers, beginning with Cyrus, to facilitate the rebuilding of the temple by extending financial resources for that purpose. This language also envisages an apocalyptic breaking in of the divine presence in sudden and violent terms and as such seems to have eschatological dimensions. This is the significance attached to Hag 2:6 by the author of the Epistle to the Hebrews, who sees here an anticipation of the messianic age. In Heb 12:26–29 he says:

> At that time his voice shook the earth, but now he has promised, "Once more I will shake not only the earth but also the heavens." The words "once more" indicate the removing of what can be shaken—that is, created things—so that what cannot be shaken may remain. Therefore, since we are receiving a kingdom that cannot be shaken, let us be thankful, and so worship God acceptably with reverence and awe, for our "God is a consuming fire."

The New Testament writer sees in Haggai's language an implicit contrast between the transitory nature of the old economy and the abiding permanence of the new economy that was initiated by the mission of Jesus.

### (2) Financial Assistance from the Nations (2:7–8)

**7I will shake all nations, and the desired of all nations will come, and I will fill this house with glory,' says the LORD Almighty. 8'The silver is mine and the gold is mine,' declares the LORD Almighty.**

---

[31] In 2:6 for MT עוֹד אַחַת מְעַט הִיא ("yet once, it is a little") the LXX has ἔτι ἅπαξ ("yet once") and P has ṭwb ḥdʾ zbn ("yet one time"). The expression in the MT emphasizes how soon the cosmic shaking Haggai announced will appear, but the LXX and P lack this stress on temporal nearness. This change may be due to a theological decision of those translators, since by their time the possibility of a quick fulfillment of Haggai's prophecy may have been regarded as no longer feasible. The text of the MT is preferable here.

[32] See J. K. Kuntz, *The People of Ancient Israel: An Introduction to Old Testament Literature, History, and Thought* (New York: Harper & Row, 1974), 405.

**2:7**    The shaking of the nations described in v. 6 will lead to (lit.) "the desirable things of all the nations" *(ḥemdat kol haggôyim)* coming into the rebuilt temple. This expression is one of the most misunderstood statements in the Book of Haggai. There are three major interpretations of this phrase: a messianic interpretation, a nonmessianic interpretation, and a blend of the two.[33] Each of these interpretations requires discussion and evaluation.

1. Many Christian interpreters, both ancient and modern, have taken Haggai's phrase to be a cryptic reference to Jesus the Messiah, in whose coming the longings of the nations find their ultimate realization.[34] This messianic understanding of the phrase is very ancient. It is found among Christian interpreters as far back as the patristic period.[35] It was canonized, so to speak, in the fourth century by Jerome, whose rendering of this part of the verse in the Latin Vulgate has been very influential: *et veniet desideratus cunctis gentibus,* "and the desire of all nations shall come." A similar understanding of the phrase, probably due either directly or indirectly to the influence of the Vulgate, is also found in a number of English versions.[36] The following translations are clearly committed to a messianic understanding of the phrase:

KJV: "and the desire of all nations shall come"
NKJV: "and they shall come to the Desire of All Nations"
LB: "and the Desire of All Nations shall come to this Temple"
Douay-Rheims: "and the Desired of All Nations shall come"

The NIV ("and the desired of all nations will come") is probably to be read with a messianic understanding as well.[37]

---

[33] André provides a helpful summary and criticism of various views held through the end of the nineteenth century (see *Le prophète Aggée,* 266–81).

[34] M. El-Meskeen, e.g., says, "The 'desire of all nations' is none other than the Son of God" ("The Desire of All Nations," *CCR* 17 [1996]: 84). In a similar way H. P. Barker comments, "But the reference is undoubtedly to Christ. The things which the nations desire, but for which they vainly seek in this direction and in that, will be found in Him" (*Christ in the Minor Prophets* [New York: Loizeaux, n.d.], 89–90).

[35] For a summary of early Christian interpretation of 2:7, along with a discussion of Jerome's translation of the phrase, see A. Škrinjar, "«Veniet desideratus cunctis gentibus» (Ag. 2,8; hebr. 2,7)," *VD* 15 (1935): 355–62.

[36] Cf. Luther's 1532 German translation of 2:7: "Da sol denn komen aller Heiden Trost" ("then the consolation of all Gentiles shall come"). This translation clearly encouraged among German-speaking peoples a messianic understanding of 2:7. On the problems of this translation see esp. G. Krause, "'Aller Heiden Trost' Haggai 2,7: Die Beweggründe für eine falsche Übersetzung und Auslegung des Textes durch Luther," in *Solange es »Heute« Heisst: Festgabe für Rudolf Hermann zum 70. Geburtstag* (Berlin: Evangelische Verlagsanstalt, 1957), 170–78. Krause rightly describes Luther's translation of the phrase as a lexically false translation (p. 170). The 1912 revision moved away from the messianic interpretation. It translates this part of v. 7: "Da soll dann kommen aller Heiden Bestes" ("then the best of all Gentiles shall come").

[37] In its introduction to Haggai the *NIV Study Bible* explains the phrase "the desired of all nations" as referring to the coming of the Messiah, although the note attached to Hag 2:7 in the same study Bible is ambivalent about this interpretation.

As a result of such translations the phrase "desired of all nations" has in many quarters assumed the status of a messianic title, as can be seen in Christian hymnody[38] and in the titles of certain books that deal with Christian messianism.[39] Those who favor a messianic understanding of this phrase usually relate it to the first advent of Jesus; it is especially common during the Christmas season to find Christological allusions to 2:7. There have been exceptions, however, to this understanding among Christians. Augustine understood the phrase to refer not to Christ's first coming but to his second coming, since "before the whole world can await him and desire His coming, it must first believe in Him and love Him."[40] Like the view that links v. 7 to the first advent of Christ, association of this verse with the second advent of Christ has also been widely held in Christendom.

But for all its attractiveness this view is highly improbable. Nothing in the context of Haggai's second sermon justifies taking these words as a messianic prediction, whether in reference to the first or second advent of Christ. It seems clear that the words refer impersonally to the wealth of the nations that the Lord will cause to flow into the temple so as to make its construction complete. The word "desire[d]" *(ḥemdat)* in v. 7 is a metonym referring to the object of their desire, namely, material wealth. There is no convincing exegetical reason for thinking that the verse has any Christological import.[41]

---

[38] The familiar messianic interpretation of 2:7 is reflected in a number of well-known Christian hymns. Charles Wesley's *Come, Thou Long Expected Jesus* has in stanza one: "Dear Desire of every nation, / Joy of every longing heart." Henry Sloane Coffin's stanza added to *O Come, O Come, Emmanuel* has "O come, Desire of nations, bind / All peoples in one heart and mind." And James Montgomery's *Angels from the Realms of Glory* has in stanza three: "Seek the great Desire of nations, / Ye have seen His natal star."

[39] A Christological understanding of this phrase is assumed in titles of several works dealing with various themes. See, e.g., R. C. Trench, *The Fitness of Holy Scripture for Unfolding the Spiritual Life of Men. II. Christ the Desire of All Nations, Or the Unconscious Prophecies of Heathendom* (Philadelphia: Hooker, 1850); E. W. Smith, *The Desire of All Nations* (Garden City: Doubleday, Doran & Co., 1928); M. von Blomberg, *The Desire of the Nations: A Timely Word for a Distressed World* (New York: Vantage, 1971); O. O'Donovan, *The Desire of the Nations: Rediscovering the Roots of Political Theology* (Cambridge: Cambridge University Press, 1996); El-Meskeen, "Desire of All Nations," 83–89.

[40] See Augustine, *De civitate Dei*, book 18, chap. 35; cf. chaps. 45, 48. For the English translation cited above see *Saint Augustine: The City of God, Books XVII–XXII*, in *The Fathers of the Church: A New Translation* (New York: Fathers of the Church, 1954), 138, 160, 168.

[41] Contrary to E. J. Young, who says of 2:7, "The promise is Messianic. The 'desire of the nations' is none other than the Messiah himself" (*An Introduction to the Old Testament*, rev. ed. (Grand Rapids: Eerdmans, 1960), 277. In a similar vein W. C. Kaiser says, "Therefore, we conclude that in verse 7 'desire' refers to the Messiah who will come. He is the preeminent 'desired One'" (*Micah–Malachi*, The Communicator's Commentary [Dallas: Word, 1992], 268). C. L. Feinberg also leans toward a messianic interpretation of this verse ("Haggai," in *The Wycliffe Bible Commentary* [Chicago: Moody, 1962], 893). In addition to these discussions E. B. Pusey has a somewhat rambling defense of this interpretation as well; see *The Minor Prophets: A Commentary, Explanatory and Practical* (reprint, Grand Rapids: Baker, 1950), 2:310–13.

2. Second, there is the nonmessianic interpretation. This interpretation finds expression in at least three very different ways of understanding the syntax of v. 7. The issue revolves around whether *ḥemdat* is an accusative of place after the verb (i.e., "they shall come to the delight of all the nations"), or whether it is the object of an understood preposition with the verb (i.e., "all the nations will arrive with riches"), or whether it is the subject of the verb *bāʾû* (i.e., "the desire of all the nations will come").

Terry understands the word to be an accusative of place after the verb, taking *ḥemdat* to refer to Zion (or more specifically to the temple) as an object of beauty or desire.[42] Much of his argument assumes the singular form of the noun *ḥemdat* as found in the MT and the related difficulty of fitting this with the plural verb *bāʾû*. But if the noun were emended to the plural *ḥămudōt* and taken to refer to valuables brought to the temple by non-Israelite nations, this difficulty disappears. Terry failed to grapple sufficiently with the possibility that the Masoretic vocalization may be mistaken here, and he certainly claims far too much when he says that his interpretation "is the only one in complete harmony with the syntax of the language."[43]

A second nonmessianic approach is that of Meyers and Meyers.[44] They maintain that the subject of the plural verb "come" *(bāʾû)* is the plural expression "all the nations" *(kol haggôyim)* and that the emended plural "desirable things" *(ḥămudōt)* should be taken as the object of an understood preposition "with," even though the verse uses no such preposition with this word. They also argue that a possessive pronominal suffix ("their") is to be supplied with the noun. For support they appeal to the following statement in v. 7 concerning the Lord's filling this house "with" glory. However, this is not really a match, since the preposition in that instance is derived from the verb, which means "to fill with." The meaning of the first half of v. 7, in their view, is this: "all the nations will arrive with (their) riches." In other words, the nations will send tribute to Jerusalem via their political representatives. This analysis of the syntax of v. 7, however, seems unnecessarily complex and encumbered by hypothetical elements that are absent from the verse.

A third nonmessianic approach seems preferable. The context leads to the conclusion that by the phrase "desire of all nations" Haggai refers not to a messianic figure but to the Lord's provision of financial resources for the temple by sovereignly inducing the nations to make their wealth available for this purpose. By "desire" Haggai refers to valuable treasures of mone-

---

[42] M. S. Terry, "'The Desire of All Nations,'" *Methodist Review* 75 (1893): 268–72.

[43] Ibid., 272.

[44] See Meyers and Meyers, *Haggai, Zechariah 1–8*, 53–54.

tary value that were prized by the nations, including such valuables as Nebuchadnezzar's army had removed from the Solomonic temple in 586 B.C. and had taken to Babylon. To facilitate the completion of the temple the Lord will so move among these nations that they will bring resources to assist in the project. Since their wealth is in fact his wealth, as v. 8 points out, the Lord is free sovereignly to dispose of it as he chooses.

Several considerations bear out this understanding. First, the context focuses on the means by which the temple project would be completed in such a way that it would be a worthy successor to the Solomonic temple. The natural expectation is that v. 7 speaks of how the temple rebuilding would occur.

Second, the word translated "desire[d]" *(ḥemdâ)* agrees with this understanding.[45] In addition to its use in 2:7 this word is used fifteen times in the Hebrew Bible, usually to describe tangible items of value or beauty. It is used in reference to stately ships (Isa 2:16), expensive houses (Ezek 26:12), choice fields (Jer 12:10), and various types of valuable vessels or utensils (Hos 13:15; Nah 2:10; Dan 11:8; 2 Chr 32:27; 36:10; Jer 25:34). Several times it is used in reference to a beautiful land (Jer 3:19; Zech 7:14; Ps 106:24). On three occasions it is used in reference to a person. In 2 Chr 21:20 Jehoram is described as one who departed life "without desire," that is, he died "to no one's regret" (NIV). In 1 Sam 9:20 Saul is described as one "to whom is all the desire of Israel," that is, the people preferred him over others as king. Daniel 11:37 speaks of a king who disregards "the desire of women," perhaps meaning "the one desired by women" (so NIV), although this is not entirely clear. The plural *ḥămudôt* (with various slight changes in spelling) occurs ten times in the Hebrew Bible. Most often it refers to valuable items or treasures (e.g., Gen 27:15; Isa 44:9; Ezra 8:27; 2 Chr 20:25; Dan 11:38,43). Once it is used of "bread of desires," that is, fine food (Dan 10:3). Several times it describes Daniel as an esteemed individual (Dan 9:23; 10:11,19). All of this suggests that, while this word may on occasion refer to an individual, it most often refers to inanimate objects of special value or worth.

A third issue concerns the verb translated "come" in v. 7. In the Hebrew text this verb is plural *(ûbā'û)*,[46] making it unlikely that an individual is in view. Oddly, however, in the MT the subject of the verb *(ḥemdat)* is singu-

---

[45] On this word see the following lexical authorities: *HALOT,* 325–26; *DCH* 3:248–49; BDB, 326.

[46] In 2:7 of the Hb. text the verb is *qal* ("they will come"), not *hiphil* ("they will bring"). However, P *(wnytwn rgt' dklhwn 'mm' )* and *Tg. Jonathan* (וייתון חמדת כל עממיא) seem to understand the verb to have a causative nuance (i.e., "they shall bring the desire of all the peoples"). This in turn leads to taking the phrase "the desire of all the nations" as the direct object of the verb rather than as its subject.

lar. This makes sense only if the subject of the verb is to be understood in a collective sense, in which case a singular subject with a plural verb is a permissible syntactical construction in classical Hebrew.[47] In such a case singular nouns used in a collective sense may be treated as plural in sense, causing the verb to appear in a plural form.[48] This happens most often when the collective noun in question refers to persons, but it may also be the case when the noun refers to inanimate things.[49] It is significant that the LXX renders *ḥemdat* by a plural *(ta eklekta)*, indicating that the Greek translators probably understood a different vocalization for the Hebrew word.[50] The Hebrew consonants in question permit either a singular or a plural vocalization (i.e., *ḥemdat* or *ḥămudōt*). In Hag 2:7 the LXX understanding of the word seems preferable to that of the MT.[51] Consequently, the clause means "the desirable things of the nations will come." It refers to the transfer of treasures to the Jerusalem temple.

3. Third, a few scholars have sought to find middle ground by combining the best of the alternative views. Wolf has argued that "desire" in 2:7 is deliberately ambiguous and that it allows for both a reference to material treasures and to personal desire.[52] In his view the former understanding is supported by the reference to silver and gold in v. 8, whereas the latter interpretation is supported by the reference to the *(shekinah)* glory in v. 9, which as he points out requires the personal presence of God.[53] According to Wolf, Haggai has carefully chosen his words in v. 7 so as to create an intentional ambiguity. In one sense the verse indicates that the wealth of nations will flow into the temple project, facilitating its rebuilding; in

---

[47] Keil retains the singular חֶמְדַּת of the MT and treats it as a collective singular agreeing in sense with the plural verb בָּאוּ (*Minor Prophets,* 192–94). So also Kessler, who says this "remains the simplest and most adequate explanation" (*The Book of Haggai,* 179–80).

[48] So, e.g., with עַם ("people"); הָאָרֶץ ("the world"). Cf. also צֹאן ("flock"); בָּקָר ("cattle").

[49] See DG §25.

[50] In 2:7 the LXX rendering (τὰ ἐκλεκτά) seems to presuppose the plural vocalization חֲמֻדֹת rather than the singular of the MT חֶמְדַּת. This understanding of the noun form is to be preferred, since the verb the noun goes with is plural in the MT (בָּאוּ). A related issue concerns the form of the verb in the LXX. Since neuter plural subjects in Gk. often take singular verbs, the LXX renders the plural Hb. verb with a singular (ἥξει). The situation in the LXX is thus the reverse of that in the Hb. text: whereas the MT has a singular subject with a plural verb, the LXX has a plural subject with a singular verb.

[51] So also GKC §145e.

[52] H. Wolf, *Haggai and Malachi* (Chicago: Moody, 1976), 37.

[53] G. R. Berry has discussed the significance of "glory" as indicating divine presence, particularly in connection with the Book of Ezekiel; "The Glory of Yahweh and the Temple," *JBL* 56 (1937): 115–17. But Berry takes a far too pessimistic view of the historical accuracy of the biblical accounts, maintaining that postexilic Jewish literature was unrealistic both in its attitudes toward prior history and in its expectations for the future; see id., "The Unrealistic Attitude of Postexilic Judaism," *JBL* 64 (1945): 309–17.

another sense "the desired of all nations" has a messianic dimension, pointing to the coming of Jesus.

It is difficult to see validity for this interpretation in the text of Haggai itself, especially if we lay aside certain faulty translations of the phrase (e.g., Vg, KJV, NKJV, LB, NIV) that influence popular understanding of the phrase. The most natural reading of Haggai's words points to a material understanding of "the desired of all nations" and not to a messianic one.[54] The point of v. 7 is that the postexilic Jews will not have to bear by themselves the financial burden of rebuilding the temple. The Lord will so move among the surrounding nations that they will underwrite to a significant degree the heavy costs of constructing and refurbishing this place of worship.[55] There seems to be no adequate reason for taking these words any other way. It is best to dispose of the messianic interpretation of 2:7 altogether.[56]

In the second half of v. 7 the Lord promises to fill this house with glory. By "glory" *(kābôd)* the manifestation of divine presence probably is intended.[57] In response to the obedience of the covenant people the Lord will once again be uniquely identified with them by virtue of his transcendent presence in the Jerusalem temple. As if to underscore the divine authority on which his message rests, Haggai again repeats the origin of this promise, "says the LORD Almighty" *(nĕʾum YHWH ṣĕbāʾôt)*. In slightly different terms the prophet will make this assertion again in vv. 8–9.

**2:8** In v. 8 Haggai cites the Lord's explanation that the monetary resources promised in v. 7 in reality belong not to the nations from which they will come but to the sovereign Lord of creation. The Hebrew text has literally "to me the silver and to me the gold."[58] The object of the preposi-

---

[54] Kaiser seems to miss the point when he says that "most translators and modern commentators are much too timid in failing to extend their understanding of the word to include the singular connotation and to see a clear Messianic reference here" (*Micah–Malachi*, 268). The problem is not one of timidity. It is the absence of exegetical support.

[55] Kessler identifies four different interpretations of the way in which the nations will participate in the temple project. Their treasures (1) will be seized as spoils of war; (2) will be contributed due to a suzerain-vassal relationship; (3) will be sent as gifts of thanksgiving; or (4) refer to the return of valuable objects of worship previously removed from the Jerusalem temple by Nebuchadnezzar in 586 B.C. (*The Book of Haggai*, 180).

[56] Although F. R. Coad is correct in noting that Christians have often linked 2:7 to Jesus' earthly ministry, it also is true that such correlation has lacked exegetical justification. He says: "But to Christian understanding the supreme fulfillment was surely when He visited it who was Himself without earthly treasure, and whose rejection brought about its destruction (Mt. 24:1,2)" "Haggai," in *The International Bible Commentary*, rev. ed. [Grand Rapids: Zondervan, 1986], 961).

[57] On this use of כָּבוֹד see *HALOT*, 458.

[58] The definite articles used with "silver" and "gold" probably should be understood in a generic sense. The implication is that Yahweh controls all the silver and gold in existence and is therefore able to dispose of it as he sees fit.

tional phrase (i.e., "me") is highlighted not only by the repetition but also by the word order, coming as it does before the subject both times.[59] The emphasis of these nominal clauses is that the money belongs to the Lord and not, as might otherwise be thought, to the nations who have possession of it (cf. Joel 4:5 [ET 3:5]). It should therefore come as no surprise that when the Lord moves upon the nations to bring these "desirable things" to his house, they will merely be returning to him what is his. Since these valuables ultimately belong to the sovereign Lord, they are his to dispose of as he sees fit.

In mentioning silver before gold, Haggai's speech aligns with earlier Hebrew idiom. A distinction in the order of listing these two precious metals appears in ancient Hebrew literature depending on the date of the material. In preexilic biblical Hebrew the normal order is "silver and gold," whereas in late biblical Hebrew the normal order is "gold and silver." The order used may reflect the relative values of these precious metals at different times.[60] Haggai, though written during the period of transition in this usage, retains here the order "silver and gold," which was more common in the earlier period. But in such texts as Dan 5:2 and Ezra 5:14 we find the order shifted to "gold and silver."[61]

Haggai's comments in this section about wealth flowing into the temple should not be misunderstood as though it were the prophet's total emphasis. Some scholars, stressing Haggai's view on the temple as a depository of valuables, have construed the prophet to mean that the temple had that purpose alone, to the exclusion of any other purpose. Carroll, for example, says:

> Thus we may read Haggai as describing the new temple as a potential storehouse or treasury of the empire. It is hardly a holy place for worship or the celebration of cultic rituals, but it is to be a place for the generating of great wealth. With its building the economic welfare of the community will be transformed (2.15–19). In Haggai 2 the essence of the divine house is that of a *bourse* or centre of the generation of wealth. It looks more like an imperial taxation centre than a holy house.[62]

This view exaggerates Haggai's emphasis. The fact that the prophet stresses the monetary requisites for moving ahead with the construction project should not be taken to mean that he had no interests other than money.

---

[59] See *GBH* §154ff.

[60] So Meyers and Meyers, *Haggai, Zechariah 1–8*, 54.

[61] M. F. Rooker documents this diachronic shift and cites numerous examples from both biblical and extrabiblical texts; see *Biblical Hebrew in Transition: The Language of the Book of Ezekiel*, JSOTSup 90 (Sheffield: JSOT Press, 1990), 174–75.

[62] See R. P. Carroll, "So What Do We *Know* about the Temple? The Temple in the Prophets," in *Second Temple Studies: Temple Community in the Persian Period*, JSOTSup 175 (Sheffield: JSOT Press, 1994), 41.

## *(3) The Splendor of the Rebuilt Temple (2:9)*

[9]"The glory of this present house will be greater than the glory of the former house,' says the LORD Almighty. 'And in this place I will grant peace,' declares the LORD Almighty."

**2:9** The prophet now underscores the anticipated glory of the rebuilt temple, perhaps with the temple scene of Isa 6:2–4 in mind.[63] In that passage the *trishagion* uttered by the seraphim ("Holy, holy, holy is the LORD Almighty") calls attention to the presence of divine glory throughout the entire earth.

The NIV translation of the first part of v. 9 is problematic. The Hebrew reads literally, "Great will be the glory of this house the latter."[64] The problem concerns which word ("house" or "glory") is modified by the adjective "latter" *(hāʾaḥărôn)*. Does Haggai mean "the glory of this latter house" (so NIV, KJV, NKJV), or does he mean "the latter glory of this house" (so NASV, NRSV, NAB, NLT)?[65] The word order in the Hebrew text is significant for determining the meaning. The demonstrative adjective "this" *(hazzeh)* immediately follows the word "house" *(habbayit)*, leaving the expression "the latter" *(hāʾaḥărôn)* outside of that construction ("the glory of this house"). This almost certainly means that the word "glory" rather than the word "house" is modified by the word "latter."[66] For the meaning "the glory of this present house" (NIV) we would expect the demonstrative to follow the word translated "present" rather than precede it.[67] It is preferable to understand the phrase in 2:9 to mean "the latter glory of this house" rather than "the glory of this latter house."[68] This understanding is confirmed by v. 3, which speaks of "this house in its former glory."

---

[63] An observation made by Meyers and Meyers; see *Haggai, Zechariah 1–8*, 54.

[64] The Hb. construction reads גָּדוֹל יִהְיֶה כְּבוֹד הַבַּיִת הַזֶּה הָאַחֲרוֹן.

[65] The construction has been rightly understood by the LXX: ἡ δόξα τοῦ οἴκου τούτου ἡ ἐσχάτη ("the latter glory of this house"). The feminine ἡ ἐσχάτη must modify the feminine ἡ δόξα, not the masculine τοῦ οἴκου. The Vg, on the other hand, has *gloria domus istius novissimae* ("the glory of this most recent house").

[66] See *GBH* §143h, which points out that in such phrases where there is an adjective, it is followed by the demonstrative. Joüon finds only one exception to this word order in the Hb. Bible, Jer 13:10 (הָעָם הַזֶּה הָרָע). See also *GBH* §139a(2), where on the basis of the placement of הַזֶּה in Hag 2:9 he rightly interprets the phrase to mean "the second glory of this house" rather than "the glory of this second house."

[67] This renders unacceptable the translation of Meyers and Meyers: "The glory of this latter House" (*Haggai, Zechariah 1–8*, 47). The same is true of the similar translation of v. 9 offered by Petersen; see *Haggai and Zechariah 1–8*, 61. Wolff (*Haggai*, 71) is indecisive on the Hb. syntax here, allowing for either possibility of meaning for the phrase. On the basis of context he takes הָאַחֲרוֹן ("the latter") to modify כְּבוֹד ("glory").

[68] As recognized, e.g., by P. A. Verhoef, *The Books of Haggai and Malachi*, NICOT (Grand Rapids: Eerdmans, 1987), 105. See also E. H. Merrill, *An Exegetical Commentary: Haggai, Zechariah, Malachi* (Chicago: Moody, 1994), 38, 40. Oddly, however, Verhoef's comment is inconsistent with his translation of the same phrase. On the one hand he rightly says, "The comparison between the 'latter' . . . and the 'former' . . . concerns the 'glory' or 'splendor' . . ., and not 'this house'" (p. 105). But he then wrongly translates the clause, "The glory of this latter house shall be greater than that of the former one" (p. 92).

Haggai does not explain exactly how this promise will come to fruition. He apparently expected the rebuilt temple to be acknowledged to some extent within a short time even by the Gentiles as a religious center deserving their honor. Many Christian interpreters recognize a more distant and complete fulfillment in the status afforded the temple by the presence of Jesus during his first advent (cf. Luke 2:25–38) and to an even greater degree at his second advent.[69]

Haggai's second sermon concludes with a promise that "in this place I will grant peace" *(ûbammāqôm hazzeh ʾettēn šālôm)*.[70] The NIV translates the Hebrew conjunction as "and," but it is probably best understood here in a causal sense: "because in this place I will give peace."[71] The statement in part is an explanation of the earlier part of the verse, showing why the latter glory of this temple will be greater than its former glory. The words may be an allusion to the Aaronic blessing found in Num 6:24–26, the final colon of which expresses a wish for the Lord's peace to rest upon the recipient of the benediction. By "peace" is meant more than the mere absence of conflict and strife. The Hebrew word *šālôm* speaks of wellness and soundness in a holistic way. Whether "this place" in v. 9 refers specifically to the temple,[72] as seems likely, or in a general way to the city of Jerusalem,[73] as is possible, is not clear.[74] The word *māqôm* is often used in the Old Testament in reference to a sacred site chosen by the Lord.[75] But the word is also used as a synonym for Jerusalem (e.g., 2 Kgs 22:16; Jer 7:3; 19:3).[76] In Hag 2:9 perhaps neither antecedent should be entirely excluded, since both city and sanctuary will be blessed objects in the fulfillment of the promise.

---

[69] See, e.g., Wolf, *Haggai and Malachi,* 39–40.

[70] At the end of 2:9 the LXX has a scribal gloss that personalizes the preceding promise of the Lord to bestow peace on the temple site: καὶ εἰρήνην ψυχῆς εἰς περιποίησιν παντὶ τῷ κτίζοντι τοῦ ἀναστῆσαι τὸν ναὸν τοῦτον ("even peace of soul as a possession for everyone who builds in order to restore this temple"). The addition is apparently intended to specify more clearly who it is who will be the recipient of Yahweh's promised blessing. According to this gloss it will be those who participate in the building project.

[71] The *wāw* used by itself in this way expresses the causal relation in what Joüon calls "a light and elegant manner" (*GBH* §170c).

[72] Cf. P. R. Ackroyd: "The indications are that *maqom* frequently has a technical meaning and this suggests that the primary reference in this passage too is to the Temple" (*Exile and Restoration: A Study of Hebrew Thought of the Sixth Century B.C.,* OTL (Philadelphia: Westminster, 1968), 156.

[73] So Keil: " 'This place' is not the temple, but Jerusalem, as the place where the temple is built" (*Minor Prophets,* 195).

[74] J. L. Mackay thinks there is a play on words here, since Jerusalem can mean "city of peace" (*Haggai, Zechariah, Malachi: God's Restored People* [Ross-shire, Scotland: Christian Focus Publications, 1994], 35). Cf. J. G. Baldwin, *Haggai, Zechariah, Malachi: An Introduction and Commentary,* TOTC (Downers Grove: InterVarsity, 1972), 49. The similarity between the word *šālôm* and the name of Solomon *(šĕlōmōh),* builder of the first temple, also may not be coincidental in this context. But Petersen discounts both of these possibilities (*Haggai and Zechariah 1–8,* 69–70).

[75] E.g., Deut 12:5; 14:23,25; 1 Kgs 8:29,30; Ps 24:3; Ezra 9:8; Exod 29:31; Lev 6:9[Eng. 16], 19[Eng. 26]; Lev 14:13; Qoh 8:10.

[76] See *HALOT,* 627.

IV. HAGGAI'S THIRD MESSAGE: *DISOBEDIENCE PRODUCES DEFILEMENT, BUT BLESSING WILL ATTEND THOSE WHO OBEY THE LORD'S COMMANDS!* (2:10–19)
1. Introduction to the Message (2:10)
    (1) Date of the Message (2:10a)
    (2) Origin of the Message (2:10b)
2. The Lord's Estimate of the People (2:11–14)
    (1) Principles of Conveyance of Purity and Defilement (2:11–13)
    (2) Condition of the People (2:14)
3. The Necessity of Obedience (2:15–19)
    (1) Evidences of the Lord's Discipline (2:15–17)
    (2) Hope for the Future (2:18–19)

## III. HAGGAI'S THIRD MESSAGE (2:10–19)

A little more than two months after his second sermon Haggai delivered a third message to the people of Judah. The theme of this message is that although disobedience to the Lord produces spiritual defilement, blessing attends those who obey the Lord. The sermon is didactic in nature, intended to communicate to Haggai's audience an important lesson concerning religious purity. This message is also foreboding, in that it warns the people of their impure condition and the resultant unacceptability of their work. The point of the message hinges on a priestly ruling concerning consequences of contact with ceremonially pure or impure items. Perhaps more concisely than anywhere else in the Hebrew Bible this sermon makes the point that impurity is more pervasive and more easily contracted than is purity.[1]

Haggai urged the people to inquire of the priests regarding a matter of ritual holiness. The priests would clarify whether, and if so under what conditions, it was possible to convey purity or impurity from one person or thing to another. This inquiry posed two questions to the priestly community. First, was it possible for a holy object to transfer its holiness from the garment in which it was wrapped to something else with which it came into contact? The answer that the priests returned to this question was negative;

---

[1] So, e.g., R. K. Harrison, *Introduction to the Old Testament* (Grand Rapids: Eerdmans, 1969), 947.

holiness cannot be transferred in this way. Second, was it possible for a holy object to be rendered impure as a result of the garment in which it was wrapped coming into contact with an impure person or object? The answer the priests returned was positive; impurity can be transferred in this way. Haggai then draws the conclusion that due to their impure spiritual condition the work of the people is unacceptable to the Lord. Nothing they do will be acceptable until first their sinful condition is resolved by repentance and forgiveness. As confirmation of this fact, Haggai again calls attention to the economic devastation that was evident throughout the land. Conditions of agricultural failure and economic depression were to be seen on every hand—no one could deny that. Haggai explains that these conditions were due to disciplinary judgment for failure to obey the Lord. Only when the people had properly addressed their spiritual condition would the Lord again extend his blessings of prosperity. The sermon concludes with an optimistic promise of the Lord's renewed blessing upon his people.

## 1. Introduction to the Message (2:10)

### (1) Date of the Message (2:10a)

**[10]On the twenty-fourth day of the ninth month, in the second year of Darius,**

**2:10a**    As is the case with the other sermons in this book, this message is preceded in v. 10 by a brief introduction that is cast in a narrative framework. This introduction provides two important pieces of background information. First, it indicates the chronological setting of the sermon. Second, it identifies the human messenger as a recipient of the divine word. Unlike Haggai's previous messages, neither Zerubbabel nor Joshua is specifically mentioned.

The date of this sermon is "the twenty-fourth day of the ninth month, in the second year of Darius." The ninth month is Kislev. The modern equivalent of this date is December 18, 520 B.C. The date holds no special significance in terms of celebration of an Old Testament feast day or commemoration of an earlier historical event. Mid-December calls to mind no such occasion. That this date falls on the day before the beginning of the celebration of Hanukkah has no significance for Haggai,[2] since Jewish observance of Hanukkah did not begin until the second century B.C.[3] We

---

[2] J. Morgenstern suggests that this fast-day mentioned by Haggai may have been an antecedent to the festival of Hanukkah that was initiated later ("The Fast in Jerusalem on the Twenty-fourth of the Ninth Month," *JBL* 66 [1947]: vii).

[3] M. A. Sweeney thinks the rededication of the temple in Maccabean times may have been viewed by some as a fulfillment of Haggai's prophecy ("Haggai," in *The Twelve Prophets*, Berit Olam: Studies in Hebrew Narrative and Poetry (Collegeville, Minn.: Liturgical Press, 2000), 2:550.

may assume that by December the winter crops had been planted, nourished by the so-called former rains that typically come to the region in the fall.[4]

### (2) Origin of the Message (2:10b)

**the word of the LORD came to the prophet Haggai:**

**2:10b** As in the previous sermons, the messenger is identified as the prophet Haggai. Unlike the previous sermons, here (and later in v. 20) the word of the Lord is said to come "to" (*'el*) Haggai rather than "by [his] hand" *(bĕyad)*. This difference is mainly stylistic, although in the former expression the emphasis may be more on Haggai as the receptor of the divine message and in the latter expression the emphasis may be more on Haggai as the intermediate agent through whom the people received the divine message.[5]

## 2. The Lord's Estimate of the People (2:11–14)

### (3) Principles of Conveyance of Purity and Defilement (2:11–13)

[11]"This is what the LORD Almighty says: 'Ask the priests what the law says: [12]If a person carries consecrated meat in the fold of his garment, and that fold touches some bread or stew, some wine, oil or other food, does it become consecrated?'"

The priests answered, "No."

[13]Then Haggai said, "If a person defiled by contact with a dead body touches one of these things, does it become defiled?"

"Yes," the priests replied, "it becomes defiled."

**2:11** Haggai now instructs the people to seek from the priests a ruling or decision (*tôrâ,* "law") concerning the possibility of conveyance of ceremonial purity and defilement according to religious standards.[6] Although Haggai's

---

[4] In Palestine the former rains usually begin sometime in mid-October or early November. The latter rains come in late March or early April. Periodic rainfall can be expected throughout the months in between. Once the latter rains have ceased, there will be no significant rainfall until the fall season. The biblical expression "former and latter rains" is a merism used to describe the entire rainy season. According to some estimates, during the months of November to February, Palestine receives approximately 70 percent of its rainfall. Normal precipitation during these months is therefore essential if crops are to have the needed moisture for growth and productivity. Persistent lack of rain at this time would obviously create severe agricultural problems. For a brief but helpful summary of patterns of rainfall in Palestine see F. S. Frick, "Rain," *ABD* 5:612.

[5] R. W. Pierce's suggestion that the expression may imply that Haggai is being associated with the Former Prophets seems to read too much into the word ("The Unresponsive Remnant: History, Structure and Theme in Haggai" [Ph.D. diss., Fuller Theological Seminary, 1984], 177).

[6] Preoccupation with issues of ritual purity and impurity eventually became a common phenomenon in rabbinical discussions of the late Second Temple period. For a helpful discussion see M. Fishbane, *Biblical Interpretation in Ancient Israel* (Oxford: Clarendon Press, 1985), 297.

question is posed with regard to both purity and defilement, it is the matter of defilement that is the focus of his interest. His first question largely functions as a foil for the second question, which strikes at the heart of the matter. Presumably these standards were part of the acknowledged Scriptures of this community. The word *tôrâ* is used here without the article in the general sense of a decision or ruling rather than as a reference to the Torah or books of Moses,[7] although it is assumed that the decision will be consistent with and based upon legal material of the Torah.[8] Haggai's appeal seems to assume a collection of authoritative religious laws whose application to specific situations was the special domain of the priestly community.

The presence of this priestly community and the acknowledgment of their religious authority may provide insight into why some of Haggai's contemporaries felt justified in neglecting the rebuilding of the temple. Perhaps there were those who wondered whether the temple was really essential, since there could be sacrifice, offerings, and priestly exposition of Torah apart from the temple.[9]

This passage also provides insight into how postexilic prophetic and priestly communities functioned together,[10] since here the prophet defers to the priests for a decision regarding cultic purity.[11] There is an implicit recognition of priestly authority in such matters.[12] The situation described in vv. 11–14 is unique in that sense; nowhere else in the Hebrew Bible is there a parallel example of priests making a similar judgment.[13] It was to proph-

---

[7] BDB cites the following parallels: Hos 4:6; Jer 2:8; 18:18; Ezek 7:26; 22:26; Mal 2:6,7,8,9; Zeph 3:4. See BDB, 436.

[8] To understand 2:11 to imply that the portion of the Torah describing the laws of sacrifice was as yet perhaps unwritten and certainly as yet uncanonized, as A. Rofé does, is to go beyond what this verse actually indicates and to read into it conclusions that have been reached by other means (*Introduction to the Prophetic Literature* [Sheffield: Sheffield Academic Press, 1997], 97).

[9] For a discussion of this possibility see S. Japhet, "The Temple in the Restoration Period: Reality and Ideology," *USQR* 44 (1991): 227–28.

[10] As E. M. Meyers points out, "Haggai presages a new role for the postexilic prophet, one that is drawn more and more closely to the priesthood" ("The Persian Period and the Judean Restoration: From Zerubbabel to Nehemiah," in *Ancient Israelite Religion: Essays in Honor of Frank Moore Cross* [Philadelphia: Fortress, 1987], 513).

[11] According to E. M. Meyers, Haggai's expression שְׁאַל תּוֹרָה ("to ask a ruling") was part of a new idiom that later developed into the common rabbinic expression פָּסַק דִּין ("to render a verdict"), used for rabbinic legal decisions ("The Use of *tôrâ* in Haggai 2:11 and the Role of the Prophet in the Restoration Community," in *The Word of the Lord Shall Go Forth: Essays in Honor of David Noel Freedman in Celebration of His Sixtieth Birthday,* ASOR Special Volume Series [Winona Lake: Eisenbrauns, 1983], 1:71, 74.

[12] Cf. Matt 8:4; Mark 1:44; Luke 5:14.

[13] J. E. Tollington's comment is accurate: "Throughout the literature of the Old Testament Hag. 2.11–14 is the only instance where the process of priestly torah actually being sought and given is recounted" (*Tradition and Innovation in Haggai and Zechariah 1–8,* JSOTSup 150 [Sheffield: JSOT Press, 1993], 81).

ets that the Lord communicated fresh disclosures of the divine will either for their own age or for the future. But it was priests who were recognized as being uniquely qualified to provide a ruling on matters of cultic purity by virtue of their role as trusted custodians of the Mosaic law.[14] Malachi 2:7–9 sheds light on the priestly function Haggai alludes to here:

> "For the lips of a priest ought to preserve knowledge, and from his mouth men should seek instruction—because he is the messenger of the LORD Almighty. But you have turned from the way and by your teaching have caused many to stumble; you have violated the covenant with Levi," says the LORD Almighty. "So I have caused you to be despised and humiliated before all the people, because you have not followed my ways but have shown partiality in matters of the law."

The distinctions alluded to in Jer 18:18 (ESV) are also instructive in this regard:

> For the law shall not perish from the priest, nor counsel from the wise, nor the word from the prophet.[15]

Although there is overlap in the domains described in this verse, it seems that teaching of the Torah is especially associated with the priestly community,[16] life instruction with the community of wisemen, and revelation with the prophetic guild. Thus the verdict of the priests on the matter posed by Haggai's questions would be regarded as authoritative.[17]

**2:12–13** Haggai's questions in vv. 12 and 13 are posed in a way that is reminiscent of similar rhetorical questions found elsewhere in the Old Testament, particularly in the Book of Jeremiah. There is first the setting forth of a hypothetical question introduced by "if,"[18] then the introduction of a

---

[14] As G. Östborn says, "The prophets reveal *tōrā* while the priests cultivate and preserve it" (*Tōrā in the Old Testament: A Semantic Study* [Lund: Håkan Ohlssons Boktryckeri, 1945], 129). On the range of priestly instruction during the preexilic period see P. J. Budd, "Priestly Instruction in Pre-Exilic Israel," *VT* 23 (1973): 1–14.

[15] Cf. Mic 3:11a: "Her leaders judge for a bribe, her priests teach for a price, and her prophets tell fortunes for money."

[16] For a helpful summary of the development of the didactic role of the priest in the OT period see R. de Vaux, *Ancient Israel: Its Life and Institutions,* Biblical Resource Series (reprint, Grand Rapids: Eerdmans, 1997), 353–55.

[17] Some scholars see this passage as reflecting a significant change in the development of OT prophecy. C. Meyers and E. M. Meyers, e.g., say, "No passage, however, is more indicative of the transformation of prophecy than this" ("Haggai, Book of," *ABD* 3:22).

[18] The particle הֵן is used here with the sense of "if." But in the following verse "if" is expressed by the common Hb. particle אִם, in what is a parallel question to the one the prophet asks in v. 12. In Hb. הֵן is a shorter form of the more common emphatic particle הִנֵּה ("behold") and is used with similar meanings. It seems likely that the use of הֵן with the sense of "if" in v. 12 is due to Aramaic influence. See *HALOT,* 251; *GBH* §167l; GKC §159w. The word may have been chosen here for stylistic variation with the later occurrence of the Hb. word אִם ("if").

complicating factor introduced by "and," and finally an appeal for adjudication of the matter introduced by the interrogative particle.[19] The use of familiar rhetorical constructions was intended to lead the audience from a familiar set of circumstances to a potential difficulty, and then to a resolution of the conflicting realities. Such verbal patterns probably were familiar to Haggai's audience.[20]

The illustration that Haggai utilizes here is tightly constructed and free of digression or elaboration. Several key questions will guide our examination of this pericope. First, in this passage what exactly is meant by holiness? Second, does the Mosaic law allow for the possibility of transfer of holiness from one entity to another, and if so, in what way and under what conditions may this take place? Third, what application of this ruling does Haggai intend with regard to the circumstances described in this message? It is to these questions that we now turn our attention.

First, a grasp of the Old Testament concept of holiness is crucial to Haggai's argument.[21] To be holy means "to be set apart," either intrinsically (e.g., in the sense that God is separate from limitation, weakness, impurity, or sin) or extrinsically (e.g., in the sense that people or objects may be consecrated for a sacred purpose). The verb *qādaš,* especially in the *piel* stem, is used with a variety of objects in the Old Testament. Holiness is a condition associated with inanimate things such as the Sabbath (e.g., Gen 2:3; Exod 20:8–11), a spatial area (e.g., Exod 19:23; 1 Kgs 8:64), parts of a sacrifice (e.g., Exod 29:27), ceremonial utensils (e.g., Exod 30:29; 40:9–11), or a period of time marked by fasting (e.g., Joel 1:14; 2:15). Even war can be sanctified in the sense that it is executed according to religious rules and for religious purposes (e.g., Jer 6:4; Joel 4:9). Holiness is a condition frequently associated with people, such as the Israelite priest (e.g., Exod 28:3,41; 29:1,33,44), the Israelites themselves (e.g., Exod 19:10,14; Josh 7:13), or a religious assembly (e.g., Joel 2:16). The primary notion of the word as used of people and things is the setting apart of someone or something for consecration to a sacred task or purpose.

Second, a grasp of the issue of transferability of holiness is crucial for understanding this section. Within the categories of the Hebrew Bible, is it possible for holiness or impurity to be conveyed from one entity to another?

---

[19] See M. Fishbane's helpful discussion in *Biblical Interpretation in Ancient Israel* (Oxford: Clarendon, 1985), 307–14.

[20] Fishbane's comment is instructive: "Thus, a prophet may involve his addressee in a question-answer scenario in order to establish a certain objective logic of inference or possibility—only to redirect the topic to the subjective condition of the listeners in order to shock them into new realizations and attitudes" (ibid., 427).

[21] Although the etymology of the root קדש ("to be holy") is not entirely clear, the semantic usage of the word in the Hb. Bible is relatively straightforward. See, e.g., *HALOT,* 1072–73.

It is clear that Old Testament teaching does allow for such transfer under certain conditions. A holy person or object may cause what comes into direct contact with it also to be holy. This is the case with the priest and his sacred vestments (Exod 29:21) and with things that have come into contact with the sacred altar (Exod 29:37) or the sacred utensils (Exod 30:29) or the sacred offering (Lev 6:11[Eng. 18],20[Eng. 27]).[22] In these examples the level of contact is secondary, that is, a holy person or object conveys holiness to another person or object by virtue of direct contact with that person or object.

Haggai's question, however, involves not a secondary but a tertiary level of contact. The consecrated meat, taken from slain sacrificial animals, is placed in the fold of a garment that subsequently comes into contact with another food item (such as bread, stew,[23] wine, oil, or some other sort of food or drink).[24] Now the question becomes, In such circumstances will the thing touched by the garment also be rendered holy? In v. 12 the priests answer this question in the negative: it will not be made holy simply by means of contact with the garment.[25]

Ritual guidelines for transfer of impurity differ somewhat from those for purity. In the case described above purity is incommunicable. But impurity in such a case is communicable, according to v. 13.[26] If a person who is ceremonially defiled through contact with a dead body comes in contact with a garment containing sacred meat, there would be transfer of impu-

---

[22] See *HALOT*, 1072–75.

[23] The precise meaning of the Hb. word נָזִיד in 2:12 is disputed. This word occurs only six times in the Hb. Bible. In Gen 25:29,34 it is used of the cooked stew that Jacob gave Esau in exchange for his birthright. In 2 Kgs 4:38,39,40 it is used of a cooked stew that Elisha's servant prepared for a group of prophets. Presumably in Hag 2:12 the word also refers to a cooked stew of some sort, probably consisting of vegetables boiled in water. This is consistent with the meaning of the verbal root of נָזִיד, which is זוד ("to boil"). In 2:12 Kessler translates the word as "vegetables," but this rendering fails to take into account the notion of cooked food as opposed to raw vegetables (*The Book of Haggai*, 197).

[24] Haggai does not clarify whether the person carrying the meat in his garment is a priest or a layperson. The suggestion that "since a priest is not specified, the person carrying meat here must be a nonpriest" is an argument from silence (C. L. Meyers and E. M. Meyers, *Haggai, Zechariah 1–8: A New Translation with Introduction and Commentary*, AB [New York: Doubleday, 1987], 55).

[25] The negative לֹא is used here with an emphatic nuance. Gesenius suggests the meaning "Certainly not!" or "No!" See GKC §152c.

[26] In this pericope Haggai emphasizes the ritual terms קֹדֶשׁ ("holy") and טָמֵא ("unclean"). The opposite of קֹדֶשׁ is usually חֹל ("profane"), and the opposite of טָמֵא is usually טָהוֹר ("pure"). Kessler suggests that in terms of their relative force these words can be placed on the following continuum: קֹדֶשׁ—טָהוֹר—חֹל—טָמֵא. He says, "Thus the two terms at the extreme ends of the continuum, קֹדֶשׁ and טָמֵא, designate the most powerful forces and the only ones which are truly contagious, whereas the middle terms חֹל and טָהוֹר represent more neutral stages, which in themselves are not communicable" (*The Book of Haggai*, 203).

rity.[27] The result is that the holiness of the garment containing a sacred object is forfeited due to such contact. The answer to Haggai's question, as reported by the priests in v. 13, is "Yes, it becomes defiled."[28] Transfer of impurity, in that sense, is easier than transfer of holiness.[29]

Third, the application that the prophet makes of this illustration is crucial.[30] Obviously he is interested in something more than just a ruling concerning holy or defiled foods. The lesson of vv. 11–13 is intended to be illustrative of the spiritual condition of his audience.[31] This point is made in v. 14: "'So it is with this people and this nation in my sight,' declares the LORD. 'Whatever they do and whatever they offer there is defiled.'"

The rhetorical effect of this assertion probably shocked Haggai's audience. After all, had they not responded to his earlier pleas to make the tem-

---

[27] The Hb. expression is טְמֵא־נֶפֶשׁ ("unclean of soul"). In this expression נֶפֶשׁ apparently has the sense of "corpse," an odd meaning for a word that normally is associated with life or vitality. Joüon-Muraoka take the genitive in a causal sense: *impure by (the fact of) a corpse* (*GBH* §129i). Here נֶפֶשׁ is apparently a shortened form of the expression נֶפֶשׁ מֵת (cf. Num 6:6; Lev 21:11). So K. Marti, *Das Dodekapropheton,* KHC 13 (Tübingen: Mohr [Siebeck], 1904), 388. Concerning impurity contracted through contact with a dead body see Num 5:2–3; 19:14–16,21–22; *Tob* 2:9. On use of the biblical expression נֶפֶשׁ מֵת to refer to a corpse see M. Seligson, *The Meaning of* נֶפֶשׁ מֵת *in the Old Testament,* StudOr 16:2 (Helsinki: Societas orientalis fennica, 1951). For a helpful discussion of this word see G. André's treatment in *TDOT* 5:330–42. See also *DCH* 5:731.

[28] Biblical Hb. does not have a word for "yes" as such. One way affirmative answers are given to questions is by repetition of a key word in the question. In 2:13 when the priests respond to Haggai's question about whether contact with a corpse conveys ceremonial impurity, they simply repeat the verb found in the question: "It is unclean." See DG §153, rem. 1.

[29] H. Wolf's analogy is instructive: "One can catch a cold from someone else, but it is impossible to catch the health of another" (*Haggai and Malachi* [Chicago: Moody, 1976], 43). J. A. Motyer draws this analogy: "If you touch something with a dirty hand you will leave a dirty mark but if you touch something with a clean hand you will not leave a clean mark" ("Haggai," in *The Minor Prophets: An Exegetical and Expository Commentary* [Grand Rapids: Baker, 1998], 3:995).

[30] Amsler identifies the following three interpretations for v. 14: (1) the moral interpretation, which emphasizes the impurity of the people as what rendered both harvest and sacrifice unclean; (2) the cultic interpretation, which stresses the need for not just the altar but also the rebuilt temple in order for holiness to be communicated to the people; and (3) the anti-Samaritan interpretation, which is based on Rothstein's arguments for dislocation with regard to 2:15–19 and which understands the unclean people referred to here to be the Samaritans rather than the Jews. It is the first of these views that seems best to fit the context. See S. Amsler, "Aggée, Zacharie 1–8," in *Aggée, Zacharie 1–8, Zacharie 9–14, Malachie,* 2d ed., CAT 11 (Genève: Labor et Fides, 1988), 36–37.

[31] Fishbane provides a helpful discussion of various techniques of what he calls inner biblical aggadic exegesis. One of these techniques is what he terms "lemmatic deduction or inference," whereby a piece of accepted religious tradition is first cited and then applied to a broader issue. The questions posed, answered, and then applied in Hag 2:11–14 provide an example of this sort of lemmatic deduction. He discusses other examples as well (see *Biblical Interpretation in Ancient Israel,* 419–25).

ple a priority? Had they not set aside their selfish pursuits in order to
accomplish the task of restoration? Were they not at that very time involved
in the project to which the prophet had called them? Should they not therefore be viewed as holy rather than as impure? Why had their prophet suddenly turned on them in this way? Haggai's illustration thus introduces to
the narrative an element of conflict. The question to be answered is this:
How can an impure people engage in a holy task? Will not their contagious
condition of impurity render impure everything with which they come in
contact?[32]

### (4) Condition of the People (2:14)

**[14]Then Haggai said, "'So it is with this people and this nation in my sight,'
declares the LORD. 'Whatever they do and whatever they offer there is defiled.**

**2:14**   The language Haggai uses in v. 14 to refer to the people is implicitly condemnatory. The expressions "this people" (hā'ām hazzeh; cf. 1:3)
and "this nation" (haggôy hazzeh) are pejorative and carry an implied element of disassociation and rebuke. The first of these words ('am, "people")
is often used in the Hebrew Bible to refer to Israel; the second term (gôy,
"nation") is most often used to refer to non-Israelite nations, although it
may on occasion refer to Israel.[33] Likewise, the expression "this people"
(hā'ām hazzeh) is often used of the Lord's people, but it frequently carries
negative connotations.[34] The expression "this nation" (haggôy hazzeh)
appears a total of only four times in the Hebrew Bible, all in reference to
the Lord's people.[35] These phrases are synonymous references to the

---

[32] D. L. Smith has recently provided a sociological analysis of vv. 10–14, understanding this
section to point to social conflict with a group of outsiders who have become a source of pollution
for Haggai's community ("The Politics of Ezra: Sociological Indicators of Postexilic Judaean Society," in *Community, Identity, and Ideology: Social Science Approaches to the Hebrew Bible,*
Sources for Biblical and Theological Study 6 [Winona Lake: Eisenbrauns, 1996], 548–56). But
since no group of outsiders has been introduced, it seems better to understand the language of pollution in this pericope to refer to the Jewish community itself and not to an outside group.

[33] For a helpful study on the use of גּוֹי to refer to Israel see A. Cody, "When Is the Chosen People Called a *Gôy?" VT* 14 (1964): 1–6. Cody identifies seven categories of usage for גּוֹי in this
sense. Hag 2:4 falls in a category he calls words of divine rejection.

[34] Among the prophets the expression הָעָם הַזֶּה ("this people") is especially common in Isaiah
and Jeremiah. See, e.g., Isa 6:10; 8:6,11,12; 9:15[Eng. 16]; 28:11,14; 29:13,14; Jer 6:19,21;
7:16,33; 8:5; 9:14[Eng. 15]; 11:14; 13:10; 14:11; 15:1; 16:5; 19:11; 21:8; 23:33; 27:16; 28:15;
29:32; 32:42; 33:24; 36:7.

[35] Exod 33:13; Judg 2:20; 2 Kgs 6:18; Hag 2:14. Cf. the similar expression גּוֹי אֲשֶׁר כָּזֶה ("a
nation that is like this"): Jer 5:9,29; 9:8[Eng. 9].

Judeans.[36] But the terms lack any sense of warmth or cordial identification of the Lord with those who are so addressed. Due to their sinful condition the Lord was unable to address them as "my people," although ultimately they were his people. Nor can he call them "my nation," although in different circumstances this expression might have been used. Instead, the Lord's words are more distant, signaling divine displeasure that is appropriate for a people insufficiently prepared for the work of God.[37]

In v. 14 Haggai concludes his illustration with an indictment: "Whatever they do and whatever they offer there is defiled."[38] As a result of their spiritual uncleanness, they contaminate everything with which they come into contact.[39] Consequently, the Lord takes no pleasure even in their undertaking of a sacred task such as the rebuilding of the temple. All they offer there is defiled, the Lord says. The verb translated "offer" *(yaqrîbû)* is standard cultic language used for presentation of sacrificial offerings. The adverb "there" *(šām)* is somewhat ambiguous. Does it refer specifically to the altar

---

[36] I see no reason to suspect either of these phrases from a text-critical standpoint. S. Talmon has suggested that a doublet was created in 2:14 by the merging of two separate but synonymous readings ("Synonymous Readings in the Textual Traditions of the Old Testament," *Studies in the Bible* 8 [Jerusalem: Magnes Press, 1961], 343). But this is a conjectural proposal that lacks manuscript support to validate it. There are many places in the Hb. Bible where Talmon has made a good case for drawing a similar conclusion, but this does not seem to me to be one of them.

[37] In 2:14 the LXX has a lengthy scribal gloss, part of which has been incorporated here from Amos 5:10: ἕνεκεν τῶν λημμάτων αὐτῶν τῶν ὀρθρινῶν, ὀδυνηθήσονται ἀπὸ προσώπου πόνων αὐτῶν· καὶ ἐμισεῖτε ἐν πύλαις ἐλέγχοντας ("[They shall be defiled] on account of their early material gains. They shall be pained because of their toils. And you hated those who reproved in the gates"). Such glosses are not uncommon in biblical manuscripts. It was relatively easy for scribes who were familiar with biblical content to incorporate readings from one text into another. Sometimes this appears to have been done intentionally, and other times it seems likely to have been accidental. For P. Haupt's view that this gloss actually belongs to v. 16, having been mistakenly relocated to v. 14 through scribal error, see "The Septuagintal Addition to Haggai 2:14," *JBL* 36 (1997): 148–50.

[38] The NIV rightly understands the time frame assumed in v. 14 to be the present; the condition of defilement on the part of the people continued up to the moment of the prophet's address. W. M. McPheeters, however, maintains that the time frame of the verbs should be understood to be the frequentative past rather than the present. He translates v. 14 as follows: "So were this people, and so was this nation before me, saith the Lord; and so was every work of their hand; and that which they offered there (from time to time) it was unclean" ("The Time of the Verbs in Haggai 2:14," *Old and New Testament Student* 12 [1891]: 304).

[39] J. G. Baldwin interprets Haggai's uncleanness as referring to the temple itself rather than to the people. She says, "The ruined skeleton of the Temple was like a dead body decaying in Jerusalem and making everything contaminated (2:10–14)" (*Haggai, Zechariah, Malachi: An Introduction and Commentary,* TOTC [Downers Grove: InterVarsity, 1972], 33). See also P. L. Redditt, *Haggai, Zechariah and Malachi,* NCB (Grand Rapids: Eerdmans, 1995), 28. But the problem was not that the unfinished temple was somehow defiling the people. The problem was that the people by virtue of their impurity were defiling everything they touched, including the holy site of the temple.

where sacrifices are offered, or does it refer in a more general sense to the temple structure? It probably has in view the specific site of sacrificial offerings, namely, the altar of the unfinished temple building.[40]

Haggai 2:10–14 thus presents a major problem with regard to efforts at rebuilding the temple. According to Haggai the people were in a deplorably sinful condition, and everything they came in contact with was thereby defiled due to their impurity. As a result, both their work on the temple and the religious sacrifices they periodically offered were unacceptable to the Lord. Like a cancer that has invaded a human body, bringing destruction and disintegration to the cells it comes in contact with, so these people were bringing spiritual defilement to everything they touched. Until the issue of their spiritual condition was resolved, no amount of religious activity they performed would be acceptable to the Lord.[41] Haggai had uncovered and laid embarrassingly bare a need for repentance on the part of the people if their efforts at restoration were to enjoy the blessing and acceptance from God for which they hoped.[42] The situation was desperate, but in the unit that follows the prophet moves the matter to a resolution.

### 3. The Necessity of Obedience (2:15–19)

The relationship between this section (vv. 15–19) and the one that precedes (vv. 10–14) is disputed.[43] As noted in the introduction, Rothstein's view that 2:15–19 actually belongs with 1:15 has serious implications for how we understand this part of chap. 2. The relocation of vv. 15–19 to a position following 1:15a permits the interpretation that vv. 10–14 are a dia-

---

[40] R. S. Sim has argued for understanding this deictic adverb to refer not specifically to the altar but to the temple itself; see "Notes on Haggai 2:10–21," *JOTT* 5 (1992): 31. See also E. R. Wendland, "Temple Site or Cemetery?—A Question of Perspective," *JOTT* 5 (1992): 44.

[41] P. R. Ackroyd's words are worth weighing: "The people who are called to be the community of the new age can nevertheless frustrate that new age by their own condition. There is no automatic efficacy in the temple, no guarantee that by virtue of its existence it ensures salvation. The effectiveness of it and its worship is determined by the condition of those who worship, that is, whether or not they are in a fit condition to receive the blessings of God" (*Exile and Restoration: A Study of Hebrew Thought of the Sixth Century B.C.,* OTL [Philadelphia: Westminster, 1968], 169).

[42] E. Achtemeier's application of Haggai's warning is instructive: "The ultimate danger of temple building, and indeed of all works of religion, is the temptation to become self-righteous: to believe that association with the things of God automatically communicates moral purity, right judgment, unconquerable power—all those qualities associated with holiness, that is, with the total otherness of God. How many futile crusades have been launched on the basis of such bland assumptions! How many communities have been split by those claiming such rightness! How many smug presuppositions of such superiority have prevented the communication or the receipt of the gospel!" (*Nahum–Malachi,* IBC [Atlanta: John Knox, 1986], 102–3).

[43] N. K. Gottwald, e.g., speaks of "the ill fit of vv. 11–14 in their present setting" (*The Hebrew Bible—A Socio-Literary Introduction* [Philadelphia: Fortress, 1985], 503).

tribe against the Samaritans rather than an indictment of the people of Judah (cf. Ezra 4:1–5). Haggai is perceived as rebuffing the desire of the Samaritans to participate in the temple project due to their unacceptable spiritual condition.

There is no adequate justification for this view, in spite of its popularity.[44] Verses 10–19 should be seen as a unit, the focus of which is not the Samaritans but the people of Judah.[45] The blame for failure in Haggai's day cannot be traced to Samaritan opposition to the building project. Instead, blame must be laid at the feet of the Judeans. In places the logical progression of this unit is a bit difficult to follow.[46] But in spite of certain awkward elements vv. 10–19 should be viewed as a unified pericope with a single referent.

### (1) Evidences of the Lord's Discipline (2:15–17)

[15]"'Now give careful thought to this from this day on—consider how things were before one stone was laid on another in the LORD's temple. [16]When anyone came to a heap of twenty measures, there were only ten. When anyone went to a wine vat to draw fifty measures, there were only twenty. [17]I struck all the work of your hands with blight, mildew and hail, yet you did not turn to me,' declares the LORD.

**2:15** The transitional word "now" *(wĕʿattâ)* begins v. 15. This word is often used in a temporal sense ("now," as opposed to later). Sometimes it has an inferential sense ("therefore," in light of what has been stated previously).[47] Neither sense can be entirely excluded here. What follows is an

---

[44] For a succinct presentation of the case against Rothstein's interpretation of the phrases "this people" and "this nation" see H. G. May, "'This People' and 'This Nation' in Haggai," *VT* 18 (1968): 190–97. May concludes that the expressions "this people" and "this nation" in Haggai refer not to the Samaritans but to Yahweh's chosen people the Jews. T. N. Townsend subsequently offered a few refinements to May's article; see "Additional Comments on Haggai II 10–19," *VT* 18 (1968): 559–60.

[45] Sellin adopts Rothstein's position, concluding that this passage marks the beginning of a separatist mind-set that was characteristic of much of later Judaism. He describes Haggai as "having rejected willing but cultically suspect helpers, thereby inaugurating the sequestration that was to be typical of later Judaism. The twenty-fourth day of the ninth month, 520 B.C., when this took place, may be called the birthday of Judaism" (E. Sellin and G. Fohrer, *Introduction to the Old Testament* [Nashville: Abingdon, 1968], 460). This conclusion is hardly justified by the text as it stands. B. S. Childs is closer to an accurate appraisal: "There is no hint in the present text to relate the antecedent of v. 14 to the Samaritans. Indeed, only one people is ever referred to within the book and that is clearly the Jewish remnant" (*Introduction to the Old Testament as Scripture* [Philadelphia: Fortress, 1979], 468).

[46] Gottwald speaks not only of difficulties in the prophet's line of argumentation, which admittedly there are, but he also refers to disorders and even *non sequiturs* in Haggai's thought (*The Hebrew Bible*, 502–3).

[47] See BDB, 773–74; *HALOT*, 901–2.

inference based on what has already been said; it also carries urgency for that present moment.

Haggai appeals to the people to identify the cause of their difficult circumstances and to adjust their lifestyle in light of recent events that have befallen them. If they are to learn from their history, they must "give careful thought to this from this day on" (vv. 15,18). The Hebrew word rendered by the NIV as "on" *(wāmā'ĕlâ)* has been understood in different ways.[48] Its basic sense is "above" or "upwards" (cf. *'ālâ,* "to go up"), but it can have either a spatial sense ("upwards") or a temporal sense ("onwards"). It is used in 2:15,18 in a temporal sense. Whether it points forward to time yet in the future for Haggai's audience or points backward to time already past is disputed. If it refers backward to difficulties previously encountered by the people as a consequence of their sin, the orientation is negative in nature. But if the word is forward-looking, it has a more positive nuance. It then anticipates the time of the Lord's renewed blessing in fulfillment of the promise of v. 19: "From this day on I will bless you."

Keil takes the word to mean two very different things in this passage: in v. 15 it means "backwards into the past," but in v. 18 it means "direction towards the future."[49] However, it seems unlikely that the word would have opposite meanings in the same context. Other scholars understand the word to mean "backward" in both verses.[50] This conclusion is based mainly on the description that follows of prior conditions of crop failure that led to economic hardship. The ASV renders the word as "backward" in both v. 15 and v. 18. But this interpretation ascribes to *mā'ĕlâ* a sense contrary to the normal usage of this word. When used temporally *mā'ĕlâ* elsewhere always means "and onward" (cf. 1 Sam 16:13; 30:25).[51] Most modern versions of Haggai rightly understand the word to be forward-looking rather than backward-looking.

The Hebrew text of v. 15 is difficult. Haggai's awkward syntax is best

---

[48] D. J. Clark describes four different understandings of וָמַעְלָה in 2:15. First, מַעְלָה is elsewhere in the Hb. Bible usually used in reference to the future, and most modern versions understand the word to have a future orientation in 2:15. Second, some commentators take מַעְלָה in 2:15 to be pointing backward to prior events. Third, some scholars view מַעְלָה in 2:15 as a scribal mistake due to the occurrence of the word in v. 18. Fourth, some scholars give מַעְלָה a future sense but understand it to go back to the construction שִׂימוּ־נָא לְבַבְכֶם ("consider"). Clark adopts the fourth approach ("Problems in Haggai 2.15–19," *BT* 34 [1983]: 432–33). See also A. Fernández, "El profeta Ageo 2, 15–18 y la fundación del segundo templo," *Bib* 2 (1921): 206–15.

[49] C. F. Keil, *Minor Prophets, Commentary on the Old Testament* (Grand Rapids: Eerdmans, 1982), 10:206–7. See also Meyers and Meyers, *Haggai, Zechariah 1–8,* 48, 58–59, 63.

[50] So, e.g., E. H. Merrill, *An Exegetical Commentary: Haggai, Zechariah, Malachi* (Chicago: Moody, 1994), 49.

[51] See *HALOT,* 613. BDB originally ascribed the sense of "and back" to the usage of מַעְלָה in Hag 2:15,18. But the editors later reversed this judgment, concluding that the more probable meaning is "and onwards." This change of opinion in BDB is often overlooked in discussions of this verse that appeal to this lexicon. See BDB, 751 (but cf. "Addenda and Corrigenda," 1125).

understood as containing two parts. First is an admonition to reflect on the
meaning of the economic difficulties and to do so both at the present
moment and in the future as well. Second is a somewhat elliptical reference
to the matter of crop failure. The NIV smooths out the construction by supplying the clause "consider how things were." This yields a satisfactory
understanding. A less desirable alternative is Mitchell's proposal to treat the
phrase "from this day on" *(min hayyôm hazzeh wāmāʿĕlâ)* as a scribal
gloss that should be deleted from the text.[52] There is insufficient textual
evidence for this suggestion.

The final part of v. 15 alludes to a time when "one stone was laid on
another in the LORD's temple." This language is similar to that of v. 18,
which speaks of "the day when the foundation of the LORD's temple was
laid." At least two interpretations have been offered for the nature and timing of the activity referred to here. One view is that of Petersen, who suggests that Haggai may be referring to an earlier ceremony of rededication
for the temple. This ceremony involved not only the laying of foundation
stones for the building but also included sacrificial liturgy performed for
that occasion (cf. Zech 4:4–6). Petersen links Israelite ceremonial practice
in this regard to what is known from Babylonian and Seleucid sources as
the *kālû* ceremony. This was a rededication ritual intended "to achieve ritual purification and cultic continuity."[53] Alternatively, it is possible that the
activity referred to in v. 15 is of a less formal nature, having in mind the
commencement of masonry construction on the temple project in a more
general sense. Since Haggai makes no direct mention in v. 15 of a ceremony, this second view seems preferable.

The word used for "temple" here and in v. 18 is *hêkal,* a word borrowed
by a number of Semitic languages from the Sumerian word *e-gal* ("large
house," "palace").[54] Elsewhere Haggai uses the more common Hebrew
word *bayit* ("house") to refer to the temple. There seems to be no significant difference in meaning intended by the choice of words. The distinction
observed elsewhere, whereby *hêkal* refers to the main room of the temple
located between the porch *(ʾêlām)* and the holy of holies *(dĕbîr)* is not in
view here, since the temple was not as yet rebuilt.

**2:16–17** The MT of v. 16 begins with the problematic expression
*mihyôtām* (lit. "from their being"). The meaning of this clause is puzzling.
Neither the nuance of the preposition *(min,* "from") nor the antecedent of
the pronominal suffix (*-ām,* "their") is clear. The KJV renders this expres-

---

[52] So H. G. Mitchell, *A Critical and Exegetical Commentary on Haggai and Zechariah,* ICC
(Edinburgh: T&T Clark, 1912), 74.

[53] D. L. Petersen, *Haggai and Zechariah 1–8: A Commentary,* OTL (Philadelphia: Westminster, 1984), 89–90. See further on Petersen's view in comments on 2:18.

[54] See *HALOT,* 244–45.

sion temporally as "since those days were." This rendering takes the preposition *min* in a temporal sense ("since" or "from the time that") and understands the pronominal suffix to refer to "those days." But it is not clear that the words should be rendered in this way. The problem is probably due to textual corruption in the MT, although some interpreters have resisted this conclusion.[55]

Two suggestions may be helpful in trying to recover the meaning of the phrase. First, the reading of the LXX seems to point to a better Hebrew text here.[56] It has *tines ēte,* which can be paraphrased "How were you?" or "How did you fare?" (RSV). The Hebrew text underlying the LXX rendering probably was *mî hĕyîtem* (or perhaps *mah hĕyîtem*). This leads to suspicion that the MT experienced graphic confusion of *yôd* and *wāw* and as a result was vocalized incorrectly. The NIV's translation "Consider how things were" (v. 15) is probably a paraphrase of this LXX rendering. Second, placement of the verse division for vv. 15 and 16 should also be reconsidered. If the LXX reading is accepted, the phrase in question does not function as a temporal clause introducing v. 16. Rather, it is a probing question asked about the economic conditions that afflicted Haggai's community. That question (i.e., "How did you fare?") invites serious reflection on difficult circumstances that should have led to significant changes in attitude and behavior. This seems to provide the best understanding of the words.

In v. 16 Haggai takes the people back to the conditions that prevailed before work was begun on the temple, that is, before the events of 1:15a. The economic consequences of the Lord's disciplinary hand were evident everywhere. With regard to the grain harvest, v. 16 indicates that productivity had been reduced by a staggering fifty percent.[57] Conditions were so

---

[55] Motyer is opposed to emending the MT here. In somewhat pejorative terms he speaks of this clause as providing "a magnet for emenders" ("Haggai," 997).

[56] The LXX has τίνες ἦτε (lit., "Who were you?"), which seems to presuppose the Hb. clause מִי־הֱיִיתֶם or, somewhat less likely, מֶה־הֱיִיתֶם. The first of these readings (מִי־הֱיִיתֶם) is preferred by D. Barthélemy, *Ézéchiel, Daniel et les 12 Prophètes, Critique textuelle de l'Ancien Testament,* OBO 50/3 (Fribourg: Éditions Universitaires Fribourg; Göttingen: Vandenhoeck & Ruprecht, 1992), 3:930. The second possibility (מֶה־הֱיִיתֶם) is favored in the apparatus of *BHS.* Clearly the context calls for a question not of identity ("Who were you?"), as though Haggai were unsure about who was present on the occasion under discussion, but for a question about their personal condition with regard to economic prosperity ("How were you?" i.e., "How did you fare?"). The Hb. interrogative pronoun מִי occasionally has this sense, in which case its meaning approximates that of the interrogative pronoun מָה ("how?"). Examples of this usage may be found in Amos 7:2; Ruth 3:16. See BDB, 566; *HALOT,* 575. It thus seems best to emend the MT מִהְיוֹתָם to מִי־הֱיִיתֶם on the basis of the LXX and to take the clause in question with v. 15 rather than with v. 16 as in the MT.

[57] Circumstances similar to those of Haggai's day have given birth to a Palestinian proverb used even in fairly modern times for situations when normal expectations go unfulfilled: "The reckoning of the threshing-floor does not tally with that of the field" (C. T. Wilson, *Peasant Life in the Holy Land* [London: John Murray, 1906], 309). For awareness of this proverb I am indebted to a citation in Mitchell, *Haggai and Zechariah,* 69.

poor that the harvest was only half of what farmers normally would have expected from comparable efforts. The grape harvest had been decimated to an even greater degree, with the result that wine-making productivity had been reduced by an astounding 60 percent.[58]

The blame could be placed on natural disasters brought about by such things as blight, mildew, and hail, according to v. 17.[59] Each of these phenomena had exacerbated the farmers' problems, and each of them had a cause greater than what met the eye. Many scholars regard v. 17 as a secondary scribal gloss added to the text (cf. Amos 4:9),[60] but the arguments

---

[58] In 2:16 the MT פּוּרָה, "winepress," presents a difficulty. Found only here and in Isa 63:3, it is one of several words for winepress, whose distinction is disputed. On the basis of location and portability, O. Borowski distinguishes three types: (1) the יֶקֶב, used for pressing both grapes and olives, was cut into rock and located in the vicinity of the vineyard; (2) the גַּת, a stone-and-mortar winepress located inside the city; (3) the פּוּרָה, possibly a portable winepress. The פּוּרָה was perhaps of sufficiently standard size to be used for measurement (*Agriculture in Iron Age Israel* [Winona Lake: Eisenbrauns, 1987], 111–12). The evidence for these distinctions is uncertain. C. E. Walsh maintains that the more general term יֶקֶב describes the press in terms of the product it yields, with a view toward the bounty of production, whereas גַּת refers particularly to the treading floor and stresses the agricultural process and the function of the press. Haggai's פּוּרָה, according to her, refers to a collecting vat and thus stresses a particular volume of liquid (*The Fruit of the Vine: Viticulture in Ancient Israel*, HSM 60 [Winona Lake: Eisenbrauns, 2000], 162–65). The problem in 2:16 is why both פּוּרָה and יֶקֶב are used for the same structure. Here the יֶקֶב apparently was a vat that included a depression cut into rock to collect liquid from processing of grapes or olives, to which one had come to draw fifty measures. פּוּרָה seems superfluous here. There are three possibilities. First, פּוּרָה is simply a variant of הַיֶּקֶב, incorporated into the text as a gloss on that word, and should be deleted (see the apparatus of *BHS*). But there is no MS support for this, and scribal transcriptional tendencies do not support this view. Second, פּוּרָה here is not the winepress but a measure of juice equal to one filling of the winepress. See Keil, *Minor Prophets*, 206–7; R. Frankel, *Wine and Oil Production in Antiquity in Israel and Other Mediterranean Countries*, JSOT/ASOR Monograph Series 10 (Sheffield: Sheffield Academic Press, 1999), 185. The NIV seems to adopt this interpretation with the translation "measures." Perhaps פּוּרָה is a metonym here (the object signifying what the object could contain), but this does not seem to be the best way to understand the word. Third, פּוּרָה may have been a part of the יֶקֶב, perhaps a tub or trough of some sort. This understanding probably would require emending the MT פּוּרָה in 2:16 to מִפּוּרָה ("from the winepress"), since it is from this container that Haggai's stipulated amount is drawn. In that case a *mêm* has been lost through haplography with the immediately preceding word (חֲמִשִּׁים). The translation would then be, "When anyone went to the wine vat to draw fifty measures from the trough, there were only twenty." See BDB, 807; *HALOT*, 920. A decision here is difficult due to lack of sufficient evidence. Overall, the third option probably is the best one.

[59] The Masoretic pointing of these nouns implies the presence of the definite article, which in this case is used in a generic sense. In a purely consonantal Hb. text the presence or absence of the article with a prefixed participle would be a matter of interpretive judgment exercised by the reader, since the consonants would be the same in either case. Here it probably is best to accept the Masoretic understanding, which reflects a common usage of the definite article in biblical Hb. But Gibson raises the question of whether in certain poetic texts this vocalization may not be entirely due to the Masoretes (DG §31 (e), rem. 1).

[60] So, e.g., P. R. Ackroyd, "Some Interpretative Glosses in the Book of Haggai," *JJS* 7 (1956): 166. This view is widely held. J. Nogalski, in fact, regards it as the majority opinion among Haggai scholars (*Literary Precursors to the Book of the Twelve*, BZAW 217a [Berlin: Walter de Gruyter, 1993], 227).

set forth for this conclusion are not convincing.

A range of agricultural problems is described in v. 17. First, "blight" (so NIV, RSV, NRSV, NKJV) or "blasting" (so KJV, ASV) refers to the scorching or burning of crops, probably due to the hot east wind that occasionally blows over Palestine from the Arabian desert (cf. Gen 41:6; Hos 13:15). This wind sometimes is referred to as the sirocco or (in Arabic) the *khamsin*. In prolonged conditions of harsh dryness vegetation had little chance of survival. Second, the "mildew" *(yērāqôn)* of v. 17 refers to a disease of plants that results in their discoloration (cf. *yāraq,* "to become green or pale"), a symptom of the unhealthy condition of the plants.[61] The word *yērāqôn* occurs only six times in the Hebrew Bible, usually in the company of the word "blight" *(šiddāpôn).* If blight is caused by conditions of dry heat, mildew is caused by conditions of excessive moisture. The two conditions seem to be mutually exclusive. The two words probably form a merism, alluding to the polar opposites of heat-related problems and moisture-related problems that at different times resulted in the ruination of crops. Third, the reference to hail in v. 17 is reminiscent of one of the plagues the Lord sent upon Egypt in the days of Moses (cf. Exod 9:13–35).[62] Hail storms were capable of causing severe damage to unprotected plant life. Given the nature of these problems it seems likely that these calamities happened at various times rather than all at once.

All these misfortunes had befallen the people of Judah. None of them could be adequately explained as mere coincidence. In v. 17 the Lord takes credit for all of these problems, attributing them to initiatives that he himself had taken. The first person verb used here is vivid: "I struck all the work of your hands." The Lord had not been a passive observer during the difficulties experienced by this community. Quite the contrary. He was the immediate cause of their problems!

In this passage Haggai adopts language found in Amos 4:9 that is reminiscent of the deuteronomic curses described in Deuteronomy 28. The promised result of covenant faithfulness was the Lord's blessing, and the promised result of covenant infidelity was the Lord's curse. The severe agricultural disasters Haggai's community experienced were due to the Lord's attempts to arrest the attention of a wayward people and draw them back into fellowship. Only now were the people beginning to awaken to the real root of their problems.

These actions had not proven to be sufficient. As v. 17 reports, "Yet you did not turn to me, declares the LORD." In spite of his discipline, which had

---

[61] For further details see R. A. Taylor, "יָרָק," *NIDOTTE* 2 (1997): 546–47.

[62] The effects of hail on agriculture are also mentioned in Ps 78:47: "He destroyed their vines with hail, and their sycamore-figs with sleet."

been exercised with therapeutic intentions, the people had persisted in their unrepentant ways. The Hebrew text of the words rendered by the NIV as "yet you did not turn to me" *(wĕʾên ʾetĕkem ʾēlay)* is very difficult.[63] A literal translation of the words is meaningless, "and there is not you to me." Many scholars regard the words as virtually untranslatable in any way that makes sense.[64] The following interpretations lack sufficient evidence in their favor.

First, some interpreters emend the text to read *wĕlōʾ šabtem ʾēlay* ("and you did not return to me"). This reading has the support of the LXX and P, which reflect here a Hebrew text that is different from the MT.[65] That Hebrew text of v. 17 is quite close to the wording of Amos 4:9, which is the passage to which Haggai alludes. However, this reading is probably the result of scribal harmonization to the Amos text. The NIV rendering "yet you did not turn to me" probably is based on this variant. Second, some interpreters take *ʾet* to mark a nominative rather than accusative construction here, as it does in certain other places in biblical Hebrew (see comments on 2:5).[66] But this does not seem to resolve the problem either, since a verb must still be supplied for the words to make sense. Third, the translation suggested by Meyers and Meyers (i.e., "nothing [brought] you to me") makes good sense and fits the context.[67] But it is doubtful that the Hebrew should be construed in this way, since supplying the verb

---

[63] The Hb. text has וְאֵין־אֶתְכֶם אֵלַי. As they stand, the words seem to make no sense, although Kessler disputes this conclusion. But it is difficult to see how he is able to arrive at the rendering "but you did not return to me" apart from emendation of the Hb. text (*The Book of Haggai*, 199).

[64] So, e.g., D. W. Thomas and W. L. Sperry, "The Book of Haggai," IB (New York: Abingdon, 1956), 1043; D. R. Jones, *Haggai, Zechariah and Malachi: Introduction and Commentary*, TBC (London: SCM Press, 1962), 51; D. A. Smith, "Haggai," in *Hosea–Malachi*, BBC (Nashville: Broadman, 1972), 7:301.

[65] The LXX has καὶ οὐκ ἐπεστρέψατε, and P has *wlʾ ʾtpḥtwn lwty*. This reading probably reflects a Hebrew text that had וְלֹא שַׁבְתֶּם אֵלַי, a reading preferred by Gesenius. See GKC §§117m, n. 3; 152n. G. R. Driver, however, has suggested that the LXX reading is actually just a paraphrase of וְאֵין־אֶתְכֶם אֵלַי ("but your inclination [or desire] was not toward me"), an understanding that he tentatively accepts ("Linguistic and Textual Problems: Minor Prophets. III," *JTS* 39 [1938]: 398–99). But that the Gk. translation is due merely to translation technique rather than textual variation does not seem likely. Rather, the LXX probably is based here on a Hebrew *Vorlage* inferior to the MT.

[66] M. Rooker understands this construction to be an example of אֵת used before a noun in the nominative case, which he thinks occurs more often in Hb. from the postexilic period than in early biblical Hb. (*Biblical Hebrew in Transition: The Language of the Book of Ezekiel*, JSOTSup 90 [Sheffield: JSOT Press, 1990], 88). R. Polzin (*Late Biblical Hebrew: Toward an Historical Typology of Biblical Hebrew Prose*, HSM 12 [Missoula, Mont.: Scholars Press, 1976], 35) and P. P. Saydon ("Meanings and Uses of the Particle אֵת," *VT* 14 [1964]: 193) draw a similar conclusion. Saydon, who calls attention to the emphasizing force of this particle, translates Hag 2:17, "and you yourself did not return to me."

[67] Meyers and Meyers, *Haggai, Zechariah 1–8*, 61–62.

"brought" seems arbitrary and without parallel.

These difficulties suggest that we probably are dealing here with a textual disturbance that has adversely affected all of our extant Hebrew evidence. The original reading of this part of v. 17 simply eludes us.[68] In the absence of further evidence to clarify the proper reading of the text, none of the existing proposals is entirely convincing. Fortunately, however, the problem with the specific wording of this part of v. 17 does not interfere with the general sense of the verse, which has the effect of underscoring the lamentable failure of the people to turn to the Lord in response to his loving but relentless discipline of them. The final words of the unit (*ně'um YHWH,* "utterance of Yahweh") once again remind the audience of the divine source of the prophet's message.

### (2) Hope for the Future (2:18–19)

[18]"From this day on, from this twenty-fourth day of the ninth month, give careful thought to the day when the foundation of the LORD's temple was laid. Give careful thought: [19]Is there yet any seed left in the barn? Until now, the vine and the fig tree, the pomegranate and the olive tree have not borne fruit.

"'From this day on I will bless you.'"

**2:18** Again the prophet calls on the people to "give careful thought" (*śîmû nā' lěbabĕkem*). These words appear twice in v. 18. The repetition underscores the urgency of the prophetic call for repentance. Appearing both at the beginning and end of the verse, the appeal for careful reflection brackets a threefold reference to the specific "day" of the oracle.[69] The reference to the date of the message ("this twenty-fourth day of the ninth

---

[68] This conclusion is similar to that reached by a number of scholars. *HALOT* (101) suggests that the text of 2:17b is corrupt and should be emended to אִתְּכֶם ("with you"). T. Muraoka regards the text as "hopelessly corrupt" (*Emphatic Words and Structures in Biblical Hebrew* [Jerusalem: Magnes; Leiden: Brill, 1985], 157). Baldwin's suggestion that since Haggai is referring to Amos we can justifiably emend the Haggai text on the basis of the Amos text minimizes the fact that inner biblical citations do not always agree precisely in wording with their source. It is exactly that sort of variation that makes Baldwin's proposal risky from a text-critical perspective (see *Haggai, Zechariah, Malachi,* 52).

[69] The Masoretic accents in v. 18 seem to require taking the final Hb. words of the verse (שִׂימוּ לְבַבְכֶם, "give careful thought") closely with what precedes in this verse. In the MT v. 18 thus begins and ends with an appeal for reflection, which forms an inclusio that frames the verse. But many Syriac, Greek, and Latin MSS delimit the verse in such a way that the second occurrence of these words goes most closely not with what precedes but with what follows in v. 19. Understood in this fashion, the second appeal for reflection focuses on whether there is yet grain in the barn (v. 19) rather than on the laying of the foundations of the temple (v. 18). For discussion of issues of delimitation in the text of Haggai see M. van Amerongen, "Structuring Division Markers in Haggai," in *Delimitation Criticism: A New Tool in Biblical Scholarship,* Pericope: Scripture as Written and Read in Antiquity (Assen: Van Gorcum, 2000), 1:51–79, esp. pp. 53–54.

month") is repeated from v. 10.[70] Haggai's reference in v. 18 to "this day" (cf. vv. 15,19) suggests a significant event or turning point. It is mentioned here in connection with recollection of the prior establishment of the foundation of the temple.

The reference in v. 18 to the foundation of the temple has been taken by some scholars to mean that Haggai was unaware of any earlier restoration of the foundations prior to 520 B.C. (cf. Zech 4:9; 8:9). If this is the case, it raises the question of what activity was engaged in following Cyrus's decree in 538 B.C. that permitted the reconstruction of the temple.[71] How could the temple be said to have been founded both in 536 B.C. and in 520 B.C.? Did Haggai (and Zechariah) have no knowledge of earlier work on the temple?[72]

The issue revolves around the interpretation of *yāsad*. Although this verb can have the sense of "to lay a foundation" (cf. Ezek 13:14; Mic 1:6), it can also mean "to restore or repair" (cf. Zech 8:9; Ezra 3:6).[73] Its emphasis may fall on the process of restoring an existing structure as opposed to the construction of an entirely new edifice. The work of restoration is in view in Haggai, and therefore the use of the verb *yāsad* does not preclude earlier work undertaken during the time of Cyrus as described in Ezra 1 and 6. It is also possible that Haggai alludes to a dedication ceremony that took place on this particular day, although this is not certain. Such a dedication ceremony would presumably provide a solemn public occasion for emphasizing the solidarity of the postexilic temple with the cherished but now destroyed Solomonic temple (see further in comments on 2:15).[74]

**2:19** The relationship between the first part of v. 19, which asks

---

[70] The words מִיּוֹם עֶשְׂרִים וְאַרְבָּעָה לַתְּשִׁיעִי ("from the twenty-fourth day of the ninth month") in 2:18 are often regarded as a secondary gloss repeating information found in v. 10. But there is no manuscript evidence that supports deleting these words from v. 18. Furthermore, since repetition is not a feature unknown to biblical writers, its presence should not necessarily lead to textual suspicion. The words should be retained as in the MT.

[71] On the earlier work at reconstruction see Ezra 1 and 6.

[72] So R. H. Pfeiffer: "The unimpeachable testimony of Haggai and Zechariah shows that in 520 nothing was known of any decree of Cyrus issued in 538. More significant still, these prophets had never heard of a considerable number of returned Exiles dwelling in Jerusalem nor of any previous plans for rebuilding the Temple" (*Introduction to the Old Testament* [London: Adam and Charles Black, 1948], 821–22). Pfeiffer concludes that the decree of Cyrus was probably a Jewish forgery by the Chronicler.

[73] For a helpful discussion of this point see A. Gelston, "The Foundations of the Second Temple," *VT* 16 (1966): 232–35. See also *DCH* 4:232–33.

[74] So, e.g., Petersen, who likens this ceremony to the Mesopotamian *kalû* ritual: "The turning point, the day when one should begin to expect those benefits, would most naturally be the day of ritual dedication, the day in which the continuity between the old and new temple was ritually declared. Hence the rededication probably occurred on 'this day'—the twenty-fourth day of the ninth month (Hag 2:18) or Nov.–Dec. 520 B.C." ("Zerubbabel and Jerusalem Temple Reconstruction," *CBQ* 36 [1974]: 369; id., "The Prophetic Process Reconsidered," *IR* 41 [1983]: 17).

whether there is seed left in the barn,[75] and the immediately following part of v. 20, which describes the failure of the crops, is strained.[76] Does Haggai intend for the question to imply a positive answer or a negative one? Presumably the answer to his question is "No, there is no seed left in the barn."[77] In that case the prophet is reminding the people of the still desolate conditions they are facing. The barns lacked the seed normally stored at this time of the year. Why so? Perhaps because the seed had been consumed as food by the people, or perhaps because it had been planted in anticipation of a coming harvest, or perhaps because the seed referred to is that of the harvest yet to come,[78] or perhaps because Persian armies passing through the region had drained these supplies.[79] What exactly had caused the barns to be empty of grain is not clear.

The NIV translates the Hebrew word *mĕgûrāh*, found only here in the Hebrew Bible,[80] as "barn." This is likely to be the correct meaning. But some scholars have suggested that the word may actually refer to "a furrow in which the seed lies embedded."[81] This meaning fits well with Joüon's suggestion that the particle *ha* in v. 19 has an exclamatory function, yielding the sense *"Surely, the seed is still in the sheath."*[82] The point of 2:19 would then be that the planted seed lies dormant in the ground, with no hope for a productive harvest. Although this interpretation yields an acceptable sense, the notion that the word refers to a barn of some sort rather than to a furrow seems to be a preferable understanding in this context.

---

[75] In 2:19 for the MT הַזֶּרַע ("the seed") the LXX has ἐπιγνωσθήσεται ("shall be known"), apparently mistaking the root זרע ("seed") for the root ידע ("to know"). This is a rather obvious case of graphic confusion of the similar letters *dālet* and *rêš*. The MT is to be preferred here.

[76] Jones regards v. 19 as Haggai's most difficult verse (*Haggai, Zechariah and Malachi*, 52). Although this may be pressing the matter too far, no exegete is likely to think it an easy passage. P. R. Ackroyd says, "Admittedly v. 19 is very difficult to translate and explain" ("Studies in the Book of Haggai," *JJS* 3 [1952]: 7).

[77] The NLT implies a positive answer to the question, but this is not likely to be correct in light of the negative features of the immediately preceding context. Cf. the NEB: "Will the seed still be diminished in the barn? Will the vine and the fig, the pomegranate and the olive, still bear fruit? Not so, from this day I will bless you."

[78] See Clark's discussion of these several options for understanding Haggai's comment ("Problems in Haggai 2.15–19," 436–37).

[79] See J. L. Berquist's discussion of this latter option (*Judaism in Persia's Shadow: A Social and Historical Approach* [Minneapolis: Fortress, 1995], 69–70).

[80] Some scholars argue in favor of emending מַמְּגֻרוֹת ("storehouses") in Joel 1:17 to מְגֻרוֹת ("storehouses"). If that emendation is accepted there are two occurrences of מְגוּרָה in the Hb. Bible.

[81] See *HALOT*, 544. מְגוּרָה is translated there as "grain pit" or "storage room," but notice is taken of the possibility that it perhaps refers to a furrow containing the planted seed. BDB takes the word to mean "store-house" or "granary." See BDB, 158.

[82] See *GBH* §161b (italics his). Joüon suggests that it is due to the frequency of *ha* for marking questions that this less frequent nuance is often overlooked.

The agricultural staples of this society—grapes, figs, pomegranates, and olives—had not yielded[83] the essential harvests the people depended on annually.[84] Without a successful yield of these agricultural staples there would be major disruptions to everyday life. It was the vine (v. 19) that produced grapes for the making of wine. The fig was used in making cakes and also in wine. The pomegranate was used for making wine and certain dyes. The olive provided oil used for cooking and a fuel source for lamps. Each of these products was essential for maintaining the lifestyle with which Haggai's audience was familiar.[85] All of these hardships—brought about by the failure of the people to seek a right relationship with the Lord—remained as painful reminders of their short-sighted choices. Though conditions might seem insurmountable, the prophet holds out hope for the future.

The sermon concludes on a surprisingly optimistic note of promise. The prophet sees in the people evidences of genuine repentance and turning to the Lord, in light of which there is the prospect of great hope for the days ahead. The people could take comfort in the promise of the Lord's renewed blessing and the attendant reversal of conditions of economic hardship. Once again the Lord would work in their behalf. The final words of v. 19 are these: "From this day on I will bless you."[86] This blessing would have temporal and tangible dimensions, since it refers primarily to renewed productivity of the land as a result of the Lord's lifting the agricultural and economic curses that had come due to the people's disobedience. But their future was brighter than their past. As surely as the deuteronomic curses had dogged the heels of their half-hearted commitment to covenant responsibilities, just as surely the Lord's blessings would reward their renewed faithfulness to those obligations. His blessings would accompany the obedience of his people.

---

[83] The verb used here, נָשָׂא, may form an inclusio with יִשָּׂא in v. 12 (Motyer, "Haggai," 994).

[84] The expression וְעַד ("and until") in 2:19 is difficult. The objects of the preposition appear to be the several agricultural items mentioned in the verse. The NIV's "until now" smooths over the problem, taking the word in a temporal sense. If וְעַד is to be retained as the correct reading, it probably should be understood in the sense of degree rather than time: "even the vine . . . has not borne" (BDB, 724). But וְעַד possibly is a mistaken vocalization for וְעֹד ("still"), which would yield the sense "the vine . . . still has not borne" (*HALOT,* 787). See also Marti, *Dodekapropheton,* 390.

[85] Similar agricultural language appears in the Book of Joel (e.g., 1:10; 2:19,24). J. D. Nogalski understands 2:19 (cf. Hag 1:11) to be expanding rather awkwardly Joel's references to such agricultural imagery ("Joel as 'Literary Anchor' for the Book of the Twelve," in *Reading and Hearing the Book of the Twelve,* SBLSymS 15 [Atlanta: Society of Biblical Literature, 2000], 102–3). But the language used by both prophets is so general as not to require this conclusion.

[86] The NIV supplies the direct object ("you"). The Hb. text concludes somewhat abruptly with the verb alone (אֲבָרֵךְ, "I will bless"). It is unusual for this verb not to have an expressed object. The LXX follows the Hb. text closely here, providing no direct object (εὐλογήσω). P supplies a third person plural object along with a final pronouncement, *brk ᵓnᵓ lhwn ᵓmr mryᵓ* ("I will bless them, says the Lord").

V. HAGGAI'S FOURTH MESSAGE: *THE LORD IS RAISING UP A NEW LEADER!* (2:20–23)
1. Introduction to the Message (2:20)
    (1) Origin of the Message (2:20a)
    (2) Date of the Message (2:20b)
2. Imminent Judgment from the Lord (2:21–22)
3. Zerubbabel and the Davidic Throne (2:23)

## V. HAGGAI'S FOURTH MESSAGE (2:20–23)

Haggai's final message is the shortest of the four sermons recorded in this book. In form it is an oracle of salvation,[1] announcing the Lord's salvific purposes to be achieved through restoration of the Davidic line.[2] The main purpose of the sermon is to announce the Lord's intentions to raise up a new leader for his people. Following an introduction that specifies its origin and date (v. 20), this oracle sets forth the Lord's twofold intention for the future. First, the oracle warns of an overthrow of human power and government (vv. 21–22). Repeated use of the first person in this announcement underscores the Lord's direct involvement in these events. Second, the oracle proclaims the Lord's choice of Zerubbabel as the agent for accomplishing his purposes (v. 23). Here too there is an emphasis on divine initiative, as indicated by the repeated use of the first person in speech attributed to the Lord. This final verse of the book bristles with language of divine selection that emphasizes Zerubbabel's role as a Davidic successor. Haggai's final message looks beyond the stark conditions that characterized the restoration community to a time of apocalyptic interruption of human history signaled by the Lord's choice of a new leader.

---

[1] On use of this form of prophetic speech in the OT see C. Westermann, *Prophetic Oracles of Salvation in the Old Testament* (Louisville: Westminster/John Knox, 1991).

[2] H. W. Wolff prefers to think in terms of two prophetic oracles that are linked by the expression יְהוָה אַיּוֹם בַּיּוֹם הַהוּא in v. 23. He labels the first of these two oracles (vv. 21b–22) a theophany announcement, and the second (v. 23) he sees as an appointment or designation (*Haggai: A Commentary* [Minneapolis: Augsburg, 1980], 98–99).

## 1. Introduction to the Message (2:20)

### *(1) Origin of the Message (2:20a)*

**²⁰The word of the LORD came to Haggai a second time**

**2:20a**  Like Haggai's previous messages, this one is framed by a historical note that identifies Haggai as recipient of the Lord's revelatory word.
As in the earlier sermons, the phrase "the word of the LORD" *(děbar
YHWH)* calls attention to the divine origin of the prophet's message. It
emphasizes that the oracle Haggai is about to announce to Zerubbabel originates not in the prophet's own imaginations or political aspirations but in
divine intentions.

As in 2:10, the Lord's word is said to come "to" *(ʾel)* Haggai rather than
"by the hand of" *(běyad)* Haggai (cf. 1:3; 2:1). As noted earlier, the difference in meaning between the two expressions is slight. The preposition *ʾel*
portrays Haggai as a passive recipient of divine revelation, while *běyad*
shifts attention to the prophet as an active agent in the communication of
that message. But the important thing is that it is the Lord's message. Haggai is simply a chosen messenger.

### *(2) Date of the Message (2:20b)*

**on the twenty-fourth day of the month:**

**2:20b**  The date of this sermon is the same as that of the previous message found in 2:10–19, namely, "the twenty-fourth day of the [ninth]
month." This date corresponds to December 18, 520 B.C. On this date the
Lord spoke to Haggai "a second time" *(šēnît),* the first time being that of
the message found in 2:10–19. Contrary to what some have suggested, there
is nothing suspect in the notion that the prophet should receive two different
oracles on a single day.

## 2. Imminent Judgment from the Lord (2:21–22)

**²¹"Tell Zerubbabel governor of Judah that I will shake the heavens and the
earth. ²²I will overturn royal thrones and shatter the power of the foreign kingdoms. I will overthrow chariots and their drivers; horses and their riders will
fall, each by the sword of his brother.**

**2:21–22**  According to v. 21 this final message is addressed solely to
Zerubbabel. Unlike Haggai's first and second sermons, which include both
the high priest Joshua and the governor Zerubbabel as named recipients,
Zerubbabel alone is mentioned here. This is due to the fact that the promises given in the following verses find their fulfillment in a royal rather than
a priestly figure; as such they are addressed specifically to governor Zerub-

babel. Unlike earlier references (1:1,12,13; 2:2), Zerubbabel's patronymic ("son of Shealtiel") is not mentioned here.[3] Some scholars have suggested that this is due to a conscious decision on Haggai's part not to emphasize Zerubbabel's Davidic connection for fear of drawing Persian attention to what might be perceived as a political threat.[4] In that case, however, one wonders why the Davidic connection was not systematically avoided throughout the entire book and not just in 2:20–23. Zerubbabel's title "governor of Judah" *(paḥat yĕhûdâ)* is employed here, as it is in 1:1,14; 2:2. The title is especially appropriate in this context, since the oracle describes an ideal rule prefigured by Zerubbabel's political position as leader of the postexilic community.

The first part of Haggai's message has a decidedly ominous tone. The shaking of heaven and earth announced in v. 21 warns of a violent disruption of normal processes in the created order. Cataclysmic earthquakes and thunderous noises in the atmosphere will herald the Lord's impending judgment. Military strength and political stability that previously provided solace will be violently altered, Haggai says. In v. 21 the prophet quotes the Lord as saying "I am about to shake the heavens and the earth."[5] The participle used here describes these events in terms of imminence.[6]

The first person verbs in v. 22 speak of violence that originates not in fortuitous events of nature but with intentional divine decisions. The repeated use of the first person is vivid: "I will overturn," "I will shatter," "I will overthrow." The sovereign Lord credits himself with the foreboding acts of judgment described here. Such language calls to mind certain prior Old Testament scenes that provide the poetic imagery and visual backdrop for this oracle.[7] In Gen 19:25 the Lord "overthrew" (same verb as "overturn" here) Sodom and Gomorrah and the surrounding plain (cf. Isa 13:19; Jer 20:16; Amos 4:11; Deut 29:23). The Song of Moses speaks of Pharaoh's

---

[3] The LXX adds τὸν τοῦ Σαλαθιηλ ("the [son] of Salathiel"), bringing the description in line with the other occurrences of this phrase. The MT is to be preferred here.

[4] So, e.g., C. Meyers and E. M. Meyers, "Haggai, Book of," *ABD* 3:22.

[5] In 2:21 MSS of the Old Greek, with the exception of Codex V, add καὶ τὴν θάλασσαν καὶ τὴν ξηράν ("and the sea and the dry land"). This probably is a secondary gloss due to harmonization with v. 6, where that phrase appears in virtually all of our MSS evidence. The shorter text of the MT is preferable in v. 21.

[6] As in 2:6 the participial construction מַרְעִישׁ אֲנִי in v. 21 is best understood as *futurum instans* ("I am about to shake heaven and earth"). On the use of the participle to indicate the imminent future see *GBH* §121e; GKC §116p; *IBHS* §37.6f. This understanding seems preferable to C. F. Keil's suggestion to take מַרְעִישׁ אֲנִי as a circumstantial clause ("If I shake heaven and earth, I overthrow . . ."; *Minor Prophets, Commentary on the Old Testament* (reprint, Grand Rapids: Eerdmans, 1982), 10:213).

[7] Haggai's language may also reflect here, as D. L. Petersen (following Sauer) suggests, some allusion to the judgmental language of national destruction as found in Psalms 2 and 110 (*Haggai and Zechariah 1–8: A Commentary,* OTL [Philadelphia: Westminster, 1984], 100).

horses and riders, along with his chariots and army, being hurled into the sea as a result of the Lord's decisive intervention at the time of the exodus (Exod 15:1,4,19,21). Haggai also speaks of the overthrow of royal thrones, the shattering of the power of foreign kingdoms,[8] and the overthrow of chariots and their drivers. The similarity of language is not coincidental.

For NIV's "royal thrones" the Hebrew text has "throne of kingdoms." Some interpreters take the singular of "throne" in this expression to be a thinly veiled threat against the Persian king Darius in particular.[9] But given the political dangers inherent in any such hint at insurrection against Persia, it is more likely that the reference is of a general nature.[10] The word "throne" *(kissēʾ)* is instead a collective singular, as confirmed by the plural *mamlākôt* ("kingdoms") to which it is linked in v. 22. The eschatological thrust of the passage reinforces the conclusion that it is not just Persia that is in view here.

The common verb *yārad* ("go down"), translated by the NIV as "will fall," is used here to describe a falling in death, as *Targum Jonathan* correctly perceives.[11] In both Exod 15:5 and Hag 2:22 this verb is used of the defeat of armies.[12] Haggai's language invokes recollection of these prior biblical scenes, and it is against this backdrop that his warning should be

---

[8] The second colon of 2:22 seems a bit overloaded due to the two genitives dependent on חֹזֶק ("strength"). The NIV translates the clause "[I will] shatter the power of the foreign kingdoms." A more literal translation is, "And I will destroy the power of the kingdoms of the nations." Some scholars regard מַמְלְכוֹת ("kingdoms"), which also occurs just three words earlier, as a gloss that may have originated as a variant to the word הַגּוֹיִם ("the nations"). But there is no MSS evidence to support this view. In spite of the awkwardness of the phrase, it seems best to retain מַמְלְכוֹת as in the MT. The twofold occurrence of מַמְלְכוֹת ("kingdoms") may in fact serve a purpose. C. L. Meyers and E. M. Meyers have suggested that a subtle distinction may be intended in this use of similar phraseology: "'Throne of kingdoms' may refer to the ruler or dynast controlling all the kingdoms composing the empire, with 'foreign kingdoms' (literally, 'kingdoms of nations') representing the constituent polities" (*Haggai, Zechariah 1–8: A New Translation with Introduction and Commentary*, AB [New York: Doubleday, 1987], 67).

[9] The Hb. phrase is כִּסֵּא מַמְלְכוֹת. Although כִּסֵּא ("throne") is singular in form, the plural of מַמְלְכוֹת extends *ad sensum* to כִּסֵּא. The LXX has θρόνους βασιλέων, acceptably rendering both words in the plural. As Wolff notes, "When a substantive *(nomen regens)* is linked with a genitive *(nomen rectum)*, the pluralizing of the nomen rectum is sufficient to indicate a plural sense in the nomen regens" (*Haggai*, 103). See also GKC §124r; *GBH* §136n.

[10] See, e.g., P. L. Redditt, *Haggai, Zechariah and Malachi*, NCB (Grand Rapids: Eerdmans, 1995), 32.

[11] In 2:22 for the MT וְיָרְדוּ ("and they will go down") *Tg. Jonathan* has ויתקטלון ("and they will be killed"), which is a correct understanding of the sense of the Hb. verb used here.

[12] Although the Hb. word יָרַד generally means "to go down," it can be used with a variety of nuances depending on the context. In 2:22 it means more than "be prostrated" (so BDB, 433). Here it refers to the mortal fall of a soldier in combat, as the following phrase "by the sword of his brother," clearly indicates. The NIV's "will fall" captures this idea only in a partial way. On the usage of this verb see *HALOT*, 435; *DCH* 4:284–89.

seen.[13] The magnitude and significance of the judgment announced in vv. 21–22 are such that only the language of unique events like the exodus seems adequate to the prophet for describing it.[14]

## 3. Zerubbabel and the Davidic Throne (2:23)

[23]"'On that day,' declares the LORD Almighty, 'I will take you, my servant Zerubbabel son of Shealtiel,' declares the LORD, 'and I will make you like my signet ring, for I have chosen you,' declares the LORD Almighty."

**2:23**  Following the warning of apocalyptic intervention in human history found in vv. 21–22, there is an announcement of the Lord's sovereign choice of Zerubbabel. This concluding promise of the Book of Haggai is extraordinary in terms of the scope of function that it envisions for Zerubbabel. The passage is replete with language used elsewhere in the Hebrew Bible for describing objects of the Lord's selection. The governor is singled out as playing a major role in the Lord's plans for the future. Haggai's description of Zerubbabel is striking, more so than in previous descriptions of Zerubbabel in this book.[15] Not surprisingly, the interpretation of v. 23 has elicited considerable discussion.[16]

The direct address in v. 23, invoking Zerubbabel's name together with his patronymic, seems to form an inclusio with the occurrence of his name in 1:1.[17] Zerubbabel is singled out as a key player not only in the reconstruction of the temple but also in the anticipated future of the Davidic kingdom. The mention of a historical figure by name in an eschatological

---

[13] Kessler thinks the panic and destruction described here may be an implicit allusion to this theme in the Behistun inscription of Darius (*The Book of Daniel*, 224).

[14] This part of Haggai's language has been viewed negatively by some scholars. W. O. E. Oesterley, e.g., speaks of Haggai's "vindictive feeling here expressed towards the Gentiles" and of his "bitterness towards the Gentiles." According to him, "Haggai belonged to the strict legalistic party among the exiles" ("The Early Post-Exilic Community," *ExpTim* 47 [1935–1936]: 397). But this is a very unsympathetic reading of Haggai's message. According to the biblical text, it is not personal frustrations that Haggai is venting against the Gentiles in a mean-spirited way. Rather, he is speaking a revelatory word from Yahweh that expresses what are actually divine intentions, not those of the prophet himself. Though not indifferent to the collapse of the Gentiles, Haggai is merely the bearer of Yahweh's message concerning the groups described in v. 22.

[15] This is, as H. G. Mitchell says, "the boldest of all his predictions" (*A Critical and Exegetical Commentary on Haggai and Zechariah*, ICC [Edinburgh: T&T Clark, 1912], 77).

[16] D. E. Gowan's laconic comment is not without basis: "Probably more has been written about the last verse of the book than is necessary" (*Theology of the Prophetic Books: The Death and Resurrection of Israel* [Louisville: Westminster John Knox, 1998], 165).

[17] So Meyers and Meyers, *Haggai, Zechariah 1–8*, 67.

setting is unusual,[18] although certain references to David elsewhere in the
Old Testament may have some similarity to this reference to Zerubbabel.[19]
The setting of v. 23 is established by the phrase *bayyôm hahû'* ("on that
day"). This phrase is frequently used with an eschatological nuance in Old
Testament prophetic literature.[20]

The language of v. 23 is characterized by terminology emphasizing uni-
lateral divine selection, such as "I will take you," "my servant," and "I have
chosen you." The piling up of such language in a short space signals that
unusual events are being described. The Hebrew verb *lāqaḥ* ("to take")
often has a very general sense, but here it is used with the specific nuance
of selecting or choosing, a usage that is attested elsewhere for this verb.[21]
The language of v. 23 is similar to that of 1 Kgs 11:37, where the Lord
addresses the following words to Jeroboam: "However, as for you, I will
take you [*w'ōtĕkā 'eqqaḥ*], and you will rule over all that your heart desires;
you will be king over Israel." The Lord will "take" (*'eqqāḥăkā*) Zerubbabel
in the sense that he has chosen him for a unique role in connection with the
momentous events described in this passage.

The term *'abdî* ("my servant"), which occurs in v. 23, is common in the
Hebrew Bible. It is often used of those whom the Lord has appointed to a
particular task, whether from among his people or the pagan nations.[22] But
*'abdî* is especially used as a designation of David as king, either in reference to the historical person of David or an eschatological figure who will
be David-like. The prophet Ezekiel, for example, says:

---

[18] Meyers and Meyers regard this phenomenon as unique, constituting "the only case in the
Hebrew Bible in which an eschatological prophecy is focused upon a known historical figure"
(*Haggai, Zechariah 1–8*, 15, 68). See also S. Japhet, "Sheshbazzar and Zerubbabel—Against the
Background of the Historical and Religious Tendencies of Ezra-Nehemiah," *ZAW* 94 (1982): 77.

[19] See, e.g., Hos 3:5, where the expression "David their king" has in view not David specifically
but a descendant in the Davidic line. Cf. Jer 30:9; Ezek 34:23–34.

[20] The expression הַהוּא בְּיוֹם occurs more than two hundred times in the Hb. Bible, often in
an eschatological sense. Among the prophets Isaiah is especially fond of this expression, using it
some forty-five times. Jeremiah uses this expression ten times; Ezekiel thirteen times; Hosea four
times; Joel once; Amos five times; Obadiah once; Micah three times; Zephaniah four times; Zechariah twenty-two times.

[21] See, e.g., Deut 1:15,23; 4:20,34; Josh 3:12; 4:2; 1 Kgs 11:37.

[22] The phrase "my servant" is used, e.g., of the following individuals: Abraham (Gen 26:24);
Jacob (Isa 43:10; 44:1,2; 44:21; 49:3; 52:13; 53:11; Jer 3:10; 46:27,28; Ezek 28:25; 37:25); Moses
(Num 12:7,8; Josh 1:2,7; 2 Kgs 21:8; Mal 3:22); Caleb (Num 14:24); David (2 Sam 3:18; 7:5,8;
1 Kgs 11:13,32,34,36,38; 14:8; Isa 37:35; Jer 33:21,22,26; Ezek 34:23,24; 35:24; 37:24; Ps
89:4,21; 1 Chr 17:4,7); Naaman (2 Kgs 5:6); Isaiah (Isa 20:3); Eliakim (Isa 22:20); Israel (Isa
41:8,9; 42:1,19); Nebuchadnezzar (Jer 25:9; 27:6; 43:10); the Branch (Zech 3:8); Job (Job 1:8; 2:3;
31:13; 42:7,8[2x]). Other permutations of this expression also appear (e.g., "servant," "your servant," "his servant," "servant of the LORD").

I will place over them one shepherd, my servant David *[ʾet ʿabdî dāwîd],* and he will tend them; he will tend them and be their shepherd. I the LORD will be their God, and my servant David will be prince among them. I the LORD have spoken. (Ezek 34:23–24)

In his use of the word "servant" Haggai is invoking Davidic associations.[23] His point is that Zerubbabel represents a restoration of the Davidic line of promise. As a result of this divine initiative, what was lost by the tragedy of the exile will in the future be regained in a manner that exceeds expectations.

The verb *bāḥartî* ("I have chosen") underscores the notion of intentional divine selection with a specific function in mind.[24] Zerubbabel represents God's renewed blessing upon the Davidic royal line. The passage holds out unusual promise for the future, although the language is somewhat guarded.[25] Neither the detailed circumstances nor the precise timing of the fulfillment of the promise is indicated.

Haggai likens Zerubbabel to a signet ring that is emblematic of divine approval.[26] By introducing imagery of the signet ring as symbolic of Zerubbabel's special relationship to the Lord, the prophet reinforces his point concerning divine selection and investiture of authority. Haggai's ring imagery is especially striking in this context.[27] The signet ring was a com-

---

[23] Haggai is, as F. M. Cross says, "reviving the old royal ideology of king and temple" ("A Reconstruction of the Judean Restoration," *JBL* 94 [1975]: 15).

[24] The word describes, as H. Seebass says, "a careful choice occasioned by actual needs, and thus a very conscious choice and one that can be examined in light of certain criteria" ("בָּחַר, *bachar,*" *TDOT* 2:74).

[25] As Wolff points out, "This promise is couched in extremely muted terms" (*Haggai,* 106).

[26] It seems best to understand חוֹתָם in v. 23 as a signet ring worn on the finger of one's hand. This is the way most versions and commentators have understood the word in 2:23, and it seems appropriate both to the context of Haggai and to the imagery of the Jeremiah passage to which Haggai is alluding. As such it is suggestive of the delegated authority residing in its bearer. But W. H. Rose has argued against this understanding. He maintains that חוֹתָם should instead be rendered here more broadly as "seal" and interpreted in terms of great personal value and protection rather than delegation of authority. In his view the oracle found in 2:20–23 is not of royal significance nor is it messianic in intent (*Zemah and Zerubbabel: Messianic Expectations in the Early Postexilic Period,* JSOTSup 304 [Sheffield: Sheffield Academic Press, 2000], 218–38). See also Kessler, *The Book of Haggai,* 229–31.

[27] It would be hard to improve on J. A. Motyer's apt description of this section: "The final verses of his book reveal Haggai as the literary equivalent of an impressionist painter—he gives general tone and effect without elaborate detail. His colors are the thunderstorm and the earthquake (2:21), revolution (2:22a), clashing armies (2:22b–c), and civil conflict (2:22d). As in a carefully composed picture, where every stroke is designed to lead the eye to what is central, so here too the focus is like a shaft of sunlight illuminating one item—a ring shining on a finger (2:23)" ("Haggai," in *The Minor Prophets: An Exegetical and Expository Commentary* [Grand Rapids: Baker, 1998], 3:1000).

mon emblem of ownership and authority in the ancient Near East; it was
used for the authentication of such things as royal directives or legal documents.[28] Missives of this sort were typically sealed with a piece of clay
impressed with the distinctive and identifying marks of the ring (cf. Jer
32:9–15). Such a ring normally was worn either suspended on a cord
around the neck (cf. Gen 38:18) or placed on a finger of the right hand (cf.
Jer 22:24), although it could be displayed on one's arm as well (cf. Song
8:6).[29] In Hag 2:23 the signet ring figuratively portrays Zerubbabel as one
who uniquely represented divine authority and who appeared as the Lord's
coregent.[30]

Haggai's allusion calls to mind Jer 22:24, where the Judean king Jehoiachin is pictured as a signet ring pulled from Yahweh's hand and cast
aside.[31] Haggai's use of the ring metaphor suggests a sovereign reversal of
fortunes for Israel's monarchy and a renewal of the Lord's blessing upon a
people that he previously disciplined through the trauma of the exile.
Although in the person of King Jehoiachin the ring was previously rejected
by the Lord and set aside, Haggai anticipates a time with Zerubbabel when
it will once again be taken up with divine pleasure. This is grounded in the
fact that the Lord sovereignly selected *(bāḥar)* Zerubbabel to accomplish
his will. The reliability of the divine promise concerning Zerubbabel is
underscored by the threefold repetition of the solemn words "declares the
LORD (Almighty)." Haggai attaches no conditions to the promise made to
Zerubbabel. Its fulfillment depends only on the ability of the sovereign
Lord to bring it about.

The magnitude of these promises to Zerubbabel poses an exegetical
problem. Were these pronouncements actually fulfilled in Zerubbabel? Did
he usher in a restoration of Israelite monarchy that was accompanied by the

---

[28] On the use of seals in general in the ANE see M. Gibson and R. D. Biggs, eds., *Seals and Sealing in the Ancient Near East,* BMes 6 (Malibu: Undena, 1977).

[29] That the signet ring was worn on one's person in order to prevent its theft or unauthorized use, as P. A. Verhoef suggests, is not entirely clear (*The Books of Haggai and Malachi*, NICOT [Grand Rapids: Eerdmans, 1987], 147). One can just as easily imagine that the signet ring may have been worn so that its owner might have convenient and ready access to it. In some instances there may also have been social advantages associated with having this emblem of authority clearly in public view.

[30] In v. 23 *Tg. Jonathan* expands the reference to Zerubbabel as a "signet ring" (הוֹתָם) to "the engraving (or setting) of a signet ring upon the hand" (כגלף דעזקא על יד), thus making the idea a bit more specific than it is in the MT.

[31] Cf. Esth 8:2, where King Xerxes removes from his finger his signet ring, which had previously been in the possession of the wicked Haman, and presents it to Mordecai as evidence of Mordecai's newly found favor with the king.

overthrow of Gentile nations in the fashion that Haggai describes?[32] The history of this period provides no evidence that he did so. Haggai's promises did not come to fruition in the person of Zerubbabel. On the contrary, not long after this prophecy was given, Zerubbabel dropped into obscurity and passed off the scene. History is silent about what became of him or under what conditions he concluded his life. Whether he was removed from office by the Persians out of concern over possible insurrection in Judah,[33] or died while in office, or continued to govern for a period of time is unknown.[34]

What is clear is that Zerubbabel did not usher in a triumphant period of rule such as vv. 20–23 describe. According to some scholars Haggai's grand predictions concerning Zerubbabel turned out to be a dismal failure.[35] What

---

[32] According to A. T. Olmstead "Haggai openly urged revolt to Zerubbabel, Yahweh's signet, and announced overthrow of the thrones of the kingdoms" ("Darius and His Behistun Inscription," *AJSL* 55 [1938]: 410–11). But this conclusion is not required by 2:20–23, and one wonders whether such an open encouragement toward revolt would even have been entertained by those who were so dependent on the good graces of Persia's foreign policy. Such an approach would have been reckless in the extreme.

[33] According to L. Waterman, Zerubbabel "became the victim of the political propaganda of Haggai and Zechariah, and it brought his immediate liquidation. He is never heard of again" ("The Camouflaged Purge of Three Messianic Conspirators," *JNES* 13 [1954]: 73). There is no hint of this liquidation in the biblical text. But according to Waterman, this lack is due to later editing of the text: "A later generation of Jews sought thus mercifully to hide from view the pitiable spectacle of two loyal and devoted prophets and a worthy governor of the royal line of David who unwittingly and solely because of inefficient means of communication were thus pilloried before the larger world and liquidated as craven conspirators" (p. 78). But this reconstruction of events takes many unwarranted liberties with the historical data. P. R. Ackroyd has discussed in detail some of the weaknesses of this view ("Two Old Testament Historical Problems of the Early Persian Period," *JNES* 17 [1958], esp. pp. 13–19).

[34] B. Uffenheimer's speculation about the outcome is possible, although it is based on silence and therefore lacks any sense of certainty: "In all probability, the excitement generated by the prophecies of Haggai and Zechariah had caused considerable suspicion among Persian officialdom, leading to his removal" (Uffenheimer, "Zerubbabel: The Messianic Hope of the Returnees," *JBQ* 24 [1996]: 225). In a similar vein J. Bright concludes: "What happened to Zerubbabel is a mystery. It is entirely possible that the Persians ultimately got wind of the sentiment in Judah and removed him. But we do not know" (*A History of Israel*, 3d ed. [Philadelphia: Westminster, 1981], 372). See also L. Boadt, *Reading the Old Testament: An Introduction* (New York: Paulist Press, 1984), 440; J. F. A. Sawyer, *Prophecy and the Biblical Prophets*, rev. ed., Oxford Bible Series (Oxford: Oxford University Press, 1993), 134.

[35] Haggai's promises for the future have been described as "an idle dream that never took shape in history" (I. G. Matthews, "Haggai," in *Minor Prophets*, An American Commentary [Philadelphia: The American Baptist Publication Society, 1935], 17). In a similar way W. H. Schmidt concludes that Haggai "was mistaken in his expectations for the immediate future" (*Old Testament Introduction*, 2d ed. [Berlin: Walter de Gruyter, 1995], 272). Cf. J. J. Collins, *Introduction to the Hebrew Bible* (Minneapolis: Fortress, 2004), 403–4.

the prophet thought would take place did not occur.[36] Haggai's predictions are therefore regarded by some scholars as an instance of prophecy failing to come to fruition, a case of what has been called cognitive dissonance within the prophetic literature.[37]

A better understanding of this matter lies in viewing Zerubbabel as a representative figure.[38] Just as the name David could carry associations of a royal figure who is in the Davidic line but who transcends the historical figure of David, so it is with Zerubbabel.[39] This governor of Judah represented a renewal of divine pleasure in a people who had returned from the disciplinary experience of the exile—a people whom the Lord was once again pleased to acknowledge and for whom he had great plans. Like many other Old Testament promises, these predictions had both a near dimension and a more distant one. Haggai's promises given to Zerubbabel, while true of him in a limited way, find their ultimate expression in a greater Zerubbabel who was to come.[40] It is not

---

[36] Meyers and Meyers conclude that even though Haggai's prophecy concerning Zerubbabel was not historically fulfilled, the prophet was nonetheless a success: "That his prophecy was not fulfilled historically only serves to confirm its authenticity. Although it was not fulfilled, it nevertheless accomplished a great deal: it helped to get the temple rebuilt on its ancient foundations and to revive and transform the mechanism of national life" (*Haggai, Zechariah 1–8*, 84). But if what he confidently announced was going to happen was not in any way fulfilled, the prophet would seem to be deserving of a more severe judgment than this opinion allows.

[37] See the following discussions: R. P. Carroll, *When Prophecy Failed: Cognitive Dissonance in the Prophetic Traditions of the Old Testament* (New York: Seabury, 1979); id., "Eschatological Delay in the Prophetic Tradition?" *ZAW* 94 (1982): 47–58.

[38] R. W. Pierce argues that since it is Zerubbabel's name that appears in vv. 21,23, any attempt to interpret the passage in a typical or representative sense fails to "deal fairly with the language of the text" ("The Unresponsive Remnant: History, Structure and Theme in Haggai" [Ph.D. diss., Fuller Theological Seminary, 1984], 188). However, as mentioned above, there is precedent elsewhere in the biblical text for doing so. In particular, David (e.g., Ezek 34:23–24) and Elijah (e.g., Mal 4:5–6) provide examples of an idealized OT individual being used to portray an eschatological figure.

[39] For a summary of messianism in key texts found in Haggai and Zechariah see R. T. Siebeneck, "The Messianism of Aggeus and Proto-Zacharias," *CBQ* 19 (1957): 312–28; A. Bentzen, "Quelques remarques surle mouvement messianique parmi les Juifs aux environs de l'an 520 avant Jésus-Christ," *RHPR* 10 (1930): 493–503; M.-J. Lagrange, "Notes sur les prophéties messianiques des derniers prophètes," *RB* 15 (1906): 67–83; K.-D. Schunck, "Die Attribute des eschatologischen Messias," *TLZ* 111 (1986): 641–52, esp. cols. 647–48; Th. Chary, "Le culte chez les prophètes Aggée et Zacharie," in *Les prophètes et le culte à partir de l'exil*, vol. 3, Bibliothèque de théologie 3, Théologie biblique (Paris: Desclée, 1955), esp. pp. 127–38; J. G. Napier, "The Historical and Biblical Significance of the Messianic Passages in Haggai" (Th.D. diss., Dallas Theological Seminary, 1984).

[40] As J. Bright remarks: "Jésus de Nazareth, affirmons-nous, est le vrai accomplissement de l'espérance d'Aggée, et son seul accomplissement. Il est le Messie de la lignée de David, plus grand que Zorobbabel, plus grand que le grand David lui-même" ["Jesus of Nazareth, we affirm, is the true fulfillment of Haggai's hope and its only fulfillment. He is the Messiah of David's lineage, greater than Zerubbabel, greater than the great David himself"] ("Aggée: Un exercice en herméneutique," *ETR* 44 [1969]: 21).

surprising that in the genealogies of Jesus provided by Matthew and Luke, Zerubbabel is mentioned as part of the messianic line.[41]

That Haggai himself necessarily expected a delayed fulfillment of his words is not likely. He had no way of anticipating the temporal distances that might exist between prediction and fulfillment. As the writer to the Hebrews says of past heroes of the faith, "These were all commended for their faith, yet none of them received what had been promised" (Heb 11:39). In that regard Haggai was no different from New Testament writers who expected the prophecies of Jesus' return to have a sooner rather than later fulfillment. They could not have anticipated the measure of time that separated their predictions from historical fulfillment. Such temporal distance, however, does not negate the validity of their prophecies. It merely confirms that at times they spoke of profound mysteries that were beyond their ability fully to comprehend.

Zerubbabel nonetheless played a crucial role in the historical events of sixth-century Judah. Along with the high priest Joshua, he was influential in leading Haggai's community to make a positive response to the Lord's instructions concerning the temple. Later generations recalled with appreciation the leadership that Zerubbabel and Joshua provided for the postexilic community. The fame of Zerubbabel and Joshua continued well into the intertestamental period, providing hope and inspiration for later generations.[42] Jesus ben Sira in the second century B.C. exclaimed:

How shall we magnify Zerubbabel?
He was like a signet on the right hand,
and so was Jeshua the son of Jozadak;
in their days they built the house
and raised a temple holy to the Lord,
prepared for everlasting glory.[43]

---

[41] See Matt 1:12–13; Luke 3:27. On the problems of the Lukan genealogy, which lists Shealtiel as the son of Neri rather than of Jeconiah (or Jehoiachin) see D. L. Bock, *Luke,* BECNT 3A (Grand Rapids: Baker, 1994), 1:355.

[42] See *1 Esdr* 3:1–5:6.

[43] *Sir* 49:11–12, NRSV.

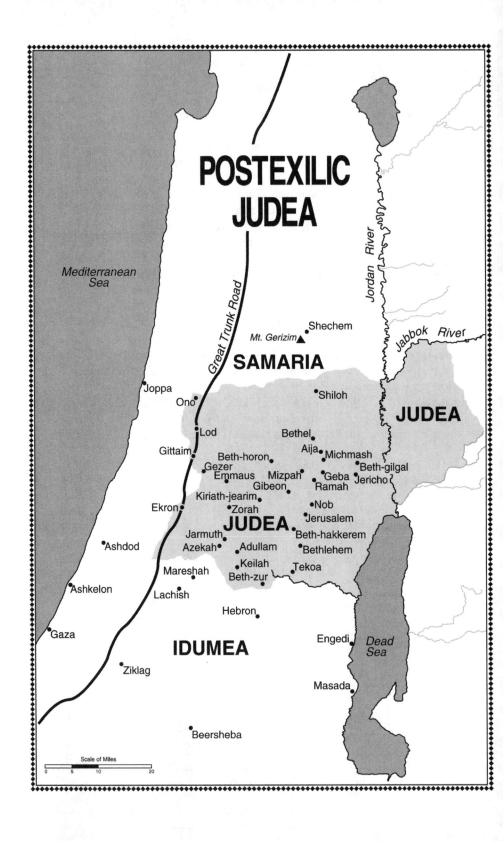

POSTEXILIC JUDEA

Mediterranean Sea

Jordan River

Jabbok River

Great Trunk Road

Shechem

Mt. Gerizim ▲

SAMARIA

Shiloh

JUDEA

Joppa

Ono

Bethel

Lod

Aija

Michmash

Gittaim

Beth-horon

Beth-gilgal

Gezer

Mizpah

Geba

Jericho

Emmaus

Gibeon

Ramah

Kiriath-jearim

Ekron

Zorah

Nob

Jerusalem

JUDEA

Jarmuth

Beth-hakkerem

Azekah

Adullam

Bethlehem

Keilah

Mareshah

Tekoa

Ashdod

Beth-zur

Ashkelon

Lachish

Hebron

Gaza

Engedi

Dead Sea

IDUMEA

Ziklag

Masada

Beersheba

Scale of Miles

0    5    10    20

# Malachi

————————— **INTRODUCTION TO THE STUDY** —————————

Malachi is an oracle from our divine Creator, Redeemer, and Lord, who loves us and deserves our honor and complete attention. It was crafted to speak to the hearts of a troubled people whose circumstances of financial insecurity, religious skepticism, and personal disappointments are similar to those God's people often experience or encounter today. Malachi is the last prophetic message from God before the close of the Old Testament period (although other books such as Ezra-Nehemiah and Chronicles may have been written later). It contains in miniature the essential message of the Old Testament, the Scriptures that Jesus revered and that his disciples used for their worship, preaching, and devotional life. It deals with the nature of God and the covenant member's relationship and responsibility to him and to other members of the covenant community, as well as with our relationship to and responsibilities for our material possessions. It also peers into God's sovereign plan for the nations of the world and the universal judgment and redemption he will bring at the end of the ages. Malachi, therefore, is a fitting conclusion to the Old Testament and provides Christians today a transition for understanding the kingdom proclamation begun by John the Baptist and continued by Jesus in the Gospels. It probably is no accident that the one prophesied in Mal 3:1 to "prepare" the way for the Lord's coming to his temple is identified as *malʾākî*, "My messenger," a word identical to the name of the book's author given in 1:1. An argument will be made in the comments on 3:1 that this prophecy was fulfilled preeminently by John the Baptist but that a further fulfillment may be expected prior to our Lord's return at the age's end. It could even be that the prophet Malachi's earliest readers considered that he and this book constituted a foreshadowing or preliminary fulfillment (cp. Isa 7:14) of this prophecy.

The Book of Malachi, then, contains a message that must not be overlooked by those who wish to encounter the Lord and his kingdom and to lead others to a similar encounter. Its message concerns God's loving and holy character and his unchanging and glorious purposes for his people. Our God herein calls his people to genuine worship, to fidelity both to himself and one another, and to expectant faith in what he is doing and will do in this world and for his people.

## 1. Author and Date

Part of the meaning of any text is to be derived from the situation in which the original communication occurred.[1] As K. Callow has written, "Communication does not take place in a vacuum but in a world of shared experiences focused in the here and now."[2] Therefore the more we know about the people, time, and place from which the Book of Malachi emerged, the better we will understand its message.

"Malachi" in Hebrew *(malʾākî)* means "my messenger." Many believe that the book is pseudonymous and that the name was taken from Mal 3:1, where the same word occurs. The Septuagint (LXX) translates the name in 1:1 as *angelou autou,* "his angel/messenger," although the book bears the title *Malachias.* If *malʾākî* is not a name but rather designates a functionary, then the book is anonymous. Some scholars hold this view because no information is

---

[1] See M. Larson, *Meaning-based Translation: A Guide to Cross-language Equivalence* (Lanham, Md.: University Press of America, 1984), 36–38, 131–39.

[2] K. Callow, *Man and Message: A Guide to Meaning-Based Text Analysis* (Lanham, Md.: University Press of America, 1998), 37.

given about the personal life of the prophet.[3] E. M. Meyers, for example, asserts that "anonymity or pseudoanonymity is a feature of late prophecy and intertestamental writing that begins with Malachi."[4] He follows J. Blenkinsopp in suggesting that the prophet "may himself have been either a priest or Temple prophet" and so had seen the corruption of the priesthood firsthand.[5]

An early Jewish tradition recorded in the Talmud (*Meg.* 15a) ascribed the Book to Ezra, although the sages rejected the view, asserting that Malachi was a personal name. Jerome stated in his prologue to his commentary on Malachi, "The Hebrews think that Malachi is Ezra the priest, because everything contained in that book this prophet also recalls" (an opinion Jerome is inclined to follow).[6] One manuscript of the Aramaic Targum to the Prophets *(Targum Jonathan)* adds after "Malachi" at the end of Mal 1:1 "whose name is Ezra the Scribe." On the other hand, Jewish tradition in general has personalized the name, regarding the title as the name of a prophet like the other prophetic works. The absence of personal information does not necessarily argue against this view since information about the prophet's birthplace or occupation is also lacking in the case of Obadiah (whose name means "Yahweh's servant") and Habakkuk. Regardless of the author's identity, the book reveals no specific details of his family, work, or circumstances. The emphasis is clearly on the message rather than the messenger since out of a total of fifty-five verses as many as forty-seven are the personal addresses of the Lord.

Although the book is not dated by a reference to a ruler or a specific event, internal evidence as well as its position in the canon favors a date during the Persian period after the rebuilding of the temple in 515 B.C.[7] Many refrain from dating the book more precisely than the fifth century, but most at least suggest a date in the early, middle, or late part of the century, depending on the supposed relationship to the ministries of Ezra and Nehemiah.[8] The

---

[3] See W. Rudolph, *Haggai-Sacharja-Maleachi.* KAT 13.4 (Gütersloh: Mohn, 1976), 247–48.

[4] E. M. Meyers, "Priestly Language in the Book of Malachi," *HAR* 10 (1986): 226.

[5] Ibid., 226–27; cf. J. Blenkinsopp, *A History of Prophecy in Israel,* rev. ed. (Louisville: WJKP, 1996), 209. Meyers dates the book to the "mid-fifth century or slightly earlier," citing A. Hill, "Dating the Book of Malachi: A Linguistic Reexamination," in *The Word of the Lord Shall Go Forth* (Winona Lake: Eisenbrauns, 1983), 77–89, although Hill actually dates the book 515-475 (p. 86).

[6] See R. Hayward, "Saint Jerome and the Aramaic Targumim," *JSS* 32 (1987): 115.

[7] Such a conclusion, however, is not universal. B. T. Dahlberg, e.g., proposed a date in the seventh century B.C. before the destruction of the Jerusalem temple ("Studies in the Book of Malachi" [Ph.D. diss., University of Columbia, 1963). See also J. O'Brien, *Priest and Levite in Malachi.* SBLDS 121 (Atlanta: Scholars Press, 1990), 118–20, 147.

[8] For a more complete catalog of views and scholars holding them, see A. E. Hill, *Malachi,* AB (New York: Doubleday, 1998), 77–80, 393–95.

majority of scholars favor a date prior to the work of Ezra and Nehemiah.[9] Of these, the ones who follow the traditional date of 458 B.C. for Ezra's arrival in Jerusalem date Malachi about 460 or earlier. Hill and Merrill, for example, date Malachi fairly early in that period,[10] and Stuart and Dumbrell place it just prior to Ezra's arrival.[11] Those who place Ezra's work after Nehemiah's, in about 428 or 398 B.C.,[12] typically date Malachi about 450 B.C., not long before Nehemiah's arrival in 445.[13] Some date Malachi's work during the time of Ezra but before Nehemiah.[14] Several scholars associate Malachi's ministry with Nehemiah, either during his first term as governor (445–433 B.C.),[15] during or just before Nehemiah's second term as governor (Neh 13:6–7),[16] or perhaps after his governorship.[17]

Reference to a governor in 1:8 (*peḥâ;* cf. Ezra 5:14; 6:7; Neh 5:15; Hag 1:1,14; 2:2,21) favors the Persian period, when Judah was a province or sub-

[9] E.g., Blenkinsopp dates the book between 486 and 445 B.C. (*A History of Prophecy in Israel,* 209).

[10] Hill, "Dating the Book of Malachi," 77–89. After "continued analysis and reflection," Hill concluded that "a round figure of 500 B.C./E. still seems most reasonable," with a *terminus ad quem* of ca. 475 (*Malachi,* 83). E. H. Merrill argues that Malachi's work preceded Ezra, "480–470 being a reasonable guess" (*Haggai, Zechariah, Malachi* [Chicago: Moody, 1994], 377–78). D. L. Petersen dates it to the late sixth or early fifth century (*Zechariah 9–14 and Malachi,* OTL [London: SCM, 1995], 6). J. F. Drinkard, Jr. places it about 500 B.C. ("The Socio-Historical Setting of Malachi," *RevExp* 84 [1987]: 389).

[11] D. Stuart dates Malachi's ministry during or "slightly in advance" of the reforms of Ezra and Nehemiah ("Malachi," in *The Minor Prophets: An Exegetical and Expository Commentary* [Grand Rapids: Baker, 1998], 3:1252–53); likewise W. J. Dumbrell, "Malachi and the Ezra-Nehemiah Reforms," *RTR* 35 (1976): 43.

[12] The view that Nehemiah preceded Ezra is argued, e.g., by J. A. Emerton, "Did Ezra Go to Jerusalem in 428 B.C.?" *JTS* 17 n.s. (1966): 1–19; H. H. Rowley, "The Chronological Order of Ezra and Nehemiah," in *The Servant of the Lord,* 2d ed. (Oxford: Blackwell, 1965), 135–68; G. Widengren, "The Persian Period" in *Israelite and Judaean History* (Philadelphia: Westminster, 1977), 503–9; J. Bright, *A History of Israel* (Louisville: WJKP, 2000), 379, 391–402.

[13] E.g., O. Eissfeldt, *The Old Testament: An Introduction* (New York: Harper & Row, 1965), 442–43. B. Glazier-McDonald dates it between 470 and 450 B.C. and dates Ezra 397 B.C. (*Malachi: The Divine Messenger* [Atlanta: Scholars Press, 1987], 16).

[14] E.g., R. K. Harrison, *Introduction to the Old Testament* (Grand Rapids: Eerdmans, 1969), 961.

[15] See J. M. P. Smith, *A Critical and Exegetical Commentary on the Book of Malachi,* ICC (Edinburgh: T&T Clark, 1912), 7.

[16] See G. L. Archer, *A Survey of Old Testament Introduction,* rev. ed. (Chicago: Moody, 1994), 479; P. A. Verhoef, *Haggai and Malachi,* NICOT (Grand Rapids: Eerdmans, 1987), 158–60; G. L. Klein, "An Introduction to Malachi," *CTR* 2 (1987): 25–26; W. C. Kaiser, Jr., *Malachi: God's Unchanging Love* (Grand Rapids: Baker, 1984), 17; C. F. Keil, *The Twelve Minor Prophets,* 2 vols (trans. J. Martin; Grand Rapids: Eerdmans, 1868[1954]), 2.427. R. B. Chisholm, Jr. dates the book to the general time of Nehemiah, but not while he was governor (*Handbook on the Prophets* [Grand Rapids: Baker, 2002], 477).

[17] G. V. Smith dates the book about 420 B.C. (*The Prophets as Preachers* [Nashville: Broadman & Holman, 1994], 327).

province of the Persian satrapy Abar Nahara, which included Palestine, Syria, Phoenicia, Cyprus, and, until 485 B.C., Babylon. The temple had been rebuilt and worship reestablished (1:6–11; 2:1–3; 3:1,10). But the excitement and enthusiasm for which the prophets Haggai and Zechariah were the catalysts had waned. As Hill proposes, "the despair and doubt triggered in the restoration community by the apparent failure of the prophetic visions of Haggai and Zechariah soon characterized the 'intellectual disposition' of the era—a disposition that pouted that Yahweh had indeed forgotten his covenant with Israel."[18] Moral deterioration and religious lethargy characterized Malachi's day. There were problems of intermarriage with foreigners (2:11; cf. Ezra 9–10; Neh 13:23–27), failure to bring tithes (3:8–10; cf. Neh 12:44–47; 13:10–14), and economic oppression (3:5; cf. Neh 5:1–13). Offering gifts to the governor (Mal 1:8) may be compared to Nehemiah's refusal of gifts (Neh 5:14,18). Whereas a date just prior to Nehemiah's second term as governor (Neh 13:4–7; c. 435 B.C.) may best fit what we know of the period, Merrill's argument is persuasive that the situation prior to Ezra's arrival is more reasonable, and Hill's linguistic data pushes the date to the first quarter of the fifth century B.C.

## 2. Historical Context[19]

### (1) The Exile

In response to the last of a series of Judean rebellions against their Babylonian overlords in 589 B.C., a Babylonian army destroyed a number of cities in southern Judah. Then after a lengthy and severe siege, it took Jerusalem in July of 586. The puppet king Zedekiah was deported to Babylon, where he soon died. His sons and many of the Jewish officials were executed, Jerusalem and the Jewish temple were looted and destroyed, and another group of citizens was deported (2 Kgs 24:18–25:21; Jer 37:1–39:10; 52:1–30; 2 Chr 36:3–21).

No longer a monarchy, Judah became a province of the Babylonian empire, administered from a new capital at Mizpah (Tell en-Naṣbeh) by a Jewish governor, Gedaliah. After an unspecified time, however, Gedaliah was assassinated along with some Babylonian soldiers by a surviving member of the royal family. As a result, there was another deportation in 582, a number of Jews fled to Egypt, and Judah may have become part of the province of Samaria (Jer 39:11–44:30).

Both literary and archaeological evidence points to severe devastation and

---

[18] Hill, *Malachi,* 83.

[19] This section is adapted from E. R. Clendenen, "The Interpretation of Biblical Hebrew Hortatory Texts: A Textlinguistic Approach to the Book of Malachi" (Ph.D. diss., The University of Texas at Arlington, 1989).

depopulation in the sixth century (cf. Lam 2:2,5,11–12,20–22; 4:9–20; 5:1–18). Although the total number deported according to Jer 52:28–30 is given as 4,600, Yamauchi suggests that this may have counted only nobles, since Kings gives the figure of 18,000 men (excluding their families) for 597 B.C. alone.[20] According to Ezra-Nehemiah, the number returning over some period of time was 42,360 (Ezra 2:64; Neh 7:66), yet we know that many remained in Babylon. In addition to those deported, thousands had certainly died either in battle or of starvation and disease, many were executed, and many had fled.

Archaeology confirms the literary evidence. E. Stern states that "the most prominent feature left by seventy years of Babylonian domination in Palestine was the total destruction and devastation of all the main cities that had flourished during the Assyrian period." The result is "an almost complete gap in the archaeology-history of Palestine, a view strengthened from one excavation to the next."[21] The only exception west of the Jordan was the region of Benjamin, that is, northern Judah, where Mizpah (Tell en-Naṣbeh), the provincial capital, was located. Many of the surviving inhabitants of Judah probably found refuge in this area.[22] The population in the rest of the country "was very small in number, and . . . large parts of the towns and villages were either completely or partly destroyed, and the rest were poorly functioning."[23]

---

[20] E. Yamauchi, "The Archaeological Background of Ezra," *BSac* 137 (1980): 196.

[21] E. Stern, *Archaeology of the Land of the Bible, Volume II: The Assyrian, Babylonian, and Persian Periods (732–332 B.C.E.)* (New York: Doubleday, 2001), 308–9. See also id., "The Babylonian Gap," *BAR* (2000) and the rejoinder (J. Blenkinsopp, "There Was No Gap") and surrejoinder (E. Stern, "Yes There Was") in *BAR* (2002): 36–39, 55, 59. What seems in particular to bother Blenkinsopp (who is not an archaeologist) about Stern's agreement with Albright's earlier conclusions (*The Archaeology of Palestine,* rev. ed. [Baltimore: Penguin, 1960], 141–42) is the idea that Judah was deserted just when critical scholars say such important compositions as Isaiah 40–66 and the final version of Deuteronomy were supposed to have been written (p. 37). Stern reaffirms that "after the Babylonian conquest, the Jews disappeared from most of Mt. Hebron and from approximately two-thirds of the area previously ruled by the kingdom of Judah." No longer having a religious center, major trade routes, or a government, the population was reduced to scattered rural settlements (p. 39).

[22] Stern, *Archaeology of the Land of the Bible,* 321. Also continuing to exist in this region during the exile were Bethel, Gibeon, and Tell el-Ful (Gibeah), although these cities too were inexplicably destroyed about 480 B.C. (pp. 321–23). East of the Jordan, Ammon also seems to have escaped severe destruction (p. 350).

[23] Ibid., 350. J. P. Weinberg estimated an exilic population of about 150,000 ("Demographische Notizen zur Geschichte der nachexilischen Gemeinde in Juda," *Klio* 54 [1972]: 45–58), but this has recently been shown to be much too large (C. E. Carter, "Opening Windows onto Biblical Worlds," in *The Face of Old Testament Studies,* D. W. Baker and B. T. Arnold [Grand Rapids: Baker, 1999], 439. J. Bright (*A History of Israel,* 3d ed. [Philadelphia: Westminster, 1981], 334), following his mentor, W. F. Albright (*The Biblical Period from Abraham to Ezra* [New York: Harper & Row, 1963], 84–87), estimated that perhaps only about 20,000 remained in Judah after the exile. For a review of opinion, see Yamauchi, "Archaeological Background of Ezra," 195–97.

Refugees drifted back gradually (cf. Jer 40:11–12), but the conditions in Judah were very poor.[24] According to D. E. Gowan, "There does not exist sufficient evidence or probability of an active, creative group in the land during the exile, although the continuance of some form of Yahwism is not to be doubted."[25] The temple site was still considered holy and was visited by pilgrims who continued to make sacrifices on perhaps a rebuilt altar (Jer 41:4–8). Nevertheless, they apparently did not welcome the exiles returning from Babylon with Sheshbazzar and Zerubbabel but joined their opponents, "the peoples around them," those in the surrounding regions of Ashdod, Samaria, and Edom, including the Arabs (Ezra 1:8–11; 3:3; 4:4; 5:14–16).

About the time of Jerusalem's destruction, the cities of Edom were also destroyed. The Edomites seem to have returned during the exile, but they were driven gradually from their homeland by Nabatean Arabs, and they began taking over southern Judah, which came to be known as Idumea.[26] The result was that Jews returning from Babylon at the end of the sixth century held little but Jerusalem and its suburbs.[27] But Edom was never again a national entity (cf. Mal 1:2–5). Abundant references to Edom in the Hebrew Scriptures indicate a profound hatred between the two nations (cf. Num 20:14–21; 1 Kgs 11:14–16). The Book of Obadiah indicates that Edomites had helped the Babylonians against Judah by cutting off their escape and delivering over many captives (v. 14). A tradition is preserved in *1 Esdr* 4:45 that it was the Edomites who burned the temple. Prophecies of the destruction of Edom are found in Obadiah, Isaiah (34:5–15), Jeremiah (49:7–22), Lamentations (4:22), Ezekiel (25:12–14; 35:1–15), Joel (3:19), Amos (1:11–12), and Malachi (1:2–5).

As for the Jews in exile in Babylon, after their recovery from the emotional and physical distress of being uprooted (cf. Pss 74; 137), conditions were good (Jer 29:4–7; Ezek 8:1; Ezra 2:65–69), although those captured in battle probably were enslaved and many of the exiles were poor. Only the king and his family captured in 597 were confined, and they were released in 562 (Jer 52:31–34//2 Kgs 25:27–30). Most of the rest were free to settle in communities near Nippur and to engage in normal agriculture or trade, as

---

[24] Stern explains that "so rudimentary must this existence have been that it has proved extremely difficult to find its traces in the material remains. Of the destroyed cities and towns, many ceased to exist entirely; others were inhabited by poorer elements, who must have salvaged material for their shelters from the rubble" (*Archaeology of the Land of the Bible*, 323).

[25] D. E. Gowan, *Bridge between the Testaments: A Reappraisal of Judaism from the Exile to the Birth of Christianity*, 3d ed. (Allison Park, Penn.: Pickwick, 1986), 37.

[26] See Stern, *Archaeology of the Land of the Bible*, 325–26, 331. See further I. Ephʿal, "Changes in Palestine during the Persian Period," *IEJ* 48 (1998): 115.

[27] See *1 Esdr* 4:50 and P. Ackroyd, *Exile and Restoration* (Philadelphia: Westminster, 1968), 20–31.

indicated by the Murashu Texts.[28] Y. Kaufmann declares that there is every indication that they experienced "economic well-being, retention of rights, and the maintenance of a certain degree of autonomy."[29] It should come as no surprise, then, considering conditions in Judah and Babylon, that later Jewish leaders had difficulty convincing large numbers to return with them to Judah.

## *(2) The Restoration*

The opportunity to return was the result of the Persian conquest of the Babylonian empire.[30] Babylon had been weakened by internal dissension caused by the absentee rulership of Nabonidus (555–539 B.C.) and his opposition to the worship of the Babylonian god Marduk.[31] The country fell easily to Ugbaru (also called Gubaru), governor of Gutium and commander of the army of Cyrus king of Persia, on October 12, 539 B.C. It was made a Persian satrapy consisting of Babylonia and their empire west of the Euphrates, ruled from Babylon by a Persian official named Gubaru from 535/4 to 525/4 B.C.

Presumably soon after the conquest of Babylon and obviously for political reasons, Cyrus issued orders for the rebuilding of walls in Babylon and the restoration of the worship of Marduk and the lesser gods of his pantheon in Babylon and the other cities of the empire. The record of this proclamation is preserved on the "Cyrus Cylinder," a piece of propaganda in the form of a Mesopotamian building text, found in Babylon in 1879.[32] According to Ezra 1:2–4; 6:2–5, in the first year after his conquest of Babylon, Cyrus issued a similar decree regarding the Jews, allowing them to return to their homeland with items from their temple looted by Nebuchadnezzar and to rebuild their sanctuary with a government subsidy.[33] This would have helped to consolidate the western frontier of his newly acquired kingdom against Egypt and the Arab tribes. It is also possible that he wished to reward Jewish aid in his takeover of Babylon. As in the case of the Cyrus Cylinder, which is written in traditional Mesopotamian form and from the point of view of a Mesopotamian ruler, the

---

[28] See M. D. Coogan, "Life in the Diaspora: Jews at Nippur in the Fifth Century B.C.," *BA* 37 (1974): 6–12. These show that "generations after the Edict of Cyrus in 538 B.C.E., many wealthy Jews remained in Babylonia and participated actively in the economy" (J. Berquist, *Judaism in Persia's Shadow: A Social and Historical Approach* [Minneapolis: Fortress, 1995], 90).

[29] Y. Kaufmann, *History of the Religion of Israel, Volume IV: From the Babylonian Captivity to the End of Prophecy* (New York: Ktav, 1977), 5.

[30] For further details on Judah in the context of the Persian empire see M. Breneman, *Ezra, Nehemiah, Esther,* NAC (Nashville: Broadman & Holman, 1993), 15–32.

[31] See I. Provan, et al., *A Biblical History of Israel* (Louisville: WJK, 2003), 285.

[32] See A. Kuhrt, "The Cyrus Cylinder and the Achaemenid Imperial Policy," *JSOT* 25 (1983): 92–93.

[33] Cf. E. Janssen, *Juda in der Exilzeit* (Göttingen: Vandenhoeck & Ruprecht, 1956), 94–104.

decree in Ezra 1:2–4 is written almost as if Cyrus were a Jew. This would indicate that it was actually written by Jews, some of whom Cyrus may have even known personally. The explicit references to Cyrus in the Hebrew Scriptures (Isa 44:28; 45:1–7) would lead many of the Jews to favor his conquests, and the passages could even have been made known to him, thus giving him the opportunity to "legitimize his conquest . . . by manipulating local traditions."[34]

### (3) The Political Situation in Judah

The nature of political authority in Judah before the appearance of Ezra and Nehemiah ca. 450 B.C. is unclear due to the scarcity and ambiguity of the evidence. Cyrus began the practice of dividing the empire into satrapies, usually ruled by Persian satraps. Satrapies, in turn, could be divided into provinces *(mĕdînôt)*, which might be further divided into smaller districts or subprovinces. Inside the satrapies, Persians tended to use whatever administrative system already existed, often including local non-Persian governors.[35] After Cyrus's conquest of the Babylonian empire, it became a new Persian satrapy including Abar Nahara ("Beyond the River"). After a revolt in Babylon in ca. 485 B.C.,[36] however (after the death of King Darius II in 486), Babylonia was joined to the satrapy of Assyria; and Abar Nahara, including Palestine, Syria, Phoenicia, and Cyprus, became a separate satrapy whose capital is still unknown.[37] Palestine included such provinces as Megiddo, Dor, Samaria, Judah, Ashdod, and Gaza,[38] though whether Judah was a separate province before the time of Nehemiah is disputed.

A. Alt advanced a theory, which has found many supporters, that from the Babylonian destruction of Jerusalem to the coming of Nehemiah, Judah was a subprovince of Samaria.[39] Zerubbabel was only an envoy, appointed for the

---

[34] Kuhrt, "The Cyrus Cylinder," 92–93.

[35] See J. M. Cook, *The Persian Empire* (London: J. M. Dent & Sons, 1983), 172–76; Berquist, *Judaism in Persia's Shadow,* 88.

[36] The exact date may have been 484 or 482, there being revolts in Babylon in both years. Most would favor the latter date. Cf. Ephʿal, "Changes in Palestine during the Persian Period," 109; but see L. L. Grabbe, *Judaism from Cyrus to Hadrian,* 2 vols. (Minneapolis: Fortress, 1992), 1:130.

[37] See A. L. Oppenheim, "The Babylonian Evidence of Achaemenian Rule in Mesopotamia," in *The Cambridge History of Iran,* vol. 2, *The Median and Achaemenian Periods* (Cambridge: Cambridge University Press, 1985), 564–67.

[38] See E. Stern, "The Province of Yehud: The Vision and the Reality," in *The Jerusalem Cathedra: Studies in the History, Archaeology, Geography and Ethnology of the Land of Israel,* vol. 1 (Jerusalem/Detroit: Yad Izhak Ben-Zvi Institute/Wayne State University Press, 1981), 12; id., *Material Culture of the Land of the Bible in the Persian Period 538–322 B.C.* (Warminster, England: Aris & Phillips, 1982), vii.

[39] A. Alt, "Die Rolle Samarias bei der Entstehung des Judentums," in *Festschrift Otto Procksch zum 60. Geburtstag* (Leipzig: Deichert & Hinrichs, 1934), 5–28.

task of rebuilding the temple. Nehemiah, then, naturally encountered opposition from Sanballat, the governor of Samaria (as well as his allies Tobiah and Geshem, perhaps governors of the provinces of Ammon and an Arab group; Neh 2:19; 4:1–3,7–8; 6:1–9), since he was coming to take over the administration of the new province of Judah as governor (*peḥâ*, Neh 5:14,18; 12:26).[40] Alt pointed out that when Tattenai, governor of Abar Nahara, questioned the renewed temple building in 520 B.C. (Ezra 4:24) and wrote to Darius about it, he complained not about a governor but only "the elders" of the Jews (Ezra 5:9). Furthermore, when Nehemiah reached Jerusalem, it was in a desperate situation physically, economically, and socially, which would be more likely if they had been administered by the Samaritans than by their own governor residing in the province.

Critics of Alt's view have pointed out that Nehemiah mentions former governors (*paḥôt*, Neh 5:15), and both Sheshbazzar (Ezra 5:14) and Zerubbabel (Ezra 6:7; Hag 1:1,14; 2:2,21) are called *peḥâ*.[41] Widengren believes that Gedeliah also served as governor of Judah under the Babylonians, though he recognizes that the word *peḥâ* is never used of him.[42] He adds that either Sheshbazzar or Zerubbabel is described by the Persian term *tiršatâ* in Ezra 2:63, a title for the governor of Judah that is also used of Nehemiah in Neh 8:9; 10:1. Furthermore, Judah is called a *mĕdînâ*, "province," in Ezra 2:1; 5:8; Neh 1:3; 7:6; 11:3.

> The term *mĕdînâ* is a term found in Imperial Aramaic and was used in the Persian chancelleries to designate a small or a large province. The term *peḥâ* was also a term in Imperial Aramaic, designating a governor, either of a great satrapy or of a small province. Accordingly, there is no doubt that Judah from the beginning of the Persian period was given the status of a province by the Persian government, and Alt's opinion seems improbable in view of these facts which were not taken into account by him.[43]

S. McEvenue counters in support of Alt that the terms *peḥâ* and *mĕdînâ* are broader than "governor" and "province." The latter is used in a ninth century B.C. context (1 Kgs 20:14,19) and perhaps later of an "administrative district," and *peḥâ* can be used of rulers at various levels. He also argues that the governors Nehemiah refers to in Neh 5:15 were more likely the governors in

---

[40] On the other hand, see the suggestion of H. Tadmor, "Some Aspects of the History of Samaria during the Biblical Period," in *The Jerusalem Cathedra*, vol. 3 (Jerusalem/Detroit: Yad Izhak Ben-Zvi Institute/Wayne State University Press, 1983), 8.

[41] Cf. M. Smith, *Palestinian Parties and Politics That Shaped the Old Testament* (New York: Columbia University Press, 1971), 196.

[42] The NIV adds "as governor" to the text of 2 Kgs 25:23.

[43] G. Widengren, "The Persian Period," in *Israelite and Judaean History* (Philadelphia: Westminster, 1977), 510–11. See also F. C. Fensham, "Medina in Ezra and Nehemiah," *VT* 25 (1975): 795–97; Ephʿal, "Changes in Palestine during the Persian Period," 117.

Samaria since he is accusing them of being greedy and tyrannical.[44] N. Avigad had noted, however, that according to Neh 5:1–13 Judah's main problems in 445 B.C. were caused not by foreign rulers but by their Jewish "brothers" (Neh 5:1,5,7–8), "nobles" and "officials" who were wealthy landowners. When Nehemiah refers to "former governors," then, they are likely Jewish governors appointed after Zerubbabel who

> administered the affairs of the province with a heavy hand, their major function being to bleed the people of the 'king's tax,' the heavy duties imposed by the Persian Empire. . . . The reconstruction of Jerusalem and its walls, of course, was not among the priorities of these earlier governors.[45]

The issue of the political status of Judah may have been settled by the discovery of postexilic bullae and seals published by Avigad. The discovery consists of a homogeneous collection of sixty-five bullae found in a jar near Jerusalem and two seals, probably found nearby. The bullae, probably from an official archive, commonly stored in pottery, were all made from twelve seals, some official, containing the name of the province Yehud (Judah), and some private. Avigad has dated the collection paleographically to "the very late 6th century B.C.E.," contemporaneous with inscribed Aramaic jar impressions found at many sites in Persian Judah, probably used for collecting taxes in wine, oil, etc.[46] One of the official bullae and one of the seals also bear the inscription "Elnathan the governor *(phw')*." Furthermore, on two of the jar impressions occur the names Yeho'ezer and Ahzai, both called "the governor" *(phw')*." On this basis, Avigad argues that Elnathan, Yeho'ezer, and Ahzai are the governors of Judea between Zerubbabel and Nehemiah

> of whom it is stated that they took a heavy tax of "food and wine" from the populace, [and] introduced an efficient tax-gathering apparatus using special jars. These, indeed, are the jars stamped with the names of the province, *yhd*, and the names of the governors and their officers, found in excavations on Judean sites.[47]

E. Meyers finds confirmation of Avigad's dating in the seal inscribed "Shelomith Maidservant *('amah)* of Elnathan the Governor," noting that a postexilic genealogy in 1 Chr 3:19 lists a woman named Shelomith (surprising in itself) who is the daughter of Zerubbabel. Her unusual mention, he says,

---

[44] S. McEvenue, "The Political Structure in Judah from Cyrus to Nehemiah," *CBQ* 43 (1981): 359–62.

[45] N. Avigad, "Bullae and Seals from a Post-exilic Judean Archive," *Qedem* 4, Monographs of the Institute of Archaeology (Jerusalem: Hebrew University, 1976), 34.

[46] Ibid., 35; see also id., "A New Class of Yehud Stamps," *IEJ* 7 (1959): 146–53; Y. Aharoni, "Some More YHWD Stamps," *IEJ* 9 (1959): 55–57; F. M. Cross, Jr., "Judean Stamps," *EI* 9 (1969): 21–27.

[47] Avigad, "Bullae and Seals from a Post-exilic Judean Archive," 35.

"seems to indicate some knowledge of her special role in society."[48] If the woman on the seal could be the daughter of Zerubbabel, Avigad's date for the governorship of Elnathan, at least, would be established. While agreeing with Avigad's interpretation of the bullae and seals, Stern questions the date and thinks it more likely they are to be associated with a reorganization of the province of Judah conducted during the second half of the fifth century, either during or shortly after Nehemiah's governorship.[49] He proposes that soon after the inception of the Persian period, the evidence favors Judah being a subprovince administered by Zerubbabel (and perhaps Sheshbazzar before him) within the province of Abar Nahara. Furthermore, it was again a province under Nehemiah and into the fourth century. However, between 515 B.C. (when the temple was completed and Zerubbabel disappeared from history) and the arrival of Ezra and Nehemiah in Jerusalem ca. 450 B.C.,

> we possess no sources attesting to the establishment of a provincial administration in Judaea. Moreover, when Nehemiah arrived in Judaea, he seems to have encountered a political vacuum with no government. Nor is there mention of any governor whom Nehemiah came to succeed. For this reason, we are obliged to hypothesize that even if there was an attempt to establish a Judaean province at the beginning of the Persian period, it was short-lived.[50]

Between Zerubbabel and Nehemiah, he says, Judah probably was ruled either from Samaria or by native priests and "landed oligarchy."[51]

Certainty about the political situation in Judah during the exile and restoration period is clearly impossible. The evidence supports Judah being a province from 538 to at least 515 B.C. and again during Nehemiah's time there. The reference in Mal 1:8 to the practice of gifts offered to the governor suggests his accessibility. If the book reflects the situation in the early fifth century, this may lend support to the presence of governors in Judah during at least part of the time between Zerubbabel and Nehemiah.[52]

### (4) The Economic Situation in Judah

Berquist argues that although Darius's policy toward the provinces "approached a laissez-faire posture, . . . encouraging local religion, and at

---

[48] E. M. Meyers, "The Shelomith Seal and the Judean Restoration: Some Additional Considerations," *EI* 18 (1985): 34.

[49] Stern, *Material Culture of the Land of the Bible,* 237; also id., "The Province of Yehud," 14. See also the discussion of the seals in Grabbe, *Judaism from Cyrus to Hadrian,* 1:68–69.

[50] Stern, "The Province of Yehud," 12–13.

[51] Id., *Archaeology of the Land of the Bible,* 355.

[52] The recent history by I. Provan et al., *A Biblical History of Israel,* 290–91, follows Avigad and tentatively dates the governors of Judah, Zerubbabel 520–510, Elnathan after Zerubbabel, Yeho'ezer 490–470, Ahzai after Yeho'ezer, Nehemiah 445–433, Bagohi after Nehemiah. "Nehemiah was clearly not the first governor of Yehud as Alt thought."

times financing local altar services," when Xerxes became king in 485 B.C., things changed dramatically. Support for local religion ceased, and "tax structures throughout the empire shifted to favor Persians and to increase the taxation upon all other ethnic and national groups." Huge financial resources were needed to support building projects as well as military ventures in the west. "Xerxes hedged the decline of the ethnic Persian economy by depleting the resources of the provinces."[53] This situation would have placed a severe strain not only on the economy of Judah but also on the temple.

Biblical evidence confirms that whoever was administrating Judah in that period, at least toward the end of the first half century, they were either inept or corrupt or both. There was severe poverty due to high taxes (Neh 5:4,15) and inflation caused by Persian economic policies and famine (Neh 5:3), resulting in confiscation of property (Neh 5:5,11) and debt slavery on a large scale (Neh 5:5,8). Interest rates had risen from about 20 percent under Cyrus and Cambyses to 40–50 percent by the end of the fifth century, which may have been a contributing factor to the inflation.[54] But Nehemiah seems to put much of the blame on "former governors" who, their income obtained by taxation, greedily "burdened the people" and allowed their subordinates to "lord it over them" (Neh 5:14–15). If these governors were foreign, then, as Williamson restates Smith's point, Nehemiah is not comparing "like with like" in 5:15, and his argument loses force.[55] It may very well be that there was no governor immediately prior to Nehemiah's coming, perhaps due to the actions of King Artaxerxes in response to the letter of two officials of uncertain rank describing Jewish efforts to rebuild the walls of Jerusalem (Ezra 4:8–23). The evidence, however, seems to point to Jewish governors of a separate province of Judah through at least much of the time in question.

## (5) The Contribution of Ezra

The part that the scribe-priest Ezra had in these events is difficult to determine. The traditional date for his coming to Jerusalem, 458 B.C., is based on understanding the reference to the seventh year of Artaxerxes in Ezra 7:8 as Artaxerxes I (464–424 B.C.). Although some would understand this reference to Artaxerxes II (404–358 B.C.), dating Ezra's return to 398 B.C., after Nehemiah,[56] and others have suggested emending the text to the thirty-

---

[53] Berquist, *Judaism in Persia's Shadow,* 89–93.

[54] See Y. Yamauchi, "Two Reformers Compared: Solon of Athens and Nehemiah of Jerusalem," in *The Bible World* (New York: Ktav, 1980), 270; see also R. P. Maloney, "Usury and Restrictions on Interest-taking in the Ancient Near East," *CBQ* 36 (1974): 1–20; Berquist, *Judaism in Persia's Shadow,* 90.

[55] H. G. M. Williamson, *Ezra-Nehemiah,* WBC (Waco: Word, 1985), 244.

[56] This is the view of Rowley and Widengren. See the previous section, Author and Date.

seventh year of Artaxerxes, resulting in a return in 428 B.C.,[57] evidence for the traditional date is strong.[58]

Regarding Ezra's purpose and function in Judah, the Aramaic letter of Artaxerxes quoted in Ezra 7:11–26 indicates that he was (1) to lead an additional group of Jewish returnees from Babylon (7:13), (2) to bring judicial reform to Judah (7:14,25–26), and (3) to restore the cultic system there (7:15–20). His and Nehemiah's mission has been compared to that of the Egyptian Udjahorresnet, a scribe-priest who with the authority of Cambyses and Darius restored cultic practices at the sanctuary of Sais and served as adviser on Egyptian affairs at Susa.[59] It is also likely that he was connected with the codification of Egyptian laws ordered by Darius in his third year (519/18). Because of this act, Darius gained the reputation of a great Egyptian legislator.

Thus the instructions to Ezra were harmonious with Persian policy elsewhere, whose purpose, of course, was to strengthen that part of the empire. They are also reasonable in view of the international situation at the time. Persia was having to deal then with a revolt in Egypt inspired by the Athenians, who captured Memphis in 459 B.C. O. Margalith argues that the Palestine-Phoenician coast came then into Greek control, possibly led by the city of Dor, a member of the Attic-Delic League and listed in the Tribute Lists in 454 B.C. During the years 460 to 454 it was especially to the advantage of Persia to have strong support from Judah, hence the mission of Ezra. After the Greeks were driven from Egypt in 454 B.C., however, and the peace of Callias was obtained in 449, Margalith suggests, "Obviously Jerusalem had ceased to be of any political or military interest to the king."[60] Therefore, when Artaxerxes heard the accusations of revolt from his officials in Palestine (Ezra 4:9–16), he ordered the reconstruction of Jerusalem to be stopped (Ezra 4:17–22). Hence, in 445 B.C. Nehemiah learned of the distress there. The subsequent mission of Nehemiah to continue the very work Artaxerxes had just halted (Neh 2:7–8) is perhaps the result of chaotic conditions in Abar

---

[57] See Bright, *A History of Israel,* 400.

[58] See E. Yamauchi, "The Reverse Order of Ezra/Nehemiah Reconsidered," *Themelios* 5 (1980): 12–13; E. H. Merrill, *Kingdom of Priests: A History of Old Testament Israel* (Grand Rapids: Baker, 1987), 503–6; D. J. Clines, *Ezra, Nehemiah, Esther,* NCBC (Grand Rapids: Eerdmans, 1984), 16–24; Williamson, *Ezra-Nehemiah,* xxxix–xliv; Breneman, *Ezra, Nehemiah, Esther,* 42–46; Provan et al., *A Biblical History of Israel,* 298–99. For a survey of the issue, cf. Grabbe, *Judaism from Cyrus to Hadrian,* 1:88–93. K. G. Hogland recently made a strong case that a 458 B.C. date for Ezra's return fits perfectly the situation in the Persian empire at that time (*Achaemenid Imperial Administration in Syria-Palestine and the Missions of Ezra and Nehemiah* [Atlanta: Scholars Press, 1992], 44, 234–44, *et passim.*

[59] See J. Blenkinsopp, "The Mission of Udjahorresnet and Those of Ezra and Nehemiah," *JBL* 106 (1987): 409–21.

[60] O. Margalith, "The Political Role of Ezra as Persian Governor," *ZAW* 99 (1987): 110–12.

Nahara caused by the revolt of Megabyzus the satrap in 448.[61]

The Book of Malachi, with its emphasis on problems of social strife (2:10; 3:5) as well as foreign influence (2:11) and laxness in the cult (1:8,10–14; 3:8–10), fits well what we know of conditions in Judah in the first half of the fifth century B.C.[62] Particularly the foreign influence (Ezra 9–10; Neh 13:1–9,23–31) and the discontinuance of the tithes (Neh 13:10–13) are known to have been matters of concern to the reformers Ezra and Nehemiah.

## 3. Text

The earliest text of Malachi is found on the fragmentary Qumran scroll of the Minor Prophets known as 4QXII[a] dating from the early Hasmonean period (ca. 150–125 B.C.). Besides portions of Zechariah (only 14:18) and Jonah, it contains four columns from Malachi comprising about 38 percent of 2:10–3:24.[63] It reflects a textual tradition between that of the MT and the LXX. This manuscript is unique in that Jonah appears to have followed immediately after Malachi.[64] In the other two known orders, that of the MT (also reflected in 8HevXIIgr) and the LXX, Malachi is last.

The only other Qumran manuscript containing a portion of Malachi (only 3:6–7) is 4QXII[c], which also contains portions of Hosea, Joel, Amos, and Zephaniah. It dates from about 75 B.C., and its textual affiliation is closer to the LXX.[65] There is also a fragment of a pesher (commentary) on Mal 1:14 (5QpMal).[66] Malachi (as well as Hosea–Obadiah) is missing from the first

---

[61] See J. M. Miller and J. H. Hayes, *A History of Ancient Israel and Judah* (Philadelphia: Westminster, 1986), 464.

[62] See also J. F. Drinkard, Jr., "The Socio-historical Setting of Malachi," *RevExp* 84 (1987): 383–90; Dumbrell, "Malachi and the Ezra-Nehemiah Reforms," 42–52.

[63] See R. E. Fuller, "The Minor Prophets Manuscripts from Qumran, Cave IV" (Ph.D. diss., Harvard University, 1988); id., "Text-Critical Problems in Malachi 2:10–16," *SBL* 110 (1991): 47–57; id., "The Twelve," in *Qumran Cave 4: The Prophets,* DJD 15 (Oxford: Clarendon, 1997), 221–32.

[64] It certainly "was placed in the second half and probably in the final third of the collection" (Fuller, "The Twelve," 222). See also id., "The Text of the Twelve Minor Prophets," *Currents in Research: Biblical Studies* 7 (1999): 83. O. H. Steck argues that the MT order is older ("Zur Abfolge Maleachi-Jona in 4Q76 [4QXII[a]]," *ZAW* 108 [1996]: 249–53). See also B. A. Jones, *The Formation of the Book of the Twelve: A Study in Text and Canon* (Atlanta: Scholars Press, 1995). Fuller acknowledges that this order "should not be taken as secondary to that of the Massoretic tradition" but "offers now a third early witness to the fluidity of order in this ancient, but still developing, collection." But "whether the placement of Jonah preserved here is older than that of the other two is as yet uncertain" ("The Twelve," 222; id., "Text of the Twelve Minor Prophets," 84).

[65] See Fuller, "The Twelve," 237–51; id., "Text of the Twelve," 86. Although officially part of 4QXII[c], Fuller believes the Malachi fragment "probably belongs to a separate, otherwise unknown manuscript of the Twelve" ("The Twelve," 251).

[66] See L. V. Montaner, *Biblia del Mar Muerto: Profetazs Menores* (Madrid: Instituto "Arias Montano," 1980), 105.

century B.C. Greek scroll of the Minor Prophets found at Naḥal Ḥever (8ḤevXIIgr)[67] and also from the first century A.D. Hebrew Minor Prophets scroll found at Murabbaʿat (Mur 88).[68] Finally, three verses from Malachi are quoted in the first century B.C. Damascus Document:[69] Mal 1:10 in CD 6:13–14[70] and Mal 3:16,18 in CD 20:18–21.[71]

The Greek Septuagint of Malachi is judged to be generally faithful and reasonably literal, as is the Syriac Peshitta.[72] Although these variant Hebrew manuscripts and translations differ from the Masoretic text (MT) at many points and often suggest how the text was understood at an early stage, I have considered the MT to be a credible testimony to the original text at each point and have not found it necessary or advisable to emend the text.

## 4. Literary Style

### (1) Genre

Malachi has a style that is unique among the Old Testament prophetic books.[73] In general it may be described as sermonic or oracular, but its frequent use of quotations, rhetorical questions, and polemical argument give it a distinctive character. It is often referred to as comprising a series of "disputation speeches," where charges are raised and evidence presented in a confrontational mood. H. Gunkel invented the form-critical term "disputation speech," in which opponents are quoted and then refuted. Considerable discussion of the form has followed Gunkel's analysis, especially in Isaiah but also to a lesser

---

[67] See E. Tov, *The Greek Minor Prophets Scroll from Nahal Ḥever (8ḤevXIIgr)* (Oxford: Oxford University Press, 1990). It does evidence Jonah's placement in the traditional order before Micah.

[68] See P. Benoit, et al., *Les grottes de Murabbaʾat* (Oxford: Clarendon, 1961).

[69] See Montaner, *Biblia del Mar Muerto,* xxii.

[70] "None who have been brought into the covenant shall enter into the sanctuary to light up His altar in vain; they shall 'close the door,' for God said, who of them shall close My door? And they shall not light up My altar in vain, that is, if they are not careful to act according to the specifications of the Law for the era of wickedness" (M. O. Wise, M. G. Abegg, Jr. and E. M. Cook, eds., *The Dead Sea Scrolls: A New English Translation* [New York: HarperCollins, 1996]).

[71] "Then each will speak to his fellow, vindicating his brother, helping him walk in God's way, and God shall listen to what they say and 'write a record-book of those who fear God and honor his name' [Mal 3:16] until salvation and righteousness are revealed for those who fear God. 'And you shall again know the innocent from the guilty, those who serve God and those who do not' [Mal 3:18]" (Wise, Abegg, and Cook, *The Dead Sea Scrolls*).

[72] See the summary of the translation evidence in Hill, *Malachi,* 4–10; Verhoef, *Haggai and Malachi,* 168–70.

[73] See my discussion of the prophetic genre in general in "Textlinguistics and Prophecy in the Book of the Twelve," *JETS* 46 (2003): 385–87.

extent in Malachi.[74] The primary argument for Malachi's identification as "disputation speech" comes from E. Pfeiffer, who cites as comparative passages Amos 5:18–20 and Isa 40:27–31.[75] He identifies six such disputation speeches in Malachi: (1) 1:2–5, (2) 1:6–2:9, (3) 2:10–16 (excluding vv. 11–12 as a later addition), (4) 2:17–3:5, (5) 3:6–12, and (6) 3:13–21 (Eng., 4:3; the last three verses of the canonical book, 4:4–6 in English, are excluded as a later addition). Each speech (with some variation and repetition) begins with a statement *(Behauptung)* charging the audience with wrongdoing, then the audience objects and demands clarification *(Einrede),* in response to which the prophet elaborates and reaches a conclusion *(Begründung).*[76]

Disagreement exists over how Malachi's disputations relate to those of the other prophets. A. Graffy has demonstrated that on the basis of form the dialogues in Malachi have a different structure and aim than the disputation genre. A proper disputation, he says, consists simply of a quotation from the people and a refutation by God or the prophet. In Malachi, however, God's view is stated, an objection of the people is raised, then God proceeds to convince the listeners of the original point. "The fundamental difference is that the aim of the forms in Malachi is to convince the listeners of the initial stated point, and not to reject the people's quoted opinion," which he considers to be an essential characteristic of the disputation.[77]

On the other hand, D. F. Murray has argued that the disputation should not be defined on the basis of formal characteristics but by the presence of "thesis, counter-thesis, dispute" in the "logical deep structure." A disputation may arise in any situation where there is a difference of opinion and may take various forms, for example, a Platonic dialogue, a debate, or the use of rhetorical questions to counter potential or actual objections to his views, as in Malachi. What makes the form in Malachi different, he says, is simply that the opening thesis of the people that the Lord is arguing against must be inferred from his initial remark.[78]

---

[74] See the summary in A. Graffy, *A Prophet Confronts His People: The Disputation Speech in the Prophets,* AnBib 104 (Rome: Pontifical Biblical Institute, 1984), 2–23. On its use in Haggai see R. Taylor's discussion of Hag 1:2–11 in this volume; B. Long, "Two Question and Answer Schemata in the Prophets," *JBL* 90 (1971): 129–37; J. W. Whedbee, "A Question-Answer Schema in Haggai 1: The Form and Function of Haggai 1:9–11," in *Biblical and Near Eastern Studies* (Grand Rapids: Eerdmans, 1978), 184–94.

[75] E. Pfeiffer, "Die Disputationsworte im Buche Maleachi," *EvT* 19 (1959): 546–68.

[76] H. J. Boecker agrees with Pfeiffer's basic analysis but prefers the term "discussion speech" since their aim is more to argue a position than to dispute the opponents' words ("Bermerkungen zur formsgeschichtichen Terminologie des Buches Malachi," *ZAW* 78 [1966]: 78–80). Boecker's analysis is followed by G. Wallis, "Wesen und Struktur der Botschaft Maleachi," *BZAW* 105 (1967): 229–37.

[77] Graffy, *A Prophet Confronts His People,* 16, 22.

[78] D. F. Murray, "The Rhetoric of Disputation: Re-examination of a Prophetic Genre," *JSOT* 38 (1987): 95–121.

Form-critical analysis can be useful for identifying textual units and for determining some of the interpretative strategies that an author would have expected a reader to employ. If a textual unit has the formal characteristics of a lament, for example, we may assume that the reader is to draw from the corresponding *Sitz im Leben* (life setting) in interpreting the unit. The use of such a genre is to have a certain rhetorical effect on the reader. But against Murray's approach, in order to be helpful, form-critical analysis depends on the identification of clear formal characteristics and the association of a particular genre with a certain *Sitz im Leben*. O'Brien accepts Graffy's argument against identifying Malachi as disputation but notes that he does not provide a useful alternative. Building on J. Harvey's 1967 study of Mal 1:6–2:9,[79] she makes an interesting case that "the entire Book of Malachi . . . employs the form of the covenant lawsuit" or *rîb*.[80] She proceeds then to analyze the book as comprising five "accusations" (1:6–2:9; 2:10–16; 2:17–3:5; 3:6–12; 3:13–21) plus a "prologue" (1:2–5), a "final admonition" (3:22), and a "final ultimatum" (3:23–24). As she notes, such an analysis accounts for the use of covenant terminology that many have observed in the book.

All that has been demonstrated, however, is that, first, Malachi employs many terms and motifs that also occur in covenant texts, suggesting that the biblical covenants are in view. This is confirmed by the explicit references to covenants in the book ("covenant with Levi" in 2:4,5,8; "covenant of our fathers" in 2:10; "marriage covenant" in 2:14; "messenger of the covenant" in 3:1). Second, the purpose of Malachi is similar to that of a "covenant lawsuit," whose purpose was either to announce or to warn of impending action against a covenant partner due to violations of covenant stipulations. It is possible that the lawsuit genre was in view, especially in 1:2–2:16. But Hill has pointed out that the "classic features" of the genre are missing and that O'Brien's identification of features is inconsistent and forced.[81]

Following a brief review of Pfeiffer, Boecker, Wallis, Graffy, and O'Brien, M. H. Floyd concludes,

> Comparison of the units on the basis of assertion plus question-and-answer format eventually breaks down because these common factors can differ in function from unit to unit. . . . Although O'Brien has refuted Pfeiffer's claim that the assertion plus question-and-answer format is the definitive factor for identifying the genre of Malachi's individual units as disputations, she continues to

---

[79] J. Harvey, *Le plaidoyer prophétique contre Israël après la rupture de l'alliance* (Paris: Desclée de Brouwer, 1967), 85–118.

[80] O'Brien, *Priest and Levite in Malachi*, 63. Cf. also E. Achtemeier, *Nahum–Malachi*, INT (Atlanta: John Knox, 1986), 172.

[81] Hill, *Malachi*, 31–33. He also claims that "the Babylonian exile rendered the formal *rîb* pattern obsolete, if not irrelevant" (p. 83, n. 5).

share his assumptions that a similarly shared common format provides a basis
on which to delimit the individual units, and that they must all thus belong to
one and the same genre. . . . Because of the limitations that are still evident in
O'Brien's much more nuanced attempt to work with these assumptions, however, the assumptions themselves appear to be dubious.[82]

### (2) Malachi as Hortatory Discourse

Rather than interpreting Malachi in terms of a certain culture-specific
genre which is highly debatable, I propose that the book be approached (at
least initially) on the basis of an inventory of universal discourse types that
has been devised by R. E. Longacre.[83] Such an inventory includes such categories as narrative, predictive, procedural, hortatory, and expository (or
descriptive). Each type may be described in terms of (1) its usual purpose
(e.g., narrative is for telling stories; procedural for telling how to do something; hortatory for changing behavior), (2) its notional or semantic structure
(e.g., a narrative will comprise certain elements such as inciting moment,
developing conflict, climax, and denouement), and (3) its grammatical/surface
structure, which is determined by the grammatical features of the particular
language, especially by the primary verb and clause types that are used. As I
have argued elsewhere, "the primary mark of the prophetic genre is its apparent intention to preserve the covenant by calling for behavioral changes on the
part of the covenant people."[84] The words of 2 Kgs 17:13 may be considered
somewhat paradigmatic of the genre.

The LORD warned Israel and Judah through all his prophets and seers: "Turn
from your evil ways. Observe my commands and decrees, in accordance with
the entire Law that I commanded your fathers to obey and that I delivered to
you through my servants the prophets."

---

[82] M. H. Floyd, *Minor Prophets: Part Two,* FOTL 22 (Grand Rapids: Eerdmans, 2000), 564–
65. The attempts of Lescow and Krieg (no works cited) to circumvent these problems "by supposing that there was originally a pristine ideal form to which all the heterogeneity secondarily
accrued," he says, also fail (pp. 565–66), as does Petersen's more flexible use of "diatribe," in part
because he retains the same units as Pfeiffer (p. 567).

[83] See, e.g., R. E. Longacre, *The Grammar of Discourse: Topics in Language and Linguistics*
(New York: Plenum, 1983); id., "Interpreting Biblical Stories," in *Discourse and Literature,* 3 vols.
(Philadelphia: John Benjamins, 1985), 3.83–98; id., *Joseph: A Story of Divine Providence—A Text-
theoretical and Textlinguistic Analysis of Genesis 37 and 39–48,* 2d ed. (Winona Lake: Eisenbrauns, 2003). Also see the excellent summary of Longacre's tagmemic approach in D. A. Dawson,
*Text-Linguistics and Biblical Hebrew,* JSOTSup 177 (Sheffield: Academic Press, 1994). Also see E. R. Clendenen, "The Structure of Malachi: A Textlinguistic Study," *CTR* 2 (1987): 3–
17; id., "Old Testament Prophecy as Hortatory Text: Examples from Malachi," *JOTT* 6 (1993):
336–41; id., "Interpreting the Minor Prophets for Preaching," *Faith and Mission* 13 (1995): 54–69;
id., "Textlinguistics and Prophecy in the Book of the Twelve," 385–99.

[84] Clendenen, "Interpreting the Minor Prophets for Preaching," 57.

Thus prophetic literature typically employs hortatory discourse. This is the case with Malachi, which can be understood as a series of hortatory addresses.[85] Hortatory discourse has three essential elements in the semantic structure: situation, change,[86] and motivation.[87] First (logically, though not always first in the text), the prophets told the people what was wrong (situation); second, they told them what they must do about it (change/command); and third, they told them why this course of action was wise or appropriate (motivation). The last structural element is easily viewed as two pronged: positive and negative. It is important to note that prophetic judgment oracles and salvation oracles are closely related, for both provide motivation, one as deterrent and the other as incentive. Furthermore, positive and negative motivation may be framed in terms of past, present, or future events or circumstances.[88]

### (3) Speech Attribution in Malachi

The Book of Malachi is in the form of speeches by Yahweh the God of Israel to his people through the agency of a prophet. Thus they are frequently referred to as oracles (unsolicited) or messenger speeches.[89] Nevertheless, they often employ the rhetorical device of quotations from the audience, which constitutes a form of interaction that can be called pseudodialogue.[90] As Baldwin explains, "Malachi reads the attitudes of his people and intuitively puts their thoughts into words, and so gains their attention before driving home his word from the

---

[85] The overall framework of the Book of Malachi as hortatory is identified by seven clear directives: two jussives (1:10; 2:15), four imperatives (3:7,10,22), and an imperfect of prohibition (2:16).

[86] The semantic element called "change" can vary in force depending on such pragmatic features as the relationship of speaker to addressee. It sometimes takes the form of exhortation, but in prophecy it can be called "command."

[87] Whereas I previously followed Longacre in proposing a fourth semantic feature, authority, I no longer consider this a separate essential element but view it as a possible form of motivation (Clendenen, "The Structure of Malachi," 6; R. E. Longacre, "Exhortation and Mitigation in First John," *Selected Technical Articles Related to Translation* 9 [1983]: 3).

[88] See the more thorough discussion in Clendenen, "Textlinguistics and Prophecy in the Book of the Twelve," 389–92, including the grammatical structure typical of each element in Hebrew hortatory discourse.

[89] Cf. J. F. Ross, "The Prophet as Yahweh's Messenger," in *Israel's Prophetic Heritage* (New York: Harper & Row, 1962), 98–107; C. Westermann, *Basic Forms of Prophetic Speech* (Philadelphia: Westminster, 1967), 98–128; J. F. A. Sawyer, *Prophecy and the Prophets of the Old Testament* (Oxford: Oxford University Press, 1987), 25–29; G. M. Tucker, "Prophetic Speech" in *Interpreting the Prophets* (Philadelphia: Fortress, 1987), 27–40.

[90] Cf. M. L. Larson, *The Functions of Reported Speech in Discourse* (Dallas: SIL, 1978), 77–85; Longacre, *The Grammar of Discourse*, 30.

Lord."[91] I understand the use of assertion–objection–response, then, not as a form-critical marker but as a rhetorical device.

Malachi can be analyzed, then, as monologue interspersed with exchanges between the Lord and his audience. Longacre has presented a useful model for the analysis of dialogue that he calls repartee.[92] A dialogue paragraph will begin with an "initiating utterance" (an utterance being the continuous words of a single speaker). This may consist of a question, a proposal, or a remark. In a simple dialogue paragraph, the initiating utterance will then be concluded by a "resolving utterance" consisting of an answer to the question, a response to the proposal, or an evaluation of the remark. Most dialogues, however, are not simple. In a complex dialogue paragraph, the initiating utterance is followed not by a resolving utterance but by a "continuing utterance," which may be followed by another and another until someone makes a resolving utterance or the dialogue ends. A continuing utterance may be a counterquestion, a counterproposal, or a counterremark. A compound dialogue consists of two or more simple or complex dialogue paragraphs linked together.[93] This model will be used in analyzing some of the paragraphs of Malachi.

Rather than speaking directly to the people of ancient Israel, the Lord normally spoke through his prophets (e.g., Jer 7:25; 25:4–6; 29:19; 35:15; 44:4; Ezek 38:17; Dan 9:6,10; Hos 12:10; Amos 2:11; 3:7; Zech 1:6; 7:3–12). These prophets sometimes would speak personally to the people, referring to the Lord in the third person and citing his words as indirect speech. Often, however, the prophet would use direct speech, acting only as the mouthpiece of the Lord, who would speak in the first person. Even then, however, we are often confused by the Lord's apparent references to himself in the third person.[94] In these cases the quotation seems to switch suddenly from direct to indirect speech, and the boundaries between the words of the Lord and those of the prophet are sometimes indistinct. In 1:4, for example, God says: "They may build, but I will demolish. They will be called the Wicked Land, a people always under the wrath of *the LORD*." Indirect speech here may be introduced by the verb *qārāʾ,* "call." God speaks to Judah in direct discourse throughout 1:2–8, marked by

---

[91] J. Baldwin, *Haggai, Zechariah, Malachi* TOTC (Downers Grove: InterVarsity, 1972), 214. Cf. Hosea's quotation of the people in Hos 1:5, which R. C. Ortlund, Jr. explains as "his creative way of articulating the national mood, the *Zeitgeist*" (*Whoredom: God's Unfaithful Wife in Biblical Theology* [Grand Rapids: Eerdmans, 1996], 57). Note that in each case of Hb. וַאֲמַרְתֶּם, "but you say," the Tg. (and all but two cases in the Peshitta) translates "and if you say," portraying the prophet as less omniscient and, more importantly, the people as less rebellious (cf. K. J. Cathcart and R. P. Gordon, *The Targum of the Minor Prophets,* The Aramaic Bible 14 [Wilmington: Michael Glazier, 1989], 229).

[92] Longacre, *Grammar of Discourse,* 43–76; id., *Joseph: A Story of Divine Providence—A Text-theoretical and Textlinguistic Analysis of Genesis 37 and 39–48,* 185–205.

[93] Longacre, *Grammar of Discourse,* 55.

[94] Cf. E. W. Bullinger, *Figures of Speech Used in the Bible* (Grand Rapids: Baker, 1968), 524–25; GKC §144p.

three uses of "says the LORD [Almighty]," one "the LORD says" (better translated "the declaration of the LORD"), and one "this is what the LORD Almighty says." Then v. 9 reads: "Now implore *God* to be gracious to *us*. With such offerings from your hands, will *he* accept you?" We would assume these to be the words of the prophet except that they are followed by "—says the LORD Almighty." Thus the words are the Lord's, but they are reported in this verse by means of indirect speech. Again God speaks throughout vv. 10–13, with four uses of "says the LORD [Almighty]." Then again in v. 14 is an indictment we would suppose was spoken by the prophet—"Cursed is the cheat who has an acceptable male in his flock and vows to give it, but then sacrifices a blemished animal to *the Lord*." But immediately following is "For *I* am a great king,' says the LORD Almighty." If divine speech is only picked up again here at the end of the verse, then God is giving justification for the curse uttered by the prophet, which is unlikely. It is more likely that vv. 10–14 switch from direct to indirect then back to direct speech (see also 2:6–7).

Another more difficult example of problems in identifying speakers in prophetic discourse is found in 1:6. Here the problem is not in the quotation itself but in the "quotation formula" or "quotative frame."[95] The NIV glosses over the problem by its rather unlikely interpretation (see the commentary at that point). The NRSV has a better and more literal rendering—"And if I am a master, where is the respect due me? says the LORD of hosts to you, O priests, who despise my name." The reader believes the divine quotation closes with "where is the respect due me?" until encountering the phrase, "O priests, who despise my name." Either we should understand the entire clause as uttered by God, who refers to himself at one point in the third person, or the sentence switches from direct to indirect and back to direct quotation again with "O priests."

In Malachi the prophet remains generally in the background, emerging only occasionally outside the quotation formulas. In a book in which most of the speeches to the people are explicitly identified as the Lord's, it is striking to find the prophet apparently speaking as himself in 3:16 and earlier in 2:10–15. The divine quotation in 2:16, however, concluding that paragraph causes one to wonder if we should understand 2:10–15 as another case of divine indirect speech, though here unmarked.[96] Another example might be found in

---

[95] "Quotation formula" is Longacre's term for the narrator's "*X* says/said." C. L. Miller refers to this as a "quotative frame." It is the device by which a speaker/writer gives information regarding the quotation. Cf. Miller, *The Representation of Speech in Biblical Hebrew Narrative: A Linguistic Analysis* (Atlanta: Scholars Press, 1996), 1 *et passim*.

[96] This would violate Miller's principle that "indirect speech in Hebrew always has a matrix clause. The obligatory status of the framing clause points to the subordinate, dependent status of indirect quotation" (*Representation of Speech in Biblical Hebrew Narrative,* 78). In the case of prophetic discourse, such as Malachi, however, perhaps the opening verse, "An oracle: The word of the LORD to Israel through Malachi," serves this purpose.

2:17, where the prophet appears to emerge again at the beginning of the next paragraph. But the Lord's direct speech fills the rest of the paragraph in 3:1–5 with no explicit indication until the end of v. 1.[97] (Also in this paragraph God appears to speak of himself in the third person, but this is a separate issue; see the commentary there.)

Although we might be tempted to explain these examples of apparent speaker overlap in prophetic discourse in terms of an identification or merging of master and messenger, S. A. Meier cautions against such an interpretation. He argues that "pronominal shifts by themselves are a shaky foundation for distinguishing divine from human speech."[98] He quotes K. Callow's observation that some languages "can slip quite naturally from direct to indirect speech in the middle of a long quotation, without any indication other than the change of a pronoun referent."[99] Meier points out that this phenomenon occurs outside prophetic books and is common in Hebrew poetry, "regardless of whether the speakers are divine, prophetic, or otherwise."[100] He describes this as the narrator or poet slipping in and out of character, citing the famous example of God speaking to Moses in Exod 24:1: "Then he said to Moses, 'Come up to the LORD, you and Aaron, Nadab and Abihu, and seventy of the elders of Israel.'"[101] Another example he mentions is in Jer 2:1–3 (RSV):

> The word of the LORD came to me, saying, "Go and proclaim in the hearing of Jerusalem, Thus says the LORD,
>> I remember the devotion of your youth,
>>> your love as a bride,
>> how you followed me in the wilderness,
>>> in a land not sown.
>> Israel was holy to the LORD,
>>> the first fruits of his harvest.
>> All who ate of it became guilty;
>>> evil came upon them,
>>>>> says the LORD."

One thing that adds to the confusion in Malachi is the uncommon style of speech attribution, in which the divine speaker (the device is only used when

---

[97] A problem with taking 2:17 to be indirect speech is the sentence fragment "By saying . . ." According to Miller sentence fragments may occur in direct speech (cf. 1:7), but not indirect speech (*The Representation of Speech in Biblical Hebrew Narrative*, 76).

[98] S. A. Meier, *Speaking of Speaking: Marking Direct Discourse in the Hebrew Bible* (Leiden: Brill, 1992), 208.

[99] K. Callow, *Discourse Considerations in Translating the Word of God* (Grand Rapids: Zondervan, 1974), 18.

[100] Meier, *Speaking of Speaking,* 209. See also Miller, *Representation of Speech in Biblical Hebrew Narrative,* 21–22.

[101] Meier, *Speaking of Speaking,* 37.

God is the speaker) is usually not identified before the speech, as in 1:6 (see also 1:8–11,13–14; 2:2,7–8; 3:5; 4:1). As Meier points out, "The book of Malachi is unique in biblical literature with an explosion of occurrences where non-initial ['amar, "he says"] is the dominant means of expressing DD [direct discourse]. This is the single most characteristic feature of the DD of Malachi."[102]

Meier notes that Malachi is similar to Haggai and Zechariah in particular in "abundantly marking divine speech," with the distinction that Malachi uses the verb āmar, "say," where they prefer něʾum yhwh, "the declaration of Yahweh [NIV, the LORD says]."[103] Twenty-six times (besides 1:1) we are given a quotation formula announcing that the Lord is speaking.[104] It varies between ʾāmar yhwh ṣĕbāʾôt, "says Yahweh of hosts" (NIV, "the LORD Almighty"; twenty-one times); ʾāmar yhwh, "says Yahweh" (NIV, "the LORD"; four times: 1:2,13; 3:13); ʾāmar yhwh ʾelōhê yiśrāʾēl, "says Yahweh the God of Israel" (NIV, "the LORD God of Israel"; once: 2:16); and něʾum yhwh, "the declaration of Yahweh" (NIV, "the LORD says"; once: 1:2). Although some of these could be understood to mark a change of speaker, at least most of them are unnecessary for that purpose, especially in their position later in the sentence or paragraph. They are better understood as markers of prominence or the boundary of a unit of text (a paragraph or subparagraph).

Beekman, Callow, and Kopesec make a useful distinction between natural and marked prominence.[105] The change element of a hortatory text, for example, has a natural prominence in that discourse type but can also be marked for special prominence by various means such as paraphrastic repetition, placing it in the center of a chiasm, or marking it with an ʾāmar yhwh clause. Other elements not naturally prominent can be marked for prominence by various means as well. Another function of the quotation formulas is to indicate the authority on which the speech is based. The quotation formulas used with speeches of Judah, however, probably do mark speaker change, since they always occur before the speech, whereas quotation formulas in divine speeches occur after what they specify (the grammatical object of the verb of speech in the quotation formula) or in the middle of a quoted sentence (2:2). The only exception is in 1:4, where the quotation formula uniquely begins with kōh, "thus."

---

[102] Ibid., 229. It does occur elsewhere (Judg 5:23; Isa 48:22//57:21; 54:1,6,8; 57:19; 59:21; 65:6–7; 66:21; Jer 30:3; 33:11; 49:18; Ezek 34:17[?]; Amos 1:15; 2:3; 5:17,27; 7:3,6; 9:15; Hag 1:8; 2:9; Zech 7:13; Ps 12:5; Eccl 1:2//12:8; Lam 3:24. The imperfect יֹאמַר is similarly used in Isa 1:11,18; 33:10; 40:1,25; 41:21; 66:9; Prov 20:14; 23:7. But by comparison the frequency in Malachi is striking (1:2,9,10,13; 2:2,4,8,16; 3:7,12,13,17; 21[4:3]).

[103] Meier, Speaking of Speaking, 229.

[104] See Blenkinsopp, A History of Prophecy in Israel, 240 for the unfounded claim that these were added later to conform the book to preexilic prophecy.

[105] J. Beekman, K. Callow, and M. Kopesec, The Semantic Structure of Written Communication, 5th ed. (Dallas: SIL, 1981), 109–10, 119–20.

## 5. Structure

To recognize the primary message of Malachi, the reader must not only identify the genre but also determine how the author has arranged the presentation of the book to highlight its central concerns. Although English versions of the prophecy of Malachi divide the book into four chapters and the Hebrew text divides it into only three (4:1–6 counted as 3:19–24), it has become almost axiomatic in Malachi studies that the book comprises six speeches, oracles,[106] or "disputations" and two appendices (4:4,5–6; Hb. 3:22,23–24) that may or may not have been added later.[107] The disputations are identified by the prophet's declaration or charge, followed by his hearers' objection introduced by *waʾămartem*, "but you say," and then the prophet's elaboration and argument (see the previous discussion of Literary Style: Genre).

| | |
|---|---|
| Speech #1—1:2–5 | God's love |
| Speech #2—1:6–2:9 | Unfaithful priests |
| Speech #3—2:10–16 | Divorce |
| Speech #4—2:17–3:5[or 3:6][108] | Divine justice |
| Speech #5—3:6–12 | Tithe |
| Speech #6—3:13–4:3 [Hb. 3:13–21] | Day of judgment |
| Appendix #1—4:4 [Hb. 3:22] | Observe the Law |
| Appendix #2—4:5–6 [Hb. 3:23–24] | Coming of Elijah |

This reality is so blatantly obvious to some that no alternative is considered.[109] Yet inconsistencies and problems with this approach have long been

---

[106] E.g., W. Neil, "Malachi," *IDB,* 3.228–32.

[107] E.g., B. S. Childs calls these appendices "later additions" (*Introduction to the Old Testament as Scripture* [Philadelphia: Fortress, 1979], 495–96). See also Eissfeldt, *The Old Testament: An Introduction,* 441–42; Hill, *Malachi,* 363–66. The latter notes that the integrity of these verses "was questioned as early as Wellhausen . . . and is now widely understood as an editorial summation of Malachi's messages appended to the book as a postscript" (p. 364). It is also regarded by many as an editorial link between the Book of the Twelve or the entire prophetic corpus and both the Torah (3:22) and the Former Prophets (3:23–24).

[108] Some conclude the fourth unit with 3:6. Cf. S. R. Driver, *An Introduction to the Literature of the Old Testament* (Edinburgh: T&T Clark, 1913), 356; G. Van Groningen, *Messianic Revelation in the Old Testament* (Grand Rapids: Baker, 1990), 927; Achtemeier, *Nahum–Malachi,* 186; E. J. Young, *An Introduction to the Old Testament* (Grand Rapids: Eerdmans, 1964), 285; and Kaiser, *Malachi,* 17, 77, 87–88, 116. Achtemeier and others do not consider the final three verses to be later additions. Van Groningen considers the six units to represent six occasions of Malachi's prophetic ministry.

[109] E.g., Chisholm, *Handbook on the Prophets,* 477–83; J. G. McConville, *Exploring the Old Testament: A Guide to the Prophets* (Downers Grove: InterVarsity, 2002), 260–65; M. A. Sweeney, *The Twelve Prophets,* Berit Olam, 2 vols. (Collegeville, Minn.: Michael Glazier, 2000), 2:716–17; Stuart, "Malachi," 3:1247–51.

noticed.[110] For example, Judah is quoted thirteen times in Malachi, not just six, and not just at the beginning of the so-called oracles. Although "oracles" one, four, five, and six begin with a statement by the Lord or the prophet followed by a question from Judah, oracles two and three begin with a statement and question (or vice versa) by the Lord or the prophet followed by a counter-question from Judah. The second and fifth oracles are more complex, with Judah responding to the Lord's answer with a second question (introduced by a second *wa'ămartem;* cf. 1:7; 3:8). Judah is also quoted two more times in 1:12–13 of the second unit, introduced by *be'ĕmārkem,* "when you say [lit., "in your saying"]" and *wa'ămartem,* "and you say." There is also another Judah quotation in 3:14 of the sixth oracle (introduced by *'ămartem*).

The third "oracle" is particularly distinctive in that the divine statement extends over four verses (2:10–13) before Judah responds. When they do respond, it is not to the entirety of God's speech but only to the last part. A similar but less striking variation occurs in the fifth unit if it begins with 3:6. A feature that causes the so-called second oracle to stand out is its length,[111] leading some to break with the traditional divisions and see 2:1–9 as a separate oracle[112] or to join it to the third oracle in 2:10–16,[113] leaving it without the formal marking as an oracle.

M. H. Floyd concludes that in view of the "impasse" caused by the false assumption that "Malachi's stylistic consistency shows the text to be generically uniform in all its main parts," the assumption that Malachi comprises a series of six oracles identifiable by the stylistic feature of statement-question-answer "must now be abandoned."[114] He also rejects "what often seems to be a corollary of this view: that generic diversity among the individual units would prevent the whole book from having any compositional integrity.[115] Floyd's alternative structure is to identify two main sections following the introduction in 1:2–5: (1) 1:6–2:16 containing two speeches about profaning the cult, and (2) 2:17–3:24[4:6] containing two speeches about Judah's cynicism.[116] The problem with this analysis is that it makes a major division at 2:17 in the middle of what I consider to be a unified discourse. I believe there

---

[110] E.g., Floyd, *Minor Prophets,* 564–66. J. Nogalski argues that the book is shaped by the question/response format but acknowledges that "the style is not fixed as an absolute pattern without deviation" (*Redactional Processes in the Book of the Twelve,* BZAW 218 [Berlin: Walter de Gruyter, 1993], 182–83).

[111] Hill explains the length of this oracle as owing to the "privileged position" of its priestly audience (*Malachi,* 173).

[112] E.g., Verhoef, *Haggai and Malachi,* 162.

[113] E.g., Kaiser, *Malachi,* 17.

[114] Floyd, *Minor Prophets,* 567.

[115] Ibid.

[116] Ibid., 568.

are in fact three main sections in Malachi corresponding to three main themes in the book.[117]

Another problem with the standard form-critical analysis is that it tends to lose sight of the book's unity, treating it as just a set of six loosely connected oracles. R. L. Alden, for example, judged that "Malachi did not start with an outline. Instead he moved from topic to topic and occasionally went back and picked up an idea touched on earlier in the book."[118] Keil attempted to indicate some unity by recognizing only three sections following the introduction:[119]

| | |
|---|---|
| 1:2–5 | Introduction |
| 1:6–2:9 | The priests are accused. |
| 2:10–16 | The people are accused. |
| 2:17–4:6 | Blessings are promised and the ungodly are warned. |

Young identified only two main divisions:[120]

| | |
|---|---|
| chaps. 1–2 | Judah's sin and apostasy described |
| chaps. 3–4 | Judgment and blessing predicted |

Kaiser employed a fivefold homiletic outline:[121]

| | |
|---|---|
| 1:1–5 | A Call to Respond to God's Love |
| 1:6–14 | A Call to Be Authentic |
| 2:1–16 | A Call to Love God Totally |
| 2:17–3:12 | A Call to Trust an Unchanging God |
| 3:13–4:6 | A Call to Take Inventory |

Whereas such structures may be pedagogically useful, they have not been generally accepted as adequately accounting for the data of Malachi's text. Hill has attempted a "rhetorical outline of Malachi" in terms of a chiastic structure with 2:17–3:5 in the center.[122] But apart from recognizing the presence of recurring themes in the book, this structure too is unconvincing. Why should 2:17–3:5 be considered the most prominent speech of the book? The command to stop breaking faith with wives is important, but it does not serve as a unifying theme for the book. His structural display also passes over 1:9–2:9, which contains the first command of the book, to cease the hypocritical offerings.

I believe that a more unified, verifiable, and satisfying structure is possible if Longacre's theory of the textlinguistic structure of hortatory discourse is

---

[117] Clendenen, "The Structure of Malachi, 3–17; id., "Old Testament Prophecy as Hortatory Text," 336–41; id., "Postholes, Postmodernism, and the Prophets: Toward a Textlinguistic Paradigm," in *The Challenge of Postmodernism* (Wheaton: Bridgepoint, 1995), 135–39.

[118] R. L. Alden, "Malachi," EBC (Grand Rapids: Zondervan, 1985), 7.708.

[119] Keil, *The Twelve Minor Prophets,* 2:427–28.

[120] Young, *An Introduction to the Old Testament,* 285.

[121] Kaiser, *Malachi.*

[122] Hill, *Malachi,* xxxvi.

taken as the starting point (see the previous section, Literary Style: Malachi as Hortatory Discourse).[123] Identifying paragraphs or subparagraphs as expressing either situation, command, or motivation (on the basis of the grammatical structure of the paragraph) uncovers a pattern of inverted repetition or chiasm. Whereas such chiasms are often identified on the basis of repeated words,[124] here the chiasm appears in the semantic structure. There are three such chiasms in the book, identifying three divisions, addresses, or embedded discourses. That is, each exhibits an *a b c b a* structure. In such chiastic structures with a single element in the center, the focus usually is assumed to be on the center element. In the first and second addresses the center element is the command, which is also the nuclear or most prominent element of hortatory, that which unifies the discourse. The element naturally prominent in hortatory, then, is also rhetorically underlined in the first two addresses. The final address, however, has two command sections that begin and end the chiasm, whereas the situation element (concerned with complacency toward serving God) is raised in prominence by placing it in the center.

|                        |                |                           |          |
| ---------------------- | -------------- | ------------------------- | -------- |
|                        | 1A Motivation  | God's Love                | 1:2–5    |
|                        | 1B Situation   | Failure to Honor God      | 1:6–9    |
| Priests Exhorted to    | 1C Command     | Stop Vain Offerings       | 1:10     |
| Honor God              | 1B' Situation  | Profaning God's           |          |
| 1:2–2:9                |                | Name                      | 1:11–14  |
|                        | 1A' Motivation | Results of Disobedience   | 2:1–9    |
|                        |                |                           |          |
|                        | 2A Motivation  | Spiritual Unity           | 2:10a,b  |
|                        | 2B Situation   | Faithlessness             | 2:10c–15b |
| Judah Exhorted to      | 2C Command     | Stop Acting Faithlessly   | 2:15c–16 |
| Faithfulness           |                |                           |          |
| 2:10–3:6               | 2B' Situation  | Complaints of God's Injustice | 2:17 |
|                        | 2A' Motivation | Coming Messenger of Judgment | 3:1–6 |
|                        |                |                           |          |
|                        | 3A Command     | Return to God with Tithes | 3:7–10b  |
|                        | 3B Motivation  | Future Blessing           | 3:10c–12 |
| Judah Exhorted to      | 3C Situation   | Complacency toward Serving God | 3:13–14 |
| Return to God          | 3B' Motivation | The Coming Day            | 3:15–21  |
| 3:7–24                 | 3A' Command    | Remember the Law          | 3:22–24  |

---

[123] Cf. my initial argument in Clendenen, "The Structure of Malachi," 3–17.

[124] E.g., see the discussion of Mal 1:11.

In each address, the parallel section (e.g., 1B′, 1A′), supplements the first. For example, the situation concerned in the first address is the priests' failure to honor God *and* their profaning his name.

The most obvious reason for arranging the elements in the third address differently is that it allows the book to conclude with the directive to "remember the law of my servant Moses" in the last paragraph (4:4). Furthermore, rearranging the elements in this concluding division causes it to stand out from the other two, thus raising it in prominence to the status of climax.[125] This prominence is also achieved by the use of two command constituents and by placing it last in the book. Finally, the third address is marked as the most prominent address by the occurrence of the verb *šûb,* "turn, return," at the beginning in 3:7 and again at the end in 4:6.

The disputation form by which the book is commonly divided into six oracles is here referred to as pseudodialogue.[126] It is found in every situation section and in the motivation sections that open the first and third divisions (it is viewed here, then, as opening a major division only twice). This suggests that it has two primary functions. One is to make vivid the charges against Judah by letting the readers hear the offensive words from their own mouths. The other is to establish a topic of discourse. In every use but one it involves Judah asking a question (the exception is in 1:13 in the situation section, where it is an exclamation).

## 6. Message and Purpose

Malachi's prophecy indicts the religious leadership of the day and chides God's people for their spiritual apathy and their skepticism and cynicism concerning God's plan for their future. It also calls the people to correct their wrong attitudes of worship by trusting God with genuine faith as living Lord. Furthermore, it warns the people of their immoral behavior toward one another and calls for their repentance lest they be terrorized at the coming of the Lord. Since Malachi's prophecy is a unified hortatory discourse, its message may be summarized by weaving together the situation, command, and motivation elements.

1. *Situation.* Malachi was faced with the failure of the priests of Judah to fear the Lord and to serve the people conscientiously during difficult times. This had contributed to Judah's indifference toward the will of God. Blaming their economic and social troubles on the Lord's supposed unfaithfulness to them, the people were treating one another faithlessly, especially breaking

---

[125] See R. E. Longacre's discussion of the principle on which this is based in "Discourse Peak as a Zone of Turbulence" in *Beyond the Sentence* (Ann Arbor: Karome, 1985), 81–92; id., *Joseph,* 18.

[126] See the previous section, "Speech Attribution in Malachi."

marriage covenants and withholding offerings in support of the Levitical priests and the landless poor.

2. *Command.* Consequently, Malachi commands them to return to the Lord by renewing their commitment to his instruction, especially by restoring worship that honored his name, loyalty to marriage covenants, and faithful handling of their material possessions.

3. *Motivation.* He bases his commands on (1) the Lord's demonstration of love for Israel (1:2), (2) their spiritual and covenant unity with God and with one another (2:10), and (3) the assurance of a coming day when the Lord will bring final redemption and judgment, blessing those who fear him and removing the wicked (3:1–6; 3:16–4:3).

The message and purpose of Malachi may also be unfolded through an ethical examination of the three addresses. In his first book on Old Testament ethics published 20 years ago, C. J. H. Wright declared his agenda "to provide a comprehensive framework within which Old Testament ethics can be organized and understood" and by that means to release "the ethical relevance and power of the Old Testament."[127] His conviction is that ethics cannot be derived from the Old Testament piecemeal ("quoting random texts that seem to be relevant"[128]) but as a systemic whole. Recognizing that ethics and theology are inextricable, his program begins by outlining "the basic framework of belief that lies behind the moral teaching of the Old Testament."[129] Wright presents that basic framework as what he calls an "ethical triangle" with a theological angle, a social angle, and an economic angle. In other words, Israel's ethics grew out of (1) the nature of *God* and their relationship to him, (2) their identity as a *people* and their relationships and responsibilities to one another, and (3) their relationship to the *land,* which represented their material environment and possessions. The parallel with Malachi is that these are the exact themes found in the three discourses and in the same order—God, people, and land.

### (1) The Theological Angle

Ethics must begin with who God is and who we are in relation to him. Wright explains that "Old Testament ethics are God-centred in origin, in history, in content and in motive."[130]

---

[127] C. J. H. Wright, *An Eye for an Eye: The Place of Old Testament Ethics Today* (Downers Grove: InterVarsity, 1983), 9, 16.

[128] Ibid., 13.

[129] Ibid., 15. He rightly considers the subject matter to be not just Israel's ethical understanding but the ethics divinely revealed in the OT. See also id., *Walking in the Ways of the Lord: The Ethical Authority of the Old Testament* (Downers Grove: InterVarsity, 1995), 111.

[130] Wright, *Eye for an Eye,* 21.

Ethical instruction in the Bible does not depend on "blind obedience" but is based on the principle that "God acts first and calls people to respond." Malachi demonstrates this principle in the opening paragraph: "I have loved you" (*ʾahavtî ʾetkem*). Malachi points to a historical event of the past, to God's choosing Jacob over Esau and to his consequent faithful treatment of Israel/ Judah in spite of their wickedness contrasted with his just treatment of Edom for their wickedness. Just as Israel's afflictions had not been accidental or merely the work of men, the same can be said of Edom's destruction. God had cursed Edom forever as a demonstration of his just administration over the entire world (1:4–5). But whereas they would become known as *gĕbûl rišʿâ*, (lit.) "a territory of wickedness" because of God's justice (1:4), Israel would be known throughout the world as *ʾereṣ ḥēpeṣ*, (lit.) "a land of delight" (3:12). This was not because they had pleased God (although they eventually would), but because God was faithful—"Because I, Yahweh, have not changed, you descendants of Jacob have not been destroyed" (3:6, HCSB). The survival of Israel's relationship with Yahweh "depended totally on his faithfulness and loyalty to his own character and promises, not on their own success in keeping the law."[131]

Old Testament ethics was founded on God's sovereignty over history, which should have enhanced Israel's motive for obedience. His sovereignty was not only manifested in redeeming his people and judging their enemies in the past but in disciplining his people in the present. Israel's bitter attitude toward God shown in their opening question in Mal 1:2 ("How have you loved us?") and throughout Malachi demonstrates that they were suffering and considered God to blame. They were whining because God was not responding favorably to their offerings (2:13).

God never denies in Malachi being the immediate cause of Judah's troubles, but he places the blame on their shoulders. He was Israel's "Father" in that he had begotten them, and thus he became their Master (1:6; cf. 2:10). It was on that basis that he demanded *kābōd* and *môrāʾ*, "honor" and "fear." The priests were charged with failing to respond in this way to God's provisions and blessings at his "table" (1:7). Their carelessness in teaching God's ways truthfully (2:6–7) and in overseeing Israel's worship had so corrupted the sacrificial system that it was an insult to God. Their treatment of his blessings gave them no right to ask for or expect God's favor (1:9). In fact, God announced that his pleasure in them was over, and their continued rituals were *ḥinnām*, "useless" (1:10). Malachi indicates that the priests had already begun experiencing the effects of the divine "curse" on them (2:2). We are not told the exact nature of their judgment, but v. 9 clarifies that they had already

---

[131] Ibid., 23. The other side of this fact, however, is that the Lord's faithful sovereignty would eventually bring about his people's conformity to his law (Jer 31:33).

begun to be "despised and humiliated before all the people."

But God's rebuke and discipline of the priests was in order that his covenant with the priestly tribe of Levi should continue *(lihyôt bĕrîtî ʾet-lēwî,* 2:4; cf. 3:3–4). This covenant was not a conditional contract but a grant. God had promised "life and peace" *(haḥayyîm wĕhaššālôm),* "and I gave them to him." It was in response to the Lord's covenant and his blessings that the Levites had initially feared him and trembled at his name (2:5). They had been faithful as his messengers (2:7), but their priestly descendants had not. Nevertheless, the Lord's control of history meant that his covenant with Levi had not been annulled any more than had his covenant with Jacob. He would "purify the Levites ["sons of Levi"] and refine them like gold and silver" so that they would present offerings to the Lord "in righteousness," and Judah's offerings would "please the LORD as in days gone by, as in former years" (3:3–4).

God's promise of a future redemption for the righteous is another aspect of his sovereignty over history that is foundational for Old Testament ethics. Strikingly in Malachi, it is the nations who are first mentioned as objects of redemption.

Third, Old Testament ethics was God-centered in content. The shape of Old Testament ethics was largely determined by God's character. As he is not only faithful but diligent and persistent in his relationships (2:4; 3:6,17), he demands that same behavior of his people in their relationships (2:10,14). As his love is equitable and impartial toward all his people, he expects his people to be impartial in their treatment of others (2:9; 3:5). As he is holy, his people must be holy (Lev 11:44–45; 19:2; 20:26; 21:8; Matt 5:48; 1 Pet 1:15–16; cf. Eph 5:1); and "God's own holiness is thoroughly practical," including generosity, justice, integrity, considerate behavior, impartiality, and honesty.[132] It was precisely because Israel during Malachi's time had lost sight of what God had done for them that they were failing to obey his law. They had lost not only the motive but also the model for obedience.[133] Idolatry was so destructive to Israel because a different "god" resulted in a different ethic.[134] This is why the ethical triangle must begin with the theological angle and why Malachi begins with a focus on how God was being viewed, treated, and portrayed by Judah's teaching leadership.

## *(2) The Social Angle*

The faithfulness God had demonstrated to Israel, his love for his people in spite of their rebelliousness, should have inspired similar faithfulness in their

---

[132] Ibid., 27, based on Lev 19. See also pp. 26–32.
[133] Cf. ibid., 29. Wright cites Isa 1:2–4; 5:1–7; Jer 2:1–13; 7:21–26; Hos 13:4–6; Mic 6:3–5.
[134] Ibid., 31.

relationships with one another (cf. Matt 18:22–35). But they responded with treachery. God's plan of redemption did not just involve the rescue of individuals and their transport to heaven. Rather, it involved the formation and redemption of a community through which God would bring global blessing and reverse the curse of Babel. This is why "so much of [the Old Testament's] ethical thrust is necessarily social." It's concern is not just to enable "the individual to lead a privately upright life before God" (though this is important), but to promote and protect "the moral and spiritual health of that whole community . . . who in their social life would embody those qualities of righteousness, peace, justice and love which reflect God's own character and were his original purpose for mankind."[135]

God had purposed that Israel should be a kingdom of priests to glorify him among the nations (cf. Exod 19:6; Rev 1:6). Although during the biblical period they mostly failed at this,[136] the Old Testament nevertheless describes the kind of society they were supposed to be and how they missed this ideal. Although the social angle of the ethical triangle is not out of the picture in Mal 1:2–2:9, it is particularly in view beginning in 2:10 ("Don't all of us have one Father? Didn't one God create us? Why then do we act treacherously against one another, profaning the covenant of our fathers?" [HCSB]). The relationship of individual Israelites to one another was grounded in their common relationship to God as their Father.

The common practice of separating 2:10–16 from 2:17–3:5 or 3:6 as two separate oracles misses the coherence of 2:10–3:6 in the theme of faithfulness and justice for one's spiritual siblings. Verse 10b is a general charge against Judah for their treachery against fellow covenant members. This general reference to treachery against "one another" is first and most prominently made specific in the issue of marital violation in 2:11–16, culminating in the charge of injustice against one's wife. But other expressions of treachery are included before this second discourse closes. The topic appears to change in Mal 2:17 ("You have wearied the LORD with your words. 'How have we wearied him?' you ask. By saying, 'All who do evil are good in the eyes of the LORD, and he is pleased with them' or 'Where is the God of justice?' "). But in fact the audience's complaints about injustice in 2:17 and the prophetic announcement of coming judgment in 3:1–6 are closely related to the theme of unfaithfulness found in 2:10–16. The link can be found not only in the "one another" of 2:10b but also in the term *ḥāmās* in v. 16, commonly rendered "violence" but best understood as "injustice." Judah's attitudes toward the Lord surface in the words Malachi

---

[135] Ibid., 34–35.

[136] Malachi shows God demonstrating his glory to Israel through the nations rather than through Israel to the nations. Cf. 1:5,11,14.

perceptively and dramatically places in their mouths in 2:17. They were justifying their own lack of just behavior by pointing to the Lord's lack of justice. Not only had they been committing treachery against their wives and others, but 3:5 charges they had also been practicing sorcery (probably to harm others; cf. Ezek 13:18,20), adultery, swearing to a lie *[šeqer]* (again probably to harm others; cf. Lev 6:2–5; 19:12), oppressing widows and the fatherless, extorting wages, and oppressing resident aliens.[137] As God had been a "witness" to the marriage covenants they broke (2:14), he was also a witness (lit. "a hurrying witness") of these crimes of injustice and would come "swiftly" to vindicate those who had been wronged. Judah's blindly hypocritical desire for justice would be satisfied when the Lord would come against all those in Judah who practiced treachery and oppression of the weak.

In 2:10b Judah's unfaithfulness is said to profane or violate Israel's covenant with God. Thus violation of social (horizontal) responsibilities of the covenant amounts to violation of the religious (vertical) responsibilities. These two dimensions of Judah's sinful behavior receive separate focus in 2:11–16 (see commentary on these verses). Judah's vertical responsibilities are again in view in 2:17–3:4 as they charge God with injustice and he responds with a commitment to purify the people and their worship. Then the discourse closes with the horizontal dimension again as the Lord's purification is said to include judgment against Judah's treacherous behavior (3:5–6).

### *(3) The Economic Angle*

The economic angle of the Old Testament ethical triangle is concerned with Israel's attitudes toward and treatment of their material possessions. This is likewise Malachi's primary concern in the final discourse (3:7–4:6[Hb. 3:24]). The focus of the economic angle is the land, representing the material aspects of God's gifts to his people. The land was "*not* just a neutral stage where the drama unfolds" but "a fundamentally theological entity."[138]

Although God gave Israel the land as their inheritance, they were to live there in dependence on him: "The land is mine and you are but aliens and my

---

[137] As A. H. Konkel points out, the *gēr* "enjoys the rights of assistance, protection, and religious participation. He has the right of gleaning (Lev 19:10; 23:22), participation in the tithe (Deut 14:29), the Sabbath year (Lev 25:6), and the cities of refuge (Num 35:15). His participation in religious feasts assumes the acceptance of circumcision (Exod 12:48; cf. Deut 16:11,14). He may bring offerings and is obligated to the regulations of purity (Lev 17:8–16). There is legislation for religious offenses (Lev 24:22), such as blasphemy of the name of Yahweh (Lev 24:16) or idolatrous practice (Lev 20:2). The sojourner is under divine protection (10:18; Ps 146:9); Israelites must love the alien as themselves (Deut 10:19), for that is what they themselves were. In daily life there was to be no barrier between the alien and the Israelite" (*NIDOTTE*, 1:837–38).

[138] Wright, *Eye for an Eye*, 50.

tenants" (Lev 25:23).[139] The land and its fruits were to be a reminder of Israel's dependence and the Lord's dependability. "He was a God *worthy* of obedience; his response to human behavior would be consistent and dependable, not a matter of arbitrary whim. He could be pleased, but not humoured."[140] The emphasis on the tithe, then, in Malachi's final discourse is directly connected to the issue of contempt for God in the first two discourses, especially to Judah's questioning of divine justice.

The situation in the final discourse is that Judah has ceased bringing their tithes to the sanctuary out of thankfulness to God for his blessings. They have in fact concluded that God has ceased to bless obedient faith. They are exhorted here to "return" to the Lord by remembering the Law of Moses and bringing their tithes and other contributions. Wright argues that one's attitude toward material possessions is a kind of thermometer that measures the health of one's relationship with God and with other people (see Neh 5:1–13; Matt 6:24).[141] This is why "failure to honour God in the material realm cannot be compensated for by religiosity in the spiritual realm."[142] This insight may suggest the relationship between Malachi's three addresses concerned with vain offerings (1:2–2:9), treachery in relationships (2:10–3:5), and the withholding of tithes (3:6–4:6 [3:24]). One's health and wholeness as a child of God is determined first by one's attitude toward and relationship with God, thus the theological angle; second by one's attitude toward and relationship with others, thus the social angle; and finally by one's attitude toward and use of one's possessions, the economic angle.

Thus, whereas the focus of Malachi's first address is on the theological angle, the social angle (i.e., the priests' poor and prejudicial instruction that "caused many to stumble," 2:6–9) and the economic angle (i.e., the best animals withheld from God, 1:8,13–14) enter as well. Likewise, the second division's focus on the social angle does not eliminate the theological angle (desecrating the sanctuary, 2:11; regarding God as unjust, 2:17; the need for righteous offerings, 3:4) and the economic angle (corruption and oppression, 3:5) from the prophet's attention.

The third and final discourse begins with the command to return to the Lord by bringing the tithes and contributions. This makes explicit the relationship between the theological and economic angles. The final refrain of the theme of divine justice and faithfulness in 3:13–4:3[Hb. 3:21] also returns to the theological angle. Judah has been withholding "the whole tithe" because of their claim that "it is futile to serve God" (3:14). Further-

---

[139] See Wright's discussion of the verse in *God's People in God's Land,* 58–64.
[140] Wright, *Eye for an Eye,* 51–53, citing 53.
[141] Ibid., 59–62.
[142] Ibid., 60.

more, the social angle is implied in the reference to the tithe as "food in my house" (3:10). The food was not for God but for the Levitical priests and the landless poor in Israel. The command is for Judah to "bring the whole tithe into the storehouse."

The Book of Malachi begins with a focus on what God had done in the past—"I have loved you." It ends with a focus on the future. The Lord declares that a historical day is coming on which "all the arrogant and everyone who commits wickedness will become stubble" (4:1[3:19]). But Malachi also assures those in Israel who fear the Lord that they are his *segullâ,* his "treasured possession." He is preparing a day when they will be abundantly and compassionately rewarded for their faithfulness (3:17). They will be healed and restored to joy and "will go out and leap like calves released from the stall" (4:2[Hb. 3:20]). They will also "trample the wicked, for they will be ashes under the soles of your feet on the day I am preparing" (4:3[Hb. 3:21], HCSB). This future dimension heightens the ethical impact of the book. Right behavior is grounded in the redemptive dimension as response of gratitude consistent with what God has done in the past. It is also grounded in the eschatological dimension as confidence that the God who began his work of righteous redemption will complete it, eliminating evil and vindicating the righteous, establishing justice and peace. God's faithful love in the past as elaborated in 1:2–5 and the coming day of the Lord announced in 3:16–4:6 together were to be the motivating factors for all the exhortations in the book.

The eschatological aspect of God's activity in history on the one hand, in judgment and also in redemption, and the past redemptive aspect on the other hand, were the two ends of God's sovereign work of design. "The combination of these two poles of Israel's historical faith gave immense ethical importance to the present. What I do here and now matters because of what God has done in the past and what he will do in the future."[143]

Malachi speaks to the hearts of a troubled people whose circumstances of financial insecurity, religious skepticism, and personal disappointments are similar to those God's people often experience or encounter today. The book contains a message that must not be overlooked by those who wish to encounter the Lord and his kingdom and to lead others to a similar encounter. Its message concerns God's loving and holy character and his unchanging and glorious purposes for his people. Our God calls his people to genuine worship, to fidelity both to himself and to one another, and to expectant faith in what he is doing and says he will do in this world and for his people.

---

[143] Wright, *Eye for an Eye,* 26.

——————————— *OUTLINE OF MALACHI* ———————————

Introduction (1:1)
  I. The Priests Are Exhorted to Honor the Lord (1:2–2:9)
    1. Positive Motivation: The Lord's Love (1:2–5)
    2. Situation: Failure to Honor the Lord (1:6–9)
    3. Command: Stop the Vain Offerings (1:10)
    4. Situation: Priests Profaning the Lord's Name by their Worship
       (1:11–14)
    5. Negative Motivation: The Results of Disobedience (2:1–9)
  II. Judah Exhorted to Faithfulness (2:10–3:6)
    1. Positive Motivation: Spiritual Kinship among Israel (2:10a)
    2. Situation: Faithlessness against a Covenant Member
       (2:10b–15a)
    3. Command: Stop Acting Faithlessly (2:15b–16)
    4. Situation: Complaints of the Lord's Injustice (2:17)
    5. Negative Motivation: Coming Messenger of Judgment (3:1–6)
 III. Judah Exhorted to Return and Remember (3:7–4:6)
    1. First Command: Return to the Lord with Tithes (3:7–10a)
    2. Positive Motivation: Future Blessing (3:10b–12)
    3. Situation: Complacency toward Serving the Lord (3:13–15)
    4. Motivation: The Coming Day (3:16–4:3)
    5. Second Command: Remember the Law (4:4–6)

INTRODUCTION (1:1)
I.  THE PRIESTS EXHORTED NOT TO DISHONOR THE LORD
    (1:2–2:9)
    1.  Positive Motivation: The Lord's Love (1:2–5)
        (1)  Love for Israel (1:2)
        (2)  End of Edom (1:3–4)
        (3)  Future of Israel (1:5)
    2.  Situation: The Priests' Failure to Honor the Lord (1:6–9)
        (1)  Indictment against the Priests (1:6)
        (2)  Evidence against the Priests (1:7–9)
    3.  Command: Stop the Pointless Offerings (1:10)
    4.  Situation: The Priests' Worship Profaning the Lord's Name
        (1:11–14)
        (1)  Prophecy of Gentile Worship (1:11)
        (2)  Indictment against the Priests (1:12)
        (3)  Evidence against the Priests (1:13–14a)
        (4)  Prophecy of Gentile Worship (1:14b)
    5.  Negative Motivation: The Results of Disobedience (2:1–9)
        (1)  Curse against the Priests (2:1–4)
        (2)  Covenant with the Priests (2:5–7)
        (3)  Corruption and Contempt of the Priests (2:8–9)

---

## INTRODUCTION (1:1)

**[1]An oracle: The word of the LORD to Israel through Malachi.**

The NIV has followed the Hebrew closely in this opening verse (except that
"through Malachi" is literally "by the hand of Malachi"). The term *maśśā᾽*,
"oracle," is also used in the first verse of Nahum and Habakkuk to introduce
their contents.[1] Otherwise it introduces smaller units within the prophetic

---

[1] M. H. Floyd cites this argument against the common view of considering Malachi as a third
appendix to Zechariah ("The מַשָּׂא *[maśśā᾽]* as a Type of Prophetic Book," *JBL* 121 [2002]: 415–
16).

books, especially Isaiah.[2] Its meaning has often been explained in the past as "burden" by association with uses where a literal "load" or "burden" is in view (cf. Exod 23:5; Num 4:24,32; 11:11; 2 Sam 15:33; Isa 22:25; 46:1–2; Jer 17:1,22,24,27). This is actually a homonym of the present word, which has no such connotation. This word is now usually translated by the more general term "oracle" or perhaps simply "utterance" or "pronouncement."[3] Dillard and Longman argue that its use predominantly in oracles against foreign nations (Isa 13:1; 14:28; 15:1; 17:1; 19:1; 21:1,11,13; 23:1; Nah 1:1; Zech 9:1) suggests that the narrower designation "war oracle" or "oracle against a foreign nation" would be more appropriate, at least in some cases.[4] But the word also is used of messages of judgment against Israel (Isa 22:1; 30:6; Ezek 12:10; Hab 1:1) or against an individual (2 Kgs 9:25). Soggin suggests "charge," which would fit most of the word's uses in prophetic contexts.[5] The word sometimes, however, could refer to a message other than one of judgment (cf. Jer 23:33,34,36,38; Zech 12:1). R. Weis has recently argued that a *maśśāʾ* is a distinct prophetic genre, and the term is better rendered, "prophetic exposition of divine revelation."[6] This genre follows a rhetorical pattern consisting of three elements that M. H. Floyd has summarized as follows:

> First, an assertion is made, directly or indirectly, about Yahweh's involvement in a particular historical situation or course of events. Second, this assertion serves to clarify the implications of a previous revelation from Yahweh that is alluded to, referred to, or quoted from. Third, this assertion also provides the basis for directives concerning appropriate reactions or responses to Yahweh's initiative, or for insights into how Yahweh's initiative affects the future.[7]

This may prove to be a helpful approach in understanding the relationship among the various biblical examples of this genre. In the case of Malachi, Floyd probably is too specific in pointing to the historical situation alluded to in Mal 3:16. He probably is correct, however, in supposing that the previous revelation in view is the Pentateuch. The question is how it should be applied "to particular situations in which the community finds itself." The directive expected in a *maśśāʾ* is summarized in the command in Mal 4:4 to remember the Torah.[8]

---

[2] It is found in 2 Kgs 9:25; Isa 13:1; 14:28; 15:1; 17:1; 19:1; 21:1,11,13; 22:1; 23:1; 30:6; Jer 23:33–38 (8x); Ezek 12:10; Nah 1:1; Hab 1:1; Zech 9:1; 12:1; Lam 2:14; 2 Chr 24:27.

[3] Cf. J. A. Naudé, "*Maśśāʾ* in the Old Testament with a Special Reference to the Prophets," *OTSWA* 12 (1969): 91–100.

[4] R. B. Dillard and T. Longman III, *An Introduction to the Old Testament* (Grand Rapids: Zondervan, 1994), 406. They do not mention this sense in their comments on Malachi.

[5] J. A. Soggin, *Introduction to the Old Testament,* OTL (Louisville: WJKP, 1989), 303.

[6] R. D. Weis, "Oracle," *ABD* 5:28–29.

[7] Floyd, "The מַשָּׂא (*maśśāʾ*) as a Type of Prophetic Book," 409.

[8] Ibid., 417–18. Thus Floyd sees "little ground for the commonly held view that 3:22–24[Eng. 4:4–6] consititutes an appendix or secondary addition to the book."

Several other prophets also are titled "the word of the LORD" (Hosea, Joel, Micah, Zephaniah). By contrast, Jeremiah and Amos are both called "the words of [the prophet]," but in both cases the heading goes on to make clear that the Lord was the prophet's source. Several prophets begin by reporting that "the word of the LORD" came to the prophet (Jeremiah, Ezekiel, Jonah, Haggai, Zechariah).[9]

The Lord's words are directed "to Israel" *(ʾel yiśrāʾēl)* elsewhere only in Jer 30:4, and there it includes Judah (lit., "These are the words Yahweh spoke to Israel and to Judah"). The recipients of the Lord's prophetic messages are more commonly given as the prophet himself (Ezek 1:3; Hos 1:1; Joel 1:1; Mic 1:1; Zeph 1:1; Zech 1:1). Those for or about whom the messages were intended are sometimes expressed by the phrase "concerning *[ʿal]* . . ." (Isa 1:1; Amos 1:1; Mic 1:1; Zech 12:1) or "about *[lĕ]* . . ." (Obad 1). Closest to the wording of Mal 1:1 is Zech 12:1 (NRSV): "An Oracle. The word of the LORD concerning *[ʿal]* Israel." The phrase "to Israel" in Malachi, then, seems to de-emphasize the prophet's importance and to portray the messages as coming more directly from the Lord to the people.

This feature is heightened by the addition of (lit.) "by the hand of Malachi." The phrase "by [or "in/into"] the hand of *X*" is a common Hebrew idiom sometimes expressing agency (Judg 15:18, "You have granted this great victory by the hand of your servant" [NRSV]) or, more commonly, authority or power over someone (Num 4:28,33; 7:8; 33:1; 2 Sam 10:10; 16:8; 18:2). One is said to speak "by the hand of" a messenger in Prov 26:6 and Esth 1:12 (cf. also 1 Sam 11:7; 16:20). God first speaks "by the hand of" a prophet in Exod 9:35, where he speaks "by the hand of Moses" (cp. Exod 34:29, where as Moses descended from Mount Sinai we are told [lit.] "the two tablets of testimony were in the hand of Moses").[10] He also spoke "by the hand of" the prophets Samuel (1 Sam 28:17; 1 Chr 11:3), Ahijah (1 Kgs 12:15; 14:18; 15:29), Jehu (1 Kgs 16:7,12), Joshua (1 Kgs 16:34), Elijah (1 Kgs 17:16; 2 Kgs 9:36; 10:10), Jonah (2 Kgs 14:25), "[all his servants] the prophets (2 Kgs 17:23; 21:10; 24:2; Ezek 38:17; Zech 7:7,12), Isaiah (Isa 20:2), Jeremiah (Jer 37:2; 50:1), and Haggai (Hag 1:1,3; 2:1).

Directing the prophetic word "to Israel" might seem somewhat anachronistic in such a postexilic situation. But Judah's leaders knew that God rec-

---

[9] J. D. W. Watts distinguishes an opening title, called a "superscription," from an opening sentence, called an "incipit" ("Superscriptions and Incipits in the Book of the Twelve," in *Reading and Hearing the Book of the Twelve* [Atlanta: SBL, 2000], 111).

[10] God also speaks בְּיַד מֹשֶׁה, "by the hand of Moses" according to Lev 8:36; 10:11; Num 17:5; 27:23; Josh 20:2; 21:2; 1 Kgs 8:53,56; 2 Chr 35:6. The phrase בְּיַד מֹשֶׁה occurs thirty-one times in the Hb. Bible, of which thirteen are with the verb צוה, "command."

ognized them as the current remnant of his covenant people.[11] M. Breneman, for example, has pointed out that "one of the chief objectives of Ezra-Nehemiah was to show the Jews that they constituted the continuation of the preexilic Jewish community, the Israelite community that God had chosen." By allusions to the exodus and by emphasizing God's continuing providential care, the temple, the Law, the feasts of Passover and Tabernacles, the writer was assuring them that "they represented the continuation of God's redemptive plan."[12] Thus the people of the restored Jewish community to whom Malachi wrote were recipients of God's promises to Israel and were obligated to obey the regulations of the covenant (4:4 specifies Moses' law was given "for all Israel").[13]

## I. THE PRIESTS EXHORTED NOT TO DISHONOR THE LORD (1:2–2:9)

Malachi's first address is governed by the ironic exhortation in 1:10, "Oh, that one of you would shut the temple doors." It is directed against the priests of the postexilic temple. Despite their responsibility under the covenant of Levi (cf. 2:4,8) to be the Lord's messengers of Torah (2:7), they were dishonoring the Lord (1:6), particularly in their careless attitude toward the offerings (1:8). Failing to take their responsibilities to the Lord seriously, they had become political pawns of the influential in Israel who used religion to maintain respectability (2:9). The priests are here exhorted to stop the empty worship and to begin honoring the Lord with pure offerings and faithful service. As motivation the Lord declares his love for them (and for all the people; 1:2–5) and threatens them with humiliation and removal from his service (cf. 2:1–3,9).

### 1. Positive Motivation: The Lord's Love (1:2–5)

These verses contain the first exchange between the Lord and Judah. Judah responds to God's affirmation of his love for them with an insolent question expressing doubt. Such an opening to the book suggests that Judah's questioning of God's love will be a major theme. Unlike preexilic

---

[11] Cf. Mal 1:1–2,5; 2:10,12; 3:6; Ezra 3:1; 6:16–17; 7:10; Neh 7:73; 9:1–2; 11:3,20; 12:47; Zech 12:1.

[12] M. Breneman, *Ezra, Nehemiah, Esther,* NAC (Nashville: Broadman & Holman, 1993), 50. Also see W. J. Dumbrell, "Malachi and the Ezra-Nehemiah Reforms," *RTR* 35 (1976): 44.

[13] See R. L. Smith, *Micah-Malachi,* WBC (Waco: Word, 1984), 302–3. G. P. Hugenberger also notes "the preponderance of 'Israel' over 'Judah' in Ezekiel and Ezra" (*Marriage as a Covenant* [Leiden: Brill, 1994], 24).

Israel, whose abundance had enticed them to forget God (Deut 8:12–14; Hos 13:4–6), the people of Judah had allowed their difficulties (see Introduction) to steal their sense of God's loving presence. In both cases the underlying problem was one of ingratitude. Such an impoverishment had resulted in moral decay. Because they failed to acknowledge God's love, they were not showing love to one another (2:10,14–16; 3:5). The remainder of the paragraph after Judah's question is the Lord's argument that his love for Judah had been abundantly demonstrated in recent history by contrast to his dealings with the nation of Edom (vv. 3–4) and that someday Israel would no longer doubt his love (v. 5).

Although this paragraph is tied primarily to Malachi's first address as motivating, together with 2:1–9, the first exhortation in 1:10, it also functions secondarily as motivation for all of Malachi's exhortations. If Judah truly recognized and understood the Lord's sovereign covenant love, not only would they come before him with the worship he deserves (1:6–2:9), they also would be faithful in their relationships (2:10–3:6) and would live in dependence on him, recognizing that all they had came from him and ultimately belonged to him (3:7–4:6).[14]

As important as God's love is to motivate his people to respond to him with worship and obedience, however, it is also a revelation of the manner of that worship and obedience. Just as the Lord's love for Israel is exclusive (1:2–5), so our worship of him must be exclusive. Since he is not only faithful but diligent and persistent in his relationships (2:4; 3:6,17), he expects that same behavior of us in our relationships (2:10,14). Because his love is equitable and impartial toward all his people, he expects us to be impartial in our treatment of others (2:9; 3:5).[15] The structure and logic of this opening section may be displayed by the following chart using the author's translation.[16] Such a chart presents paragraph logic in terms of multiple layers of embedding, that is, subparagraphs used as constituents of other paragraphs or other subparagraphs. The most prominent element of a paragraph is typically marked as "Thesis." This chart shows that the overall paragraph is a

---

[14] P. J. Botha focuses on Judah's failure to honor the Lord as a unifying theme of the book. "The relationship between Yahweh and his people is defined predominantly, almost exclusively, in terms of his honour and their failure to recognise it and to display their respect for him publicly" ("Honour and Shame as Keys to the Interpretation of Malachi," *OTE* 14 [2001]: 395). Even this opening paragraph, he says, contrasts Yahweh's faithfulness with their lack of honor given to him. "The book must be understood as a formal complaint of a senior partner in a treaty who is not honored as he had the right to expect. Yahweh is in fact shamed by his subjects and this constitutes a covenant violation" (pp. 395–96).

[15] Cf. C. J. H. Wright, *An Eye for an Eye: The Place of Old Testament Ethics Today* (Downers Grove: InterVarsity, 1983), 26–32.

[16] This is a much simplified version of the paragraph analysis of R. E. Longacre. See *Joseph: A Story of Divine Providence,* 2d ed. (Winona Lake: Eisenbrauns, 2003), 81–134.

complex dialogue[17] focused mainly on God's answer, which is an embedded paragraph with an antithesis (an "although" element) and a thesis. That thesis, in turn, is an embedded paragraph with a thesis and a result. Each of those elements is itself an embedded paragraph, etc. The various layers of embedding are reflected by the amount of indentation.

God speaks: *I have loved you,*                                                                    *1:2*
      *says Yahweh.*
Judah asks: *And you say, How have you loved us?*
God answers:
  Antithesis: *Was Esau not Jacob's brother?—*
        *Declaration of Yahweh.*
  Thesis:
    Thesis:
      Thesis: *Yet I loved Jacob,*
      Antithesis: *And Esau I hated.*                                           *1:3*
    Result:
      Thesis: *I made his mountains a wasteland*
        *and his inheritance for the jackals of the wilderness.*
      Amplification:
        Thesis:
          Quotation formula: *Although Edom should say,*         *1:4*
            *"We have been battered, but we shall rebuild the ruins,"*
            *thus Yahweh of hosts says:*
          Quote:
            Antithesis: *They may build,*
            Thesis: *But I shall demolish.*
        Result: *And they will be called a territory of wickedness*
          *and the people which Yahweh has cursed forever.*
        Result: *And your eyes will see,*                               *1:5*
          Result: *And you will say,*
            *"Great is Yahweh over the territory of Israel."*

### (1) Love for Israel (1:2)

**²"I have loved you," says the LORD.**
**"But you ask, 'How have you loved us?'**
**"Was not Esau Jacob's brother?" the LORD says. "Yet I have loved Jacob,**

**1:2**    Malachi begins by affirming God's love for the benefit of those who were questioning it, either by their words or their actions. The modern reader will wonder whether an affection or an action is in view and whether the time of God's love is past or present. Like most versions, the NIV has translated the Hebrew verb form (a *qāṭal* or perfect conjugation) with a present perfect (cf.

---

[17] See the Introduction: "Literary Style."

REB, "I have shown you love"), suggesting a past situation or activity in continuity with the present.[18] Terms for "love" were common in ancient Near Eastern treaties as synonyms for covenant loyalty.[19] In Mesopotamian texts, divine love also motivated selection of a king (see also Neh 13:26).[20] Likewise in the Hebrew Bible, especially in Deuteronomy, *'āhab,* "love," often is found in texts dealing with choosing[21] and with faithfulness.[22] Wallis explains that it involves "the passionate desire to be intimately united with a person," but it also has "a strikingly pragmatic character" and "includes a conscious act in behalf of the person who is loved or the thing that is preferred."[23] Here in Malachi it refers to the Lord's election of Israel for a special and exclusive relationship, redeeming them from bondage in Egypt and from exile in Babylon, and continually acting in faithfulness to that relationship (cf. Deut 7:6; Amos 3:2).[24] Although God certainly had affection for Israel,[25] the focus here is on his repeated actions in accordance with a continuing relationship.

It is appropriate that Malachi, the last of the writing prophets, should contain an echo of God's affirmations of love from the beginning of Israel's history in Deuteronomy.[26] This echo also encompasses all the demonstrations of that

---

[18] See the discussion of such "quasi-fientive" verbs in *IBHS* §22.2.3b.

[19] See W. L. Moran, "The Ancient Near Eastern Background of the Love of God in Deuteronomy," *CBQ* 25 (1963): 77–87; N. Lohfink, "Hate and Love in Osee 9,15," *CBQ* 25 (1963): 417; J. Bergman, A. O. Haldar, G. Wallis, "אָהַב," *'āhabh,*" *TDOT* 1:101.

[20] See Bergman et al., "אָהַב," *'āhabh,*" 1:100.

[21] Cf. Deut 4:37; 7:6–8; 10:14–15; Ps 78:68; Isa 41:8. In Isa 48:14 the Persian king Cyrus is called God's "chosen ally," translating a form of אָהַב. See also Matt 12:18; 17:5; Rom 1:7; 11:28; Eph 1:4–5; 2:4–5; Col 3:12; 1 Thess 1:4; 2 Thess 2:13,16; 1 John 3:1; Jude 1.

[22] Cf. Exod 21:5; Deut 5:10; 6:5; 7:13; 10:12; 11:1,13,22; 13:3; 15:16; 23:5; 30:6,16,20; 1 Sam 18:1–4; 20:14–17; 1 Kgs 5:1[15]; 2 Chr 2:11[10]; Jer 31:3; Hos 11:4.

[23] Bergman et al., "אָהַב," *'āhabh,*" 1:105. E. Stauffer asserts that OT religion was distinguished from surrounding fertility cults and the Greek world in that "the love of God for Israel . . . is not impulse but will; the love for God and the neighbour demanded of the Israelite . . . is not intoxication but act" ("Love in Judaism," *TDNT* 1:38).

[24] As J. I. Packer has written, "The love of the God who is spirit is no fitful, fluctuating thing, as the love of man is, nor is it a mere impotent longing for things that may never be; it is, rather, a spontaneous determination of God's whole being in an attitude of benevolence and benefaction, an attitude freely chosen and firmly fixed. There are no inconstancies or vicissitudes in the love of the almighty God who is spirit" (*Knowing God* [Downers Grove: InterVarsity, 1973], 110). Also see the survey of OT expressions of God's love for Israel in G. Quell, "αγαπαω, αγαπη, αγαπητος," *TDNT* 1:31–34. He stresses too much, however, love as "spontaneous feeling" (pp. 22, 25) and so denigrates the term's use in Malachi and Deuteronomy (pp. 33–34).

[25] See the excursus on "Divine Impassibility" at 2:17.

[26] On the generally Deuteronomic character of Malachi see J. Blenkinsopp, *A History of Prophecy in Israel* (Philadelphia: Westminster, 1983), 242; Dumbrell, "Malachi and the Ezra-Nehemiah Reforms," 45–47. Dependence on the Book of the Covenant (cf. Exod 23:20–26) and on "priestly legislation," however, is also evident. Cf. D. L. Petersen, *Late Israelite Prophecy: Studies in Deutero-Prophetic Literature and in Chronicles* (Missoula, Mont.: Scholars Press, 1977), 43; E. M. Meyers, "Priestly Language in the Book of Malachi," *HAR* 10 (1986): 229.

steadfast love from the time of Moses to the end of Old Testament revelation. The reader of Malachi should also recall the Lord's affirmation of love with which "the Book of the Twelve" or Minor Prophets begins. Watts notes that God's love (*'āhabâ*)for Israel is only explicit in the Twelve in Hosea (3:1; 9:15; 11:1,4; 14:3–4) and here in Mal 1:2.[27] All that has happened in and to Israel has not overturned the Lord's love for his people (cf. Mal 3:6). The reminder here at the end of the prophets (and the end of the OT in the *Protestant Christian Bible*) serves as a summary of God's faithfulness that would be preeminently demonstrated by his provision of a messianic deliverer in Jesus Christ.[28]

Like a Pauline epistle, the Book of Malachi begins in the indicative mood before moving to the imperative.[29] Biblical faith includes both, but obedience is always a response to what God has already done. As C. J. H. Wright explains, "God did not send Moses down to Egypt with the law already tucked under his cloak."[30] Rather, the giving of the Law is prefaced by "You yourselves have seen what I did to Egypt, and how I carried you on eagles' wings and brought you to myself" (Exod 19:4). The knowledge that one has been chosen by God for an intimate relationship and that God will always act in accordance with that relationship should make a profound difference in the way we handle obstacles, failure, disappointment, strife, and human antagonism (cf. Rom 5:1–11). As someone has said, "Smile, God loves you—and after all you've put him through, that's really something" (cf. Hos 3:1). To a large extent spiritual health and growth consist in a growing appreciation for God's love (cf. Eph 3:14–19).

The people of Israel who returned from exile in Babylon had been awe-struck by God's faithfulness to his covenant with Abraham. "You have kept your promise because you are righteous," the Levites had prayed (Neh 9:8). Even when Israel had rebelled against him, God had demonstrated his forgive-ness, grace, compassion, patience, and love in not deserting them (Neh 9:17; cf. Mal 3:6). Even when their rebellion occurred over and over, the Lord "delivered them time after time" (Neh 9:28). Though Israel had repeatedly refused warnings to "return to your law" (Neh 9:29; cf. Amos 4:6–11), in his great mercy the Lord "did not put an end to them or abandon them" (Neh 9:31). Therefore, in the presence of continuing hardship, the restoration community had confessed their sins, praised God for his grace, and reaffirmed their com-mitment to him (Neh 9:32–38; esp. vv. 32–33):

---

[27] J. D. W. Watts, "A Frame for the Book of the Twelve: Hosea 1–3 and Malachi," in *Reading and Hearing the Book of the Twelve* (Atlanta: SBL, 2000), 212.

[28] Cf. John 3:16; Rom 5:5–8; Gal 2:20; Eph 2:4; Titus 3:4; 1 John 4:9–10; Rev 1:5.

[29] R. H. Mounce notes that it was only after five and a half chapters of Romans that Paul exhorted his readers for the first time in 6:11. It was important to build "a strong theological base before turning to the ethical implications that flow from it" (*Romans,* NAC [Nashville: Broadman & Holman, 1995], 152).

[30] Wright, *Eye for an Eye,* 22.

Now therefore, O our God, the great, mighty and awesome God, who keeps his covenant of love, do not let all this hardship seem trifling in your eyes—the hardship that has come upon us, upon our kings and leaders, upon our priests and prophets, upon our fathers and all your people, from the days of the kings of Assyria until today. In all that has happened to us, you have been just; you have acted faithfully, while we did wrong.

But the community's appreciation for God's love, faithfulness, and justice in the face of their sin had not lasted. The prophet introduces this first insight into the people's changed attitude with the first of eight uses of "But you say [NIV "ask"]."[31] God's love is what spans the chasm between the beauty of his holiness and the ugliness of human sin (cf. Isa 6:3–7), but Judah had lost sight either of God's holiness or of their wickedness, or more likely both.[32] Like self-centered children who had begun taking love for granted, Judah became blind to it and responded to the Lord's discipline with, "You don't love me."[33] As evidence, they pointed to others who had it better and said, "All who do evil are good in the eyes of the LORD, and he is pleased with them" (2:17), and, "It is futile to serve God. What did we gain by carrying out his requirements . . .?" They began to "call the arrogant blessed" and to say, "Certainly the evildoers prosper, and even those who challenge God escape" (3:14–15). They had allowed a skewed perception of their experience to divert their attention from the clear declaration of Scripture that God hates evil, idolatry, and hypocritical worship and rejects the wicked; on the other hand, he loves righteousness and welcomes the upright.[34]

Yet God graciously condescended to prove his love to Judah by pointing to the nation of Edom, which had descended from Judah's (i.e., Jacob's) twin brother Esau (cf. Gen 25:25–26; 36:1,9,19,40–43). The question "Was not Esau Jacob's brother?" furnishes the basis for the rest of the Lord's remarks in this section (vv. 2–5). Therefore, its prominence is underlined by the divine quotation formula "the LORD

---

[31] The term וַאֲמַרְתֶּם is found twenty-seven times in the OT, usually in passages instructing someone what to say (e.g., Gen 32:20). The only other examples of this use in Malachi (1:2,6,7,13; 2:14,17; 3:8,13) introducing an objection are found in Ezek 18:19,25; 33:20.

[32] A. T. Robertson wrote: "One's theory of God and sin decides his theology and his life. Tell me your view of God and sin and I can fill out the rest" (*Keywords in the Teaching of Jesus* [Philadelphia: American Baptist Publication Society, 1906], 43).

[33] M. Luther explains, "He is upbraiding the Israelites for their ingratitude, because when God had loved them, they in return neither loved Him as their Father nor feared Him as their Lord (cf. Mal. 1:2–6) . . . . [They] fail to see what God has bestowed on them, and what He has taken from their brothers the Edomites, for no other reason than His hatred of the one and His love for the other" (*Bondage of the Will* [Old Tappan, N.J.: Revell, 1957], 227).

[34] E.g., Deut 12:31; 16:22; Jer 44:4; Pss 5:4–5; 11:4–7; 45:7; Prov 6:16–19; 8:13; Isa 1:14; 61:8; Hos 9:15; Amos 5:21; Zech 8:17; Mal 2:16. See also Heb 1:9; Rev 2:6.

says"[35] and by its form as a rhetorical question (its significance is discussed in the comments on vv. 3–4).[36]

### (2) End of Edom (1:3–4)

**³but Esau I have hated, and I have turned his mountains into a wasteland and left his inheritance to the desert jackals."**

**⁴Edom may say, "Though we have been crushed, we will rebuild the ruins."**

**But this is what the LORD Almighty says: "They may build, but I will demolish. They will be called the Wicked Land, a people always under the wrath of the LORD.**

**1:3–4** God had given Judah a demonstration of his hatred of evil in the way he had dealt with Edom, a pagan nation noted in the Bible for its pride, treachery, greed, and violence.[37] They had made themselves especially odious to the Jews when Babylon had conquered and plundered Jerusalem.[38] Edom's actions that had brought about God's destruction of their nation are not mentioned here, but they would have been common knowledge.

As a result, God had devastated their land. In fulfillment of prophecy[39] the nation of Edom had been conquered and its people driven out, perhaps

---

[35] The Hb. expression here, נְאֻם יְהוָה, is lit. "announcement [or "utterance" or "oracle"] of Yahweh." It occurs 268 times in the Hb. Bible, נְאֻם [אֲדֹנָי] יְהוָה, "announcement of Lord Yahweh," occurs an additional 94 times, and נְאֻם הַמֶּלֶךְ יְהוָה צְבָאוֹת, "announcement of the King, Yahweh of hosts," three more times. They are most prominent in Haggai (12x), Amos (21x), Jeremiah (175x), Obadiah (2x), Zephaniah (5x), Zechariah (20x), Ezekiel (85x), and Isaiah (25x). Outside this expression the term נְאֻם is used sixteen times with the human agent of revelation, whether Balaam (Num 24:3,4,15,16), David (2 Sam 23:1) or Agur (Prov 30:1). Although variations on נְאֻם יְהוָה are usually translated "declares/says the LORD," its function is not to identify the speaker but to insist that Yahweh is their source (cf. Jer 23:41; 9:21[E 22]; Ezek 13:7). Cf. T. L. Wilt, "'Oracle of Yahweh': Translating a Highly Marked Expression," *BT* 50.3 (1999): 301–4; L. J. Coppes, "נָאַם," *TWOT* 541–42; S. A. Meier, *Speaking of Speaking: Marking Direct Discourse in the Hebrew Bible* (Leiden: Brill, 1992), 298–314.

[36] Waltke and O'Connor explain, "*Rhetorical* questions aim not to gain information but to give information with passion" (*IBHS* §18.2g). See also R. Gordis, "A Rhetorical Use of Interrogative Sentences in Biblical Hebrew," *AJSL* 49 (1933): 212–17; GKC §150e; L. J. de Regt, "Functions and Implications of Rhetorical Questions in the Book of Job," in *Biblical Hebrew and Discourse Linguistics* (Dallas: SIL, 1994), 361–73.

[37] Cf. 2 Chr 20:10–11; 25:14,20; Jer 49:16; Amos 1:9,11; Obad 3.

[38] Cf. Ps 137:7; Ezek 25:12; 35:15; 36:5; Joel 3:19; Obad 10–14. Cf. also *1 Esdr* 4:45,50. The attitude of the Jews toward Edom may be part of the reason Malachi attaches the expression נְאֻם יְהוָה to it, which would be better translated, "This is the Lord speaking."

[39] Cf. Isa 34:5–17; Jer 49:7–22; Lam 4:21; Ezek 25:12–14; 35:1–15; Amos 1:11–12; Obadiah.

by the Nabatean Arabs late in the sixth century.[40] At least by the time of
Malachi their cities had become ghost towns populated only by desert creatures. The reference to jackals connotes desolation.[41]

Although it is true, then, that the term "love" when contrasted with "hate"
can mean "prefer" (as one wife could be preferred over another[42]), and
"hate" can mean to "slight" or "think less of,"[43] that is not the meaning of
the word pair here in Malachi.[44] Here God's hatred involved his determined
response of opposition to Edom's wickedness, resulting in their destruction.
The point is not that God loved Jacob *more than* Esau but that he loved him
*rather than* Esau.[45] Just as the political sphere serves as the background of
God's "love" for Israel, so it does for his hatred of Edom.[46] As J. A. Thompson has demonstrated, Israel's allies could be referred to as "lovers" and

---

[40] See N. Glueck, *The Other Side of the Jordan* (Cambridge, Mass.: American Schools of Oriental Research, 1970), 126. P. K. McCarter, Jr. concluded his discussion of dating the destruction
of Edom, "The precise date of the final expulsion of the Edomites is undetermined, but is placed
late in the sixth century by general agreement. The archaeological evidence, still regrettably mea-
ger, shows the last part of that century to have been a period of general collapse in Edomite culture"
("Obadiah 7 and the Fall of Edom," *BASOR* 221 [1976]: 89). See also J. M. Myers, "Edom and
Judah in the Sixth–Fifth Centuries B.C.," in *Near Eastern Studies in Honor of William Foxwell
Albright* (Baltimore: The Johns Hopkins Press, 1971), 379–80; P. Bienkowski, "The Edomites: The
Archaeological Evidence from Transjordan," and B. Glazier-McDonald, "Edom in the Prophetical
Corpus," in *You Shall Not Abhor an Edomite for He Is Your Brother: Edom and Seir in History and
Tradition* (Atlanta: Scholars Press, 1995), 41–92, 30.

[41] Cf. Job 30:29; Ps 44:19; Isa 13:21–22; 34:13; Jer 9:11; 10:22; 49:33; 51:37; Lam 5:18. Cf.
D. Hillers, *Treaty Curses and the Old Testament Prophets,* BibOr (Rome: Pontifical Biblical Institute, 1964), 29, 53. On the wilderness motif in the Bible see D. A. Garrett, *Hosea, Joel,* NAC
(Nashville: Broadman & Holman, 1997), 88–91. The feminine plural for "jackals" (תַּנּוֹת) is
anomalous, since elsewhere the plural is masculine. The LXX has δόματα, a corruption of δώ-
ματα, "dwellings." Hence the Hb. is often emended to נְ(א)וֹת, "pasture" (cf. נְאוֹת מִדְבָּר in Jer
9:9). For other suggestions cf. Hill, *Malachi,* 155, who concludes that תַּן, "jackal," has both masculine and feminine plurals.

[42] Cf. Gen 29:30–33 and Deut 21:15–16, where "not love[d]" is lit. "hated." See also Gen
25:28.

[43] See W. C. Kaiser, Jr., *Malachi: God's Unchanging Love* (Grand Rapids: Baker, 1984), 27.
Cf. Gen 39:30–31; Deut 21:15; 22:13; 24:3; Luke 14:26; 16:13. See also O. Michel, "μισέω,"
*TDNT* 4.690. W. G. T. Shedd explains the "Hebrew sense" of "hate" as "loving less" or "showing
less favor towards." "Love," he says, is here "the exercise of compassion," and "hate" is its "non-
exercise" (*A Critical and Doctrinal Commentary upon the Epistle of St. Paul to the Romans* [New
York: Scribners, 1893], 286).

[44] Cf. J. Murray, *The Epistle to the Romans,* NICNT (Grand Rapids: Eerdmans, 1968), 21–23;
C. E. B. Cranfield, *A Critical and Exegetical Commentary on the Epistle to the Romans,* ICC
(Edinburgh: T&T Clark, 1979), 2:480.

[45] Note *2 Esdr* 3:16: "You set apart Jacob for yourself, but Esau you rejected."

[46] Cf. Lev 26:17; 2 Sam 5:8; 19:6–7; 2 Chr 1:11; Ps 44:8; Ezek 16:36–37; 23:28.

their enemies as "haters."[47] God had demonstrated himself to be Edom's enemy by devastating them.

If the prophet had used the term "Edom" in v. 3 as he did in v. 4, this explanation of God's hatred would be sufficient. But Malachi connects God's treatment of the Edomites to the divine rejection of Esau that occurred before he and his twin brother Jacob were born (cf. Gen 25:23; Rom 9:10–13). The point is that God in the sovereignty of his will had chosen to enter into a covenant relationship with Jacob and his descendants rather than with Esau and his descendants. This did not mean that all Jacob's descendants would be spiritually and eternally "saved" (since the spiritual benefits of election would belong to a subset of physical Israel; cf. Rom 9:6) or that all Esau's descendants necessarily would be "lost." The finality of Edom's judgment (see v. 4) does not mean that individual Edomites were forbidden from entering a covenant relationship with Israel's God by faith. Deuteronomy 23:7–8[Hb. 8–9] states, "Do not abhor an Edomite, for he is your brother. . . . The third generation of children born to them may enter the assembly of the LORD" (see also Amos 9:12). Even the apparent individuality of Deut 23:3 ("No Ammonite or Moabite or any of his descendants may enter the assembly of the LORD, even down to the tenth generation") had not kept Ruth the Moabite from becoming a member of the covenant by swearing allegiance to the Lord (cf. also Rahab in Josh 6:17,23,25).

Furthermore, God's hatred of Esau did not mean that Esau or his descendants would be excluded from all acts of divine benevolence (cf. Gen 4:15–24; 33:9; 36:7,31–42), just as in the case of Ishmael, also rejected by God (Gen 21:11–21). Such passages as Ps 145:8–9,13–17; Ezek 18:23,32; 33:11; Matt 5:44–45; 23:37; Acts 14:17; 1 Tim 2:4; and 2 Pet 3:9 teach that there is a sense in which the love of God is universal.[48] He bestows his

---

[47] J. A. Thompson, "Israel's 'Lovers,'" *VT* 27 (1977): 475–81; id., "Israel's 'Haters'," *VT* 29 (1979): 200–205. Cf. M. E. Tate, "Questions for Priests and People in Malachi 1:2–2:16," *RevExp* 84 (1987): 395, who notes that English, like Hebrew, uses the terms "love" and "hate" with varying degrees of emotional involvement.

[48] Failure to distinguish between God's love for all and his love for his elect results either in unbiblical universalism or in an equally unbiblical subjugation of the divine will to the perverted and capricious human will. This fallacy leads F. Guy (who defines divine love simply as God's willing the best for "every created entity") to state: "It is unthinkable that the divine love is restricted to a fortunate part of creation and that another (perhaps even larger) part is excluded. In regard to human reality, the divine love includes absolutely all, intending the ultimate good—that is, the eternal salvation—of every person" ("The Universality of God's Love," in *The Grace of God, the Will of Man: A Case for Arminianism* [Grand Rapids: Zondervan, 1989], 36). But this view cannot stand before Mal 1:2–3, especially as it is expounded in Rom 9. In the face of human depravity, such a "divine love" that "respects human freedom, even to the extent of allowing humanity to be utterly irrational and perverse—that is, to reject the love that has created, sustained, and redeemed it" (p. 45) is a love without arms and legs, that is, not divine at all.

blessings on all and grieves over those who are lost.[49] Nevertheless, Esau's descendants would be excluded *as a nation* from that special electing love that would belong to Israel. God's choosing Jacob and his descendants meant that he established a permanent relationship with Israel as a whole, in which he would instruct them with truth, train them with righteousness, care for them with compassion, bless them with goodness, and discipline them with severity;[50] regardless of how often they strayed from him, he would be faithful to them by his grace until his work in them was complete and "all Israel" (Rom 11:26, referring back to true Israel in Rom 9:6) would enjoy the righteousness, peace, and joy that come from knowing God (Jer 33; Ezek 36; Acts 13:16–41; Rom 9–11).[51] As Jeremiah declared, "The people who survived the sword found grace in the wilderness; when Israel sought for rest, the LORD appeared to him from far away. I have loved you with an everlasting love; therefore I have continued my faithfulness to you" (Jer 31:2–3, NRSV). God's choice of Israel also meant that they would be his primary instruments for bringing salvation to the sinful world and glory to himself (Gen 12:2–3; Isa 49:3; Ezek 36:23; 37:28; 39:7; 1 Pet 2:9). This perpetual alliance with God made the difference between Israel and the other nations.

Although God is at least as troubled by the sins of his elect as he is by those of the nonelect, his response to the former takes the shape of discipline (i.e., corrective punishment), but to the latter it is eternal wrath ("a people always under the wrath of the LORD"). Whereas Judah's devastation by the Babylonians had been a temporary situation, Edom would never return to their land.[52] Any hopes they might have had to do so (lit. "if Edom should

---

[49] L. Berkhof explains: "A father who is also a judge may loathe the son that is brought before him as a criminal, and feel constrained to visit his judicial wrath upon him, but may yet pity him and show him acts of kindness while he is under condemnation . . . . General Washington hated the traitor that was brought before him and condemned him to death, but at the same time showed him compassion by serving him with the dainties from his own table. Cannot God have compassion even on the condemned sinner, and bestow favors upon him?" (*Systematic Theology*, 4th ed. [Grand Rapids: Eerdmans, 1941], 445). See also J. Piper, *The Pleasures of God: Meditations on God's Delight in Being God* (Portland: Multnomah, 1991), 143–46.

[50] Regarding the judgment of Israel, G. J. Wenham wrote, "Judgment does not prove that God has rejected his people. Rather he punishes them because they are his own (Amos 3:2)" (*The Book of Leviticus*, NICOT [Grand Rapids: Eerdmans, 1979], 332). Contrast God's words regarding Edom with Lev 26:43–44; Deut 30:3; Ezek 20:32–44.

[51] Cf. J. Piper's careful study of Rom 9:4–5 in *The Justification of God: An Exegetical and Theological Study of Romans 9:1–23*, 2d ed. (Grand Rapids: Baker, 1983), 21–44. Note especially his opinion that "Paul's intention is missed if these privileges are described as mere antiquarian, theocratic distinctives or as simply passing over from Israel to the Church" (p. 40).

[52] The verb יִבְנוּ, "may build," is interpreted as a modal expressing a hypothetical case (cf. *IBHS* §31.4e). The contrast in the two clauses between human effort and divine decree is strengthened by the use of fronted pronoun subjects, "they" and "I."

say"[53]) were futile.[54] God's verdict regarding the permanence of Edom's judgment is solemnly underlined by the introductory "this is what the LORD Almighty says." The translation "we will rebuild" is literally "we will return, and we will build." The verb *šûb* ("turn, return") can serve adverbially with the idea of doing something again, but the context and its use later in the book suggest that it may refer here to a determination to return to their land. The verb recurs three times at the beginning of the last division of Malachi, in 3:7 (twice) and 3:8, referring to Judah's repentance. Then it occurs again in 4:6 at the end of the book ("He will *turn* the hearts of the fathers to their children"). Its use with Edom as the subject may be a foreshadowing of its later application to Judah, since the focus here is on a contrast between Edom and Judah. Whereas Edom will be unable to return, being "a people always under the wrath of the LORD," Judah is later commanded to return spiritually and is threatened with cursing if they refuse.

The conclusion of v. 4 is literally, "They will call them a territory of wickedness and the people whom Yahweh has cursed forever." The interdict here was against the restoration of the people to their homeland and assumed the continuation of their opposition to God. God's dealing with Edom is clearly in response to their "wickedness." Depending upon who is speaking, to curse means "to predict, wish, pray for, or cause trouble or disaster on a person or thing."[55] A curse uttered by God would clearly involve the causation of trouble.

This reference to cursing is the first of several in the book, using three different roots: *z'm* here (connoting God's anger or indignation), *'rr* in 1:14, three times in 2:2 and twice in 3:9, and *ḥrm* in 4:6. The other occurrences have Judah as the object. Here Edom would be "called"[56] a "territory of wickedness," that is, a symbol of what happens to the wicked (cf. Jer 49:17–18). Judah, on the other hand, is promised in 3:12 that the nations would someday "call them blessed" (*'šr*, to "call happy" or "consider fortunate," an antonym of "curse"), for they would become a "delightful land" (lit. a "land of joy"). A time is coming, God says, when appearances will no longer be deceiving. According to 3:15, Judah was calling "blessed" (*'šr*) those "doers of wickedness" (the same word for "wickedness" used in 1:4; the NIV has "evildoers") who "build" (the

---

[53] The NKJV translation is "even though Edom has said." There is no justification for translating the Hb. imperfect with a present perfect, but the concessive "even though" or "even if" is a possible translation of כִּי introducing a subordinate clause preceding the main clause. But see the caution in A. Aejmelaeus, "Function and Interpretation of כִּי in Biblical Hebrew," *JBL* 105 (1986): 198–99; B. Bandstra, "The Syntax of Particle *ky* in Biblical Hebrew and Ugaritic" (Ph.D. diss., Yale University, 1982), 130–33.

[54] Hillers sees here an example of a treaty curse he calls a "futility curse" (*Treaty Curses and the Old Testament Prophets,* 78–79).

[55] D. Stuart, "Curse," in *ABD* 1.1218–19.

[56] This is an impersonal passive construction, in which an active third person verb is used whose subject has no specified referent (GKC §121a).

same verb used of Edom in 1:4 but in the sense "prosper" in 3:12; cf. NIV) and so test God's patience and seemingly get away with it.

What had happened to Edom was a sign that all evildoers will someday receive justice (e.g., Ps 28:4–5). There is likely more to the mention of Esau and the Edomites than reference to Israel's archenemy. In Isa 34:5–17 Edom clearly is representative of the arrogant nations of the world who oppose the purposes and ways of God and will receive the divine judgment of destruction (also 63:1–6; Ezek 36:5).[57] As Oswalt states, "God is sovereign of all things and the world which opposes him is irrevocably doomed."[58] Judah was wrong about God's justice as well as about his love (cf. 2:17). The first paragraph, then, not only introduces the theme of the Lord's love but also sets up the theme of God's justice that is dealt with in some detail later in the book.

One further question must be addressed regarding Mal 1:2–4. What is the significance of Malachi's argument that Esau was Jacob's brother (v. 2)? What part did this fact play in the demonstration of God's love for the Jewish people Malachi was addressing? God's treatment of Israel in contrast to his treatment of Edom and the other nations demonstrates the significance of his "everlasting love," but this argument alone would not depend on Esau's filial relationship with Jacob. One effect of this fact is to heighten the striking character of God's election of Jacob and his descendants, since Esau too was a descendant of blessed Abraham and even of Isaac, his promised seed. Like light in opposition to darkness, love takes on special significance only when it is restricted (cf. 2 Sam 19:6). The closeness of the relationship between Jacob and Esau serves to define and so to intensify the demonstration of love, much like a spotlight in

---

[57] J. A. Motyer points to Pss 60:8[10]; 83:6[7] as early evidence that Edom had "a symbolic place in the theme of the hostile alliance against Zion" (*The Prophecy of Isaiah* [Downers Grove: InterVarsity, 1993], 269). He notes that Ezek 35 sees Edom's overthrow "as part of the kingdom of the future." It will also be "the exact fulfilment of what was promised at the beginning (Gn. 25:23). The purposes of God according to election stand." B. C. Cresson, "The Condemnation of Edom in Postexilic Judaism," in *The Use of the Old Testament in the New and Other Essays* (Durham: Duke University Press, 1972), 139–40, notes that postbiblical Jewish writings used Edom as a symbol for Rome.

[58] J. N. Oswalt, *The Book of Isaiah Chapters 1–39,* NICOT (Grand Rapids: Eerdmans, 1986), 617. D. W. Baker calls Edom "the paradigm of all the nations" ("Obadiah" in *Obadiah, Jonah, Micah,* TOTC [Downers Grove: InterVarsity, 1988], 39). See also J. R. Bartlett, *Edom and the Edomites,* JSOTSup 77 (Sheffield: Sheffield Academic Press, 1989), 184–86; Cresson, "The Condemnation of Edom in Postexilic Judaism," 132; and B. Dicou, *Edom, Israel's Brother and Antagonist: The Role of Edom in Biblical Prophecy and Story,* JSOTSup 169 (Sheffield: JSOT, 1994), esp. 13–17,41–42. Amos 9:12 indicates, however, that there is more to the biblical symbolism of Edom than judgment. What is left of Edom and the nations after God's judgment will be included in the people of God (see also Jer 49:11; Obad 21). See B. K. Smith, "Amos," in *Amos, Obadiah, Jonah,* NAC (Grand Rapids: Broadman & Holman, 1995), 167–68.

a darkened theater focuses attention on the appointed spot.[59]

More than this, however, probably is involved. When the people respond to the Lord's declaration of love with (in effect), "Show us the evidence," they seem to assume that they have a claim on his love, and they are bitter because they are not receiving it. So the Lord points them to Esau, who as Isaac's son and Jacob's brother might be expected to have as much claim on God's favor as Jacob did.[60] Then God reminds them that he chose Jacob for an intimate relationship but rejected Esau." They knew very well that the distinction between the two had been made before either of them was born, the point Paul calls attention to in Rom 9:11. Jacob and his descendants had an enduring relationship with God only by God's sovereign grace. Then God points them to the desolation of Edom to show them the results of wickedness in those not covered by his mercy. Their response to this display of God's righteousness in preserving them alive in spite of their rebellion should have been to praise the glory of his grace, as v. 5 declares their response someday would be.

Some interpreters of the Jacob and Esau discussion in Rom 9:10–13 have argued that the topic is not individual election to eternal salvation but national election to temporal privileges.[61] As we have seen, corporate election is in view, but individual election to a divine relationship is as well, as indicated by reference to the individuals, Jacob and Esau. It is to this divine election of individuals that the apostle Paul refers in Romans 9. As J. Piper has argued, "The interpretation which tries to restrict this predestination or unconditional election to nations rather than individuals or to historical tasks rather than eternal destinies must ignore or distort the problem posed in Rom 9:1–5, the individualism of 9:6b, the vocabulary and logical structure of 9:6b–8, the closely analogous texts elsewhere in Paul, and the implications of 9:14–23."[62] Does the conclusion that the topic of Rom 9:10–13 is individual election to eternal salvation, however, mean that Mal 1:2–4 must be understood in the same way?

---

[59] E. Stauffer asserts that "the distinctive character of Israelite אַהֲבָה [love] is . . . its tendency to exclusivism. . . . The love extolled in the OT is the jealous love which chooses one among thousands, holds him with all the force of passion and will, and will allow no breach of loyalty. It is in קִנְאָה [jealousy] that there is revealed the divine power of אַהֲבָה. . . . It is a love which makes distinctions, which chooses, which prefers and overlooks. It is not a cosmopolitan love embracing millions" ("Love in Judaism," *TDNT* 1:38).

[60] Note the claim that Esau makes on Isaac's love in Gen 27:34–38, but he receives the "antiblessing" of vv. 39–40 instead. I owe this observation to K. A. Mathews.

[61] E.g., Cranfield, *Romans,* 479; H. L. Ellison, *The Mystery of Israel* (Grand Rapids: Eerdmans, 1966), 43; F. Godet, *Commentary on St. Paul's Epistle to the Romans* (New York: Funk & Wagnalls, 1883), 351; F. J. Leenhardt, *The Epistle to the Romans, A Commentary* (London: Lutterworth, 1961), 249; W. Sanday and A. C. Headlam, *The Epistle to the Romans,* ICC (Edinburgh: T&T Clark, 1902), 245; G. Schrenk, "ἐκλέγομαι," *TDNT* 4.179.

[62] Piper, *Justification of God,* 73 (this concludes his argument on pp. 56–73). See also Murray, *Romans,* 15–24; D. J. Moo, *The Epistle to the Romans.* NICNT (Grand Rapids: Eerdmans, 1996), 571–72, 585–87; T. R. Schreiner, *Romans* (Grand Rapids: Baker, 1998), 501–3.

Malachi focuses on Edom's desolation, not on Esau's condemnation, as the result of God's "hating" Esau. Furthermore, Gen 25:23 declares Jacob and Esau to be representatives of "two nations" and "two peoples" and that the result of the divine decree will be that "the older will serve the younger." Käsemann, who argues that Paul is concerned "timelessly . . . with the election and rejection of two persons who are elevated as types," nevertheless concludes that in Romans "the quotations are taken out of their context and its sense is disregarded."[63]

This, however, is not the case. The collective function of Jacob and Esau is dependent on something that was true of them individually. Furthermore, the patriarchal narratives demonstrate repeatedly that divine blessing is not automatic, the result of physical descent or prevailing customs, nor can it be obtained by human effort. It is a work of sovereign grace, as God would later declare to Moses in Exod 33:19: "I will have mercy on whom I will have mercy, and I will have compassion on whom I will have compassion," which Paul quotes in Rom 9:15. Furthermore, the narrative in Gen 25:24–34, which Malachi is reflecting, shows how the character and lives of Jacob and Esau as individuals were the outworking of the divine word pronounced before their birth.[64] Esau's despising (*bzh,* used in Mal 1:6–7,12; 2:9) of his birthright (v. 34) amounted to his despising the Lord's promises (Heb 12:16–17). As Sailhamer explains, although it occurred before they were born, "God's choice of Jacob over Esau did not run contrary to the wishes of either of the two brothers."[65] Thus the Old Testament explains the destiny of Esau and the Edomites both by the divine word and by their own wickedness, as it also explains the destiny of the remnant of Israel both by the divine word and by their faith. The message is that no one deserves God's favor. Shedd is right that in a sense God initially "hates" both Jacob and Esau insofar as they are "in Adam."[66] Never-

---

[63] E. Käsemann, *Commentary on Romans* (Grand Rapids: Eerdmans, 1980), 264–65. Of Jerome's similar view that "things have a force in Paul which they do not possess in their own places," M. Luther says, "This is just to say that when Paul lays the foundations of Christian doctrine, he does nothing but corrupt the Divine Scriptures, and delude the souls of the faithful, with an idea conceived in his own brain, and violently thrust into those Scriptures!" (*Bondage of the Will,* 223).

[64] J. Sailhamer also suggests that their conflict, as well as others in Genesis, was the outworking of God's word of judgment to "put enmity between you and the woman, and between your offspring and hers" (Gen 3:15). But more than judgment, these conflicts had a divine, redemptive purpose, as expressed by Joseph in 50:20, "You intended to harm me, but God intended it for good to accomplish what is now being done, the saving of many lives." Sailhamer draws back, however, from what seems to be the significance of Gen 3:15 for these conflicts and explains only that "God's will was accomplished in spite of the conflict" ("Genesis," EBC, 2:182).

[65] Sailhamer goes on to point out that "in few cases in Genesis do we find such a clear and forthright statement of the writer's own understanding of the sense of the individual stories. . . . Esau, though he had the right of the firstborn, did not value it over a small bowl of soup. Thus, when in God's plan Esau lost his birthright and consequently his blessing, there was no injustice dealt him. The narrative has shown that he did not want the birthright. He despised it" ("Genesis," 2:183–84).

[66] Shedd, *Romans,* 286.

theless, God is glorifying his name by graciously placing his electing love on some, transforming their hearts (cf. Deut 4:29–31; 30:6; Jer 31:33; Ezek 36:26–27,31–32), while passing by others (Exod 33:19; 34:5–7).[67] So also Paul declares that "God's purpose in election" is "to make the riches of his glory known to the objects of his mercy, whom he prepared in advance for glory" (Rom 9:11,23).

This is exactly God's purpose in Malachi. He is making the riches of his glory known among the restored community of Israel by demonstrating the sovereignty of his electing love. They deserved nothing from him and would wind up in the same state as Edom for their wickedness, were it not for his changeless and sovereign love (3:6–7; a love declared by a word that cannot fail, Rom 9:6). God had demonstrated that love upon Jacob and his descendants by his faithfulness and mercy in preserving them thus far. And he would continue to preserve a faithful remnant of those who feared him and honored his name (3:16; a "remnant chosen by grace," Rom 11:5), who would "bring offerings in righteousness" (3:3). Then after removing from them "all the arrogant and every evildoer" (4:1), his people whose names were on his "scroll of remembrance" (3:16) would be healed (4:2) and would become his "treasured possession" (3:17). Then the knowledge of God's glory will fill the earth (Hab 2:14), and as Mal 1:5 assures, Israel will cry out with exuberant delight, "Great is the LORD—even beyond the borders of Israel!"

### (3) Future of Israel (1:5)

**⁵You will see it with your own eyes and say, 'Great is the LORD—even beyond the borders of Israel!'**

**1:5**    The point of v. 5 is that someday a repentant Israel will see God's judgment on all his enemies and will praise God for the greatness of his covenant faithfulness and sovereign power. He is not just "our God"; he is the God of all creation, the God with whom all must reckon. The history of every culture, society, people, nation, community, clan, family, and individual who has ever lived or will ever live leads inevitably to an encounter with the sovereign God. There is a theme of universality in the Book of Malachi, as some have claimed (see comments on 1:11; 2:10), but it is not a theme of God's acceptance of all peoples. It is rather that of his universal lordship, his sovereign

---

[67] This corollary of divine election, by which God chooses in his infinite wisdom and not without compassion to leave some to the destiny of condemnation and judgment determined by human sin, is called "reprobation." As J. P. Boyce declares, "It is neither as an effect of Election or Rejection or of Preterition that man has fallen, or sins, or is condemned, or will be destroyed. The simple effect is that he is not rescued, and consequently is left where he would have been without these acts. They do not lead to destruction. They simply do not rescue from it" (*Abstract of Systematic Theology* [Louisville, Ky.: Dearing, 1882], 362).

intention to subdue the earth to the praise of his glory, removing the wicked and exalting those who fear him (cf. 3:12–4:3).

The subject "you" is reintroduced emphatically in Hebrew to make the connection to the "you" in v. 2.[68] God will turn Israel's doubt into praise. "Your own" as reflecting this emphasis should not be understood as referring necessarily to Malachi's immediate audience. We may suppose that some in Malachi's day may have seen the validity of the prophet's argument and praised God for repeated demonstrations of his faithfulness to his people. But the way Edom functions in Scripture as a symbol of all God's enemies suggests that the ultimate fulfillment of this prophecy will be eschatological. Whereas Judah was doubting God's love, someday all Israel will see the evidence of it and submit to the Lord with words of praise (cf. Zech 12:1–10; Rom 11).[69]

The word translated "borders" here *(gĕbul)* can also mean "territory." It is the same word translated "land" in v. 4 ("Wicked Land," lit. "territory of wickedness"), and it likely has the same meaning here in v. 5. Israel's recognition of the Lord's greatness will evidently follow his great judgment on the nations in which they too will recognize his greatness (cf. Pss 67:1–7; 72:8–11; 99:1–3; 102:15–22).[70] One may compare such prophecies of eschatological judgment as Ezekiel 38–39, which announces a divine intervention that will cause all creatures, including "all the people on the face of the earth," to "tremble at my presence" (Ezek 38:20; cf. Isa 64:1–2). Through the devastation of Gog's armies and "the many nations with him," the Lord declares: "I will show my greatness and my holiness, and I will make myself known in the sight of many nations. Then they will know that I am the LORD" (Ezek 38:22–23). This same judgment will also have an effect on Israel: "I will make known my holy name among my people Israel. I will no longer let my holy name be profaned" (Ezek 39:7; cf. Mal 1:6–14); "I will display my glory among the nations, and all the nations will see the punishment I inflict and the hand I lay upon them. From that day forward the house of Israel will know that I am the LORD their God" (Ezek 39:21–22; cf. Joel 3:1–21; Zech 14:1–21; Rom 11:11–12,25–27).

---

[68] Israel's quote is introduced by two clauses that would be lit., "Your eyes will see, and you will say." The fronting of the subjects serves to bring the "you" back into focus.

[69] On "your eyes will see" as a covenant formula see J. Muilenburg, "The Form and Structure of the Covenantal Formulations," *VT* 9 (1959): 355; also M. Weinfeld, "The Covenant of Grant in the Old Testament and in the Ancient Near East," *JAOS* 90 (1970): 200.

[70] The word "even" is an interpretative addition. The prepositional construction מֵעַל לְ usually means "above," as some translate it here (including LXX, ὑπεράνω), yielding the sense that Yahweh is "enthroned over Israel in majesty and power and attracting the wonder and reverence of the world at large" (J. M. P. Smith, *A Critical and Exegetical Commentary on the Book of Malachi*. ICC [Edinburgh: T&T Clark, 1912], 23; also Verhoef, *Haggai and Malachi*, 194, 206). But this is contrary to the context of Israel seeing the judgment on Edom. Tate notes that the sense "beyond" or "outside" for מֵעַל לְ that best fits here is also found in 1 Sam 17:39 and Neh 12:37 ("Questions for Priests and People," 405).

## 2. Situation: The Priests' Failure to Honor the Lord (1:6–9)

The audience of this paragraph is specified in 1:6 as the priests. The reference to priests again in 2:1, in the last paragraph of the first address, identifies them as the primary audience of the entire address. The effect of saving this identification until the second paragraph is that the motivation of God's love in the first paragraph applies not only to the priests and to the first address but to the entire book and to all Israel. Nevertheless these first two paragraphs are closely related as forming a contrast between the Lord's love and Israel's failure to respond appropriately by honoring him. Whereas we would expect love to be the appropriate response to love, in the father-child and master-servant relationship in view here love would be exhibited in obedience from the heart.

The topic of this paragraph is announced by God's rhetorical question, "Where is the honor/respect due me?" Here is the first explicit indication in the book of the problem that the prophet was addressing—the failure of Judah, beginning with the priests, to honor/fear the Lord (cf. Neh 9:16–17,26,29). Again the audience objects, however, and again the Lord presents evidence to substantiate his thesis. The theme of honoring or fearing the Lord will appear again several times in Malachi (1:11,14; 2:2,5; 3:5,16; 4:2), making it a major theme of the book. In spite of the Lord's love, Judah failed to honor him. The book, however, contains no explicit command to honor the Lord. Instead, the audience is furnished with examples of what happens to those who honor or who fail to honor him (2:2; 3:5,16; 4:2). The command given in 3:7 to return to the Lord and the command in 4:4 to remember the law may be understood to include the command to honor the Lord.

Verses 6–14 are unified rhetorically and thematically, particularly by the repetition of terms, synonyms, and similar sounds throughout the passage. References to the fear of the Lord and his name in vv. 6,14 mark the boundaries of the whole. Except for the exhortation in v. 10 that divides the section into two parts (a division confirmed by the A-B-C repetition), the verses describe the situation the prophet was confronting in the first address. Its structure can be displayed with a literal translation that allows the repetitions to be more apparent:[71]

A–A son honors a father and a servant his master.
Now if I am a father, where is my honor?
And if I am a master, where is my fear *[môrā'î]?*
*Says Yahweh of hosts* to you O priests, despising *[bzh]* my name?
And you say, "How have we despised *[bzh]* your name?" (v. 6)

---

[71] With a few exceptions each line translates a Hb. sentence. Note that each of the A sections contains one divine quotation formula that heightens reference to the Lord's name; neither of the B sections contains a divine quotation formula; and the two outside C' sections in vv. 8–9 and v. 13 contain two divine quotation formulas.

B–Presenting *[ngš]* on my altar defiled *[g'l]* food *[leḥem]*.
And you say, "How have we defiled *[g'l]* you?"
By your saying, "Yahweh's table, it is despised *[bzh]*." (v. 7)

C–And when you present *[ngš]* blind to sacrifice *[zbḥ]*, is it not
   wrong?
And when you present *[ngš]* crippled and sick, is it not wrong?
Bring *[qrb]* it to your governor.
Would he accept *[rṣh]* you?
Or would he lift your face? *says Yahweh of hosts.* (v. 8)
So now beseech *[ḥlh]* God's face that he may be gracious *[ḥnn]* to
   us.
From your hand has this come?
Will he lift the face on your account? *says Yahweh of hosts.* (v. 9)

D–Who is also among you that he would shut the doors,
   that you might not kindle fire *[tā'îrû]* on my altar for nothing
   *[ḥinnām]?* (v. 10a)

C–I have no pleasure *[ḥpṣ]* in you, *says Yahweh of hosts,*
   and an offering *[minḥâ]* I will not accept *[rṣh]* from your hand.
   (v. 10b)

A–Because from east to west great will be my name among the nations,
   everywhere incense is going to be presented *[ngš]* to my name;
And pure offerings *[minḥâ]*,
   for great will be my name among the nations, *says Yahweh of hosts.* (v. 11)

B–But you are profaning *[ḥll]* it
   by your saying, "The Lord's table, it is defiled *[g'l]*,
   and its fruit, despised *[bzh]* is its food *['oklô]*." (v. 12)

C–And you say, "Behold, what a nuisance!"
   And you sniff at it, *says Yahweh of hosts.*
   And you bring *[bw']* stolen, the crippled and the sick.
   And you bring *[bw']* the offering *[minḥâ]*.
   Will I accept *[rṣh]* it from your hand? *says Yahweh.* (v. 13)

A–And cursed *['rr]* is the deceiver in whose flock is a male,
   and though making a vow, he sacrifices a blemished one to the Lord.
   Because I am a great king, *says Yahweh of hosts,*
   my name is going to be feared *[nôrā']* among the nations. (v. 14)

The theme of these verses is that the priests were manifesting their careless attitude toward the Lord and dishonoring his name in the kinds of offerings they were bringing to him. A secondary theme also appears in vv. 11–14 that heightens the first by contrast—the foreign nations who have been strangers to God's redemptive covenants and hostile to his purposes will someday give him the honor/fear that he deserves and desires. Verses 6–10 also contain a balancing contrast between offerings being made to God and those being made to their human ruler.

The passage uses several words to describe Judah's offerings and how they affected the Lord. Specifically the priests were allowing animals to be offered that were "blind," "stolen [NIV, injured]," "crippled," and "sick" (1:8,13). These offerings are also referred to more generally as "blemished" (1:14) and as such were unacceptable to God (e.g., Deut 17:1). To allow such violation of cultic law was "wrong" (*rā*ʿ, v. 8) or displeasing to the Lord. The opposite kind of offerings, which the Lord said the nations would someday bring (1:11), were "pure," that is, ceremonially clean (*ṭāhôr;* cf. the same root in 3:3). Thus by implication the offerings that Judah was bringing were unclean, a term referring to something unacceptable to God or inappropriate for cultic use. Finally, the offerings are referred to in this passage as "food" (*leḥem* in 1:7 and *ʾōkel* in 1:12) that was "defiled" (1:7) and "despised" (1:12; the semantic ranges of these two words overlap). The effect of such offerings on the Lord's "table" (1:7,12), that is, the "altar" (1:7,10), was that it too was "despised" (1:7) and "defiled" (1:12; note the reversal of the modifiers, "defiled . . . despised," that stresses the relationship between Judah's offerings and their altar). The effect of such careless practices did not stop with the "table," however, but also amounted to "despising" (1:6) and "profaning" (1:12; a synonym of both "despise" and "defile" but closer to the latter) the Lord's name. The prophet also expresses this idea even more directly in that they are said to have "defiled" the Lord himself (1:7; cf. Ezek 13:19; 43:7).

### (1) Indictment against the Priests (1:6)

**⁶"A son honors his father, and a servant his master. If I am a father, where is the honor due me? If I am a master, where is the respect due me?" says the LORD Almighty. "It is you, O priests, who show contempt for my name.**

**"But you ask, 'How have we shown contempt for your name?'**

**1:6** If Judah was blind to God's love, they should at least have recognized that God as their father and Lord deserved their honor. This paragraph is based on the accepted norm that a father deserves "honor" *(kābôd)* from his son (cf. Exod 20:12/Deut 5:16) and a master deserves honor and "respect" or fear (*môrāʾ* from the root *yrʾ* "to fear") from his servant (cf. Jer 34:5). It is also based on a doctrine understood by all, especially the priests, that God as Israel's Creator and Lord of the covenant was Israel's "father"[72] and their "master" (*'ădônîm*, a plural of respect). That God was Israel's father is also the assumption of 2:10a; 3:17 (see comments there). The term for "master" is elsewhere translated "Lord" when used of God.[73] But it could also designate a human master (who owned/directed servants), a husband, or a political ruler.[74]

As Israel's father and master the Lord deserved and demanded that they honor him (cf. 1 Sam 2:30; Dan 5:23; Hag 1:8). The noun *kābôd* ("honor"), which occurs in Mal 1:6 and 2:2, is used in two senses: (1) the perceivable manifestation of one's worth (hence "wealth, glory, splendor, reputation"), whether human (1 Kgs 3:13; 1 Chr 29:28; Prov 22:4; Isa 10:18; 16:14)[75] or divine (e.g., Exod 16:7; 24:16; 33:18–23; 40:34–35; Deut 5:24; Pss 24:7–10; 26:8; 63:2[Hb. 3]; Isa 40:5; 59:19; Ezek 1:28; 3:23; 39:21; 44:4; Hab 2:14,16; cf. John 1:14; 17:5),[76] and (2) the recognition of that worth with acts of deference or praise (e.g., Pss 22:23[Hb. 24]; 29:1,2; 50:15,23; Isa 42:8,12; 43:20–

---

[72] E.g., Exod 4:22–23; Deut 32:5–6,18–20; Ps 103:13; Isa 1:2; 43:1,15; 44:1–2; 45:11; 63:8,16; 64:8–12; Jer 3:19; 31:9,20; Hos 1:10; 11:1–4; Rom 9:4. Father-son terminology was used in covenants in the ANE. Note 2 Kgs 16:7, where Ahaz calls himself Tiglath-pileser's "son" (NIV, "vassal"). See D. J. McCarthy, "Notes on the Love of God in Deuteronomy and the Father-Son Relationship between Yahweh and Israel," *CBQ* 27 (1965): 144–47; F. C. Fensham, "Father and Son as Terminology for Treaty and Covenant," in *Near Eastern Studies in Honor of W. F. Albright* (Baltimore: Johns Hopkins, 1971), 121–25. Note also the NT doctrine of God as Father, esp. in Jesus' instructions (Matt 6:6,9) to the children of God to pray for their Heavenly Father's name to be honored ("hallowed"; also note the connection in the prayer between God as Father and God as King). G. R. Beasley-Murray explains, "In this context the prayer for the sanctification of the divine name denotes a plea for God to act in such a manner that his name be acknowledged in all the world as 'holy and terrible' (Ps. 111:9 RSV)," and the prayer "implies a desire for the sovereign God to unveil his glory in the judgment and salvation that initiate his kingdom in order that men may see who he is and give him the glory due to his name" (*Jesus and the Kingdom of God* [Grand Rapids: Eerdmans, 1986], 150). G. E. Ladd explains that our relationship to God as Father determines our relationship to his kingdom, and vice versa. "Those who know God as their Father are those for whom the highest good in life is the Kingdom of God and its righteousness" (*A Theology of the New Testament*, rev. ed. [Grand Rapids: Eerdmans, 1993], 83). Also C. F. D. Moule, "Children of God," *IDB* 1:558–61. On fatherhood of God see also Matt 13:43; Luke 12:32; John 1:11–12; Rom 8:14–23; 9:26; Gal 3:23–4:7; 2 Cor 6:17–18; Eph 1:5; 1 Thess 1:5; Heb 2:10; 12:5–8.

[73] E.g., Mal 1:12,14; Gen 18:27f.; Exod 4:10; Josh 7:8; 1 Kgs 3:10; Pss 2:4; 66:18; Isa 6:1,8,11; 29:13. It is also used many times as a title preceding God's name—יְהוִה אֲדֹנָי (NIV translates "Sovereign LORD"; e.g., 2 Sam 7:18).

[74] E.g., Gen 18:12; 24:9; 39:2f.; 45:8–9; Exod 21:4f.; 1 Sam 25:10; 26:15; 2 Sam 2:7; Ps 45:11; Isa 26:13; Jer 34:5; Amos 4:1.

[75] E.g., the priestly garments were to display or declare the dignity of the priestly office (Exod 28:2,40).

[76] H. D. Preuss observes, "In earthly as well as heavenly worship (Psalm 29), and also in nature (Psalm 19), God's *kābôd* is experienced and then praised" (*Old Testament Theology* [Louisville: WJKP, 1995], 1:167). He speaks of it as "the sign and the means of his [God's] active presence."

24; 48:11; Jer 13:16).[77] It is the second meaning that is reflected in the verb and that is in view in Malachi. The Lord's worth deserves praise and worship (e.g., Isa 66:19; Ezek 3:12). This is what the priests and people were not doing. Like Judah before the exile, "their words and deeds are against the LORD, defying his glorious presence [lit. 'the face of his glory']" (Isa 3:8).

Many times in Scripture "fear" is said to be the appropriate response to God,[78] before whom everyone's thoughts as well as actions are exposed (e.g., Gen 16:13; Pss 11:4; 33:13; Prov 15:3; Isa 29:15). The practical result of the fear of God is covenant loyalty (e.g., Deut 5:29; 6:2,13,24) and restraint from sin.[79] Thus the fear of God can be equated with wisdom, which should be the guiding principle of one's life (Job 28:28; Ps 111:10; Prov 1:7; Mic 6:9). According to Isa 33:6 the fear of the Lord is the key to the divine treasure of "salvation and wisdom and knowledge." It is the beginning of faith (cf. Isa 50:10). S. R. Driver wrote, "The foundation of the religious temper is the fear of God; this brings with it a natural disposition to 'walk in all his ways' ([Deut] 8:6), and ends with the devotion of the entire being to His love and service."[80] W. Eichrodt argued that although the fear of God does not involve "a naked feeling of terror," the term "reverence" alone "may be too refined to keep one aware of the intended element of inward terror."[81] Certainly "respect" does not adequately express what God's holiness should arouse in us (see, e.g., Isa 8:13 for the relationship between holiness and fear). Respect calls for politeness and such gestures as taking off one's hat, but fear results in awe and obedience. What keeps God's awesome holiness and unapproachable majesty from producing "naked terror" is the revelation of his will, the knowledge that he is not capricious,[82] and the knowledge that he is also a God of love. According to J. Gerhard, "The fear of God is to be united with the love of God; for love without fear makes men remiss, and fear without love makes them servile and des-

---

[77] W. Dyrness explains, "The idea of glory is used in the double sense of showing respect (or glorifying) and of that which inspires such respect" (*Themes in Old Testament Theology* [Downers Grove: InterVarsity, 1979], 42).

[78] E.g., 2:5; 3:16; Gen 22:12; Exod 20:20; Deut 4:10; 10:12–13,20; Josh 24:14; Pss 2:10–12; 33:18; 34:7–11; 76:7–12; 103:11–17; 145:19; 147:11; Prov 1:7; 14:27; 19:23; Isa 8:13; Jer 5:22; Matt 10:28; Acts 9:31; 10:34–35; 2 Cor 5:11; 7:1; Col 3:22; 1 Pet 1:17; 2:17; Rev 19:5.

[79] Cf. 3:5; Gen 20:11; 22:12; 42:18; Exod 1:17; 18:21; 20:20; Lev 19:14; 25:17,36,43; Deut 25:18; Jer 3:8; 32:40; Neh 5:15. Cf. M. Weinfeld, *Deuteronomy and the Deuteronomic School* (Oxford: Clarendon, 1972), 274–81. "Fear" was part of the "diplomatic vocabulary of the Near East" used in treaties to demand "exclusive allegiance" (pp. 83–84; see also p. 332).

[80] S. R. Driver, *A Critical and Exegetical Commentary on Deuteronomy* (Edinburgh: T&T Clark, 1895), 125. See also V. H. Kooy, "The Fear and Love of God in Deuteronomy," in *Grace Upon Grace* (Grand Rapids: Eerdmans, 1975), 106–16.

[81] W. Eichrodt, *Theology of the Old Testament* (Philadelphia: Westminster, 1961, 1967), 2:269.

[82] Eichrodt, *Theology of the Old Testament*, 2:273.

perate."[83] R. H. Pfeiffer wrote, "Religion in general is the tension between opposite feelings of fear and longing; at its highest level (as in Deuteronomy), religion is love accompanied by a humble sense of inferiority, reverent trust in an immensely powerful and fearful deity, who is at the same time just and benevolent."[84]

But the priests were showing the opposite attitude to honor, fear, and love. Following the divine quotation formula, "says the LORD Almighty," the audience is clarified in the phrase (lit.) "to you, O priests, despising of my name." The verb translated "show contempt" (from $bāzâ$) is a participle, indicating an ongoing or characteristic attitude. It was not an attitude of revulsion but of treating something as if it were insignificant or worthless (parallel to $qālal$, "be slight, trifling" in 1 Sam 2:30). They were not taking God seriously, with the result that they considered their service to him as unimportant, not worth much time or trouble. According to 2:9 God's judgment of the priests was that "all the people" had come to have this same attitude toward them (the judgment also announced to Eli in 1 Sam 2:30). It was the attitude of Esau to his birthright, which he considered less important than a bowl of soup (Gen 25:34; Heb 12:16). The term also described one who disregarded God's word by defiantly breaking his commands (Num 15:30–31; 2 Sam 12:9), as the priests were doing in placing defiled food on the altar (vv. 7–8).[85]

The object of their contempt was God's "name." One's "name" *(šēm)* was understood to be a manifestation, expression, or representation of one's nature or character, similar to one's $kābôd$ ("honor, glory"). The term ranged in meaning from being equivalent to the person himself (in the case of God's "name"; e.g., Gen 4:26; 12:8; Exod 20:24; Lev 24:11; Prov 18:10; Isa 30:27) to one's reputation.[86] Calling or placing one's name over or on something expressed not only one's sovereignty over it but also that it was considered an extension of oneself and thus a display of one's glory (e.g., 2 Sam 12:28; 2 Kgs 21:7; 2 Chr 7:14; Isa 4:1; 43:7; Jer 7:9–15; 14:9).[87] To speak or act in someone's

---

[83] J. Gerhard, quoted by C. F. Keil, *The Pentateuch*, in *Commentary on the Old Testament* (Grand Rapids: Eerdmans, 1976), 3:343.

[84] R. H. Pfeiffer, "The Fear of God," *JBL* 5 (1955): 41–48.

[85] Note that David, whom 2 Sam 12:9 charges with despising the Lord's word, is charged in v. 10 with despising the Lord himself, which apparently amounts to the same thing.

[86] E.g., in Gen 6:4 "men of renown" is lit. "men of name"; also 11:4; 12:2; Deut 22:14,19; Josh 9:9; 2 Sam 7:9,23; 8:13; Isa 63:12,14; Jer 32:20). Cf. Amarna letters nos. 287:60-61; 288:5-7 in *ANET,* 488.

[87] R. de Vaux says the phrase "place where I put My name" in Deuteronomy refers to claiming ownership. He traces the idea to kings inscribing their names at a site as a claim to sovereignty over the conquered area or at a temple they had built ("Le lieu que Yahvé a choisi pour y établir son nom," in *Das ferne und nahe Wort*, ed. F. Maas [Berlin: Alfred Töpelmann, 1967]: 219–29, cited in Weinfeld, *Deuteronomic School,* 194). On the close relationship between God's name and his glory see Piper, *The Justification of God,* 88. He also argues that they "consist fundamentally in his propensity to show mercy and his sovereign freedom in its distribution."

name involved *becoming* their name, a representative and extension of the person, having their authority (e.g., Exod 5:23; 1 Sam 17:45; 1 Kgs 21:8). How one behaved who bore the name would bring either honor or shame and defilement on that name and on the person whose name one bore (cf. Ezek 13:19; 36:20–23; see also comments on Mal 1:12). How one regarded or treated the name showed how one regarded the person. Since Moses and the prophets spoke in God's name (Deut 18:19), how one responded to their words betrayed one's regard for God.

Thus God's "name" here refers to his nature or character as revealed in his words and acts (cf. Exod 20:24; 23:20–21; Deut 12:5; 28:58; 1 Sam 25:25; 2 Sam 7:13; Pss 8:1[2]; 22:22[23]; 54:1,6[3,8]; Prov 18:10; Isa 30:27; 56:6; Mic 4:5;[88] John 12:28; 17:6,26).[89] In other words, what they knew of God did not impress them. The most precious truth in all God's Word is that the Lord has made himself known to us, grasping us in his redeeming love (e.g., Gen 28:12–15; John 1:9–18,51; 3:13–16). But bitterness in the hearts of the priests had numbed their spiritual senses. God to them was like a customer who enters a place of business but who does not appear to have any money for a purchase. He was neglected, given as little attention as possible, with the hope that he would soon be on his way. Or else he was like a silent partner, assigned a place in the corner where he could lend the establishment an air of respectability, as long as he kept quiet and did not get in the way. Israel continued to offer sacrifices in his name and to call upon his name to bless Israel (cf. Num 6:27), but they honored him with their lips rather than their hearts (Isa 29:13). This amounts to a violation of the third commandment, "You shall not misuse the name of the LORD your God" (Exod 20:7), one aspect of which is to use the divine name lightly, thoughtlessly, insincerely, or wickedly.[90] The priests reacted to this charge with shock and unbelief, "How have we shown contempt for your name?" This introduces the Lord's explanation.

*(2) Evidence against the Priests (1:7–9)*

> [7]"You place defiled food on my altar.
>
> "But you ask, 'How have we defiled you?'
>
> "By saying that the LORD's table is contemptible. [8]When you bring blind animals for sacrifice, is that not wrong? When you sacrifice crippled or diseased animals, is that not wrong? Try offering them to your governor! Would he be pleased with you? Would he accept you?" says the LORD Almighty.

---

[88] To "walk in the name of the LORD" means to live in accordance with his character as it is revealed in his precepts.

[89] On the significance of the divine "name" see also Eichrodt, *Theology of the Old Testament,* 1:206–8. Also note G. F. Oehler's definition, "the whole side of the divine nature which is turned toward man" (*Theology of the Old Testament* [Minneapolis: Klock & Klock, 1978], 125).

[90] Cf. W. C. Kaiser, Jr., *Toward Old Testament Ethics* (Grand Rapids: Zondervan, 1983), 87–88.

**9"Now implore God to be gracious to us. With such offerings from your hands, will he accept you?"—says the LORD Almighty.**

**1:7** "You place" translates an active participle (pointing to an ongoing practice) meaning "presenting"[91] and is parallel to the active participle in v. 6 translated "show contempt." Both modify "O priests." Because of their ignorance of God's Word and carelessness of his character, they could despise his name and defile his altar and yet deny it. The word describing the food as "defiled" is also used of the Lord's table in v. 12 and of the Lord himself in the next clause in v. 7.[92] It is from the verb $gā\dot{}al$, which is almost identical to the verb $gāʿal$ that meant "abhor, loathe, feel disgust." The latter is in the same semantic range as the verb $bāzâ$, "show contempt," in the previous verse.[93] We could argue that the verb $gāʾal$ is used here with the meaning of $gāʿal$ and translate "How have we loathed you?" in v. 7 and "saying of the Lord's table, 'It is loathed'" in v. 12.[94] Although this would be reasonable, such a meaning in v. 7 would yield "you place loathed food on my altar," which is less likely. The meaning "defiled," however, appears difficult too when applied to the Lord in v. 7, "How have we defiled you?"[95] The previous clauses have said nothing about defiling the Lord, only about despising his name and offering defiled food. The solution seems to be that the verb $gāʾal$ is functioning in both semantic ranges "defile" and "loathe." It is, in fact, a play on words.[96] It is used both in the sense "defile" and as a synonym for $bāzâ$, "show contempt." The effect is to strengthen the point that presenting "defiled" offerings was betraying the priests' contempt for the Lord and his worship and polluting everything that they did.

---

[91] The verb is a *hiphil* from נגשׁ and occurs also in 1:8,11 *[hophal]*; 2:12; 3:3. Its more general meaning is "bring" (cf. Exod 21:6; 1 Sam 14:18; 15:32; 23:9; 1 Kgs 5:1 [Eng., 4:21]; Amos 6:3), and it is frequently used of bringing offerings (Exod 32:6; Lev 2:8; 8:14; Judg 6:19; 1 Sam 14:34; 2 Chr 29:23; Amos 5:25).

[92] The word translated "defiled" in v. 7 (מְגֹאָל) is a *pual* (passive) participle from גאל (II), "to desecrate, defile" *(HALOT)*. The offerings desecrated the altar because they were defiled or impure themselves. The LXX translates it by an aorist passive, ἠλισγημένους, "polluted." The root is used of hands "stained" with blood in Isa 59:3 (see also Lam 4:14; Isa 63:3; Dan 1:8).

[93] The verbs occur together in Ezek 16–17.

[94] *HALOT* explains it as a by-form of געל, "abhor, loathe, feel disgust" (cf. J. Blau, "Über Homonyme und angeblich Homonyme Wurzeln," *VT* 6 (1956): 244–45.

[95] But the concept is found in the expression "profane" (חלל) the Lord's "name" in 1:11–12. See also Ezek 13:19; 22:26; 43:7–8. The LXX translates ἐν τίνι ἠλισγήσαμεν αὐτούς, "How have we defiled *them?*" Targum translates, "How is it polluted/abominable?" (except in Codex Reuchlinianus, which reads, "How have we repudiated you?" (Cathcart and Gordon, *The Targum of the Minor Prophets*, 230). Contra J. M. P. Smith (*Malachi*, 42) these translations are clearly trying to avoid the theological problem and do not reflect a variant reading (cf. R. P. Gordon, "The Citation of the Targums in Recent English Bible Translations," *JJS* 26 [1975]: 57).

[96] It may also be called a "portmanteau word" (cf. W. G. E. Watson, *Classical Hebrew Poetry*, JSOTSup 26 [Sheffield: JSOT, 1986], 244).

Offering defiled sacrifices would have the effect of defiling the altar. The priests showed their contempt for the Lord's name by offering him food that desecrated the very sanctuary whose holiness they were responsible to maintain (cf. Num 18:1–7).[97] The violation by Aaron's sons, Nadab and Abihu, in offering "unauthorized fire before the LORD" was interpreted as a failure to honor the Lord and was punished by death (Lev 10:1–3). The priests of Judah had apparently forgotten this vivid lesson on God's holiness and the serious nature of their responsibility. The question "How have we defiled you?" may be understood as virtually identical to "How have we shown contempt for your name?" in v. 6. "Your name" is a less direct equivalent of "you." The sense of the second question is then, How does presenting defiled food amount to loathing/defiling you? The priests are claiming not to understand how their improper offerings would affect *the Lord*. This is a call for the Lord to explain his initial answer, as he proceeds to do in vv. 7b–8.

The Lord's explanation relies on an implied comparison between the altar and a ruler's table at which guests were served (see also Ezek 39:20; 41:22; 44:16).[98] In the various other places in Scripture where reference is made to someone's "table," the person named (e.g., "the king's table" in 1 Sam 20:29 and 1 Kgs 4:27 [Hb. 5:7]; "David's table" in 2 Sam 9:7–13; and "Jezebel's table" in 1 Kgs 18:19) is the host.[99] For his family, friends, and guests he provides food that is brought by his servants (cf. 1 Kgs 4:27 [5:7]; 10:5). In this paragraph in Malachi the Lord is pictured as the host, the altar is the table, the offerings are the "food" (not a term commonly used in the OT for temple offerings[100]), and the priests are the servants who bring the food. The people of Judah are perhaps the guests who are to enjoy God's fellowship at

---

[97] J. Pedersen says "the priest was the servant of a sanctuary" whose duty it was "to maintain the holiness of the place" (*Israel: Its Life and Culture,* 2d ed. [London/Copenhagen: Oxford University Press/Branner og Korch, 1959], 3–4:157). According to R. Abba, "The essential function of the Levitical priesthood is . . . to assure, maintain, and constantly re-establish the holiness of the elect people of God" ("Priests and Levites," *IDB,* 3:877–78). W. Harrelson says that "priests were first of all guardians of sanctuaries, charged to see that when the Holy appeared the community was helped, not harmed, by that appearance" (*From Fertility Cult to Worship* [Garden City: Doubleday, 1969], 46).

[98] The quotation is lit., "Yahweh's table—it is despised." This is a grammatical construction variously known as casus pendens, nominative absolute, or extraposition. See especially G. Khan, *Studies in Semitic Syntax* (New York: Oxford University, 1988), xxvi–xxvii; also GKC §143; *GBH* §156; T. Muraoka, *Emphatic Words and Structures in Biblical Hebrew* (Jerusalem: Magnes, 1985), 93–99. Its function here is to heighten the discourse prominence of its clause in the paragraph and to call attention to the identification of the altar as "the LORD'S table."

[99] See also 2 Sam 19:29 [Eng. v. 28]; 1 Kgs 2:7; Neh 5:17; Job 36:16.

[100] Offerings are referred to as "food" (לֶחֶם) in Lev 3:11; 21:6,8,21; 22:25; Num 28:2; Ezek 44:7. The figurative interpretation offered here is the opposite of Tate's, who supposes that the term "recalls the idea of sacrifices and offerings as food for the deity" ("Questions for Priests and People," 396).

his table and also those who furnish the food that was prepared for the king (or governor; see v. 8).

The table is a symbol of hospitality and relationship, and the attitude toward someone's table would betray the attitude toward the person and the relationship. Although the priests would not likely have used the term "contemptible" for the Lord's table, their actions spoke for them.

**1:8** Judging an offering's acceptability was the priest's responsibility (cf. Lev 27:11–12,14). The kinds of sacrifices that the people were bringing to the temple and that the priests were declaring acceptable and offering to the Lord were in clear violation of the Mosaic cultic law (cf. Lev 22:18–25; Deut 15:21).[101] That the temple personnel were lax in their responsibilities during this period is also expressed in Ezra (9:1; 10:5) and Nehemiah (13:4–9,22,29–30). But according to Ezek 22:26, this was not a new problem in Israel: "Her priests do violence to my law and profane my holy things; they do not distinguish between the holy and the common; they teach that there is no difference between the unclean and the clean; and they shut their eyes to the keeping of my Sabbaths, so that I am profaned among them."

The term translated "wrong" in Mal 1:8 (*rā*) can also mean "unpleasant, displeasing, evil" and is used of an animal that was "bad" or unacceptable for offering (Lev 27:10,12,14,33; see also Deut 23:9[10]; Prov 20:14).[102] God's love for his people should have stirred up their love for him, especially in his priests, but their disobedience demonstrated their lack of love.[103] It even demonstrated that they placed no value upon him—they despised his name. Those bringing food to a ruler's table would bring only the best available. If they did not, it would be because they despised him and cared nothing for his favor. Yet the very purpose for offering gifts to a "governor" was to please him and gain his favor. Valuable gifts would declare the glory of the recipient. The point made here ironically by an imperative (lit. "bring it to your governor" but implying an underlying condition) is that if such pitiful gifts were made to the governor, he would be insulted and angry. The following questions expect negative replies. The governor would not be pleased or favorable toward them, and they would not be so foolish as to think otherwise.[104] But God's people had

---

[101] Vv. 8,13 have only one term, עִוֵּר, "blind," in common with the list in Lev 22:22. Deut 15:21 shares the term פִּסֵּחַ, "crippled," as well as עִוֵּר. רַע is used there modifying מוּם, together translated "serious flaw."

[102] The word may be used here because of its double meaning of "bad/wrong" (suggestion from K. A. Mathews). The question "Is that not wrong?" (אֵין רָע) can also be translated as a statement, "It is not wrong." This could make sense in the context if it expresses either the priests' attitude or the judgment they render when such animals are presented (Tate, "Questions for Priests and People"). For the use of רַע meaning "wrong" see 1 Sam 24:11.

[103] Cf. 1:2; Exod 20:6; Deut 5:10; 7:12; 11:1,13; Josh 22:5; Neh 1:5; Dan 9:4; John 14:15,21–24; 1 John 5:3.

[104] The verb translated "be pleased" is from רָצָה and occurs in vv. 10,13, translated "accept." "Accept" in v. 8 translates the idiom "lift up the face," which can mean to "show partiality" (as in 2:9; see fuller discussion there) or, as in vv. 8–9, to "accept, be favorable toward" someone.

greater respect for their earthly rulers than for the Lord (cf. Matt 10:28). A primary function of the sacrificial system was as a testimony to the glory and grace of God. But the priests of Judah were conducting so-called worship that not only obscured God's character but misrepresented it. It was a false testimony, full of lies and unrighteousness, that profaned God's name.[105]

**1:9** The second imperative "implore" is also ironic. It translates an expression that literally means "soften the face." The verb *ḥālâ* with object "face" (here "the face of God") means to "pacify, appease, entreat the favor of" someone.[106] On the human level it is used in Prov 19:6 of trying to gain ("curry") the favor of a "ruler" in order to obtain some benefit. The parallel line there speaks of befriending "a man who gives gifts." It can have a similar meaning when God is the object. King Saul used the term when explaining to Samuel why he had inappropriately offered sacrifices—in order to obtain God's help against the Philistines (1 Sam 13:12). Like the priests in Malachi, he claimed to be seeking God's favor, but his disobedience in fact showed a disregard for God. In several cases when this verb is used, the subjects are trying to move God to turn from wrath (cf. Exod 32:11; 1 Kgs 13:6; 2 Kgs 13:4; Jer 26:19; 2 Chr 33:12), but the prophet Daniel understood that this was to be accomplished not just with sacrifices but "by turning from our sins and giving attention to your truth" (Dan 9:13).

The imperative in v. 9, followed by a one-word clause meaning literally "that he may be gracious/show favor to us *[wîḥānēnû]*," could be an exhortation for the priests to seek God's favor by appropriate means—prayer and repentance rather than by unacceptable sacrifices.[107] Yet the following question, "Will he accept you?" (lit., "Will he lift the face on your account?"), demands a negative reply.[108] The preceding clause probably is also to be

---

[105] According to Piper, "unrighteousness" (ἀδικία) in Pauline usage (e.g., Rom 1:18,29; 1 Cor 13:6; 2 Thess 2:10,12) refers to "a disposition and conduct which contradict truth, particularly the truth about God" (*The Justification of God,* 94). In contrast, God's righteousness or truth, he explains, is "his unswerving commitment always to bring his actions into accord with the reality of his infinitely worthy glory" (p. 95).

[106] *HALOT* gives the meaning of פָּנִים חִלָּה as "to soften by caressing; to appease, flatter." The *qal* of חלה means "be/become weak," so the *piel* expression (occurring 16x in the OT) would mean to change an angry, fixed, or disagreeable face into a more agreeable one. Note the idiomatic use of the *niphal* in Amos 6:6 (translated "grieve"), the *qal* in 1 Sam 22:8 (translated "is concerned"), in Isa 57:10 ("faint"), and especially in Jer 5:3 ("felt pain"), where it is parallel to "made their faces hard" (פְּנֵיהֶם חִזְּקוּ). Cf. also עוז / עַז, "strong/be strong," with פָּנִים in Deut 28:50; Dan 8:23; Eccl 8:1 (where "brighten the face" is the opposite); Prov 7:13; 21:29. For an alternate explanation see K. Seybold, "חָלָה, *chālāh*," *TDOT* 4.407–9.

[107] Note the NEB translation: "But now, if you placate God, he may show you mercy; if you do this, will he withhold his favour from you?"

[108] Note that the divine quotation formula, "says the LORD Almighty," concluding both vv. 8 and 9 is attached in each case to the clause using the "lift up the face" idiom. This helps call attention to the comparison between the governor and God as recipients of gifts. The thrice-repeated use of פָּנִים, "face," in vv. 8c–9 may also mark the climax of vv. 6–9. The idiom is also used in Gen 4:7 (observation from K. A. Mathews).

understood as a question, but it reads literally, "From your hand came [was] this." "From your hand" is also used in vv. 10,13 of their unacceptable offerings. Finally, the verb translated "implore" (the imperative, *ḥallû*) echoes the participle *(ḥōleh)* from the same root *(ḥlh),* translated "diseased" in vv. 8,13,[109] thus suggesting (with sarcasm) that they continue offering these unclean sacrifices (note similar sarcastic instructions to sacrifice in Amos 4:4–5). So, as with the imperative in v. 8, we should understand as ironic the exhortation in v. 9 to seek God's favor.[110] M. Fishbane thinks there is an allusion to the blessing the priests offered according to Num 6:25–26 (lit.): "May Yahweh brighten his face toward you and be gracious to you *[wîḥunnekā].* May Yahweh lift up his face toward you and give you peace."[111] The prophet is saying: "Go ahead with your beseeching God's favor with these pitiful offerings. He won't accept you. He won't respond favorably on your account. Your governor would be insulted by such gifts. Yet you think that with them you can turn God's head and cajole him."

## 3. Command: Stop the Pointless Offerings (1:10)

**[10]"Oh, that one of you would shut the temple doors, so that you would not light useless fires on my altar! I am not pleased with you," says the LORD Almighty, "and I will accept no offering from your hands.**

**1:10** Here occurs the first true directive in the book.[112] It is based on the grounds presented in vv. 6–9 (echoed in v. 10b), and elaborated in vv. 11–14, that the priests demonstrated by their improper offerings an attitude of contempt for the Lord. Although the exhortation is given to shut down the temple, this is tragic irony. What the Lord actually desired can be inferred from 1:6–14:

---

[109] חַלּוּ ("implore") is a *piel* imperative; וְחֹלֶה ("or diseased") is a *qal* active participle.

[110] The function of the initial וְעַתָּה, "so now," is probably to introduce the climax or punch line of the author's illustration. It may be that "Implore God to be gracious to us" was what the offerers said to the priests when they brought their putrid presents to the temple.

[111] M. Fishbane, *Biblical Interpretation in Ancient Israel* (Oxford: Clarendon, 1985), 333. He also thinks that מְחַלְלִים ("profane") in v. 12 echoes חַלּוּ ("implore") in v. 9. The priests thought they were beseeching God, but all they were doing was profaning him. Fishbane argues (pp. 332–34) that Mal 1:6–2:9 is "a remarkable post-exilic example of the aggadic exegesis of Num 6:23–27," having "more than casual, terminological similarities" with it (p. 332).

[112] The Eng. clause, "Oh, that one of you would shut the temple doors," translates two Hb. clauses: a desiderative clause (cf. GKC §151a; *IBHS* §18.2f) that could be translated, "Would that one were also [גַּם] among you?" followed by a clause with a *waw* plus jussive, "that he might shut the doors." T. Muraoka notes that גַּם "is frequently employed when giving an exaggerated, aggravated or extreme case" (*Emphatic Words and Structures in Biblical Hebrew*, 143). Its common additive force makes sense here, serving to contrast the wished-for priest who would shut the gates with those priests just mentioned who were bringing improper sacrifices. According to GKC §153 גַּם here "is placed before two co-ordinate sentences, although, strictly speaking, it applies only to the second."

fear and honor manifested in proper sacrifices from pure hearts. But he preferred no ritual to the empty ritual they were orchestrating. Not long before, he
had summoned the Babylonians to destroy the city and temple for Judah's violations of his holiness. Prior to those drastic measures he had solemnly and fer-
vently cried out against their "evil deeds" and declared to Judah in a similar
fashion through the prophet Isaiah (Isa 1:10–17) that he had had "more than
enough" of "meaningless" offerings *(minḥâ)* and "detestable" incense
*(qĕṭōret)* from their hands, that he had "no pleasure" *(ḥpṣ)* in the multitude of
their sacrifices, and that he hated even their assemblies for feast days and found
them to be a "burden" that he was "weary of bearing," calling them "evil" (see
also Amos 5:21–23). In the face of their wicked lives God had implored them
with anger and grief to cease the clamor and frenzy of their religious activity:
"When you come to appear before me, who has asked this of you, this trampling of my courts? Stop bringing meaningless offerings!" (Isa 1:12–13a).

According to 2 Chr 28:24, idolatrous King Ahaz of Judah "shut the doors of
the LORD's temple and set up altars at every street corner in Jerusalem" (cf.
2 Chr 29:3,6–7).[113] The present verse may be an allusion to that event, the
point being that what the priests of Judah were doing was no better than Ahaz's
idolatry. God ironically wished for another King Ahaz who would construct a
visible barrier between God and his people like the one they already had constructed in their hearts (cf. Isa 59:1–3). After Judah's great wickedness had
brought about the devastating punishment of exile, it is amazing that the abundance of Judah's gratitude for the Lord's restoration should have reverted so
quickly to empty ritual.

Many have claimed that the prophets opposed ritual itself as a devolution
from heartfelt religion.[114] This reading of the prophets is based on a denial of
the Pentateuch as verbal revelation and on a reconstruction of Israel's history
that is at variance with the biblical account. The prophets are then read in the
context of that reconstruction. That Samuel, one of the prophets cited as verbally opposing sacrifice (1 Sam 15:22–23), also offered sacrifice (1 Sam 9:13)
shows that the prophets' objection was not to the principle of sacrifice but to
particular sacrifices being offered.[115] From the beginning the essence of
Israel's revealed religion was to be wholehearted trust in and devotion to the
Lord (e.g., Deut 6:4–6), manifested in and authenticated by obedience to God's
revealed will (Deut 5:29; cf. John 14:15; Rom 1:5). Sacrificial ritual that did

---

[113] M. J. Selman explains that "shutting the temple doors . . . does not contradict Ahaz' worship
on the new altar [cf. 2 Kgs 16:10–18], since the latter was outside the temple" (*1,2 Chronicles,*
TOTC [Leicester: InterVarsity, 1994], 482). On דְלָתַיִם referring to the temple doors see also
1 Kgs 6:34; 2 Kgs 18:16; Ezek 41:25; Neh 6:10.

[114] E.g., G. J. Botterweck, "חָפֵץ, *ḥāpēṣ*," *TDOT* 5:101–3.

[115] See T. E. McComiskey, "Hosea," in *The Minor Prophets, Vol. 1, Hosea, Joel, Amos* (Grand
Rapids: Baker, 1992), 92.

not arise from wholehearted devotion to the Lord was sin (Prov 15:8; Isa 1:13; Amos 4:4; cf. Rom 14:23; Heb 11:6), and ritual that masked a perversion of biblical ethics did not arise from wholehearted devotion, nor did ritual that violated biblical instructions. God hates acts and words of "worship" rendered hollow by acts of disobedience (Amos 5:21–24; Mic 6:6–8; Matt 23:23). The prophets never opposed ritual *as* meaningless but ritual *that was* meaningless. Authentic worship can be expressed in formal ritual acts as well as in spontaneous acts, and either can be sham or hypocrisy. Israel's ritual properly performed was for expressing their faith, learning and proclaiming the nature of their holy God, and receiving atonement. It was never intended to replace obedience or to hide a disregard for God's instructions (cf. Pss 40:6–8; 51:16–19).

The word "useless" translates the adverb *ḥinnām*, which is from the same root (*ḥnn*) as the verb "be gracious" in v. 9 and is related to the word *ḥēn*, "favor, grace."[116] It describes something done either (1) gratuitously or undeservedly, without recompense or justification (cf. Gen 29:15; Exod 21:2; Num 11:5; Jer 22:13; Lam 3:52), or (2) without purpose or effect, that is, "in vain" (cf. Prov 1:17, "How *useless* to spread a net in full view of all the birds!" and Ezek 6:10, "I did not threaten *in vain* to bring this calamity on them"). The second sense is the one that fits here. Although the priests would have had some purpose in mind—to appeal for God's favor or perhaps just to maintain the tradition—the Lord of the temple was declaring that their activity was not only pointless but counterproductive. It was making him angry.[117]

The absoluteness of his response might be conveyed better by translating more literally, "I have no pleasure [*ḥēpeṣ*] in you."[118] Because the priests

---

[116] Fishbane argues that this is an intentional wordplay. He notes the similarity of תָּאִירוּ, "light fires," in 1:10, נוֹרָא, "to be feared," in 1:14, and הַמְּאֵרָה, "a curse," and וְאָרוֹתִי, "and I will curse," in 2:2 to יָאֵר, "make shine," in the priestly blessing of Num 6:26. Thus "the gift . . . of a brightened divine countenance which leads to divine favour . . . and the raising of the divine countenance . . . which leads to . . . peace . . . [in Num 6:25–26] are punningly countered by the prophet's wish that the priests will no longer ignite . . . the alter [sic] in vain . . . and by the anticipated divine curse" (*Biblical Interpretation in Ancient Israel,* 333).

[117] M. Horton likens contemporary religiosity to Adam and Eve's fig-leaf religion: "Fearful of judgment, we devise new ways of dealing with our sins and consequent guilt. Our coverings may be more sophisticated, gilded with psychological or spiritual terminology, but they are still nothing more than fig leaves. We want to find 'the spiritual,' perhaps, but the last person we want to meet up with is the God who is always there, for he knows what we are really like and will certainly judge us. Thus, we prefer encounters with 'the sacred' to encountering God himself. Sacredness is ambiguous, open, free, and boundless. God himself is a particular person—Yahweh—who holds us responsible for our sins" (*In the Face of God* [Dallas: Word, 1996], 6–7).

[118] אֵין־לִי חֵפֶץ בָּכֶם. The noun חֵפֶץ, "pleasure," also occurs with אֵין, "there is not," and בְּ, "in," in Eccl 5:3[4]; 12:1; Jer 22:28; 48:38; Hos 8:8. In the last three of these no "pleasure" means no "value" in one's eyes, i.e., being "despised" (בָזוּה in Jer 22:28). When negated, the verb חָפֵץ ("is pleased") "comes to mean rejection" (G. J. Botterweck, "חָפֵץ *ḥāpēṣ*," *TDOT* 5:98; cf. Job 21:14; Prov 18:2; Jer 6:10). In the context of desired friendship see its use in 1 Sam 18:22; 19:1. The verb occurs in Mal 2:17 and 3:1. See also 2 Sam 15:26; Isa 62:4; 65:12; Jer 9:24.

despised the Lord, he despised them and rejected their hypocritical expressions of devotion. The statement is then underlined by the divine quotation formula, "says the LORD Almighty," and by the elaboration, "I will accept no offering from your hand."[119] The verb here translated "accept" (from *rāṣâ*) is rendered "be pleased with" in v. 8. It is from a root synonymous with that of *ḥēpeṣ* in the preceding clause.[120] In v. 8 the object of *rāṣâ* is the one bringing gifts; here and in v. 13 ("should I *accept* them from your hands?") it is the gifts themselves. The priests' sinful attitudes were displayed in their improper sacrifices, and the Lord was displeased with both. Verse 10b echoes and intensifies vv. 8–9, surrounding and thus heightening the directive of v. 10a and effectively concluding the first half of vv. 6–14 with a somber and ominous crescendo of divine displeasure. For the Lord's servant who longs to hear from him, "Well done, good and faithful servant" (Matt 25:21), the evaluation "I have no pleasure in you" would be a sickening word. But apparently they did not care.

The Lord is not dependent upon human offerings or service. They are a means of testifying to his greatness and exalting his name, and he is pleased with sincere praise and worship. Worship also benefits the worshipers, serving to nourish their relationship with God individually and to encourage one another in the faith.[121] But religious activity performed without genuine love and gratitude to God is not only useless but repulsive to him because it slanders his character. God does not need our gifts or our service, and his favor cannot be bought. Gifts that are offered "reluctantly or under compulsion" (2 Cor 9:7) humiliate the recipient and place him under obligation. The God who can transform stones into followers (Matt 3:9) wants no part in such a transaction.

---

[119] The three divine quotation formulas in vv. 8,9,10 all mark expressions of displeasure. The first two mark questions; and the last, the divine pronouncement. The result is emphatic repetition: Would the governor be pleased? Was God pleased? God was not pleased.

[120] Cf. Quell, "αγαπαω, αγαπη, αγαπητος," *TDNT* 1:22. The last two clauses of v. 10 are poetically parallel, though separated by the divine quotation formula (the parallelism explains the position of *ûminḥâ* in its clause):

| ʾên- | lî | ḥēpeṣ | bakem | ʾāmar | yhwh | ṣĕbāʾôt |
|------|------|--------|--------|--------|--------|--------|
| There-is-not | to-me | pleasure | in-you | says | Yahweh-of | hosts. |
| ûminḥâ | lōʾ- | erṣeh | miyyedkem | | | |
| and-offering | not | I-will-accept | from-hand-your | | | |

חפץ and רצה also occur as a word pair in Pss 51:18[16]; 147:10. The use of the jussive וְיִסְגֹּר, "would shut," the divine quotation formula, and the elaboration or paraphrase all help mark this verse as the most prominent in the first division.

[121] G. H. Mallone notes, however, that the casual question, "Did you enjoy the worship service today?" may betray an improper self-centered attitude to worship. "Whether we enjoy it or not, are comfortable or not, are built up or not, none of these areas is a sufficient criterion for measuring worship. Rather, the test of any worship should be, 'What did God receive from it? What did I put into it? Did God enjoy the worship? Was he pleased by the sacrifice of our praise and our service? Or was he discontent because our wills, emotions and intellects were disengaged in the process?'" (*Furnace of Renewal: A Vision for the Church* [Downers Grove: InterVarsity, 1981], 51–52).

## 4. Situation: The Priests' Worship Profaning the Lord's Name (1:11–14)

The most prominent verb in this paragraph is "profane" in v. 12. It is a Hebrew participle (lit. "are profaning") and serves to describe further the priests' behavior that necessitated the prophet's words. This paragraph shares a common theme with vv. 6–9 that the priests were showing contempt for the Lord by their careless sacrifices (see chart in introduction to vv. 6–9 showing the repetitive structure of vv. 6–14). But whereas the earlier section draws a contrast to gifts made to the governor, this one relies on a contrast with the pure worship the Lord would someday receive from the Gentiles (see also comments on 1:5). The paragraph is marked off by references in vv. 11 and 14 to the Lord's name "among the nations," in both cases made prominent by the divine quotation formula "says the LORD Almighty." Both verses are also structurally parallel to v. 6, which also refers to the Lord's "name." The point of the paragraph is that although a time is coming when even Gentiles all over the world will fear the Lord, God's own chosen people of Judah were profaning him. The antithetical prophecy of Gentile worship begins and ends the paragraph in vv. 11 and 14b, enclosing the thesis in v. 12 and two arguments demonstrating the thesis in vv. 13 and 14a.

### (1) Prophecy of Gentile Worship (1:11)

**[11]My name will be great among the nations, from the rising to the setting of the sun. In every place incense and pure offerings will be brought to my name, because my name will be great among the nations," says the LORD Almighty.**

**1:11**   Whereas among the priests of Judah the Lord's name was "despised," that is, considered of little value (see comments on v. 6), among the nations, God's name someday would "be great." The prophecy of future Gentile worship is stated in two clauses in this verse, then is repeated chiastically (i.e., in reverse). The repetition is more pronounced in Hebrew (see the following literal translation), where both clauses that prophesy the exalting of God's name begin with *kî*, "for, because":[122]

---

[122] Neither כִּי clause has a clear causal relationship to the preceding. The excellent study by A. Aejmelaeus explains that כִּי clauses preceding the main clause can be conditional, temporal, or causal ("Function and Interpretation of כִּי in Biblical Hebrew," *JBL* 105 [1986]: 197; also see *GBH* §170n). The parallel with the second כִּי and the similar use of כִּי in v. 14 indicates that the first use of כִּי here is not temporal. Translating the second כִּי clause "when I am a great king" would make little sense. Preposed causal כִּי may be a shorthand version of יַעַן כִּי, which almost always introduces a preposed causal clause (1 Kgs 13:21; 21:29; Isa 3:16; 7:5; 8:6; 29:13) or תַּחַת כִּי (Deut 4:37; Prov 1:29). Typically circumstantial clauses with בְּ + inf. const. are usually understood causally in 1 Kgs 10:9; 1 Chr 15:26; 2 Chr 2:10[11]; 9:8; 12:12; 16:7; 19:2; 28:9; Neh 10:1; see also כִּי in 2 Chr 20:37. Greater ambiguity exists between causal and temporal כִּי in present and future contexts because narrative is often marked by the use of וַיְהִי, whereas וְהָיָה (e.g., Exod 1:10) less often marks future clauses.

A       Because (*kî*) from the rising of the sun even to its setting
        *great [will be] my name among the nations,*
   B       in every place *incense* is going to be brought to my name;
   B′      and pure *offerings,*
A′      for (*kî*) *great [will be] my name among the nations,*
        says Yahweh of hosts.

The third clause is abbreviated to only the subject, "pure offerings," and depends for its predicate upon the previous clause (hence the NIV translation as a single clause).[123]

Such a repetitive structure is used in Malachi for rhetorical underlining to strengthen either the beginning of a new section, as here (see also 1:6; 2:10; 3:1,7), or the center of one of the chiastic divisions (cf. 1:10; 2:15–16). Here it stresses the antithesis of the paragraph, that the Gentiles, who had not had the biblical covenants and the long history of God's faithfulness to them, who had not been the recipients of God's special love since the time of Abraham, and of God's instruction since the time of Moses (cf. Eph 2:12), would nevertheless one day lift up the name of the Lord in praise and honor.[124] This verse reminds us of God's promise to make Abraham's name great among the nations, who would be blessed through him (Gen 12:2–3). God had purposed that Israel in return should be a kingdom of priests to glorify him among the nations (cf. Exod 19:6; Rev 1:6). Although God's purpose to make himself known and worshiped among the nations would not be thwarted, he would do it differently from the way Moses may have expected (cf. Ezek 36:20–36; 39:7; Rom 3:1–8; 11:11–12). The Hebrew Scriptures continue to declare what Israel was supposed to be and how they failed.[125] Furthermore, through Israel would come the Messiah (e.g., Rom 9:5), who would himself be a light to the nations (Isa 42:6) and through whom Israel will finally become the light they were intended to be (Isa 60:1–3).[126]

The future setting of vv. 11 and 14b is indicated more by the situation than

---

[123] That this is grammatically a separate clause is made likely by the two כִּי clauses and the placement of the subject "pure offerings."

[124] Cf. 1 Kgs 8:41–42; Ps 86:9–10; Isa 2:2–3; 19:19–25; Jer 3:17; 16:19–20; Amos 9:12 [cp. Acts 15:17]; Mic 7:17; Zeph 2:11; 3:9; Zech 2:15 [Eng. 11]; 8:20–23; 14:16; Rev 21:24; *Tob* 13:11; *1 Enoch* 90:30–36.

[125] Cf. Wright's discussion of Israel as God's ethical paradigm in *Eye for an Eye,* 40–45.

[126] This is not to demean Israel's role as the divinely chosen path for the Messiah. As Piper argues, the Gk. construction in Rom 9:5 ("from them is traced the human ancestry of Christ") stresses that "with the coming of Christ, the privileges of Israel have reached their decisive climax" (*The Justification of God,* 43). R. L. Saucy also shows from Ezek 36:23 (also Jer 16:14–20) that Israel will continue to serve as God's revelatory instrument in that "Gentile recognition of Israel's God" will be brought about by "the vindication of the name of God through the restoration of Israel under the new covenant" (*The Case for Progressive Dispensationalism* [Grand Rapids: Zondervan, 1993], 123).

by the grammar. The main clauses are either verbless (lit. "my name great among the nations") or employ participles ("will be brought" in v. 11 and "is to be feared" in v. 14, probably better translated "is going to be brought/presented"[127] and "is going to be feared"). When participles are used as predicates, the time is often future (but not always; see vv. 7,12) and the stress is on the certainty of the event.[128] In the present case the future time is clear from the fact that the Gentile nations in general were not then recognizing the Lord's greatness and worshiping him.

Some have attempted to interpret 1:11,14b as pointing to something true in Malachi's day, often arguing for a universalistic perspective in the book (also see comments at 1:5; 2:10). Y. Kaufmann cites some (Wellhausen, Marti, Sellin, Horst, Kittel, Torrey, Lindblom, Oesterley-Robinson, Margolis, Segal) who have taken the verses as "acknowledgement of the 'monotheism of the pagan faiths'" and that "idol worship is really worship of one God."[129] Besides absurdly contradicting much of the rest of the Old Testament as well as the thrice-repeated reference to "my name" in 1:11 itself and the apparent rejection of pagan religion in 2:11, this interpretation violates the structure of Malachi's argument, in which Gentile worship of the Lord must be an assumed fact acknowledged by all his hearers. It would seriously weaken his argument regarding the strikingly antithetical and foolish nature of Judah's careless worship if the premise were such a new, highly debatable (even heretical) assertion.[130] It would also be totally illogical and utterly confusing to the readers that pagan worship in the name of pagan gods in pagan temples could be "pure" and acceptable to God, while Judah's own sacrifices to the Lord in the Jerusalem temple were "useless" (v. 10). Malachi's supposed universalist perspective is also at odds with the declaration in 1:4 that Edom was "a people always under the wrath of the LORD" and with the commitment to the law of Moses in 4:4[Hb. 3:22].[131]

---

[127] The verb is passive of נגשׁ. The active participle occurs in 1:7 ("place") and the imperfect in 1:8 ("bring"). The meaning "present" fits the context better throughout this chapter.

[128] According to Waltke and O'Connor, when the participle has a future orientation, "it denotes the full range of ideas connoted by English 'I am going to . . .,' namely, certainty, often with immanency" (*IBHS* §37.6f).

[129] Y. Kaufmann, *History of the Religion of Israel* (New York: Ktav, 1977), 4:442–43.

[130] G. A. Smith, for example, applauds the assertion in 1:11 that "the very sacrifices of the heathen are pure and acceptable to Him" as "perhaps the most original contribution which the Book of Malachi makes to the development of prophecy" (*The Book of the Twelve Prophets*, rev. [Garden City: Doubleday, Doran & Co., 1929], 2:350–51). R. H. Pfeiffer also claims that Malachi's "religious liberalism [is] unparalleled in the Old Testament" (*Introduction to the Old Testament* [N.Y.: Harper & Brothers, 1948], 613). Others have rejected 1:11–14 as original in the book largely because of its alleged uncharacteristic universal perspective (K. Elliger, *Das Buch der zwölf kleinen Propheten*, ATD [Göttengen: Vandenhoeck & Ruprecht, 1967], 2:198–99).

[131] Although Kaufmann rejects such a "universalistic" perspective in Malachi, he retains the present tense by understanding the verses as hyperbolic, "literary flourishes" expressing "the same idealistic, unrealistic universalism" found elsewhere in the Bible, as in Jonah 1:16; 3:5; Pss 47:3; 113:3; Ezra 1:2; Dan 4:11–34; 6:21,26–28 (*History of the Religion of Israel*, 4:442–43). M. Smith, *Palestinian Parties and Politics* (New York: Columbia University Press, 1971), 93–94, considers it a reference to "an extensive private cult of Yahweh carried on by gentiles" in the postexilic period.

Baldwin also makes the point that the phrase "from the rising to the setting of the sun" is found elsewhere in the Bible "in contexts which look towards an eschatological demonstration of the Lord's person to the whole inhabited earth" (cf. Pss 50:1; 113:3; Isa 45:6).[132] Malachi 1:11,14b especially echo Isa 59:19a: "From the west, men will fear the name of the LORD, and from the rising of the sun, they will revere his glory." Jesus alluded to these prophecies when he declared in Matt 8:11 (cf. Isa 25:6–8) that "many will come from the east and the west, and will take their places at the feast with Abraham, Isaac and Jacob in the kingdom of heaven." Saucy affirms that "the messianic kingdom is never equated with Israel alone, but always has a universal dimension that encompasses the nations also."[133] Whereas it is possible Malachi might have considered the growing number of Gentile proselytes and God-fearers as a foreshadowing of an eschatological phenomenon, the prophet's language goes beyond a foreshadowing.[134] Furthermore, as Hugenberger has pointed out, an eschatological "reminder" in this passage "of Yahweh's purpose for the conversion of the nations, a plan entailed in Israel's calling to be a blessing to the nations (cf. Mal. 3:12) and one which features the temple as its focus, would not be out of place in the light of Malachi's prominent interest in eschatology (cf., e.g., Mal. 3:1–5,17,19–24[ET 4:1–6])."[135]

Taking as figurative the references to "incense" and "offerings," Malachi's prophecy can be understood as being fulfilled in the present age (cf. Heb 13:15–16; 1 Pet 2:4–5).[136] Nevertheless, such a limited fulfillment does not

---

[132] J. G. Baldwin, "Malachi 1:11 and the Worship of the Nations in the Old Testament," *TynBul* 23 (1972): 122. See also Achtemeier, *Nahum-Malachi*, 177–78; B. Glazier-McDonald, *Malachi: The Divine Messenger*. SBLDS (Atlanta: Scholars Press, 1987), 55–61.

[133] Saucy, *The Case for Progressive Dispensationalism*, 129–30. These passages serve as part of his argument that "Gentiles were to be included [in the new covenant] without becoming a part of Israel" (p. 122). He points to Isa 19:25, for example, as an indication that whereas the Gentiles will be "part of the people of God along with Israel," a distinction will be retained (p. 124).

[134] See Hugenberger, *Marriage as a Covenant*, 39; contra C. von Orelli, *The Twelve Minor Prophets* (Edinburgh: T&T Clark, 1893), 389; T. C. Vriezen, "How to Understand Malachi 1:11," in *Grace upon Grace* (Grand Rapids: Eerdmans, 1975). Equally unsatisfying is the view that Malachi was referring to the worship of diaspora Jews, which "retains its value in relation to temple sacrifices even when the temple sacrifices themselves are offered unworthily in Jerusalem" (J. Swetman, "Malachi 1:11: An Interpretation," *CBQ* 31 [1969]: 207). As Tate argues, this interpretation "depends on sources much later than Malachi and seems to lack any support in the text" ("Questions for Priests and People," 398; see also R. P. Gordon, *Studies in the Targum to the Twelve Prophets: From Nahum to Malachi* [Leiden: Brill, 1994], 56–58).

[135] Hugenberger, *Marriage as a Covenant*, 39.

[136] D. A. Garrett explains that "the language about incense and grain offerings . . . need not be taken as a prediction of literal offerings to God by Gentile worshipers. It is simply Malachi's way of saying that the worship by the Gentiles would be pure and holy." He understands Malachi, then, to refer to "the repentance and turning to God by the nations of the present era" ("Israel's Unfaithfulness: The Priests. Malachi 1:6–2:9" *Mid-America Journal* 11 [1987]: 27). Cf. also the interpretation in *Didache* 14:1–3 and the discussion in N. E. Nagel, " 'The Word of the Lord to Israel through Malachi': Liturgically Received in the *Didache*," in *"Hear the Word of Yahweh": Essays on Scripture and Archaeology in Honor of Horace D. Hummel* (St. Louis: Concordia Academic Press, 2002), 193–203.

fully satisfy the biblical prophecies of Gentile salvation.[137] A universal and all-inclusive worship of the Lord awaits the return of Christ. Just as the Old Testament did not foretell two comings of the Messiah, so also it did not foretell a dawning of the messianic age with accompanying spiritual benefits of the new covenant preceding a later complete fulfillment.[138]

### (2) Indictment against the Priests (1:12)

[12]"But you profane it by saying of the Lord's table, 'It is defiled,' and of its food, 'It is contemptible.'

**1:12** "Profane" is a participle, here describing a present activity (as in 1:7, "place"). The verb (*ḥālal*) is a synonym of *gāʾal*, "defile," in v. 7 (also v. 12), which adds to the many parallels between the two verses (also see chart in introduction to vv. 6–9):

| v. 7 | v. 12 |
|---|---|
| defiled *[gʾl] food [leḥem]* | profaned *[ḥll] the name* |
| defiled *[gʾl] the Lord* | defiled *[gʾl] table* |
| despised *[bzh] table* | despised *[bzh] food [ʾoklô]*[139] |

Whereas the verbals occur in the same order in vv. 7 and 12, the order of their

---

[137] While the OT can speak of the present age as eschatological, passages such as Matt 8:11–12 surely refer to a distant future time. See B. Witherington III, *Jesus, Paul and the End of the World* (Downers Grove: InterVarsity, 1992), 66–68, 136–38. He also compares Mark 4:31–32. Also see J. Jeremias, *Jesus' Promise to the Nations* (Philadelphia: Fortress, 1982), 46–73. He understands Matt 8:11 as showing Jesus' eschatological interpretation of Mal 1:11 (p. 62). On Gentile salvation cf. Pss 22:28; 47:10; 68:30,32; 72:9–11; 96:8; Isa 2:3; 18:7; 19:23–25; 25:6–8; 45:23; 49:12,23; 56:7; 60:1–16; 66:18; Jer 3:17; Dan 7:14; Mic 7:12,17; Zeph 3:9; Hag 2:7; Zech 8:21–23; 9:10; 14:16.

[138] R. L. Saucy declares, "The fulfillment of the [new] covenant in the church is in perfect harmony with the Old Testament promises of eschatological salvation for both Israel and the nations. Only the spiritual provisions of the new covenant are applied at present" (*The Case for Progressive Dispensationalism*, 135). He also explains that whereas the apostle Paul "*does see* the fulfillment of these Old Testament texts in the present salvation of both Jews and Gentiles, . . . he looks forward to a time of even greater blessing for the Gentiles as a result of Israel's redemption" (p. 137).

[139] This parallel with v. 7 makes less likely the view that אָכְלוֹ, "its food," is to be deleted as an error or explanatory gloss (E. Sellin, *Das Zwölfprophetenbuch übersetzt und erklärt*, KAT [Leipzig: A. Deichertsche, 1930], 597). Nor is it necessary to excise וְנִיבוֹ, "and its fruit," as dittography (S. R. Driver, *The Minor Prophets*, NCB [New York: Oxford University Press, 1906], 308; W. Rudolph, *Haggai-Sacharja 1–8/9–14-Maleachi*, KAT [Gütersloh: Gütersloher Verlagshaus Gerd Mohn, 1976], 251). וְנִיבוֹ נִבְזֶה אָכְלוֹ, lit. "and its fruit, despised is its food," has a poetic quality with its sound repetition. Its grammatical structure matches the previous clause as well as its parallel in v. 7. Both words are an example of casus pendens, as also in v. 7 (see also 3:9). Thus Glazier-McDonald is correct: "Simply because two synonymous words appear in the same line, it does not follow that one of them must be superfluous" (*Malachi*, 62). See the discussion of the casus pendens at 1:7.

objects changes from *a-b-c* to *b-c-a,* a rhetorical way of referring the hearer/ reader back to the earlier text.[140]

"Profane" is used again in 2:10 of profaning "the covenant of our fathers" and in 2:11 of desecrating the sanctuary "by marrying the daughter of a foreign god." According to Ezek 13:19 the women of Judah had profaned even the Lord himself (cf. Mal 1:7) by making and selling instruments of idolatry. To "profane" means to desanctify, to make or treat something as unholy, that is, as common, insignificant, or worthless.[141] Someone's "name" is what makes them unique, special, or significant. To lose that quality is the ultimate humiliation. So besides the concept of rendering something ritually impure, unacceptable, or useless, the word "profane" could convey the idea of bringing dishonor or disgrace to someone by associating their name with something shameful. According to Lam 2:2, in judgment against Judah the Lord "has brought her kingdom and its princes down to the ground *[lāʾāreṣ]*in *dishonor.*" It might be likened to ceremoniously removing the insignia of rank from a military officer, publicly demoting him in disgrace. Similarly, Ps 89:39[40] describes how because of the abundant treacheries of Judah's king the Lord had humiliated him and "*defiled* his crown in the dust *[lāʾāreṣ]*" To "profane" someone's name meant to ruin their reputation (cf. Ezek 36:20–23, and see the discussion of "name" at Mal 1:6). Scripture repeatedly declares God's purpose of making known, protecting, or redeeming the glory of his great name, acting for his "name's sake," whether in judgment or deliverance.[142] God's name is holy because he is holy—utterly unique and perfect in every way. This quality of holiness is also acquired in a limited and derivative sense by those persons or things that belong to him, including Israel and its priesthood, the temple and its furnishings, and the sacrifices and worship events. Such things acquired holiness from God's presence and the association of his name. But acquired or derivative holiness had to be maintained by personal holiness. Such impure and unnatural behavior as sacrificing children to Molech (Lev 18:21; 20:3), swearing falsely by the Lord's name (Lev 19:12; Jer 34:16), committing incest (Amos 2:7), or idolatry (Ezek 20:39) carried the ultimate penalty of death because it involved contact between the unclean and the holy. It not only would desanctify the participants, it also defiled Israel and the sanctuary as God's dwelling place and disgraced his name. Furthermore, it profaned the covenant made with him in that it involved breaking the oath sworn before him (2:10).

---

[140] Repetition alone might be thought sufficient for this, but reverse repetition is often used for back reference. Cf. M. Greenberg, *Ezekiel, 1–20,* AB (New York: Doubleday, 1983), 198; K. A. Mathews, *Genesis 1–11:26,* NAC (Nashville: Broadman & Holman, 1996), 114.

[141] See the helpful discussion of holiness in Wenham, *The Book of Leviticus,* 18–25.

[142] E.g., 1 Sam 12:22; Pss 23:3; 79:9; 106:8; Isa 48:9; Jer 14:21; Ezek 20:9,14,22,44; 36:20–23; Dan 9:19; Rom 1:5. See on "the pleasure of God in his fame" J. Piper, *The Pleasures of God* (Portland: Multnomah, 1991), 101–21.

Priests could profane his name by failing to keep themselves holy (Lev 21:6), by coming into contact with or practicing mourning rites for the dead (Lev 21:1–5,10–12), or by marrying a prostitute, a divorced woman, or a widow (i.e., anyone but a "virgin"; Lev 21:7,13–14). A priest's failure to marry properly would also "defile *[ḥālal]*his offspring among his people" (Lev 21:15). If a priest's daughter became a prostitute, she would "defile herself" *(ḥālal)*[143] and also "disgrace" *(ḥālal)* her father and thus was to be "burned in the fire" (Lev 21:9). According to Lev 21:17–23 a priest who had a "defect" was not to "come near to offer the food of his God," or he would "desecrate" *(ḥālal)* the sanctuary and apparently also profane the Lord's name.

Here in Malachi this was also the effect of bringing blemished offerings and thus defiling the altar, treating it with contempt (the rest of Mal 1:12 is essentially a restatement of 1:7—see comments there and chart in the introduction to 1:6–9), and thus disgracing the name of the Lord. In Lev 22:2 priests were told to "treat with respect" *(nāzar)* the holy offerings "so they will not profane my holy name." Improper behavior is specified as approaching the offerings in a state of uncleanness (Lev 22:3–8). A priest's failure to keep the Lord's "requirements" is then said to be "treating [those requirements] with contempt" *(ḥālal),* resulting in guilt and death, "for I am the LORD, who makes them holy" (Lev 22:9).

The Lord was very particular about who was qualified to serve him in the sanctuary and how that service was to be conducted. There are also instructions in the New Testament about qualifications for church office and the way worship is to be conducted (e.g., 1 Cor 11–14; 1 Tim 2–3; Titus 1:5–9). Whenever we disregard or circumvent the Lord's instructions and requirements, such as his requirements for elders and deacons, we profane his name and desecrate his worship.

### (3) Evidence against the Priests (1:13–14a)

**¹³And you say, 'What a burden!' and you sniff at it contemptuously," says the LORD Almighty.**

**"When you bring injured, crippled or diseased animals and offer them as sacrifices, should I accept them from your hands?" says the LORD. ¹⁴"Cursed is the cheat who has an acceptable male in his flock and vows to give it, but then sacrifices a blemished animal to the Lord.**

Two lines of evidence support the charge that the priests were profaning the Lord's name, defiling the altar, and despising the offerings and fellowship with the Lord (v. 12).

---

[143] Note in Ezek 22:5 הַשֵּׁם טֻמְאַת (lit. "unclean of the name") is translated "O infamous city" (NIV) or "you infamous one" (NRSV).

**1:13** The first line of evidence is found in v. 13.[144] The first statement expresses the words the priests would utter, silently or under their breath or perhaps in secret to one another, "What a burden!" This exclamation consists of two Hebrew words, *hinnê* (traditionally translated "behold") and another that combines the interrogative "what?" (*mâ*, used as an exclamation[145]) with a noun (*tĕlāʾâ*) meaning "hardship, burden" (cf. Exod 18:8; Num 20:14; Lam 3:5; Neh 9:32). It is derived from a verb root (*lʾh*) that means to become weary (and give up; cf. Jer 6:11; 20:9; Isa 7:13; Jer 12:5). There is perhaps an allusion to the Lord's words in Isa 1:14: "Your New Moon festivals and your appointed feasts my soul hates. They have become a burden to me; *I am weary* of bearing them." The priests were tired of offering sacrifices to the Lord; it had become a nuisance to them (cf. Isa 43:22, "You have been weary of me, O Israel!" [NRSV]). As a result, the Lord was tired of receiving them (cf. v. 10).

Another way the priests were profaning the Lord's name is expressed in the statement "you sniff at it contemptuously."[146] The verb *nāpaḥ*, "blow," occurs in this form (the *hiphil* stem) only here and in Job 31:39. It may be translated "sniff at in contempt, disdain,"[147] or "enrage."[148] The pronoun antecedent could be the Lord's "table" from v. 12, or it could be his "name" from v. 11 and so parallel to "you profane it" in v. 12. If the meaning "enrage" is followed (or even perhaps "disdain"), the antecedent would be "the Lord," yielding the translation "you enrage him" (see the NRSV, which follows the scribal notation that the pronoun was originally "me"[149]). The tendency of the book to

---

[144] The verse begins with four clauses (not counting the embedded quote "what a burden!"), each containing a *waw*-plus-perfect tense verb. The third and fourth clauses I interpret with the NIV as circumstantial ("when . . ."), supporting the following question ("should I accept them?"), although they are independent in form. The NIV, however, translates the verbs as sequential ("bring . . . and offer"). This is illegitimate, however, for two reasons. First, the verbs are identical (וַהֲבֵאתֶם, "and you bring"). The first verb has the three types of blemished sacrifices as its object, and the object of the second is the general word הַמִּנְחָה, "the offering," which comprises the animals mentioned in the previous clause. Second, in expository discourse, as here (vv. 12–14a), the *waw*-plus-perfect does not function sequentially (see Longacre, *Joseph,* 107, 121; E. R. Clendenen, "The Interpretation of Biblical Hebrew Hortatory Texts: A Textlinguistic Approach to the Book of Malachi" [Ph.D. diss., The University of Texas at Arlington, 1989], 95),. The fourth clause should be interpreted as supporting the third, yielding the translation, "When you bring as an offering injured, crippled, or diseased animals, should I accept them from your hands?"

[145] See *GBH* §162a.

[146] Note the somewhat similar concept expressed by the verb בָּעַט, "kick," in 1 Sam 2:29.

[147] BDB, 656. The REB translates, "You sniff scornfully at it."

[148] *CHAL,* 241. *HALOT* gives the metaphorical meaning as "put in a rage, undervalue."

[149] Likewise the NJB has, "You . . . sniff disdainfully at me." In his study of the *tiqqune sopherim,* C. McCarthy considered this to be a "false correction" (*The Tiqqune Sopherim and Other Theological Corrections in the Masoretic Text of the Old Testament* [Göttingen: Vandenhoeck & Ruprecht, 1981], 113–15). Some believe the "scribal corrections" represent midrashic interpretation rather than text history. See the discussions in I. Yeivin, *Introduction to the Tiberian Masorah,* SBLMS (Missoula, Mont.: Scholars Press, 1980), 49–51; E. Tov, *Textual Criticism of the Hebrew Bible* (Minneapolis: Fortress, 1992), 64–67.

associate the divine quotation formula with personal references (cf. 1:2,6,9,10, 11,14; 2:2,4,16; 3:1,5,7,10,13,17,21) would lend support to the latter interpretation. But the close association assumed in the passage between the Lord, his name, and his "table" makes the end result the same. The priests' "worship" was nothing but insincere religious activity that insulted the Lord (cf. Hos 6:6; Amos 8:5; Mic 6:6–8).[150] It was the opposite of what the apostle Paul observed in the churches of Macedonia. In spite of "the most severe trial, their overflowing joy and their extreme poverty welled up in rich generosity"; and "they gave themselves first to the Lord and then to us" (2 Cor 8:2,5). "If the willingness is there," Paul said, "the gift is acceptable" (8:12). The principle is that gifts should be given "not reluctantly or under compulsion, for God loves a cheerful giver" (9:7). The reason, Piper explains, is that "God is most glorified in us when we are most satisfied in him."[151] But Judah's gifts and the priests' service at the altar were being given with the opposite attitude. They had not always been contemptuous toward the Lord's worship. But their failure to respond to life's trials in wisdom and faith had led to a loss of the delight in the Lord that produces genuine worship. The professional minister and every believer must constantly guard against developing such a cold heart toward God that maintains the activity without the gratitude and love behind it. Mallone quotes G. K. Chesterton's comment that the absence of praise reveals that our religion is "more a theory than a love affair." Mallone then exhorts: "A man must respond to the One who has given him everything. Not to do so is the highest form of ingratitude and self-sufficiency."[152] Such loss of gratitude and delight in worship is a sign of spiritual decay that could lead to a shipwrecked life.

The priests' disdain for their sacrificial duties was reflected in the carelessness with which they conducted them. The rest of v. 13 continues to echo phrases from vv. 6–10. The priests were disregarding sacrificial regulations in bringing "injured, crippled or diseased animals" to the altar.[153] The sacrifices are described here by three adjectives identical to those used in v. 8 except for the first. In place of *'iwwēr*, "blind," they are described as *gāzûl*, which means

---

[150] D. Haack likens such religious activity to a snakeskin full of ants. "The snake itself has long been dead, eaten out from within, . . . but the skin moves, filled with busy life" (*The Rest of Success* [Downers Grove: InterVarsity, 1989], 110).

[151] J. Piper, *Let the Nations Be Glad! The Supremacy of God in Missions* (Grand Rapids: Baker, 1993), 26.

[152] Mallone, *Furnace of Renewal*, 46–47. He also quotes C. S. Lewis (p. 47): "Except where intolerably adverse circumstances interfere, praise almost seems to be inner health made audible. . . . Just as men spontaneously praise whatever they value, so they spontaneously urge us to join them in praising it: 'Isn't she lovely? Wasn't it glorious? Don't you think that magnificent?'" But Malachi's priests were far from such "inner health."

[153] The verb "bring" (causative of בוֹא, "come") is a synonym of the verb (קָרַב) in "try offering them to your governor" in v. 8 and also of the verb (נָגַשׁ) translated "bring" in vv. 8 and 11 and "place" in v. 7.

either "injured" or more probably "stolen." It is a passive participle of the verb meaning "tear away, seize, rob."[154] If "stolen" is the sense, it contrasts with King David's statement, "I will not sacrifice to the LORD my God burnt offerings that cost me nothing" (2 Sam 24:24). The unacceptability of such sacrifices is stressed by the rhetorical question demanding a negative reply. The verb translated "accept" (*rāṣâ*) occurs earlier in v. 8 ("be pleased") and in v. 10, where it is followed as here by the phrase "from your hands."[155]

**1:14a** In this verse is the second line of evidence that God's name was being profaned. The indictment is directed against the offerers here rather than the priests.[156] That it was not the priests alone who were guilty of treating the Lord with contempt is implicit in vv. 6–13, since the priests were only offering the Lord what the people were bringing them. The fault was primarily with the priests because they were responsible for temple worship and also for teaching the people about the Lord and his Law. But the offerers who were defrauding the Lord with their sacrifices are also said to be "cursed" (cf. Deut 27:16). This is the second of seven references in Malachi to "curse" (see comments at 1:4).[157] Of the four Hebrew synonyms used, the word here *('ārar)* is the only one used more than once and is applied to the priests three times in 2:2. Here it is a passive participle[158] describing the "cheat"[159] who has a male

---

[154] According to BDB, 159–60, it refers to "that rescued after seizure by wild beasts, therefore mutilated," hence the RSV "taken by violence." Cf. Exod 22:31[Hb. 30]; Lev 17:15. But "taken by robbery" is more likely. Cf. Deut 28:29,31; Jer 21:72; 22:3; Isa 61:8 (See J. Schupphaus, "גָּזַל *gāzal*," *TDOT* 2:456–58; Tate, "Questions for Priests and People," 406; Kaiser, *Malachi*, 49.

[155] The verb is also preceded in v. 10 as here by the noun מִנְחָה, "offering." See the chart of parallels in the introduction to 1:6–9.

[156] Tate takes this as evidence that all of vv. 11–14 are directed to the people rather than the priests ("Questions for Priests and People," 397).

[157] See also S. Gevirtz, "Curses," *IDB* 1:750; W. J. Urbrock, "Blessings and Curses," *ABD* 1:755–61.

[158] This form occurs eighteen times in Deut 27:15–26; 28:16–19. The word is often used as the opposite of בָּרַךְ, "bless" (cf. Gen 9:25–26; 12:3; 27:29; Num 22:6; 24:9). V. P. Hamilton comments that all the "curse-sayings" employing this word are directed against "one violating his relationship to God" (*TWOT* 75). It may be that אָרוּר is used in part because of its similarity in sound/form to נוֹרָא, "feared," in v. 14b (note also מוֹרָאִי, "my fear," in v. 6). The word תָּאִירוּ ("light fires") in v. 10a is also similar. Those refusing to fear (יָרֵא) the Lord were cursed (אָרַר) and had no right to light fires (אוּר) on the altar. The placement of these roots may also be structurally significant (see chart in introduction to vv. 6–9).

[159] The word נוֹכֵל is a *qal* active participle from נכל, "be crafty, deceitful." The *qal* occurs only here, but the *piel* in Num 25:18 describes an act of the Midianites ("they deceived you") that incited the priest Phinehas to exercise God's judgment against an Israelite idolater. In response God made with Phinehas and the tribe of Levi "a covenant of peace" (Num 25:12–13), the covenant referred to in Mal 2:4–5. In Gen 37:18 the *hithpael* describes Joseph's brothers' plot to kill him, and in Ps 105:25 it is used of the Egyptian oppression of Israel. In Exod 1:10 pharaoh uses a form of חכם, "deal shrewdly," to describe his plan. What one considers shrewd or "good business" may in fact be nothing but deceitful and "cursed" in the eyes of God.

animal[160] in his flock that is presumed to be "acceptable" (there is no Hb. word for "acceptable" in the clause; it is inferred from the opposite word "blemished"[161] that follows). He vows to give it to the Lord if he answers his prayer (on vow offerings cf. Lev 27:9–10; Num 30:2; Deut 23:21–23); but when the Lord answers the prayer, the offerer breaks his vow, reneges on his promise, and offers a "blemished" animal (cf. Eccl 5:1–7).

The sense of the person's being "cursed" may be suggested by J. Scharbert's comment that "the intention of the one pronouncing this expression was to vigorously keep himself aloof from that person and his action." It spoke, then, of separation from God. It also spoke of being "expelled from a community relationship" and from the "security, justice, and success" that had been enjoyed there. Being cursed by God meant being "delivered over to misfortune."[162]

### (4) Prophecy of Gentile Worship (1:14b)

**For I am a great king," says the LORD Almighty, "and my name is to be feared among the nations.**

**1:14b** As in 1:11 (see note there), it is better to understand the causal clause here as referring to what follows rather than to what precedes, thus translating, "'Because I am a great king,' says the LORD Almighty, 'my name is going to be feared among the nations.'" The envelope structure of vv. 11–14 thus concludes by repeating the declaration from v. 11 that someday the nations were going to have the opposite attitude toward the Lord that Judah did. Whereas the priests and people of Judah honored their earthly leader more than the Lord (1:8), the nations would acknowledge the Lord as king.[163] The main verb in this sentence is a participle here translated "is to be feared." As the participle in v. 11 translated "will be brought" (better, "is going to be brought"), it refers to a future event that is certain. Whereas here the Lord's name is going to be "feared among the nations," according to v. 11 it will be "great among the nations" and will arouse the offering of

---

[160] K. Elliger (*BHS* text note) suggests an original זָכֵּה, "pure," for the MT זָכָר, "male."

[161] The word מָשְׁחָת is a *hophal* participle from the root שׁחת, which also occurs in 2:8 (a *piel* translated "violated") and 3:11 (a *hiphil* wrongly translated "cast") and refers to something "spoiled" or "ruined." Elsewhere the concept "blemish" or "defect" uses the noun מוּם/מְאוּם (cf. Lev 21:17; 24:19; Num 19:2; Deut 15:21; 17:1; Dan 1:4). For the NT concept see Eph 5:27; Col 1:27; 1 Pet 1:19; 2 Pet 2:13; Jude 12.

[162] J. Scharbert, "ארר, *'rr*," *TDOT* 1:408–11. Or as Urbrock explains, it connoted "a sort of banning or barring of benefits" ("Blessings and Curses," *ABD* 1:756).

[163] S. L. McKenzie and H. N. Wallace note that the title "great king" is used of suzerains in ANE treaties ("Covenant Themes in Malachi," *CBQ* 45 [1983]: 558).

incense (cf. Jonah 1:16). The expressions are essentially synonymous. Because the nations will recognize the Lord's greatness as King of the earth, they will respond appropriately with fear, expressed in offerings of incense (see the comments at 1:6 on the fear of God). Piper begins his book on missions with the bold declaration:

> Missions is not the ultimate goal of the church. Worship is. Missions exists because worship doesn't. Worship is ultimate, not missions, because God is ultimate, not man. When this age is over, and the countless millions of the redeemed fall on their faces before the throne of God, missions will be no more. It is a temporary necessity. But worship abides forever.[164]

### 5. Negative Motivation: The Results of Disobedience (2:1–9)

The recurrence of "O priests" (cf. 1:6; 2:1) here in the last paragraph of Malachi's first division helps to mark off this division of Malachi's prophecy as a unit (1:2–2:9), as well as to identify its primary audience. Like the second division (2:10–3:6), the first begins with positive motivation (1:2–5) and closes here with negative motivation. If the priests would not alter their behavior, the Lord would curse them and remove them disgracefully from service. The Lord's command to the priests is also implied, however, in the condition in v. 2: "If you do not listen, and if you do not set your heart to honor my name." The description of the Lord's covenant with Levi in vv. 5–7 also contains implied commands for the postexilic priests, especially the explanation in v. 7 that "the lips of a priest ought to preserve knowledge, and from his mouth men should seek instruction—because he is the messenger of the LORD Almighty." Furthermore, the Lord's charge against the priests is referred to in vv. 8–9. This concentration of mitigated hortatory elements in the final paragraph of the first division adds to the climactic nature of the paragraph, as the same concentration marks the final paragraph (3:1–6) of the second division as climactic.[165]

The structure of the paragraph is indicated by the verb forms and pronouns. It begins with second person pronouns and a series of six future tense

---

[164] Piper, *Let the Nations Be Glad,* 11. He also declares: "All of history is moving toward one great goal, the white-hot worship of God and his Son among all the peoples of the earth. Missions is not that goal. It is the means. And for that reason it is the second greatest human activity in the world" (p. 15).

[165] The climactic nature of the section is also marked by the הִנֵּה "behold" clause in v. 3; the initial וְעַתָּה introducing the topicalizing clause (lit.), "And now for you is this decree, O priests"; and the section's grammatical complexity. On ways of marking the "peak" of a discourse see R. E. Longacre, "Discourse Peak as Zone of Turbulence," in *Beyond the Sentence* (Ann Arbor: Karome, 1985), 81–92.

verbs in vv. 1–4, marking what may be called predictive discourse.[166] Then follows narrative through the rest of the paragraph, marked by the past tense verbs.[167] This division is confirmed by the framing repetition of "this admonition" in vv. 1 and 4 and by the divine speech formula, "says the LORD Almighty," that begins the admonition in v. 2 and recurs in v. 4. The repetition of "covenant with/of Levi" in vv. 4,8 is also a framing device, so that v. 4 serves both to conclude the first part of the paragraph and to introduce the second part. The most prominent statements in the first part of the paragraph are the warning, "I will send a curse upon you," in v. 2 and the result, "And you will know that I have sent you this admonition so that my covenant with Levi may continue," in v. 4 (both underlined by the divine speech formula). The reference to the covenant with Levi in v. 4 leads to the third person narrative elaborating upon the covenant in vv. 5–7, then the return to second person in vv. 8–9 (note also the third use of the divine speech formula in v. 8) shows how the postexilic priests had violated it.[168]

### (1) Curse against the Priests (2:1–4)

[1]"And now this admonition is for you, O priests. [2]If you do not listen, and if you do not set your heart to honor my name," says the LORD Almighty, "I will send a curse upon you, and I will curse your blessings. Yes, I have already cursed them, because you have not set your heart to honor me.

[3]"Because of you I will rebuke your descendants; I will spread on your faces the offal from your festival sacrifices, and you will be carried off with it. [4]And you will know that I have sent you this admonition so that my covenant with Levi may continue," says the LORD Almighty.

**2:1** This concluding paragraph of the first division begins with *wĕ'attâ*, "and now," an expression that often in the Old Testament begins a speech or marks a climax or conclusion.[169] In Gen 4:11 it introduces God's judgment on

---

[166] The verbs are *wĕqāṭal* forms and a participle.

[167] These are especially the two *waw*-consecutive imperfects (*wayyiqṭōl* forms) in v. 5. Most of the rest of the verbs are perfects, used in narrative of backgrounded actions.

[168] See also E. Wendland, "Linear and Concentric Patterns in Malachi," *BT* 36 (1985): 11.

[169] See its use in 1:9. It is often followed by הִנֵּה ("behold"), which occurs in v. 3. Cf. Gen 41:33; 45:5; Exod 3:9; Deut 10:12; 26:10; 2 Sam 7:25; 14:15; 1 Kgs 8:26; 2 Chr 13:8; Isa 52:5. Its first uses in Genesis are to introduce consequences (3:11; 11:6; 12:19; 20:7; 21:23, etc.). In 4:11 it introduces the consequential curse on Cain for his treachery. On עַתָּה ("now") Andersen and Freedman say, "When this adverb is used for transition, rather than specifying the time when something happens, it is usually followed by a command or exhortation, or . . . by what may be a precative" (*Hosea*, AB [Garden City: Doubleday, 1980], 500). D. Slager notes that וְעַתָּה ("and now") before an exhortation may mean "therefore," citing Gen 20:7; 34:21 ("The Use of 'Behold' in the Old Testament," *Occasional Papers on Translation and Textlinguistics* 3 [1989]: 62). B. Glazier-McDonald calls it "a word of transition" and cites its use to introduce announcements of punishment, although the passages she cites use עַתָּה rather than וְעַתָּה (*Malachi: The Divine Messenger*, SBLDS [Atlanta: Scholars Press, 1987], 64). M. Weinfeld says that "in the oration [וְעַתָּה] generally indicates a turning-point, such as the transition from the parable to the moral lesson that is to be drawn from it" and that it is common in "deuteronomic orations" (*Deuteronomy and the Deuteronomic School* [Oxford: Clarendon, 1972], 175). It is also frequently associated with a vocative, "O Israel" or "O sons" (e.g., Deut 4:1; 10:12; 1 Sam 12:13; Prov 5:7; 7:24).

Cain: "*[So] now* you are under a curse and driven from the ground." Here the particle introduces a sentence announcing the paragraph topic: a decree of warning or "admonition" to the priests.[170] The content of the decree is given and elaborated in vv. 2–3, and its purpose is given in v. 4 in terms of God's covenant with Levi.

**2:2** There are serious consequences for anyone foolish enough to ignore the Lord's words (cf. Lev 26:14–39; Zech 1:4–6; 7:12–14). Yet the conditional nature of v. 2a declares that a possibility of the Lord's mercy remained for this generation of religious leaders.[171] A decisive change of attitude is called for in the expression "set your heart," which is literally "place upon the heart." The word "heart" *(lēb / lēbāb)* denotes in Hebrew what may be called the command center of a person's life, where knowledge is collected and considered and where decisions and plans are made that determine the direction of one's life.[172] In view of the 814 occurrences of the word in the Old Testament in reference to the human "heart" ("the commonest of all anthropological terms"[173]) and the common usage of "heart" in English of emotions, it is important to differentiate the Hebrew meaning from the English and so to "guard against the false impression that biblical man is determined more by feeling than by reason."[174] The expression "place upon the heart" is found a dozen times in the Old Testament. It means *to determine a course of action in response to one's knowledge or awareness of something.*[175] Sometimes "words" are placed on the heart (Deut 11:18; 1 Sam 21:12[Hb. 13]; Job 22:22), in which case the sense is similar to writing (Prov 3:3; 7:3; Jer 17:1; 31:33) or binding upon the heart (Prov 6:21), or simply to "remember" (cf.

---

[170] Contra Hill (*Malachi*, 197), Verhoef (*The Books of Haggai and Malachi*, 237), and others, Glazier-McDonald is correct that this is not an oracle of command or instruction but of warning and judgment. Therefore "decree" or "admonition" is a better translation of הַמִּצְוָה than "commandment." This use of the term also occurs in Nah 1:14. The repetition of הַמִּצְוָה in 2:4 is not a cataphoric reference to the covenant with Levi (Hill) but an anaphoric reference to these words of warning.

[171] According to D. J. McCarthy, such a conditional statement was typical of an introduction to a list of blessings and curses in ancient Near Eastern treaty documents (*Treaty and Form: A Study in Form in the Ancient Oriental Documents and in the Old Testament* [Rome: Pontifical Biblical Institute, 1963], 3, 76).

[172] Cf. H. W. Wolff, *Anthropology of the Old Testament* (Philadelphia: Fortress, 1974), 40–55.

[173] Ibid., 40.

[174] Ibid., 47.

[175] Seventeen times לֵב / לֵבָב ("heart") is the direct object of שִׂים ("place"). In these cases the sense is to observe, notice, or pay attention to something and to reflect upon it. Resulting action is assumed, but the acquiring of knowledge is primarily in view. The object of attention is specified by the context (Ezek 44:5a; Hag 2:15,18[2x]) or in a prepositional phrase using עַל, "upon" (Job 1:8; Hag 1:5,7), אֶל, "to" (Exod 9:21; 1 Sam 25:25; 2 Sam 18:3[2x]; Job 2:3; 34:14), or לְ, "to" (1 Sam 9:20; Deut 32:46; Ezek 40:4; 44:5b). Similar to the expression "place upon the heart" is one that uses the verb נָתַן, "give" (cf. Ezra 7:27; Neh 2:12; 7:5).

Exod 17:14; Num 15:39; Ps 119:49,52; Isa 46:8; Mal 4:4).[176] In other cases as well, "place upon the heart" focuses on the knowledge that is to determine actions (2 Sam 19:19[Hb. 20]; Song 8:6; Isa 42:25; 57:1,11; Jer 12:11). Other uses as here in Mal 2:2, however, focus on the actions themselves, and their basis in knowledge is assumed. The closest equivalent to the use here is in Dan 1:8, where what is placed on the heart is specified by a succeeding clause (there a relative clause, here an infinitival clause). Daniel responded to instructions to eat unclean food by deciding not to defile himself. Malachi's priests were to respond to the Lord's greatness by repenting and giving him the honor he deserved (see comments at 1:6 on "honor").[177] If questioned, these priests would have testified to knowing and believing the Lord's greatness. But their actions betrayed the superficial nature of their supposed faith.

The Hebrew word translated "a curse" is literally "the curse." It is apparently an allusion to the covenant curses of Deut 28:15–68, which soberly warned Israel that the consequence of disobedience would be God's blocking of every normal artery of blessing and his opening of the floodgates of disaster (see also Neh 10:28–29).[178] The initial warning is followed by an elaboration in three climactic stages, continuing through the end of v. 3. First is the immediate consequence that the Lord would turn their blessings into curses ("I will curse your blessings"), that is, every aspect of their lives would become plagued by trouble (cf. Amos 8:10).[179] The Lord confirmed this warning by pointing out to them that they had already begun experiencing the curse,[180] one aspect of which, according to v. 9, was that they had already begun to be "despised and humiliated before all the people." Their failure to honor the Lord was resulting in their loss of honor.

---

[176] For the latter meaning compare the expression "ascend [עלה] upon the heart" in Isa 65:17; Jer 3:16; 7:31; 19:5; 32:35; 44:21.

[177] The expression "give honor/glory" is also associated with repentance in Josh 7:19; 1 Sam 6:5; and Jer 13:16. See also Rev 16:9.

[178] The term הַמְּאֵרָה, "the curse," occurs elsewhere only in Deut 28:20; Prov 3:33; 28:27; and Mal 3:9. Deut 28:20a reads lit., "Yahweh will send on you the curse, the confusion, and the rebuke on all the work of your hand that you do."

[179] See Verhoef, *Haggai and Malachi,* 239; Garrett, "Israel's Unfaithfulness: The Priests," 29. H. C. Brichto relates אָרַר to Akk. *arāru,* "to ban, block off," and defines it as involving a "ban or barrier, a paralysis on movement or other capabilities" (*The Problem of 'Curse' in the Hebrew Bible* [Philadelphia: Society of Biblical Literature and Exegesis, 1963], 17, 216–17. B. Glazier-McDonald relates בִּרְכוֹתֵיכֶם ("your blessings") to 3:10 (and to Gen 3:17–19) and interprets it as "the earth's produce" that God is threatening with drought (*Malachi: The Divine Messenger,* 66). But this would affect more than just the priests. To M. Fishbane it refers to the priestly privilege of pronouncing blessings upon others (*Biblical Interpretation in Ancient Israel,* 332–34; also J. M. O'Brien, *Priest and Levite in Malachi,* SBLDS [Atlanta: Scholars Press, 1990], 33, 35).

[180] The LXX translator apparently did not understand this and retains the plural: "And I will curse it; and I will scatter [διασκεδάσω] your blessing, and it will not be among you, for you are not placing to your heart."

**2:3**  The second stage of the elaboration is that the curse would also affect the priests' descendants (lit., "Behold, I am rebuking to you the seed").[181] This aspect of the warning is given considerable emphasis. Verse 3 begins with the particle *hinnê* (untranslated in NIV), often translated "see" or "behold."[182] This is the first of five "behold" clauses in the book (cf. 3:1[2x]; 4:1,5). They all occur, as here, at the end of a division and give prominence to a declaration of the Lord about the future.[183] In each case it occurs with a participle (here translated "will rebuke"). The grammatical construction *hinnê* plus a participle describes an event as occurring in the imminent future (suggesting the translation "am about to rebuke") or with such certainty that it may be considered "on the way."[184] As such, Slager explains, it also can serve, as here, to "call special attention to a ground(s) that leads to an exhortation."[185] Thus, it adds a sense of urgency to the Lord's appeal to the priests.

---

[181] לָכֶם, "to you," can be understood either as causal ("on your account") or as possessive ("which belongs to you"). Glazier-McDonald relates the threat (הִנְנִי גֹעֵר לָכֶם אֶת־הַזֶּרַע) to 3:11 (וְגָעַרְתִּי לָכֶם בָּאֹכֵל, "and I will restrain the devourer for you"; NIV, "I will prevent pests from devouring your crops"), viewing it as a threat to agricultural productivity. J. M. P. Smith ("Malachi," 36–37) and P. Verhoef (*Haggai and Malachi*, 241) argue that this would have been an inappropriate punishment for the priests and does not fit the use of זֶרַע ("seed") elsewhere. Some emend the object to הַזְּרֹעַ, "the arm," yielding "I will rebuke [i.e., stop the effective action of, as in 3:11; Pss 9:5[Hb. 6]; 119:21; 106:9; Nah 1:4] the arm," making them "powerless to officiate as priests, especially in lifting their arms over the people to bless them (Tate, "Questions for Priests and the People," 400, 406). Others, following the LXX and 1 Sam 2:31, also emend the participle to גֹּדֵעַ, yielding "I will cut off your arm/strength" (NEB; *BHS*) with the same effect (Achtemeier, *Nahum–Malachi*, 180). Although it is possible in view of parallels between 1 Sam 2:12–17,27–29 and Mal 1:6–2:9, the emendations are unnecessary and weaken the connection to Deut 28:20 and to 3:11. Changing "seed" to "arm" also eliminates the semantic/phonetic connection between הַזֶּרַע and the following verb וְזֵרִיתִי from זרה, "to spread, scatter, winnow" (cf. the possible wordplay between the two roots in Isa 30:22–24).

[182] It is actually הִנְנִי, "behold me," which furnishes the subject for the following participle.

[183] According to T. Muraoka, "The primary function of these particles [הִנֵּה and הֵן] lies in indicating that the speaker or the writer wants to draw the special attention of the hearer or the reader respectively to a fact or object which can be said to be important, new, unexpected, etc." (*Emphatic Words and Structures in Biblical Hebrew*, 138). Slager explains similarly: "Basically *hinnēh/hēn* is used to *highlight* the noun/proposition(s) that follows it. It *raises the relative prominence* of the information after, so that the information has an *impact* on the reader/listener. Usually it calls upon the reader/listener to *pay attention*" ("The Use of 'Behold' in the Old Testament," 50). See also C. J. Labuschagne, "The Particles *hēn* and *hinnê*," in *Syntax and Meaning: Studies in Hebrew Syntax and Biblical Exegesis*, OTS 18 (Leiden: Brill, 1973), 1–14; D. McCarthy, "The Uses of *wĕhinnēh* in Biblical Hebrew," *CBQ* 40 (1978): 330–42; S. Kogut, "On the Meaning and Syntactical Status of הִנֵּה in Biblical Hebrew," in *Studies in Bible* (Jerusalem: Magnes, 1986), 133–54.

[184] Cf. GKC §116p; Williams §214; *GBH* §121e; W. F. Stinespring, "The Participle of the Immediate Future and Other Matters Pertaining to Correct Translation of the Old Testament," in *Translating and Understanding the Old Testament* (Nashville: Abingdon, 1970), 64–70.

[185] Slager, "The Use of 'Behold' in the Old Testament," 59–64.

J. M. O'Brien notes that the word for "descendants" (*zera'*, "seed") "frequently describes future offspring who will share in the benefits granted to the original recipient," as the descendants of Aaron and Phinehas were given the priesthood (Exod 28:43; Num 17:5; 25:13; Lev 21:17; 22:4).[186] Here the term broadens the recipients of the curse. O'Brien also calls attention to a parallel in Hos 4:6–8, which declares that the priests of Israel would be punished along with the people: "Because you have rejected knowledge, I also reject you as my priests; because you have ignored the law of your God, I also will ignore your children." That parallel, together with the next stage in the elaboration of the curse, suggests that Malachi was warning of a similar rejection for these priests and their descendants.

The final stage of the elaboration is in the sequence, "I will spread [or "scatter"[187]] on your faces the offal from your festival sacrifices, and you will be carried off with it."[188] The word "offal" *(pereš)*, emphasized here by repetition (lit., "I will spread offal on your faces, the offal of your festivals"), refers to the entrails and also the bodily waste that would litter the area where animals had been sacrificed after a "festival."[189] Elsewhere the term is used of the entrails of the bull for the sin offering that was brought to consecrate Aaron and his sons to the priesthood. After the bull was slaughtered and its blood and fat offered at the altar, the flesh, hide, and "offal" (i.e., everything that remained) were burned "outside the camp" (Exod 29:14; Lev 8:17). The same procedure was followed in the case of the sin offering "if the anointed priest sins, bringing guilt on the people" (Lev 4:3; cp. 4:11 with Exod 29:14) and also for the bull and goat offered as sin offerings on the Day of Atonement (Lev 16:27). The only other place where the term occurs is in the passage describing the ritual for making the waters of purification from the ashes of the red heifer (Num 19:5).[190]

---

[186] O'Brien, *Priest and Levite in Malachi*, 34.

[187] The verb זָרָה elsewhere means to "winnow" (i.e., to separate and eliminate chaff by blowing it away) or "scatter," especially in the sense of "disperse, dispel, dissipate." It is often used (mainly the *piel*, as here) of God's judgment in scattering Israel among the nations (cf. Lev 26:33; Pss 44:11[Eng. 12]; 106:27; 1 Kgs 14:15; Jer 31:10; Ezek 5:10,12; 12:14–15; 20:23; Zech 2:2,4 [Eng. 1:19,21]), to "put an end to your uncleanness" (Ezek 22:15). Its use here of scattering and so removing the offal from the temple courts may allude to these contexts of divine judgment. The similarity of זָרָה to זֶרַע ("seed") implies that their seed would be defiled and scattered.

[188] With Verhoef (*Haggai and Malachi*, 243) and others, the literal "he will carry you" should be understood as an impersonal passive.

[189] The term חַג is used especially of the three great pilgrimage feasts where numerous sacrifices were brought: Passover and Unleavened Bread, Harvest or Weeks, and Ingathering or Tabernacles (Exod 23:14–19; 34:18–26; Lev 23:4–44; Deut 16:1–17). In Ps 118:27 it refers as here to animal sacrifice.

[190] These waters served as a kind of instant sin offering in cases where someone had been defiled by coming into contact with death. O'Brien translates פֶּרֶשׁ as "dung" and notes that it is found elsewhere only in "P texts" (*Priest and Levite in Malachi*, 34).

The "offal" from the sacrificed animals had to be taken "outside the camp" because it was unclean and otherwise would defile the Lord's dwelling place with his people (cf. Lev 10:4–5; 13:46; 24:14; Num 5:3; Deut 23:10,12; Heb 13:11–13). For Miriam's sin of jealousy and rebellion against Moses, the Lord struck her with leprosy and confined her "outside the camp" for seven days. The time set for her discipline of quarantine was derived by comparison (Num 12:14; cf. 31:19): "If her father had spit in her face, would she not have been in disgrace for seven days?" Spreading the defiled waste on the priests' faces and carrying them away as so much waste themselves was a figurative way of saying they would be removed from office in utter disgrace.[191] The use of such vivid imagery expresses both the degree of revulsion the Lord felt for the priests' behavior and also his attitude toward their hypocritical religious festivals. As they had treated the Lord with contempt (1:6) and defiled his altar with their corrupt and useless sacrifices (1:7), so the Lord would treat them with contempt and defile them, rendering them useless. Since they considered it such a burden to serve the Lord (1:13), he would free them from their burden by removing them and their descendants from his service.[192]

**2:4** Reference to "this admonition," repeated from 2:1, serves to conclude vv. 1–4, and reference to a "covenant with Levi," repeated in 2:8, introduces the discussion of the covenant in vv. 5–9. The purpose of the admonition or decree and of the threatened curse was the preservation of the covenant with Levi (which the behavior of these priests had placed in jeopardy) and their restoration, if possible, to faithfulness to that covenant. If the priests failed to correct their sinful attitudes and behavior and to begin honoring the Lord, he would remove them from the priesthood as he had the descendants of Eli (1 Sam 2:30–33). At least then they would know that he was serious about

---

[191] "You will be carried off with it" is literally "and he will carry you to it" (וְנָשָׂא אֶתְכֶם אֵלָיו). This is an "impersonal passive," i.e., an active third person verb whose subject has no referent in the context and serves as a passive. It is similar to the English expression "They say," when what is meant is "It is said." Cf. *IBHS* §4.4.2, 22.7. "To it" means "to the same place that it is taken," i.e., the dung heap. If Fishbane is correct that this rebuke is constructed on the basis of Num 6:23–27, the use of נָשָׂא, which also means "lift up," may allude ironically to the blessing, "May Yahweh lift up his face to you and give you peace" (Tate, "Questions for Priests and the People," 400).

[192] J. Milgrom cites a parallel in a Hittite text (*ANET*, 209, lines 600–618): "If . . . the kitchen servant . . . gives the god to eat from an unclean (vessel), to such a man the gods will give dung (and) urine to eat (and) to drink." The same text, he notes, elsewhere reads: "Does the god take revenge on him alone? Does he not take revenge on his wife, his children, his descendants, his kin, his slaves, his slave-girls, his cattle (and) sheep together with his crop and will utterly destroy him?" (*ANET*, 208, lines 35–38). Also citing the imprecation in Mal 2:12, Milgrom claims that "these resemblances (and others) between the two documents are so remarkable that the possibility must be entertained that this Hittite text lay before Malachi" (*Leviticus 1–16*, AB [New York: Doubleday, 1991], 459, citing P. Segal, "Further Parallels between the Priestly Literature in the Bible and the Hittite Instructions for Temple Servants," *Shnaton* 7–8 [1983–84]: 265–73).

maintaining his covenant with Levi.[193] The privilege of association with a group blessed by God does not assure the individuals in that group of God's favor. One's personal faith is necessary to avoid disqualification and to appropriate the lasting benefits of membership in the group. This principle applied to the descendants of Abraham, Isaac, and Jacob (cf. Matt 8:11–12/Luke 13:28; John 8:39–47; Rom 9:6–8); to the generation of Israel who were delivered from Egypt (cf. Josh 5:5–6); and also to the descendants of Levi, Aaron, and Zadok (cf. Lev 10:1–3; 1 Sam 2:29–36; Ezek 44:6–14). It also applies today both to unbelievers who have attached themselves to a Christian fellowship and to unbelieving members of a Christian family (cf. Acts 5:1–11; 1 Cor 8–11, esp. 9:24–10:13; 11:27–34; Heb 10:26–39).

To one familiar with the biblical distinction between priests and Levites, this connection of the priests of Judah to a covenant with Levi may be surprising. The Bible presents Levi as a tribe of Israel within which the clan descending from Aaron was to serve as priests (cf. 1 Chr 6:1–53). In the Mosaic legislation the rest of the tribe is referred to as "Levites," who were responsible for assisting the priests in the service of the tabernacle (Num 3–4). During the monarchy that relationship continued in the service of the temple and also after the exile in the second temple.[194]

### Excursus: Priests and Levites in Critical Perspective

Critical scholars use the evidence of Malachi in developing various theories for the history of Israel's priesthood and even of the OT canon. Most consider the distinction between priests and Levites, familiar to Bible students, to be a postexilic development promoted by "P" (the priestly history). If the postexilic book of Malachi treats them as identical, as Deuteronomy is commonly thought to do, that may have implications for the dating of "D" and "P."[195]

J. Wellhausen's extremely influential rewriting of the history of Israel's priesthood rejected any genealogical connection of the Levites to Levi or the "sons of Aaron" to Aaron. He declared that the "Levites" were only members of a priestly guild that officiated at cult centers ("high places") in Israel until they

---

[193] "So that my covenant . . . may continue" translates לִהְיוֹת בְּרִיתִי. For הְיֹה meaning "remain, continue" cf. Ruth 1:2; Dan 1:21. בְּרִיתִי can be either the complement of the infinitive, yielding the translation "to be my covenant" (cf. 1 Kgs 1:35; Neh 5:14; Jer 29:26; Jonah 4:6), or its subject, producing "that my covenant may be/continue to be" (cf. 1 Kgs 8:16,29,52; 2 Kgs 15:19; Esth 1:22; 3:14; Isa 10:2; Ezek 17:14). Verse 5 shows that the covenant referred to is one already in force, so the translation "may continue" is appropriate. Cf. Baldwin, *Haggai, Zechariah, Malachi,* 233–34; R. L. Smith, *Micah–Malachi,* 309. Efforts to emend or explain otherwise the verb לִהְיוֹת "are deemed necessary only when one assumes that the deity is destroying the covenant," which 3:3 indicates is not the case (O'Brien, *Priest and Levite in Malachi,* 40).

[194] Cf. 1 Kgs 8:4–6; 1 Chr 23:28–32; 2 Chr 7:6; 8:14–15; 13:9–10; 24:5–6; 29:16,34; 30:15–17; 35:11–15 for the first temple and Ezra 6:18; 8:15; Neh 12:47 for the second temple.

[195] For a summary of the various views see O'Brien, *Priest and Levite in Malachi,* 27–29.

were disenfranchised by Josiah's centralization of worship in Jerusalem in the seventh century B.C. The "sons of Aaron," he said, were actually descendants of the non-Israelite (Jebusite!) Zadok, whom David appointed as priest in Jerusalem.[196] It was the postexilic "Priestly source" that assigned them the fictitious pedigree. After summarizing modern approaches, O'Brien concludes that "a post-exilic date for P no longer can be merely assumed," and "in the wake of discussions of the term 'sons of Aaron' by scholars such as Cody, Haran and Cross and the suggestion that Chronicles may preserve some reliable traditions, Wellhausen's view that 'sons of Aaron' is an artificial creation must also be questioned."[197]

Perhaps the most unlikely part of Wellhausen's scenario is that the Deuteronomist, whose document gave warrant to Josiah's reform shutting down the high places as idolatrous, also sanctioned giving the Levites equal status with the Zadokites at the Jerusalem temple.[198] The Zadokites, he claimed, were unwilling to give the Levites a place, however, leaving them at the mercy of Israelite charity (cf. 2 Kgs 23:9, though it does not mention "Levites"). To solve this problem Ezekiel demoted the Levites to the role of temple servants because of their participation in worship at the high places, and thus he gave them a livelihood in the temple.[199]

J. R. Spencer followed Wellhausen at many points, assuming the Bible to be a mixture of conflicting traditions. He concluded that Levites, Zadokites, and Aaronites were not related by family but were competing priestly factions in ancient Israel. The Levites, he argues, controlled the priesthood before the monarchy but were supplanted and dismissed by the Zadokites during Solomon's time. Josiah's reform (reflected by the Deuteronomist) attempted to reinstate the Levites as priests alongside the Zadokites. Joshua 21, which distinguishes priests and Levites, is suspected as a later addition. (Note also 1 Kgs 12:31 assumes that priests were always to be from the tribe of Levi.) Although the Zadokites were discredited and lost power after the Jerusalem temple was destroyed, he says, Ezekiel tried but failed to reinstate them with the Levites as

---

[196] On difficulties with Zadok's lineage cf. Cody, *History of Old Testament Priesthood,* 88–93. He accepts arguments for a non-Levitical (perhaps Jebusite) Zadokite priesthood in Jerusalem that was in tension with the Levites (pp. 111, 113–14). Although Wellhausen and others rejected the Levitical descent of the Zadokites, some critical scholars have defended either their Levitical or even Aaronic lineage. See R. Abba, "Priests and Levites," *IDB,* 3:882; Haran, *Temples and Temple Service in Ancient Israel,* 77–78; Cross, *Canaanite Myth and Hebrew Epic,* 207–15; T. Polk, "The Levites in the Davidic-Solomonic Empire," *Studia Biblica et Theologica* 9 (1979): 10. See the survey of the discussion in G. W. Ramsey, "Zadok," *ABD* on CD-ROM. Version 1.0.

[197] O'Brien, *Priest and Levite in Malachi,* 23.

[198] Citing Deut 18:6–8; on this point cf. M. Haran, *Temples and Temple Service in Ancient Israel* (Oxford: Clarendon, 1978), 100.

[199] J. Wellhausen, *Prolegomena to the History of Ancient Israel* [Gloucester, Mass.: Peter Smith, 1983], 121–51, 171–72. See the critiques of Wellhausen in J. G. McConville, *Law and Theology in Deuteronomy,* JSOTSup (Sheffield: JSOT, 1984), 124–53 and M. S. Moore, "Role Preemption in the Israelite Priesthood," *VT* 46 (1996): 316–29.

their subordinates. Finally, the postexilic "P" writer and the Chronicler ignored the Zadokites and reflected the rise of the Aaronites with the Levites as their servants.[200] This reconstruction, which builds on work by Wellhausen, Gunneweg, Cody, Cross, Haran, and others, is based on assumptions of biblical discord[201] and the critical reconstruction of the history of the Old Testament canon.[202]

Despite numerous references in Scripture to priests and Levites as separate groups,[203] Scripture also speaks of the tribe of Levi as the priestly tribe. It uses the term "Levites" at times to speak of the entire tribe, including the priests (cf. Josh 21:4; 2 Chr 30:21–22), and even of the priests in particular. J. G. McConville has demonstrated that the Book of Deuteronomy knows the distinction between priests and Levites (e.g., Deut 10:6,8) but does not always reflect it in its terminology.[204] He demonstrates, for example, from passages like Deut 27:9–14 that the term "Levites" can be used specifically of priests.[205] There the tribe of Levi is stationed on Mount Gerizim to bless the people (v. 12), yet the "Levites" join those on Mount Ebal to pronounce the curses (v. 14). "Levites" in this case is a shorthand reference to "the priests, who are Levites," mentioned in v. 9.[206] Also Deut 31:9 refers to "the priests, the sons of Levi, who carried the ark," and v. 25 refers to "the Levites who

---

[200] J. R. Spencer, "Priestly Families (or Factions) in Samuel and Kings" in *The Pitcher Is Broken,* JSOTSup 190 (Sheffield: Academic Press, 1995), 387–400.

[201] Thus explaining, e.g, the Bible's failure to present Aaron in a consistently positive light (ibid., 389).

[202] He considers it significant, then, that "Zadok really only appears in the Deuteronomistic History, Ezekiel, and Chronicles" (ibid., 391).

[203] The phrase "priests and Levites" occurs twenty-seven times in the NIV, mostly in Chronicles and Ezra-Nehemiah. Beyond that the two terms occur in the same verse sixty-six more times. Note the distinction is also assumed in Josh 21:1; Judg 17:12.

[204] McConville shows that Deuteronomy in general "is not so precisely technical in its use of cultic terminology as P is" (*Law and Theology in Deuteronomy,* 136). On distinctions between "upper and lower clergy" see pp. 138–39. He also argues that Deuteronomy tends deliberately to avoid reference to priests vis-à-vis Levites as it does other divisions within the people as part of its stress on "the wholeness or brotherhood" of Israel standing "directly before God" (pp. 148–49).

[205] Ibid., 138.

[206] The passage also manifests a clear distinction between those Levites on Mt. Ebal who were priests and those on Mt. Gerizim who were not. Yet according to O'Brien, Wellhausen's view that the Deuteronomist champions that any Levite could serve as priest "has become almost axiomatic in biblical studies, as frequently assumed as it is argued" (*Priest and Levite in Malachi,* 12).

carried the ark."[207] The term "Levites" is also described in the broader sense in Josh 18:7 as those who "do not get a portion among you, because the priestly service of the LORD is their inheritance." In Mal 1:6–2:9 (cf. also 3:3), Malachi likewise uses the term "Levi" of the tribe to which the priesthood belonged. As in Deuteronomy, the author would have been quite familiar with the distinction between priests and Levites, but he chose to view the tribe as a whole, as the descendants of Levi to whom God had entrusted by covenant the spiritual well-being of Israel under the authority of the sons of Aaron (cf. Num 25:11–13).[208] One aspect of Malachi's message was to assure that God was not finished with the tribe of Levi.

## Excursus: The Levitical Covenant

The Levitical covenant is by no means as prominent in Scripture or in biblical theological studies as the Abrahamic, Mosaic, Davidic, and new covenants. Hebrews 7–8 seems to depict it as a corollary of the Mosaic covenant. In order to understand Malachi's reference to the "covenant with/of Levi" (2:4,8), it is necessary to rehearse the history of God's relationship with the tribe. The background for the covenant began in the patriarchal period. Following the rape of their sister Dinah by a Canaanite prince named Shechem, who subsequently begged for her hand in marriage, Jacob's sons hatched a deceitful plot for revenge (Gen 34). Having tricked the men of the Canaanite town into being circumcised, two of the brothers, Simeon and Levi, instigated an attack on them while the men were recuperating and killed every male (Gen 34:25,30). Although

---

[207] McConville, *Law and Theology in Deuteronomy,* 137–38. Whether "who carried the ark" is understood as restrictive or nonrestrictive depends on one's presuppositions regarding the relationship of priests and Levites. Regarding Deut 18:1–8 McConville notes that nowhere does it explicitly call the Levites "priests," especially where it might be expected in v. 7 (p. 128). Also the entire passage refers to the whole tribe of Levi, and its concern is with their livelihood (not with the relative status of priests and Levites, as Wellhausen argued, nor is it associated with the centralization of the cult; see pp. 142, 145–47). Verse 1 refers literally to "the priests, the Levites, all the tribe of Levi." Verse 5 says the Lord chose them "out of all your tribes," which would describe the tribe of Levi. On the basis of the other passages mentioned, then, he interprets "Levite(s)" in vv. 6–8 as "a kind of shorthand for the fuller expression which has recently occurred in the context" (p. 143). The passage speaks of the whole tribe of Levi as the priestly tribe, not understanding all Levites as priests but that "priesthood belongs to the tribe of Levi, in the sense of Josh. 18.7" (pp. 144–45).

[208] E. M. Meyers follows G. E. Wright ("The Levites in Deuteronomy," *VT* 4 [1954]: 325–30) in recognizing a distinction in Deuteronomy between altar clergy on the one hand, called either "the priests the Levites" or "priests," and teachers on the other hand, called "Levites." Meyers asserts that this "twofold division of labor within the priesthood . . . is a feature that is characteristic of the priesthood from the beginning. The prophet Malachi . . . seems to reflect not only the language of D but of P also, while at the same time alluding to the twofold role of priesthood" ("Priestly Language in the Book of Malachi," *HAR* 10 [1986]: 229). The Bible, however, does not portray the "twofold role" in the priesthood as congruent with the terms "priest" and "Levite." Thus Meyers is incorrect that Malachi's reference to "Levi" is to "the teaching clergy and not altar clergy." The association of the term here with "priest," he says, is "because the altar functions of the priesthood in a theocratic environment had grown closer and closer to that of a teacher."

Jacob's other sons participated in plundering the town, for their bloodthirsty revenge God cursed Simeon and Levi with landlessness (Gen 49:5–7).[209]

Simeon's tribe was eventually absorbed into Judah (cf. Josh 19:9 and the blessing of Moses in Deut 33, which omits Simeon), but because of the Levites' faithfulness at Mount Sinai, Levi's curse was changed into blessing.[210] In response to Israel's idolatry with the golden calf, when Moses summoned "whoever is for the LORD," the tribe of Levi rallied to him and carried out God's judgment (Exod 32:26–29; cf. Deut 33:9). Moses assured them of God's blessing for their holy zeal as they dedicated themselves wholly to the Lord (Exod 32:29; following the MT with NKJV, JPSV, NASB rather than the LXX with NIV). The exact nature of the blessing is unclear at this point, although the phrase translated "set apart to the LORD" could refer to ordination to priesthood (see NRSV).[211]

Priests in Israel are first mentioned in Exod 19:22,24, but their identity is not disclosed. Then Aaron and his sons Nadab and Abihu are found in Exod 24:1–2 worshiping the Lord "at a distance" along with seventy elders and then are allowed to see God and live (vv. 9–11). But they are referred to only as "leaders

---

[209] Critics reject the biblical explanation for Levi's landlessness. E.g., A. Cody explains that if there was a secular tribe of Levi it was either decimated by the time of the settlement or was slow in becoming sedentary, thus failing to obtain territory in the land, resulting in their status as גֵּרִים, "strangers" (*A History of Old Testament Priesthood* [Rome: Pontifical Biblical Institute, 1969], 56). He explains the development of their cultic specialization by reason of their landlessness and based on traditions of their involvement in the beginnings of Israel's religion (pp. 59–60).

[210] Note the threat in Mal 2:2 of another reversal, cursing their blessings. An imaginative Jewish priestly tradition reinterpreted Gen 34 as the basis for Levi's personal elevation to the priestly office by his father Jacob. This tradition can be traced back to the third century B.C. and is reflected in *Aramaic Levi, Jub.* 30:1–32:9, and the *T. Levi*. R. A. Kugler argues that this picture of Levi can be derived from a synoptic reading of Exod 32:25–29; Num 25:6–13; Deut 33:8–11 together with Gen 34 and that Malachi "construct[s] a covenant with Levi" on this basis (*From Patriarch to Priest: The Levi-Priestly Tradition from Aramaic Levi to Testament of Levi* [Atlanta: Scholars Press, 1996], 3–4, 18–22). His hermeneutic of "reading texts together" may explain how the post-biblical tradition was created, but it does not apply to Malachi, whose reference to "Levi" is not to "the *individual named Levi*" but to his descendants. Kugler denies this because of the form לֵוִי without the article in Mal 2:4 and אִתּוֹ, "with him," in 2:5 (p. 19). But this reflects the usage of Moses' blessings in Deut 33 (לֵוִי is also used as the name of the tribe in Num 1:49; 3:6 [cp. 3:9]; "the staff of Levi" in Num 17:13 does not refer to a staff belonging to the individual Levi; also cf. Num 26:59; Deut 10:9; 27:12; Ezek 48:31; 1 Chr 21:6). Malachi is speaking of the same covenant in 2:8 when he refers to the בְּרִית הַלֵּוִי, "covenant of Levi."

[211] A more literal rendering of the MT is, "Today fill [the LXX reads ἐπληρώσατε, "you filled"] your hands to Yahweh who gives you a blessing, for each of you went against his son and his brother." The expression "fill the hands" refers elsewhere to ordination to the priesthood (Exod 28:41; 29:9,29,33,35; Lev 8:33; 16:32; 21:10; Num 3:3; Judg 17:5,12; 2 Chr 13:9; 1 Kgs 13:33), although in Ezek 43:26 reference is to consecrating the altar. So the NRSV renders Exod 32:29, "Today you have ordained yourselves [reading with LXX as NIV] for the service of the LORD, each one at the cost of a son or a brother, and so have brought a blessing on yourselves this day." But the identical expression "fill the hand to Yahweh" only occurs elsewhere in 1 Chr 29:5, where it is used of dedicating oneself to Yahweh by giving to the temple project, and in 2 Chr 29:31, where it refers to the assembly's renewed dedication to Yahweh.

of the Israelites." The first specific mention of Aaron's priesthood comes in the Lord's instructions regarding a permanent Aaronic priesthood in Exodus 28–29 (cf. 27:21), but no connection is made there between his priesthood and his Levitical descent (cf. Exod 4:14; 6:16–20). It appears that cultic service came first to Aaron and his descendants and then was broadened to involve the whole tribe of Levi, probably because of the golden calf incident.

Soon after Aaron's death (Num 20:22–29), a second wilderness incident occurred, in many respects parallel to the one involving the golden calf. At that time a covenant was explicitly announced, making the permanent connection between priesthood and the tribe of Levi.[212] When Israel worshiped Baal of Peor in Shittim and engaged in sexual immorality there, Aaron's grandson Phinehas pleased the Lord by putting to death one of the offenders together with a Midianite woman he had brought to his tent.[213] The Lord commended his zeal (Num 25:11–13; cf. Ps 106:28–31), declaring that Phinehas

> has turned my anger away from the Israelites; for he was as zealous as I am for my honor among them [lit., "by his being zealous/jealous with my zeal/jealousy in their midst], so that in my zeal I did not put an end to them. Therefore tell him I am making *my covenant of peace* with him. He and his descendants will have *a covenant of a lasting priesthood*, because he was zealous for the honor of his God [lit., he was zealous/jealous for his God] and made atonement for the Israelites.

Probably on the basis of Deut 33:8–11 (see below), Malachi considers this "covenant of peace" to have been a covenant not just with Phinehas and his descendants or the priestly descendants of Aaron but with the whole tribe of Levi (i.e., Levi and his descendants; cf. 2:5).[214] This interpretation had also been given in Deut 10:8, where, apparently referring to the same incident, Moses wrote, "At that time the LORD set apart the tribe of Levi" (likewise Neh 13:29 would identify the covenant as "the covenant of the priesthood and of the Levites"). Their purpose as given there would be "to carry the ark of the covenant of the LORD, to stand before the LORD to minister and to pronounce blessings in his name" (cf. 21:5).

A more theologically explicit purpose, however, may be derived from the incident itself. The verb translated in Num 25:11,13 "was zealous" *(qānā')* and the noun "zeal" *(qin'â)* often refer elsewhere to jealousy, either human or divine

---

[212] The right of the Aaronites to Israel's "most holy offerings" (cf. Num 18:8–18) is also declared in Num 18:19 to be "an everlasting covenant of salt" and is connected to their landlessness in v. 20. Note vv. 21–24 specify the Levites' provision of tithes as "a lasting ordinance" and connect it to their landlessness.

[213] Note the similarity of the sin there to Malachi's situation expressed in 2:11. For studies of the precise nature of the sin in Num 25, cf. S. C. Reif, "What Enraged Phinehas?—A Study of Numbers 25:8," *JBL* 90 (1971): 100–106; F. M. Cross, *Canaanite Myth and Hebrew Epic* (Cambridge: Harvard University, 1973), 202.

[214] T. R. Ashley considers the blessing that went specifically to Phinehas's descendants would be the high priesthood (Eli being an exception; *The Book of Numbers,* NICOT [Grand Rapids: Eerdmans, 1993], 523). See Glazier-McDonald's argument (*Malachi: The Divine Messenger,* 79–80) that Mal 2:4–5 is based primarily on Num 25:12–13.

(e.g., Gen 30:1; 37:11; Exod 20:5; 34:14; Deut 4:24; 6:15; 32:16,21; Josh 24:19).[215] When Scripture speaks of God's "jealousy," it speaks not of envy, however, but of his determination to preserve from corruption his relationship with his wayward people. As such it is the other side of his love (cf. Song 8:6), which motivates him to exercise his wrath against any threats to the covenant relationship he has established for the benefit of his people. Phinehas was commended because he acted with that same zeal to defend and preserve from corruption God's relationship with Israel by eliminating unfaithfulness. He thus protected Israel's life by turning away God's anger.[216] That was the kind of zeal the Lord was looking for from the priests of Malachi's day, rather than the careless neglect he was receiving. And the Lord continues to be pleased with holy zeal not only to extend and strengthen his church but also to preserve its purity. He continues to desire shepherds who will defend his church with diligence, self-sacrifice, humility, and tears from "savage wolves" who "will arise and distort the truth in order to draw away disciples after them" (Acts 20:18–35, esp. vv. 28–31).

The ministry of the priests and Levites then would be "to bear the responsibility for offenses against the sanctuary" (Num 18:1). That is, through the sacrificial system they would serve as spiritual lightning rods or insulators to avert disaster when the people violated cultic law and so to enable a perfectly holy God to dwell with an unholy people (cf. Num 16:22; 17:12–13; 18:5). This would be the means by which they would convey God's blessing upon the people (Num 6:22–27; Deut 10:8; 21:5).[217] The "nonpriestly" Levites were informed that their new role would be to care for and to guard the Lord's house and to assist the descendants of Aaron in worship and in making atonement for Israel through the sacrifices (Num 1:50–53; 3:6–10; 8:19; 16:8–10; 18:2–7; 1 Chr 9:26–33; 15:2; 23:24–32; 2 Chr 23:18–19; 31:2; 34:12–13).[218]

The tribe of Levi also came to belong to the Lord in a special sense as substitutes and symbols of the firstborn children of Israel, whom the Lord had purchased by redeeming them on the night he struck the firstborn of Egypt (Num

---

[215] See the studies by L. Coppes, קָנָא *(qānāʾ)*, *TWOT* 2:802–3; A. Stumpff, "ζῆλος," *TDNT* 2:878–80, 883–84; and N. J. Opperwall and R. J. Wyatt, "Jealous," *ISBE*, rev., 2:972.

[216] Ashley suggests that the deaths of these two offenders served as a "ransom price" to reduce the deserved death sentence upon the whole nation. Phinehas thus obtained "peace," or "wholeness," for Israel and was rewarded with God's promise of "wholeness," which would take the shape of an "everlasting priesthood" (*Numbers,* 522–23). See also Milgrom, *Numbers,* 217.

[217] Cf. J. C. Kelly, *The Function of the Priest in the Old Testament* (Rome: Pontificum Athenaeum Antonianum, 1973), 23.

[218] Before the temple was built, the Levites were assigned to carry the tabernacle and its furnishings (Num 1:50; 4:15; 1 Sam 6:15; 2 Sam 15:24). The significance of the sprouting of Aaron's rod (Num 17) in the context is the confirmation of God's selection of the tribe of Levi and, more importantly, Aaronic authority over the tribe. Placing the rod in the ark signified that Aaronic authority would be a permanent feature of the Mosaic covenant. The NT doctrine of the non-Levitical Christ as our High Priest entails as radical a departure from the old covenant as the cessation of animal sacrifices (Heb 3:1; 4:14; 5:1–10; 7:1–28). P. D. Hanson, following Wellhausen's basic approach, considers Num 16–17 to have been edited by the postexilic Zadokite (=Aaronite) priests as an attack on the Levites (*The Dawn of Apocalyptic* [Philadelphia: Fortress, 1975], 267–69).

3:12–13,40–43; 8:16–19). This special relationship to the Lord, rather than the curse on Levi, came to be the explanation for their landlessness. As the Lord's possession they would be provided for from the offerings (Lev 6:14–7:36; Num 18:8–32; Deut 10:9; 18:1–8; Josh 13:14; 18:7).[219]

Moses alluded to the Lord's covenant with Levi in his mediatorial blessing of the tribe in Deut 33:8–11.[220]

About Levi he said:

Your Thummim and Urim belong to the man you favored.[221]
You tested him at Massah;
    you contended with him at the waters of Meribah.
He said of his father and mother,
    'I have no regard for them.'
He did not recognize his brothers
    or acknowledge his own children,
but he [MT "they"] watched over your word
    and guarded your covenant.
He teaches [MT "They teach"] your precepts to Jacob
    and your law to Israel.
He offers [MT "They offer"] incense before you
    and whole burnt offerings on your altar.
Bless all his skills, O LORD,
    and be pleased with the work of his hands.
Smite the loins of those who rise up against him;
    strike his foes till they rise no more.

The phrase "the man you favored" refers to God's election of Levi as the priestly tribe (pointing specifically to their possession of the "Thummim and Urim"[222])

---

[219] McConville argues persuasively that the tribe was intended to serve as instructive examples of the principle of devotion to and dependence on the Lord alone. The Levite was "an ideal representation of how the whole people should stand both to Yahweh and to the land" in that "he personifies the dependent spirit" (*Law and Theology in Deuteronomy,* 150–51).

[220] For a summary of critical opinion on the contribution of this passage to the history of Israel's priesthood, see O'Brien, *Priest and Levite in Malachi,* 10–11; Cody, *A History of Old Testament Priesthood,* 114–20.

[221] The LXX and 4QDeut[h] contain an addition that would change the rendering to "Give to Levi your Thummim, and your Urim to the man you favored." Cf. J. Duncan, "New Readings for the 'Blessing of Moses' from Qumran," *JBL* 114 (1995): 273–90.

[222] J. C. Kelly explains (citing Judg 18:5; 1 Sam 14) that this symbolized the priestly office "in that they represent what was apparently the original function of the *kohen* in Israel, oracular consultation" (*Function of the Priest,* 11). He argues that the priestly role of oracular consultation eventually evolved into their role as teachers of *Torah* (pp. 12–13). That oracular consultation could not function alongside *Torah* instruction, however, is an unnecessary assumption. J. Pedersen says, "The oracle would merely come in to supplement the law in individual instances or to apply it" (*Israel: Its Life and Culture,* 3–4:160).

and means, according to Merrill, "the man brought into your (covenant) loyalty."[223] Moses went on to remind the Lord that the Levites had proved themselves in the wilderness by their zeal for his "word" and "covenant" (i.e., the Mosaic covenant). The two wilderness incidents are most likely referred to as the occasions when Levi "watched over" the Lord's word and "guarded" his covenant (unless one assumes a postexilic date for the "priestly source").[224] Then he pointed to the two primary functions of the tribe: to teach his "precepts" *(mišpaṭîm)* and "law" *(tôrâ)* in Israel and to officiate at the altar. J. C. Kelly calls v. 10 "the essential verse for an understanding of the function of Levi among the tribes of Israel."[225] The teaching ministry is specifically entrusted to the priests in Lev 10:11 and is surely related to their responsibility for the ark, where the *Torah* was kept (cf. Deut 10:1–2; 31:9–13). As Merrill notes, the priests and Levites appeared in this role "to a greater or lesser extent in subsequent history . . ., especially in post-Old Testament times when teaching of Torah became the very center of Judaism."[226] Whereas the priests' cultic role is the topic in Mal 1:6–14, their instructive role is in view in 2:5–9 (see esp. comments on vv. 6–7).

In spite of the Lord's later displeasure with much of the priesthood,[227] he renewed his covenant with Levi in Jer 33:17–22, associating it explicitly with the Davidic covenant, implicitly with the Abrahamic covenant, and contextually with the new covenant. First, the Lord declared through the prophet that after the restoration "David will never fail to have a man to sit on the throne of the house of Israel, nor will the priests, who are Levites, ever fail to have a man to stand before me continually to offer burnt offerings, to burn grain offerings and to present sacrifices" (vv. 17–18). Second, he declared that his covenants with David and with

---

[223] E. H. Merrill, *Deuteronomy,* NAC (Nashville: Broadman & Holman, 1994), 438. The Hb. phrase is לְאִישׁ חֲסִידֶךָ, lit. "are to the man of your loyalty." Tate's observation that "nothing is said of a covenant" in Deut 33:8–10 ("Questions for Priests and the People," 400; also Garrett, "Israel's Unfaithfulness: The Priests," 30) is an overstatement, especially if the events and instructions of Numbers are acknowledged as preceding and furnishing background for those of Deuteronomy. Besides, M. Weinfeld argues for the synonymy of חֶסֶד and בְּרִית ("בְּרִית *bᵉrîth,*" *TDOT* 2:270).

[224] Kelly takes the reference to "Massah" and "Meribah" as an allusion to Moses' and Aaron's faithfulness in opposing Israel's complaining and rebellion after leaving Egypt (Exod 17; Num 20:1–11) and the reference to Levi's impartial and courageous zeal as to Exod 32:25–29 (*Function of the Priest,* 14). The term "Meribah" (meaning "quarreling"; cf. Gen 13:8) is used both of Rephidim in Exod 17:7 and of Kadesh in Num 20:13,24. Rephidim is also called "Massah" (meaning "testing") in Exod 17:7 and Num 14:22. Moses' point in Deut 33:8 may be understood as a general affirmation of the Levitical tribe's faithfulness throughout Israel's trials and disappointing behavior between Egypt and Canaan.

[225] Kelly, *Function of the Priest,* 15.

[226] Merrill, *Deuteronomy,* 439–40. Rejecting the Mosaic origin of this passage, Cody (*A History of Old Testament Priesthood,* 116) claims that "the giving of *tôrâ* by priests does not appear in any texts earlier than the eighth century or early ninth century (Hos. 4:6; Mic. 3:11; cf. also 2 Kgs. 12:3), but from that time on down to the Exile it is closely associated with priests (Dt. 31:9,26; Jer. 2:8; 18:18; Ezek. 7:26; Zeph. 3:4)." See also Jer 8:8; Hos 8:12.

[227] Cf. Jer 1:18; 2:8,26–28; 5:31; 6:13; 8:1–12; 23:11; Lam 4:13; Ezek 22:26; Hos 4:6–8; 6:9; Mic 3:11; Zeph 3:4.

"the Levites who are priests ministering before me" were as sure and permanent as the day and the night (vv. 20–21; cf. 31:35–37), and third, that the Lord would "make the descendants of David my servant and the Levites who minister before me as countless as the stars of the sky and as measureless as the sand on the sea-shore" (v. 22). Thus the "lasting priesthood" *(kĕhunnat 'ôlām)* promised to Phinehas in Num 25:13 would find fulfillment in connection with the Davidic covenant.

It may be that Jeremiah's reference to Levitical priests is figurative. Some believe that this promise regarding the Levites, like the Davidic promise, has been or is being fulfilled in Christ, who is not only the messianic King but also the Priest of the new covenant (cf. Ps 110:4; Zech 6:13; Heb 7:23–28).[228] Thus the continual offerings and sacrifices referred to would be fulfilled by the eternal effects of the one sacrifice of Christ. As F. H. Klooster declares: "The offering of the one sacrifice for all time by the eternal priest also fulfilled the Levitic (Phine-has) Covenant and made the Sinaitic Covenant 'obsolete' (Heb 8:13)."[229] The promise of countless descendants of David and the Levites would presumably be fulfilled by the multitudes of "those who believe," who are not only "children of Abraham" (Gal 3:7) but also of David and Levi. Perhaps they are the "kingdom and priests" (note the conjoining of the two spheres) who are to "serve our God" and "reign on the earth," who were "purchased . . . from every tribe and language and people and nation" by the Lamb that was slain, who is also the Lion of the tribe of Judah (Rev 5:5–10).

Against viewing Christ as the direct fulfillment of the covenant with Levi, however, is his human descent from the tribe of Judah and the argument in Heb 7:11–19 that his priesthood is like that of Melchizedek and involves a change from the Levitical one.[230] Whereas Feinberg allows that "in the highest sense Christ as King-Priest will, of course, fulfill these promises (cf. Ps 110:4)," he asserts that "in the priestly realm the primary emphasis is on Levi's line, which must not be confused with Christ's priesthood after the order of Melchizedek."[231] Also, Jer 33:15–16 seems to place the time of fulfillment after Christ's return, when he "will do what is just and right in the land" and when

---

[228] See F. B. Huey, Jr., *Jeremiah, Lamentations,* NAC (Broadman & Holman, 1993), 302; R. K. Harrison, *Jeremiah and Lamentations,* TOTC (Downers Grove: InterVarsity, 1973), 145; T. Laetsch, *Bible Commentary: Jeremiah* (St. Louis: Concordia, 1965), 268–73. But G. Van Groningen's conclusion is that "the Aaronic house is also to continue. The levitical priesthood, in charge of the worship ritual and especially of the sacrifices and the rites accompanying these, is to remain in effect" (*Messianic Revelation in the Old Testament* [Grand Rapids: Baker, 1990], 727).

[229] F. H. Klooster, "The Biblical Method of Salvation: A Case for Continuity," in *Continuity and Discontinuity: Perspectives on the Relationship between the Old and New Testaments* (Westchester, Ill.: Crossway, 1988), 157.

[230] J. A. Thompson suggests that the expression "the priests, who are Levites" in Jer 33:18 may be simply a way of designating "legitimate priests" who would serve the Lord (*The Book of Jeremiah,* NICOT [Grand Rapids: Eerdmans, 1980], 602–3). But it is difficult to see how this would fulfill "my covenant with the Levites" in 33:21.

[231] C. L. Feinberg, "Jeremiah," EBC (Grand Rapids: Zondervan, 1986), 6:592.

"Jerusalem will live in safety" and be called "The LORD Our Righteousness," that is, during the Millennium.[232]

A revival of sacrifices and priesthood is also considered part of the Millennial restoration in Ezekiel, which narrows the priesthood to the descendants of the Levitical priest Zadok (cf. Ezek 40:46; 43:19). Zadok, a descendant of Aaron through Eleazar (1 Chr 24:3), had remained loyal to David and Solomon (2 Sam 15; 1 Kgs 1) and was consequently appointed high priest following the removal of the treacherous Abiathar (1 Kgs 2:26–27,35), who was descended from Aaron through Ithamar and the cursed house of Eli (1 Sam 2:29–33).[233] According to Ezek 44:15, the Zadokite priests also remained faithful during the course of Israel's growing idolatry (see also 48:11). Late in the preexilic period the non-Zadokite priests became involved with idols and desecrated the temple, for which in the Millennial restoration they will be demoted to the role of Levites (44:6–14).[234] In the future, then, only the descendants of Zadok will be allowed to enter the sanctuary, to offer sacrifices, and "to come near my table to minister before

---

[232] See W. C. Kaiser, Jr., "Evidence from Jeremiah," in *A Case for Premillennialism: A New Consensus* (Chicago: Moody, 1992), 114–16.

[233] According to P. D. Hanson, 1 Sam 2:27–36 was "a Zadokite addition to the history of Eli" intended "to discredit the lineage of their Levitical opponents." The Zadokites interpreted the fall of Shiloh as "a pronouncement of divine judgment upon Eli and his descendants" (*The Dawn of Apocalyptic*, 224). His hermeneutic of sociological conflict is another attempt to turn the biblical data on its head. E.g., he interprets God's words of judgment on the Jerusalem cult in Jer 7:13–14 as a bitter polemic of Jeremiah the Levite against the Zadokites of Jerusalem (p. 225). See the summary of Hanson's views in O'Brien, *Priest and Levite in Malachi*, 15–16. J. O. Akao argues that the Deuteronomic movement originated with the descendants of Abiathar in their opposition to the Zadokite priesthood of Jerusalem ("In Search of the Origin of the Deuteronomic Movement," *IBS* 16 [1994]: 174–89).

[234] This is interpreting "Levites" in v. 10 as "Levitical priests" and interpreting the disobedience of Israel in vv. 6–9 as at least closely related to that of the "Levites" in vv. 10–14. It is unlikely that vv. 10–14 deal with the Levites who served the priests, since the judgment involved no longer serving as priests or approaching the "holy things" (also mentioned in v. 8) or the "most holy offerings" but rather "having charge of the gates of the temple" and "of the duties of the temple and all the work that is to be done in it," which is precisely what the Levites had always done. The alternative is to say with Wellhausen that all Levites had been priests at the high places, while the Zadokites were Jerusalem priests (*Prolegomena to the History of Ancient Israel*, 123–24). But this contradicts Exod 28–29; Num 3–4; 16:8–11 and other texts. Dating the pentateuchal "priestly document" after Ezek 44 involves changing it to a work of historical fiction and causes more problems than it solves. For a discussion of those problems see J. G. McConville, "Priests and Levites in Ezekiel: A Crux in the Interpretation of Israel's History," *TynBul* 34 (1983): 3–31. See esp. his discussion of terms for clerical classes on pp. 22–25. Hanson views Ezek 44 as part of the Zadokite revision of Ezekiel and as constituting "heated polemic where the sole object is to malign the opposing party so as to support the accuser's claim to sole legitimacy." Whereas Ezekiel had assigned their duties "because they were the honored possession of Yahweh, here their duties are *their punishment for idolatry!*" (*The Dawn of Apocalyptic*, 266). Cody also claims that "the levites are tendentiously and unfairly accused of abandoning the worship of Yahweh for the worship of idols" (*Ezekiel with an Excursus on Old Testament Priesthood* [Wilmington: Michael Glazier, 1984], 261).

me and perform my service" (44:16; the only other place besides Mal 1:7,12, where the altar is identified as the Lord's "table").

Based on 1 Kgs 2:27, it seems that we should understand Zadok as the "faithful priest" prophesied in 1 Sam 2:35, to whom the Lord promised, "I will firmly establish his house, and he will minister before my anointed one always" (cf. 2 Sam 7:11–13).[235] The parallel between Jer 33:18 and 1 Sam 2:35 (esp. the phrase *kol-hayyāmîm,* lit. "all the days," translated "always" in 1 Sam 2:35 and "continually" in Jer 33:18) suggests that Jeremiah may have been alluding to the Samuel prophecy. If so, there is an additional reason why Jeremiah's "man to stand before me continually" should not be understood as Christ, since this "faithful priest" is distinguished in Samuel from "my anointed one." Therefore it seems that we should interpret Jer 33:17–22 as a prophecy of the Zadokite priesthood that will serve under the divine King-Priest during the Millennium in fulfillment of the covenant with Levi.[236]

One additional reference to the Levitical covenant occurs in Neh 13:29. There the "men of Judah" had committed a "terrible wickedness" and been "unfaithful to our God by marrying foreign women" as Solomon had done (13:26–27; cf. Ezra 9:14). Even one of the sons of the high priest had married the daughter of Sanballat the Horonite, who had ridiculed and plotted against God's people (13:28; cf. Neh 2:19; 4:1–8; 6:1–14). Nehemiah responded to the people with righteous anger and to the priests with prayer: "Remember them, O my God, because they defiled the priestly office and the covenant of the priesthood and of the Levites" (13:29).[237] The covenant that began with Phinehas as "a covenant of a lasting priesthood" (Num 25:13) came to be considered a covenant with the whole tribe, which was uniquely related to God and to which the priesthood belonged. The tribe of Levi would be blessed in that the whole tribe would be occupied with the Lord's service and would be provided for from the tithes and offerings and by being the tribe from which the priesthood came. Thus while the Levitical covenant focused especially on the priesthood, it involved privileges and responsibilities for the whole tribe and so could be designated by Nehemiah as "the covenant of the priesthood and of the Levites."[238]

Although the restoration under Zerubbabel, Ezra, and Nehemiah occurred as an outworking of the prophets' words (cf. Ezra 1:1), the fulfillment was far from complete due to the people's persistence in sin (cf. Neh 9:36–37).[239] And

---

[235] Cf. R. P. Gordon, *1 & 2 Samuel: A Commentary,* Library of Biblical Interpretation (Grand Rapids: Zondervan, 1986), 88; R. D. Bergen, *1, 2 Samuel,* NAC (Nashville: Broadman & Holman, 1996), 84.

[236] For an explanation of the necessity for rebuilding the temple and reinstituting the priesthood and sacrifices in the Millennium, see L. E. Cooper, *Ezekiel,* NAC (Nashville: Broadman & Holman, 1994), 353, 376–81.

[237] "Because they defiled the priestly office" is lit. "because of the defilements of the priesthood." The term for "defilements" is גֹּאֲלֵי, from the same root as the verb used in Mal 1:7,12.

[238] Term for "the Levites" here is הַלְוִיִּם, which can be synonymous with לֵוִי and בְּנֵי לֵוִי, referring to the whole tribe or can refer to a segment within the tribe.

[239] Cf. J. G. McConville, "Ezra-Nehemiah and the Fulfillment of Prophecy," *VT* 36 (1986): 206–22.

although Nehemiah "purified the priests and the Levites of everything foreign, and assigned them duties, each to his own task" (13:30), according to the gospel writers, by the time of Jesus the Jerusalem priesthood was under God's curse (cf. Matt 16:21; 21:23–46). But the promise of a lasting Levitical priesthood was still in effect, as well as the promise in Mal 3:3–4 that the Lord would "purify the Levites and refine them like gold and silver" and that they would "bring offerings in righteousness, and the offerings of Judah and Jerusalem will be acceptable to the LORD, as in days gone by, as in former years."

Could these prophecies be finding fulfillment in the church as a "holy priesthood, offering spiritual sacrifices acceptable to God through Jesus Christ" (1 Pet 2:5; see also v. 9; Heb 13:15–16)? That some type of fulfillment is already occurring is perhaps suggested in Acts 6:7, which indicates that some Levitical priests had become Christians. But if a Jewish Millennial kingdom is necessary to fulfill some of the aspects of the Abrahamic covenant (e.g., prophecies of Israel's prominence among the nations in Isa 11:14; 14:1–4; 49:22–26; 60:5–7; Jer 31:7; Mic 4:1–8),[240] then it seems that a literal Levitical (Zadokite) priesthood is necessary during that time to complete God's promises to the tribe. It is doubtful that Phinehas and his descendants would feel that God's covenant with them of a "lasting priesthood" had been fulfilled by a holy priesthood of non-Levites and Gentiles, however sanctified and legitimate they were. Likewise, would the priests of Jeremiah's day be satisfied by such a fulfillment or the Zadokites who heard or read the prophecies of Ezekiel? Furthermore, if a nonliteral fulfillment is sufficient for Ezekiel's prophecies of a holy priesthood, then what would be the meaning of Ezekiel's narrowing the priesthood to the Zadokites?

On the condition of Israel's obedience and faithfulness to the covenant, God had promised a special relationship with them as his "treasured possession," a "kingdom of priests," and a "holy nation" (Exod 19:5–6). As the tribe of Levi had a special relationship with God within Israel, so the entire nation had a special relationship with God over against the nations (cf. Deut 7:6–16; 14:2; Ps 135:4; Isa 41:8–20; 43:20–21; 44:1–5). In the ancient Near East priesthood was considered a highly privileged position, believed to have the ear of the god and to receive the special love and care of that god. As long as Israel was faithful to the Lord as a nation, they would have such a position of being wholly set apart for him, privileged with continual access to his presence and involvement in his service.[241]

---

[240] Cf. Saucy, *Progressive Dispensationalism*, 221–45, 272–96. He argues for an earthly Millennial kingdom of Christ on the basis of certain prophetic elements that fit neither the present age nor the eternal state, especially the need for a "historical display of the glory of Christ" (cf. 1 Cor 15:24–28) and "for the completion of his messianic salvation" in causing peace and righteousness to prevail among the peoples of the earth (p. 291).

[241] W. E. Glenny notes that while Israel's mediatorial office of being a light to the nations may be implicit in their role as priests, "it is not emphasized [in Exod 19:6] as it is later in Isa. 61:1–9" (also Isa 42:6). "Kingdom of priests" rather emphasizes Israel's "worship and priestly service to Yahweh" ("The Israelite Imagery of 1 Peter 2," in *Dispensationalism, Israel and the Church* [Grand Rapids: Zondervan, 1992], 171).

Israel's disobedience, however, brought them cursing rather than blessing (Lev 26; Deut 28). They failed to obey the Lord and keep the covenant, and rather than being a kingdom of priests and a holy nation, they became a sinful kingdom, were temporarily abandoned by the Lord, and their very temple was destroyed (Lam 2:2–10; Ezek 8:6; 10:4,18–19; 11:22–23; Amos 9:8). Nevertheless, God did not abandon his plans for Israel nor for all the peoples of the earth to be blessed through them (Gen 12:3). As Paul the apostle wrote regarding Israel, "God's gifts and his call are irrevocable" (Rom 11:29). Thus God has promised a restored temple in Jerusalem again full of his glory, where he will dwell among his people forever, never again to be defiled by them, and from which he will reign over the earth in an everlasting kingdom (Ezek 20:39–41; 43:1–7; 48:35; Dan 7:22,27). Furthermore, all the nations of the earth will stream to the everlasting light of God's glory in Jerusalem and worship him there in righteousness (Isa 2:1–4; 56:6–8; 60:1–22), and his nation of Israel "will be called priests of the LORD" and "ministers of our God" (Isa 61:6; cf. 66:19–24).

If a complete fulfillment of the Levitical covenant must await the Millennial kingdom, then how are we to understand Peter's explanation that Christian believers "are being built into a spiritual house to be a holy priesthood, offering spiritual sacrifices acceptable to God through Jesus Christ" (1 Pet 2:5) and that we are "a royal priesthood, a holy nation, a people belonging to God" (2:9)? Similarly, how are we to understand the apostle John's praise of Christ, who "has made us to be a kingdom and priests to serve his God and Father" (Rev 1:6)? The explanation that accounts on the one hand for Israel's continuing distinctiveness in God's program and on the other hand for the New Testament's insistence that the day of fulfillment has already dawned is that the spiritual benefits of the new covenant are being fulfilled in the church at the present time but that a more complete and literal fulfillment involving Israel as a nation awaits the Millennial reign of Christ (see comments on 1:11).[242]

### (2) Covenant with the Priests (2:5–7)

**[5]"My covenant was with him, a covenant of life and peace, and I gave them to him; this called for reverence and he revered me and stood in awe of my name. [6]True instruction was in his mouth and nothing false was found on his lips. He walked with me in peace and uprightness, and turned many from sin.**

**[7]"For the lips of a priest ought to preserve knowledge, and from his mouth men should seek instruction—because he is the messenger of the LORD Almighty.**

The first division of Malachi begins with a contrast between the people of Israel/Judah and their forefather Jacob on the one hand and the nation of Edom and their forefather Esau on the other hand (1:2–5). It ends here with a contrast, narrower in scope, between the priests at the beginning of Israel's history and those of Malachi's day. The covenant with Levi referred to in v. 4 is elaborated

---

[242] See ibid., 183; and esp. C. A. Blaising and D. L. Bock, *Progressive Dispensationalism* (Wheaton: Bridgepoint, 1993), 232–83.

in vv. 5–7 by describing what the Lord demanded from the Levitical priesthood and at first had received. Then vv. 8–9 rehearse how the priests of Malachi's day were failing in their responsibilities and how the Lord was responding to their unfaithfulness.

Verse 5 is a general statement of the Levitical covenant: what the Lord promised and delivered and what he expected and received initially from the priestly tribe in response. Verse 6 then gives some specifics of how at first the Levitical priests faithfully carried out their duties of biblical instruction and spiritual leadership. Finally the Lord's history lesson is applied in v. 7 with a brief explanation of the priests' instructional role.

**2:5** A more literal rendering of this elliptical verse would be: "My covenant was with him: life and peace, and I gave them to him; fear, and he feared me. And from the presence of[243] my name he was terrified." "Life and peace" was the Lord's covenant promise, and "fear" was Levi's obligation; both were fulfilled. J. M. O'Brien understands the covenant with Levi to be a "grant" type.[244] She employs Weinfeld's distinction between the grant type covenant (as God made with Abraham), which emphasizes "an obligation of the master to his servant," and the treaty (as he made with Israel), which emphasizes "an obligation of the servant, the vassal, to his master the suzerain."[245] Weinfeld explains that "while the grant is a reward for loyalty and good deeds *already performed,* the treaty is an inducement to future loyalty."[246] But "while the grant is mainly a promise by the donor to the recipient, it presupposes the loyalty of the latter."[247]

---

[243] The term מִפְּנֵי, lit. "from the face of," often occurs with verbs of fearing. It usually expresses causation and can be translated "because of" or "for fear of" with verbs of hiding, escaping, fleeing, expelling, destroying, etc. (BDB, 818).

[244] O'Brien, *Priest and Levite in Malachi,* 40. There is no object "them" in the LXX (or the Vg.), which apparently understands ἔδωκα αὐτῷ ἐν φόβῳ φοβεῖσθαί με, "I gave to him to fear me with fear," as a charge to respond to God with fear (T. Muraoka, *A Greek-English Lexicon of the Septuagint* [Louvain: Peeters, 2002], 585). The Tg. likewise does not have "them" but reads "My covenant was with him (for) life and peace, and I gave him *the perfect teaching of my law* and he feared *from before* me and *feared* from before my name," interpreting "fear" as "the perfect teaching of my law" (K. J. Cathcart and R. P. Gordon, *The Targum of the Minor Prophets,* The Aramaic Bible 14 [Wilmington/Edinburgh: Michael Glazier, 1989], 232), which identifies some Hb. MSS also lacking the object suffix "them"). In his *Studies in the Targum to the Twelve Prophets* (Leiden: Brill, 1994), 67, however, Gordon expresses the opinion that the Tg. *Vorlage* probably agreed with the MT.

[245] Weinfeld, *Deuteronomy and the Deuteronomic School,* 74. On the concept of covenant generally see id., "בְּרִית *bᵉrîth,*" TDOT 2:253–79.

[246] Weinfeld, *Deuteronomy and the Deuteronomic School,* 75. He also notes that the words of Mal 2:6, "He walked with me in peace and uprightness," like the expression "walked before me" in Gen 24:40; 48:15, are equivalent to an expression in Assyrian grants (pp. 75–76).

[247] Ibid., 74.

The Lord had blessed the priestly tribe of Levi with full, happy life[248] and with well-being (*šālôm,* "peace" or "wholeness").[249] The two concepts of life and peace occur together in David's greeting to Nabal (1 Sam 25:6). The sage also promises them to the one who listens to his wise instruction (Prov 3:2). Together they constitute the blessings of divine favor: length of days, health, and prosperity. A "covenant of peace" is referred to in Num 25:12; Isa 54:10; Ezek 34:25; 37:26 (cf. also Lev 26:6; 1 Kgs 5:12; Job 5:23; Pss 29:11; 85:8). A bilateral "treaty of peace" (Josh 9:15; 10:1) would mean that both parties promised to refrain from hostilities against the other and furthermore would seek the other's welfare, including a pledge of aid if the treaty partner were attacked. God's "covenant of peace" with the tribe of Levi or with Israel would involve the assurance of an enduring relationship with himself and a pledge to secure and protect their welfare by his divine grace, wisdom, and power.

In response the Lord had expected and received fear (*môrāʾ,* "reverence"; see comments on 1:6).[250] Emphasis in the last clause is on the Lord's "name" and on "he" (as opposed to "you"), resulting in the sense that the early priesthood, in contrast with those of Malachi's day, had wisely feared nothing but God. Thus Malachi's indictment of the priests in 1:6–14 resounds here (see comments on "name" at 1:6). At first things had been different. The verb here translated "stood in awe" *(ḥātat)* can mean either to "be shattered, destroyed"[251] or to "be disheartened, dismayed, terrified."[252] The idea of

---

[248] On the meaning of "life" as happiness, "that is to say, life in its fullest sense," cf. Weinfeld, *Deuteronomy and the Deuteronomic School,* 307–13. J. C. Kelly says, "For Deuteronomy, as for the Old Testament in general, life is blessing, initial blessing of being, together with the increase of goods and family, and peace and security, in short what might be described as well being, fullness of life" *(Function of the Priest,* 22).

[249] J. Pedersen explains that the Hb. concept of "peace" was not a negative or passive one but involved wholeness and completeness. It meant harmony between friends, triumph in war, success in one's endeavors, good health, and security. The Hb. equivalent of the Eng. greeting "How are you?" is "Do you have 'peace'?" (cf. Gen 29:6; 2 Sam 18:29; 2 Kgs 4:26). See *Israel: Its Life and Culture,* 1–2:311–29. See also G. L. Carr, "שָׁלֵם *(shālēm)," TWOT* 2:930–31; G. von Rad, "שָׁלוֹם in the OT," *TDNT* 2:402–6; H. Tadmor, "Treaty and Oath in the Ancient Near East: A Historian's Approach," in *Humanizing America's Iconic Book* (Chico, Calif.: Scholars Press, 1982), 131.

[250] In v. 2:5a (lit., "My covenant was with him the life and the peace, and I gave them to him fear and he feared me") Garrett understands "them" to include "fear" as God's gift ("Israel's Unfaithfulness: The Priests," 31). I prefer an analysis (like the NIV) as two pairs of clauses hinged before "fear": "My covenant was with him [promising] life and peace, / and I gave them to him; / / [the covenant called for] fear, / and he feared me."

[251] Cf. 1 Sam 2:10; Isa 7:8; 8:9; 30:31; 51:6; Jer 48:1,20,39 for the intransitive "be shattered" in *qal* and *niphal* (with no discernible difference in meaning). The transitive "shatter" is expressed by the *hiphil* in Isa 9:3[Eng. 4] and Jer 49:37.

[252] Cf. 2 Kgs 19:26//Isa 37:27; Job 32:15; 39:22; Isa 20:5; 31:4,9; Jer 1:17; 8:9; 10:2; 17:18; 50:2,36; Obad 9 for the intransitive "be dismayed, disheartened, terrified" in *qal* and *niphal.* The transitive "dishearten, terrify" is expressed by the *piel* or *hiphil* (also apparently indistinguishable in meaning) in Job 7:14; 31:34; Jer 1:17.

"going to pieces" either physically or emotionally (as in the English idiom) may not be far from the surface in all its uses.[253] It occurs many times together with the verb to "fear" in exhortations *not* to "be afraid" (*yārēʾ*) or "discouraged" (*ḥātat*) because of Israel's enemies.[254] In disregard of this divine assurance "Saul and all the Israelites were dismayed *[ḥātat]* and terrified *[yārēʾ]*" at the words of Goliath the Philistine (1 Sam 17:11; cf. also Jer 23:4). Only here in Malachi are the two verbs used together of the fear of God. Those who have God's law in their hearts (cf. Isa 51:7) and thus have an appropriate and healthy fear of the true God,[255] as did the early Levitical priests, have no need to fear anything else (cf. Isa 8:12–13; 51:12–13; 1 Pet 3:14–15). According to Deut 11:25, God promised Israel that if they would be loyal and obedient to him their enemies would be unable to stand against them (*bipnêkem*, lit. "in your face"), for he would "put the terror *[pḥd]* and fear *[môrāʾ]*" of them "on the whole land" (also see Deut 7:17–21,24; Josh 2:11; 21:42). The Assyrians used various means (e.g., public impalement) to place fear and dread in the hearts of their enemies in order to subvert resistance.[256] As those who know the Lord, we must realize that we live every moment of every day in the immediate presence of a God whose limitless grace is all that protects us from being destroyed by the boundless conflagration of his righteous wrath. Only a fool could respond with anything but fear and love, which together should motivate diligent faithfulness and obedience.

**2:6** The fear of the Lord motivates not only moral obedience in general but also the fulfillment of divinely assigned roles within the community of faith. Verses 6–7 describe the teaching role of priests within ancient Israel. Besides performing ritual sacrifice and otherwise officiating at the sanctuary, they were responsible for instructing the people in the deeds and words of God (cf. Lev 10:9–11; Deut 33:8–11; 2 Chr 15:3; 17:7–9; Mic 3:11; Jer

---

[253] The verb נֵחַת is *niphal* perfect from חָתַת (cf. *HALOT;* GKC §67u). The two meanings "be shattered, destroyed" and "be dismayed, disheartened, terrified" may be traced to two Akk. terms, *ḥatû* II, "strike down," and *ḥātu, ḥattu* I, "terror, panic." With the meaning "broken," it also has Ug. and Arab. cognates (F. Maass, "חָתַת *ḥātat,*" *TDOT* 5:277–78). Maass gives the basic meaning of the Hb. as "terrify, be terrified" (p. 278), but this does not seem to satisfy all the uses.

[254] Cf. Deut 1:21; 31:8; Josh 1:9; 8:1; 10:25; 1 Chr 22:13; 28:20; 2 Chr 20:15,17; 32:7; Jer 30:10//46:27; Ezek 2:6; 3:9. O'Brien explains that these two terms occurring together "indicate extreme awareness of the power of another" (*Priest and Levite in Malachi,* 41).

[255] Cf. Isaiah's response in Isa 6:5 to his vision of God "high and exalted." H. H. Rowley observes that what makes him tremble for his life as he stands before God is "not the consciousness of his humanity in the presence of divine power, but the consciousness of his sin in the presence of moral purity" (*The Faith of Israel* [London: SCM Press, 1956], 66).

[256] Weinfeld notes the use of the equivalent word pair *ḥattu puluḥtu,* "fear and dread," in neo-Assyrian royal inscriptions (*Deuteronomy and the Deuteronomic School,* 50–51).

18:18; Ezek 7:26; Hos 4:6; Hag 2:11).[257] C. J. H. Wright explains that it was especially as teachers of the law that the priests represented God to the people. He points out that this function is mentioned before their sacrificial role in the blessing of Moses in Deut 33:10 and is "the sole, almost proverbial, function" attributed to them in Jer 18:18. King Jehoshaphat as part of his reform also called on the Levitical priests "to administer the law of the LORD and to settle disputes," warning them to "serve faithfully and wholeheartedly in the fear of the LORD" (2 Chr 19:8,9).[258]

"True instruction" here is *tôrat 'ĕmet,* literally "instruction of truth." The term *tôrâ,* often translated "law," is used both of the content of God's instruction to his people (from specific regulations and their explanation to the entire Old Testament as the Torah; cf. 4:4[Hb. 3:22]; Hos 8:12) and also of the process of teaching itself.[259] Here the latter is probably intended, since "Torah of truth" would be somewhat redundant. Nevertheless "truth" would be understood to refer to God's special revelation through appointed spokesmen like Moses.

The word *'ĕmet* can refer to something or someone that is sound and stable and therefore can be counted on as reliable, dependable, or faithful.[260] Hezekiah was grateful "there will be peace and security [*'ĕmet,* stability]" in his lifetime (Isa 39:8). The reliability of something described as *'ĕmet* can be a result of its corresponding to the facts (e.g., Gen 42:16; Deut 13:14[Hb. 15]). A judge was to refuse bribes, making decisions not only in accordance with God's revealed truth, the Torah, but also the relevant facts of the situation, regardless of the persons involved (cf. Exod 18:21; Prov 29:14).[261] Nothing in

---

[257] T. F. Torrance asserts, "All that the priest does, all liturgical action, answers to the Word given to the priest who bears that Word and mediates it to man, and only in relation to that primary function does he have the other functions of oblation and sacrifice" (*Royal Priesthood: A Theology of Ordained Ministry,* 2d ed. [Edinburgh: T&T Clark, 1993], 1).

[258] C. J. H. Wright, *Walking in the Ways of the LORD: The Ethical Authority of the Old Testament* (Downers Grove: InterVarsity, 1995), 134, 141–42.

[259] See the helpful study of תּוֹרָה *(tôrâ)* by B. Lindars, which is nevertheless hindered by faulty method as well as critical assumptions regarding the history of OT literature ("Torah in Deuteronomy," in *Words and Meanings* [Cambridge: Cambridge University Press, 1968], 117–36). He says the term originally designated cultic regulations given in response to questions, then general instruction as in the wisdom tradition, then was applied in Deuteronomy to the whole body of law. E. M. Meyers states, "Of the total of 220 occurrences of *tôrāh* in the Bible only 52 may be translated as 'law,' 'statute,' 'judgment' or 'ruling' and hence may be viewed as independent of the book or law of Moses's statutes and judgments" ("Priestly Language in the Book of Malachi," 230).

[260] It is related to the verb אמן, which in the *niphal* means "to be permanent, reliable, faithful" and in the *hiphil* "to believe, trust." It overlaps in meaning with אֱמוּנָה, "faithfulness, honesty." For the use of אֱמֶת as "faithfulness" see, e.g., Gen 24:49; 32:10; Josh 2:14; 1 Kgs 2:4; 3:6; Ps 30:9; Isa 61:8; Hos 4:1; Mic 7:20.

[261] Similar to the phrase תּוֹרַת אֱמֶת is מִשְׁפַּט אֱמֶת, "decision of truth" (NIV "judges fairly") in Ezek 18:8 (cp. מִשְׁפְּטֵי־צֶדֶק, "just decisions," in Isa 58:2).

this world is as reliable as the revealed truth of God's written Word, which in the form of "stipulations" *('ēdōt),* "decrees" *(ḥuqqîm),* "laws" *(mišpāṭîm),* and "commands" *(miṣwōt;* cf. Deut 4:40,44–45) were entrusted to the priests who were to teach them faithfully in Israel (Deut 17:18; 31:9–13,26). The priests' knowledge of the Torah enabled them to equip God's people proactively with the truth and so to train them in righteousness (cf. 2 Tim 3:16–17). It also equipped the priests to act as judges in settling disputes (e.g., Deut 17:8–13; 2 Chr 17:7–9; 19:4–11; Ezek 44:24) as Moses had done (Exod 18:13–20)[262] and so to respond to difficult situations with counsel, rebuke, and correction. Instruction that is "true" must be true in both content and in application. A faithful teacher's instruction must be consistent, always corresponding to reality, never adjusted according to the situation to favor the interests of teacher or student.

The word *'ĕmet,* "truth," is opposed here to *'awlâ,* (NIV "false"), which denotes injustice, treachery, or some other form of wickedness involving falsehood or deceit (cf. 2 Sam 3:34; Job 6:30; 13:7; 27:4; 36:22–23; Ps 37:1; 119:3; Isa 59:3–4; Zeph 3:5,13).[263] Such things were not to be "found" on their lips.[264] Those entrusted with teaching and counseling God's people must be careful and faithful guides to truth and righteousness. To do otherwise is to be a "false" teacher who imparts lies about God and encourages wickedness.[265] Israel's leaders were rebuked by the prophet Micah because they sought to "build Jerusalem" with "bloodshed" and "wickedness *['awlâ]*" (also Hab 2:12). Their wickedness involved "despis[ing] justice and distort[ing] all that is right." More specifically, "her leaders judge for a bribe, her priests teach for a price, and her prophets tell fortunes for money" (Mic 3:9–11; also 2 Chr 19:7, which connects justice with the fear of the Lord). They had forsaken the truth for what would be advantageous. Such wickedness

---

[262] Note that in the process of judging, Moses "inform[s] them of God's decrees and laws" (Exod 18:16b) and "show[s] them the way to live and the duties they are to perform" (18:20).

[263] *HALOT* gives the meaning as "Badness, malice, injustice." Derivatives are עוּל (I), "act unjustly," עָוֶל, "perversity, injustice, dishonesty" (e.g., Lev 19:15; Ps 7:3–4[Hb. 4–5]; Ezek 18:8), and עַוָּל, "criminal, sinner." The use of עַוְלָה in Ps 92:15[Hb. 16] ("The LORD is upright; he is my Rock, and there is no *wickedness* in him.") shows it to be an appropriate opposition to that which was reliable and could be trusted. The psalm praises Yahweh's "steadfast love in the morning, and [his] faithfulness by night" (v. 2[Hb. 3]). Also in Ps 43, hounded by "deceitful and *wicked* men" the psalmist pleads for God's "truth" to guide him (v. 3).

[264] The term "found" (Hb. מָצָא) was sometimes used in judicial contexts. Cf. Exod 21:16; 22:2–8; Deut 22:28. See the discussion of the term εὑρεθήσεται (2 Pet 3:10; cf. also 3:14) in T. R. Schreiner, *1, 2 Peter, Jude,* NAC (Nashville: Broadman & Holman, 2003), 385–87.

[265] On prophets, teachers, and apostles who are false in that they presumptuously claim to speak for God but utter lies, cf. Deut 18:22; Jer 8:8; 14:13–15; 28:9; Lam 2:14; Ezek 13:1–23; 22:28; Matt 7:15–23; 24:11,24; Acts 13:6; 2 Cor 11:13–15; 2 Pet 2:1–3; 1 John 4:1. Such are guilty of violating the Third Commandment (Exod 20:7; Deut 5:11) by using the Lord's name for falsehood (שָׁוְא, also "emptiness, futility"; NKJV, "in vain").

God hates (cf. Isa 61:8). Against such a background the apostle Paul would have considered very serious the charges that his preaching was "in vain" (NRSV) because he employed "deceit," "trickery," or "flattery," trying to "please mortals," or because he taught with "impure motives" or "with a pretext for greed" (1 Thess 2:1–6). If he had done so, he would have qualified as a false teacher who came with words of men rather than of God (1 Thess 2:13). Like God's true prophets of old, Paul knew that failure to impart God's Word with care and integrity was a serious matter, so he also instructed Timothy to be a "workman" who "correctly handles the word of truth" (2 Tim 2:15; cf. 1 Tim 1:3–7; 4:1–16; 5:21; 6:3–5,20–21; 2 Tim 1:13–14; 2:14–19).

The priests were to make sure Israel knew what God required of them— how they were to live as members of his covenant community and how to avoid defiling his dwelling among them. In the context of Aaron's sons' deaths for violating the Lord's holiness, Aaron and his surviving sons were instructed to "teach the Israelites all the decrees the LORD has given them through Moses" (Lev 10:11; cf. also 2 Kgs 12:2). Since obedience to the Lord's *Torah* defined Israel's faithfulness to their covenant with him, the life of Israel depended largely on the priests faithfully performing their duties of instruction. As J. C. Kelly explained, "The aim, the raison d'etre, of the duty and privilege of the Levitical *kohen* to transmit knowledge of the *Torah* to Israel was none other than to preserve her life."[266] Thus instruction in God's truth was to be "in his mouth," meaning, as Verhoef explains, that priests and Levites were to be "capable and motivated to dispense their knowledge of the Law in all circumstances and according to the needs of the people."[267]

Being careful and faithful guides to truth and righteousness, however, calls for more than talk (cf. Matt 5:19; 1 Thess 2:10). It calls for walking with the Lord "in peace and uprightness," that is, maintaining harmony with him by obedience (cf. Job 21:25; on "peace" see 2:5).[268] The term for "uprightness" *(mîšôr)* refers elsewhere either to level ground (Pss 26:12; 27:11; 143:10; Isa 40:4; 42:16) or to fairness (Ps 67:4[Hb. 5]; Isa 11:4). The lack of fairness is in view in Mal 2:9, where the priests are said to have "shown partiality in matters of the law." Perhaps the best way to comprehend the lifestyle of "peace and uprightness" is to consider its opposite, which Isa 59:7–15 (esp. vv. 7–

---

[266] Kelly, *Function of the Priest*, 17; also see p. 20. He defines this "life" more fully on pp. 18–19. Also see the study of תּוֹרָה *(tôrâ)* in J. E. Hartley, "יָרָה *(yārâ),*" *TWOT* 1:403–5.

[267] Verhoef, *Haggai and Malachi*, 247.

[268] Other passages speaking of walking with God are Gen 5:22,24; 6:9; Hos 11:12; Mic 6:8. Comparable is the more frequent reference to walking "before [לִפְנֵי]" God. Cf. Gen 17:1; 24:40; 48:15; 1 Kgs 2:4; 8:23,25; 2 Kgs 20:3; 2 Chr 6:14,16; Pss 56:14[Eng. 13]; 116:9; Isa 38:3.

8,15 below) describes (cf. also Luke 1:79; Rom 3:17; note that "the way of peace" here is dependent on maintaining "truth"; author italics):

> Their feet rush into sin;
>     they are swift to shed innocent blood.
> Their thoughts are evil thoughts;
>     ruin and destruction mark their ways.
> The *way of peace* they do not know;
>     there is no justice in their paths.
> They have turned them into crooked roads;
>     no one who *walks* in them will know *peace*.
>
> . . . . . . . . . . . . . . . . . . . . . . . . . . . . . . . .
>
> *Truth* is nowhere to be found,
>     and whoever shuns evil becomes a prey.
> The LORD looked and was displeased
>     that there was no justice.

Such is the condition of a society that has abandoned truth: with its loss go peace, justice, direction, and the knowledge of God (cf. Dan 9:13). So Malachi concludes his nostalgic lament in v. 6 by reminding that God's teachers must be lighthouses, continually and faithfully proclaiming and practicing the truth, and by that means "turn[ing] many" from destruction on the rocks of iniquity (*ʿāwōn*, NIV "sin").[269]

**2:7** Verse 6 having narrated the priests' teaching responsibilities, v. 7 explains that these result from their role as "messenger [*malʾak*, sometimes translated "angel"] of the LORD Almighty."[270] Elsewhere the Lord's "messengers" are either supernatural beings or prophets.[271] But whereas those messen-

---

[269] Cf. Isa 53:6; Jer 23:22; 36:3; Ezek 3:19–20; 33:8–9; Acts 3:26. See also Mal 4:6 and its use in Luke 1:16–17.

[270] Note the significance given this concept by its structural location, as displayed in the chart introducing vv. 8–9. V. 7 consists formally of three dependent clauses related to the last (independent) clause of v. 6 and introduced by an initial כִּי. The third clause is further embedded as a dependent clause inside the second by another introductory כִּי. The parenthetic nature of the clauses is marked not only by their dependent form but also by the verb switch from perfect to imperfect. The semantic repetition in the first two clauses from the first two clauses of v. 6 indicates that v. 7 is semantically related not just to the last clause of v. 6 but to the whole verse. It also indicates that the primary point of v. 7 is in the third (doubly embedded) clause. The two uses of כִּי may be understood as working together, the second essentially resumptive of the first. The sense may be paraphrased: The reason a priest should diligently fulfill his responsibility of dispensing knowledge and instruction is that he is the messenger of Yahweh of hosts.

[271] In Eccl 5:6[Hb. 5] it may also refer to a priest. The designation is used of supernatural beings in Gen 16:7–13; 19:1,15; 21:17; 22:11,15; 24:7,40; 28:12; 31:11; 32:1[Hb. 2]; 48:16; Exod 3:2; 14:19; 23:20,23; 32:34; 33:2; Num 20:16; 22:22–35; Judg 2:1,4; 5:23; 6:11–12,20–22; 13:3–21; 1 Sam 29:9; 2 Sam 14:17,20; 19:27; 24:16–17; 1 Kgs 13:18; 19:5,7; 2 Kgs 1:3,15; 19:35; 1 Chr 21:15; 2 Chr 32:21; Job 4:18; 33:23; Pss 34:7[Hb. 8]; 35:5–6; 78:25,49; 91:11; 103:20; 148:2; Isa 37:36; 63:9; Dan 3:28; 6:22; Hos 12:4[Hb. 5]; Zech 1–6; 12:8; Mal 3:1b. It refers to prophets in 2 Chr 36:15–16; Isa 44:26; Hag 1:13 (see also Mark 1:2–8).

gers conveyed new words or instructions from God, priests were his messengers in that they informed his people of the words of his law previously revealed and also applied that law to their lives and situations as Malachi was doing (whose name means "my messenger"). Malachi's time near the end of Old Testament prophecy and the completion of the Old Testament canon would make the term's use here especially significant.[272] That teachers of God's Word could be described as "messengers" implies the ongoing relevance of God's past instructions and shows the continuing importance of the role of biblical teacher (and translator) among God's people. Those who proclaim God's written Word are no less important to his redemptive program than those who previously served as "prophets," since both carry God's message (cf. 2 Pet 1:19–21).[273]

A messenger was expected to "preserve" (*šāmar*, "watch, guard, keep") the "knowledge" that had been entrusted to him, making sure that it was faithfully delivered in its unchanged entirety at the proper place and time. According to J. E. Hartley "the basic idea of the root *[šmr]* is 'to exercise great care over.'"[274] As the life of a community depends upon the keeper of its water supply to guard that supply from loss or contamination, so the life of Israel depended upon its priests to preserve God's written word and effectively to dispense it when "men should seek" it.[275] Such continues to be the responsibility of those called to be teachers of God's Word. If we permit its sense to be contaminated or its power to be restricted by the intellectual currents of the day or by our own convenience or sinful carelessness, then we have betrayed our trust and violated our calling and deserve the same "curse" threatened upon these

---

[272] E. M. Meyers cites the identification of the priest with "the messenger of the LORD" ("a quasi-prophetic individual who figures centrally in the prophecies of First Zechariah") as evidence that "the boundaries between teaching priest and prophet-sage were fading in the Persian period" ("Priestly Language in the Book of Malachi," 231).

[273] Those who lament the passing of the age of prophecy or who try to recapture it by reinventing "prophets" who receive "words from God" today would do well to ponder the significance of the doctrine of Scripture's sufficiency. See, e.g., W. Grudem, *Systematic Theology* (Leicester/ Grand Rapids: InterVarsity/Zondervan, 1994), 127–37.

[274] J. E. Hartley, "שָׁמַר," *TWOT* 2:939.

[275] The second clause of v. 7 is better rendered "and instruction may be sought from his mouth." Note the repetition of תּוֹרָה, "instruction," echoes the beginning of v. 6, as does more deliberately the reverse echo of "lips . . . mouth." Thus v. 7 is explanatory of the whole of v. 6. Meyers understands the expression "seek [בקשׁ] instruction" as a "typical postexilic idiom" meaning to "seek a ruling" (cf. Hag 2:11, which uses שׁאל, "ask," rather than בקשׁ). The idiom describes "the function of a teaching priest to whom individuals turn for specific advice on religious matters" ("Priestly Language in the Book of Malachi," 229–30). Also see E. M. Meyers, "The Use of *tôrâ* in Haggai 2:11 and the Role of the Prophet in the Restoration Community," in *And the Word of the Lord Shall Go Forth* (Winona Lake: Eisenbrauns, 1983), 69–76. He finds this meaning of תּוֹרָה as "ruling" also in Exod 12:49; Lev 7:7; Num 15:16,29.

priests, to be "despised and humiliated before all the people" (v. 9) and finally removed from service as false teachers.

### (3) Corruption and Contempt of the Priests (2:8–9)

**⁸But you have turned from the way and by your teaching have caused many to stumble; you have violated the covenant with Levi," says the LORD Almighty. ⁹"So I have caused you to be despised and humiliated before all the people, because you have not followed my ways but have shown partiality in matters of the law."**

The focus on the covenant with Levi in vv. 5–9 turns in vv. 8–9 from past obedience to present disobedience. The turn is signaled by the initial "but you" (plural, *wĕ'attem*) in v. 8, the change from "he" to "you," and by the recurrence of the divine speech formula, "says the LORD Almighty" (note the structural significance of its use in vv. 2,4,8). Also structurally significant is that both vv. 5–7 and vv. 8–9 end in dependent causal clauses. Furthermore, the statements in vv. 8–9 echo in contrast those of vv. 5–7:

A—I *gave [nātan]* them [life and peace] to him;
  B—He . . . *stood in awe [niḥat]* of my name
    C—He *walked [hālak]* with me in peace and uprightness
      D—and turned *[šûb] many* from sin.
        E—For *[kî]* the lips of a priest ought to *preserve [šāmar]* knowledge,
          and from his mouth men should seek *instruction [tôrâ]*—
          F—because *[kî]* he is the messenger of the LORD Almighty.
    C'—**But you** have turned *[sûr]* from the *way [derek]*
      D'—by your teaching you have caused *many* to stumble;
  B'—you have *violated [šiḥat]* the covenant with Levi
A'—So I have *caused [nātan]* you to be despised and humiliated before all the people,
        E'—because *[kî]* you have not *followed [šāmar]* my ways
          but have shown partiality in matters of the *law [tôrâ]*."

Rather than being beacons of truth urgently summoning God's people to remain on the smooth but narrow path of righteousness and rather than being diligent shepherds faithfully retrieving the Lord's sheep from the destructive sideroads of sin, Malachi's priestly "messengers" had forsaken the path themselves and had treacherously led many to stumble along paths of their own choosing. Rather than faithful shepherds who protect and guard the sheep, they had been "shepherds who destroy and scatter the sheep of my pasture" (Jer 23:1).

**2:8** Here the prophet turns back to his audience, the priests, with a threefold indictment. First, rather than walking with the Lord "in peace and uprightness" (v. 6), they had "turned from the way" (cf. 3:7). Their failure in the ministry began with failure in their own lives. This first indictment echoes earlier charges of apostasy against Israel, as in the time of the judges, when they had "prostituted themselves to other gods and worshiped them" and had *"turned from the way* in which their fathers had walked, the way of obedience to the LORD's commands" (Judg 2:17; cf. Exod 32:8; Deut 9:12,16; 11:28; 13:5; 31:29).

Second, instead of turning "many from sin" (v. 6), their instruction had "caused many to stumble." "Stumbling" is how the Bible often describes the failure of sin and its disastrous effects (Prov 24:17–18; Isa 3:8; 8:14–15; 59:10; Jer 6:19–21; 20:10–11; Hos 14:1). It is a trouble typical of those who follow the "way of the wicked" (Prov 4:19) but avoided by those who love the law of the Lord and thus have "great peace" (Ps 119:165; cf. Prov 3:23; 4:11–12). In Jer 18:15 the Lord laments how "my people have forgotten me; they burn incense to worthless idols, which made them stumble in their ways and in the ancient paths. They made them walk in bypaths and on roads not built up" (cf. also 2 Chr 28:23; Ezek 36:15; Hos 4:5). The wicked may cause others to stumble by placing in their way an obstacle they cannot see or avoid, by leading them onto a path full of such obstacles, or by failing to warn them of such dangers (Lev 26:37; Job 18:7; Prov 4:16). Those trusted with the task of instruction are thus partly responsible for the failure of those in their charge if they give false instruction by word or example (Ezek 44:12) or if they fail to give adequate instruction regarding potential dangers ahead (Ezek 3:20; Hos 4:5–6).[276] Jesus would have strong words of judgment against such false teachers (Luke 17:1–2; cf. Rom 14:13,21; 1 Cor 8:9; Rev 2:14).

The third and most prominent charge (marked by the divine speech formula) was that instead of standing in awe (*niḥat* in v. 5) of the Lord's name the priests had "violated *[šiḥat]* the covenant with Levi."[277] The verb *šḥt* refers to the state of something being so damaged as to render it useless or out of commission (i.e., "ruined") or to the causing of such a state. Such is the state of a cloth belt left out in the elements (Jer 13:7), a malformed pot on the potter's wheel (Jer 18:4), an eye rendered useless by injury (Exod 21:26), a city wall breached by enemies (Ezek 26:4), a land rendered unlivable by insects (Exod 8:24[Hb. 20]) or by violence (Gen 6:11–12),[278] or by people corrupt with sin (Ps 14:1; Ezek 16:47; 23:11). When the object is people or

---

[276] Wright states, "The prophets' quarrel with the priests was precisely that they had failed in their teaching role, and thus the people, deprived of knowledge of the law, were understandably living in disobedience to it" (*Walking in the Ways of the LORD*, 142).

[277] Although בְּרִית הַלֵּוִי could be translated either "covenant with Levi" or "covenant with the Levites," the previous context makes the former preferable (O'Brien, *Priest and Levite in Malachi*, 37–38).

[278] Note the wordplay in Gen 6:11–13 with four uses of the verb שָׁחַת in its various senses. Human behavior had become so "corrupted" by violence as to ruin the earth, rendering it so useless that God decreed to ruin it utterly by a flood and then to start again (cf. Jer 18:4).

other living things, the verb refers to the ultimate ruin of death (e.g., Gen 6:13,17; 9:11,15; 13:10; 1 Chr 21:15; 2 Chr 12:7; 21:7; 36:19; Ezek 5:16; 9:8; 26:4). In Mal 1:14 it describes an animal unacceptable for sacrifice because of a defect, and in 3:11 it is used of crops ruined by pests. Here it is a covenant *(bĕrît)* that was ruined or rendered inoperative by being broken.[279] The expression "violate the covenant" apparently is similar in meaning to "profane *[ḥll]* the covenant" in v. 10 (cf. Num 30:2; Pss 55:20[Hb. 21]; 89:31,34[Hb. 32,35]),[280] "defile *[gʾl]* the covenant" in Neh 13:29 ("defiled the priestly office and the covenant of the priesthood and of the Levites"), "break *[prr]* the covenant" in Gen 17:14,[281] and "transgress [ʿbr, NIV "violate"] the covenant" in Deut 17:2.[282] A covenant was a relationship between two parties established by an oath of obligation.[283] When one party failed to fulfill his covenantal obligation, the covenant was said to be "broken" in that the other party was no longer obligated to fulfill his obligations. But the second party could "forgive" the covenant breach and restore or renew the covenant. This is the case with the Levitical covenant in Malachi, where 2:4 and 3:3 make clear that the covenant was not "destroyed," but broken.

**2:9** The divine consequences of the three charges had already commenced (cf. v. 2). Following the Hebrew particle *(gam)*, rendered "so,"[284] is the emphatic (because of word order) divine pronoun *ʾănî*, "I," which stands in opposition to "but you" at the beginning of v. 8. The sense is "Now here is

---

[279] O'Brien notes that the term is used in the Phoenician Kilamuwa inscription (KAI 24) of breaking a treaty (*Priest and Levite in Malachi*).

[280] Note that in Zeph 3:4 the priests are said to "profane the sanctuary [קֹדֶשׁ, NRSV "what is sacred"] and do violence to [חָמְסוּ] the law." See Mal 2:11.

[281] Also Lev 26:15 (where NIV translates it "violate"),44; Deut 31:16,20; Judg 2:1; 1 Kgs 15:19//2 Chr 16:3; Isa 24:5; 33:8; Jer 11:10; 14:21; 31:32; 33:20–21; Ezek 16:59; 17:15–16,18–19; 44:7; Zech 11:10 (NIV "revoke"). פָּרַר is used with מִצְוֹת, "commands," in Num 15:31; Ezra 9:14 and with תּוֹרָה, "law," in Ps 119:126. The understanding of רָשַׁע (*Hiph.*) with בְּרִית in Dan 11:32 (NASB "act wickedly toward the covenant") seems to be different in the context (cf. vv. 28,30), contrary to the NIV translation ("violate[d] the covenant").

[282] Also Josh 7:11,15; 23:16; Judg 2:20; 2 Kgs 18:12; Jer 34:18; Hos 6:7; 8:1. In Deut 29:11 [Eng. 12] עָבַר is used with בְּרִית to mean "enter a covenant."

[283] See, e.g., G. P. Hugenberger, *Marriage as a Covenant: Biblical Law and Ethics as Developed from Malachi*, (Grand Rapids: Baker, 1998), 168–215.

[284] The NIV translation "so" renders the initial Hb. וְגַם (lit. "and also"; in v. 2 it is rendered "yes . . . already"). Muraoka (*Emphatic Words and Structures in Biblical Hebrew*, 63–65, 143–46) argues, against Labuschagne ("The Emphasizing Particle GAM and Its Connotations," in *Studia Biblica et Semitica* [Wageningen: Veenman en Zonen, 1961], 193–203), that גַּם seldom has anything but an "additive" force, i.e., a coordinating conjunction. Waltke and O'Connor note, however, "It can signal a final climax in an exposition . . . and is the only Hebrew adverb that marks a discourse ending—all others mark beginnings or middles" (*IBHS* §39.3.4d). Also see *BHRG* §41.4.5.

what *I* have done."[285] In Amos 4:6, as here, the phrase *gam ʾănî* begins a reminder of the Lord's discipline, which had already been inflicted in order to turn Israel from sin before more severe punishment became necessary (see also Mic 6:13).

The verb translated "despised" (participle from *bzh*) is the same one that describes the priests' treatment of the Lord in 1:6 (translated "show contempt"; see also 1:7,12). When Aaron's sons Nadab and Abihu failed to glorify the Lord "before all the people" (Lev 10:3), the Lord incinerated them. His grace had lessened the penalty, however, toward Malachi's priests, who had begun suffering the same contempt they were showing for the Lord. The Lord who specializes in bringing down the proud and exalting the humble (cf. 1 Sam 2:1–10; Isa 2:11–17; 57:15; Ezek 17:24) had begun showing up their proud professionalism for the emptiness it was.

The cause for their humiliation is expressed here more generally as their failure to be the Lord's loyal servants. Loyal service is frequently the sense of the verb *šmr* ("guard, watch, keep"; NIV "followed") with *derek* ("way"; cf. Gen 18:19; Judg 2:22; 2 Sam 22:22; Job 23:11; Pss 18:21[Hb. 22]; 37:34; Prov 8:32), since it involves a servant's carefully following his master's instructions.[286] The interpretation of the last clause of v. 9 depends on the sense of the idiom to "lift the face" (which the NIV understands as "show partiality") and on whether the negation beginning the previous clause governs both clauses.[287] The two clauses could be translated literally "according to your not keeping [participle] my ways and lifting [participle] faces *in the instruction* [*battôrâ,*the same word that occurs in v. 8]." There is no explicit indication of a contrast as interpreted by the NIV "but" (although the conjunction *wĕ* sometimes joins contrasting clauses). As a fallen face indicates displeasure or unhappiness (Gen 4:6), lifting one's face indicates a gladdened heart (Job 11:15) or pleasure with someone (Num 6:26; Job 22:26). Lifting the face of another means to please them by receiving them in a friendly manner or granting their request as in 1:8–9 (also Gen 32:20[Hb. 21]; Deut 28:50; Job 42:9; Prov 6:35; 1 Sam 25:35; Lam 4:16). If the negation in the previous clause in 2:9 governs this clause as well, the sense is that the priests were not adminis-

---

[285] אַף גַּם also introduces divine punishment in Judg 2:21; Isa 66:4; Jer 4:12; 13:26; Ezek 5:11; 8:18; 9:10; 16:43; 24:9; Amos 4:6; Mic 6:13; Prov 1:26. In Hos 4:6 it occurs emphatically at the end of the clause after the announcement of punishment. In Hos 3:3 it introduces divine reward.

[286] Cf. O'Brien, *Priest and Levite in Malachi*, 38. שָׁמַר ("keep") is more commonly used with חֹק ("statute") or מִצְוָה ("command"); and דֶּרֶךְ ("way") is used with הָלַךְ ("walk"; cf. Deut 11:22; 13:4–5; 19:9; 26:17; 28:9; 30:16; Josh 22:5; 1 Kgs 2:3; 8:58; 11:33,38; Zech 3:7). Using שָׁמַר with דֶּרֶךְ could be an abbreviated way of combining the concepts.

[287] Cf. M. Gruber, "The Many Faces of Hebrew נָשָׂא פָנִים 'Lift up the Face'," *ZAW* 95 (1983): 252–60. He translates Mal 2:9, "I also have made you contemptible and lowly in the estimate of the whole people because you do not keep My ways and because you show partiality in judicial decision" (258).

tering the grace of God to people in their instruction so that their hearers might find acceptance and favor with God.[288]

The idiom, however, also can mean to regard someone with special honor or favor (cf. 2 Kgs 3:14; 5:1; Job 32:21; 34:19; Isa 3:3; 9:15[Hb. 14], where "prominent men" are lit. those "lifted of face"). This sense occurs particularly in judicial contexts and involves giving preference or showing partiality to someone, sometimes in connection with a bribe, so that justice is perverted (Lev 19:15 [parallel to *hdr*, "to honor"]; Deut 10:17; 2 Chr 19:7; Ps 82:2). It then overlaps the use of the idiom "recognize [*hiphil* of *nkr*] the face" (as in Deut 1:17; 16:19; Prov 24:23; 28:21). Although the context here in Malachi is not unambiguously judicial, its connection to seeking priestly instruction (v. 7) suggests that the NIV is correct in interpreting the idiom as involving prejudicial priestly activity.[289] This is confirmed by the parallel between vv. 8 and 9 (rendered lit.):[290]

v. 8—But you turned from *the way*
       You caused many to stumble *in the instruction [battôrâ]*
. . . . . . . . . . . . . . . . . . . . . . . . . . . . . . . . . . . . . . . . . . . .
v. 9—according to your not keeping *my ways*
       and lifting faces *in the instruction [battôrâ]*

Seemingly it was by not applying the law equitably to all that the priests were causing "many to stumble."[291] Perhaps it was the influential, whose favor the priests wanted to curry or retain, that they allowed to bring unacceptable sacrifices to the altar (cf. 1:14). Their efforts to gain favor without integrity, however, had only resulted in their loss of the people's respect (cf. Prov 24:23–25).

Impartiality in teaching (or careless frankness) is what the Jewish "spies" claimed to value about Jesus in Luke 20:21.[292] He always spoke and taught

---

[288] So Glazier-McDonald, *Malachi*, 73.

[289] Note also the warning in 1 Tim 5:21 to (lit.) "guard these things [instructions in vv. 17–20, esp. vv. 19–20 regarding elders accused of sin] without prejudice, doing nothing according to partiality" (ἵνα ταῦτα φυλάξῃς χωρὶς προκρίματος, μηδὲν ποιῶν κατὰ πρόσκλισιν).

[290] This parallel overlaps broader connections within vv. 5–9. See introduction to vv. 8–9.

[291] O'Brien argues that this understanding leaves the participle נֹשְׂאִים with no explicit antecedent (*Priest and Levite in Malachi*, 39). But the same is true of מַגִּשִׁים, "placing," in 1:7, whose antecedent "you" is supplied by the context.

[292] Luke used the Hebraism λαμβάνειν πρόσωπον (lit. "to take up/receive the face"), which the LXX also uses for פָנִים נָשָׂא ("lift up the face") in Lev 19:15; 2 Kgs [4 Kgdms] 3:14; Ps 82[81]:2; Mal 1:8–9; 2:9. According to the parallel passage in Matt 22:16 they said Jesus "did not care for anyone [i.e., did not court anyone's favor], for [he] did not see the face of men [NIV, 'you pay no attention to who they are']" (οὐ μέλει σοι περὶ οὐδενός, οὐ γὰρ βλέπεις εἰς πρόσωπον ἀνθρώπων). See also Gal 2:6; *Sir* 7:6; 35:14–16. Several NT passages employ words from the root *prosōpolēmp-*, which is based on the words λαμβάνειν and πρόσωπον, appearing first in the NT (cf. Acts 10:34; Rom 2:11; Eph 6:9; Col 3:25; 1 Pet 1:17; Jas 2:1,9). Cf. E. Lohse, "πρόσωπον," *TDNT* 6:779–80; E. Tiedtke, "Face," *DNTT* 1:587. Jas 2 declares the complete incompatibility of any kind of "favoritism" with biblical faith.

"what is right [*orthōs*, 'straight']" and "the way of God in accordance with the truth," regardless of who was involved. By this he exhibited the divine character or "ways" since impartiality was a consistent characteristic of God's dealings. It was also one which he expected his people to exhibit as they patterned themselves after his "ways" (Lev 19:15;[293] Deut 10:17; 2 Chr 19:7; Job 34:19; Jas 3:17; 1 Pet 1:17). Whenever teachers of God's Word sacrifice the message of that Word because it is inconvenient, offensive, or politically incorrect for some or all of their hearers in the contemporary context, they have betrayed both their divine Master and those entrusted to their care, whom they are leading to disaster (1 Tim 5:21).[294] They also show that they really despise and profane the Lord's name and his worship (1:6,12–13) and so invite upon themselves the Lord's curse as false teachers (2:1–2). At the very least, this could involve the eventual loss of respect among the people once dependent on them. At worst, the penalty could involve the woes that Jesus left unspecified but compared to being thrown into the sea attached to a millstone (Luke 17:1–2).

---

[293] C. J. H. Wright points out that the behavior in Lev 19 is motivated by the refrain "I am the LORD," which is to say, "This is what I require of you because it is what I myself would do" (*An Eye for an Eye: The Place of Old Testament Ethics Today* [Downers Grove: InterVarsity, 1983], 27).

[294] There is often truth to charges that even evangelicals sometimes sacrifice the truth of the biblical message for "relevance," conforming the Bible to secular models of wisdom like approaches to self-worth, self-recovery, and self-help. W. Willimon, for example, has written: "The psychology of the gospel—reducing salvation to self-esteem, sin to maladjustment, church to group therapy, and Jesus to Dear Abby—is our chief means of perverting the biblical text" ("Been There, Preached That," *Leadership* [Sept., 1995], 74–78). It also dishonors God, as Piper declares: "The steady diet on Sunday morning of practical 'how to's' and psychological soothing and relational therapy and tactical planning seem dramatically out of touch with Reality—the God of overwhelming greatness" (*Let the Nations Be Glad*, 12–13).

## II. JUDAH EXHORTED TO FAITHFULNESS (2:10–3:6)

The audience of the second address broadened beyond the religious leadership to the entire nation of Judah. The prophet's concern was the people's indifference to the Lord's will. They were blaming their economic and social troubles on the Lord's supposed injustice and unfaithfulness to them (2:17) and were being unfaithful to one another, especially their wives, many of whom may have been abandoned for pagan women. Consequently the temple and the covenant were being profaned (2:10b–15a). The prophet's command, which governs and unifies this address, was for them to stop their treachery (2:15b–16). To motivate their obedience the prophet reminded them of their spiritual and covenant unity (2:10a), and he warned them that the Lord of the covenant was coming in judgment (3:1–6).

### 1. Positive Motivation: Spiritual Kinship among Israel (2:10a)

**¹⁰Have we not all one Father? Did not one God create us?**

This address begins, like the first, with rhetorical questions about Judah's lineage (see comments on 1:2, "Was not Esau Jacob's brother?"), though here it is their spiritual lineage in view. Although the opening three questions at first appear parallel, the first two (as in 1:2) begin with the interrogative particle *hălô'* ("is it not/did not?") and describe a state or existing situation, whereas the third begins with *maddûaʿ* ("why?") and describes an ongoing activity considered illogical and reprehensible in that existing situation.[1] The first two questions (forming an antithesis) set up the contrasting third question (the thesis), which introduces another section charging Judah with wrongdoing. NRSV renders the third question, "Why then are we faithless to one another, profaning the covenant of our ancestors?" (similarly HCSB, ESV, NLT). The function of the first two questions is to stress the seriousness of the following charge in 2:10b–15a and thus to motivate the command in vv. 15b–16 not to "break faith."[2]

**2:10a** The dual concepts of God as Father[3] and Creator, while not synonymous, should be understood as complementary (cf. Isa 64:8). The verb "create" translates the Hebrew *bārāʾ,* as in Gen 1:1,21,27, etc. This should not be taken to mean that the group Malachi had in mind by "we" and "us" was all mankind.[4] The "one another" in v. 10b refers to participants in "the covenant of our fathers" and thus the people of Israel.[5] Besides, as C. F. D. Moule wrote, the phrase "children of God" in the Bible "is not, with only very few exceptions, applied to mankind as such, as though they were actually God's children, even if they are such potentially."[6] The fatherhood of God in the Old

---

[1] The first two questions exhibit features of a poetic couplet, with parallel elements and alliteration. Note *hălôʾ // hălôʾ, ʾāb ʾeḥād // ʾēl ʾeḥād,*and *lĕkullānû // bĕrāʾānû.*The third question contrasts sharply with the first two structurally: (1) two clauses rather than one; (2) interrogative "why?" asks for explanation rather than affirmation; (3) different word order in main clause; and (4) imperfect conjugation main verb.

[2] K. W. Weyde points to a similar structure in Jer 14:19 and Hab 1:12–13 (*Prophecy and Teaching: Prophetic Authority, Form Problems, and the Use of Traditions in the Book of Malachi,* BZAW 288 [Berlin: Walter de Gruyter, 2000], 221).

[3] The "father" has often been interpreted as Adam, Abraham, Jacob, or Levi. This interpretation apparently led to the reversing of the clauses in some MSS of the LXX to place first the reference to God (A. S. van der Woude, "Malachi's Struggle for a Pure Community: Reflections on Malachi 2:10–16," in *Tradition and Re-Interpretation in Jewish and Early Christian Literature* [Leiden: Brill, 1986], 67). The clauses' parallel structure, their order in the MT, and the antithetical "daughter of a foreign god" in v. 11 argue for the identification of "one Father" and "one God." Cf. also M. E. Tate, "Questions for Priests and People in Malachi 1:2–2:16," *RevExp* 84 (1987): 401; G. P. Hugenberger, *Marriage as a Covenant: Biblical Law and Ethics as Developed from Malachi,* (Grand Rapids: Baker, 1998), 40; P. A. Verhoef, *The Books of Haggai and Malachi,* NICOT (Grand Rapids: Eerdmans, 1987), 265. Reference to the "covenant of our fathers" also makes it unlikely that the singular "father" would refer to one with whom God made a covenant (M. A. Shields, "Syncretism and Divorce in Malachi 2,10–16," *ZAW* 111 [1999]: 70).

[4] This verse should not be used, then, as evidence for a universalistic perspective in the Book of Malachi, as some have done (see comments on 1:11). J. J. Collins argues from v. 10 that Malachi was open to marriage with Gentiles and that he was writing in opposition to Ezra's reform ("The Message of Malachi," *TBT* 22 [1984]: 212). For a refutation see Hugenberger, *Marriage as a Covenant,* 95–98.

[5] So Hugenberger, *Marriage as a Covenant,* 40.

[6] C. F. D. Moule, "Children of God," *IDB* 1:559. On p. 560 he states: "The NT does not seem to present a doctrine of all men as such being children of God, any more than the OT sees others than the chosen people . . . in this status." He mentions as exceptions Luke 3:38; Acts 17:28.

Testament is an expression of the unique and exclusive relationship the Lord established with Israel by his sovereign grace in choosing them through Abraham, redeeming them from Egypt, and forming his covenant with them at Sinai (cf. Exod 4:22–23; Isa 44:1–2; 63:16; Hos 11:1; John 8:41).[7] In the New Testament it is primarily those in Christ who are described as "sons" of God, who can call God their "Father" (cf. John 1:12–13; Rom 8:14–17; Gal 3:26–4:7; Eph 1:5; Heb 2:10–12; 1 John 3:1).[8] This New Testament teaching should not be understood simply as an extension of Israel's sonship. In the first place, the Christian usually is said to be God's child by adoption, whereas Israel is God's son because he brought them into existence as a nation (note the conception and birth image of Num 11:12).[9] Furthermore, Christian sonship is related to the Old Testament teaching that David and his royal descendants were "sons" of God as precursors or types of the perfect messianic King who would sit on David's throne forever, who is the unique Son of God (cf. 2 Sam 7:14–16; Pss 2:6–7,12; 89:26–29; Isa 9:6–7; Rom 1:3–4; 2 Cor 6:18; Heb 1:5; 5:5). The Christian's sonship is derived from our relationship with Christ as adopted sons.[10] On this basis New Testament believers typically identified one another as "brothers" (cf. Matt 5:22–24; 23:8; 28:10; Acts 15:1,23,36; 18:18; Rom 1:13; 8:29; 1 Cor 5:11; 6:6; 7:12; Col 1:2; 4:15; 1 Tim 6:2).

The significance of the verb *bārā'* in Mal 2:10 is that Israel owed its existence to God as did the heavens and the earth and all it contained. Also, since

---

[7] See also Deut 1:31; 8:5; 14:1; 32:5–6,18–20; Ps 103:13; Prov 3:12; Isa 1:2; 30:1,9; 43:6; 45:11; 63:8; 64:8; Jer 31:9,20; Hos 1:10; Rom 9:4. Note Jer 3:4,19–22 combines the images of Israel as unfaithful son and as unfaithful wife. On God as Israel's father see D. McCarthy, "Notes on the Love of God in Deuteronomy, and the Father/Son Relationship between Yahweh and Israel" (*CBQ* 27 [1965]: 144–47); G. Fohrer, *History of Israelite Religion* (New York: Abingdon, 1972), 81; P. A. H. de Boer, *Fatherhood and Motherhood in Israelite and Judean Piety* (Leiden: Brill, 1974), 14–25.

[8] See also Matt 5:9,44–45; 6:6,9; 12:48–50; 13:43; Luke 6:35; 12:30,32; Rom 9:8,26; Eph 4:6; Phil 4:20; Col 1:2,12–13; 1 Thess 1:3; 3:11,13; 5:5; 2 Thess 1:1; 2:16; Phlm 3; Heb 12:5–8; Jas 1:27; 3:9; 1 Pet 1:17; 1 John 2:1,13,15–16,23–24; 5:1–2.

[9] Cf. C. J. H. Wright, *God's People in God's Land: Family, Land, and Property in the Old Testament* (Grand Rapids/Exeter: Eerdmans/Paternoster, 1990), 16–17; also de Boer, *Fatherhood and Motherhood*, 23.

[10] Moule sees as early as Matt 11:25–27//Luke 10:21–22 the thought that "Christ as Son, in a unique sense, is able to make known the fatherhood of God to others, who are thus (it may be deduced) to become sons by adoption" ("Children of God," 1:560). He then cites John 3:3; 1 Pet 1:3; 2:2; Jas 1:18. Another difference between the Father-son relationship of Israel in the OT and that of the church in the NT is that the former tended to be corporate or nationalistic and the latter individualistic and thus more intimate. See D. Guthrie and R. P. Martin, "God," in *Dictionary of Paul and His Letters* (Downers Grove: InterVarsity, 1993), 357–58. This is not to say that Israelites could not be designated the Lord's sons and daughters as members of Israel and as being individually responsible for loyalty and obedience. Cf. Wright, *God's People in God's Land*, 18.

in its forty-five uses God is always the subject, the verb suggests his sovereignty (cf. Isa 45:7–8). As a son was under his father's authority, much more was Israel under the Lord's authority. The verb is used here in its redemptive sense, often associated with Israel's relationship with God by covenant.[11] Isaiah 43:1–7, which begins and ends with reminders that the Lord had "created" Israel, reassures Israel of his faithfulness and his enduring love for them (cf. Mal 3:6). Though the Lord's wrath had scattered them (Isa 42:24–25), his love would gather them: "Bring *my sons* from afar and *my daughters* from the ends of the earth" (Isa 43:6; cf. Deut 32:19; 2 Cor 6:18).[12] His people should not fear, "for I have redeemed you; I have summoned [called] you by name; you are mine" (Isa 43:1). But those called by name also received his name ("called by my name") and were created for his glory (Isa 43:7). In these terms, Motyer explains, Isaiah describes a "crowning intimacy," a "direct personal relationship involving having a specific plan and place for the one named."[13]

The theme of the Lord as Israel's father runs through Malachi's prophecy. It is implied in the opening declaration of God's love for Jacob (1:2), then used in 1:6 to rebuke priestly carelessness—"If I am a father, where is the honor due me?" It is alluded to in 3:17 in a promise of God's future compassion on Israel—"I will spare them, just as in compassion a man spares his son who serves him" (cf. 2 Cor 1:3). Here in 2:10 the Lord's fatherhood is recalled and used to rebuke unfaithfulness, echoing Deut 32:6.[14]

> They have acted corruptly toward him;
> > to their shame they are no longer his children,
> > but a warped and crooked generation.
> Is this the way you repay the LORD,
> > O foolish and unwise people?
> Is he not your Father, your Creator [*qnh,* a different word from Mal 2:10, can also mean "acquire"],
> > who made you and formed you? (Deut 32:5–6)

Whereas in Deut 32:6 and in Mal 1:6 the message regards proper response to God as one's Father/Redeemer, here the message regards proper treatment of fellow Jews as one's spiritual siblings. The phrase translated "with one

---

[11] Cf. its use in Exod 34:10 (obscured by the common translation "done" or "performed"), which connects it to the formation of Israel by covenant. See also Ps 102:18; Isa 43:1,7,15.

[12] Num 21:29 identifies the "destroyed" Moabites as sons and daughters of Chemosh, apparently because they considered him responsible for their lives and welfare.

[13] J. A. Motyer, *The Prophecy of Isaiah* (Downers Grove: InterVarsity, 1993), 331.

[14] Weyde, *Prophecy and Teaching,* 222, notes that Deuteronomy 32:6 and Isa 64:8[Hb. 7] are the only other passages in which Yahweh is explicitly said to be both Creator and Father of Israel.

another" in v. 10b is literally "a man with his brother."[15] The Bible consistently assumes that ill-treatment of a brother is particularly heinous. Judah
pled for his brother Joseph's life with the argument, "For he is our brother, our
flesh" (Gen 37:27).[16] As C. Blomberg explains (commenting on Matt 5:22),
"brother" in Matthew's Gospel, "when not referring to a biological sibling,
consistently means *a fellow member of the religious community* and usually
refers to Jesus' disciples . . . against whom anger is most inappropriate. That is
to say, it is particularly bad for Christians to get angry at other Christians who
have themselves also been spared God's wrath."[17] Using a similar argument,
the apostle Paul exhorted truthfulness in speech, "for we are all members of
one body" (Eph 4:25).

The charges and commands of 2:10–3:6 are based in part on the relationship
shared by the people of Israel as the offspring and creatures of the one God.
Realizing that God brought them into existence as a united whole in a covenant
relationship to himself should have produced faithfulness not only to him, but
also to one another. Their unity should have motivated mutual understanding,
caring, and support. As 1 John 5:1 declares, "Everyone who loves the father
loves his child as well."

## 2. Situation: Unfaithfulness against Covenant Members (2:10b–15a)

The first charge against Judah in this second address is introduced by the
third rhetorical question in v. 10, then explained and elaborated in vv. 11–15a.
These verses are the most challenging in the book for the interpreter, presenting many textual, syntactical, and exegetical difficulties. The passage is unified by the use of the verb *bāgad,* translated "break faith," which occurs in vv.
10b,11 and again in v. 14 (also in vv. 15b,16). Verse 10b is a general charge
against Judah for their unfaithfulness against fellow covenant members. Such

---

[15] The expression אִישׁ בְּאָחִיו ("each/one with his brother; NIV "with one another") is often
used idiomatically (with various prepositions besides בְּ) of individuals other than brothers. So the
NIV may be right in not stressing the meaning here (but cf. Jer 23:35; 31:34), although it does fit
the context. Note the similarity between אִישׁ בְּאָחִיו here and אִישׁ אֶת־רֵעֵהוּ ("each/one with his
friend"; NIV "with each other") in 3:16. The former construction (with only slight variation) is also
found in Gen 26:31; 37:19; 42:21,28; 43:33; Exod 16:15; 25:20; 37:9; Lev 25:14; 26:37; Num
14:4; 2 Kgs 7:6; Ezek 4:17; 24:23; 33:30; Joel 2:8; Mic 7:2; Zech 7:9,10. The latter construction
is also found in Gen 11:3,7; 15:10; 31:49; Exod 18:7; Judg 6:29; 7:22; 10:18; 1 Sam 10:11; 14:20;
20:41; 2 Kgs 3:23; 7:3,9; 2 Chr 20:23; Esth 9:19,22; Isa 13:8; 41:6; Jer 23:27,30; 34:15; 36:16;
Jonah 1:7; Zech 3:10; 8:16,17.

[16] See also Gen 4:8–11; 38:8; Deut 25:5–10; Judg 9:56; Neh 5:1–8; Pss 50:20; 133:1–3; Prov
17:17; Isa 58:7; Jer 12:6; Amos 1:11 (note v. 9 refers to בְּרִית אַחִים, "a treaty of brotherhood);
Obad 10; Matt 5:22–24; Acts 7:26; Rom 14:10,15,21; 1 Cor 6:6–8; 1 Thess 4:6; Heb 13:1; 1 Pet
1:22; 3:8; 1 John 2:9–11; 3:10–17; 4:20–21.

[17] C. Blomberg, *Matthew* (Nashville: Broadman & Holman, 1992), 107. [author's italics]

unfaithfulness is said to profane or violate Israel's covenant with God, just as the priests' behavior was violating (or corrupting) the Levitical covenant (2:8). Thus violation of social (horizontal) responsibilities of the covenant amounts to violation of the religious (vertical) responsibilities. Failure to love one's "neighbor" evidences failure to love God. These two aspects of Judah's sinful behavior receive separate focus in the following verses. Verses 11–12 focus on the vertical aspect of Judah's unfaithfulness. By "marrying the daughter of a foreign god," they had committed a "detestable" act (*tôʿēbâ,* an "abomination"), which "desecrated" (the same verb *ḥālal* translated "profaned" in v. 10) the Lord's sanctuary. Such unfaithfulness to God also involved a horizontal dimension in that it introduced a spiritually destructive element into the covenant community. Verses 13–15a then focus on the horizontal aspect of Judah's unfaithfulness—the breaking of marriage covenants. But this had a vertical dimension as well in that God was "witness" to those covenants. Such structural unity argues strongly against those who would simplify the passage by either excising verses or by one-dimensional interpretations (discussed later).

### (1) Charge of Unfaithfulness to Brothers (2:10b)

**Why do we profane the covenant of our fathers by breaking faith with one another?**

**2:10b**   Contrary to the NIV translation, the focus is not on profaning the covenant but on being unfaithful to one's brother. Profaning the covenant is the result.[18] Unlike the first two sentences of v. 10, this third sentence consists of two clauses, whose literal translation is, "Why do we break faith [or "act unfaithfully"] a man with his brother to profane the covenant of our fathers?"

The verb *bāgad,* "break faith," occurs forty-three times in the Old Testament, five of which are in Malachi (2:10,11,14,15,16; a frequency exceeded only by Proverbs [nine] and Jeremiah [seven]).[19] The word describes either violation of a covenant (Judg 9:23; cf. 9:3,6) or an act of betrayal or treachery in a relationship that calls for loyalty, kindness, and service (cf. Job 6:15; Jer 12:6; Lam 1:2).[20] Erlandsson explains that the word is used "of a man [who] does not honor an agreement, or commits adultery, or breaks a covenant or some other ordinance given by God."[21] Verhoef suggests that its relationship to *beged,* "garment, covering," may suggest the sense "to cover or cloak things

---

[18] Note the order of clauses in the Hb. text is also reversed in the NIV. The Hb. order forms a chiastic pattern with vv. 11–12 and vv. 13–15a: social/religious//religious/social.

[19] Cf. S. Erlandsson, "בָּגַד *bāghadh," TDOT* 1:470. Note also the nouns for "treachery," בֶּגֶד (Isa 24:16; Jer 12:1), and בֹּגְדוֹת (Zeph 3:4), and the adjective בָּגֹד, "treacherous" (Jer 3:7,10).

[20] Cf. *DCH* 2:90–91, which suggests the meaning "betray, be disloyal."

[21] Erlandsson, "בָּגַד *bāghadh*," 1:470.

over, and so to act falsely, perfidiously, to break faith."[22] The verb *bāgad* (and its related words) occur most often in reference to Israel's covenant with the Lord (Mal 2:11), usually in contrast to his faithfulness. In Hos 6:7 it is used synonymously with covenant transgression ("Like Adam, they have broken the covenant—they were unfaithful to me there").[23] Israel's betrayal of the Lord in violating their covenant with him is compared in Ps 78:57 to a bow for which someone reaches in a time of need but finds broken (see also 1 Sam 14:33; Prov 25:19). The word connotes shattered hopes and often suggests deceit (note Jer 9:2 ["unfaithful people"] in context with vv. 3–6) and disaster (cf. Prov 11:3,6; Isa 24:16; 33:1). The participle form used as a noun refers to a "traitor" (e.g., Isa 21:2). Such ideas can appropriately be applied to acts of marital unfaithfulness such as adultery, desertion, and divorce (cf. Exod 21:8; Prov 23:28; Jer 3:8,11,20; 5:11; 9:2[Hb. 1]; Hos 5:7).

According to Malachi, not only were the men of Judah guilty of committing acts of treachery such as betrayal of the marriage covenant (v. 14), but their behavior involved a violation and thus a betrayal of their covenant with God (see the discussion of covenant violation in 2:8). This covenant is identified here as "the covenant of our fathers." Since the audience of 2:10–3:6 has broadened from the priests to the whole nation, this does not refer to God's covenant with Levi specified in 2:4,8.[24] The reference could be to God's covenant with Abraham, Isaac, and Jacob, the "patriarchal" or "Abrahamic" covenant.[25] Yet the charge of unfaithfulness to one's brother is more fitting in the context of the Mosaic covenant, which constituted Israel as a nation.[26] In Judg 2:20 the Lord's covenant (*běrîtî*, "My covenant") that Israel had "violated"

---

[22] Verhoef, *Haggai and Malachi,* 267. *HALOT* considers these two words homonyms, from two separate roots. But N. Sarna suggests the homonymous relationship may account for the six uses of בֶּגֶד, "garment," in the account of Joseph's encounter with Potiphar's wife in Gen 39:12–18 (*The JPS Torah Commentary: Genesis* [Philadelphia: The Jewish Publication Society, 1989], 274).

[23] Thus it can be used synonymously with such words as חָטָא, "sin" (H.-J. Zobel, "בָּגַד, *bāghadh;* בֶּגֶד, *beghedh,*" *TDOT* 1:471).

[24] Contra G. S. Ogden, "Figurative Language of Mal 2:10–16," *BT* 39 (1988): 223–30. Use of such "religious or liturgical vocabulary" as "abomination," "sanctuary of Yahweh," "bring offerings," and "altar of Yahweh" shows continuity with the first address but, as most commentators agree, is insufficient to demonstrate that the audience is still the priests.

[25] This is the tentative view of S. L. McKenzie and H. N. Wallace ("Covenant Themes in Malachi," *CBQ* 45 [1983]: 551–52), who point out that the phrase is used in this way in Deut 4:31; 7:12–14; 8:18. Against taking "fathers" in Deut 5:3 to refer to the earlier generation of the exodus see E. R. Clendenen, "Life in God's Land: An Outline of the Theology of Deuteronomy," in *The Church at the Dawn of the 21st Century* [Dallas: Criswell, 1989], 164).

[26] Cf. W. Rudolph, *Haggai–Sacharja 1–8/9–14–Maleachi,* KAT (Gütersloh: Gütersloher Verlagshaus Mohn, 1976), 272; Verhoef, *Haggai and Malachi,* 267; D. L. Petersen, *Zechariah 9–14 and Malachi,* OTL [Louisville: Westminster John Knox, 1995], 197. Van der Woude understands both uses of בְּרִית, "covenant," in vv. 10,14 as having the "covenant community" in view ("Malachi's Struggle for a Pure Community," 67).

*(ʿbr)* is said to have been "laid down for their forefathers," literally, "commanded *[ṣwh]* their fathers," an expression that would apply most appropriately to the Mosaic covenant. Even more clearly, Solomon referred in 1 Kgs 8:21 to "the covenant of the LORD that he made with our fathers when he brought them out of Egypt" (cf. also Deut 29:25; 2 Kgs 17:15; 2 Chr 34:32; Jer 31:32; 34:13). Also the term "fathers" (NIV "forefathers") in Mal 3:7 refers to the exodus generation. Of course, the Mosaic covenant should be viewed as an extension and development of the patriarchal covenant.

The charge of profaning the covenant (using the verb *ḥālal* but translated "violate") is also made in Pss 55:20(Hb. 21) and 89:34(Hb. 35; see 89:31[Hb. 32], where it is the Lord's "decrees" that are profaned). The verb *ḥālal* occurs in Mal 1:12 of profaning the Lord's name and in 2:11 of desecrating the sanctuary. To "profane" meant to make something unholy, that is, to rob it of its significance or worth (see discussion at 1:12). In Num 30:2[Hb. 3] someone who makes a vow to the Lord or swears an oath but fails to fulfill it is said to "profane [NIV, "break"] his word." Thus to profane a covenant would be to disregard it or to treat it with contempt by violating it. Since this was a covenant made not only before God but with God, profaning it involved the most serious repudiation of faith.

The use of first person plural "we" in this charge against Israel is surprising since it seems to imply the prophet's participation in the crime.[27] Outside this verse only Malachi's audience employs first person plural (1:2,6–7,9; 2:17; 3:7–8,13–15; the exception is Edom in 1:4). Its use by the prophet in the charge against Judah is made appropriate by its use in the previous two rhetorical questions stressing the unity of God's people. It recalls the concept of corporate responsibility found elsewhere in the Old Testament as well as a prophet's identification with his audience (e.g., Josh 7:11–13; Ezra 9:6–15; Neh 1:6–7; Jer 14:7,20; Dan 9:4–19).[28]

### (2) Charge of Unfaithfulness to God (2:11–12)

**[11]Judah has broken faith. A detestable thing has been committed in Israel and in Jerusalem: Judah has desecrated the sanctuary the LORD loves, by marry-**

---

[27] The LXX has τί ὅτι ἐγκατελίπετε ἕκαστος τὸν ἀδελφὸν αὐτοῦ τοῦ βεβηλῶσαι τὴν διαθήκην τῶν πατέρων ὑμῶν, "Why have you forsaken each man his brother, to profane the covenant of your fathers?" The vocalization of נִבְגַּד as *niphal* creates an unusual usage. It may be a scribal attempt to remove the difficulty by repointing the word (Hugenberger, *Marriage as a Covenant,* 87), though the verb occurs elsewhere only in *qal,* and a *niphal* would make little sense.

[28] Cf. Rudolph, *Haggai–Sacharja 1–8/9–14–Maleachi,* 272, n. 4. Petersen's view (*Zechariah 9–14 and Malachi,* 196) that all three questions are put into the mouths of the people so that they "call into question their own behavior" is unnecessary and violates the practice elsewhere in the book of introducing quotations of Malachi's audience with a quotation formula (so Weyde, *Prophecy and Teaching,* 224).

ing the daughter of a foreign god. **¹²As for the man who does this, whoever he may be, may the LORD cut him off from the tents of Jacob—even though he brings offerings to the LORD Almighty.**

Verses 11–15a, which elaborate the charge of betrayal in v. 10b, are divided into two parts by the clause beginning v. 13: "Another thing you do." A few have proposed that vv. 11–12 (and the beginning clause of v. 13) are a later addition and that the prophet originally addressed only the problem of divorce.[29] The argument is that v. 10 sets up the problem of divorce, not the problem of intermarriage that concerns vv. 11–12. Also, concern for mixed marriages is claimed to have postdated the time of Malachi and violates the universalism of 1:11 (see comments there). Furthermore, it is claimed that in a society permitting polygamy the forming of new marriages would not require divorce.[30] The descriptive style of vv. 11–12 also is supposedly foreign to the book. As it has been frequently demonstrated, this paragraph is coherent as it stands,[31] and interpretation that involves altering the text is always suspect (as reflected in the dictum "to emend is not to explain"), as are prescriptive arguments regarding "style," which is notoriously difficult to delineate.[32] Concern for mixed marriages and other kinds of relationships that would jeopardize spiritual purity in Israel in fact runs through the Old Testament beginning in Genesis (e.g., 24:3). Regarding the incompatibility of polygamy and divorce, the time of Malachi at least yields no evidence of polygamy, and even if it were common in Israel, we do have evidence that divorce was known as well (Deut 22:19,29; 24:1–3; Ezra 10; Isa 50:1; Jer 3:8).[33]

---

[29] Cf. G. A. Smith, *The Book of the Twelve Prophets,* 2d ed. (Garden City: Doubleday, Doran & Co., 1929), 2:340, 363–65. E. Pfeiffer, "Disputationsworte im Buche Maleachi," *Evangelische Theologie* 19 (1959): 554; K. Elliger, *Das Buch der zwölf kleinen Propheten,* ATD 25/2, 7th ed. [Göttingen: Vandenhoeck & Ruprecht, 1964], 189; O. Eissfeldt, *The Old Testament: An Introduction* (New York: Harper & Row, 1965), 442; R. Mason, *The Books of Haggai, Zechariah, and Malachi,* CBC (New York: Cambridge University Press, 1977), 149–50. Some consider only part of vv. 11–12 to be a late addition, e.g., van der Woude, "Malachi's Struggle," 66. See the arguments against excising vv. 11–12 in Hugenberger, *Marriage as a Covenant,* 85–94.

[30] This argument is also used by those who argue against a literal interpretation of 2:10–16, e.g., C. C. Torrey, "The Prophecy of Malachi," *JBL* 17 (1898): 9; A. Isaksson, *Marriage and Ministry in the New Temple* (Lund: Gleerup, 1965), 30.

[31] E.g., Rudolph, *Haggai–Sacharja 1–8/9–14–Maleachi,* 272–73; Verhoef, *Haggai and Malachi,* 264. Weyde shows that by using traditions particularly from Lev 19 and Deut 7 and 32, vv. 11–12 explain v. 10, that the men of Judah "profane the covenant of our fathers" first by intermarriage with women who worship a foreign god (*Prophecy and Teaching,* 225–36).

[32] Van der Woude notes that 3:16 employs the same descriptive style ("Malachi's Struggle," 66).

[33] See Hugenberger's survey of the evidence for "polygyny" (having multiple wives) in Israel and the ANE (*Marriage as a Covenant,* 84–123, esp. 106–18). He concludes that "although polygyny was never illegal, monogamy is seen as the marital ideal in a number of texts and that actual marital practice was monogamous with few, if any, exceptions, particularly in the post-exilic period" (p. 122).

**2:11**   After restating the charge from v. 10b ("Judah has broken faith"), the prophet elaborates in v. 11 that Judah's sin amounted to an "abomination" (*tôʿēbâ*, NIV "detestable thing"). The following Hebrew particle *kî*, "for," introduces why Judah's behavior was an abomination: first in its effect (lit., "Judah has profaned [*ḥālal*, cf. 1:12; 2:10b] the Lord's holiness") and then in its nature as tending toward idolatry (lit. "and married the daughter of a foreign god").[34] The term "abomination," whose root meant to "hate" or "abhor,"[35] referred to activity that would cause the most serious defilement requiring destruction or death.[36] It was used of various immoralities, including those notable among the Canaanites (whom God had condemned to extinction), such as homosexuality, prostitution, child sacrifice, witchcraft, dishonesty, violence, and perversion of justice.[37] It was also used of reprehensible religious behavior such as idolatry,[38] sacrificing blemished animals (Deut 17:1), and hypocritical worship (Prov 15:8; 21:27; 28:9; Isa 1:13). In Jeremiah's temple sermon the Lord charged those coming to "this house, which bears my Name" with such abominations as oppressing the helpless, idolatry, theft, murder, adultery, and perjury, thus making his house a "den of robbers" (Jer 7:6–11). In Ezek 5:11–12 God had declared that "because you have defiled [*ṭmʾ*] my sanctuary with

---

[34] We should note that יְהוּדָה is treated as feminine in the first clause of v. 11, as subject of בָּגְדָה, then as masculine in the subordinate clauses with חִלֵּל and וּבָעַל. There is no need to emend בָּגְדָה to בָּגַד with *BHS* and Petersen (*Zechariah 9–14 and Malachi*, 194). As feminine יְהוּדָה refers to the country as a whole, whereas the masculine is used of the people (van der Woude, "Malachi's Struggle," 67; Verhoef, *Haggai and Malachi*, 267–68). Glazier-McDonald explains the effect (although probably overstating the situation): "The feminine-masculine shift here . . . stresses the enormity of the people's offense by enunciating that betrayal is practiced everywhere in the country, 2:11a, and profanation by every one of its inhabitants, 2:11c" (*Malachi: The Divine Messenger.* SBLDS [Atlanta: Scholars Press, 1987], 89).

[35] E. Gerstenberger, "תעב *tʿb*," *TLOT* 3:1328–31. Note the word תּוֹעֵבָה, "abomination," can be used in conjunction with שָׂנֵא, "hate" (Deut 12:31; Prov 6:16; Jer 44:4) or in opposition to רָצֹן, "pleasure, delight" (Prov 11:1,20; 12:22; 15:8) or to אָהֵב, "love" (Prov 15:9).

[36] Regarding the defiling (טמא) nature of תּוֹעֵבָה see esp. Lev 18:24,27,30; 2 Chr 36:14; Ezra 9:11 (also using נִדָּה, "impurity"); Jer 2:7; Ezek 5:11; 43:7–8. For the use of חלל see Jer 16:18; Ezek 44:7. For the requirement that תּוֹעֵבָה required removal by death or destruction see Lev 18:29 ("cut off," כרת), Lev 20:13; Deut 13:9–10[Hb. 10–11]; 17:5; 2 Chr 36:17 ("put to death," הרג or מות), Deut 7:25; 13:16[Hb. 17] ("burn in the fire," שׂרף בָּאֵשׁ); Deut 13:16[Eng. 15] ("completely destroy," חרם), 2 Kgs 21:12; Jer 44:23 ("disaster," רעה).

[37] Cf. Lev 18:22–30; 20:13; Deut 12:31; 18:9–12; 22:5; 23:17–18; 25:13–16; 1 Kgs 14:24; 2 Kgs 16:3; Prov 3:31–32; 6:16–19; 11:1; 12:22; 17:15; 20:10,23; Jer 6:13–15=8:10–12; 32:35; Ezek 18:5–13; 22:2–12; 33:25–26,29. Note the term could describe violations other than idolatry and so cannot be used to interpret the nature of the violation here in Malachi (contra J. M. O'Brien, *Priest and Levite,* SBLDS [Atlanta: Scholars Press, 1990], 68; Glazier-McDonald, *Malachi*, 89–90; Petersen, *Zechariah 9–14 and Malachi*, 198).

[38] Cf. Deut 7:25–26; 13:14; 17:2–5; 27:15; 32:16; 2 Kgs 23:13; 2 Chr 34:33; Isa 44:19; Jer 2:7; 16:18; 44:4,22; Ezek 6:9,11; 7:3–9,20; 8:1–17; 9:4–6; 11:18,21; 14:3–11; 16:2,15–26,36–59; 23:36–39.

all your vile images and detestable practices *[tô'ăbōt]*," two thirds of the people would die by plague, famine, and sword, and a third "I will scatter to the winds and pursue with drawn sword." Furthermore, for the sake of his name the Lord would "destroy," "demolish," "smash," "lay waste," "devastate," and "wipe out" all their high places and altars of idolatry and would "lay the dead bodies of the Israelites in front of their idols" and scatter their bones around the altars (Ezek 6:3–7). One of the many "abominations" rebuked by the prophet Ezekiel (in a passage with several parallels to Malachi) was that the priests had profaned *[ḥālal]* God's temple and broken *[prr]* his covenant by bringing (lit.) "sons of a foreigner *[nēkār]* uncircumcised in heart and uncircumcised in flesh to be in my holy place" (Ezek 44:7; cf. Neh 13:4–9). According to 2 Chr 36:14 it was for the "unfaithfulness" *[ma'al,* a synonym of *bgd]* of the priests and people who were "following all the detestable practices *[tô'ăbōt]* of the nations and defiling *[ṭm']* the temple of the LORD, which he had consecrated in Jerusalem" that the Lord had brought the Babylonians against them to enslave, kill, and destroy. Therefore Malachi's charges were extremely serious. The same kind of reprehensible behavior that had condemned the Canaanites to extinction (cf. Ezra 9:1–14) and brought death, destruction, and exile on treasonous, apostate Israel was being practiced by the restored covenant community.

Locating the abomination "in Israel" (rather than in Judah) might seem surprising except that, as noted at 1:1, the people to whom Malachi spoke and wrote would have recognized themselves as the remnant of Israel and as such were obligated to keep Israel's covenant with the Lord, as indicated in the reference in v. 10 to "the covenant of our fathers."[39] Weyde may also be correct that Malachi is alluding to Deut 17:4 ("this detestable thing has been done in Israel") and simply adds "and in Jerusalem" to specify in which "town" the covenant was being violated (Deut 17:2).[40]

Locating the abomination in Jerusalem means that the violation was committed even in the spiritual center of the nation, thereby profaning "the sanctuary the LORD loves." This is literally "the holiness of Yahweh *[qōdeš yhwh]* which he loves." Some have argued that rather than an explicit reference to the temple the point, as in 1:7,12, is that Judah's actions amounted to profaning the Lord, treating him as of no significance, the opposite of glorifying or sanctifying his name and demonstrating him to be holy (cf. Lev 10:3; see discussion of

---

[39] We agree with Verhoef (*Haggai and Malachi,* 268) that deletion of "in Israel" (e.g., *BHK*) or "in Jerusalem" (e.g., D. R. Jones, *Haggai, Zechariah and Malachi,* TBC [London: SCM, 1962]) or both *(BHS)* is without warrant. M. Breneman has observed that "the prayers of Ezra 9:6–15; Neh 1:5–11; and Neh 9:5–37 demonstrate their deep consciousness of the covenant. 'You are the LORD God, who chose Abram . . . and you made a covenant with him. . . . You have kept your promise' (Neh 9:7–8)" (*Ezra, Nehemiah, Esther,* NAC [Nashville: Broadman & Holman, 1993], 51).

[40] Weyde, *Prophecy and Teaching,* 226.

"profane" in comments on 1:12).[41] But this sense would not likely be followed by "which he loves."[42] Others have suggested that "the holiness of Yahweh" refers to Judah, so that by their behavior they were defiling themselves.[43] Another view is that the covenant itself was profaned. Supporting this view is the parallel of v. 10, which explicitly says that Judah's actions have "profaned" (same verb) the covenant.[44] The more common view is that the sanctuary is in view, the place where the Lord manifested his presence and was to be worshiped.[45]

The phrase *qōdeš yhwh* occurs elsewhere only in Lev 19:8, where it refers to an offering that is "holy to the LORD," having been consecrated to him.[46] Nevertheless the related word *miqdāš,* (lit.) "holy place," was clearly used of the sanctuary, as in the phrases *miqdĕšê ʾēl,* "the sanctuary of God," in Ps 73:17, *miqdāš ʾădōnāy,* "the sanctuary of the Lord" in Lam 2:20, and *miqdāš yhwh,* "the sanctuary of the LORD" in Ezek 48:10. Also, since it was the Lord's

---

[41] S. Schreiner, "Mischehen-Ehebruch-Ehescheidung. Betrachtungen zu Mal 2,10–16," *ZAW* 91 (1979): 210; Petersen, *Zechariah 9–14 and Malachi,* 198.

[42] Hugenberger, *Marriage as a Covenant,* 42. Petersen solves this by emending אֲשֶׁר, "which," to אֲשֵׁרָה, "Asherah," and attaching it to what follows rather than what precedes. Hill favors Schreiner's view but interprets אֲשֶׁר as a causal conjunction, translating "because he loved and married the daughter of a strange El" (*Malachi,* 221,231). This involves a rejection of the Massoretic tradition of accentuation and employs the less common causal use of אֲשֶׁר (but cf. Mal 3:19 [4:1]). Also these two verbs "loved" and "married" are not used together anywhere else.

[43] J. G. Baldwin, *Haggai, Zechariah, Malachi,* TOTC (Downers Grove: InterVarsity, 1972), 238–39; Verhoef, *Haggai and Malachi,* 268–69; D. Stuart, "Malachi," in *The Minor Prophets: An Exegetical and Expository Commentary* (Grand Rapids: Baker, 1988), 3:1332; Mason, *Haggai, Zechariah, and Malachi,* 150; C. von Orelli, *The Twelve Minor Prophets* (Edinburgh: T&T Clark, 1893), 394. The Tg. reads, "For [some] of the house of Judah have profaned their soul, which was sacred in front of Yahweh, and they have enjoyed taking women from the daughters of the nations" (L. Kruse-Blinkenberg, "The Peshitta of the Book of Malachi," *ST* 20 [1966]: 110). Van der Woude ("Malachi's Struggle," 67–68) sees as a parallel the use of חלל with בְּרִית in v. 10, which he interprets as a charge against violating the "covenant community." Like Hill, he considers it likely that "Judah" is the subject of both אָהֵב, "he loves/loved," and וּבָעַל, "and he married."

[44] E. H. Merrill, *An Exegetical Commentary: Haggai, Zechariah, Malachi* (Chicago: Moody, 1994), 418. Cf. the view of van der Woude ("Malachi's Struggle," 67–68). A view that seems to have little in its favor is that the divorced wife was what the Lord loved and Judah had profaned (C. Stuhlmueller, "Malachi," in *The Jerome Biblical Commentary* [Englewood Cliffs, N.J.: Prentice-Hall, 1968], 400).

[45] J. M. P. Smith, *A Critical and Exegetical Commentary on the Book of Malachi* (Edinburgh: T&T Clark, 1912), 48; R. L. Smith, *Micah–Malachi,* WBC (Waco: Word, 1984), 319; Glazier-McDonald, *Malachi,* 90; P. L. Redditt, *Haggai, Zechariah, Malachi,* NCBC (Grand Rapids: Eerdmans, 1995), 171.

[46] Also in both passages the penalty is being "cut off from his people/the tents of Jacob." Stuart asserts that Lev 19:8 "surely refers to ruining God's people" ("Malachi," 1332). But this is not clear there at all. The text does not say the violator is cut off because by eating the fellowship offering on the third day he has profaned his people. The offering is what is profaned there.

dwelling place, Mount Zion or more specifically the tabernacle or temple could be referred to as *hammiqdāš,* (lit.) "the holy place" (Exod 15:17; 25:8; Lev 12:4; 19:30; 20:3; 21:12,23; 26:2; Num 3:38; 18:1; 19:20; 1 Chr 22:19; 28:10; 2 Chr 20:8; 30:8; Ps 68:35[Hb. 36]; Ezek 43:21; 45:3,4), *miqdāšekā,* (lit.) "your holy place" (Ps 74:7; Isa 63:18; Dan 9:17), *miqdāšô,* (lit.) "his holy place" (Ps 78:69; Lam 2:7), *miqdāšî,* (lit.) "my holy place" (Isa 60:13 Ezek 5:11; 8:6; 9:6; 23:38,39; 24:21; 25:3; 37:26,28; 44:7,8,9,11,15,16), *mĕqôm qodšô,* (lit.) "the place of his holiness" (Ezra 9:8), and *har qodšekā,* (lit.) "the mountain of your holiness" (Ps 15:1). But it could also be designated as *(haq)qōdeš,* (lit.) "the holiness" (Exod 36:1,3,4,6; Lev 4:6; 10:4,18; Num 3:28,31,32; 4:12; 8:19; 18:3,5; 28:7; 31:6; 1 Chr 24:5; 2 Chr 29:5,7; Pss 20:2[Hb. 3]; 63:2[Hb. 3]; 68:24[Hb. 25]; 74:3; 134:2; Ezek 44:27; 45:2,3; Dan 8:13,14; 9:26; Zeph 3:4), *qodšô,* (lit.) "his holiness" (Pss 60:6[Hb. 8]; 114:2 [referring to Judah]; 150:1), *qodšî,* (lit.) "my holiness" (Isa 62:9), and *qodšekā,* (lit.) "your holiness" (Isa 63:18).[47] In Ps 78:68–69 the psalmist declares that God "chose the tribe of Judah, Mount Zion, which he loved" (the clause "which he loved" being identical to the one in Mal 2:11[48]) and "built his sanctuary *[miqdāšô]*." "The holiness of Yahweh which he loves" in Mal 2:11 probably refers, then, to the newly rebuilt temple that Judah's behavior had profaned,[49] although a reasonable alternative is that it refers to God's people with the intended reference back to his declaration of love for them in 1:2.[50]

Whether the sin actually involved temple personnel or was committed in or around the temple is not specified, but Malachi's words against the priests in 1:6–2:9 would lead us to expect priestly involvement. Furthermore, the seemingly parallel passage in Ezra 9 makes such involvement explicit:

> After these things had been done, the leaders came to me and said, "The people of Israel, *including the priests and the Levites,* have not kept themselves separate from the neighboring peoples with their detestable practices *[tô'ābôt],* like those of the Canaanites, Hittites, Perizzites, Jebusites, Ammonites, Moabites, Egyptians and Amorites. They have taken some of their daughters as wives for themselves and their sons, and have mingled the holy race with the peoples around them. And the leaders and officials have led the way in this unfaithfulness *[ma'al].*" (Ezra 9:1–2).

The interpretative crux in Mal 2:11 is the clause "by marrying [lit. "and married"] the daughter of a foreign god." One question arising from this verse

---

[47] Note that in several passages מִקְדָּשׁ ("place of holiness") and קֹדֶשׁ ("holiness") are both used of the Lord's sanctuary.

[48] This makes more unlikely Petersen's emendation of אֲשֶׁר, "which," to אֲשֵׁרָה, translating: "Judah has profaned the very holiness of Yahweh. He loves Asherah; he has married the daughter of a foreign god" (*Zechariah 9–14 and Malachi,* 194).

[49] Glazier-McDonald points out that "of the nearly 310 occurrences of קֹדֶשׁ . . . eighty-two bear the concrete sense of 'temple, sanctuary'" (*Malachi,* 91).

[50] See Weyde, *Prophecy and Teaching,* 230–34.

is whether an ongoing practice or a single incident is in view, especially because of the singular *ʾēl nēkār,* "foreign god." The use of the plural "we/us" in v. 10 and especially the phrase "one another" suggest that Malachi had in mind numerous instances.[51] The phrase "foreign god," which also occurs in Deut 32:12 and Ps 81:9[Hb. 10] (also note the almost identical *ʾělôah nēkār,* "foreign god," in Dan 11:39), refers to any god other than Yahweh the God of Israel,[52] the God who delivered them from Egypt and entered into an exclusive covenant relationship with them, the God who "Father[ed]" and "create[d]" them (Mal 2:10). The plural (*ʾělōhê hannēkār,* "the foreign gods") occurs many times, as when Jacob tells his household to rid themselves of their "foreign gods" in preparation to worship the Lord (Gen 35:2,4), as one would sever former courting relationships in preparation for marriage.[53] The term "foreign" should not be assumed to have had a neutral connotation as it does in our pluralistic society. It rather described something dangerous and threatening, as suggested by its cognates in Ugaritic (*nkr,* "strange") and Akkadian (*nakru, nakiru,* "hostile, enemy"). Nevertheless, this was not merely an expression of xenophobia (note the words of judgment in 3:5 against those who "deprive aliens of justice"). The Old Testament repeatedly demonstrates that the presence of such "foreign gods" threatened a relationship with Yahweh the loving God and obstructed his worship. The phrase "foreign god" is equivalent to *ʾēl zār,* "strange god" (Ps 44:20[Hb. 21]), with which it occurs in Ps 81:9 [10], where Israel is told (lit.), "Let there not be among you a strange god, and do not worship a foreign god."[54] It is also equivalent to *ʾēl ʾaḥēr* in Exod 34:14, where Israel is told not to "worship any *other god,* for the LORD, whose name is Jealous, is a jealous God" (although the singular occurs only there, the plural *ʾělōhîm ʾăḥērîm,* "other gods," occurs many times; e.g., Exod 20:3; 23:13; Deut 6:14).

Some, while interpreting the marriage figuratively, interpret the phrase "the daughter of a foreign god" literally, as designating a pagan goddess. Thus "the wife of your youth" in v. 14 is understood as the Lord, and Judah's sin, in line with their preexilic history, was idolatry and so apostasy. Their "divorce" (assuming a connection between vv. 11–12 and vv. 14–16), would have been

---

[51] Except when the context specifies that only two individuals are involved (e.g., Gen 36:31; Exod 25:20), the use of "one another" ( אִישׁ בְּאָחִיו and variations) always implies more than one occurrence (e.g., Gen 37:19; 42:21; 43:33; Exod 16:15; Lev 26:37; Ezek 4:17; Mic 7:2).

[52] The "foreign gods'" lack of true substance is made clear in such passages as Jer 8:19 with its divine query, "Why have they provoked me to anger with their images, with their worthless foreign idols [בְּהַבְלֵי נֵכָר]?" See also Deut 28:36,64; 32:16–17,21,39.

[53] See also Deut 31:16; Josh 24:20,23; Judg 10:16; 1 Sam 7:3; 2 Chr 33:15; Jer 5:19.

[54] Note too the use of זָרִים (*zārîm*) in Hos 5:7 with "children" in the sense "illegitimate," also in context with בָּגַד (*bāgad*).

from the Lord or from their covenant with him.[55] But this interpretation does not suit the context established by the reminder in v. 10 that the Lord is Israel's one "Father" ("the children of the LORD" in Deut 14:1 are clearly not gods[56]) or by the charge that "brothers" were committing acts of treachery against "one another."[57] At least in v. 14 the Lord's role is "witness" to rather than participant in the broken covenant, thus making it difficult to see the "covenant" in that verse as either the Mosaic or Abrahamic covenants between God and Israel (even though "the covenant of our fathers" in v. 10 refers to such a national covenant). the Lord is also distinguished in v. 14 from "the wife of your youth" and (lit.) "the wife of your covenant [NIV "marriage covenant"]." Also, whenever Scripture uses marriage imagery to depict the relationship between Israel and the Lord, Israel rather than the Lord is the wife.[58] Besides, the adjective "foreign" would be unnecessary if "daughter of a god" meant "goddess," since biblical faith sanctioned no goddess in Israel.[59]

---

[55] See F. F. Hvidberg, *Weeping and Laughter in the Old Testament* (Leiden: Brill, 1962), 120–23; Isaksson, *Marriage and Ministry in the New Temple,* 31–33; G. W. Ahlström, *Joel and the Temple Cult of Jerusalem,* VTSup 21 [Leiden: Brill, 1971], 49; O'Brien, *Priest and Levite,* 68–69; id., "Judah as Wife and Husband: Deconstructing Gender in Malachi," *JBL* 115 (1996): 241–50; Petersen, *Zechariah 9–14 and Malachi,* 202–3. S. Erlandsson (*TDOT* 1:471) asserts: "In Mal. 2:10ff., covenant ideology and marriage symbolism are combined in order to express the apostasy of the people from Yahweh." Isaksson's argument that "Malachi is a priestly reformer, not a prophetic renovator of the ethics of marriage" (*Marriage and Ministry,* 32) overlooks the prophet's point that personal and social behavior had cultic effects in that unfaithfulness to "one another" profaned the covenant and desecrated the sanctuary. Note also the concern with ethics in 3:5.

[56] See Glazier-McDonald, *Malachi,* 92.

[57] The latter point also argues against the attempt of M. A. Shields to interpret 2:11–12 figuratively but 2:13–16 literally. His suggested chiastic structure of 2:10–16 disregards the crucial third question in v. 10 ("Syncretism and Divorce in Malachi 2,10–16," 7).

[58] See Hugenberger, *Marriage as a Covenant,* 31–32. J. J. Collins declares that "there can be little doubt that the reference [to divorce in vv. 13–16] is to the breakup of actual marriages" ("Marriage, Divorce, and Family in Second Temple Judaism," in *Families in Ancient Israel* [Louisville: WJKP, 1997], 124). Torrey ("Prophecy of Malachi," 4–5) and B. Vawter ("The Biblical Theology of Divorce," *Proceedings of the Catholic Theological Society of America* 22 [1967]: 223–43) try to avoid these objections by considering the marriage to depict Israel's relationship with the covenant, and the "daughter of a foreign god" as depicting a foreign cult. Hugenberger observes that besides being unique this imagery is implausible since "the most prominent obligation of Israelites toward the covenant is obedience and this would hardly typify an Israelite husband's obligation toward his wife" (*Marriage as a Covenant,* 32).

[59] See Kruse-Blinkenberg, "Peshitta," 100. The Peshitta translated, "Judah has defiled the sanctuary of the mighty Lord and has loved and worshipped strange gods," similar to the LXX (ἐπετηδευσιν εἰς θεοὺς ἀλλοτρίους, "went after other gods"). But Kruse-Blinkenberg concludes that "P does not seem to grasp the historical background and besides P does not understand the verb בעל." Verhoef explains the LXX rendering as avoiding the issue of mixed marriages, which were common among Hellenistic Jews (*Haggai and Malachi,* 269).

More likely, then, "daughter of a foreign god" refers collectively to women[60] outside the community of faith, foreign pagans who worshiped a god other than the Lord.[61] Foreigners are elsewhere referred to as children of their god (Num 21:29), as the people of Israel were considered the Lord's offspring (see comments on Mal 2:10). Judah's sin was literal marriage outside the community of faith; the Lord's sons (v. 10) were marrying the daughters of pagan gods and thus treacherously introducing into the covenant family of Israel the elements of its destruction.[62] Although there is no indication that idolatrous behavior had yet been introduced into Judah,[63] the problem was not unrelated to idolatry.[64] Marriage outside the covenant community (specifically with the Canaanites) was forbidden by Moses, not for reasons of racial or ethnic exclusivism but because "they will turn your sons away from following me to serve other gods, and the LORD's anger will burn against you and will quickly destroy you" (Deut 7:3–4; cf. Exod 34:11–16; Neh 13:26). The corruption of the human heart is already a strong enough foe to righteousness without inviting enticement to sin into one's home through marriage to one who is still in bondage to the spiritual powers of wickedness (cf. Deut 13:6–11; 31:20–21). Israel's history offers abundant examples of the spiritual dangers of entering relationships with unbelievers (cf. Josh 23:7,12–13; Judg 2:1–3; 3:5–7; Ps 106:35; 1 Kgs 11:4–10; Jer 44:15–19; see also 2 Cor 6:14–17). Nevertheless, Ezra 9 and Neh 13:23–30 confirm that the

---

[60] The singular "daughter" is used rather than plural not because it refers to a goddess (J. M. P. Smith, *Malachi,* 49) but because the one taking in marriage is the collective singular "Judah" (cf. Deut 33:7; Jer 14:2; 33:16; 52:27; Nah 1:15[Hb. 2:1]).

[61] J. Morgenstern likens it to a marriage between Menahem and a Tyrian princess ("Jerusalem—485 B.C.," *HUCA* 28 [1957]: 15–47).

[62] See M. Zehnder, "A Fresh Look at Malachi 2:13–16," *VT* 53 (2003): 227–28.

[63] Contra Glazier-McDonald (*Malachi,* 98–99) et al. Some have claimed that this is suggested by the use of the verb בעל, "marry," rather than לקח, "take" (cf. e.g., Gen 19:14; 28:1; Lev 21:7; Deut 20:7; 24:4,5; 1 Sam 25:43; 1 Kgs 3:1; 16:31; Jer 16:2; 29:6; Ezek 44:22; Hos 1:3; Neh 6:18) or *hiphil* of ישׁב (only in Ezra 10:2,10,14,17,18; Neh 13:23,27); but see the use of בעל, "marry," in Gen 20:3; Deut 21:13; 24:1 (which uses both expressions—[lit.] "if a man should take a woman and marry her"); Isa 62:4–5; Prov 30:23. Nowhere does the use of the verb בעל, "marry," seem to connote idolatry. Glazier-McDonald illogically claims that because בעל means "become master," to "marry the daughter of a foreign god" would mean that her god would become his master (p. 91). On the contrary, if that meaning of בעל is pressed, it would mean that the man becomes the master. Glazier-McDonald correctly points out, however, that intermarriage "had both religious and social consequences" ("Intermarriage, Divorce, and the *bat-'ēl nēkār:* Insights into Mal 2:10–16," *JBL* 106 [1987]: 610). She asserts that "the *bat-'ēl nēkār* was neither foreign woman nor goddess; she was both at once."

[64] Cf. Collins, "Marriage, Divorce, and Family," 123; Weyde, *Prophecy and Teaching,* 233.

problem continued in the postexilic community, even among the priests.[65] Malachi gave no indication of how many were guilty of this treachery, only that the problem and the guilt could be described collectively as "Judah's."

**2:12** Translation of this verse is extremely difficult. A literal rendering would be something like "May Yahweh cut off to the man who does it, waking and answering, from the tents of Jacob, and presenting an offering to Yahweh of hosts." It begins as a parenthetical curse against "the man who does it," but it is unclear whether the parenthesis includes the entire verse. The concluding clause may connect more directly to v. 11. Its point seems to be that the violation of Judah or of "the man" was being committed while at the same time continuing to worship the Lord as if nothing had changed.[66] This is especially why the temple was being defiled. The NIV (also REB) interpretation that the penalty would be exacted "even though" the person should bring an offering to the temple is possible but unlikely.[67] This relationship would usually be expressed differently, and as Waltke-O'Connor explains, the participle usually "describes an ongoing state of affairs, involving repeated . . . or continuous . . . action."[68]

The curse itself is complicated by a phrase of uncertain meaning, which the NIV has translated "whoever he may be."[69] The phrase consists of two coordinated participles *('ēr wĕ'ōneh)* that are variously derived and translated: "him that waketh and him that answereth,"[70] "he that calls and he that makes

---

[65] Van der Woude suggests that "by marrying foreign women Judaeans tried to share the privileges of their alien overlords" ("Malachi's Struggle," 66). Similarly, Hugenberger explains: "In a world where property frequently was inalienable and where wealth and status were primarily in non-Israelite hands, the temptation for the returned exiles to secure these through intermarriage must have been significant" (*Marriage as a Covenant,* 103–4; cf. also G. A. Smith, *Book of the Twelve Prophets,* 344).

[66] A parallel situation might be found in 1 Cor 5.

[67] Although Verhoef's translation is identical to the NIV, he explains, "The detestable thing was to act piously while at the same time desecrating the sanctuary of the Lord" (*Haggai and Malachi,* 271). O'Brien translates the clause as part of the coordinate object of the verb, understanding the curse against the man as his being deprived of three categories of persons: "the *'ēr,* the *'ōneh,* and the *maggîš minḥâ"* (*Priest and Levite,* 71). Besides the massoretic vocalization being against understanding the final clause in this way, the third term is separated from the others by the phrase "from the tents of Jacob." Besides, O'Brien offers no parallel for depriving someone of one to present offerings on his behalf.

[68] *IBHS* §37.6d. The concessive or contrastive relationship expressed by "even though" is usually indicated either by כִּי with a dependent clause (e.g., Gen 8:21; 44:18; 48:14) or by a disjunctive independent clause (e.g., Gen 31:50; Lev 26:37; 1 Sam 12:12). Weyde supports the same interpretation as the NIV, citing GKC §141e (*Prophecy and Teaching,* 247–49). But of the verses cited in GKC, only Gen 18:27; 2 Sam 3:39; Ps 28:3 offer possible parallels.

[69] Likewise Verhoef, *Haggai and Malachi,* 270.

[70] S. R. Driver, *The Minor Prophets* (New York: Oxford University, 1906), 314; cf. R. C. Dentan, "Malachi," *IB* (New York: Abingdon, 1956), 6:1135. Baldwin says this is based on an Arabic expression and "envisages a nomadic custom of keeping watch round the tents at night." It "agrees with the mention of *the tents of Jacob"* (*Haggai, Zechariah, Malachi,* 239).

reply,"[71] "the master and the scholar" (KJV, cf. Vg, *magistrum et discipulum*"),[72] "the aroused one and the lover,"[73] "protector and appealer,"[74] "protector and oppressor,"[75] "whether nomads or settlers" (REB). It is also frequently explained and translated through emendation: "(hostile) witness and (defending) counsel,"[76] "anyone who gives testimony" on behalf of the guilty (NIV margin), "any to witness or answer" (NRSV), "witness and advocate" (NJB), "root and branch,"[77] "nakedness and improper cohabitation."[78] However the individual words are understood, the expression is usually taken to be an idiom employing opposites to depict the whole range of men in Judah (a merism; cf. Ps 139:2–3), thus "anyone."[79]

---

[71] von Orelli, *The Twelve Minor Prophets*, 394.

[72] This understanding is supported in two talmudic passages cited by R. P. Gordon, *Studies in the Targum to the Twelve Prophets* (Leiden: Brill, 1994), 126.

[73] B. Glazier-McDonald, "Malachi 2:12: *ʿēr wĕʿōneh*—Another Look," *JBL* 105 (1986): 295–98; id., *Malachi*, 98. Citing M. Pope's interpretations of Song 2:7–8; 3:5; 4:16; 5:2; 8:4–5 for עוּר, and extrapolating an additional meaning for the *qal* of עָנָה II ("be wretched" in the *qal*, "oppress, humiliate, do violence to, rape" in the *piel* according to *HALOT*) from a *piel* use, she understands the phrase as "the one who is aroused (from sexual inactivity, i.e., the aroused one) and the lover." She believes that it refers to "the syncretistic phenomena that have entered the Yahweh cult through intermarriage." She thus relates it to the interpretation of a "daughter of a foreign god" in v. 11 as a goddess and the weeping in v. 13 being part of a fertility rite. The penalty the prophet announces against this idolatrous fornication, she argues, is barrenness (see her interpretation of v. 15), the opposite of its intent. Here she translates, "May Yahweh cut off the man who does this—the aroused one and the lover—from the tents of Jacob, and the one who brings near an offering to Yahweh of Hosts." "The man" would supposedly be not the "aroused one" but "the lover."

[74] Rudolph derives the participle עֵר from עִיר, "protect" (cf. *HALOT*) rather than עוּר, "awake," yielding "protector and appealer" ("Beschützer und Gesprächspartner"; *Haggai–Sacharja 1–8/9–14–Maleachi*, 268–69). Against this cf. Schreiner, "Mischehen-Ehebruch-Ehescheidung. Betrachtungen zu Mal 2,10–16," 211.

[75] Cf. *HALOT*, "עָנָה II."

[76] See G. R. Driver, "Confused Hebrew Roots," in *Occident and Orient: Gaster Anniversary Volume* (London: Taylor's, 1936), 80, following J. Wellhausen (Kläger und Verteidiger") in *Die kleinen Propheten übersetzt und erklärt* (Berlin: Walter de Gruyter, 1963 [1892]), 207. The reading עֵד, "witness," rather than עֵר is based on the LXX (ἕως καὶ ταπεινωθῇ, "until he is also humiliated," reading עַד, "until") and is supported by 4QXII^a (cf. R. E. Fuller, "The Minor Prophets Manuscripts from Qumran, Cave IV," [Ph.D. diss., Harvard University, 1988], 10–11; id., "Text-Critical Problems in Mal 2:10–16," *JBL* 110 [1991]: 47–57). J. M. P. Smith cites Marti's objection to this emendation that "witness" would require the legal context of the city "gates" rather than the "tents of Jacob" (*Malachi*, 71).

[77] Torrey, "The Prophecy of Malachi," 5. From 3:19 he reconstructed the original text as שֹׁרֶשׁ וְאָנָף. He later abandoned the view in "ʿēr wĕʿōneh in Mal 2:12," *JBL* 24 (1905): 176–78.

[78] Petersen, *Zechariah 9–14 and Malachi*, 194. He repoints the phrase עוּר וְעֹנָה; but עוּר means "skin," not "nakedness" (Lev 13:5; Jer 13:23; Ezek 37:6,8; Job 7:5) and never occurs in a sexual context. The word עֹנָה only occurs in Exod 21:10, and its meaning is uncertain, although it is usually taken to refer to a wife's "conjugal rights."

[79] Note in a similar context in 1 Kgs 14:10 the merism עָצוּר וְעָזוּב, "bound or free." See the discussion of that expression in *HALOT*, 871.

Also unclear is whether the phrase functions adjectivally or nominally. If "the man" serves as the object of the verb *yakrēt,* "cut off," then the phrase would modify it in some way (as in the KJV, NRSV, NLT, REB, and others). The preposition *lĕ,* "to," with "the man" in this case would serve, as it does occasionally, as a direct object marker.[80] The phrase almost certainly functions nominally, however, as the object of the verb. The prepositional phrase "to the man" either modifies the object of the verb as a possessive, yielding the sense "belonging to the man,"[81] or could serve as a kind of indirect object, yielding "cut off from the man."[82] Either of the latter two senses is supported by the structurally parallel passage in 1 Kgs 14:10, whose literal translation would be:

> Therefore behold I am going to bring disaster to the house of Jeroboam, and I will cut off to Jeroboam *[lĕyārābĕ'ām]* one urinating against a wall [NIV, "every last male"], bound or free *['āṣûr wĕ'āzûb],* in Israel. And I will burn up the rest of the house of Jeroboam just as dung is burned until it is gone.

Here too the verb "cut off" is followed by a nominal with the preposition "to" and then a participle phrase, "urinating against a wall," serving as the object (followed by another participle phrase, "bound or free").[83] The following verse uses "to Jeroboam" *[lĕyārābĕ'ām]* in a possessive sense: "Anyone belonging to Jeroboam who dies in the city, the dogs shall eat" (14:11a, NRSV). Another parallel is God's warning to Israel in Jer 44:7 (lit.): "Why are you doing great harm to yourselves, to cut off to you man and woman, child and infant, from the midst of Judah, so as not to leave to yourselves a remnant?" Furthermore, Isa 14:22 contains the Lord's promise to "cut off from Babylon [lit. "to Babylon"] her name and survivors, her offspring and descendants." These parallel passages suggest that the otherwise inexplicable phrase *'ēr wĕ'ōneh* likely refers to the man's family and descendants who would disappear from the "tents of Jacob" (a phrase used elsewhere only in Jer 30:18, with "tents of Judah" only in Zech 12:7[84]), taking with them the name of the

---

[80] Verhoef, *Haggai and Malachi,* 270 and Glazier-McDonald, *Malachi,* 94, citing GKC §117n. Also cf. *GBH* §125k.

[81] On this use of לֹ cf. *IBHS* §11,2,10d; *GBH* §130g, citing an interesting parallel, יִמּוֹל לָכֶם כָּל־זָכָר, lit. "shall be circumcised to you every male" = "all your males shall be circumcised" (Gen 17:12).

[82] Cf. NAB. This could be considered the *dativus commodi* expressing *for* whom (or against whom) something is done. Cf. *GBH* §133; O'Brien, *Priest and Levite,* 71; Weyde, *Prophecy and Teaching,* 236–40.

[83] In no other passage where לֹ is used with כרת does לֹ introduce the direct object. Also see 1 Sam 2:33; 1 Kgs 21:21; 2 Kgs 9:8; Jer 47:4. In Isa 9:13[14] "Yahweh will cut off from Israel head and tail."

[84] Cf. also 2 Sam 20:1; 1 Kgs 12:16; Job 18:14; Pss 52:7[5]; 78:55. Weyde favors the view that עֵר וְעֹנֶה, though a word pair expressing the totality of punishment, does so by alluding to the Jacob tradition of the death of Judah's sons עֵר וְאוֹנָן, Er and Onan, the offspring of Judah and a Canaanite woman (*Prophecy and Teaching,* 241–46).

treacherous man. This meaning of *'ēr wĕ'ōneh* is also found in the Peshitta and Targum, which translated "son and grandson."[85] J. M. P. Smith likewise suggests that the phrase refers to "the whole of the transgressor's family," citing a parallel Arabic expression, "There is not in the city a caller, nor is there a responder," meaning that "none have been left alive."[86] In any case, as O'Brien has argued, recognizing that *'ēr wĕ'ōneh* must be the object of the verb precludes understanding it as explaining the sin of "the man who does it," whether sexual (with Glazier-McDonald and Petersen) or otherwise.[87] Verse 12, then, can perhaps best be translated as part of the previous verse: "Judah has acted treacherously so that an abomination has been committed in Israel and in Jerusalem. For Judah has profaned the Lord's sanctuary, which he loves, and married the daughter of a foreign god (may Yahweh cut off from the tents of Jacob any descendants of the man who does such a thing), while presenting offerings to Yahweh of hosts."

The curse here with its use of the verb "cut off" and the phrase "from the tents of Jacob" echoes the penalty formula found mainly in the Pentateuch: "that soul shall be cut off from his people/from the congregation of Israel" (KJV; Gen 17:14; Exod 12:15,19; 31:14; Lev 7:20,21,27, etc.) or "I [God] . . . will cut him off from among his people/from the midst of my people" (KJV; Lev 17:10; 20:3,6; Ezek 14:8). J. Milgrom lists seven different views of *kārēt* ("cutting off").[88] Jewish exegesis defined it as (1) childlessness and premature death, (2) death before age sixty, (3) death before age fifty-two, (4) "extirpation," that is, termination of one's line of descent, or (5) loss of life in the hereafter, that is, exclusion from "resting" with one's "fathers" or from being "gathered" to one's "people" after death (e.g., Gen 15:15; 47:30; 49:29; Num 20:24; 27:13; Deut 31:16; Judg 2:10; 2 Sam 7:12). In addition, most modern interpreters, he says, favor either (6) excommunication[89] or (7) human execution. He dismisses the modern interpretations on the grounds that all the instances involve deliberate sins against God, which necessitated punishment by God.[90] Wenham adds that often the crimes involved were "secret sins" that

---

[85] Kruse-Blinkenberg, "Peshitta" 101; Gordon, *Targum to the Twelve Prophets*, 126. As Baldwin states, "Though the Targum interprets rather than translates . . . this is the meaning the prophet wanted to convey. The idolater, left with no-one belonging to him in his old age, would so obviously not be blessed that other people would be discouraged from following his example, and no children of his would survive to perpetuate his sin" (*Haggai, Zechariah, Malachi*, 239).

[86] J. M. P. Smith, *Malachi*, 50. "The destruction of the sinner and all his kin is apparently asked for," he explains. D. Barthélemy et al. explain: "The expression is proverbial. In the destroyed camp there is no longer any one [sic] who is conscious and able to answer anyone drawing near the camp and shouting to let his presence be known. For everybody in the camp is dead" (*Preliminary and Interim Report on the Hebrew Old Testament Text Project* [New York: UBS, 1980], 5:433).

[87] O'Brien, *Priest and Levite*, 71.

[88] J. Milgrom, *Leviticus 1–16*, AB (New York: Doubleday, 1991), 457–60.

[89] E.g., Glazier-McDonald, *Malachi*, 93.

[90] See also W. Horbury, "Extirpation and Excommunication," *VT* 35 (1985): 13–38.

only God could prosecute (cf. Exod 30:38; Lev 7:20–21; Num 15:30–31).[91] Also divine "cutting off" is distinguished from human execution in Lev 20:2–3 ("Any Israelite or any alien living in Israel who gives any of his children to Molech must be put to death. The people of the community are to stone him. I will set my face against that man and I will cut him off from his people; for by giving his children to Molech, he has defiled my sanctuary and profaned my holy name").[92] Milgrom also points out that death did not always occur right away, and the concept of "premature" death is difficult to define. He concludes that *kārēt* meant that "the person's line will be terminated by God and, possibly, that he will be denied life in the hereafter."[93]

Milgrom's confidence in his evidence that "cutting off" did not involve physical death may be excessive. He claims that the imprecation of David's enemies in Ps 109:13 ("May his descendants be cut off, their names blotted out from the next generation") "both equates *kārēt* with extirpation and states explicitly that *kārēt* need not be carried out upon the sinner himself but will affect his descendants." But the expression in question (the pentateuchal curse calling for cutting off an *individual*, not explicitly his descendants) is not used in Psalm 109. It only calls for cutting off "his descendants." Furthermore, David's enemies were calling for his death: "May his days be few; may another take his place of leadership. May his children be fatherless and his wife a widow" (vv. 8–9). Likewise in Ruth 4:10, the second passage Milgrom cites, Boaz does not refer explicitly to Ruth's former husband *Mahlon's* being cut off but "that *his name* will not disappear [lit. "be cut off"] from among his family or from the town records." Even if the expression in question were explicitly used here, the passage does not support Milgrom's contention that physical death was not necessarily involved, since Mahlon was in fact dead.[94] As Milgrom admits, two other passages he cites as evidence for his view (Num 16:33 and Deut 29:19) do not even use the verb *kārat*. That leaves Mal 2:12, which he translates, "May the Lord cut off *(yakrēt)* from the one who does this all descendants from the tents of Jacob." Although the only justification he gives for the translation "descendants" is the "context" of 2:3 ("because of you I will rebuke your descendants"), which is from a different section of Malachi's prophecy, we have already shown from parallel passages that this is a credible translation. Whether family and descendants were implied even when they were not mentioned is unclear, but the weight of evidence seems to be that they

---

[91] G. Wenham, *The Book of Leviticus* (Grand Rapids: Eerdmans, 1979), 242.

[92] Milgrom, *Leviticus 1–16,* 460. Although Exod 3:14 ("Observe the Sabbath, because it is holy to you. Anyone who desecrates it must be put to death; whoever does any work on that day must be cut off from his people") does not make clear the distinction, that passage should be read in light of Lev 20:2–3.

[93] Ibid., 424.

[94] Note in Josh 7:9 having one's "name" cut off means being exterminated.

usually were. The term "cut off" describes radical removal or eradication (cf. Gen 9:11; Josh 11:21; Isa 9:14[Hb. 13]; Pss 12:3[Hb. 4]; 109:15). As a penalty it seems to have been a divine sentence of condemnation that would eventually result in the cessation of one's name from the family of Israel (cf. Num 27:4; 1 Sam 24:21) and implied exclusion from peace in the afterlife. Although physical death might not occur immediately, it would continually hang over the condemned person with its threat of eternal ruin.[95]

### (3) Charge of Unfaithfulness to Wives (2:13–15a)

**[13]Another thing you do: You flood the LORD's altar with tears. You weep and wail because he no longer pays attention to your offerings or accepts them with pleasure from your hands. [14]You ask, "Why?" It is because the LORD is acting as the witness between you and the wife of your youth, because you have broken faith with her, though she is your partner, the wife of your marriage covenant.**

**[15]Has not [the LORD] made them one? In flesh and spirit they are his. And why one? Because he was seeking godly offspring.**

Whereas vv. 11–12 concentrate on instances of Judah's violation of their covenant with God, involving marriage to pagan women, vv. 13–15a focus on violations of the marriage covenant. Again we are not told how many instances had occurred, only that "you" (plural except in the prophet's reply in v. 14) were guilty. An important question is how the instances of intermarriage were related to the instances of divorce. On the one hand each is treated separately and condemned. The charge of marital unfaithfulness in these verses is introduced by the clause (lit.), "And this [is] a second [thing] you do." This argues against those who would see vv. 10–16 as concerned with only one issue, either spiritual apostasy, marriage to pagan women, or divorce.[96]

As discussed in the introduction to vv. 10–15a, however, v. 10 as well as the repetition of the verb *bāgad* force us to see the behavior condemned in vv. 11–12 and vv. 13–15a as related. It may be that both intermarriage and divorce are

---

[95] Cf. Wenham, *Leviticus,* 242.

[96] While some excise the clause as secondary (see comments on vv. 11–12), R. Althann suggests that שֵׁנִית, "second," means "gnashing of teeth" and that זֹאת, "this," means "insult, indignity," translating, "Even indignity, gnashing of teeth you perform" ("Malachy 2,13–14 and UT 125,12–13," *Bib* 58 [1977]: 418–19). The case for such an interpretation is weak. Although van der Woude considers that זֹאת may mean "shame, shameful act," he regards deletion of שֵׁנִית as "unwarranted (despite the LXX) and only based on the false thesis that the prophecy of Malachi originally spoke of divorce only" ("Malachi's Struggle," 68). The LXX has read שֵׁנִית as שָׂנֵאתִי, "I hate," which Hugenberger (*Marriage as a Covenant,* 33) and Verhoef (*Haggai and Malachi,* 262) think was probably in its *Vorlage,* having arisen under influence of שָׂנֵא, "hate," in v. 16. Hugenberger notes that if the LXX reading were original, we would expect also אֲשֶׁר, "which," since it occurs eleven times in Malachi. Fuller, noting the agreement of 4QXII[a] with the MT, believes the LXX has simply misread שֵׁנִית as a perfect of שׂנא ("Minor Prophets Manuscripts from Qumran, Cave IV," 11).

simply examples of unfaithfulness.[97] On the other hand, intermarriage can only indirectly be described as "breaking faith with one another." Consequently, many understand the practice of divorce condemned in vv. 13–15a as logically related to the intermarriage of vv. 11–12—Jewish men were divorcing their Jewish wives *because* they were entering advantageous marriages with pagan women.[98] Otherwise the question remains unanswered about why the men were divorcing their wives. Nevertheless, the passage never makes explicit this connection between intermarriage and divorce, and the rejected women are not explicitly identified as Jewish. The correct interpretation must maintain both the unity of vv. 11–15a and the distinctiveness of vv. 11–12 and 13–15a. It seems likely that the prophet had in mind the entire scenario of Jewish men abandoning their Jewish wives for pagan ones but that he wanted to condemn each aspect of this behavior separately since not all who were guilty of abandoning their wives were doing so for purposes of intermarriage (although all surely had remarriage in mind), and not all those who were intermarrying had to abandon wives to do so.

But why is the problem of divorce dealt with *after* the problem of intermarriage? Zehnder notes that whereas the paragraph on intermarriage uses "perfect" verb forms ("Judah *has broken faith*. A detestable thing *has been committed*"), the paragraph on divorce shifts to the "imperfect" with "Another thing you *do*." He may be right in suggesting this has an "intensifying effect" ('not only have you done that, but now you even do the second thing')." It is the problem of divorce that Malachi was especially concerned with.[99]

**2:13** The NIV rendering of v. 13 could suggest that Judah's objectionable behavior amounted to flooding the altar with tears, which some consider to have been part of a pagan ritual reintroduced into postexilic Judah (cf. Ezek 8:14).[100] But it is "the LORD's altar" rather than a pagan one that is in view. The claim that Judah was "practicing pagan-style worship" at the Lord's altar[101] would mean that the problem of divorce introduced in v. 14 was yet a

---

[97] So Von Orelli, *The Twelve Minor Prophets*, 397; Baldwin, *Haggai, Zechariah, Malachi*, 237; Hugenberger, *Marriage as a Covenant*, 98–100; Collins, "Marriage, Divorce, and Family," 124.

[98] Cf. Zehnder ("A Fresh Look at Malachi 2:13–16," 230), who also cites the agreement of C. F. Keil, H. G. Reventlow, J. M. P. Smith, P. A. Verhoef, and G. P. Hugenberger.

[99] Ibid., 231–32. He suggests one reason may be that Ezra/Nehemiah had "already denounced" the problem of mixed marriages.

[100] Most who interpret this section as directed against the reappearance of pagan cultic worship in Judah see here a reference to the ritual of weeping for Tammuz/Adonis/Baal. Cf. J. G. Matthews, "Tammuz Worship in the Book of Malachi," *Palestine Oriental Society Journal* 11 (1931): 42–50; Hvidberg, *Weeping and Laughter*, 121–22; Ahlström, *Joel and the Temple Cult of Jerusalem*, 49; Petersen, *Zechariah 9–14 and Malachi*, 201–2. Glazier-McDonald considers this verse to describe a second aspect of the intermarriage issue, in which the man is said to "bring his wife's cultic rites to Yahweh's altar" (*Malachi*, 99). But v. 13 clearly explains the reason for the weeping.

[101] Stuart, "Malachi," 1334.

*third* activity the prophet was condemning. Besides, as O'Brien has noted, "the people in 2:14a inquire of the reasons of His displeasure, a fact suggesting that their transgression has not yet been named."[102] The reply they receive says nothing about ritual weeping. The focus is on the betrayal of "the wife of your youth"; "a second thing" refers to the entirety of vv. 13–14.[103]

Contrary to the NIV, the first independent clause following the paragraph introduction is "you say," which is modified by a preceding adverbial clause, itself modified by a causal clause.[104] More literally it would be "covering with tears the altar of Yahweh, with weeping and groaning,[105] since there is no

---

[102] O'Brien, *Priest and Levite in Malachi*, 72. Glazier-McDonald illogically suggests that "although the question has already been answered—'because you served him with the wrong cult' (2:13)—, a second reason is tendered here" (*Malachi*, 100).

[103] Another problem with the view of Hvidberg and others is that if v. 13 referred to the pagan ritual of weeping at the death of a *god*, there would be an awkward switch from the surrounding verses that are claimed to concern worship of a pagan *goddess*. Although Zehnder argues for a third view, the weeping of the women victimized by the treacherous men, he acknowledges that the more common view supported here is legitimate and "cannot be totally dismissed." His main argument against this is that his view allows a more "sensible connection" to the introductory "This is a second thing you do." But this objection is negated by his view also requiring v. 13 be understood as "an intentional rhetorical device by which the drama of the situation is made more impressively visible" by reserving the actual accusation for v. 14 ("A Fresh Look at Malachi 2:13–16," 233).

[104] The infinitive construct כַּסּוֹת from כסה, "cover," is serving as if it were בְּכַסּוֹת or כְּכַסּוֹת, "when/while covering." On causal מִן see *IBHS* §11.2.11d. Petersen (et al.) reverses the causal sense and makes the Lord's unwillingness to accept the offering the result of the (ritual) weeping (*Zechariah 9–14 and Malachi*, 202). מֵאֵין is found twenty-eight times in the OT In twenty-five of these it is followed by a noun or substantival participle. In twenty-one cases it has a privative sense—e.g., "without inhabitant" (13x, e.g., Isa 5:9; 6:11; Clines [*Classical Hebrew Dictionary*, 1:217] identifies all of these as introducing a final clause, "so that there is not," but this sense is not required in any and in some it is a strain). In two cases NIV and NRSV translate "until there is no" (Jer 7:32; 19:11), although BDB, *HALOT*, and Clines identify these as causal uses, and RSV translates "because there is no." In two of the twenty-five it is clearly causal (Isa 50:2; Ezek 34:8). Of the remaining three uses of מֵאֵין one is here in 2:13 governing an adverb and an infinitive. The other two uses are in Jer 10:6–7 in the expression מֵאֵין כָּמוֹךָ, "there is no one like you." Clines lists Mal 2:13 as a causal use. BDB, 35 (also *HALOT*, 42, but with the alternative "because") identifies the use in 2:13 as final ("so that there is no"). Some emend מֵאֵין to מָאֵן, *piel* perfect of מאן, "refuse" (*HALOT*, 540; NEB). R. Althann emends to מֵאֵין, a "double emphatic negative" with the interrogative מָה. He translates the clause as giving the divine penalty for the weeping: "There will no longer be a turning to the gift" ("Malachy 2,13–14 and UT 125,12–13," 419–20).

[105] The noun אֲנָקָה from the root אנק is a synonym of the more frequent אֲנָחָה, "sighing, groaning" *(HALOT)* from the root אנח. The two verbs are used together in Ezek 9:4 (perhaps "moaning and groaning"). The noun אֲנָקָה occurs elsewhere only in Pss 12:6[5]; 79:11; 102:21 [20], and the verb אנק only in Jer 51:52; Ezek 9:4; 24:17; 26:15 (see also the metathesized נאק in Ezek 30:24; Job 24:12 and נְאָקָה in Exod 2:24; 6:5; Judg 2:18; Ezek 30:24). Like אנח and its derivative, the words represent the sounds of those who are full of pain, grief, and anguish due to injury, loss, or other distressing circumstances. Although the root אנק often refers to the distress of God's people, nowhere does it refer to pagan worship, despite Stuart's claim that "His use of the term *groaning (ʾănāqâ)* demonstrates that temple worship in the 460s B.C. went far beyond a simple (and acceptable) attitude of contrition. It was pagan worship, emphasizing manipulative mourning and misery (Hos. 7:14)" ("Malachi,' 1334). Weyde likewise asserts that in none of the passages where these terms occur (דִּמְעָה, "tears"; בְּכִי, "weeping"; אֲנָקָה, "groaning") "is there any indication that they refer to a ritual in the fertility cult" (*Prophecy and Teaching*, 250–51).

longer a turning[106] to the offering and accepting with pleasure from your hand,[107] you say, 'Upon what [basis]?'" The terse question, then, expresses Judah's complaint that the Lord was not accepting their offerings, which apparently represented prayers for help (cf. 1 Kgs 8:22,28–30//2 Chr 6:12,19–21; Isa 56:7). In Ps 6:6[Hb. 7] David declares, "I am worn out from groaning; all night long I flood my bed with weeping and drench my couch with tears." Then in v. 9[10] he rejoices that "the LORD has heard" his tearful repentance and "cry for mercy" and "*accepts* my prayer," although he does not indicate how he has learned of the Lord's gracious response, whether by a prophetic word or a divine act. The weeping and groaning of Malachi's contemporaries did not result as it should have from their repentance (cf. 1 Kgs 8:33–39//2 Chr 6:24–31; Pss 80; 126; Isa 22:12; Joel 1:13; 2:12–17) but from their grief or even anger at the Lord's refusal to accept their offerings (cf. Cain's response in Gen 4:4–5). We assume the manner of acceptance they were anticipating was the reversal of their difficult circumstances (cf. 3:11,14; Judg 2:18; Job 23:2; 24:12; Pss 6:6–10; 39:12; Jer 45:3; Lam 1:11). As so often occurs among those who claim to follow the Lord, they were complaining because the Lord was not meeting their demands. They never imagined that the failure was their own (compare the situation at the first battle of Ai in Josh 7).

This passage picks up from 1:6–14 the theme of useless offerings. The noun here rendered "pleasure" *(rāṣôn)* is from the same root *(rṣh)* as the verb rendered "be pleased with" in 1:8 and "accept" in 1:10,13. It is almost always used of God's pleasure (or lack of it), especially in certain offerings (e.g., Lev 1:3; 19:5; 22:19–21; Isa 56:7), human actions (Ps 19:14[Hb. 15]), or persons (Deut 33:16,23; Ps 5:12[Hb. 13]). It also refers to the divine will (Pss 103:21; 143:10; Ezra 10:11). If kings have the power to do what "pleases" them (Dan 8:4; 11:3), much more so does God. The opposite of God's "pleasure" would be his "anger" (cf. Pss 19:14[15]; 30:5[6]; Prov 19:12), and what was furthest removed from "pleasing" him was "detestable" to him (Prov 11:1,20; 12:22; 15:8). Whereas Judah had expected the Lord to receive their offerings "with pleasure," the offerings were actually detestable to him because Judah's behavior was "detestable" (v. 11; cf. Rom 8:8; 1 Thess 4:1; Heb 11:6). Malachi would echo the thought of Isa 58:3–10, where God charges (v. 3b), "on the day

---

[106] The NIV "pays attention to" renders the infinitive construct of פְּנָ, "turn," with the preposition אֶל, "to." This construction is also found with the meaning "respond to [usually with favor]" in Lev 26:9; Num 16:15; Deut 9:27; 2 Sam 9:8; 1 Kgs 8:28 // 2 Chr 6:19; 2 Kgs 13:23; Pss 25:16; 69:16[Hb. 17]; 86:16; 102:17[Hb. 18]; 119:132; Ezek 36:9.

[107] The NIV "accepts" translates the infinitive construct of לְקַח, "take, seize, accept." For the meaning "accept" cf. Ps 15:5. For the use with מִיַּד, "from the hand of," cf. 2 Kgs 5:20; Isa 40:2. The verb is used with the metaphorical sense of heeding instructions in Prov 2:1; 10:8. Verhoef states that "the *pleasure* of the Lord is the very *raison d'être* of every offering. When an offering is not accepted with pleasure, it fails in its intention to restore or affirm the communion with God" (*Haggai and Malachi*, 273).

of your fasting, you do as you please and exploit all your workers." God's people had not yet learned the lesson that religious activity in itself cannot please God (cf. Jer 6:20; 14:10–12; Hos 8:13; Amos 5:21–24). If it is used as a substitute for obedience, then like the manna that Israel disobediently kept until morning it begins to smell (Exod 16:20).

**2:14** The answer to the people's question and complaint is that the men have betrayed their wives. The striking characteristic of v. 14 is the skewed relationship between the grammatical and semantic structures in v. 14b. The answer to the question "Why?" (lit. "Upon what [basis]?") is expressed by three clauses: a causal clause (beginning with ʿal kî, "because"[108]) followed by a relative clause and then an adverbial clause. The clauses and the proposition expressed by each may be described as follows (author translation):

> Clause 1: *because Yahweh served as witness between you and the wife of your youth*
> Proposition 1: *Yahweh witnessed the covenant between you and "the wife of your youth."*
>
> Clause 2: *against whom you have acted treacherously*
> Proposition 2: *You acted treacherously against her.*
>
> Clause 3: *though she was your partner, even the wife of your covenant*
> Proposition 3: *She was your partner in that she was your wife by covenant*

What is apparently the primary answer to "Why?" is found not in the main initial clause but in the embedded relative clause introduced by the particle *ʾăšer,* "who, which" (NIV, "because").[109] The men of Judah (or some of them; assuming a collective singular "you") are guilty of treachery. The third clause, the adverbial (concessive, "though") clause, elaborates upon the second: the reason the men's behavior can be called treachery is that their wives had entered a covenant with them. The assumption is that the men have violated that covenant.

To the initial argument in v. 10 that one's wife was a spiritual sibling, a member of the covenant community of Israel, the third clause adds that these wives had allied themselves with their husbands by a marriage covenant. The feminine word rendered "partner" *(ḥăberet/ḥăbērâ)* occurs only here in the Old Testament, but its masculine counterpart *(ḥābēr)* occurs a dozen times. Sometimes it refers only to a "friend, companion" (e.g., Song 1:7; 8:13), but it could also point to a closer relationship sometimes involving an agreement or covenant. In Judg 20:11 it is used of a representative group of men from the tribes of Israel who were united by a commitment to avenge a vile act of immorality. It is also used of tribal unity in Ezek 37:16,19. In Eccl 4:10 it refers to

---

[108] Cf. *IBHS* §38.4a. Note that as in 1:7 the answer to the question under consideration is given in a subordinate clause dependent on the information given in the question.

[109] Although אֲשֶׁר can mean "because," its much more common use as a relative makes perfect sense here. The clause אֲשֶׁר אַתָּה בָּגַדְתָּה בָּהּ, "against whom you acted treacherously," is missing in 4QXIIᵃ (see R. Fuller, "Text-Critical Problems in Malachi 2:10–16," *JBL* 110 [1991]: 52). But it is found in all other textual witnesses, and the question of v. 14 goes unanswered without it.

business partners (cf. Prov 28:24; Isa 1:23; 44:11; also cf. the related word *ḥabbār,* "guildsman," in Job 41:6 [Hb. 40:30]). The root also occurs as a verb meaning "bind, associate" (e.g., Gen 14:3; Exod 26:3; 28:7; 2 Chr 20:35–37; Dan 11:6,23) and occurs in *Sir* 7:25 meaning "marry."[110] Although the designation of a wife as a "partner" does not negate the subjection of her marital role to that of her husband, it certainly counters the concept that she was to be viewed as a mere possession to be disposed of at will.[111] Though more than a friend or companion, she was not to be regarded as less than that.

The nature of the "partnership" is defined further by the appositional phrase (lit.) "the wife of your covenant." Hugenberger has argued soundly for the traditional view that the covenant referred to here is the marriage covenant and not the national covenant of v. 10; he renders it "your wife by covenant."[112] He presents five initial arguments: (1) Malachi uses the term "covenant" variously, speaking of God's covenant with Israel in 2:10 and perhaps 3:1, and of his covenant with Levi in 2:4–5,8; (2) the LORD is said to be a "witness" (cf. Gen 31:44–50) of this covenant, not a covenant partner; (3) the term designating the wife a "partner," with which the phrase is in apposition, is from a root that "frequently designates persons who have come into association by an agreement or contract";[113] (4) the expression translated "break faith with" suggests infidelity against a covenant partner (although, as he admits, the covenant partner can be the Lord; cf. Jer 3:20); and (5) in expressions parallel to "wife of your covenant," the covenant is always between the governing noun ("wife" in this case) and the genitive noun or pronoun ("your" in this case): "keepers of his covenant" in Pss 25:10; 103:18, "possessors of Abram's covenant" in Gen 14:13, and "men of your covenant" in Obad 7.[114] Other Old Testament passages that

---

[110] See also H. Cazelles, "חָבַר *chābhar,*" *TDOT* 4:193–97; M. O'Connor, "Northwest Semitic Designations for Elective Social Affinities," *JANESCU* 18 (1986): 73–80; P. Kallaveettil, *Declaration and Covenant: A Comprehensive Review of Covenant Formulae from the Old Testament and the Ancient Near East,* AnBib 88 (Rome: Biblical Institute, 1982), 51–53.

[111] See Zehnder, "Fresh Look at Malachi 2:13–16," 236.

[112] Hugenberger, *Marriage as a Covenant,* esp. 27–30. Contra Milgrom and others who deny that marriage was viewed as a covenant in the OT (e.g., id., *Cult and Conscience: The Asham and the Priestly Doctrine of Repentance* [Leiden: Brill, 1976], 134; M. Greenberg, *Ezekiel 1–20,* AB [New York: Doubleday, 1983], 278).

[113] Hugenberger elaborates: "There are no cases where fellow Israelites are designated with the term חָבַר (verbal or nominal forms) merely on the basis of their mutual involvement in Yahweh's covenant with Israel" (*Marriage as a Covenant,* 28; contra van der Woude, "Malachi's Struggle," 68).

[114] Against Isaksson's claim (*Marriage and Ministry,* 31) that "marriage was not a compact entered into by man, wife and Yahweh as witness but a matter of commercial negotiation between two men [husband and father-in-law]" (see also S. L. McKenzie and H. N. Wallace, "Covenant Themes in Malachi," *CBQ* 45 [1983]: 553), Glazier-McDonald notes that covenants could be established between any two entities including man and wife (cf. Ezek 16:8; Prov 2:17). She also notes that "although a written marriage contract is not attested in the OT, both Greengus and de Vaux maintain that since bills of sale and divorce (Deut 24:1f; Jer 3:8; Isa 50:1) were written up, it would be surprising if contracts of marriage did not exist at the same time" (*Malachi,* 102–3; S. Greengus, "The Aramaic Marriage Contracts in the Light of the Ancient Near East and the Later Jewish Materials" [master's thesis, University of Chicago, 1959] 116; R. de Vaux, *Ancient Israel,* 2 vols. [New York: McGraw-Hill, 1965], 1:33).

explicitly indicate the marriage relationship was covenantal are Prov 2:17;
Ezek 16:8,59–62; Hos 2:16–20.[115]

The first clause expresses the proposition that the Lord had served as witness of these marriage covenants. Although Judah's treachery, the topic of the
second clause, modifying "the wife of your youth," is the primary answer to the
question why the Lord was not responding to Judah's offerings, the first clause
explains why their actions were an affront to God: he had acted as witness to
that covenant.[116] What is logically the third proposition is the one the author
chose to spotlight by placing it first and by syntactically subordinating the
other two propositions to it. The phrase "the wife of your youth" in itself
heightens the heinousness of the treachery since it implies a long history of the
wives' faithfulness to their husbands (cf. 1 Sam 17:33; Ps 71:5; Prov 2:16–17;
5:18; Isa 54:6; Jer 3:4; Joel 1:8; Zech 13:5).[117] Like a river rushing down a
mountain, fed by many streams, such extended faithfulness creates a logical
and ethical force against which to respond with treachery requires a determination of sin that would rival a salmon's fight to return to its spawning ground.

Hugenberger draws four significant implications from the fact that marriage
was viewed as a covenant between husband and wife formed before the Lord:

> 1) First, if a covenant existed between a husband and his wife, any offence against the
> marriage by either the husband or the wife may be identified as sin . . ., perfidy . . ., or infi-
> delity . . . against the other.
>
> 2) Second, if a covenant existed between a husband and his wife, because God is
> invoked in any covenant-ratifying oath to act as guarantor of the covenant, any marital
> offence by either the husband or the wife may be identified as sin . . . against God.

---

[115] See Hugenberger's discussion of these passages and of others that point to a marriage covenant (*Marriage as a Covenant,* 294–312). He also argues that 1 Sam 18–20 offers "a narrative
analogy between David's covenant with Jonathan and David's (marriage) covenant with Michal"
(pp. 311–12). G. E. Mendenhall and G. A. Herion also observe that in Malachi "Yahweh is explicitly acknowledged to be a (third-party) 'witness' between the two parties of the marriage, and there
are clear allusions to (violated) obligations and to resultant curses (2:13). As we have seen, these
elements also appear in LB suzerainty treaties" ("Covenant: 2. Marriage as a Covenant," in *ABD*
1.1179–1202). For examples of fifth century B.C. Jewish marriage covenants see B. Porten and
J. C. Greenfield, eds., *Jews of Elephantine and Arameans of Syene: Aramaic Texts with Translation*
(Jerusalem: Hebrew University, 1974), 114–19.

[116] On the Lord as covenant witness see Judg 11:10; 1 Sam 12:5; 20:23,42; Jer 29:23; 42:5; Mic
1:2; Rom 1:9; 2 Cor 1:23; 1 Thess 2:5; Rev 3:14.

[117] This is supported by the emphatic אַתָּה, yielding "against whom *you* have acted unfaithfully." T. T. Perowne cites "the binding force of years since spent together in intimate companion-
ship" (*Malachi, with Notes and Introduction,* CBSC [Cambridge: University Press, 1890], 26). R.
Hayward summarizes Jerome's interpretation that "the returned exiles had put away their Jewish
wives who were tired, jaded, weak, and deformed as a result of the long journey home from exile,
and had taken instead the fresh, young and attractive Gentile women whom they found living
around Jerusalem" ("Saint Jerome and the Aramaic Targumim," *JSS* 32 [1987]: 117). Hugenberger
wisely rejects the suggestion that the phrase "wife of your youth" gives the motive of divorce as
the lost beauty of their wives (*Marriage as a Covenant,* 103).

3) Third, . . . any marital infidelity ought to prompt God's judgment against the offending party.

4) Finally, . . . intermarriage with pagans ought to be prohibited because idolatry would necessarily ensue when a ratifying oath is sworn.[118]

Judah's behavior was an insult and outrage against the God before whom they had formed their covenants. As in the covenant between Jacob and Laban in Gen 31:50, the Lord being witness meant that he would act as "judge" (note v. 53) to ensure that if the covenant was violated the guilty party would be punished (also see Mal 3:5): "If you mistreat my daughters or if you take any wives besides my daughters, even though no one is with us, remember that God is a witness between you and me."[119] Not only does the Lord appear here in his role of Defender of the defenseless and Helper of the helpless, invisible but powerful witness of every injustice, but he also watches over covenants made before him and judges those who break vows. Since it involved breaking oaths sworn before the Lord, these men's treatment of their wives was also another act by which Judah was defaming the God of Israel, like the insulting sacrifices described in 1:6–14.

**2:15a** Many would concur with J. M. P. Smith's assessment that the beginning of this verse in the Hebrew text "is hopelessly obscure."[120] Kruse-Blinkenberg considers the best solution is "to put some dots instead of a translation and to make a note: Unintelligible."[121] Although these may be overstatements of the difficulties, the situation is such that any interpretation and translation must be understood to be tentative. The following necessarily tedious discussion will lead to a conclusion that may be expressed by the following paraphrase: "Don't you know that God made you one with your wives?

---

[118] Hugenberger, *Marriage as a Covenant*, 281–82. He then presents evidence that the Bible itself draws these implications (pp. 282–94).

[119] See also Zeph 3:8. In Gen 31 the concurrence of a marriage and a covenant between husband and father-in-law should not be taken as paradigmatic. The covenant between Jacob and Laban here was not the marriage covenant itself, which was between husband and wife. Nevertheless, one might regard as a corollary of the marriage covenant a husband's responsibility to the wife's family faithfully to care for his wife. At least in a practical sense divorce often involves a breach between two families as well as between a husband and wife.

[120] J. M. P. Smith, *Malachi*, 54. After citing a few of the various interpretations including some involving emendation, he concluded, "No satisfactory solution of the problem of this verse has yet been found" (p. 55). Torrey also wrote that vv. 15–16 are "hopelessly corrupt" ("Prophecy of Malachi," 10, n. 20). Hvidberg has asserted that "nothing definite can be said about Verses 15 and 16, the text being completely unintelligible" (*Weeping and Laughter in the Old Testament*, 123). Isaksson agrees and continues, "When scholars construe from them that Yahweh hates divorces or that the purpose of marriage is to procreate children, they can only do so, as I have already pointed out, by resorting to quite arbitrary emendation of the text" (*Marriage and Ministry*, 34).

[121] Kruse-Blinkenberg, "Peshitta," 102. He notes that although the Peshitta tends to "make obscure passages of the MT understandable," here "P seems to be almost as obscure as MT." He translates the version "why is [?was?] there not a man?; and the rest of his spirits; this [?] one sought seed from God."

And in spite of your treachery in divorcing your wives, there is still a remnant
of that spiritual bond. And what is the purpose of that oneness? It is to produce
godly offspring with God's help."

A literal rendering would be "And not one [he] did/made, and a remnant of
spirit [is/was?] to him [i.e., "and he has/had a remnant of spirit"]. And what [is/
was] the one? Seeking seed of God." The difficulties here suggest to many the
likelihood of textual corruption.[122] As it stands, the syntactical and exegetical
problems are legion. Is "one" (ʾeḥād) in the first clause the subject or object (or
predicate adjective) of "did/made" (ʿāśâ)? Does it refer back to ʾeḥād in v. 10?
If it is the subject, what is the understood object (perhaps "it," "her," or
"them")? Does "one" refer to God (or to Adam or Abraham,[123] especially if
"one father" in v. 10 refers to one of these) or to the marital relationship of
v. 14 (perhaps alluding to Gen 2:24) or to the one guilty of unfaithfulness (noting similarities to the curse in v. 12, especially "to the man who does it")? Or
is it pronominal with lōʾ, "not," with the sense "no one" (cf. Job 14:4)? If "one"
is the object, who is the understood subject of the verb? Does the verb ʿāśâ here
mean "do" or "make"? Is the clause a statement (e.g., "And no one did [it]" or
"And he did not make one") or a question (e.g., "And did he not make [them]
one?")? In the second clause is the "spirit" (rûaḥ) here human or divine? If
human does it refer to spiritual insight or creative power? Does the pronoun
"him" refer back to "one" or to the subject of "did/made" (if that is different)
or to someone or something else? How is this second clause related to the first
(adjectival modifying ʾeḥād or concessive ["although . . ."])? Should "seeking"
(mĕbaqqēš) be read (against the massoretic accentuation) with the previous
words ("what is the one seeking") or the following words ("seeking seed of
God")? Does "the one" (hāʾeḥād) have the same referent as "one" at the beginning of the verse (i.e., God, Adam, Abraham, the guilty person, etc.), or does it
refer to someone or something else? What relationship does "of God" have to
"seed"?[124] Attributive ("godly seed") or source ("seed from God")? The

---

[122] Baldwin states, "Here the text becomes difficult, having suffered perhaps at the hand of
scribes who took exception to its teaching" (*Haggai, Zechariah, Malachi,* 240). Cf. also L. Kruse-
Blinkenberg, "The Book of Malachi according to Codex Syro-Hexaplaris Ambrosianus," *ST* 21
(1967): 79.

[123] Tg. identifies both occurrences of "one" in the verse as Abraham (cf. Isa 51:2; Ezek 33:24),
who sought "that offspring should be established for him from the Lord." Gordon explains the
probable background for this view as the tradition mentioned by Rashi and Kimchi that the prophet
was responding to an objection pointing to Abraham's relationship with Hagar: he was only trying
to fulfill God's promise of an heir (K. J. Cathcart and R. P. Gordon, *The Targum of the Minor
Prophets,* The Aramaic Bible, vol. 14 [Wilmington/Edinburgh: Michael Glazier, 1989], 234). Jerome also identifies the "one" as Abraham, citing Isa 51:2 (R. Hayward, "Saint Jerome and the Aramaic Targumim," *JSS* 32 (1987): 117–18). See Zehnder's explanation and refutation of the view
that identifies הָאֶחָד with Abraham ("Fresh Look at Malachi 2:13–16," 237–38).

[124] Rudolph would insert כְּרַע, "according to the will of," between זֶרַע, "seed," and אֱלֹהִים,
"God," but with no manuscript support (*Haggai-Sacharja 1–8/9–14-Maleachi,* 270).

almost limitless multiplicity of interpretations of this verse result from the various combinations of answers to these many questions.[125] Even more interpretations result from various proposals for emending the verse.[126]

Nevertheless, if our structural analysis is correct, v. 15a serves as the final expression of the situation addressed in this second discourse, describing the reprehensible nature of Judah's behavior that needed correction to avoid God's judgment threatened in 3:1–6. Whatever the specific content of this text portion, it should lead to the command in 2:15b–16 to "guard . . . your spirit" and remain faithful to "the wife of your youth."

The two most widely held interpretations (or family of interpretations) involve (1) considering *'eḥād*, "one," as the pronominal subject of its clause, or (2) considering it a predicate referring to the divinely intended oneness of the marriage relationship. Verhoef, advocating the first option, translates: "No one with a residue of spirit [sound judgment] would act that way. What does the one [someone with sound judgment] do? He is seeking godly offspring."[127] Such an interpretation is contextual and avoids the temptation of emending the text. It is not, however, without difficulties. For example, Hugenberger has demonstrated that no example of *lō'* ("not") + *'eḥād* "offers clear support for the pronominal rendering posited for Mal. 2:15." In all the clauses where the two words both occur, "the numerical sense of 'one' is clearly prominent."[128]

A second difficulty is that Verhoef understands the first clause to be demonstrative because it contains no indication that it is interrogative.[129] Such an

---

[125] van der Woude remarks: "Mal. 2:15 is one of the most difficult passages of the whole Old Testament. It would be a hopeless task to record all the attempts that have been made to explain this verse" ("Malachi's Struggle," 69).

[126] E.g., reading הֲלֹא, "did not?" rather than וְלֹא, "and not" (Wellhausen, *Die kleinen Propheten*, 240; Sellin, *Das Zwölfprophetenbuch*, 605); שְׁאֵר(וֹ), "(and) flesh," rather than וּשְׁאָר, "and a remnant of" (Sellin; Rudolph, *Haggai-Sacharja 1–8/9–14-Maleachi*, 270; Baldwin, *Haggai, Zechariah, Malachi*, 240); and אַחֵר, "another," in place of אֶחָד, "one," and/or הָאֶחָד, "the one," on the basis of the LXX ἄλλος/ἄλλο. Fuller argues from line length that the lacuna in 2:15 of 4QXII[a] between וּשְׁאָר and הָאֶחָד probably contained the word וַאֲמַרְתֶּם, "but you say," after לְ, "to him" (see LXX καὶ εἴπατε), but that "both witnesses are attempting to understand a disturbed text" ("Text-Critical Problems," 53–4).

[127] Verhoef, *Haggai and Malachi*, 262. See also Schreiner, "Mischehen-Ehebruch-Ehescheidung. Betrachtungen zu Mal 2,10–16," 216–17. Shields similarly translates, "But no one doing this has any integrity" ("Syncretism and Divorce," 76). Zehnder's translation of the text as it stands is similar: "And no one, who has done this, has a remnant of spirit. But what does the One require? a godly seed!" ("Fresh Look at Malachi 2:13–16," 241).

[128] Hugenberger, *Marriage as a Covenant*, 130. He also notes that "in the vast majority of instances when an OT author intends to say 'no one' with some verb in the perfect, this is accomplished by employing אִישׁ + לֹא + perfect . . . or more simply לֹא + perfect . . . or even לֹא + third person plural perfect."

[129] Verhoef, *Haggai and Malachi*, 276.

indication, however, is not always necessary.[130] Most consider Mal 1:8 to contain (twice) an unmarked interrogative clause: "Is that not wrong?" Also, the interrogative clause "and what is the one . . .?" can be viewed as parallel.

A third difficulty with Verhoef's view is that he understands "spirit" as "intelligence, sound judgment," citing Num 27:18; Deut 34:9; Josh 5:1; 1 Kgs 10:5; and Isa 19:3. In other words, "the person who seeks a godly offspring has spiritual insight and does not violate the marriage as a divine institution. Such a person will not send his legal wife away in order to marry a heathen girl, because he has consideration for the elevated character and purpose of marriage." Such a person understands his responsibility to the covenant to "procreate citizens not only for the kingdom of Israel but above all for the kingdom of God."[131] Although the meaning "intelligence, sound judgment" is a possibility for *rûaḥ* in Num 27:18 and Deut 34:9, it does not easily fit the other passages he cites (see, however, Gen 41:38; Job 32:8; Isa 11:2).[132] Without some clue to the contrary we would expect the presence of "spirit" to indicate not wisdom but life.[133]

A fourth problem is with the interpretation of *hāʾeḥād*, "the one." As van der Woude explains, "It is unlikely that the author of the verse could refer to 'no one' by 'that one.' "[134] A final problem with *ʾeḥād* being the subject is that one must supply an object ["that way'] for the transitive verb *ʿāśâ*, "do, make."[135]

---

[130] See GKC §150a; *GBH* §161a. Hugenberger notes that "the word order of an unmarked interrogative verbal clause is frequently inverted," as is Mal 2:15 (whether אֶחָד is subject or object), and "in every case there is a passionate rhetorical character to the unmarked interrogative with the expected answer never in doubt" (*Marriage as a Covenant,* 146). He agrees with H. G. Mitchell's definitive study that "the purposeful omission of the interrogative ה lends to the clause an element of incredulity, sarcasm, or irony" ("The Omission of the Interrogative Particle," in *Old Testament and Semitic Studies in Memory of William Rainey Harper,* vol. 1 [Chicago: University of Chicago, 1908]: 115–29). Hugenberger also observes (*Marriage as a Covenant,* 147) that an interrogative sense for the first clause of Mal 2:15 is supported by the major versions (LXX, Peshitta, Tg., Vg).

[131] Verhoef, *Haggai and Malachi,* 277.

[132] Shields points out that BDB has a category "moral character" for רוּחַ and cites Isa 57:15; 66:2; Ps 32:2; Prov 11:13 ("Syncretism and Divorce," 81). But none of these support the translation "integrity" he proposes for the word in Mal 2:15.

[133] H. W. Wolff explains רוּחַ, "spirit, wind, breath" especially as man's vital power (derived from God), that which animates his physical and emotional life, empowering him for effectiveness (*Anthropology of the Old Testament* [Philadelphia: Fortress, 1974], 32–39). E.g., see Judg 3:10; 15:19; Job 34:14–15; Ps 146:4; Isa 42:5. Hugenberger also argues (*Marriage as a Covenant,* 135) that this meaning also would be inconsistent with the use of רוּחַ in vv. 15b,16 (lit. "so keep watch over your spirit"), but as we will see consistency here is not really necessary.

[134] van der Woude, "Malachi's Struggle," 69.

[135] This is also a problem for Petersen's interpretation that considers אֶחָד and הָאֶחָד as both referring to God. He treats the problematic וּשְׁאָר רוּחַ as being in apposition to the unexpressed object of עָשָׂה, translating, "Has not (the) One made (us), his vigorous remnant? What is the One seeking but a godly progeny?" (*Zechariah 9–14 and Malachi,* 194).

Glazier-McDonald likewise interprets *lō' 'eḥād* as pronominal; but she emphasizes a contrast with v. 10 and interprets *rûaḥ* as the ability to procreate: Whereas God exercises his creative power sovereignly and independently, man's ability to procreate is derivative, coming to him from God. No one who intermarries (i.e., commits the sin under discussion) will retain the power to procreate, that is, to obtain "seed of [i.e., from] God." She translates the verse (with interpretative glosses) as follows: "And not one does it (intermarries) and has a remnant of spirit (reproductive potential). And what is the one seeking? A seed of (given by) God? So, if you value your creative ability, be on your guard and do not deal deceitfully with the wife of your youth."[136] This interpretation has many of the same problems as Verhoef's. In addition, the expression "has a remnant of spirit" is an unlikely way to refer to the ability to produce offspring. The word "remnant" seems to have no meaning in such an expression unless it refers to the ability to produce *additional* children, an idea completely missing from the context. Although God's "spirit" is elsewhere said to impart life (Gen 1:2; 6:3 [NRSV]; Ps 104:29–30; Eccl 12:7), power, and ability (mental or physical; Gen 41:38; Exod 31:3; 35:31; Num 11:17,25; Deut 34:9; Judg 3:10; 6:34; 11:29), and the condition of a person's "spirit" can describe his emotional and physical health (Gen 45:27), nowhere else is it associated with "man's reproductive potential."[137] From the use of *rûaḥ* elsewhere, the most likely sense of the expression that one "has a remnant of spirit" would be that he remains alive.

An entirely different (and preferable) interpretative path is taken by those who consider *'eḥād*, "one," in the initial clause to be part of the predicate and the Lord (from v. 14) to be the understood subject of *'āśâ*, "make." The verse would allude then to Gen 2:24 and the original divine intention for marriage.[138] As v. 10 argues filial unity against treachery on the basis of God's covenant with Israel at Sinai, so here Malachi more pointedly argues against marital treachery on the basis of the marital "one flesh" relationship, which was set forth in the account of the original paradigmatic couple.[139] Some further consider the second clause as concessive ("although. . . "), with *rûaḥ*, "spirit,"

---

[136] Glazier-McDonald, *Malachi,* 109.

[137] In some cases one's "spirit" is said to determine his will and the direction of his life and actions (Num 14:24; Deut 2:30; Judg 9:23).

[138] See the extended discussion of this allusion and of the paradigmatic nature of Adam and Eve's marriage in Hugenberger, *Marriage as a Covenant,* 148–67. But note Shields' rejection of this allusion in "Syncretism and Divorce," 79–80 (though he exaggerates the difficulties).

[139] See N. Lohfink, "אֶחָד," and N. P. Bratsiotis, "בָּשָׂר," *TDOT;* W. Neuer, *Man and Woman in Christian Perspective* (London: Hodder & Stoughton, 1990). These see "one flesh" as the bondedness produced and expressed by the sexual union. Hugenberger argues on the basis of the Bible's use of בָּשָׂר as a kinship term (e.g., Gen 29:14; 37:27; Lev 18:6; 25:49; 2 Sam 5:1; Isa 58:7) rather that it "refers to the establishment of a new family unit," i.e., "the familial bondedness of marriage which finds its quintessential expression in sexual union" (*Marriage as a Covenant,* 162–63).

referring to God's ability to create other wives for Adam, and the antecedent of the pronoun in *lô,* "to him/it" to refer to the Lord. W. C. Kaiser, for example, translates, "Did not he [God] make them one?—even though he had the residue of the spirit [i.e., "enough creative power in reserve"; presumably "to supply many partners"]. So why only one [partner]? Because he was seeking godly offspring."[140] But Hugenberger correctly points out that this interpretation would only make sense if the issue in the context were polygyny (multiple wives) rather than divorce and the permanence of the marriage bond, clearly the concern of vv. 14 and 16. Polygyny is nowhere mentioned in the paragraph, which in fact assumes that Malachi's contemporaries were monogamous. Furthermore, Hugenberger notes that such an interpretation would virtually require the feminine form *ʾaḥat,* "one," referring to Eve, rather than the masculine *ʾeḥād,* referring to the marital "one flesh" relationship.[141]

Hugenberger, on the other hand, considers the second clause to describe the "one flesh" relationship of the marriage "between you and the wife of your youth" in v. 14. The pronoun, he says, refers not to God but to "one." He thus translates, "Did He not make [you/them] one, with a remnant of the spirit belonging to it? And what was the One[142] seeking? A godly seed! Therefore watch out for your lives and do not act faithlessly against the wife of your youth."[143] He considers "spirit" to refer to "the spirit of God which resides in man" (cf. Num 11:25a, "Then the LORD . . . took some of the spirit that was on him [Moses] and put it on the seventy elders") but perhaps at the same time "the breath of life." He seems to favor the view that the clause is "an implied threat of being completely deprived of 'life-spirit,'" perhaps alluding to Gen 6:3, "where God determined that his holy life-giving spirit would not continue to strive with [or "abide in," NRSV with the LXX] mankind . . . as a result of the marital infractions described in that context." So in Malachi "men who have similarly transgressed have only a residue of his spirit . . ., which now they must guard."[144]

Some would emend the second clause, as in the NIV, based on the similarity of *šěʾār,* "remnant," to *šěʾēr,* "flesh." Although the words differ only in a vowel, the emendation usually also involves moving the conjunction from its position prefixed to *šěʾār* to the following word, *rûaḥ,* "spirit," producing

---

[140] W. C. Kaiser, Jr., *Malachi: God's Unchanging Love* (Grand Rapids: Baker, 1984), 139.

[141] Hugenberger, *Marriage as a Covenant,* 132–33.

[142] Note this interpretation considers הָאֶחָד, "the one," to refer to God, whereas אֶחָד, "one," refers to the marital relationship. Hugenberger does not consider this aspect essential, however, to his overall interpretation (ibid., 134).

[143] Ibid., 133.

[144] Ibid., 136–37. Zehnder charges that in Hugenberger's view the clause translated "with a remnant of the spirit belonging to it" "lacks any real sense." He also charges that the connection to Gen 6:3 is too tenuous to be plausible ("A Fresh Look at Malachi 2:13–16," 239).

"flesh and spirit belonging to him/it."[145] The versions, however, which differ at several points from the MT, all reflect the MT *šĕʾār*, "remnant." It is preferable, then, to follow the MT reading if sense can be made of it, which Hugenberger's interpretation manages to do, at least in part, although he admits that "the expression ["the remnant of the spirit"] is problematic on virtually every interpretation."[146]

One problem with Hugenberger's interpretation of the second clause is that if *rûaḥ* refers to the threatened "life-spirit" of the men who were violating the marriage covenant, would not a second person pronoun fit better—"with a remnant of spirit belonging to *you*"? If as seems likely the third person *lô* ("to it") refers back to the marriages that were being dissolved, then the function of the "spirit" in view was in giving life not to the men but to their marriages, witnessing to the union and filling them with the divine presence. What may be in view, then, is not a threat but a reality that was being neglected. Marriage is not only a union of flesh that can be dissolved but one of the divine Spirit, who "remained," maintaining a unity that survived human efforts to sever it. I would translate v. 15a, "Did He not make [you] one [with your wives], (and a remnant of that Spirit-created unity [still] belongs to the relationship)." That is, in spite of the men's treachery there was yet a remnant of the spiritual bond.

The following clause according to this interpretation is a rhetorical question asking about the nature or purpose of that oneness.[147] This is in accordance with the massoretic tradition that groups *mĕbaqqēš*, "seeking," with the following clause,[148] and it also considers both uses of *ʾeḥād* in the verse to refer to marital oneness. The answer to the question is given in terms of fruitfulness. The nature or purpose of marital unity is "seeking seed of [i.e.,

---

[145] According to Hugenberger (*Marriage as a Covenant*, 132) this was first proposed by A. van Hoonacker (*Les douze petits prophètes* [Paris: Gabalda, 1908], 726, 728), who translated, "Did he not make 'them' to be a single [being], which has its flesh [and] its life? And what does this unique [being] seek? A posterity for God! Therefore take care of your life, - And 'do not be' faithless to the wife of your youth." See also J. J. Collins, "Marriage, Divorce, and Family," 126.

[146] Hugenberger, 134.

[147] The article with הָאֶחָד, "the one," is thus an article of previous reference. The word מָה, which the NIV translates "why?" almost always means "what?" Hugenberger finds only seventeen times of 554 occurrences that it means "why?"—and never in a verbless clause (*Marriage as a Covenant*, 139). Also see his discussion (pp. 137–38) and rejection of a proposed emendation that supplies a supposed original "and you say" before this question, yielding, "And you say, 'what does he desire?'"

[148] Note the NIV follows the MT cantillation in interpreting 2:15 but considers God the understood subject of the participle מְבַקֵּשׁ, "seeking." Hugenberger points out that "it is extremely rare in Hebrew to elide the pronominal subject of a participle. . . . The single other example in Malachi, namely 2:9, differs significantly from the present case" (*Marriage as a Covenant*, 139).

"from"] God."[149] Concluding the description of the situation here with a reference to the importance of a godly seed points ahead to the book's conclusion where a relational revival is predicted in the eschatological future, with "the hearts of the fathers" turning to their children and "the hearts of the children" turning to their fathers (4:6).

Too often do contemporary married couples think of children as an option; they regard their own personal happiness or fulfillment as the primary goal in marriage. This was never to be the case according to the biblical revelation. The first divine command given to the first human couple was to "be fruitful and increase in number; fill the earth and subdue it" (Gen 1:28). God intended that a man's purpose in departing from his father and mother and in joining himself to a wife by covenant, thus becoming one with her in flesh (Gen 2:24), should be fruitfulness.[150] By that means were God's people to spread his rule throughout the whole earth, producing and discipling children who would manifest the divine glory in their obedient lives and continue the process until the earth was full of his glory (Gen 22:17). Although sin interfered with the process, the purpose has not been superseded. Although couples can no longer be assured of bearing children (as the theme of barrenness in Genesis makes clear), they are still to "seek" them and can reproduce themselves in other ways if necessary, through adoption and/or spiritual discipleship.

Malachi's contemporaries, however, like many modern couples, had disregarded their divine responsibilities. The men, engrossed in their own selfish goals, were seemingly interested in acquiring wives they could use to achieve them. Certainly "marrying the daughter of a foreign god" (v. 11) was not the way to "seek seed of God."

A paraphrase of 2:10–15a may help to summarize our comments on this difficult section:

> Do we covenant members not all have the same Father? Did not one God create us? Why then are we acting treacherously against one another and so violating and desecrating the covenant God made with our fathers at Sinai, by which he constituted us one people of faith? In the first place the men of Judah are committing an abomination that has desecrated God's holy and beloved dwelling place among us: they are introducing into this people of

---

[149] "Godly seed/offspring," as with the NIV, is equally possible, but reference to God as "Father" in 2:10 would favor "seed of God." The use of זֶרַע, "seed," for "children," could be because of the context of Gen 1, where זֶרַע occurs three times, but it is more likely because of its use of the redemptive "seed" in Gen 3:15 (cf. also 4:25) and in God's covenants of grace with mankind (Gen 9:9; 12:7; 13:15–16; 15:5,18; 17:7–10). Note also the use of זֶרַע הַקֹּדֶשׁ, "seed of holiness," in Ezra 9:2 and זֶרַע יִשְׂרָאֵל, "seed of Israel," in Neh 9:2. The meanings of "seed from God" and "godly seed" would overlap, since what one seeks from God are children of grace (John 1:12–13; 3:3–8; 1 John 5:1,4; see the discussion in Hugenberger, *Marriage as a Covenant,* 140–41).

[150] It may not be insignificant in this regard how often biblical references to marriage are immediately followed by references to childbirth. E.g., Gen 38:2–5; Exod 2:1–2; 6:20,23,25; Ruth 4:13; 2 Sam 5:13; 1 Chr 2:19,21; 4:18; 2 Chr 11:20; Jer 29:6; Hos 1:3,6,8.

faith the destructive element of paganism by marrying women who worship foreign gods. Do they think they can do this and continue to bring offerings to the Lord of hosts, pretending that all is well? Make no mistake about it. The Lord will obliterate from the habitations of Israel even the memory of any man who does such a thing. What is more, you are acting treacherously against the wives of your youth, your partners, who are your wives by covenant. Then you whine and complain because the Lord is not responding to your prayers and offerings. Don't you know he acted as witness to those marital covenants you have broken? Do you think there will be no consequences? And don't you know that he made you *one* with your wives? And in spite of your treachery in putting away your wives, there is still a remnant of that spiritual bond. And what is the nature and purpose of that oneness? It is to seek a godly seed from God.

## 3. Command: Stop Acting Unfaithfully (2:15b–16)

**So guard yourself in your spirit, and do not break faith with the wife of your youth.**
**[16]"I hate divorce," says the LORD God of Israel, "and I hate a man's covering himself with violence as well as with his garment," says the LORD Almighty.**
**So guard yourself in your spirit, and do not break faith.**

**2:15b–16**   The beginning and end of the command section is marked by commands not to "break faith" (on *bāgad* see comments on 2:10b), each of which is preceded by instructions to "guard yourself in your spirit." Inside this "envelope structure" are two clauses, each of which is punctuated by a divine quotation formula. Like the paraphrase in the command section of the first address in 1:10, this repetitive structure marks the turning point of the chiastic second address. The following more literal translation serves to clarify the structure:

a—So *you shall be on guard* in your spirit,
  b—and with the wife of your youth let him not *act faithlessly*.[151]
    c—If he hates so as to divorce,[152]

---

[151] Some have emended the MT on the basis of the versions to avoid the confusion of person in this clause, either changing the verb to second person (with the LXX, *Tg. Jon,* Vg, and a few Hb. MSS) or the pronominal suffix on "youth" to third person (Peshitta). But Hugenberger correctly points out that such person shifts apparently did not bother the native Hb. speakers as they do us (*Marriage as a Covenant,* 142–43; cf. GKC §144p). Note esp. his point: "It is only on the assumption of the originality of the MT, which has both second and third person references in tension, that a reasonable account can be given for the simpler uniform third person reference of the Peshitta as well as the simpler uniform second person reference of the LXX, Targum Jonathan, and Vulgate" (similarly Fuller, "Text-Critical Problems," 56). Since the "him" is unspecified, it is perhaps best rendered "with the wife of your youth let no one break faith" or as an impersonal passive, "the wife of your youth must not be treated faithlessly." Note that in the command section of the first address there is also a person shift: "Oh that there were among *you* that *he* would shut the doors" (1:10).

[152] Or "hates/hated and so divorces/divorced." This nontraditional understanding is defended below.

      d—says the LORD God of Israel,
     c′—he covers his garment with violence,
      d′—says the LORD of hosts.
a′—So *you shall be on guard* in your spirit,
  b′—and do not *act faithlessly.*

The verb translated "guard yourself" (*šāmar*, "watch, guard, keep") in its basic form *(qal)* is used in 2:7 of the priest's responsibility to tend or "preserve" the divine revelation and in 2:9 of "following" instructions. The passive/reflexive form (*niphal*, occurring thirty-seven times, twenty-four of which are imperative) is used twice here in 2:15b–16 followed by the phrase "in your spirit" *(běrûăhkem)*. Elsewhere this form of the verb means to "be on one's guard" against[153] some danger or to "pay careful attention" regarding (preposition *bě*, "in" as here) certain instructions (e.g., Exod 23:13). The verb can be used with another in a command to add a sense of special care, or diligence to certain instructions (e.g., Isa 7:4), or to stress the importance of the instructions.[154] Here the form is not imperative but a future oriented form (*waw* plus perfect, *wěnišmartem*) prominent in procedural and predictive discourse but also used for less prominent directives in hortatory discourse, as here.[155] A similar grammatical situation (employing the identical form *wěnišmartem*) is in Deut 4:4–5, where the instruction to "be . . . careful" immediately precedes and qualifies the command, "Do not provoke them to war." Elsewhere the verb *šāmar* is used with *rûah,* "spirit," only in Job 10:12 (in Eccl 11:4 *rûah* means "wind")—"You gave me life and showed me kindness, and in your providence *watched over my spirit.*" In the basic stem *šāmar* is used with a synonym of *rûah, nepeš,* "breath, throat, desire, life, soul, person, self,"[156] as a direct object in Deut 4:9 ("*watch yourselves* closely so that you do not forget"); Pss 25:20; 86:2 ("guard my life"); Prov 19:16 ("guards his life"). In the passive/reflexive form *šāmar* is found with *nepeš* and the preposition *lě,* "to" ("*watch yourselves* very carefully") in Deut 4:15 (followed by "so that you do not become corrupt") and Josh 23:11 (followed by "to love the LORD your God") and with the preposition *bě* in Jer 17:21 (NIV "Be careful" or NRSV "For the sake of your lives,[157] take care."). The phrase "be on guard in your spirit" here

---

[153] E.g., with preposition *bě* in 2 Sam 20:10; *min*, "from" as in Jer 9:3; *'el*, "to," in Exod 10:28.

[154] Judg 13:4; Job 36:21; fifteen times with the added element *lěkā/lākem*, "to you [sg./pl.]," as in "make sure" in Gen 24:6.

[155] Other uses of *niphal waw* plus perfect of שָׁמַר may be found in Deut 2:4; 4:15; Josh 23:11 (וְנִשְׁמַרְתֶּם as here); Deut 23:10[Eng. 9] (תָּ וְנִשְׁמַרְ); 2 Kgs 6:10 (וְנִשְׁמַר).

[156] See B. K. Waltke, " נֶפֶשׁ," *TWOT* 2:587–91.

[157] This is suggested in BDB, 1037, as perhaps the sense of the expression used by Malachi, noting the use of the preposition בְּ to mean "at the cost/price of, in payment for" (Gen 30:16; Exod 34:20; Deut 19:21 [with נֶפֶשׁ]; Josh 6:26; 2 Sam 3:14; 23:17 [with נֶפֶשׁ]; 24:24; 1 Kgs 2:23; 1 Chr 12:19; Prov 7:23; Lam 5:9;

probably means "watch yourselves carefully" or "be very careful." It is unnecessary, then, for the use of *rûaḥ* in vv. 15b–16 to be identical to its use in v. 15a,
although the word *rûaḥ* may have been used here rather than its synonym
*nepeš* because of its use in v. 15a.[158]

The traditional interpretation of v. 16 as a general condemnation of divorce,
reflected in the NIV translation (and in most translations; e.g., KJV, NRSV,
NASB, NJB, NCV, NLT) is strained when compared to Moses' permission for
divorce in Deut 24:1–4 (see also Lev 22:13; Num 30:9; Deut 22:13–19,28–
29).[159] It also appears to conflict with Ezra's insistence on marital dissolution
in Ezra 10:5,11 and with Jesus' allowance for divorce in Matt 19:9.[160] Concerning the latter passage that touches on the case of divorce on the basis of
sexual immorality, we should note that Mal 2:10–16 is primarily directed
against a man who breaks his marriage vows. The issue of breaking faith is
made explicit in vv. 10,11,14,15, and 16. The passage does not deal with the
case of a man divorcing a wife who has already broken her marriage vows, so
it also does not apply to the case of a woman divorcing her husband who has
already broken his marriage vows. This is another reason the passage should
not be understood as an absolute condemnation of divorce under any circumstances.[161] In fact, according to Jer 3:8 the Lord himself had divorced the
Northern Kingdom of Israel because of her adulteries (cf. Hos 2:2).[162]

Some regard Malachi's words as a "protest" against Ezra's dissolving of

---

[158] C. H. J. Wright (*God's People in God's Land*, 221) follows van Hoonacker (*Les douze petits
prophètes*, 726–27) in understanding Malachi's point being that divorce is "an attack on one's own
'life,' as well as being against God."

[159] See J. M. Sprinkle, "Old Testament Perspectives on Divorce and Remarriage," *JETS* 40
(1997): 529–33. Those who argue for a figurative interpretation of vv. 10–16 do so in part to avoid
such a conflict, especially in view of the influence of Deuteronomy on Malachi. Cf. Isaksson, *Marriage and Ministry in the New Temple*, 34; Petersen, *Zechariah 9–14 and Malachi*, 204; Ogden,
"Figurative Language in Mal 2:10–16," 224. For this same reason van der Woude argues that
divorce is not the issue in v. 16 but rather mistreating one's Jewish wife after taking a foreign second wife ("Malachi's Struggle for a Pure Community," 71).

[160] Hugenberger agrees that such an unconditional prohibition "would place that verse in intol-
erable and unnecessary tension with the testimony of the rest of the Old Testament concerning the
practice of divorce" (*Marriage as a Covenant*, 93). To attempt a harmonization between Moses,
Ezra, and Malachi is not illegitimate special pleading. If someone known to be intelligent and trust-
worthy says something today that seems to contradict something he said yesterday, one must
assume until it is proven otherwise that there are circumstances not immediately apparent that reconcile the two statements. All the more, if Moses, Ezra, and Malachi were all spokesmen for the
one faithful and true God (cf. Mal 3:6), it is reasonable to assume that their words do not contradict
each other. To assume otherwise is to deny the divine character of Scripture (or to impugn the character of the divine) that Scripture itself teaches and that traditionally has been a pillar of Judeo-
Christian religion.

[161] See D. Instone-Brewer, *Divorce and Remarriage in the Bible: The Social and Literary Context* (Grand Rapids: Eerdmans, 2002), 57.

[162] Ibid., 39–43.

mixed marriages.[163] The relationship between the two, however, could have
been just the opposite, with Ezra's crisis resulting at least in part from the situation found in Malachi. Marriage relationships had been formed with pagan
wives, perhaps often at the expense of former Jewish wives.[164] The situation in
Ezra can be viewed as exceptional, justifying Ezra's "extreme measures" on
the basis of his position in salvation history.[165]

Another way to resolve the tension between Ezra and the traditional reading
of Mal 2:16 is by arguing that what occurs in Ezra is not really divorce but the
annulment of illegitimate unions.[166] In support of this approach Hugenberger
points to Ezra's unusual vocabulary both for the unions and for their dissolution. "In particular, it should be noted that Malachi's terms in 2:16 are not those
employed by Ezra."[167] He further notes that unlike the pattern of Deut 24:1–4
and Malachi, the action in Ezra is not initiated by the husbands or even by the
wives and that thus "they resemble the dissolution of Michal's invalid 'marriage' to Paltiel at the instigation of Ishbosheth (2 Sam 3:15)."[168] But however
we understand what happened in Ezra, there are other cases in the Old Testament (all dealing with the situation of a slave-wife) where divorce appears to

---

[163] So Kruse-Blinkenberg, "Peshitta," 103–4. He argues that the Peshitta, the Tg., and the LXX
(ignoring the inner septuagintal conflict on this point) all corrected v. 16 to avoid conflicting with
Deut 24. See also J. J. Collins, "Message of Malachi," 212; id., "Marriage, Divorce, and Family,"
123–27; L. G. Perdue, "The Israelite and Early Jewish Family," in *Families in Ancient Israel* (Louisville: WJKP, 1997), 187. The Peshitta translator apparently skipped the first clause of v. 16
because of its difficulty (a common practice in the Peshitta), making it necessary to insert a negative in the second line, yielding "and he should *not* conceal wickedness in his garment" (Gordon,
*Targum to the Twelve Prophets*, 126–27).

[164] See J. G. McConville, *Ezra, Nehemiah, and Esther,* DSB (Philadelphia: Westminster, 1985),
70. H. G. M. Williamson also considers the situation in 2:10–16 as preceding that of Ezra 10, perhaps causing the majority of Ezra's audience to have less sympathy for the non-Jewish families
(*Ezra, Nehemiah,* WBC [Waco: Word, 1985], 160). But he argues that the steps taken by Shecaniah
and Ezra were racist in motivation and supported by poor exegesis of OT law (p. 161). But the
nature of Scripture is such that we must conclude with Sprinkle that "as tragic and painful as these
divorces were it was nonetheless God's will that they occurred" ("Old Testament Perspectives,"
538).

[165] So Sprinkle, "Old Testament Perspectives," 548. D. Wilson argues that the divorces required
by Ezra were cases of an offense having been committed that normally would have required the
death penalty ("detestable practices"), which could not be applied "because the returned exiles
were under the legal authority of the Persian empire" (*Reforming Marriage* [Moscow, ID: Canon,
1995], 136–37).

[166] See H. Wolf, *Haggai and Malachi: Rededication and Renewal*, EBC (Chicago: Moody,
1976), 95; W. A. Heth and G. J. Wenham, *Jesus and Divorce: Towards an Evangelical Understanding of New Testament Teaching* (London: Hodder & Stoughton, 1984), 162–64; W. F. Luck,
*Divorce and Remarriage: Recovering the Biblical View* (San Francisco: Harper & Row, 1987), 282.

[167] For the original unions, Hugenberger notes, Ezra uses *hiphil* forms of שׁב in 10:2,10
"rather than the expected לקח. For the dissolution Ezra uses "לְהוֹצִיא" in 10:3 and וְהִבָּדְלוּ in
10:11, rather than שׁלח, גרשׁ, or even שׂנא" (*Marriage as a Covenant*, 96).

[168] Ibid., 96.

be required (Gen 21:8–14; Exod 21:10–11; Deut 21:10–14).[169] In none of these cases is divorce depicted as a good thing; it is only necessary under certain circumstances created by sin.

One might be inclined to make peace between the traditional interpretation of Mal 2:16 and the rest of the Bible's teaching on divorce if that interpretation emerged easily from the text. But in fact a translation such as "'I hate divorce,' says the LORD God of Israel," is very difficult without resorting to emendation.[170] A more literal translation of v. 16a would be "If [or "for"] he hates sending away [i.e., "divorce"], says Yahweh God of Israel, then [or "and"] violence covers [or "he covers/will cover with violence"] his garment, says Yahweh of hosts." A translation such as the ESV ("For the man who hates and divorces, says the LORD, the God of Israel, covers his garment with violence, says the LORD of hosts") or HCSB ("'If he hates and divorces [his wife],' says the LORD God of Israel, 'he covers his garment with injustice,' says the LORD of Hosts") makes more sense of the Hebrew text as it stands than the various traditional translations.

The first problem one notices with the NIV rendering is that the first verb is third person, "he hates/hated" *(śānēʾ),* rather than first person, "I hate." The translation "I hate" requires emending the text.[171] It could be inferred from the following quotation formula that this is an indirect divine quote (or the Lord speaking of himself in the third person; cf. 1:9),[172] but this is awkward and

---

[169] See Sprinkle, "Old Testament Perspectives," 533–36.

[170] C. J. Collins states, "The chief problem with the customary translations . . . is that it is only possible to get them by *emending the Masoretic text*" ("The [Intelligible] Masoretic Text of Malachi 2:16 or, How does God feel about divorce?" *Presbyterion* 20.1 (1994): 36. Sprinkle likewise states that the traditional rendering "is an impossible translation of the MT, one that can only be retained on the basis of conjectural emendation without any manuscript support" ("Old Testament Perspectives," 539).

[171] Some would emend the perfect form שָׂנֵא (without textual evidence) to שָׂנֵאתִי (R. L. Smith, *Micah-Malachi.* 320), or to the imperfect אֶשְׂנָא (Wellhausen; cf. Hugenberger, *Marriage as a Covenant,* 63), or to the participle, שֹׂנֵא (Verhoef, *Haggai and Malachi,* 278), whose subject could be supplied by the context (GKC §116s). Some would leave the form as is but understand it as an alternate form of the participle (C. F. Keil, *The Twelve Minor Prophets* [Grand Rapids: Eerdmans, 1980], 454; W. C. Kaiser, "Divorce in Malachi 2:10–16," *CTR* 2 [1987]: 77; W. Rudolph, "Zu Mal 2,10–16," *ZAW* 93 [1981]: 85–90; id., *Haggai-Sacharja 1–8/9–14-Maleachi,* 270). But such a participle form occurs nowhere else, whereas the participle form שֹׂנֵא occurs eight times. Also the predicate use of the participle almost always has an expressed subject. According to *IBHS* §37.6, exceptions are after הֲנֵה, "or if the referent has just been mentioned," neither of which is the case here. Petersen treats it, without argument, as a verbal adjective whose subject is שַׁלַּח, translating, "Divorce is hateful!" (*Zechariah 9–14 and Malachi,* 204). Petersen concludes a somewhat confusing discussion by denying that 2:10–16 involves "a negative judgment on human divorce" (pp. 204–5).

[172] Although Hb. tolerates such disparity, especially in prophetic speech (see "Introduction: Literary Style and Structure"), in sixteen out of seventeen other verses in Malachi reference to God when followed by a divine quotation formula uses the first person (1:2,4,6,10,11,13; 2:2,4; 3:1,5,7,10, 11,13,17,21 [Eng. 4:3]. The one exception is in 1:9, but there "God" is explicitly referred to whereas here we only have "he."

requires a confusing switch to a new unannounced third person in the next clause, "and violence will cover *his* garment." The KJV/NKJV treats the statement as an indirect quote, adding "that" and reversing the clauses: "For the LORD God of Israel says that He hates divorce, for it covers one's garment with violence" (NKJV). This translation attempts to make sense of the text without emendation, but it employs an unlikely interpretation of the second clause in the statement, treating it as a kind of relative clause modifying "divorce" and in effect explaining why God hates it: "God hates divorce, which covers *his* [one's] garment with violence." This would be more reasonable if "says Yahweh God of Israel" did not intervene. The KJV/NKJV interpretation agrees with almost every other in reaching for an antecedent back to the third person prohibition at the end of v. 15 (lit.), "Let him [the unfaithful husband] not act faithlessly." But it makes this difficult with the intervening "he hates divorce" referring to God. Therefore this explanation, though possible, must be rejected if a better one can be found.

The NIV follows several translations in understanding the second clause of the statement (lit. "then [or "and"] violence covers [or "he covers/will cover with violence"] his garment") as a noun clause further describing what God hates (see NRSV, JPS, NAB, NASB, NJB). The NIV clarifies by repeating "and I hate." But the Hebrew construction, which uses a finite verb, "he covers," rather than, for example, a participle ("and the one who covers"), does not fit the pattern for an object clause in Hebrew.[173] The simplest interpretation is to see the perfect conjugation verb "he covers" as parallel (i.e., on the same syntactic level) to the preceding perfect conjugation verb "he hates," yielding, "he hates . . . and/then/so he covers."

This leads to the question of the initial particle *kî*, left untranslated in the NIV but usually translated "for." Its use here could be logical ("for, because") or emphatic ("indeed" or untranslated as in the NIV), either of which is com-

---

[173] It does not fit the examples of object clauses with *waw* plus a finite verb in *GBH* §177h–k. In all these examples the object clause follows immediately a transitive clause having no other object. That is not the case in Mal 2:16, where, according to the traditional interpretation, the object of שֹׂנֵא is already supplied by שַׁלַּח, and there is an intervening clause, אָמַר יְהוָה אֱלֹהֵי יִשְׂרָאֵל, "says Yahweh, God of Israel." S. Schreiner interprets the clause as contrastive, translating "Senn einer nich mehr liebt, Ehe scheiden . . .; aber der jenige besudelt mit Schande sein Gewand" ["If one no longer loves, divorce . . .; but such a one covers his garment with shame"] ("Mischehen-Ehebruch-Ehescheidung. Betrachtungen zu Mal 2,10–16," 217–18). This has most of the same problems as other views that consider שַׁלַּח to be imperative (see below), plus the unlikely logic of permission combined with condemnation. Also there is no grammatical clue that the clause is contrastive, such as a disjunctive clause and/or at least clear lexical opposition (as in 1:3,4; cf. F. I. Andersen, *The Sentence in Biblical Hebrew* [The Hague: Mouton, 1974], 68,179–80). For further critique of Schreiner's view see Hugenberger, *Marriage as a Covenant,* 61–62; W. Rudolph, "Zu Mal. 2:10–16," *ZAW* 83 (1981): 85–90; C. Locher, "Altes und Neues zu Maleachi 2,10–16," *Mélanges Dominique Barthélémy* (Göttingen, 1981), 241–71. The latter nevertheless affirms that the verse supports divorce of foreign non-Yahwistic wives.

patible with the traditional interpretation; but it could also be conditional ("if, when"; cf. Mal 1:4, NRSV; 1:8),[174] an understanding favored by several interpreters (also NEB, REB).[175] All the ancient textual witnesses support this interpretation. The Targum has, "But if you hate her, divorce her, says the Lord God of Israel, and do not conceal sin in your garment."[176] The Vulgate is similar.[177] The Septuagint tradition is split, but both translate with a conditional conjunction.[178] One (LXX^ℵABQV) reads, "But if, having hated, you divorce, says the Lord God of Israel, then iniquity will cover his garments."[179] The other (LXX^LW) reads, "But if having hated [or "you hate," LXX^W], divorce! says the Lord God of Israel, and iniquity will cover his garments [*endumata autou* with LXX^W; LXX^L reads "your thoughts" *enthumēmata sou*]." According to the latter reading, the text seems to grant permission for divorce, at least in the first clause (the Targum carries this through by adding the negative in the last clause), although it is difficult to make sense of the whole sentence. The readings of the Targum, LXX^LW, 4QXII^a, and Vulgate are surely a case of harmo-

---

[174] See A. Aejmelaeus, "Function and Interpretation of כִּי in Biblical Hebrew," *JBL* 105 (1986): 197; *HALOT,* 471; *IBHS* §38.2d.

[175] E.g., Schreiner's translation cited previously. See also Hugenberger, *Marriage as a Covenant,* 67–70. Baldwin believes that although it originally expressed God's hatred for divorce, the Hb. text "suffered early at the hands of some who wanted to bring Malachi's teaching into line with that of Deuteronomy 24:1," and so "the Hebrew in fact reads 'if he hates send (her) away'" (*Haggai, Zechariah, Malachi,* 241).

[176] Cathcart and Gordon, *The Targum of the Minor Prophets,* 235. Gordon argues that the Tg.'s insertion of the negative in the final clause is not uncommon in the ancient versions and does not prove oral or literary dependence on the Peshitta (*Targum to the Twelve Prophets,* 127). 4QXII^a reads כִּי אִם שְׂנֵתָהּ שַׁלַּח, which also should probably be rendered, "But if you hate (her), divorce" (Fuller, "The Minor Prophets Manuscripts," 15–16; id. "Text-Critical Problems in Malachi 2:10–16," 55. Shields, however, suggests that שְׂנֵתָהּ could be read as an infinitive construct with feminine suffix, and שַׁלַּח could be read as perfect, yielding, "If hating her, he divorces," though he acknowledges Fuller's reading is more probable ("Syncretism and Divorce," 84).

[177] *Cum odio habueris, dimitte.*

[178] Either interpreting the MT כִּי or reading אִם כִּי with 4QXII^a.

[179] ἀλλὰ ἐὰν μισήσας ἐξαποστείλῃς, λέγει κύριος ὁ θεὸς τοῦ Ισραηλ, καὶ καλύψει ἀσέβεια ἐπὶ τὰ ἐνδύματα αὐτοῦ, λέγει κύριος παντοκράτωρ (J. Ziegler, ed., *Septuaginta: Vetus Testamentum Graecum. Vol. 13. Duodecim Prophetae.* [Göttingen: Vandenhoeck & Ruprecht, 1984]). Some overlook this tradition and speak of the LXX as justifying divorce (e.g., Verhoef, *Haggai and Malachi,* 279; Glazier-McDonald, *Malachi,* 109), even though this is the reading in the text in both Ziegler and Rahlfs (*Septuaginta,* rev. ed. [Stuttgart: Württembergische Bibelanstalt/ Deutsche Bibelgesellschaft, 1979], although Rahlfs reads ἐνθυμήματά σου rather than ἐνδύματα αὐτοῦ). As D.C. Jones points out, then, Isaksson's claim that "no instance can be quoted of these verses being understood in earlier times as an attack on divorce" (*Marriage and Ministry,* 32–34) is false (Jones, "Malachi on Divorce," *Presbyterion* 15 [1989]: 21).

nizing the verse with current practice and with the accepted interpretation of Deut 24:1–4[180] since it rather clearly violates the context of Mal 2:10–16. Nevertheless, the tradition of interpreting the sentence as conditional is very strong, and it is possible to do so without understanding it as commending divorce if the result is in the clause "then violence covers/will cover his garment" (or "then he covers/will cover his garment with violence"). With the intervening divine quotation formula ("says the LORD God of Israel") between the condition (protasis) and the result (apodosis), this would match the pattern of the conditional sentence in 2:2.[181]

Finally, one must deal with the word *šallaḥ,* which the NIV and most translations read as a verbal noun (infinitive construct), meaning "sending away, divorce," and treat as the object of "he hates."[182] This is the word used for "divorce" in Deut 22:19,29; 24:1,3,4; 1 Chr 8:8; Isa 50:1; Jer 3:1,8.[183] But because of the various problems with the traditional interpretation, van Hoonacker reads *šallaḥ* as the perfect conjugation verb *šillaḥ,* "he divorces," and the perfect verb *śānēʾ* as the participle *śōnēʾ,* "hating," which he treats as the indeterminate subject of *šillaḥ,* yielding "if one who hates divorces," or as he translates, "if someone divorces for aversion [i.e., "hatred" or "dislike"]." The result of the condition is taken to be "he covers his garment with injustice."[184] This

---

[180] J. J. Collins believes the Qumran text "must be read as a correction of the text preserved by the Masoretes, attempting to clarify its sense and reconcile it with Jewish tradition" ("Marriage, Divorce, and Family," 125). Cathcart and Gordon call the Tg. reading "a straightforward example of Targumic 'converse translation'. . . by which MT is made to say the opposite of what is intended and so, in this case, conform to rabbinic orthodoxy in relation to the divorce question" (*Minor Prophets,* 235). See also Kruse-Blinkenberg, "Peshitta," 104, 111; Fuller, "Text-Critical Problems," 56.

[181] Noted by D. C. Jones, "Malachi on Divorce," 18. C. J. Collins, who otherwise agrees with Jones's interpretation, rejects the interpretation of כִּי as conditional largely because he is "not persuaded that *kî* can introduce a conditional clause except with an imperfect verb" ("Masoretic Text of Malachi 2:16," 39). But although the majority of cases of conditional כִּי occur with the imperfect, it arguably occurs with the perfect as well: Lev 13:51; Num 5:20; Isa 16:12; 28:15; 30:4; 63:16; Jer 12:5; Ezek 3:19,21; 33:9; Mic 7:8; Mal 3:14; Pss 21:12; 119:83; Job 7:13; 22:29; Prov 11:15; 23:22; 27:13; Ruth 1:12.

[182] Although the form is morphologically identical to the imperative, as interpreted by the ancient versions previously mentioned, this violates the context and is awkward with the preceding third person כִּי־שָׂנֵא, "if he hates," as well as the clause "and he covers," which furthermore seems to condemn divorce. It also requires supplying an object "her" with both verbs.

[183] In some cases (Deut 24:1; Isa 50:1; Jer 3:8) the verb שׁלח also has the literal meaning "send away," as the NIV translates (cf. also Gen 21:14; Deut 21:14). But the context, esp. in Deut 24:4 with reference to "a certificate of divorce" (סֵפֶר כְּרִיתֻת), makes clear that divorce is in view, as the NIV reflects in translating שׁלח as "divorce" in that passage. Other terms for divorce are גֵּרֵשׁ, "drive out" (Lev 21:7,14; 22:13; Num 30:9[Hb. 10]; Ezek 44:22) and כְּרִיתוּת (Deut 24:1,3; Isa 50:1; Jer 3:8), related to the verb כָּרַת, "cut."

[184] van Hoonacker, *Les douze petits prophètes,* 728–29.

interpretation is supported by the strong Septuagint tradition mentioned above. Glazier-McDonald favors this interpretation because (1) it fits the context, continuing the string of perfect tense verbs beginning in v. 11 that describe what the "errant spouse" has done, and (2) it reflects the use of the verbs "hate" and "send away" in Deut 24:3 ("and her second husband *dislikes [lit., 'hates'] her* and writes her a certificate of divorce, gives it to her and *sends her [wĕŝillĕḥāh]* from his house").[185] D. C. Jones suggests that "Malachi is aiming his protest directly at the practice falsely assumed to be morally permissible from the merely descriptive terms" of Deut 24:3.[186]

R. Westbrook's interpretation is similar, although he does not understand v. 16 as a conditional sentence and does not emend *śānēʾ*. Understanding both *śnʾ* and *šlḥ* as finite verbs (emending the second verb from an infinitive to a perfect), he translates, "For he has hated, divorced . . . and covered his garment in injustice."[187] His interpretation of Mal 2:16 is based on his observation that Deut 24:1–4 reflects two different motives for divorce. One is the first husband's, who divorces his wife for "something indecent" *('erwat dābār)*in her, which he argues was justifiable grounds permitting divorce without financial settlement; the other is the second husband's, who divorces his wife because he "dislikes her," which was considered subjective and unjustified and required a

---

[185] Glazier-McDonald, *Malachi*, 111. Hugenberger adds that "hate" is also used in a marriage context in Gen 29:31; Deut 21:15–17; 22:13,16; Judg 15:2; Prov 30:23; Isa 60:15 (*Marriage as a Covenant*, 70). The Aramaic expression שׁנאה מפסם, which can be translated "provisions of divorce," occurs in a fifth century B.C. Jewish marriage contract from Elephantine (Porten and Greenfield, *Jews of Elephantine and Arameans of Syene*, 16–17). An Elephantine marriage law dating 449 B.C. reads, "Tomorrow or (the) next day, should Anani stand up in an assembly and say: 'I hated Tamet my wife,' silver of hatre(d) is on his head. He shall give Tamet silver, 7 shekels, 2 q(uarters), and all that she brought in her hand she shall take out, from straw to string" (B. Porten, *The Elephantine Papyri in English* [Leiden: Brill, 1996], 209). Zehnder agrees that "an outright rejection of divorce by YHWH" here "would be astonishing," since it would ignore "the parallel usage of שׁנא and שׁלח not only in Deut 24:3, but also in Deut. 22:13,19; it seems to be unlikely that in two contexts dealing with the same subject matter and using the same combination of words . . . in one case שׁנא refers to the aversion of a husband against his wife . . ., while in the other . . . it refers to YHWH's rejection of divorce" ("A Fresh Look at Malachi 2:13–16," 254).

[186] Jones, "Malachi on Divorce," 19. Shields also favors van Hoonacker's interpretation ("Syncretism and Divorce," 84–86).

[187] R. Westbrook, "The Prohibition on Restoration of Marriage in Deuteronomy 24:1–4," in *Studies in Bible, 1986*, Scripta Hierosolymitana (Jerusalem: Magnes, 1986), 403. He follows J. M. P. Smith (*Book of Malachi*, 60) in emending שׁלּח to שׁלּח (Smith, van Hoonacker, and others actually give the perfect form as שׁלּח, but as C. J. Collins notes ["The (Intelligible) Masoretic Text of Malachi 2:16," 37], this is incorrect. Smith translates (inexplicably), "For one who hates and sends away covers his clothing with violence" (p. 55).

financial compensation to the estranged wife.[188] Westbrook argues for the reasonableness of this supposition based on the recognition of this distinction in ancient Near Eastern and postbiblical Jewish law. He shows on the one hand that "there is a tradition spanning the whole length of ancient Near Eastern law that upon dissolution of the marriage, whether by divorce or death of the husband, the wife was entitled to a financial settlement consisting at least of the restoration of her dowry but generally also of a payment from the husband's resources."[189] On the other hand, such payment was not necessary in cases where the wife was guilty of misconduct such as "in the sphere of her financial and household duties" or "sexual misconduct not amounting to adultery [for which death was the penalty] but rather in the sphere of indecency or immodesty."[190] Malachi's objection, then, is to divorce that could not be justified on objective grounds but resulted only from the husband's whim. Westbrook finds a parallel to the asyndetic (without conjunction) construction, "hates, divorces," in a Neo-Assyrian marriage contract: "If H[usband] hates, divorces, he must pay." He suggests, therefore, that the prophet has taken the phrase "from a standard legal idiom."[191]

Hugenberger correctly notes first that the position of the divine quotation formula favors construing v. 16 as a conditional sentence, since it is less intrusive between the protasis and apodosis than in Westbrook's interpretation.[192]

---

[188] Westbrook reconstructs the scenario: "The first husband has divorced his wife on the grounds of her 'indecency' and has therefore escaped the normal financial consequences—he paid her no divorce-money and most probably kept her dowry. The woman nonetheless managed to find another husband, and that marriage has ended in circumstances which leave her well provided for: her dowry (if she had received a second one from her family), possibly marital gifts from the second husband, plus divorce money or the widow's allowance. Now that she is a wealthy widow or divorcée, the first husband forgets his original objections and seeks to remarry her" ("Prohibition on Restoration of Marriage," 404–5). In Deut 22:13–21 is a law dealing with similar fraudulent activity on the part of a husband who, "looking for a pretext to divorce his spouse and recover the marriage fee, brings an accusation of premarital sexual irregularity against a newly married wife" (J. Blenkinsopp, "The Family in First Temple Israel," in *Families in Ancient Israel* [Louisville: WJKP, 1997], 61 [see also p. 65]). For a correction to Westbrook's scenario, cf. J. H. Walton, "The Place of the *Huṭqaṭṭēl* within the D-Stem Group and Its Implications in Deuteronomy 24:4," *HS* 32 (1991): 7–17.

[189] Westbrook, "Prohibition on Restoration of Marriage," 396.

[190] Ibid., 398.

[191] Ibid., 400, 403. J. J. Collins favors Westbrook's understanding of the syntax but argues that "'to hate' in this context is simply a technical term for divorce, for whatever reason." He translates, "For one repudiates, divorces . . . and covers his garment with violence"—i.e., a general condemnation of divorce ("Marriage, Divorce, and Family," 125–26). He suggests, however, that what appears as a general condemnation may have been intended more specifically, just as Amos's "sweeping dismissal of the sacrificial cult" was not intended to be applied so broadly. We can only say, then, that Malachi "viewed the practice of divorce in his day as excessive and unjust" (p. 126).

[192] Hugenberger also points out that each of the twenty-one uses of אמר יהוה in Malachi occurs in "a major break in the grammar of the verse" (*Marriage as a Covenant,* 68).

Second, Hugenberger argues that subordinating v. 16a to v. 15b increases the awkwardness of the person shifts:

> v. 15b—"Take heed to *your*selves, and let *none* be faithless to the wife of *your* youth."
> v. 16a—"For *he* has hated, divorced, says Yahweh, God of Israel, and covered *his* garment in injustice."
> v. 16b—"So take heed to *your*selves, and *do* not be faithless."

The logic of the subordination is also unclear in that "one is left to puzzle over the precise antecedent of the 'he'" in v. 16a, and "it is not obvious how the assertion, 'for he has hated, divorced . . .' actually explains the command, 'Take heed to yourselves.'"[193] One might have expected an explanatory relationship such as "Expel such a man, for he has hated" or "Take heed to yourselves . . . for I will judge all such faithless husbands."[194] Therefore, Hugenberger prefers van Hoonacker's view, while drawing on Westbrook's explanation of its background in Deut 24:1–4. He finds it unnecessary to emend the text, however, explaining *šallaḥ* as a variant form of the infinitive absolute,[195] which can function as a finite verb, in this case a perfect.[196] He argues persuasively that the sense is that if a man "hates and so divorces" his wife he thereby covers his garment with violence.[197]

---

[193] This objection applies equally to other views such as C. J. Collins ("Masoretic Text of Malachi 2:16," 39) that translate כִּי as "for."

[194] Hugenberger, *Marriage as a Covenant*, 68–69. Even if "let none be faithless" in v. 15b is not emended to second person with the versions, he explains, it "appears inadequate to account for the wholesale shift to the third person in v. 16a" (p. 69). It should be noted that Hugenberger's view does not remove the person shift but may relieve its awkwardness somewhat. Concerning the causal/explanatory relationship, he mentions the possibility that v. 16a could be a fronted explanation for v. 16b (as we have argued for 1:11 and 1:14), but the supposed emphatic nature of such a clause reversal (tentatively citing *GBH* §170n) is inappropriate in this case (p. 69).

[195] Cf. GKC §52o; *GBH* §52c. Elsewhere the *piel* infinitive absolute of שׁלח occurs three times in the Hb. Bible, twice as שַׁלֵּחַ (Deut 22:7; 1 Kgs 11:22) and once as here, שַׁלַּח (Isa 58:6).

[196] Hugenberger, *Marriage as a Covenant*, 72–73. Cf. *IBHS* §35.5.2; *GBH* §123x. See also *BHRG* §20.2.4. C. J. Collins suggests that שַׁלַּח is an alternate form of the perfect by analogy with נַשַּׁנִי in Gen 41:51 and וְכָרַכַר in Num 24:17, citing *GBH* §52a ("Masoretic Text of Malachi 2:16," 37). It may be better to understand שַׁלַּח as infinitive construct completing the meaning of the preceding perfect as in Gen 8:12; Exod 2:18; Ps 109:16 or as a result ("hate so as to divorce") as suggested by Sprinkle ("Divorce and Remarriage," 539). See also Gen 31:28, where a perf. + inf. const. occurs (הִסְכַּלְתָּ עֲשׂוֹ) that is literally "you were foolish in acting," i.e., "you acted foolishly." By analogy Mal 2:16 would mean "he divorced hatefully." (I thank my colleague D. K. Stabnow for this reference.)

[197] Note the translation of Mal 2:16 in *The Complete Bible: An American Translation* (Chicago: University of Chicago Press, 1939): "'For one who hates and divorces,' says the LORD God of Israel, 'covers his clothing with violence.'" Also see the almost identical ESV. D. C. Jones notes two fifth century B.C. Elephantine papyri that refer to the case of a Jewish wife dissolving her marriage by "disliking and leaving" *(sene' unepaq)* her husband ("Malachi on Divorce," 18, citing D. Daube, *The New Testament and Rabbinic Judaism* [New York: Arno, 1973], 366). See also Zehnder, "Malachi 2:13–16," 254–55.

Although the details are less than certain, the view that accounts best for the data of the text understands the issue to be unjustifiable divorce, that is, for reasons other than "something indecent" in the wife (Deut 24:1). This would include divorce for personal convenience or advantage or for any other reasons related to self-satisfaction. The result of the husband's treachery is that "he covers his garment with violence" (or that "violence covers his garment," which would amount to the same thing). The NIV translation "covering himself with violence as well as with his garment" is very unlikely (although similarly in JPS). Although the verb "cover" can be reflexive ("cover himself," Gen 38:14), the translation "as well as with his garment" is difficult to justify from the Hebrew, which reads simply "upon his garment." Also unlikely is the KJV translation that treats "violence" as the object of the verb and "his garment" as the instrument: "one covereth violence with his garment" (similarly NJB). The Hebrew preposition 'al, "upon," can precede the object of the verb "cover" (Deut 13:9; Isa 26:21), but it is not used to identify the instrument.

The word translated "violence" *(ḥāmās)* is found sixty times in the Old Testament. According to H. Haag, although all *ḥāmās* "is ultimately directed against Yahweh" (cf. Ezek 22:26; Zeph 3:4), it is used of "cold-blooded and unscrupulous infringement of the personal rights of others, motivated by greed and hate and often making use of physical violence and brutality."[198] It sometimes involves false accusation (e.g., Ps 27:12) and usually describes the strong doing wrong or injury to the weak (e.g., Ps 72:14; Isa 53:9; Jer 22:3; Mic 6:12). The word is also one of many in the Old Testament used to describe human wickedness in a somewhat general sense and is the sin charged against corrupt mankind before the flood (Gen 6:11,13),[199] the Edomites, archvillains of Israel and of God (Joel 3:19; Obad 10), the people of Nineveh (Jonah 3:8), and even Israel when they were ripe for judgment (Hab 1:3,9). As such it is found closely related to words such as "sin," "iniquity," "pride," "malice," "wickedness," and especially "oppression."[200] A "man of violence" is also a "wicked man" (Ps 140:4[Hb. 5]; Prov 3:33), an "evil man" (Ps 140:3[Hb. 2]), a "worthless man" (Prov 16:27), and a "perverse man" (Prov 16:28). The opposite of *ḥāmās* is "blessings," "good," "salvation," "praise," "right," and especially "peace" and "justice" (Prov 10:6; 13:2; Isa 59:6,8; 60:18; Amos 3:10; Hab 1:2–

---

[198] H. Haag, "חָמָס *chāmās*," *TDOT* 4:480, 482.

[199] On the meaning of חָמָס in Gen 6:11,13, U. Cassuto states: "All the commentators, both ancient and modern, are accustomed to explain the word to mean lawlessness perpetrated by force. But this interpretation does not suit the context, for there is no reason to suppose that the text speaks of a particular kind of wrongdoing. . . . In the language of the Bible [חָמָס] signifies generally anything that is not righteous. The reference is to wickedness generally, to unrighteousness as a whole" (*Commentary on the Book of Genesis* [Jerusalem: Magnes, 1974], 52–53).

[200] Haag, *TDOT* 4:480. Cf. Pss 12:5[Hb. 6]; 55:11[Hb. 12]; 73:8; Isa 59:6–7; 60:18; Jer 6:6–7; 20:8; Ezek 45:9; Amos 3:9–10; Hab 2:17.

3).[201] In Ps 73:6 the arrogant and wicked are said to "clothe themselves with violence," that is, it is a characteristic of their lives and they practice it shamelessly (cf. also Jer 2:34).

The one who divorces his wife out of hate or greedy desire, then, according to the prophet joins a devilish fraternity. The very things he is responsible as her husband to pursue on her behalf—blessings, good, salvation, praise, right, peace, and justice—he is wickedly and unscrupulously robbing from her.[202] As Gamberoni writes, his "garment" (*lĕbûš* rather than *beged*) that is said to be defiled with his violence could be "a faint allusion to the practice of covering a woman with the edge of one's garment as a token of marriage" (Ruth 3:9; Ezek 16:8).[203] Thus, according to D. C. Jones, *lĕbûš* "would then be a metonymy for the marriage relationship, which is radically abused through arbitrary divorce."[204] But since one's clothing was especially important to cover shame and also to help identify one's role in society, and since, as Gamberoni says, "representatives of the powers of wickedness" are often seen as "dressed in the consequences of their total failure,"[205] the point is probably more that such a treacherous man will wear his shameful character for all to see (cf. Zech 3:3–5).[206] As D. C. Jones has stated, "Divorce for 'hatred' is a radical breach of fidelity; it is 'violence' against the companion to whom one has been joined in marriage. It therefore stands condemned by the God of justice, mercy, and troth."[207]

The prophet's concluding exhortation, "So guard yourself in your spirit, and do not break faith" is a strong warning to every husband that he must be constantly on his guard against developing a negative attitude toward his wife. C. J. Collins admonishes, "He who is wise will watch for the first stirrings of resentment, which might turn into dislike, and repent of it immediately, lest he deal treacherously with her whom the Lord has given to be a blessing."[208]

---

[201] Haag, *TDOT* 4:481. I. Swart concludes rightly that the word in Mal 2:16 should probably be translated "unrighteousness" or "injustice" ("In Search of the Meaning of *ḥamas*: Studying an Old Testament Word in Context," *JSem* 3 [1991]: 160–61).

[202] Note the words of Sarai to Abram in Gen 16:5: "You are responsible for the wrong [חֲמָסִי] I am suffering [because of Hagar]."

[203] J. Gamberoni, "לָבֵשׁ *lābēš*," *TDOT* 7:467.

[204] D. C. Jones, "Malachi on Divorce," 19. He acknowledges the equal likelihood that the term refers to the "'clothing' in which one appears before the Lord, now covered with the cruelty of divorce on one's marital companion."

[205] Gamberoni, "לָבֵשׁ *lābēš*," 7:461, 464.

[206] Baldwin explains it as "a figurative expression for kinds of gross injustice which, like the blood of a murdered victim, leave their mark for all to see" (*Haggai, Zechariah, Malachi,* 241). As Keil expresses it, "a soiled garment is a symbol of uncleanness of heart" (*The Twelve Minor Prophets,* 454). Cf. also Hugenberger, *Marriage as a Covenant;* Merrill, *Haggai, Zechariah, Malachi,* 424; Shields, "Syncretism and Divorce in Malachi 2,10–16," 85.

[207] D. C. Jones, "Malachi on Divorce," 22.

[208] Collins, "Masoretic Text of Malachi 2:16," 40.

The summary of Mal 2:13–16 by Zehnder may serve well as a conclusion to this section. He concludes that the passage "contains an argument which in its *Tendenz* not only favors monogamy as the kind of marriage relationship which alone corresponds to God's creational intentions, but which ultimately can be understood as a basis for a fundamental questioning of the acceptability of divorce. If man and woman form a unity in their marriage relation that is established in creation itself, this unity and consequently the marriage covenant is not to be dissolved either by taking another woman in addition to the first one or by divorce."[209]

## 4. Situation: Complaints of the Lord's Injustice (2:17)

[17]You have wearied the LORD with your words.
"How have we wearied him?" you ask.
By saying, "All who do evil are good in the eyes of the LORD, and he is pleased with them" or "Where is the God of justice?"

**2:17** This verse is generally thought to begin the fourth oracle or disputation of the book (2:17–3:5 or 3:6; see introduction). This is due to the threefold form of prophetic challenge–audience reaction–prophetic elaboration sometimes said to be typical of the disputation form. It is also due to the apparent change of topic from intermarriage and divorce to theodicy and coming judgment. As discussed previously, however, the disputation form in Malachi is a literary device to describe the hortatory situation. Furthermore, the structural pattern we have observed in the book would suggest a parallel relationship between 2:10b–15a and 2:17, the two situation elements of the second address. It also suggests that the complaints of the audience about injustice in 2:17 and the prophetic announcement of coming judgment in 3:1–6, although rightly considered a new paragraph, are closely related to the theme of unfaithfulness found in 2:10–16. The link can be found in v. 16 in the term *ḥāmās*, "violence, injustice." The sin of unfaithfulness that was widespread in Judah was in fact a case of injustice, failing to give someone his due. Yet Judah, unable to recognize its own corruption, saw its current economic and social troubles (cf. Hag 1:6,9–11; 2:16–19; Neh 9:32–37) as a sign of God's unfairness or unfaithfulness. They deserved divine blessings, they thought, but were receiving divine afflictions instead. Ignoring their own sins and aggravated by the sins of others, either within or around Judah, which they perceived were going unpunished, they were complaining of divine injustice (cf. Mal 1:2). It appeared that "all who do evil are good in the eyes of the LORD" (cf. 3:15), implying the corollary that they, on the other hand, were being ill treated. This was a blatantly blasphemous denial of the Mosaic teaching that "anyone who does these [evil]

---

[209] Zehnder, "Fresh Look at Malachi 2:13–16," 259.

things is detestable to the LORD" (Deut 18:12; cf. 25:16; Isa 5:20).[210] If this is not so, they said, then "Where is the God of justice?" That is, why does he not act (cf. Isa 40:27)?[211]

The Lord had amply demonstrated his immanence and his justice throughout the history of his relationship with Israel. It was in response to their cries for help that the Lord had delivered them from oppression in Egypt by "a mighty hand" (Exod 3:19) in faithfulness to his covenant with Abraham, Isaac, and Jacob (Exod 2:23–25; 3:6–10, etc.). He had given them the sacrificial system so that he could dwell among them and righteous laws which if Israel followed would bring glory to them and to him before the nations.

> What other nation is so great as to have their gods near them the way the LORD our God is near us whenever we pray to him? And what other nation is so great as to have such righteous decrees and laws as this body of laws I am setting before you today? (Deut 4:7–8)

The Lord had guided the people with attentive righteousness throughout the period of the judges and the monarchy, alternately delivering them or disciplining them as was necessary, climaxing in the exile and restoration. Governor Nehemiah in his public prayer in Nehemiah 9 recognized these things, confessing the Lord's righteousness, faithfulness, and compassion since the time of Moses (see esp. Neh 9:8,13,17,19,28–32). Nehemiah also knew that Judah's present hardships were the result not of the Lord's unfaithfulness but of their sins.

> In all that has happened to us, you have been just; you have acted faithfully, while we did wrong. . . . Because of our sins, its abundant harvest goes to the kings you have placed over us. They rule over our bodies and our cattle as they please. We are in great distress. (Neh 9:33,37)

But Malachi's audience had concluded (as we sometimes do), in effect, that God was either unjust or negligent—either way, he was not being faithful to his covenant. No wonder the Lord was weary of them! (Cp. Moses' complaint of "the burden of all these people" in Num 11:11–17.)

The term "weary" *(yg‘)* can refer to being physically spent as a result of prolonged labor, travel, or other activity. It can also refer to emotional disturbance (i.e., a sense of being annoyed) or exhaustion resulting from the persistent stresses, sorrows, and trials of life (cf. Pss 6:6; 69:3; Isa 49:4; Jer 45:3). In the

---

[210] Petersen declares that "the similarities between the statement in Mal. 2:17 and those in Deuteronomy are so striking that they cannot be accidental" (*Zechariah 9–14 and Malachi,* 208). Also note God's accusing Israel in Psalm 50 for hypocritically continuing their sacrifices though "when you see a thief, you are pleased *[rṣh]* with him,//And you associate with adulterers" (v. 18, NASB).

[211] The common rendering of אוֹ, as "or" joining two quotations of the people, suggests that these are two alternatives. People were saying either one thing or the other. It is more likely that the אוֹ should be rendered "or else" (with NAB, JPS, Verhoef, *Haggai and Malachi*) and be considered part of the one quotation. In this case it is equivalent to וְאִם לֹא ("but if not," Gen 42:16; 1 Sam 2:16; cf. 1 Kgs 20:39; Isa 27:5).

sense of having diminished physical or emotional energy, the Lord cannot become "weary"; he is a source of strength to the weary (Isa 40:28–31). But since being "weary" may imply prolonged and often unpleasant activity that is soon to stop, the verb can be used figuratively of God. His weariness represents the fact that God's patience is near an end, as it had also been in Isa 43:22–24, a passage to which Malachi may be alluding.

> Yet you have not called upon me, O Jacob, you have not *wearied* yourselves for me, O Israel. You have not brought me sheep for burnt offerings, nor honored me with your sacrifices. I have not burdened you with grain offerings nor *wearied* you with demands for incense. You have not brought any fragrant calamus for me, or lavished on me the fat of your sacrifices. But you have burdened me with your sins and *wearied* me with your offenses.

The term, then, vividly conveys God's patient and gracious endurance of their rebellious and insulting attitude toward him and that the time for his patience is almost over.

### Excursus: Divine Impassibility

Does God really become "weary"? Is there a sense in which God can be said to experience emotional frustration, disappointment, and even pain because of sin? We could ask a similar question concerning the assertion in 1:2–3 that the Lord "loved" Jacob/Israel but "hated" Esau/Edom. There too we considered the expressions to be figurative, pointing to God's sovereign election in choosing by his grace to form a relationship with some of his creatures and to leave others to pursue their rebellious desires to their own destruction. God's "love" also denotes the faithful care with which he providentially maintains his relationship with those who are his, and his "hate" denotes his persistent rejection of the aims and ways of sin and his sovereign determination ultimately to destroy wickedness from his creation.

But can it appropriately be said not only that God's acts are analogous to human acts that are typically motivated by emotions of affection and pleasure on the one hand or revulsion and displeasure on the other hand, but also that he actually experiences those emotions? Numerous biblical texts ascribe just such feelings to God. For example, Gen 6:6 states that "The LORD was grieved that he had made man on the earth, and his heart was filled with pain." Judges 10:16b informs us that God "could bear Israel's misery no longer." Isaiah 63:9–10 declares: "In all their distress he too was distressed. . . . In his love and mercy he redeemed them; he lifted them up and carried them all the days of old. Yet they rebelled and grieved his Holy Spirit. So he turned and became their enemy and he himself fought against them" (see also Eph 4:30). According to Ps 2:4 in the face of human pride and opposition "the One enthroned in heaven laughs; the Lord scoffs at them." In Jesus' parable of the "prodigal son" he portrays the father, who represents God, as "filled with compassion." At the sight of his returning son he "ran to his son, threw his arms around him and kissed him" (Luke 15:20).

Yet classical theism has affirmed that God is "impassible" *(apathēs)*, which some have taken to mean that he "is not capable of being acted upon or affected emotionally by anything in creation."[212] The doctrine is more commonly defined in terms of God's immunity to being driven by the capricious world of emotion or passion and especially his immunity to suffering. As G. L. Prestige expresses it, God, being "supreme in power and wisdom," is "incapable of being diverted or overborne by forces and passions such as commonly hold sway in the creation and among mankind."[213] H. P. Owen explains the doctrine as meaning "particularly that [God] cannot experience sorrow, sadness, or pain."[214] Athenagoras, the second-century Athenian apologist, distinguished God from the Greek gods of Homer as having "neither anger, nor desire, nor yearning."[215] This doctrine had its roots largely in the doctrine of God's transcendence and absolute independence (or aseity), that is, that he is "self-sufficient in *everything:* in his existence, in his attributes, in his decrees, and in his works."[216] As expressed in the *Westminster Confession* (2.2):

> God hath all life, glory, goodness, blessedness, in and of Himself; and is alone in and unto Himself all-sufficient, not standing in need of any creatures which He hath made, nor deriving any glory from them, but only manifesting His own glory in, by, unto, and upon them. He is the alone fountain of all being, of whom, through whom, and to whom are all things; and hath most sovereign dominion over them, to do by them, for them, or upon them whatsoever Himself pleaseth.

God's independence was taken to imply his immutability[217] and his absolute perfection and incorruptibility, from which was inferred his eternal blessedness. If God can be affected emotionally by his creatures, it was argued, then he is not independent and immutable but is subject to the same passions and suffering that disturb and encumber us. Tertullian could not conceive of God experiencing anger or exasperation because "God alone is happy in view of His incorruptible nature."[218] Calvin commented on the divine "repentance" in Gen 6:6, "Certainly God is not sorrowful or sad, but remains forever like Himself in His celestial and happy repose."[219] The eternal God of purpose and constancy does not act capriciously, impulsively, or irrationally. He cannot be swayed by emotional appeals

---

[212] G. R. Lewis, "Impassibility," *Evangelical Dictionary of Theology* (Grand Rapids: Baker, 1984), 553. G. MacGregor explains that God cannot be acted upon, nor can he change internally, "nor can he experience the sensations of pleasure or pain that we humans experience" (*Dictionary of Religion and Philosophy* [New York: Paragon, 1989], 331).

[213] G. L. Prestige, *God in Patristic Thought* (London: SPCK, 1952), 6.

[214] H. P. Owen, *Concepts of Deity* (New York: Macmillan, 1971), 23.

[215] *Legatio* 21; see also 8,10.

[216] H. Bavinck, *The Doctrine of God* (Grand Rapids: Eerdmans, 1951), 144–45. As Irenaeus wrote, God is "rich and complete, lacking nothing" (*Adv. Haer.* 4.14.1; cf. also 3.8.3).

[217] As C. F. H. Henry states, "[God] wills eternally to be himself in the fullness of his independent vitality, and never ceases to be himself" ("The Living God of the Bible," *SBJT* 1.1 [1997]: 19). See further our excursus, "Immutability of the Everlasting God," at 3:6.

[218] *Adv. Marc.* 2.16.

[219] J. Calvin, *Commentary on Genesis,* trans. and ed. J. King, 1554. Online: http://ccel.wheaton.edu.

to act contrary to his eternal will, nor can circumstances so affect him that he would act in disharmony with his eternal knowledge and wisdom.[220] The church fathers derived the doctrine of God's independence in part from the meaning of the divine name, Yahweh ("I AM WHO I AM" in Exod 3:14; see also Exod 33:19), which they interpreted as defining God as "being itself" and therefore as eternally and immutably the same.[221]

Prior to the Enlightenment, virtually all, orthodox and "heretics" alike, affirmed God's essential impassibility,[222] an assumption many today argue they inherited from Greek philosophy rather than from Scripture.[223] Some even argue that classical theism's foundational doctrine of God's absolute independence is the product of the hellenization of Christian thought.[224] Certainly the Greeks held some beliefs in common with biblical faith,[225] and in its efforts to make itself understood by the pagan culture, the early church employed language that, as J. Pelikan says, "still bears the marks of its struggle." Nevertheless, "the charge that one's theological opponent has subordinated the truth of divine revelation to the philosophy of the Greeks is a common one in the history of theological polemics."[226] The issue is not whether classical theism is similar to Greek philosophy but rather to what extent it conforms to Scripture, which declares that the Lord God is absolute constancy and faithfulness. He depends upon nothing outside himself, but rather all things depend upon him. His creative work arose from no necessity or need on his part but only from the absolutely free exercise of his sovereign will.[227] The Creator's purpose for all his creation reflects his infinite knowledge, wisdom, and fatherly care, and it will be fulfilled perfectly in

---

[220] Cf. Augustine, *Confessions* 12.15; *City of God* 11.21.

[221] E.g., Augustine, *On the Trinity* 5.2. Bavinck correctly points out, however, that God is really not defining his essence here but is declaring his unchangeable character: "God is and remains the God of his people, immutable in his grace and truthfulness" (*Doctrine of God*, 106).

[222] E. L. Mascall notes, "There are few doctrines that can claim in their support so long and consistent a witness in the tradition of Christian theology as the doctrine of the impassibility of God" (*Existence and Analogy* [New York: Archon, 1967], 134).

[223] E.g., J. Moltmann, *The Trinity and the Kingdom* (San Francisco: Harper & Row, 1981), 22; A. E. McGrath, *Christian Theology: An Introduction* (Oxford, UK/Cambridge, U.S.A.: Blackwell, 1994), 213–15.

[224] E.g., C. Pinnock, *The Openness of God* (Downers Grove: InterVarsity, 1994), 107.

[225] Note Plato's defense of divine immutability in *The Republic* II.381 and Aristotle's in *Metaphysics* XII.5–9.

[226] J. Pelikan, *The Christian Tradition: A History of the Development of Doctrine,* vol. 1, *The Emergence of the Catholic Tradition (100–600)* (Chicago: University of Chicago Press, 1971), 45. Pelikan does admit that "what later generations of the church . . . inherited in the dogma of the church included more than a little of Greek philosophy as well." Nevertheless, he calls Harnack's claim a "distortion" that Christian dogma is "in its conception and development a work of the Greek spirit on the soil of the gospel." "Christian doctrine," Pelikan says, "proved again and again that it could not live by philosophy alone, but had to turn to the word of God in the Old and New Testament" (p. 55).

[227] See esp. Pss 33:10–11; 102:25–27; Isa 46:9–10; John 5:26; Acts 17:24–25; Rom 11:34–36. Cf. J. Edwards, "Dissertation Concerning the End for Which God Created the World," in *The Works of Jonathan Edwards,* vol. 8, *Ethical Writings* (New Haven: Yale University Press, 1957), 462.

every case. He rules from eternity over all time and space and is continually at work in the lives of his creatures.

Whereas some in the early church, like Clement of Alexandria, were surely too gracious in receiving into their belief systems what Greek thought had to offer, the claim of C. Pinnock and others that Greek philosophy is responsible for Christian theology's "tilt toward transcendence" is a blatant overstatement of the historical data and a denial of clear biblical evidence in support of classical theism.[228]

One could argue on the one hand for almost a deistic exercise of God's sovereign will, that he is like a great Computer Programmer who has begun a program that runs his universe with infinite complexity, responding to every circumstance with predetermined efficiency. Yet the Bible does not allow such a picture of a detached and passionless Creator-Designer. But neither does it allow the image of a purely responsive God for whom the future is infinite possibility. Whereas modern theology, with pressure from process theology, is leaning in the latter direction, the ancient and medieval church leaned the other way.

Classical theism has taught that God is only passible *(pathētos)* in Christ. As Ignatius of Antioch wrote to Polycarp ca. A.D. 107, "Look for Him that is above the times, Him who has no times, Him who is invisible, Him who for our sakes became visible, Him who is impalpable, Him who is impassible, Him who for our sakes suffered, Him who endured everything in every form for our sakes."[229] It was in part to deliver man from being subject to our "passions" that God became "passible man" in Christ.[230] Gregory of Nyssa wrote, "As God, the Son is certainly impassible and incapable of corruption; and whatever suffering is asserted concerning Him in the Gospel, He assuredly wrought by means of His human nature which admitted of such suffering."[231]

On the other hand, to Clement of Alexandria passionlessness is a goal of the Christian life, and even Christ "was altogether impassible; into Him no movement

---

[228] Against the revelation of a sovereign, omnipotent, and omniscient God who decrees the end from the beginning, presented in Ps 33:10–11; Isa 45:7; 46:9–10, and elsewhere, Pinnock proposes that "God sets goals for creation and redemption and realizes them 'ad hoc' in history. If Plan A fails, God is ready with Plan B" (p. 113). Elsewhere he contends that "the Bible does not represent God in possession of exhaustive knowledge of all future contingents. On the contrary, it presents God as a dynamic agent who deals with the future as an open question" (*Predestination and Freewill: Four Views of Divine Sovereignty and Human Freedom* [Downers Grove: InterVarsity, 1986], 139). See Pinnock's discussion in A. Mohler, "The Eclipse of God at Century's End: Evangelicals Attempt Theology without Theism," *SBTJ* 1.1 (1997): 6–15. P. R. Johnson has noted that in their desire for a God responsive to human pain and need rather than the *apathetic* God of classical theism, open theists have produced a *pathetic* "God in the hands of angry sinners" ("God without Mood Swings," in *Bound Only Once: The Failure of Open Theism* [Moscow, Ind.: Canon, 2001], 113.

[229] *Ad Poly.* 3. Cf. also Irenaeus, *Adv. Haer.* 3.17.6.

[230] Irenaeus, *Adv. haer.* 3.19.1.

[231] *Adv. Eunom.* 6.1. Irenaeus had earlier explained, "The Word indeed was quiescent in the temptation and crucifixion and death, but assisted the humanity in the victory and endurance and benevolence and resurrection and assumption" (*Adv. Haer.* 3.20.3).

of passion could find its way, neither pleasure nor pain."[232] Augustine defined "passion" (Lat. *passio*) as "a movement of the mind contrary to reason," and so impassibility is "life without those feelings which take place contrary to reason and disturb the mind."[233] "It is in the freedom from all disturbance, from all the weaknesses and defects which in human experience are associated with the various phases of the emotional life, that Augustine sees the divine impassibility."[234] Biblical references to divine feelings, he held, actually refer to divine actions that men commonly associate with those feelings. "The anger of God is His vengeance upon sin; the pity of God is the goodness of His help; the jealousy of God is that providence whereby he does not allow those whom He has in subjection to Himself to love with impunity what he forbids."[235] Anselm likewise meditated, "You are compassionate in terms of our experience, but not in terms of your being. . . . For when you see us in our wretchedness, we experience the effect of compassion, but you do not experience that feeling. So you are compassionate, in that you save the wretched and spare those who sin against you; and yet you are not compassionate, in that you are affected by no sympathy for wretchedness."[236]

The same line of thought was followed by Aquinas, who explained biblical references to God's anger or mercy or repentance as metaphorically ascribing to God the human emotions commonly associated with a particular effect. Thus "God is called merciful in so far as out of His loving-kindness He takes away the miseries of men, just as we do the same thing through the passion of mercy. . . . God is said to repent in so far as according to the eternal and immutable order of His providence He makes what He previously had destroyed, or destroys what He had previously had made—as those who are moved by repentance are found doing."[237] Emotions or passions to Aquinas were "acts of the sensitive [i.e., "sensual"] appetite" and as such involved bodily change of some sort (e.g., increased heart rate), which God would not experience since he has no body. God only loves, for example, as an act of the will (or "intellectual appetite") in that he wills good for his creatures.[238] He can be said to love some more than others in that he wills the greater good for some than for others.[239] Calvin did not depart from this

---

[232] *Stromateis* 7.11–14; 5.11; 6.9; 7.2. Similarly Origen, *de Principiis* II.4.4; *Contra Celsus* 4.71–72; *Num. Hom.* 23.2.

[233] *De Civ. Dei* 8.17; 14.8.4. Note in Harper Lee's novel, *To Kill a Mockingbird,* Atticus Finch says to the jury, "I am confident that you gentlemen will review without passion the evidence you have heard" ([New York: Lippencott, 1960], 208). That is, he wants their evaluation of the facts to be objective and rational, free of personal prejudice.

[234] J. K. Mozley, *The Impassibility of God: A Survey of Christian Thought* (Cambridge: University Press, 1926), 104.

[235] *Cont. adv. leg. et prophet* 1.40.

[236] *Proslog.* 8.

[237] *Summa Contra Gentiles* I.91.16. Similarly *Summa Theologica* q. 21, art. 3: "Mercy is especially to be attributed to God, as seen in its effect, but not as an affection of passion" since mercy involves "being affected with sorrow at the misery of another as though it were his own," which "belongs not to God."

[238] *Summa Theologica* q. 20, art. 1.

[239] Ibid., q. 20, art. 3.

viewpoint, commenting on Isa 63:9, "God, in order to alleviate the distresses and afflictions of His people, Himself bore their burdens; not that He can in any way endure anguish, but by a very customary figure of speech, He assumes and applies to Himself human passions."[240]

W. G. T. Shedd, defining "passion" not as synonymous with feeling or emotion but as "the working of mere appetite," flatly declared, "God has no passions."[241] As he explained further, whereas men and angels act and react in relation to the external universe they inhabit, "this does not apply to God. He is not operated upon and moved from the outside, but all his activity is self-determined."[242] Shedd denies that "the Divine nature is destitute of feeling altogether."[243] But he limits those emotions that can be *literally* attributable to God by the criterion of "divine blessedness": "God cannot be the subject of any emotion that is intrinsically and necessarily an unhappy one." This limits God's actual emotions, he says, to love, awakened by righteousness, and wrath, awakened by sin.[244] Although we usually associate wrath with unhappiness, "when the wrath falls upon only the sin and uncleanness of hell, and burns up nothing but filth in its pure celestial flame; then the emotion is not merely right and legitimate, but it is beautiful with an august beauty."[245]

The doctrine of God's transcendence at times has been emphasized to such a metaphysical extent that he seems almost isolated and callous. The ninth century theologian John Scotus Erigena claimed that all that is said of God is said metaphorically. "In truth God neither acts nor is acted upon, neither moves nor is moved, neither loves nor is loved."[246] Such a description of a static God does not match the living God encountered in Scripture. Also if this were the essential nature of God, it would be difficult to reconcile the doctrine of the incarnation with the unity of the Godhead. Can it be said that the acts and experiences of Christ are not also *God's* acts and experiences?[247] And what about the unity of the person of Christ? Can we speak of Christ's suffering as taking place in his

---

[240] J. Calvin, *Commentary on the Book of the Prophet Isaiah,* trans. and ed. W. Pringle, 1550. See also Turretin, *Institutio Theologiae elencticae* loc. 3, qu. 2.

[241] W. G. T. Shedd, *Dogmatic Theology* (Grand Rapids: Zondervan, 1971), 1:170–71.

[242] Ibid., 1:171.

[243] Ibid., 1:172.

[244] Ibid., 1:174.

[245] Ibid., 1:177.

[246] *De Divisione Naturae* p. 504, sec. 62B.

[247] Cf. T. F. Torrance, *The Christian Doctrine of God, One Being Three Persons* (Edinburgh: T&T Clark, 1996), 243–44: "There is a relation of complete fidelity and reliability between what God is in Jesus Christ toward us and what he is eternally in his unchangeable being. . . . God is not one thing in himself and another thing in Jesus Christ. . . . The constancy of God in time and eternity has to do with the fact that God really is like Jesus, for there is no other God than he who became man in Jesus and he whom God affirms himself to be and always will be in Jesus." He also quotes Athanasius: "One cannot say that [Jesus' pain, agitation and distress in soul] are natural to Godhead, but *they came to belong to God by nature,* when it pleased the Word to undergo human birth and to reconstitute in himself, as in a new image, that what he himself had made but which had been disorganised by sin, corruption and death" (p. 248).

human but not his divine nature?[248] Is not the efficacy of the cross owed in part
to the deity of the Christ as well as his humanity?[249] As D. Brown wrote, "To say
that the divine nature [of Christ] remains entirely impassible in the union would,
I think, undermine any claim to there being a single person present since there is
no way of distinguishing between God the Son's relationship to that particular
human nature and any other human nature."[250] Whereas Luther agreed in principle with the traditional doctrine of impassibility, he believed that in Christ the
two natures shared characteristics to the extent that it was possible to say that in
him God suffered and died.[251]

Mozley has chronicled the reaction to the classical doctrine of divine impassibility in Britain in the late nineteenth and early twentieth centuries.[252] A. J.
Mason expressed the thoughts of many today that it is possible to maintain
impassibility only in the sense that although God experiences emotion he is not
controlled by emotion. "No storms of grief can shake the permanent serenity of
God in its inmost depths, inasmuch as God sees the end from the beginning and
knows Himself to be able to overcome at last all that now causes sorrow to Him
and to those whom He loves." Nevertheless, biblical expressions of divine emotions, he said, are not metaphorical. "If words mean anything, God is capable of
grief and joy, of anger and of gratification; though there is nothing which can
force such states of feeling upon Him without His being willing to undergo
them." [253]

Furthermore, many have maintained that Jesus' words, "I and the Father are
one" and "If you have seen me you have seen the Father," force us to conclude
that the emotion and suffering we see in the incarnate Christ is an essential and
eternal aspect of the divine nature. According to W. Temple the cross reveals
"what selfishness in us means to God. . . . He displays his utter alienation from
evil by showing us the pain that it inflicts on Him."[254] Although in a "highly technical sense" he acknowledged that God is "without passion" in that as "Creator
and Supreme" he "is never 'passive' in the sense of having things happen to Him
except with His consent" and also "is constant, and free from gusts of feeling
carrying Him this way and that," nevertheless since the term "impassibility"

---

[248] Cf. Owen, *Concepts of Deity,* 24.

[249] As Cyril of Alexandria asserted, "If the Word did not suffer for us humanly, he did not
accomplish our redemption divinely; if he who suffered for us was mere man and but the organ of
Deity, we are not in fact redeemed" (quoted in Torrance, *Christian Doctrine of God,* 247). Torrance
echoes, "It is in his perfect oneness in being with God that the passion of Christ is saving" (*Christian Doctrine of God,* 252).

[250] D. Brown, *Divine Trinity,* 264, quoted in Torrance, *Christian Doctrine of God,* 251.

[251] J. Pelikan, ed., *Luther's Works* (St. Louis: Concordia, 1959), 23.104–5; also Heidelberg Disputation [1518]).

[252] Mozley, *The Impassibility of God,* 127–66. G. R. Lewis notes that even in 1786 the Anglican
Bishops Conference dropped the word "passions" from the Thirty-nine Articles' affirmation that
God is without body, parts, or passions ("Impassibility of God," 553).

[253] A. J. Mason, *The Faith of the Gospel: A Manual of Christian Doctrine* (New York: Dutton,
1907), 32f.

[254] W. Temple, *Christus Veritas,* 1924, 184.

means "incapable of suffering" he rejected it as "almost wholly false."[255] H. Bushnell wrote, "It is as if there were a cross unseen, standing on its undiscovered hill, far back in the ages, out of which were sounding always, just the same deep voice of suffering love and patience, that was heard by mortal ears from the sacred hill of Calvary."[256] On the other hand, although H. R. Mackintosh agreed that "a deity of stoical apathy is not the God whom Christ reveals," nevertheless he objected to placing "suffering *qua* suffering in the psychosis of God Himself." Only in Christ did God come to know "suffering as suffering." Trying to supplement the redemptive efficacy of Christ's suffering by positing "age-long pain in heaven" would be in danger of "losing a Christ who saves."[257]

Many have noted that the very idea of love carries with it the possibility of suffering when the beloved should suffer or should make choices that would lead to suffering (cf. 2 Cor 2:4). As Moltmann wrote, "If God were incapable of suffering in every respect, then he would also be incapable of love."[258] The idea that a loving divine Father could not see wayward and rebellious humanity without grief and personal suffering became especially important after the beginning of World War I when men called for a doctrine of God that made sense of intense misery and suffering.[259] Archbishop C. F. D'Arcy wrote in 1919, "If we have reason to believe that God shares in every human grief, that no lonely sufferer endures his agony apart from the sympathy and fellowship of God, that every sacrifice made is a sacrifice on God's part as well as on man's, and that, in suffering, God is calling on us to join Him in His age-long struggle against evil, we have a view of the world and of human life which gives to all genuine moral effort, whether pleasurable or painful, an intrinsic worth which cannot be estimated."[260]

As we observe Christ's reaction to Lazarus's death in John 11, we can agree that human misery receives much more from God than serene contemplation from a distance. Jesus was "deeply moved in spirit and troubled" and even wept

---

[255] Ibid., 269.

[256] H. Bushnell, *The Vicarious Sacrifice* (New York: Scribners, 1866), 23. Even more poignantly, C. A. Dinsmore wrote: "There was a cross in the heart of God before there was one planted on the green hill outside of Jerusalem. And now that the cross of wood has been taken down, the one in the heart of God abides, and it will remain so long as there is one sinful soul for whom to suffer" (*Atonement in Literature and Life* [Boston: Houghton Mifflin, 1906], 229–33).

[257] H. R. Mackintosh, *Historic Theories of Atonement* (London: Hodder & Stoughton, 1920), 252–56. Mozley asserted, "The significance of the Cross cannot be confined within the limits of time, but it does not follow that the actual pain of the Cross can be transferred backwards into the life of God and viewed as always associated with His love" (*The Impassibility of God,* 183). Nevertheless, Mackintosh declared that the atonement was "something done by God; it is an expression of his nature, for the atonement really is the cost to God of forgiveness" (*Some Aspects of Christian Belief* [London, 1924], 93).

[258] Moltmann, *The Trinity and the Kingdom*, 23. See also D. Ngien, "The God Who Suffers," *Christianity Today* (1997): 38.

[259] Cf. Moltmann, *The Trinity and the Kingdom*, 34–36.

[260] C. F. D'Arcy, "Love and Omnipotence," in *God and the Struggle for Existence* (New York: Association Press, 1919), 33.

as Mary and the others did (John 11:33–38). Surely this was not just a drama to assure us of God's intention to alleviate suffering and death. Nevertheless, the idea of some that human suffering involves cooperation with God's struggle against evil seems to lose sight of suffering's origin in human sin and to reverse the redemptive relationship we bear to Christ. In the first place evil is an intrinsic quality of fallen humanity, not a common enemy we share with God. Similarly, Whitehead's description of God as "the great companion—the fellow sufferer who understands" is blasphemously inadequate.[261] The only sense in which evil exists apart from man is in Satan, whom Christ conquered at the cross and will entirely eliminate in the eschaton—without our help. Second, Christ came to take upon himself the guilt of sin and its consequent penalty of suffering and death. His vicarious redemption is sufficient and effective for the redemption of all who believe and requires no supplementation by our suffering.[262] If "age-long pain in heaven" is inadequate and unnecessary to supplement the redemptive efficacy of Christ's suffering, as Mackintosh charged, certainly human suffering cannot do so.

According to John 11, this particular case of human suffering, into which Christ entered, could have been prevented by Christ himself. Even though "Jesus loved Martha and her sister and Lazarus" (v. 5), "when he heard that Lazarus was sick, he stayed where he was two more days" (v. 6). Why did Jesus intentionally delay when he could have returned in time to prevent the pain and grief Lazarus's death would cause not only to Lazarus's family and friends but also to Jesus? Jesus' own explanation was that "it is for God's glory so that God's Son may be glorified through it" (v. 4). Jesus' raising of Lazarus from the dead was the most amazing miracle that Jesus performed, and his anticipated joy in glorifying God by doing so made worthwhile the precursory grief ("for your sake I am glad I was not there, so that you may believe," v. 15). We may say five things, then, about human suffering: (1) it was caused by the fall, (2) it causes grief to God as well as to man, (3) it will be eliminated in the future according to God's plan, (4) in the meanwhile it results (in ways usually hidden from man) in God's glory,[263] and (5) it also serves to build up believers and prepare them for glory.[264]

---

[261] Cf. A. N. Whitehead, *Process and Reality,* corrected ed. (New York: Free Press, 1978), 497.

[262] As R. Melick explains, "The fellowship of sharing in his sufferings" in Phil 3:10 does not mean that the Christian contributes to Christ's sufferings but that Christ's sufferings are counted as our own as we are identified with him (*Philippians, Colossians, Philemon,* NAC [Nashville: Broadman, 1991], 136). Melick also explains Col 1:24 in terms of Acts 9:16. Paul would complete Christ's afflictions in that his afflictions would further the gospel and build up the body of Christ, bringing greater glory to Christ (pp. 237–40).

[263] The beginning of the Book of Job raises the question, Does God deserve to be worshiped for who he is, despite our circumstances? Job's suffering glorifies God at least because in all Job's arguing and complaining he never deserts his faith in God or even takes his eyes from him. Cf. also Acts 5:41; 9:16; 2 Cor 1:5–9; Phil 1:29; 2 Tim 1:8–12; 1 Pet 2:19–21; 4:12–19.

[264] Rom 5:3–5; 8:17–18; 2 Thess 1:5; 1 Pet 1:6–9. For a more detailed discussion of the purpose of suffering see J. S. Feinberg, "Pain," *Evangelical Dictionary of Theology* (Grand Rapids: Baker, 1984), 815–17.

The answer, then, to our original question must be subtly stated. As man, the image of God, is an emotional as well as a rational being, so too is God emotional as well as rational.[265] Although grief only entered human experience as a result of the fall, there is no reason to suppose that the "positive" emotions such as joy, pleasure, or affection were not an original part of man's experience, as when Adam saw his wife Eve for the first time. And if they were intrinsic to humanity, then they must also be intrinsic to deity. But what about grief? It seems that when grief became part of man's experience because of sin, it also became part of God's experience. This did not, however, reduce God to finiteness. The alternatives of "essential incapacity for suffering, or a fateful subjection to suffering" comprise a false dichotomy.[266] The original and essential divine experience of blessedness that was humanity's before the fall and that we are promised through Christ's redemption entails not "incapacity for suffering" but freedom from suffering and so inclusion in the divine rest, peace, and imperturbability. And whereas man was *subjected* to pain and suffering because of sin, there is every reason to conclude that God, whose character is not violated by the experience of emotion as it is in perfect harmony with divine rationality and will, freely and sovereignly experiences grief as well as joy in his relationship with his creatures as part of his plan of redemption.[267]

Moltmann's statement that God "remains master of the pain that love causes him to suffer"[268] is suggestive but imprecise. In the first place, even God's love is a result of his will to love. It is not just a "cause" of his action. Human experience often proceeds from emotion to will and then to act. But divine action always has its source in the divine will, then in divine emotion. It can be said that this distinction is part of what the doctrine of impassibility is all about. Second, in view of the uniqueness of Christ's atoning work, it is probably better to reserve the term "suffering" for the incarnate Christ, who endured physical as well as emotional pain.[269] It is sufficient to say that God grieves at sin, rejoices at righ-

---

[265] Cf. Mozley, *The Impassibility of God,* 180. He concludes, "Even if 'feeling,' owing to its associations, is an unfortunate word, it still may be much truer to say that God feels than that He does not" (p. 181).

[266] Moltmann, *The Trinity and the Kingdom*, 23.

[267] Mozley wrote, "It makes much difference whether, given the notion of a suffering God, God is thought of as suffering because the world leaves Him no option, in which case God's nature must be regarded as rendered passible by the constraint exercised upon it by the world, or whether God is said to suffer because in His love He freely associates Himself with the world's suffering by means of a true compassion. So one must bring in another of theology's relatively valuable distinctions, and ask whether God suffers because of His nature, or because of His grace" (*The Impassibility of God,* 181).

[268] Moltmann, *The Trinity and the Kingdom*, 23.

[269] Torrance denies that "Christ suffered only in his humanity and not in his divinity," but he asserts that "certainly the kind of physical and emotional suffering Christ endured in his incarnate historical existence in body and spirit is not the kind of suffering that we may attribute to God" (*Christian Doctrine of God,* 252). So "in Christ God both suffered and did not suffer: through the eternal tranquillity of his divine impassibility he took upon himself our passibility and redeemed it"; i.e., "he masters and transmutes it within the embrace of his own immutable peace and serenity" (p. 251).

teousness, and delights to satisfy the needs of his children. As he watches and cares for every sparrow, much more is he compassionately attentive to the smallest details of our lives (Matt 10:29–31). It is not without genuine emotion that God works in the lives of his creatures either in wrath and judgment or in love and blessing. What emotion God can experience is only limited by the perfections of his nature. For example, in view of his infinite knowledge, wisdom, and power, he cannot truly be surprised, frustrated, or disappointed, even though he is clearly grieved by our sin.[270] Nor does he ever experience anxiety, fear, or dread of the future. God's eternal "blessedness" of which theologians used to speak is the unavoidable result of the effectiveness with which God accomplishes his plans. Thus, since God can see the end simultaneously with the beginning, even his grief is not identical to human grief but is analogous to it (or vice versa).

Understood within these parameters, then, the doctrine of God's impassibility can be maintained. As Prestige has explained, "It is clear that impassibility means not that God is inactive or uninterested, not that He surveys existence with Epicurean impassivity from the shelter of a metaphysical insulation, but that His will is determined from within instead of being swayed from without."[271] It is, in fact, a corollary of his immutability. "Since God is in every way perfect, he cannot be altered by the influence of external things."[272] Or as Bavinck expressed it, "There is change round about him; there is change in the relations of men to God; but there is no change in God."[273] God has no need or cause to change; therefore his people have no need or cause to fear (cf. Mal 3:6 and discussion there).

Judah's charges against the Lord in Mal 2:17, that he either delights in all who do evil or at least refuses to exercise justice, are refuted in 3:1–6. The word for "justice," *mišpāṭ*, appears again in 3:5 but in the related sense of "judgment."

## 5. Negative Motivation: Coming Messenger of Judgment (3:1–6)

Like the first address, the second ends with a section that motivates the command (to faithfulness in this case) by describing what unpleasant things will happen if it is disobeyed. Like the climactic negative motivation section of 2:1–9, it uses *hinnê* ("see," "look," "behold") clauses (note the literal rendering of 3:1 below) to underline what is being said about the future.[274] The threat cen-

---

[270] Cf. Tertullian's statement, "God may be wrathful, but he is not irritated" (*Against Marcion* 2.16.7). On God's knowledge of the future See further our excursus, "Immutability of the Everlasting God," at 3:6.

[271] Prestige, *God in Patristic Thought*, 7. A similar definition is given in *The New Dictionary of Theology* (Wilmington: Michael Glazier, 1987), 510.

[272] M. Erickson, "God and Change," *SBJT* 1.2 (1997): 39.

[273] Bavinck, *The Doctrine of God*, 151.

[274] On the use of הִנֵּה see the notes on 2:1–3. The climactic nature of 3:1–6 is indicated by the striking rhetorical features: the chiasm in v. 1 and especially the extensive use of paraphrase throughout the section.

ters around the coming of the messenger of the covenant, whose arrival will bring a judgment of fire on the "great and dreadful day of the LORD" named in 4:5 and introduced in 3:2. Within the paragraph 2:17–3:6, these verses present the result of the sins described in 2:17. Weary of Judah's hypocritical pleas for justice and their complaints of divine inaction, the Lord announces a coming day of justice that will be different from what they expect or desire.

Verses 1–6 comprise a series of four main predictions (i.e., announcements regarding the future). The first three are each followed by resultant predictions, and the fourth is followed by an antithesis.[275] The structure may be displayed as follows (literal translation):

Prediction 1: *"See, I am sending my messenger.*                                     v. 1
    Result:    And he will clear a path before me.
Prediction 2: *And suddenly the Lord whom you are seeking will come to his temple.*
        [Paraphrase: And the messenger of the covenant in whom you delight,
            see, he is coming, <u>says Yahweh of hosts</u>.]
    Result:    And who will endure the day of his coming,                          v. 2
        [Paraphrase: and who is the one who stands when he appears?
            For he is like a smelting fire and like cleansing lye.]
Prediction 3:
        [Illustration: And he will sit {as one} smelting and purifying silver.]    v. 3
        *And he will purify the sons of Levi.*
        [Paraphrase: And he will refine them like gold and silver.]
    Result:    Then they will be to Yahweh presenters of offerings in righteousness.
        [Paraphrase: And pleasing to Yahweh will be the offerings of Judah    v. 4
            and Jerusalem as the days of old and as former years.]
Prediction 4: *And I will come near you for judgment.*                              v. 5
        [Amplification: And I will be a hurrying witness against sorcerers and adulterers
            and those who swear falsely
            and those who extort the wages of the wage earner, widow, and fatherless
            and those who turn aside a sojourner and do not fear me,
            <u>says Yahweh of hosts</u>.]
    Antithesis: Because I, Yahweh, have not changed,                               v. 6
        you the sons of Jacob have not perished."

## *(1) The Coming Lord (3:1–2)*

**[1]"See, I will send my messenger, who will prepare the way before me. Then suddenly the Lord you are seeking will come to his temple; the messenger of the covenant, whom you desire, will come," says the LORD Almighty.**

**[2]But who can endure the day of his coming? Who can stand when he appears? For he will be like a refiner's fire or a launderer's soap.**

---

[275] The so-called fifth oracle or disputation is usually said to begin with 3:6, partly on the basis of the divine quote formula at the end of v. 5 (e.g., Hill, *Malachi,* 284–85; Stuart, "Malachi," 1361). But since אָמַר יְהוָה, "says the LORD," occurs twenty-five times in Malachi, it cannot be said necessarily to conclude an oracle.

**3:1** The primary challenge of this verse is to identify the agents involved. There are four potential agents: "I/me," "my messenger," "the Lord *[hāʾādôn]* you are seeking," and "the messenger of the covenant." Most identify "I/me" with "the Lord you are seeking." Some consider "my messenger" and "the messenger of the covenant" to be two different agents distinct from "the Lord."[276] Petersen, on the other hand, thinks it likely that the two messengers are the same and are to be identified with "the Lord," a "prophetic messenger endowed with the same sorts of powerful abilities that Elijah received according to Mal. 3:23–24."[277] But was it not God himself the people had been "seeking" (2:17)? Furthermore, the fact that this "Lord" *(hāʾādôn)* would come to "his temple" indicates "the Lord" is no mere Elijah.[278]

The structure of the verse must be considered in sorting out the identifications. The chiastic (reverse) repetition, more clearly observed in a literal rendering, gives strong emphasis to this prophecy of the coming judge. This structure, together with the final quote formula, "says the LORD Almighty," and the adverb "suddenly,"[279] mark this as the most prominent part of the paragraph (2:17–3:6).

a— "**See**, I am sending my messenger.
And he will clear a path before me.
And suddenly **he will come** to his temple,
  b — the Lord **whom you are seeking** *[ʾăšer-ʾattem mĕbaqšîm]*.
  b′— And the messenger of the covenant **in whom you delight** *[ʾăšer-ʾattem ḥăpēṣîm]*,
a′ — see, he is coming."
  says Yahweh of hosts.

The verb *pānâ,* "clear" (NIV "prepare"), in this form *(piel)* means to "clear away, remove," and the object specifies either what is to be removed (Zeph 3:15) or (as here) what place is to be cleared (Gen 24:31; Lev 14:36; Ps 80:10). As Isa 57:14 and 62:10 clarifies, the sense is to clear away obstacles in the path.

This verb with the object *derek* means "prepare the way" or better "clear a path" and is used as a command in Isa 40:3; 57:14; 62:10. Only in Isa 40:3, however, is the Lord the one who is coming (in the other passages it is the people returning to the land), but there it is the people rather than a "messenger" who is to prepare for the Lord's arrival. Malachi apparently interprets the "messenger" here as identical with the "voice" in that passage, which the New

---

[276] E.g., Y. Kaufmann, *The History of the Religion of Israel, vol. 4: From the Babylonian Captivity to the End of Prophecy* (New York: Ktav, 1977), 444–45.

[277] Petersen, *Zechariah 9–14 and Malachi,* 210–12.

[278] See D. Stuart, "Malachi," in *The Minor Prophets: An Exegetical & Expository Commentary* (Grand Rapids: Baker, 1988), 3:1351–52.

[279] Baldwin, *Haggai, Zechariah, Malachi,* 243, explains that "suddenly" is associated with ominous conditions or imminent calamities.

Testament sees as fulfilled in John the Baptist (Matt 3:3; Mark 1:3; Luke 3:4; John 1:23). John the Baptist is also understood in the New Testament (Matt 11:14; 17:10–13//Mark 9:11–13; Luke 1:13–17) to fulfill the prophecy of Elijah in Mal 4:5, who is announced there to precede "that great and dreadful day of the LORD." If this verse may be understood in light of Isa 40:3, the task of "my messenger" would be to summon the people to prepare for the Lord's coming by clearing away the obstacles of unbelief.[280]

What is confusing is that the first person "before me" (identified at the end of the verse as Yahweh of hosts) changes to third person "he will come to his temple, the Lord whom you are seeking." Furthermore, this person ("the Lord") seems to be identified structurally with "the messenger of the covenant in whom you delight." So a messenger is to clear the way for Yahweh, who is coming to his temple and is "the messenger of the covenant." One explanation for this conundrum is to reject the proposed structure and understand the second half of the verse as essentially repeating the content of the first. This would identify "the messenger of the covenant" with "my messenger," reflected in a translation such as, "and/so the messenger of the covenant . . ."[281] But this neglects the parallel between "the Lord whom you are seeking" and "the messenger of the covenant in whom you delight," making the two relative clauses (*ʾăšer-ʾattem mĕbaqšîm* / *ʾăšer-ʾattem ḥăpēṣîm*) refer to different things.[282] These relative clauses probably should be understood as alluding to the question in 2:17 to which the Lord is responding, "Where is the God of justice?" If our understanding is correct, then this is one of those enigmatic Old Testament passages in which God and his unique angel/messenger ("the angel of the LORD") are spoken of as if they are one and the same (Gen 16:7–14; 18:1–19:1; 22:12; Exod 3:1–6).[283] From a Christian perspective its meaning is elucidated only in the New Testament through the coming of Jesus, God's Son, the Sent One (John 3:17; 3:34; 4:34; 5:23–24,30,36–38; 6:29,38–39,44,57; 7:16,18,28–29,33; 10:36; 12:44–45,49; 13:20; 14:24; 17:3, etc.). Especially

---

[280] W. C. Kaiser, Jr. explains that "under the oriental figure of an epiphany or arrival of the reigning monarch, the text urged for a similar removal of all spiritual, moral, and ethical impediments in preparation for the arrival of the King of Glory" ("The Promise of the Arrival of Elijah in Malachi and the Gospels," *GTJ* 3 [1982]: 225).

[281] Or as in REB ("I am about to send my messenger to clear a path before me. Suddenly the Lord whom you seek will come to his temple; the messenger of the covenant in whom you delight is here, here already, says the Lord of Hosts") or JPS ("Behold, I am sending My messenger to clear the way before Me, and the Lord whom you seek shall come to His Temple suddenly. As for the angel of the covenant that you desire, he is already coming").

[282] See also D. L. Bock, *Proclamation from Prophecy and Patterns,* JSNTSup (Sheffield: Academic Press, 1987), 322; Verhoef, *Haggai and Malachi,* 298.

[283] G. Van Groningen, *Messianic Revelation in the Old Testament* (Grand Rapids: Baker, 1990), 930. Note the NJB: "And suddenly the Lord whom you seek will come to his Temple; yes, the angel of the covenant, for whom you long, is on his way, says Yahweh Sabaoth."

significant for the context of judgment is John 8:16—"But if I do judge, my decisions are right, because I am not alone. I stand with the Father, who sent me."

The irony in the phrase "whom you desire/delight in" is apparent in its connection to the same word in 2:17. The wearisome people complain that God seems to be "pleased with" *(ḥāpēṣ)* those who do evil. They, on the other hand, pretend to hate evil and "desire" (the same Hebrew word) the messenger of the covenant to come with justice. They have charged that God is pleased with evil, whereas they are pleased with justice. The sense could be expressed by the translation "whom you (claim to) desire."

The phrase "messenger of the covenant" should be understood against the background of ancient Near Eastern covenant negotiations, which were usually carried out through messengers. One might argue that whenever a messenger of God appears in the Old Testament, the covenant between the Lord and Israel is always the issue.[284] Strongly in the background of this passage is Isaiah's message concerning the Lord's servant:

> "Here is *my servant*, whom I uphold, my chosen one *in whom I delight*; I will put my Spirit on him and he will bring justice to the nations. He will not shout or cry out, or raise his voice in the streets. A bruised reed he will not break, and a smoldering wick he will not snuff out. . . "I, the LORD, have called you in righteousness; I will take hold of your hand. I will keep you and will make you to be a covenant for the people and a light for the Gentiles, to open eyes that are blind, to free captives from prison and to release from the dungeon those who sit in darkness. (Isa 42:1–3,6–7)

In a narrow sense, the covenant that this divine servant messenger would come to administer would be that made with Israel in the wilderness of Sinai, the covenant that promised judgment for unbelief. But in a broad and ultimate sense he would be sealing that covenant that God made with Abraham promising vindication to God's people and blessing to all the nations of the earth.

**3:2** This verse expresses through rhetorical questions the result of the Lord's coming announced in the second prediction of v. 1. The verb translated "endure" sometimes means "contain" (cf. 1 Kgs 8:27; 2 Chr 2:6; 6:18). It is also used figuratively of things such as preaching, divine wrath, or grief that cannot be contained or endured (Prov 18:14 [NRSV]; Jer 6:11; 20:9; Joel 2:11; Amos 7:10). The participle is used here in a future sense: literally, "Who will endure . . .?" But how was this question to be answered? Could any endure? The answer is not given until v. 6.

Following the initial clause of v. 2 is another rhetorical question that paraphrases the first and is then is expanded by an explanatory comparison. The second question also employs a participle but with a prefixed article: literally, "Who is the one who stands . . .?" The expression "Who can stand . . .?" (using

---

[284] Cf. Gen 31:11–13; Exod 23:20–23,32; Judg 2:1–4,20; 1 Sam 11:7; 2 Sam 3:12–14; 5:11; 1 Kgs 20:1–9,34; 2 Kgs 17:4,13; Ps 78:49; Isa 33:7; 44:26; Ezek 17:15; Mal 2:7.

an imperfect rather than a participle) is also used regarding the Lord's wrath in Nah 1:6 ("Who can withstand his indignation?"); Pss 76:7[Hb. 8] ("Who can stand before you when you are angry?"); 130:3 ("If you, O LORD, kept a record of sins, O Lord, who could stand?"); 147:17 ("Who can withstand his icy blast?"). The question "Who can stand?" also echoes verses with a battle imagery: Josh 10:8; 2 Kgs 10:4; Jer 46:15; 46:21; Ezek 13:5; Dan 11:15; Amos 2:15 (see also Job 8:15). It is perhaps with this background that the verse is applied in a context of divine judgment (Pss 1:5; 5:5).

The "day of his coming," that is, "when he appears," is the "day of the LORD" made explicit in 4:5. The danger faced by the wicked is the Lord himself, who in the last clause of v. 2 is compared to a smelting fire used to remove metal impurities,[285] then to the lye soap used to wash clothes. The Lord's work as a refiner of men is also described in Isa 1:25; 48:10; Jer 6:29; 9:7[Hb. 6]; Zech 13:9; Dan 11:35; 12:10. Sometimes the sense is testing rather than removal of wickedness (Pss 17:3; 26:2; 66:10; 105:19). The comparison between the Lord and fire is made more explicitly in Deut 4:29 ("For the LORD your God is a consuming fire, a jealous God") and Heb 12:29 ("for our God is a consuming fire"; cf. Deut 9:3; Isa 30:27; Ps 50:3). The "smoking firepot with a blazing torch" in Gen 15:17, then, is an appropriate divine symbol, as is the burning bush of Exod 3:2.[286] The appropriateness of this symbol for God owes itself to mankind's dependence on various manifestations of fire for life, light, and protection (cf. Exod 13:21; 2 Kgs 6:17; Isa 4:5; Zech 2:5) but especially for purification and destruction (cf. Gen 19:24; Lev 10:1–2; Num 11:1; 2 Kgs 1:10; Ezek 39:6). Fire's use for purification and destruction overlap since purification is accomplished by the destruction of the undesirable (cf. 1 Cor 3:10–15). Although vv. 2–4 deal explicitly with purification, especially of the Levites (v. 3), judgment is also involved, as indicated by the questions "Who can endure?" and "Who can stand?" and by the declaration in v. 5, "So I will come near to you for judgment." That judgment will be against "sorcerers, adulterers and perjurers, against those who defraud laborers of their wages, who oppress the widows and the fatherless, and deprive aliens of justice, but do not fear me." Against such as these the Lord's anger burns (Exod 22:24; Deut 31:17; 2 Kgs 23:26; Job 42:7; Ps 97:3; Isa 30:33; 66:15,24; Jer 15:14; Hos 8:5; Nah 1:6; Zeph 3:8; Zech 10:3; Heb 10:27; 2 Pet 3:7; Rev 20:10,14–15). Sharing many features with the present passage is Ezek 22:18–22:

---

[285] For a summary of the refining process, see D. I. Block, *The Book of Ezekiel, Chapters 1–24,* NICOT (Grand Rapids: Eerdmans, 1997), 717.

[286] See also Exod 19:18; 2 Sam 22:9; Ezek 1:27; 10:1–7; Dan 7:9–10; Acts 2:3–4; 2 Thess 1:7). Cf. L. Ryken et al. eds., *Dictionary of Biblical Imagery* (Downers Grove: InterVarsity, 1998), 287.

Son of man, the house of Israel has become dross to me; all of them are the copper, tin, iron and lead left inside a furnace. They are but the dross of silver. Therefore this is what the Sovereign LORD says: 'Because you have all become dross, I will gather you into Jerusalem. As men gather silver, copper, iron, lead and tin into a furnace to melt it with a fiery blast, so will I gather you in my anger and my wrath and put you inside the city and melt you. I will gather you and I will blow on you with my fiery wrath, and you will be melted inside her. As silver is melted in a furnace, so you will be melted inside her, and you will know that I the LORD have poured out my wrath upon you.

It has been suggested that Jesus' "baptism of fire" alludes to "an eschatological stream of fire by which the wicked are consumed and the righteous refined (cf. Zech 13:9)."[287]

The word for "soap" is *bōrît* (note the similarity to *běrît,* "covenant"), referring to a cleansing agent made of alkali or potash.[288] The word occurs elsewhere only in Jer 2:22 ("Although you wash yourself with soda [*neter,* "natron, lye"] and use an abundance of *soap,* the stain of your guilt is still before me"). A synonym, *bōr,*[289] from the same root, occurs in Job 9:30–31 ("Even if I washed myself with soap and my hands with *washing soda,* you would plunge me into a slime pit so that even my clothes would detest me") and Isa 1:25 ("I will turn my hand against you; I will thoroughly [lit., "as *lye*"[290]] purge away your dross and remove all your impurities"). The word translated "launderer" is a participle from the verb *kbs,* "wash." It is used forty-eight times in the Old Testament, usually of removing ritual uncleanness by washing clothes.[291] The emphasis on washing in the Old Testament was a continual reminder of the separation between sinful man and the holy God (cf. Exod 19:10). "Physical washing became associated with the need for cleansing of the sinful soul" (cf. Job 9:28–31; Ps 51:2,7[Hb. 4,9]; Isa 1:16; 4:4–5; Jer 2:22; 4:14).[292] Unfortunately, it eventually was regarded as a substitute for it. These verses promise a time of judgment when the Lord would remove and discard the wicked like dross or dirt and refine his people. Cleansing ultimately can be accomplished only through Christ (John 13:10; 1 Cor 6:11; Titus 3:5; Heb 9:9–14; 10:1–22; 1 John 1:7–9; Rev 7:14; 22:14).

---

[287] Ibid., 288.

[288] *DCH* 2:267. *HALOT* renders it "alkaline salt, extracted from soap-plants, *Mesembrianthemum cristallinum.*"

[289] *HALOT* renders this word "potash, lye (alkali obtained from the ash of wood and plants, chemically $K_2CO_3$)."

[290] Likewise J. N. Oswalt, *The Book of Isaiah Chapters 1–39,* NICOT (Grand Rapids: Eerdmans, 1986), 103. *DHC,* however, renders this phrase, "so that it becomes like soap" (2:258).

[291] On the practice of washing clothes see J. D. W. Watts, *Isaiah 1–33,* WBC (Waco: Word, 1985), 91. כבס is used with בֶּגֶד thirty-six times, all but one (2 Sam 19:25) in Leviticus and Numbers (e.g., Lev 6:20; 11:25,28,40; 13:6,34,56,58; Num 8:7,21). It is also used once with לְבוּשׁ (Gen 49:11), twice with שִׂמְלָה (Exod 19:10,14), and once with בָּשָׂר (Lev 17:16).

[292] Ryken et al., eds., *Dictionary of Biblical Imagery,* 927.

## *(2) The Purifying Lord (3:3–4)*

**³He will sit as a refiner and purifier of silver; he will purify the Levites and refine them like gold and silver. Then the LORD will have men who will bring offerings in righteousness, ⁴and the offerings of Judah and Jerusalem will be acceptable to the LORD, as in days gone by, as in former years.**

**3:3** The third prediction of 3:1–6 is preceded by an illustration. We are told to picture a metalworker seated at his work. Such will be the Lord's activity as he purifies the Levites. Here the Lord is compared not with the fire as in v. 2 but with the artisan. As a silversmith purifies silver,[293] the Lord will purify the sons of Levi, that is, the priests. Whereas v. 2 expresses the unpleasantness of the process, this verse suggests the skill and attentiveness of the divine artisan seated at his work.[294] The quality of the product and thus the value of the process are emphasized by the repetition and expansion of the illustration in the clause, "and refine[295] them like gold and silver." According to G. A. Klingbeil, "God's refining of his people always involves a concrete goal or purpose, i.e., cleansing and purification. Something precious will result from the process."[296]

The reference to Levites[297] and offerings in vv. 3–4 stitches this second division to the first (cf. 2:1–9). The Lord's coming will deal not only with the problem of unfaithfulness, the particular concern of this division of the book, but also with the problem of laxness in worship, which was targeted in the first division. If there is to be a cleansing of God's people, it must begin with the temple and the priesthood, those "responsible for the religious decline of the people."[298] Their need for cleansing was made vivid in 2:3, where the Lord threatened to "spread on your faces the offal from your festival sacrifices."

The clause giving the result of the Lord's refining work may be understood syntactically in two different ways. A literal rendering would be "then they will

---

[293] Though there is no preposition "as" here in Hb. as there is in v. 2, the messenger of the covenant will not literally be "a refiner and purifier of silver"; a comparison must be in view. The participles are best understood as adverbial accusatives describing "the *manner* in which an action or state takes place" (GKC § 118m; cf. 118p,r; *IBHS* § 10.2.2d). I fail to see the advantage Hill claims for the rendering "he will remain a refiner and purifier of silver" (*Malachi,* 274–75).

[294] See Verhoef, *Haggai and Malachi,* 290. To explain the priority of silver over gold at this time cf. A. Robinson, "God, the Refiner of Silver," *CBQ* 11 (1949): 188–90. Note also his comment, "There is a dramatic moment when [the refiner] knows that all dross has gone from it. Peering over it, the silver suddenly becomes a liquid mirror in which the image of the refiner is reflected. Then he knows that his task is done" (p. 190).

[295] Unclear in the NIV, the word for "refine" here is not צָרַף, as earlier in the verse, but the less frequent זָקַק, "to filter, purify" (cf. Ps 12:7[Eng. 6]; Job 28:1).

[296] G. A. Klingbeil, "זָקַק," *NIDOTTE* 1:1141.

[297] The בְּנֵי־לֵוִי, "sons of Levi," here refers especially to the priests, as it does in Deut 21:5; 31:9. See also the discussion of Levites at 2:4.

[298] Verhoef, *Haggai and Malachi,* 291.

be/become to the LORD presenters of offerings in righteousness" (v. 3b). The interpretation depends on whether "to the LORD" is taken with the verb or with the complement. If taken with the verb, it yields the idiomatic sense "then they will belong to the LORD." In this case "presenters of offerings in righteousness" would be in apposition to the subject.[299] The NIV is one of the few translations that follows this interpretation, though it is favored by the masoretic "punctuation."[300] The alternative is to disregard the masoretic tradition and to understand "to the LORD" as modifying the substantival participle, yielding "presenters to the LORD of offerings in righteousness." In this case the word order places the focus on "to the LORD." The Levites have been presenting offerings (2:3), but they have not been offering them "to the LORD," that is, in a righteous state or manner (cf. 1 Kgs 3:6; Isa 9:7; 48:1; 63:1; Zech 8:8; Ps 5:8[Hb. 9]).[301] The NRSV, for example, follows this second alternative except that it translates the clause as circumstantial, "until they present offerings to the LORD in righteousness." This, however, fails to bring out the progressive sense of the participle construction, "be/become presenters," and it fails to account for the focus on "to the LORD." However the syntax is construed, the result of the Lord's refining will surely be a priesthood who belongs to the Lord and has changed their attitude "from disdain, contempt, and carelessness to honesty and integrity."[302] It is important to note by comparison with Jer 2:22 ("Although you wash yourself with soda and use an abundance of soap, the stain of your guilt is still before me") that a process of self-purification is not in view here. The Lord must do the purifying if right worship will be the outcome.[303]

**3:4** The result of the third prediction, like the result of the second (v. 2), is followed by paraphrase. The righteous offerings of v. 3 are said in v. 4 to be pleasing to the Lord. By referring to "the offerings of Judah and Jerusalem" this verse suggests that the cleansing will extend beyond the priesthood. In contrast to the Lord's attitude of "weariness" or exasperation in 2:17, his purifying work will result in offerings that will please him (cf. 1:11).[304] The verb (*ʿārab*)

---

[299] See Glazier-McDonald, *Malachi,* 153; O'Brien, *Priest and Levite in Malachi,* 44; Hill, *Haggai and Malachi,* 277.

[300] I.e., the disjunctive accent *(zaqeph)* with לַיהוה.

[301] As D. A. Garrett noted on Hos 3:4 (*Hosea, Joel,* NAC [Nashville: Broadman & Holman, 1997], 103): "'Sacrifice' could be good or evil, depending on to whom and with what attitude the sacrifice was made. Sacrifice to Yahweh with a broken heart is good, but sacrifice to Baal is always evil, and even sacrifice to Yahweh without true faith is corrupting (1 Sam 15:22)."

[302] Hill, *Malachi,* 278. The verb נֹגֵשׁ, "present," earlier occurred in 1:7,8,11; 2:12. The noun מִנְחָה, "offering," occurred in 1:10,11,13; 2:12,13.

[303] On the possible allusion to Mal 3:1–4 in 1 Pet 4:12, see T. R. Schreiner, *1, 2 Peter, Jude,* NAC (Nashville: Broadman & Holman, 2003).

[304] Glazier-McDonald notes the parallel between וְהָיוּ לַיהוָה, "and they will belong to the LORD" in v. 3, and וְעָרְבָה לַיהוָה, "and it will be pleasing to the LORD" in v. 4 (*Malachi,* 153).

means "to be pleasant" or "pleasing" and occurs only seven times.[305] In three other cases it refers to sacrifices (Jer 6:20; Hos 9:4) or meditation (Ps 104:34) as pleasing to the Lord. Elsewhere it describes the pleasantness of sleep (Ezek 16:37; Prov 3:24), of one's lover (Ezek 16:37), or of a fulfilled desire (Prov 13:19). It is a synonym of *rṣh* and of *ḥpṣ* in Mal 1:8,10,13; and 2:17.

> "When you bring blind animals for sacrifice, is that not wrong? When you sacrifice crippled or diseased animals, is that not wrong? Try offering them to your governor! Would he be pleased *[rṣh]* with you? Would he accept you?" says the LORD Almighty. (1:8)
> "Oh, that one of you would shut the temple doors, so that you would not light useless fires on my altar! I am not pleased *[ḥpṣ]* with you," says the LORD Almighty, "and I will accept *[rṣh]* no offering from your hands. (1:10)
> "And you say, 'What a burden!' and you sniff at it contemptuously," says the LORD Almighty. "When you bring injured, crippled or diseased animals and offer them as sacrifices, should I accept *[rṣh]* them from your hands?" says the LORD. (1:13)
> You have wearied the LORD with your words. "How have we wearied him?" you ask. By saying, "All who do evil are good in the eyes of the LORD, and he is pleased *[ḥpṣ]* with them" or "Where is the God of justice?" (2:17)

So the situation described in the first division will be reversed by the Lord's purifying work.

Like the paraphrase in v. 2, this one is expanded, here with a comparison to "days gone by" and "former years" (cf. Amos 9:11; Mic 7:14). We may assume this to be the same time as in 2:5–6, which describes the priests' former faithfulness:

> My covenant was with him, a covenant of life and peace, and I gave them to him; this called for reverence and he revered me and stood in awe of my name. True instruction was in his mouth and nothing false was found on his lips. He walked with me in peace and uprightness, and turned many from sin.

### (3) The Vindicating Lord (3:5–6)

**5"So I will come near to you for judgment. I will be quick to testify against sorcerers, adulterers and perjurers, against those who defraud laborers of their wages, who oppress the widows and the fatherless, and deprive aliens of justice, but do not fear me," says the LORD Almighty.**

**6"I the LORD do not change. So you, O descendants of Jacob, are not destroyed.**

**3:5** This verse begins with the fourth and last main prediction in 3:1–6 and indicates that after purifying the sons of Levi, the Lord will exercise judgment against the people's wickedness.[306] Six sins (or seven with NIV; see

---

[305] According to *HALOT*, four other identical roots (homonyms) also occur, meaning (I) "stand surety for," (II) "be involved with someone," (III) "offer," and (IV) "turn into evening."

[306] I see no need to interpret the *waw* on וְקָרַבְתִּי as introducing "a statement of exclamation and certitude" or of being emphatic (thus Hill, *Malachi*, 279). Nor is the JPS translation "But first" justified. Having dealt with the priests, God will deal with the people in general.

comments on "those who defraud laborers of their wages" below) are listed, culminating in the general indictment that they "do not fear me." The word for "judgment" here is the same word, *mišpāṭ*, used by the people in their impertinent question in 2:17, "Where is the God of justice?" Thus the people are reminded that the "justice" they sought is the very thing the Lord was going to bring. But the Lord's justice is evenhanded and is impossible for hypocrites to control. It would bring condemnation and punishment against the sins of the very people who were calling for it. The verb "come near" is used in a forensic sense as often in Isaiah, but there it is always others called to come before God (34:1; 41:1,5; 48:16; 57:3). Only here is God the one who comes.

Like predictions two and three, the fourth is expanded by the following clause. The phrase "quick to testify" is literally "a hurrying witness."[307] The term "witness" *('ēd)* calls to mind the covenant between God and Israel, which Israel swore to uphold.[308] The Book of the Law was a witness against them (Deut 31:26), as was Israel's God, who had pledged to enforce the covenant (Deut 28:15–68). The related verb *'wd*, "to witness, warn" (cf. Mal 2:14) could also mean "accuse" (e.g., 1 Kgs 21:10,13; Ps 50:7; Amos 3:13). As R. Chisholm explains, when God acted as witness, "he did not merely testify to the truth, but also served as the vindicator of wronged parties and the judge of wrongdoers."[309] When the time comes for God to judge, Malachi says, he will do so quickly, without hesitation. Like Isaiah's audience, who wanted God to hurry up and prove himself (Isa 5:19), Malachi's disputants would wish they had not spoken so rashly.

The first sin listed is Sorcery or witchcraft *(kšp)*,[310] the attempt to control the physical and spiritual world through magical incantations, charms, and rituals. It is encountered about a dozen times in the Bible, beginning with the Egyptian practitioners of magic (Exod 7:11).[311] If a sorceress or witch was found in Israel, she was to be executed according to Exod 22:18. In Deut 18:9–

---

[307] "Hurrying" is the *piel* participle of מהֹר. The form is used only two other times. In Prov 6:18 it describes one who is "swift" to do evil; and in Gen 41:32, something that will happen "soon."

[308] On the connection between "covenant" and "witness" see Gen 31:44–52; Deut 31:19,21; Josh 22:27–34; Jer 42:5.

[309] R. B. Chisholm, "עוּד," *NIDOTTE* 3:337. He notes further (3:338) that Yahweh's dual role as "witness-judge" is especially clear in this passage from Malachi, where he serves as both witness and "enforcer" (i.e., "messenger"). Cf. Jer 29:21,23, which describes the sins (viz., adultery and lying) of two Jewish false prophets among the exiles in Babylon. Yahweh declares, "I know it and am a witness to it," and he announces that they will be executed.

[310] Cf. the Akk. term, *kišpû*, "magic, witchcraft," referring to magic intended to bring harm. On the use of magic in the ANE see J. A. Scurlock, "Magic," *ABD* 4:464–68. "Sorcerers" and "adulterers" are both masculine plural *piel* participles in Hb. but are both translated by feminine nouns in the LXX: τὰς φαρμακοὺς, "sorceresses," and τὰς μοιχαλίδας, "adulteresses."

[311] Other terms for various forms of magic or sorcery are used in Lev 19:26,31; 2 Kgs 21:6//2 Chr 33:6, etc. See the discussion of these terms in G. André, "כָּשַׁף *kāšap*," *TDOT* 7.360–66.

11 sorcerers are lumped together with those who sacrificed their sons and daughters in the fire, who practiced divination, gave oracles, interpreted omens, cast spells, were mediums or spiritists, or who consulted the dead. God viewed such practices as evil and was provoked to anger by them (2 Chr 33:6). It was for such detestable sins that the Canaanites had been under God's judgment. Jezebel, the Phoenician wife of king Ahab, is charged with sorcery or witchcraft in 2 Kgs 9:22. Sorcery had been unable to prevent the downfall of Judah (Jer 27:9–10; cf. Mic 5:12) or of Babylon itself (Isa 47:8–15; Dan 2:2; cp. Acts 8:9–13; 13:6–12). Sorcery is also condemned in the New Testament, where it is specifically listed as a disqualification from the future blessings of divine fellowship (Gal 5:20; Rev 9:21; 21:8; 22:15). True biblical faith is unique in zealously pressing the fact of divine freedom from any kind of human manipulation (cf. Acts 8:18–23). In the context of Malachi's list, however, what may be especially in view is the use of sorcery to harm others (cf. Ezek 13:18,20).

The second sin listed is adultery. The seriousness of the sin of adultery is nowhere more vivid than in Job 31:11–12. Verse 11 describes it as *zimmâ*, defined as "indecent and disgusting sexual conduct"[312] and a "criminal offense" (NRSV; *ʿāwōn pĕlîlîm*). In v. 12 it is called "a destructive, hellish fire, consuming everything I have" (TEV; cf. Prov 6:27–33). Not surprisingly, then, it was one of the sixteen capital crimes in Israel (Lev 20:10; Deut 22:22).[313] Some may be surprised, however, that the definition of adultery in the Old Testament is a matter of some controversy. The view of what may be the majority of Old Testament scholars is that adultery in the Old Testament and in ancient Israel was defined as "sexual intercourse between a married or betrothed woman and any man other than her husband. The marital status of the woman's partner is inconsequential since only the married or betrothed woman is bound to fidelity. The infidelity of a married man is not punishable by law but is criticized" (as in Mal 2:14–15 and Prov 5:15–20).[314] E. Neufeld even claimed that

---

[312] M. H. Pope, *Job*, AB (New York: Doubleday, 1965), 203.

[313] The other capital crimes were murder, kidnapping, striking or cursing one's parents, magic or divination, bestiality, sacrificing to false gods, profaning the Sabbath, offering human sacrifice, incest, homosexuality, blasphemy, false prophecy, incorrigible rebelliousness, fornication, and rape of a betrothed virgin. See W. C. Kaiser, Jr., *Toward Old Testament Ethics* (Grand Rapids: Zondervan, 1983), 91–92. See also Hos 4:2; Jer 7:9.

[314] E. A. Goodfriend, "Adultery," *ABD* 1:82. Similarly, J. Milgrom declares that "it is the bride, not the husband, who is subject to the laws of adultery" (*Cult and Conscience* [Leiden: Brill, 1976], 134). O. J. Baab declared that "adultery was not so much evidence of moral depravity as the violation of a husband's right to have sole sexual possession of his wife and to have the assurance that his children were his own" (*IDB* 1.51). G. H. Hall says adultery in the OT "involves the sexual liaison of a man with a married woman . . . a married woman with a man . . . or a man with a betrothed girl" ("אַף," *NIDOTTE* 3:3). This leads to the view that adultery was considered wrong primarily because it threw into question or corrupted the line of descent (cf. D. R. Mace, *Hebrew Marriage: A Sociological Study* [London: Epworth, 1953], 242; A. Phillips, *Ancient Israel's Criminal Law* [Oxford: Blackwell, 1970], 117), from which one might reach the abominable conclusion that such an act only counts as adultery if children are produced.

"the husband was under no obligation whatsoever to his wife to refrain from extramarital intercourse, nor had the wife any ground for complaint, at all events as long as he did not deprive her of her necessary maintenance and her right to marital intercourse. This seems to be an implication of Ex. 21:10."[315] It is true that the Old Testament repeatedly condemns any man who would have relations with his neighbor's wife.[316] Furthermore, although the term "adultery" *(n'p)* is often used of a woman (e.g., Hos 4:14), there are no indisputable cases in which she is clearly unmarried.[317] Her marital status, however, is not always specified (Job 24:15–16; Prov 30:20).

According to Prov 5:3–5, however, a young man is to avoid the "strange woman" (Hb. *zārâ*; NIV "adulteress"; NRSV "loose woman"), that is, a woman other than his wife,[318] because going with her will lead to anguish and death (cf. also Prov 7:5–27). Judicial punishment is not mentioned, but this is more than "criticism" (see also Hos 4:14). As we have seen from Mal 2:14–15, a man's divorcing his wife is sin because it is a betrayal of his marriage covenant. In fact, as Hugenberger pointed out, "If a covenant existed between a husband and his wife, then any offence against the marriage by either the husband or the wife may be identified as sin *(ḥṭ', pš', etc.)*, perfidy *(m'l)*, or infidelity *(bgd)* against the other, as these terms are employed elsewhere in analogous cases of covenant violation (e.g., 2 Kgs. 1:1; 18:14; etc.)."[319] He also demon-

---

[315] E. Neufeld, *Ancient Hebrew Marriage Laws* (London: Longmans, Green & Co., 1944), 163.

[316] Exod 20:17; Lev 18:20; Deut 5:21; 22:22,24; Job 31:9; Prov 6:29; Jer 5:8; Ezek 18:6,11,15; 22:11; 33:26. D. N. Freedman and B. E. Willoughby argue that "since nothing is said [in Lev 20:10] about whether the adulterer is married, this question clearly does not matter in the situation" *(TDOT* 9.114). But that is true not because the marital status of the man is of no importance but because the case is of a man committing adultery with another man's wife, which itself renders the act adulterous and therefore a transgression. Freedman and Willoughby also state that the violation in this case is not against the woman or against the man's own wife (if he is married) but against the woman's husband. This is not stated in the passage, however, which only says, "If a man commits adultery with another man's wife—with the wife of his neighbor."

[317] Hugenberger, *Marriage as a Covenant,* 314.

[318] The term נָכְרִיָּה, "strange woman," outside Proverbs refers to a "foreign woman" (1 Kgs 11:1,8; Ruth 2:10; Ezra 10:2,10,11,14,17,18,44; Neh 13:26,27). It is usually said to refer to another man's wife in Proverbs (M. V. Fox, *Proverbs 1–9,* AB [New York: Doubleday, 2000], 139–41), but this exceeds the evidence. Fox himself says "the antithesis of the *zarah-nokriyyah* [strange or foreign woman] is not an Israelite woman or a woman of proper social standing, but rather one's own wife" (p. 140). He also notes that in Ezek 16:32 Judah is called an adulteress who prefers "strangers" to her own husband, meaning she "tak[es] other men instead of her husband." Therefore the "strange woman" would be any woman other than the man's wife (note JPS "forbidden woman" in Prov 6:24; 23:27, "unfamiliar woman" in 20:16; 27:13, and RSV's "adventuress"). Whether or not she is married to another would be an additional qualification. Thus the NIV's translation of נָכְרִיָּה in Proverbs as "wayward wife" (2:16; 6:24; 7:5; 23:27), "another man's wife" (5:20) is unjustified (note the translation "wayward woman" in 20:16; 27:13).

[319] Hugenberger, *Marriage as a Covenant,* 282. He points out that in Num 5:12,27 adultery is identified as מַעַל, "perfidy," apparently because it was considered an oath violation (cf. Num 5:6–7; p. 283). Note his refutation of Milgrom's four reasons for rejecting this inference on pp. 283–88. He also points out that the term בָּגַד, "infidelity, treachery," which usually refers to covenant violation, is used of a husband as well as a wife as in Exod 21:8; Jer 9:1[Eng. 2]; Mal 2:14–16.

strates that it was regarded as sin against God, inviting judgment (see Gen 39:9).[320] The marital status of the man, therefore, is most assuredly not "inconsequential." Marital fidelity is as much an obligation of the husband in the Old Testament as the wife, and infidelity, whether on the part of the husband or the wife, is a sin, regardless of whether the term "adultery" (the root *n'p*) is used of it.

Furthermore, in Matt 19:9 (par. Mark 10:11; Luke 16:18) Jesus explains that divorcing one's wife and marrying another amounts to adultery (*moixao*, "commit adultery") because it breaks the one-flesh relationship established at marriage. And in Matt 5:27–28 he elaborates on the law of adultery: "You have heard that it was said, 'Do not commit adultery.' But I tell you that anyone who looks at a woman lustfully has already committed adultery with her in his heart." No suggestion is given that Jesus was assuming the woman lusted after as well as the other woman in Matt 19:9 were married.

The common view that sexual relations between a married man and an unmarried woman was not condemned is based on an argument from silence and on the assumption that Israelite marriage law and custom would have followed that of the surrounding cultures, in which adultery was forbidden primarily because it involved infringement of a husband's rights and property.[321] The biblical evidence may be misleading because of our modern assumption that there was a significant group of unmarried women in Israelite society. Even the "prostitute" is often said to be married, and marriages usually took place soon after puberty. Although "adultery" is commonly used of the marital infidelity of a wife or of her lover, a married man's visit to a prostitute also seems to involve adultery in Jer 5:7–8: "Why should I forgive you? Your children [or "sons"] have forsaken me and sworn by gods that are not gods. I supplied all their needs, yet they committed adultery and thronged to the houses of prostitutes. They are well-fed, lusty stallions, each neighing for another man's wife." Adultery and promiscuity erodes human dignity and reduces us to beasts. "A man who bears the image of God and yet treats sex as a mere

---

[320] Ibid., 291–93.

[321] Against the view that the OT condemned adultery because it involved the infringement of property rights, Wright (*God's People in God's Land,* 201–2) notes that this assumption would make illogical the death penalty for both parties (Why destroy the property?). He also points out that characteristically "the death penalty was not applied to offenses involving property" (e.g., see Lev 19:20). Elsewhere he explains that the common translation "bride-price" for "מֹהַר" is very misleading in giving rise to the idea that marriage in Israel was solely a matter of purchase. . . . This view, and its oft-repeated correlates, that wives in Israel were chattel property and that adultery was simply a property offense, cannot be supported from a careful study of the laws and narratives about wives in the OT" ("Family," *ABD* 2.761–68*).*

biological phenomenon is degraded and blind."[322] We would do well to heed the words of S. H. Kellogg:

> Marriage and the family are not merely civil arrangements, but divine institutions; so that God has not left it to the caprice of a majority to settle what shall be lawful in these matters. . . . God has declared not merely the material well-being of man, but *holiness*, is the moral end of government and of life; and He will find ways to enforce His will in this respect. 'The nation that will not serve Him shall perish.' All this is not theology, merely, or ethics, but history. . . . Despite the unbelief of multitudes, the Holy One still governs the world, and it is certain that He will never abdicate His throne of righteousness to submit any of His laws to the sanction of a popular vote.[323]

As stated in Heb 13:4, "Marriage should be honored by all, and the marriage bed kept pure, for God will judge the adulterer and all the sexually immoral."

Third, the Lord also promises judgment against "perjurers," literally "those who swear to a lie *[šeqer]*." An oath involved a guarantee of the truthfulness of one's word (but see Matt 5:37; Jas 5:12), sometimes a promise of loyalty, as when King Abimelech asked for an oath from Abraham in Gen 21:23: "Now swear to me here before [lit. "by"] God that you will not deal falsely *[šāqar]* with me or my children or my descendants. Show to me and the country where you are living as an alien the same kindness *[ḥesed,* "faithful love"] I have shown to you" (see also Josh 2:12; Isa 19:18; Zeph 1:5). A mutual agreement sealed with such reciprocal oaths constituted a covenant (Gen 26:28–29). An oath might also include a conditional curse on oneself (e.g., 1 Sam 20:13; Matt 26:74). To make such an oath "by the name of" or simply "by" God (Gen 24:3; Deut 6:13; 10:20; Josh 23:7) meant that one was inviting God's anger should one fail to act in accord with one's word (as in the expression, "May God deal with me, be it ever so severely," 2 Sam 3:35).[324] To swear to the truthfulness of

---

[322] D. Wilson, *Fidelity: What It Means to Be a One-Woman Man* (Moscow, Ind.: Canon, 1999), 54. We should also note Wilson's caution: "Happily married men do not wake up one morning and decide they are going to commit adultery that day. Particularly with Christians, the consummation of infidelity usually comes as the last in a series of mild compromises and unobtrusive self-deceptions" (p. 59). D. Willard proposes that "one of the most telling things about contemporary human beings is that they cannot find a reason for not committing adultery. Yet intimacy is a spiritual hunger of the human soul, and we cannot escape it. . . . We now keep hammering the sex button in the hope that a little intimacy might finally dribble out. In vain. For intimacy comes only within the framework of an individualized faithfulness within the kingdom of God. Such faithfulness is violated by 'adultery in the heart' as well as by adultery in the body" (*The Divine Conspiracy* [New York: HarperCollins, 1998], 163).

[323] S. H. Kellogg, *The Book of Leviticus* (3d ed.; 1899; repr., Minneapolis: Klock & Klock, 1978), 430–31.

[324] God could also take an oath, but he could only swear "by himself" (Gen 22:16; Heb 6:13). Perhaps the equivalent to swearing "by God" was to swear "as the LORD lives" (e.g., 1 Sam 19:6; 28:10). Cf. God's oath in Num 14:21: "As I live . . ." On the language of oaths in the Hb. Bible cf. S. A. Meier, *Speaking of Speaking: Marking Direct Discourse in the Hebrew Bible* (Leiden: Brill, 1992), 201–5.

a lie (e.g., 1 Kgs 8:31–32; Jer 5:2), therefore, was a serious offense against God, profaning his name (Lev 19:12; Num 30:2) by implying that God was powerless or did not care how his name was treated. It amounted, in fact, to a violation of the Third Commandment (Exod 20:7; Deut 5:11; Jer 7:9; Zech 5:3–4). Worshipers of the Lord, on the contrary, are to pursue the "hallowing" of his name (Matt 6:9; John 12:28).

More particularly in view here, however, is the use of false oaths to defraud or harm others. For example, false oaths are included with violations requiring the *Asham* or "guilt offering" in Lev 6:2–5:

> deceiving his neighbor about something entrusted to him or left in his care or stolen, or if he cheats him, or if he finds lost property and lies about it, or if he swears falsely, or if he commits any such sin that people may do—when he thus sins and becomes guilty, he must return what he has stolen or taken by extortion, or what was entrusted to him, or the lost property he found, or whatever it was he swore falsely about.

The same is suggested by Lev 19:12 read in the context of vv. 9–18, which lists it along with laws concerning care for the poor and strangers, theft, deceit, oppression, withholding pay from a laborer (the same concept as here in Mal 3:5, though different terms are used except for "laborer"), taking advantage of the helpless, injustice, slander, injury to a neighbor, and vengeance. In Jer 7:9 it is listed along with the sins of theft, murder, adultery, and burning incense to Baal, and Zech 5:3–4 pairs it with theft (see also 1 Tim 1:9–11, which lists "perjurers" after "liars").

The fourth sin listed is "those who defraud laborers of their wages [or "who extort the *wages of a wage earner*," *śĕkar śākîr*],[325] who oppress the widows and the fatherless." No Hebrew word corresponds to "who oppress" in the phrase "who oppress the widows and the fatherless." "Widow and fatherless" (*'almānâ wĕyātôm*) is usually taken as the expanded object either of the preceding words, yielding "against those who oppress the hired workers in their wages, the widow and the orphan" (NRSV),[326] or of the following words, yielding "who subvert the cause of the widow, orphan, and stranger" (JPS).[327] The Hebrew accentuation favors the latter, though the word order makes this view unlikely. The interpretation followed by the NIV, that an additional verb is to be understood, is also followed by the REB, the NAB, and some commentaries.[328] The LXX supplies two verbs, reading "and who oppress *[katadunasteuontas]* the widow and strike *[kondulizontas]* the fatherless." Otherwise it follows the Hebrew closely, which groups the sins in v. 5 into four categories by four uses of the preposition *bĕ*, "on, against" (followed by four uses of the Greek preposition *epi* in the LXX):

---

[325] The phrase שְׂכַר שָׂכִיר, "wages of a wage earner," occurs elsewhere only in Deut 15:18, although פְּעֻלַּת שָׂכִיר is found in Lev 19:13.

[326] Stuart, "Malachi," 1357; Petersen, *Zechariah 9–14 and Malachi*, 207.

[327] Cf. Rudolph, *Haggai–Sacharja 1–8/9–14–Maleachi*, 276.

[328] Merrill, *Haggai, Zechariah, Malachi*, 429; Verhoef, *Haggai and Malachi*, 282.

> I will come near you for judgment, and I will be a swift witness
> against those who (masc., but fem. in LXX) practice sorcery
> and against those who (masc., but fem. in LXX) practice adultery
> and against those who (masc.) swear (LXX adds "in my name") to a lie
> and against those who (masc.) extort the wages of a wage earner
>      widow and fatherless
>      who (masc.) divert (justice from) a stranger
>      and do not fear me.

It is easy to see poor treatment of the wage earner, the widow or fatherless, and the stranger as similar in kind, whether the widow and fatherless fits more closely with the preceding or the following. Glazier-McDonald suggests that since the preceding verb *('āšaq)* can mean either "extort" or "defraud, rob, oppress," in its former meaning it governs the object, "wages," and in its latter meaning it governs the object, "widow and fatherless," as it does in Zech 7:10.[329] This may be the most reasonable explanation, though the difference in meaning is minimal.

This list of sins builds to a climax in contempt for the Lord. As failure to fear the Lord had resulted in religious activity that actually insulted him (1:6–14), so here it resulted in wickedness and injustice toward the helpless. In fact, according to Isaiah, if Israel's temple worship had been meticulous, it would still have been meaningless and even detestable in view of the absence of the essential ethical component that included justice for the fatherless and the widow (Isa 1:13–17; cf. Isa 10:1–3; Jer 7:11). The widow, the fatherless, and the stranger are also treated together in such passages as Exod 22:21–22 (in whose context the sin of sorcery is also listed, 22:18).[330] The Mosaic law included the stranger with the poor as those who should not be harmed in any way but deserved gracious provision and even "love." Israel was to consider and treat them with kindness, remembering that they themselves had been strangers in Egypt before the Lord freed them and that they remained strangers in that the land continued to belong not to them but to the Lord (Lev 19:10,33–34; 23:22). This attitude toward the land should have inhibited the development of a society highly stratified between a landed nobility and the poor.[331] But as King Ahab's treatment of Naboth illustrates, such an attitude was increasingly replaced by greed in preexilic Israel, necessitating such prophetic words of grief and anger as those of Isaiah and also Amos, who rebuked those who would steal grain from the poor and then "hate the one who reproves in court and despise him who tells the truth" (Amos 5:7,10). Amos also charged,

---

[329] Glazier-McDonald, *Malachi*, 164–5; also Hill, *Malachi*, 283.

[330] M. Fishbane considers that Mal 3:5 makes explicit reference to Exod 22 (*Biblical Interpretation in Ancient Israel* [Oxford: Clarendon, 1985], 293–94). See also Deut 10:18; 14:29; 16:11,14; 24:17–21; 26:12–13; 27:19; Jer 7:6; 22:3; Ezek 22:7; Zech 7:10; Pss 94:6; 146:9.

[331] Cf. C. J. H. Wright, *An Eye for an Eye: The Place of Old Testament Ethics Today* (Downers Grove: InterVarsity, 1983), 37–38, 51–62.

"You oppress the righteous and take bribes and you deprive the poor of justice in the courts" (5:12). The expression "deprive the poor of justice" is the same Malachi uses of the treatment of strangers, literally, "those who divert strangers," meaning those who keep strangers from receiving justice.[332] The sin is also listed as one of the Levitical curses that came to describe so much of Israel's history: "Cursed is the man who withholds justice from the alien, the fatherless or the widow" (Deut 27:19). So in Malachi's postexilic Judah some had returned to the kind of greed and corruption that had invited the devastation and deprivation of exile from which they had so lately been delivered.

What may be especially significant here is that, as Wright argues, one's attitude toward material possessions is a kind of thermometer that measures the health of one's relationship with God and with other people (see Neh 5:1–13; Matt 6:24).[333] This is why "failure to honour God in the material realm cannot be compensated for by religiosity in the spiritual realm."[334] This insight may suggest the relationship between Malachi's three addresses concerned with vain offerings (1:2–2:9), treachery in relationships (2:10–3:5), and the withholding of tithes (3:6–4:6). One's health and wholeness as a child of God is determined first by one's attitude toward and relationship with God, thus the "theological angle"; second by one's attitude toward and relationship with others, thus the "social angle"; and finally by one's attitude toward and use of one's possessions, the "economic angle." These three angles are part of an "ethical triangle" and are interrelated. Thus, whereas the focus of Malachi's first address is on the theological angle, the social (i.e., the priests' poor and prejudicial instruction that "caused many to stumble," 2:6–9) and economic (i.e., the best animals withheld from God, 1:8,13–14) angles enter as well. Likewise, the second division's focus on the social angle does not eliminate the theological (desecrating the sanctuary, 2:11; regarding God as unjust, 2:17; need for righteous offerings, 3:4) and economic (corruption and oppression, 3:5) angles from the prophet's attention.

**3:6** Malachi ends this negative motivation section (3:1–6) that climaxes his second address with an echo of the book's first paragraph. Many commentators regard v. 6 as beginning the fifth oracle or disputation.[335] But this would break the pattern of the preceding three predictions, each of which is balanced by a following proposition. Whereas the first three predictions are each bal-

---

[332] The expression is also used with the explicit object מִשְׁפָּט, "justice," in Exod 23:6; Deut 16:19; 24:17; 27:19; 1 Sam 8:3. A similar expression occurs in Isa 10:2: לְהַטּוֹת מִדִּין דַּלִּים, "to deprive the poor of a legal claim," which is parallel to וְלִגְזֹל מִשְׁפַּט עֲנִיֵּי עַמִּי, "and to rob justice from the afflicted of my people." The way justice was diverted was probably usually through bribes (cf. Job 36:18; Prov 17:38).

[333] Wright, *An Eye for an Eye*, 59–62.

[334] Ibid., 60.

[335] E.g., Hill, *Malachi,* 291; Stuart, "Malachi," 3:1361.

anced by a result, however, the fourth prediction is balanced by an antithetical sentence. Although the Lord is coming in judgment (v. 5), Jacob (see 1:2) will not be destroyed because their charges of his faithlessness (2:17) are false. The Lord is not a capricious God who may change his plans on a whim. Jacob is mentioned only twice more in Malachi, in 1:2 and 2:12. Therefore the reference to Jacob here at the end of the second division unifies the first two divisions and also the second division itself, which begins at 2:10.

The Hebrew text consists of two clauses,[336] the first clause beginning with the particle *kî*, which has many different uses in various contexts: "for, because; when, if; that; indeed." Several translations render the particle "for," apparently treating the clause as furnishing the reason or explanation for the preceding (NASB, NKJV, NRSV, ESV, JPS). Other translations treat it as emphatic, rendered "surely" (NAB), "no" (NJB), or left untranslated (NIV, REB, TEV).[337] The second clause is often considered the logical result of the first, the connection rendered "so" or "therefore" (cf. NIV, NRSV, NASB, NKJV). No word in the Hebrew text corresponds to "so," although this does not preclude such a translation. Other versions treat the two clauses as coordinate, rendering the connection by "and" or "nor." The second clause begins literally "and/but you." The word order suggests a contrast or comparison with the "I, Yahweh" of the first clause.

There are two problems with rendering *kî* as "for." One is that it subordinates the idea of God's changelessness to his coming in judgment in v. 5, meaning that what does not change is his opposition to sinners.[338] Although this is true and appropriately answers the charge in 2:17 that God delights in evildoers, it leaves the final clause (lit. "and/but/though you, sons of Jacob, have not perished") only tenuously connected to its paragraph.[339] The second problem is that it again would break the pattern of the preceding three predictions, leaving v. 5 without a balancing proposition.

The three propositions for which some connection must be recognized are as follows:

---

[336] Although Hill (*Malachi*, 294–95) and others consider יְהוָה אֲנִי a verbless clause (cf. KJV), it is almost certainly an appositional subject of the following negated perfect verb שָׁנִיתִי. Although אֲנִי יְהוָה occurs about two hundred times, in almost every case it is an appositional subject when followed by a finite verb (e.g., Num 14:35; Isa 42:6; 45:8; Ezek 5:13,15,17; 14:4,9; 17:21; 21:4,10,22,37). The only exception seems to be Ezek 17:24.

[337] Cf. Verhoef, *Haggai, Malachi*, 299.

[338] A. van Hoonacker, *Les douze petits prophètes* (Paris: Gabalda, 1908), 733; Glazier-McDonald, *Malachi*, 176.

[339] J. M. P. Smith agreed that it "hardly satisfies the demands of the context." He tried to solve the problem by omitting לֹא as dittography or by interpreting it as emphatic, producing, "You will surely be destroyed" (*Malachi*, ICC [Edinburgh: T&T Clark, 1912], 66–68).

a—I will come near you for/in judgment.
b—I, Yahweh, have not changed/do not change.
c—You, the sons of Jacob, have not come to an end.

Propositions *b* and *c* are closely related semantically, both negating some sort of change. Lack of change in Yahweh is related to lack of change in the sons of Jacob. It is reasonable to suppose, as most commentators and translations recognize, that the intended connection is that the latter is dependent on the former, hence the common translation "so" or "therefore." The dependent relationship, however, could be marked by the initial *kî*, and since a causal or explanatory relationship between *b* and *a* is difficult to find, this alternative is a more likely explanation of the syntax.[340] Although causal *kî* clauses normally follow the main clause, Malachi has used causal *kî* clauses preceding the main clause twice before (see comments at 1:11,14 and note at 1:11).[341]

The verse may be translated then, "Because I, Yahweh, have not changed, you, the sons of Jacob, have not perished." The point is that if Yahweh were the kind of unfair and unfaithful God they charge him with being, who acted capriciously on the basis of momentary convenience, he would have put an end to them long ago. The verb for "change," *šānâ*, is used of David changing his "sense," that is, pretending to be mad out of fear of the Philistines (1 Sam 21:14); it is used of Jeroboam's wife changing or disguising her appearance to gain information from a prophet (1 Kgs 14:2); and it is used of Israel opportunistically changing their allegiance, first to Assyria then to Egypt, depending on what seems most advantageous at the time (Jer 2:36). The Hebrew word is related to an Akkadian word *šanû*, which "is used of altering contracts, agreements, words, and texts."[342] Closely related to the message of Malachi, *šānâ* is used of God in Ps 89:34[Hb. 35]: "I will not violate my covenant or *alter* what my lips have uttered." As VanGemeren explains, the point there is that "the love of God outweighs his judgment. Though he may discipline even acrimoniously, his 'love' (*ḥesed,* Ps 89:33; cf. v. 28) will still extend to the offspring of David. Though man may show contempt for the covenant, the Lord will never 'violate' . . . his own covenant. What he has promised by oath stands (v. 34)."[343]

---

[340] Likewise Stuart, "Malachi," 3:1361.

[341] Of the many examples of preposed causal כִּי clauses given in the note on 1:11, the most common form is כִּי + perfect, which is the form used here. The closest parallel to the syntax here is found in Job 30:11: "Because God has loosed my bowstring and humbled me, they have cast off restraint in my presence" (NRSV; see also Isa 15:1).

[342] R. B. Chisholm, "שָׁנָה," *NIDOTTE;* cf. N. Waldman, "Some Notes on Malachi 3:6; 3:13 and Psalm 42:11," *JBL* 93 (1974): 543.

[343] W. VanGemeren, "Psalms" in EBC on CD-ROM. Accordance 6.0. See also Jer 30:11: "I will make a full end of all the nations among whom I scattered you, but of you I will not make a full end. I will discipline you in just measure, and I will by no means leave you unpunished" (ESV). Also note Deut 4:30–31.

The term "sons of Jacob" here confirms that the point of 3:6 is very similar to that of Mal 1:2–5, where Jacob and Esau are contrasted and where continuity is made explicit between God's people at the time of Malachi and their ancestor Jacob.[344] Of the fifteen occurrences of "sons of Jacob" in the Old Testament, all but three (1 Kgs 18:31; 2 Kgs 17:34 besides here) are found in Genesis (seven of them in Gen 34–35) since the term is strongly associated with Israel's origins under God's covenant grace. It is God's promise to the patriarchs, then, that is in view, his promise to create a people for himself from the seed of Abraham, Isaac, and Jacob.[345] His commitment to his people does not change (cf. Rom 11:1–6,11–12,25–29). God's faithfulness to his covenant with Israel is similarly taught in Hos 11:9: "I will not carry out my fierce anger, nor will I turn and devastate Ephraim. For I am God, and not man—the Holy One among you. I will not come in wrath." And Neh 9:31 declares, "But in your great mercy you did not put an end [the noun form of the verb "destroyed" in Mal 3:6] to them or abandon them, for you are a gracious and merciful God."

The unbounded persistence of God's love is also taught in Heb 13:8 in terms of God's unchangeableness. The assurance that Jesus Christ does not change is given in the context of the confidence God's children should have in his spiritual presence and aid:

> Keep your lives free from the love of money and be content with what you have, because God has said, "Never will I leave you; never will I forsake you." So we say with confidence, "The Lord is my helper; I will not be afraid. What can man do to me?" Remember your leaders, who spoke the word of God to you. Consider the outcome of their way of life and imitate their faith. Jesus Christ is the same yesterday and today and forever. (Heb 13:5–8)

Whereas the focus in verses such as Heb 13:8 is on the future, the context of Mal 3:6, like Neh 9:31, suggests its focus is on the past, although the perfect tense can be translated either "have not changed" or "do not change." The use of another perfect in the second clause (NRSV, "you, O children of Jacob, have not perished") suggests that "have not changed" would be a preferable rendering of the first perfect. If the immediate sense were that Jacob *would* not perish because God *did* not or *would* not change, then the two verbs would more likely be imperfects. The use of two perfects suggests the sense that Jacob *had* not perished because God *had* not changed. Even so, however, there is nothing

---

[344] This is a more likely explanation of the reference to "Jacob" here than Kruse-Blinkenberg's view that there is a pun on the name, which means "deceiver" (Gen 27:36). He translates the second clause, "and you have not stopped being sons of Jacob" ("The Pesitta of the Book of Malachi," 104–5), a possible but unlikely interpretation.

[345] The Tg. to Mal 3:6 adds an object to the verb in the first clause, rendering "For I the LORD have not changed my ancient covenant." In the second clause, however, the sense is changed considerably to an argument for divine punishment after death: "but you, O house of Israel, you think that if a man dies in this world his judgment has ceased." This sounds like anti-Sadducean polemic (R. P. Gordon, *Studies in the Targum to the Twelve Prophets: From Nahum to Malachi* [Leiden: Brill, 1994], 58–61).

to suggest that God's consistency in the past will cease at any time in the future. In fact, God's changelessness seems to be an inference (or even an assumption) of the previous verse. The God who revealed his displeasure in the past at "sorcerers, adulterers and perjurers, against those who defraud laborers of their wages, who oppress the widows and the fatherless, and deprive aliens of justice, but do not fear me" is the same God the Judahites were dealing with in Malachi's day. But just as his holiness had not changed (and so would not change), his faithfulness had also not changed (and so would not change). As the prophet Micah declared in 7:18–20,

> Who is a God like you, who pardons sin and forgives the transgression of the remnant of his inheritance? You do not stay angry forever but delight to show mercy. You will again have compassion on us; you will tread our sins underfoot and hurl all our iniquities into the depths of the sea. You will be true to Jacob, and show mercy to Abraham, as you pledged on oath to our fathers in days long ago.

God's faithful love to the sons of Jacob could not change because of the oath he swore to Abraham and the other Patriarchs. Even the curses God declared against Israel in the case of their future disobedience (Lev 26; Deut 28) did not include final rejection. What resulted, rather, was a new covenant with them (Jer 31:31–34). Paul's answer to the question, "Did God reject his people?" in Rom 11:1 is *mē genoito,* "By no means!"[346] God's assurance through the prophet Isaiah encompassed future as well as past: "Listen to Me, house of Jacob, all the remnant of the house of Israel, who have been sustained from the womb, carried along since birth. I will be the same until your old age, and I will bear you up when you turn gray. I have made you, and I will carry you; I will bear and save you" (Isa 46:3–4, HCSB).

We might ask, however, whether the very point derived from God's immutability is in fact valid. Israel's continuing existence as a people is secure because God does not change. If God changes, Jacob's descendants are doomed. His purposes and his covenant promises are as solid and permanent as the nature and character of God. But where is Israel now? Some have argued that Israel's continuing disobedience annulled God's promises to ethnic Israel and that he is fulfilling his promises in spiritual Israel, the church.[347] But Paul deals with this in Romans 9–11. Ethnic Israel's relative absence from the redeemed community had resulted from their spiritual pride and self-

---

[346] See W. E. Glenny's argument that although passages such as 1 Peter 2 indicate that the church is the fulfillment of OT prophecies, it is not the final and complete fulfillment, which must be in the nation of Israel ("The Israelite Imagery of 1 Peter 2," 184).

[347] E.g., W. Grudem, *1 Peter,* TNTC (Grand Rapids: Eerdmans, 1988), 113; M. H. Woodstra, "Israel and the Church: A Case for Continuity," in *Continuity and Discontinuity: Perspectives on the Relationship between the Old and New Testaments* (Westchester, Ill.: Crossway, 1988), 231, 234–37; P. Barnett, *Jesus and the Rise of Early Christianity: A History of New Testament Times* (Downers Grove: InterVarsity, 1999), 220.

sufficiency, but their failure was not total (Rom 11:1–10), nor was it final (Rom 11:11–32). Rather, there will come a time when "all Israel will be saved, as it is written: 'The deliverer will come from Zion; he will turn godlessness away from Jacob. And this is my covenant with them when I take away their sins'" (Rom 11:26–27).[348] The New Testament writers considered that in spite of Israel's apostasy the Abrahamic covenant remained valid (cf. also Luke 1:46–55,67–80).

## Excursus: Immutability of the Everlasting God

In answer to the question, Is there ever any change in God? the church has traditionally given an unequivocal answer: No. Since Mal 3:6 has traditionally been a key verse for establishing the doctrine of God's "immutability," it is appropriate to ask at this point whether Scripture can bear the weight of this doctrine. The answer to this question may seem obvious until one begins to define the doctrine in more detail and to consider its corollaries and ramifications. Is it sufficient to say that God *does* not change, or is it the case that God *cannot* change? And what is there about God that does not change? Is it only his essential being and attributes, or does the doctrine also apply to his purposes, plans, and desires—both long term and short term; his methods of accomplishing his purposes; his standards, principles, and practices of judgment (including the penalties for disobedience); his relationships, attitudes, and behavior toward his creatures; his knowledge, etc.

These questions also raise the issue of God's relationship to time. Do we have a transcendent God who lives above the human fray in a timeless eternity, for whom time does not exist, and whose timeless decree renders certain whatsoever comes to pass? Or do we have an immanent God who is infinitely good, wise, and powerful and who has a goal for human history but who pursues that goal within the fray, constantly and resourcefully responding to, countering, and encouraging human actions? If the latter, does he know with certainty what those human actions are going to be, or is he limited to perfect knowledge of the past and present and what his infinite intelligence can predict about the future? These questions will surely continue to challenge God's people until we see him face-to-face, and we must openly acknowledge that as finite creatures we will never fully comprehend the infinite God. We can know "but the outer fringe of his works; how faint the whisper we hear of him!" (Job 26:14; cf. Job 42:3; Ps 145:3; Isa 40:28; 55:8–9). But these questions must nevertheless be answered at the present time as best we can because they determine a great deal of how we live as Christians.

Limitations of space as well as knowledge and skill preclude a thorough handling of these issues here. Simply stated, the view of the present author is that those who limit the implications of Mal 3:6 and related texts to only one aspect

---

[348] For a defense of the view that Paul is arguing for the future salvation of ethnic Israel, see S. L. Johnson, Jr., "Evidence from Romans 9–11," in *A Case for Premillennialism: A New Consensus* (Chicago: Moody, 1992), 199–223.

of the divine nature, such as his moral character or his loyalty to his covenant, are mistaken.[349] Although God's faithfulness is the focus of this passage, the divine attributes do not operate in isolation but are interrelated. God does not go back on his word and reject his people because, as the Westminster divines concluded, he is "infinite, eternal, and unchangeable, in his being, wisdom, power, holiness, justice, goodness, and truth."[350] He is not capricious because it is not in his character to be so. "If we are faithless, he will remain faithful, for he cannot disown himself" (2 Tim 2:13). On an individual level, the godly sufferer of Psalm 102 finds hope in God's faithfulness to his people. Though everything else may change, Israel's God will remain the same (Ps 102:25–27 quoted in Heb 1:10–12; see also Num 23:19; Ps 103:17; Jas 1:17; Heb 6:17–18). Passages that seem to speak of God "changing his mind" must be understood in the context of such verses as Ps 33:10–11: "The LORD foils the plans of the nations; he thwarts the purposes of the peoples. But the plans of the LORD stand firm forever, the purposes of his heart through all generations" (see also Isa 14:24; 46:9–10).[351] God's plans and purposes do not change. As Hodge wrote, "Infinite in wisdom, there can be no error in their conception; infinite in power, there can be no failure in their accomplishment."[352] H. Blocher declares: "We ought to bow before the biblical authority of these themes. Immutability is not first Platonic, it is Scriptural. There is a vibrant witness to that truth, and not only in peripheral passages."[353]

On the other hand, we may hesitate to extend the concept of God's immutability to say that nothing about God ever changes.[354] For example, he deals in one way with the wicked and unrepentant and in another way with those who turn from their sinful rebellion in humility and trust (Jer 18:7–10). Thus there is often an implicit conditionality about his declarations of impending judgment (e.g.,

---

[349] J. M. P. Smith, e.g., declares that Mal 3:6 "is not an abstract proposition that Yahweh cannot change in any respect . . . but simply a positive affirmation" that "the moral character of Yahweh remains unchanged; hence, sinners must undergo the punishment they so richly deserve" (*Malachi*, 66); see also Glazier-McDonald, *Malachi*, 179; Hill, *Malachi*, 295.

[350] *Westminster Shorter Catechism*, Q. 4.

[351] On the use of the verb נחם, often (misleadingly) translated "change the mind," see H. Van Dyke Parunak, "A Semantic Survey of *NḤM*," *Bib* 56 (1975): 512–32. In such passages as Exod 32:12,14; Num 23:19; 1 Sam 15:29; Jer 18:8,10; 26:3,13,19; 42:10; Ezek 24:14; Joel 2:13–14; Amos 7:3,6; Jonah 4:2; Ps 110:4 he argues that the meaning (of the *niphal* or *hithpael*) is "retract a previously declared action," either punishment or blessing. In such passages as Gen 6:6; 1 Sam 15:11,35 it means "suffer emotional pain."

[352] C. Hodge, *Systematic Theology* (Grand Rapids: Eerdmans, 1940), 1.390.

[353] H. Blocher, "Yesterday, Today, Forever: Time, Times, Eternity in Biblical Perspective" *TynBul* 52.2 (2001): 195; see also id., "Divine Immutability," in *The Power and Weakness of God* (Edinburgh: Rutherford House, 1990), 1–22.

[354] This view of such theological giants as Augustine, Anselm, Aquinas, and Calvin has been called the strong view of God's immutability: by virtue of his absolute existence or aseity, the simplicity or indivisibility of his nature, and his absolute perfection, there is in God an eternal oneness of being, knowledge, and will. Cf. R. Swinburne, *The Coherence of Theism* (Oxford: Clarendon, 1986), 212; P. Helm, *Eternal God* (Oxford: Clarendon, 1988), 85–86; J. S. Feinberg, *No One Like Him: The Doctrine of God* (Wheaton: Crossway, 2001), 264.

Exod 32:10; Num 14:12; Jonah 3:4). God's character does not change, but the situation changes, just as the sun that warms and enables life is the same sun that burns and scorches.[355] When God declares his intentions in a certain situation, it may be conditioned upon the situation remaining unchanged. But if conditions change, such as by human repentance or intercession, God's immediate attitudes and intentions in that situation can change, although his ultimate purposes remain the same (Prov 19:21). It is in this sense proper to refer to him as "a graciously flexible God."[356] But if the only variable that changed in a situation were God's will, then the declaration of passages such as Num 23:19–20 ("God is not a man, that he should lie, nor a son of man, that he should change his mind. Does he speak and then not act? Does he promise and not fulfill?") or 1 Sam 15:29 ("He who is the Glory of Israel does not lie or change his mind; for he is not a man, that he should change his mind") would be false.[357]

The question whether God's knowledge changes must be answered emphatically, No. Traditional Christianity has always affirmed that just as God's knowledge of the past and present is exhaustive, so is his knowledge of the future. According to Isa 41:23, an essential attribute of deity is the ability to "tell us what the future holds" (see also Deut 18:22; Isa 42:9; 44:7; 48:3–7).[358] The God who created us knows everything we are going to say before we say it (Ps 139:4; Isa 65:24). He even wrote out our days in his book "before one of them came to be" (Ps 139:16). We may disagree over whether God determines who will believe and be saved or merely knows it beforehand, but at least the latter has been almost universally acknowledged as explicitly taught in Scripture.[359] God is never uncertain before the event or mistaken or surprised afterwards (see Deut 31:20–

---

[355] Cf. Bavinck, *The Doctrine of God,* 152.

[356] G. A. Boyd, *God of the Possible* (Grand Rapids: Baker, 2000), 77.

[357] It is not difficult to answer Boyd's challenge (ibid., 77–78): "Suppose . . . that God wanted to tell us in Scripture that he *really does* sometimes intend to carry out one course of action and that he *really does* sometimes change his mind and not do it. How could he tell us this in terms clearer than he did in this passage [i.e., Jer 18:8]?" The answer is that God would have avoided telling us in other passages that he does not change!

[358] J. M. Frame cites prophetic histories of God's people (Gen 9:26–27; 13:13–16; 27:27–29,39–40; 49:1–28; Num 23–24; Deut 32:1–43; 33:1–29) and explains, "Here God announces (categorically, not conditionally) many centuries ahead of time the character and history of the patriarchs and their descendants. These prophecies anticipate countless free decisions of human beings, long before any had the opportunity to form their own character." He also cites other detailed predictive prophecies (1 Sam 10:1–7; 1 Kgs 13:1–4; Isa 44:28–45:13; Jer 37:6–11) as examples of God's exhaustive knowledge of the future ("Open Theism and Divine Foreknowledge," in *Bound Only Once: The Failure of Open Theism* [Moscow, Ind.: Canon, 2001], 93–94). See also 1 Sam 23:11–12; Jer 38:17–23.

[359] E.g., Gen 17:19; Jer 1:5; Dan 12:1; Matt 25:34; Luke 1:13–16; John 6:64,70–71; 10:26–29; Rom 8:29–30; 9:11–13; 2 Thess 2:13–14; 1 Pet 1:1–2.

21).[360] Nevertheless, some in the past and present have been unable or unwilling to tolerate the tension this perspective on God places on their understanding of human freedom. The argument is that if God's knowledge of the future is exhaustive, then human actions are rendered already certain before they occur. If this is the case, they argue, human freedom is only an illusion.[361] On the other hand, if man is free of any constraints on his actions, then since the future does not yet exist, it is incapable of being known. So God's ignorance of future human actions is not a limitation of God but is a logical impossibility comparable to God's inability to make a stone too heavy for him to lift.

It seems to me the simplest way to reconcile God's omniscience with human freedom is by way of the doctrine of the eternality of God.

> Not in our way does God look forward to the future, see the present, and look back upon the past, but in a manner remotely and profoundly unlike our way of thinking. God's mind does not pass from one thought to another. His vision is utterly unchangeable. Thus, He comprehends all that takes place in time—the not-yet existing future, the existing present, and the no-longer-existing past—in an immutable and eternal present. (*City of God* 11.21)[362]

Just as theologians have affirmed God's ubiquity or omnipresence, that he is not limited by the dimension of space but is everywhere immediately present, so they have traditionally affirmed that God is also not limited by the dimension of time but is immediately present at every moment. Although a history of man's encounter with God could in principle be written, it would be impossible to write a history of God because we cannot truly speak of God as having a past, a present, and a future. Augustine's expressions are excessive, and it is unwise to say that time does not *exist* for God, since "if time does not exist for God, it does not exist. God is the only Measure of truth and reality."[363] Nevertheless, all time is simultaneously present with him. By his very nature God cannot change, nor does he need to.

---

[360] Passages that appear to describe God gaining new information (e.g., Gen 22:12; Deut 13:3; Jer 32:35) or uncertain about the outcome of a situation (e.g., Jer 26:3; Ezek 12:3) must be either considered in hopeless contradiction to other portions of Scripture or must be acknowledged as figurative or rhetorical, as is commonly done with God's seeming not to know where Adam is after the fall (Gen 3:9) and his need to "go down and see" if the sins of Sodom and Gomorrah are as bad as he has heard (Gen 18:20–21). Cf. J. M. Frame, "Open Theism and Divine Foreknowledge," 88–92. Scholars sometimes seem to make every effort to uncover divine ignorance, as when P. Enns conjures up from Exod 33:3 ("I might destroy you [Hb. "lest I destroy you"] on the way") the charge that "the Lord does not know how he might react at some point in the journey; he does not seem to trust himself to control his anger . . . . We should resist the temptation to gloss over this description of God. This is God's Word and this is how he is described. We should not dismiss it on the basis of what we 'know' God to be like" (*Exodus*, NIVAC [Grand Rapids: Zondervan, 2000], 578; note also pp. 591–92). For further response to Open theism see Frame, *No Other God: A Response to Open Theism* (Phillipsburg, N.J.: P&R, 2001); B. A. Ware, *God's Lesser Glory: The Diminished God of Open Theism* (Wheaton: Crossway, 2000).

[361] E.g., Pinnock, *The Openness of God,* 121.

[362] See also Augustine, *Confessions* 11.13.16; 11.31.41; 12.15; Anselm, *Monologium* 21–22; *Proslogium* 19; Aquinas, *Summa Theologica* I.10.4.

[363] Blocher, "Yesterday, Today, Forever," 196.

This view of the eternality of God has fallen on hard times recently but is worth reconsidering. Some have argued that time and space are not really comparable and that if God were immediately present at every point of time, he would be unable to know the difference between then and now or before and after.[364] These issues are well beyond the scope of this study and must be left for others to handle, but I believe this view of the relationship of God and time provides the most coherent and consistent explanation of the data of revelation. Whereas God transcendently exists outside the bounds of history and can "make known the end from the beginning" (Isa 46:10), he also condescends to enter the flow of history to deal with situations on a human level, providing incentives, deterrents, and remedies for human actions as well as comfort and compassion for human pain.[365]

But however one understands God's relationship to time, a particular understanding of human freedom (i.e., "libertarian"), which is not even explicitly taught in Scripture (although human responsibility is explicitly taught, which requires *some* form of human freedom), should not be used to deny Scripture's explicit teaching that God not only knows the future exhaustively but in some sense determines it. For example, according to Prov 16:9, "In his heart a man plans his course, but the LORD determines his steps," and 21:1 states that "the king's heart is a stream of water in the hand of the LORD; he turns it wherever he will." Finally, Eph 1:11 tells us that "in him [Christ] we were also chosen, having been predestined according to the plan of him who works out everything in conformity with the purpose of his will."[366]

---

[364] For various ways of dealing with this issue, see G. E. Ganssle, ed., *God & Time: Four Views,* (Downers Grove: InterVarsity, 2001). P. Helm has noted that although the classical view has "an impressive pedigree," it is probably the minority view among contemporary theologians and philosophers of religion ("Divine Timeless Eternity," *God & Time,* 28). The reason is that such a view seems at odds with the interactive God of Scripture who responds to human sin and also to prayers and needs. Even Helm, who supports the classical view, admits that whereas biblical passages concerning God's timelessness are consistent with such a view, the language of Scripture is not sufficiently precise to say that such a view "is entailed" by Scripture, which can also support the more contemporary view that whereas God's existence is temporally boundless, he exists in time (p. 31). Helm considers the classical view, however, "a better approach to the relevant scriptural data than any of its rivals," and "it prevents us from making certain types of false inferences about God."

[365] Cf. Hodge, *Systematic Theology,* 1.385–89. Hodge, who affirms the classical view of God's eternality and that he "is absolutely immutable in his essence and attributes," nevertheless is not happy with the language of Augustine and others when they seem to confuse "immutability with immobility. In denying that God can change, they seem to deny that He can act." Although God is immutable, he is also "perpetually active." And any explanation of immutability must be consistent with God's activity. Hodge is also unwilling to deny to God succession in thought, since this is to him a necessary attribute of personhood. God "is not a stagnant ocean, but ever living, ever thinking, ever acting, and ever suiting his action to the exigencies of his creatures, and to the accomplishment of his infinitely wise designs" (1.890).

[366] See also Gen 45:7; 50:20; Exod 4:21; Deut 2:30; Josh 11:18–20; 2 Sam 24:1/1 Chr 21:1; 1 Kgs 12:15; 13:1–3; 22:19–23,34; Ezra 1:1; 6:22; Pss 105:25; 139:16; Isa 6:9–10; 63:17; Jer 1:5; Lam 3:37–38; Dan 1:9; Hab 1:6; Luke 22:22; John 13:18–19; 17:12; Acts 2:23; 4:27–28; 13:27,48; 17:26; 27:24,31; Rom 9:18; 11:36; Eph 2:10; Rev 17:17.

III.  JUDAH EXHORTED TO RETURN AND REMEMBER (3:7–4:6)
 1.  First Command: Return to the Lord with Tithes (3:7–10a)
     (1)  Call for Repentance (3:7)
     (2)  Call for Tithes (3:8–10a)
 2.  Positive Motivation: Future Blessing 3:10b–12)
     (1)  Blessing from Heaven (3:10b)
     (2)  Blessing from the Land (3:11)
     (3)  Blessing from the Nations (3:12)
 3.  Situation: Complacency toward Serving the Lord (3:13–15)
     (1)  Strong Words (3:13)
     (2)  Worthless Worship (3:14)
     (3)  Bitter Blessing (3:15)
 4.  Motivation: The Coming Day (3:16–4:3)
     (1)  A Book of Remembrance (3:16)
     (2)  A Day of Distinction (3:17–18)
     (3)  A Day of Burning (4:1–3)
 5.  Second Command: Remember the Law (4:4–6)

## III.  JUDAH EXHORTED TO RETURN AND REMEMBER (3:7–4:6)

This final division is marked off by the use of the verb *šûb,* "return," in 3:7 and 4:6 (see comments at 1:3–4). The order of sections in this division is altered from the previous pattern so that it begins and ends with commands. The result is that the book concludes with the command to remember the law. The situation section is made prominent by placing it in the center of the division. It also contains the longest speech of Judah in the book, which affords deeper insight into the people's sinful attitudes that called for Malachi's prophecy. The general effect of the rearrangement of sections in this last division is that it stands out as the most prominent of the three, forming a climax to Malachi's prophecy. Also, although the explicit commands of the first two divisions are negative because Judah was guilty of active disobedience, those of this division are positive because Judah was guilty of passive disobedience. The overall effect is, "Stop doing those things and begin doing this."

## 1. First Command: Return to the Lord with Tithes (3:7–10a)

This first section is marked as command by the imperative verb "return" opening the section in v. 7 and by the imperative "bring" at the end of the section in v. 10a. The second command elaborates the first. Israel's return to the Lord is to manifest itself in bringing to him the tithes they have been withholding. The structure and logic of this opening section may be displayed by the following chart using the author's translation. As in the case of similar previous charts, the paragraph is portrayed in terms of multiple layers of embedding, indicated by levels of indentation (see the introduction to 1:2–5). The most prominent element of a paragraph or subparagraph is typically marked as "Thesis."

God speaks:
  Reason:
    Thesis: *Since the days of your fathers, you have turned from my statutes.*  *v. 7*
    Paraphrase: *And you have not kept [them].*
  Thesis:
    Thesis: *Return to me.*
    Result: *And I will return to you,*
        *says Yahweh of hosts.*
The people request clarification:
  *And you say, How shall we return?*
God elaborates:
  *Will a man rob God? For you are robbing me.*  *v. 8*
The people request further clarification:
  *And you say, How have we robbed you?*
God elaborates further:
  Reason:
    Thesis: *[You have robbed me of] the tithe and the contribution.*
    Amplification:
      Antithesis: *You are being inflicted with a curse.*  *v. 9*
      Thesis: *Yet you are robbing me—the nation, all of it.*
  Thesis:
    Thesis: *Bring all the tithe to the treasure house.*  *v. 10a*
    Result: *That it may be nourishment in my house.*

### (1) Call for Repentance (3:7)

**[7]Ever since the time of your forefathers you have turned away from my decrees and have not kept them. Return to me, and I will return to you," says the LORD Almighty.**

  **"But you ask, 'How are we to return?'**

**3:7** Like the last section of division one (2:1–9), this verse in the first section of division three is packed with all three hortatory elements, neatly expressed here as nowhere else in the book.

> Situation: "Ever since the time of your forefathers you have turned away from
>      my  decrees and have not kept them.
> Command: Return to me,
> Motivation: and I will return to you," says the LORD Almighty.

The occurrence of the divine quotation formula, "says the LORD Almighty," marks this speech by the Lord as the most prominent part of the paragraph (vv. 7–10a). Although the command is the most prominent part of the speech and is appropriately what Judah responds to, it is accompanied by expressions of the situation and motivation. This suggests that this "packed" verse may be considered a key verse in Malachi's prophecy. Some expression of the situation is necessary at this point because the main situation section has been reserved for the center of the discourse (3:13–15). As with most commands, however, the situation in view can be inferred at least in part from the command itself.

The prophet's opening expression, "Ever since[1] the time of your forefathers," covers considerable time, about a thousand years.[2] The term "forefathers" is *ʾābōt,* "fathers." Although "your fathers" is first used in Scripture of the patriarchs Abraham, Isaac, and Jacob (Gen 48:21; Exod 3:13–16), the first time it is used in a negative way is in Num 32:14, referring to the refusal of the exodus generation to trust God and conquer the promised land (see also Mal 2:10). It is used later of Israel during the time of the Judges when they abandoned Yahweh for the Canaanite gods (1 Sam 12:15). Then the prophet Isaiah announced God's judgment for "your sins and the sins of your fathers. . . . Because they burned sacrifices on the mountains and defied me on the hills, I will measure into their laps the full payment for their former deeds" (Isa 65:7). The Lord condemned Israel through the prophet Jeremiah (Jer 7:25–26) in terms similar to those of Malachi:

> From the time your forefathers left Egypt until now, day after day, again and again I sent you my servants the prophets. But they did not listen to me or pay attention. They were stiff-necked and did more evil than their forefathers.

---

[1] The Hb. term translated "ever since the time of" combines the word יוֹם, "day," with the prepositions לְ, "to," and מִן, "from." It is similarly used in Judg 19:30 ("since the day"); 2 Sam 7:6 ("from the day"); 2 Kgs 19:25 ("in days of old" with קֶדֶם); Isa 7:17 ("since"); and 1 Chr 17:10 ("ever since"; cf. Ezra 9:7 without לְ).

[2] The sentence opens with an adverbial phrase whose closest parallel in Malachi is in 1:11, which begins the situation section of the first address: כִּי מִמִּזְרַח־שֶׁמֶשׁ וְעַד־מְבוֹאוֹ, "Because from the rising of the sun even to its setting . . ."

Israel, like the human race in general, has had a long history of disobedience.

The verbs *sûr,* "turn away," and *šāmar,* "kept,"[3] which may be understood as antonyms, occur together several times in the so-called Deuteronomic History (Deuteronomy–Kings). There the life of faithfulness and success is described as a path marked by God's laws and statutes on the one hand (cf. Mal 4:4)[4] and by his own footsteps on the other hand (i.e., his presence).[5] The path is the same in either case, and failing to follow either sign means abandonment of God's path. Here too, by turning from the Lord's "decrees" the people have turned from the Lord himself. We cannot follow God without the guidance of his Word, which must be carefully heeded to avoid stumbling or turning from the path (Deut 5:32; 11:16; Josh 1:7; 23:6; 2 Kgs 18:6; Hos 7:14; see also Mal 2:6,8).[6]

The first figurative use of the Hebrew verb *šûb,* "return," is in Solomon's prayer in 1 Kgs 8:33: "When your people Israel have been defeated by an enemy because they have sinned against you, and when they *turn back* to you and confess your name, praying and making supplication to you in this temple . . ." (cf. also v. 48; 2 Chr 6:38; Jer 3:10). Such "turning back" in repentance involves a renewal of loyalty to the Lord expressed in confession and prayer.[7] Similar to Mal 3:7 with its two occurrences of the verb *šûb* is Jer 15:19 (lit.): "If you come back, I will take you back."[8] The closest parallel to Malachi, however, is found in Zech 1:3: "Therefore tell the people: This is what the LORD Almighty says: 'Return to me,' declares the LORD Almighty, 'and I will return to you,' says the LORD Almighty."[9] The result of sincerely returning to the Lord is clarified in Jer 24:7: "They will be my people, and I will be their God,

---

[3] There is no object with the verb שָׁמַר, "kept," in Hb. Although one is often supplied by emendation, A. E. Hill correctly points out that this is not necessary since the context easily supplies it (*Malachi,* AB [New York: Doubleday, 1998], 300). As he notes, Malachi elsewhere employs such "gapping" (cf. 1:3,7,12; 2:9,17; 3:8).

[4] P. Enns probably is correct that in these contexts חֹק, "statute," used here, shares roughly the same semantic domain with מִצְוָה, "commandment," מִשְׁפָּט, "judgment," and תּוֹרָה, "instruction, law" ("חקק," *NIDOTTE* on CD-ROM. Version 1.0).

[5] Of course, this portrayal of the godly life as one of following Yahweh and his laws is not confined to the Deuteronomic History. See, e.g., Lev 18:4; Num 14:24,43; 2 Chr 34:33; Job 34:27.

[6] J. A. Thompson and E. A. Martens explain that "the term סוּר ["turn away"] describes defection, a shift in loyalties and allegiance, mostly in the sense of religious apostasy" ("שׁוּב," *NIDOTTE* on CD-ROM. Version 1.0).

[7] Thompson and Martens elaborate on the elements of repentance from Jer 3:22–4:2: "acknowledging God's lordship (3:22); admitting wrongdoing (3:23), including the verbal confession, 'We [I] have sinned' (3:25); addressing the shame (3:25); and affirming and adhering to new conduct (4:1–2)" ("שׁוּב," *NIDOTTE*). See also Hos 14:1–3.

[8] There, however, the second use of שׁוּב is in the *hiphil.*

[9] The difference in Zech 1:3, besides the intervening נְאֻם־יְהוָה צְבָאוֹת, "declares the LORD Almighty," is that the second occurrence of שׁוּב is an imperfect rather than a cohortative as here, making explicit here the purpose/result relationship (*IBHS* §34.6).

for they will return to me with all their heart" (cf. also 2 Chr 30:6,9; Neh 1:9). Wholehearted repentance would result in such divine blessing that any doubt of God's favor and compassion would be removed (cf. 3:14–15).

For the fifth time, Malachi uses pseudo-dialogue to express Judah's attitude toward the Lord's message (cf. 1:2,6–7; 2:14,17; 3:7–8,13). The problem was that Judah failed to recognize that they had strayed from the divine path. Although they had noticed the absence of God's blessings (1:2; 2:13–14,17; 3:14–15), they had not noticed the absence of their God. They were like the stereotypical husband who has failed to recognize that his relationship with his wife has deteriorated. The interrogative word "how" (*bammeh/bammâ*, lit. "by what?") occurs twenty-nine times in the Hebrew Bible, more frequently in Malachi (6x) than in any other book except Judges (8x).[10] In Malachi these obtuse and obstreperous people ask, "*How* have you loved us?" (1:2), "*How* have we shown contempt for your name?" (1:6), "*How* have we defiled you?" (1:7), "*How* have we wearied him?" (2:17), and now, "*How* are we to return?" (3:7), and "*How* do we rob you?" (3:8). Their other questions are similar: "*Why* [*al-mâ*] [do you not accept our offerings]?" (2:14), and, "*What* [*mâ*] have we said against you?" (3:13). In each case Judah's question is not just for information (as in 2 Sam 21:3) but contains an element of complaint and disputation. Here they arrogantly question why they should need to repent. As the NLT renders it, "How can we return when we have never gone away?"[11] The Lord's patience with his people is indeed amazing.

One reason for Judah's confusion may have been the strong vein of Old Testament teaching going back to Moses' messages even before entering the land. He had declared in Deut 4:25–31 that Israel would one day act corruptly, engage in idolatry, and be driven from the land. Then from among the idolatrous nations Israel would again seek the Lord with all their heart and "in later days you will return to the LORD your God and obey him" (4:30). Having experienced now the Babylonian exile, the release by the Persians, and the return and restoration under Zerubbabel and then Ezra and Nehemiah, naturally the people would have thought all this was behind them. "Return to the Lord? We thought we already did!" A quick read through the Books of Ezra and Nehemiah, however, as well as Malachi, shows that the prophecies of national repentance and spiritual restoration and blessing have not yet been fulfilled.[12]

---

[10] Judg 6:15; 16:5,6,10,13,15.

[11] The TEV misses this sense in its rendering, "What must we do to turn back to you?"

[12] J. G. McConville argues that Ezra and Nehemiah "express deep dissatisfaction with the exiles' situation under Persian rule, that the situation is perceived as leaving room for a future fulfillment of the most glorious prophecies of Israel's salvation and that the cause of the delayed fulfillment is the exiles' sin" ("Ezra-Nehemiah and the Fulfilment of Prophecy," *VT* 36 [1986]: 223).

## (2) Call for Tithes (3:8–10a)

> [8]"Will a man rob God? Yet you rob me.
> "But you ask, 'How do we rob you?'
> "In tithes and offerings. [9]You are under a curse—the whole nation of you—
> because you are robbing me. [10]Bring the whole tithe into the storehouse, that
> there may be food in my house.

**3:8** The Lord might have responded to Israel's question by pointing again to their insulting so-called worship (1:4); their treachery against one another (2:10), especially their wives (2:14); their profaning the Lord's sanctuary by intermarriage with pagan idolators (2:11); or their toleration or practice of sorcery, adultery, perjury, and economic exploitation of the defenseless (3:5). Instead, he brought to their attention another area in which their rebellion against God was manifesting itself—the withholding of tithes.[13] As discussed in the comments on 3:5, we may suggest that Malachi's third address focuses on what C. J. H. Wright calls "the economic angle." That is, Israel's attitude toward and use of their possessions was one indication of the health of their relationship with God.[14]

The Old Testament refers to "the land" over a thousand times, and the vast majority of these references are to the land of Canaan, the land that God promised the fathers, the land he gave Israel, the land where he would bless his people. How Israel regarded and treated the land and its produce was a central feature of their responsibilities under God's covenant. Ownership of land came to represent participation in the covenant community to whom God had given the land. But that ownership had to be *legitimized* by an attitude of faith and gratitude toward God shown by one's proper use of the land. This especially involved keeping the Sabbath and participation in festivals of joy with gifts to God. It also involved the bringing of tithes through which the landless priests and Levites were provided for.

Although God gave Israel the land as their inheritance, he made it clear that it was actually a stewardship: "The land is mine and you are but aliens and my tenants" (Lev 25:23). One reason for this was the sinful human tendency to disconnect the gift from the giver (Deut 6:10–12). W. Brueggemann pointed out that "the land, source of life, has within it seductive power. It

---

[13] Against the majority, M. A. Sweeney begins the so-called fifth speech at 3:8. The fourth speech, he says, is an accusation of wearying Yahweh and a summons to return (2:17–3:7). But that invents a hiatus in the middle of a pseudo-dialogue between the prophet and the people and begins a new speech with the answer to the question concluding the previous one (*The Twelve Prophets*. Berit Olam [Collegeville, Minn.: Liturgical, 2000], 2.722).

[14] Cf. C. J. H. Wright, *An Eye for an Eye: The Place of Old Testament Ethics Today* (Downers Grove: InterVarsity, 1983), 46–62. R. Warren writes: "The Bible is very clear: God uses money to test your faithfulness as a servant. That's why Jesus talked more about money than he did about either heaven or hell" (*The Purpose-Driven Life* [Grand Rapids: Zondervan, 2002], 267).

invites Israel to enter life apart from covenant. . . . Israel does not have many resources with which to resist the temptation. The chief one is memory."[15] So if they should be tempted pridefully to say, "My power and the strength of my hands have produced this wealth for me," they were to remember that it was Yahweh their God "who gives you the ability to produce wealth, and so confirms his covenant, which he swore to your forefathers, as it is today" (Deut 8:17–18). How they regarded and treated the land would demonstrate whether they acknowledged his lordship over them, their dependence on him, and their gratitude toward him. This acknowledgment was to be expressed in Israel's festivals, especially Firstfruits, Weeks, and Tabernacles (Lev 23:9–22,33–43), in the weekly Sabbath observance of rest (Exod 20:8–11; Deut 5:12–15),[16] in the observance of a Sabbath year (Exod 23:10–11; Lev 25:1–7,18–22) and of the year of Jubilee (Lev 25:8–17,23–55), and in their sacrifices and offerings, especially the consecration of the firstborn (Exod 13:11–16; 34:19–20; Num 18:15–17), and in the tithe. These were not only acknowledgments, however, but also reminders that God had been faithful to his promises. Moses told Israel, "Eat the tithe of your grain, new wine and oil, and the firstborn of your herds and flocks in the presence of the LORD your God at the place he will choose as a dwelling for his Name, *so that you may learn to revere the LORD your God always*" (Deut 14:23). We should understand God's material blessings as intended to glorify him and to enrich not individuals but the entirety of God's people.

The term for "tithe" is *ma'ăśēr,* meaning "tenth part." Moses had instructed Israel that "a tithe of everything from the land, whether grain from the soil or fruit from the trees, belongs to the LORD; it is holy to the LORD" (Lev 27:30). Also "the entire tithe of the herd and flock—every tenth animal that passes under the shepherd's rod—will be holy to the LORD" (Lev 27:32). After Israel settled in the land they were to bring the tithe annually to the sanctuary and consume a portion of it, leaving the remainder with the Levites, who were to share a tithe with the priests (Num 18:21–32; Deut 12:5–19; 14:22–27).[17] Moses instructed Israel in Deut 12:17–19:

---

[15] W. Brueggemann, *The Land* (Philadelphia: Fortress, 1977), 53. H. G. M. Williamson points out from the context of Lev 25:23 that the immediate implication of God's ownership was that wealth should never be concentrated in the hands of a few ("The Old Testament and the Material World," *EvQ* 57 [1985]: 10).

[16] R. de Vaux calls the Sabbath "a tithe on time" (*Ancient Israel* [New York: McGraw-Hill, 1961], 480). It was thus an acknowledgment that all one's time belonged to Yahweh. Cf. also R. R. Ellis, "Divine Gift and Human Response: An Old Testament Model for Stewardship," *Southwestern Journal of Theology* X.X (1994): 10.

[17] Cf. J. G. McConville, *Law and Theology in Deuteronomy,* JSOTSup 33 (Sheffield: JSOT, 1984), 76–78, 86–87.

You must not eat in your own towns the tithe of your grain and new wine and oil, or the firstborn of your herds and flocks, or whatever you have vowed to give, or your freewill offerings or special gifts. Instead, you are to eat them in the presence of the LORD your God at the place the LORD your God will choose—you, your sons and daughters, your menservants and maidservants, and the Levites from your towns—and you are to rejoice before the LORD your God in everything you put your hand to. *Be careful not to neglect the Levites* as long as you live in your land.

Every third year, however, the tithe was to be dispensed in the person's hometown to be consumed by the local landless inhabitants—Levites, foreign residents, the fatherless, and widows (Deut 14:28–29; 26:12). The tithe, like the Sabbath year, was to benefit the poor and the landless, thereby showing love to both God and neighbor.[18] The Hebrew phrase in Deut 12:19 translated "be careful" occurs nine times in Deuteronomy (and only twelve times elsewhere).[19] J. G. Millar notes that in Deuteronomy it

> is normally reserved for remembering the events of Horeb (4:9), the exodus (6:12) and even God himself (11:16). Remembering the Levites is just as important, for this is a mark of a proper loving response to God within Deuteronomic theology. If they are neglected, and prevented from joining in the celebration in God's presence, then God's relationship with the entire nation would be affected, in keeping with their failure to obey the laws and statutes.[20]

The term "offerings" translates the word *těrûmâ*, which is traditionally translated "heave offering" (e.g., Exod 29:27–28, Lev 7:14,32; Num 15:19–21). It is found seventy-six times in the Hebrew Bible (mostly in Exodus, Numbers, and Ezekiel) and is usually related to the causative of the verb *rûm,* "be high," suggesting the raising of an offering to God. It is often found with the term *těnûpâ*, traditionally rendered "wave offering." The rabbis understood the *těrûmâ* to be a ritual act involving raising and lowering an offering and the *těnûpâ* as moving an offering forward and back. Some still favor a similar interpretation,[21] although others, while rendering *těnûpâ* as "wave

---

[18] E. E. Carpenter, "Tithe," *ISBE*, rev. (Grand Rapids: Eerdmans, 1988), 4:863.

[19] הִשָּׁמֶר ֹ[וּ] לְךָ/לָכֶם.

[20] J. G. Millar, *Now Choose Life: Theology and Ethics in Deuteronomy* (Grand Rapids: Eerdmans, 1998), 113. He further asserts (p. 120), "Throughout these laws [Deut 12–26], along with aliens, orphans and widows, the way in which the Levites are treated provides an index of Israel's obedience. Self-preoccupation can have no place in the life of Israel." Giving to these dependents amounted to giving to Yahweh (cf. Matt 25:34–46).

[21] J. I. Durham translates תְּנוּפָה as "symbolic offering" but understands that it was manipulated or waved in some way. He translates תְּרוּמָה as "offering" or "the gift held aloft" (*Exodus.* WBC [Waco: Word, 1987], 349, 393).

offering," consider *těrûmâ* as "offering" or "contribution."[22]

J. Milgrom argues that the causative form of the verb *rûm*, "be high," in ritual texts refers to setting aside something or donating a gift (Exod 35:24; Lev 2:9; 4:8,10,19; 6:3; Num 15:19–21; 18:19,26–32; 31:28). The noun *těrûmâ* he understands to mean "gift" and the act as "the setting aside of an object from its owner's domain to transfer it to God's domain," that is, an act of dedication.[23] Whereas a *těnûphâ* is made almost always "before the Lord," that is, a ritual act performed at the sanctuary, a *těrûmâ* is always made "to the LORD." It "is not a ceremony at all" and is often not brought to the sanctuary but given directly to the priest.[24] R. E. Averbeck has observed, however, that such a rigid distinction "forces [Milgrom] to argue for diachronic revision in two passages," Lev 9:21 and 10:14–15. Averbeck demonstrates from Lev 10:15 that

> the same materials on the same occasion could be referred to as both a contribution *[těrûmâ]* and a wave offering *[těnûpâ]* because the former refers simply to the fact that something was turned over to the Lord as a contribution while the latter refers to the manner in which the contribution was presented to the Lord. The manner of presenting a wave offering was apparently a conspicuous act meant to draw attention to the parts actually offered to the Lord in contexts where this needed to be communicated ritually.[25]

That the *těrûmâ* did not require a literal lifting before the Lord is suggested from its use of a portion of land in Ezek 45:1,6–7; 48:8–21.

The relationship of the *těrûmâ* to the tithe is suggested by Num 18:8–24. The offerings the Lord had reserved for the priests, since he was giving them no land, are specified in vv. 8–20: all the *těrûmâ*, the holy offerings brought to the Lord, the portions of the grain, sin, and compensation offerings that were not burned, the wave offerings, and firstfruits. Then the provision of the tithes is designated for the Levites in v. 21 for the same reason. After specify-

---

[22] B. S. Childs, *The Book of Exodus* (Philadelphia: Westminster, 1974), 519, 523; W. Brueggemann, "Wave Offering," *IDB* 4:817. *HALOT* defines תְּרוּמָה as "consecrated gift," "offering," or "contribution." H.-P. Stähli explains ("רום to be high," *TLOT,* 1223): "It may have originally referred to a particular kind of sacral presentation of gifts in which a portion was consecrated and symbolically transferred—not burned but placed at the priest's disposal—through *těrûmâ* 'elevation,' i.e., by being lifted high before the altar of Yahweh," but it also "appears in the OT as a general term for various cultic contributions that go to the priests (Lev 7:14, 32; 22:12; Num 5:9; 18:8, 11, 19, 28; Ezek 44:30; 2 Chr 31:10, 12, 14; perhaps Mal 3:8) and the Levites (Num 18:24), in Ezek also to the prince (*nāśî'* Ezek 45:16)."

[23] J. Milgrom, *Leviticus 1–16*, AB (New York: Doubleday, 1991), 474–75. He finds corroboration in the Akk. root *rāmu*, "give a gift," and related nouns meaning "gift."

[24] Ibid., 474. He also argues that it was actually the תְּנוּפָה, traditionally the "wave offering," that was lifted before the Lord, hence an "elevation offering" (pp. 469–73). "The wave offering is a fiction that should be stricken from the cultic lexicon of the ancient Near East" (p. 473).

[25] R. E. Averbeck, "נוף," *NIDOTTE* on CD-ROM. Version 1.0.

ing the Levites' responsibility at the Tent of Meeting in vv. 22–23, the explanation is given that "I give to the Levites as their inheritance the *tithes* that the Israelites present as an *offering [tĕrûmâ]* to the LORD." The tithes, then, were considered a particular type of *tĕrûmâ.* If so, then God's explanation to the people in Malachi probably meant that they were holding back the offerings that belonged to him, especially the tithes, and that were supposed to be given to the temple personnel as their livelihood.

If the land and its produce belonged to God as Lev 25:23 declares, then all the more so did the tithe. Therefore to withhold it amounted to robbing not only the poor but also God (cf. Ps 51:4; Matt 25:45).[26] The charge is initiated with a question whose sense seems to be, "Is it right [rather than "Is it possible?" or "Is it conceivable?"] for a man to rob God?"[27] The particle *kî* beginning the next clause can be rendered "yet" (as in NIV and most translations), or "surely" (as in NET) or "for." The usual rendering assumes the understood point of the question as, "It is not right to rob God, *yet* you are robbing me [the second use of the verb is a participle]." This makes sense, although the more frequent meaning of the particle as "for" makes sense here too if the clause is explaining the reason for the question.[28]

The word used in 3:8–9 for "rob" *(qāba')* occurs elsewhere only in Prov 22:23, where it is used as a synonym for *gāzal,* "to take by force, rob, plunder" (cf. Isa 10:2; Jer 21:12; Mal 1:13).[29] As the priests in 1:6–7 had not considered their carelessness with the sacrifices to be a personal insult to God, so the people here claim unawareness that in withholding from the temple and its priesthood they were robbing God. The term for "man" here is *'ādām.* The creature dares to rob from the Creator (Gen 1:27; 2:7; 5:1; 9:6; Deut 4:32).

**3:9** This verse amplifies the charge that Judah was robbing God by pointing out two additional facts. The first is that they were doing this even though,

---

[26] The third use of the verb "rob" is a perfect, so the clause probably should be rendered, "How have we robbed you?" (Hill, *Malachi,* 305).

[27] Cf. TEV; similarly, the use of "ought/should" in NJPS and NLT.

[28] Contrary to Hill (*Malachi,* 304–5), I see no reason to consider the use of כִּי here as emphatic.

[29] The meaning of קָבַע is disputed. The LXX translates it with πτερνιζω, "deceive," perhaps confusing it with עָקַב. See NJPS and REB ("defraud") and NJB, NLT, and TEV ("cheat"). *BHS* would emend on the basis of the LXX, but Hill notes that three recensions of the LXX as well as the Vg and the Syriac all support the MT (*Malachi,* 303; cf. J. Ziegler, *Septuaginta: Duodecim Prophetae* [Göttingen: Vandenhoeck & Ruprecht, 1984], 336). The meaning seems clear from its use in Prov 22:23. J. M. P. Smith cogently argues that Malachi would hardly have said Judah had "deceived" God, since this is not possible ("Malachi" in H. G. Mitchell, J. M. P. Smith, and J. A. Bewer, *A Critical and Exegetical Commentary on Haggai, Zechariah, Malachi, and Jonah* [Edinburgh: T&T Clark, 1912], 70). An intentional allusion to עֲקֹב, "Jacob," in 2:6 is unlikely, as D. Stuart explains ("Malachi," 3.1367).

like the Levites in 2:2, God had already begun to discipline them with the curses he had warned them about a thousand years before (and as he had disciplined them time after time since then).[30] "You are under a curse" uses a participle and could be more literally translated "by the curse you are being cursed." The verse begins in Hebrew with two clauses in strong and almost poetic contrast. Each clause contains three words, the second word being the pronoun "you" (plural), and the last word being a verb ending in the sound *-îm* (i.e., a masculine plural participle). The clauses can be literally rendered:

> By-the-curse you are-being-cursed,[31]
> yet-me[32] you are-robbing.

In spite of the self-destructive nature of their behavior, they continued inviting the divine curses of Deut 28:15–68 by plundering the divine storehouse.[33] The painful experiences referred to here are perhaps first alluded to in 1:9, then again in 2:13 and in 2:17. Not until 3:11 is a specific difficulty mentioned— something was devouring their crops. Whether that was their only crisis we do not know. But clearly their failure to give what they owed to God was resulting in his withholding from them what they thought he owed them.

The second additional fact added by v. 9 to the accusation of v. 8 is that the entire nation was guilty. Outside the syntactical symmetry of the two clauses just examined is a noun phrase at the end of the verse that is in apposition to the "you" of those clauses—"the nation, all of it." Such awkward Hebrew has invited attempts to correct the text, but this grammatical device was well known to the book's author, who also used it in 1:7,12.[34] Its function is to call attention to the clause where it is found and to emphasize here that Judah's waywardness was not limited to a few. The whole nation was guilty before God and therefore was in a dangerous spot.[35] Were it not for the Lord's faith-

---

[30] See the discussion of the curse motif in Malachi in the comments on 1:3–4. The same term that occurs here, הַמְּאֵרָה, "the curse," occurs in 2:2. See the comments there.

[31] I.e., Judah was suffering severely under the curse. The LXX rendering, καὶ ἀποβλέποντες ὑμεῖς ἀποβλέπετε, "and you surely look away," may find support in 4QXII^a (R. E. Fuller, "The Twelve," in *Qumran Cave 4: The Prophets*, DJD 15 [Oxford: Clarendon, 1997], 226–27): וּמֹראִים אֹתֶם רָאִים, but the reading of the scroll is far from certain, and the Tg. supports the MT (R. P. Gordon and K. J. Cathcart, *The Targum of the Minor Prophets*, The Aramaic Bible 14 [Wilmington: Michael Glazier, 1989], 237).

[32] The NIV rendering as causal, "because you are robbing me" (similarly most translations), is mistaken. There is no causal particle here, only the clause initial וְאֹתִי, whose disjunctive *waw* should be understood adversatively, "yet" (Hill sees the *waw* here as "epexegetical" but also "emphatic" [*Malachi*, 308]). The sense is that even though they were suffering under the divine curse, they continued to rob God.

[33] So also Hill, *Malachi*, 307.

[34] See the discussion at 1:7. K. Elliger, the Hebrew editor of Hosea to Malachi in *BHS*, wishes to correct the text there as well.

[35] Hill suggests that this "fifth disputation" is more general in its application than the previous ones (*Malachi*, 308). This would support my argument that the final division of the book is climactic. However, 2:11 is also stated in general terms: "Judah has broken faith."

fulness, of which he reminded them even at the beginning of the prophecy, Israel would be ruined (see also 3:6).

Although Israel is typically referred to as a "people" rather than a "nation" and the term "nation" is sometimes used of Israel in a derogatory sense (Zeph 2:1), this is not always the case (Exod 19:6; Zeph 2:9). Therefore, although Malachi's use of the term could mean that Israel was acting toward the Lord the way all the nations acted, disregarding his ownership of all things, this understanding is tenuous.[36]

**3:10a**    As the paragraph begins in v. 7 with a reason (Israel's turning away) followed by a command (to return) with a result (God's return), so it ends in vv. 8–10 with a reason (Israel's robbing God) followed by a command with a result. The command is for God's people to "bring the whole tithe into the storehouse," and the result is "that there may be food in my house."

As Hill explains, the reference to the "storehouse" is to "an extended hallway divided into numerous rooms or cubicles . . . for storage of tithes consisting of grain, wine, and (olive) oil."[37] The phrase "the whole tithe" is almost identical to that which occurs in Lev 27:30, "*Every tenth* of the land's produce, grain from the soil or fruit from the trees, belongs to the LORD," and Num 18:21, "I have given the Levites *every tenth* in Israel as an inheritance" (HCSB). But an even closer parallel is found in Deut 14:28, "At the end of every three years, *bring all the tithes* [lit. "tithe"; but a different word for "bring" is used there] of that year's produce and store it in your towns" (similarly Deut 26:12).[38] Specifying "the whole tithe" suggests that many were either withholding part of the tithe or were bringing nothing.[39] Reference to the "whole" tithe also echoes the guilt of the "whole" nation in v. 9.

Immediately following in Deut 14:29 is the purpose—"so that the Levites (who have no allotment or inheritance of their own) and the aliens, the fatherless and the widows who live in your towns may come and eat and be satisfied, and so that the LORD your God may bless you in all the work of your hands." This is clearly the background for the twin purposes of "food" (or "nourishment") in Mal 3:10a and divine blessing in vv. 10b–12. The interpre-

---

[36] *Contra* B. Glazier-McDonald, *Malachi: The Divine Messenger* (Atlanta: Scholars Press, 1987), 192; Hill, *Malachi,* 308. J. A. Motyer explains, "Generally speaking, עַם specifies Israel in relation to its history with God, while גּוֹי (nation") depicts the people as a national entity among other nations" ("Zephaniah" in *The Minor Prophets: An Exegetical and Expository Commentary* [Grand Rapids: Baker, 1998], 3.935). See also Stuart, "Malachi," 3.1368–69.

[37] Hill, *Malachi,* 310.

[38] In Lev 27:30,32; Num 18:21,28 the phrase is כֹּל מַעֲשֵׂר, "every tithe/tenth." Malachi adds the article and the definite object marker: אֵת כֹּל הַמַּעֲשֵׂר, "all the tithe/tenth" or "the whole tithe/tenth." The phrase in Deut 14:28; 26:12 differs from Malachi only in the absence of the article, which in fact is missing from Mal 3:10 in DSS 4QXII^a (Fuller, *DJD* XV, 226–27). The LXX has καὶ εἰσηνέγκατε πάντα τὰ ἐκφόρια, "and you shall bring in all the produce (pl.) of the earth."

[39] J. M. P. Smith, "Malachi," 72.

tation of "food"[40] as intended for the priests and Levites is made explicit in
the Aramaic Targum, which renders "and there shall be *provision for those
who serve in my Sanctuary*"[41] (see also 2 Chr 31:4–10). The term "storehouse" (lit. "house of treasure"[42]) is also used in Neh 10:38[Hb. 39]: "A priest
descended from Aaron is to accompany the Levites when they receive the
tithes, and the Levites are to bring a tenth of the tithes up to the house of our
God, to the storerooms of the *treasury*." A similar phrase is also used in Neh
12:44: "At that time men were appointed to be in charge of the storerooms for
the contributions, firstfruits and tithes. From the fields around the towns they
were to bring into the storerooms the portions required by the Law for the
priests and the Levites, for Judah was pleased with the ministering priests and
Levites."

Caring for landless inhabitants, especially the Levites, involved more than
a lesson in compassion. As the Nazirites were to be occasional reminders that
Israel was to be holy and dedicated to the Lord (Num 6:1–21), the Levites
were to be a constant reminder that Israel was to be dependent on the Lord.
Millar, stressing a point made previously by McConville, explains that
"Israel's spiritual appropriation of the inheritance can come only when she
sees the landless Levite, with only the Lord himself to enjoy, and models her
life on him." Therefore, "the function of Levi in the land is to remind Israel
that her ultimate calling is not merely to enjoy its produce, but relationship
with him." So "if the Levites are neglected, it is not simply a sign of disobedience, but of a falling away from the relationship which the Levites themselves
model."[43]

## 2. Positive Motivation: Future Blessing (3:10b–12)

This section looks at first like part of the preceding command section
because of the imperative in v. 10b, "Test me." This is only a rhetorical
device, however, whose purpose is to introduce what the Lord would do for
Judah if they would return to him, and so it furnishes motivation. If they
would bring their tithes in faithfulness to the Lord, he would demonstrate his
faithfulness to them with abundant blessings. Whereas positive motivation in

---

[40] Although the term טֶרֶף usually means "prey" (e.g., Num 23:24; Isa 5:29), it can also mean
"food" (Ps 111:5; Job 24:5; Prov 31:15).

[41] Gordon and Cathcart, *The Targum of the Minor Prophets,* 237.

[42] The phrase without the article refers to the temple treasury in pagan Babylon (Dan 1:2). The
term אוֹצָר is elsewhere used figuratively of God's storehouse or treasury from which he sends his
bounty on the earth (Deut 28:12; Isa 45:3; Jer 10:13; but cf. Deut 32:34; Jer 50:25) or of a place
where valuables were kept that had been dedicated to God (Josh 6:19,24; 1 Kgs 7:51; 14:26; 15:18;
2 Kgs 12:18, etc.), or of the royal treasury (2 Kgs 20:13,15; 24:13).

[43] Millar, *Now Choose Life,* 128–29.

the first two addresses takes the form of past incentives to present behavior, both motivation sections in this final address have a future orientation. Supporting the parallel relationship of the two motivation sections, three divine quotation formulas are found in each. Here they underline the positive statement of blessing in v. 10b, the negative statement of blessing in v. 11 ("I will prevent pests"), and the result in v. 12 ("all the nations will call you blessed"). The structure and logic of the passage may be pictured as follows (author's translation):

Thesis: *And test me in this,*                                                      *v. 10b*
   *says Yahweh of hosts.*
Result:
   Thesis: *[See] if I will not open for you the floodgates of heaven.*
      Amplification #1: *And I will pour out for you a blessing*
      *until there is no more need.*
      Amplification #2: *And I will rebuke for you the devourer*          *v. 11*
         Result #1: *And it will not ruin for you the produce of the ground*
         Result #2: *And the vine in the field will not be barren for you,*
         *says Yahweh of hosts.*
   Result: *Then all the nations will consider you fortunate,*              *v. 12*
      *for you will be a delightful land,*
      *says Yahweh of hosts.*

### (1) Blessing from Heaven (3:10b)

**Test me in this," says the LORD Almighty, "and see if I will not throw open the floodgates of heaven and pour out so much blessing that you will not have room enough for it.**

This section begins with the Lord's command to "test" or prove him and discover that he is faithful. The verb used *(bāḥan)* is one of three common verbs in the Old Testament for testing. The others are *nāsâ* and *ṣārap*.[44] The synonym *nāsâ* occurs with the sense "test" (it can also mean "attempt") in thirty-one verses. In ten of these it refers to divine testing either of individuals (Abraham in Gen 22:1, the psalmist in Ps 26:2, and Hezekiah in 2 Chr 32:31) or more often of the people of Israel (Exod 15:25; 16:4; 20:20; Deut 8:2,16; 13:3; Judg 2:22–3:4) or the tribe of Levi (Deut 33:8). In ten verses it refers to testing God in the sense of challenging or disputing his presence or power and thus provoking him to anger (Exod 17:2,7; Num 14:22; Deut 6:16; Pss 78:18,41,56; 95:9; 106:14; Isa 7:12). The other passages refer to human testing as when David needed to try out the armor (1 Sam 17:39) or the queen of

---

[44] See Ps 26:2, where the three verbs occur together as synonyms. Other related words are חקר, "search, examine," as in Jer 17:10; Ps 139:1,23, and ברר, "purge, sift," as in Eccl 3:18; Dan 11:35.

Sheba came to test Solomon with questions (1 Kgs 10:1; 2 Chr 9:1).

The word ṣārap occurs in twenty-nine verses and usually refers to the process of refining. The active participle is used of literal metalworkers in gold or silver (e.g., Judg 17:4; Isa 40:19; 41:7; 46:6). Otherwise it is used as a metaphor for the divine work of removing impurities, as in Mal 3:2–3 (see also Isa 1:25; 48:10; Jer 6:29; 9:7). The passive participle is used metaphorically of the "pure" result of the refiner's work (Ps 18:30; 119:140; Prov 30:5).

The verb used here, bāḥan, also occurs in twenty-nine verses. In nineteen of those, God is testing man, often his heart (lit. "kidneys") or mind (1 Chr 29:17; Jer 11:20; 12:3; 17:10; 20:12; Pss 7:9; 17:3; 26:2; Prov 17:3). Though the word usually has a "theological" sense, according to Brensinger, in cases where this is lacking (Gen 42:15–16; Job 12:11; 34:3; Ezek 21:13 [18]) "the key concern involves evaluating the dependability of something."[45] In Ps 95:9 it is used of man testing or provoking God, but only in parallel to nāsâ. It also has this sense in Mal 3:15, where it probably was used instead of nāsâ because bāḥan had been used in v. 10. The NIV translation "test me in this" is literal and urges or commands the Judean community to give God the opportunity to prove his faithfulness in response to their faith.

The expression "in this" conveys the sense "by this means" and is used similarly along with the verb bāḥan in Gen 42:15 to describe Joseph's test of his brothers: "And this is how [lit. "by this"] you will be tested: As surely as Pharaoh lives, you will not leave this place unless your youngest brother comes here" (also see v. 33). The expression "by this" also occurs without a verb of testing but in situations where God is offering a "test" or demonstration of his presence or character. Moses is to tell Pharaoh, "*By this* you will know that I am the LORD: With the staff that is in my hand I will strike the water of the Nile, and it will be changed into blood" (Exod 7:17). And Joshua tells the Israelites, "This is how [lit. "By this"] you will know that the living God is among you" (Josh 3:10; see also Num 16:28; Ps 41:11).[46] Although it is wrong to test God with complaining, rebellion, and unbelief (Exod 17:2–7; Num 14:22; Deut 6:14–18; Pss 78:17–19,40–42,56–58; 95:8–9; 106:6–29), it is not wrong to test him with obedience, especially when he commands it.[47]

The divine response to the people's faithful obedience would be the opening of "the floodgates of heaven" and his "pour[ing]" on them an abundance of blessing. This promise is expressed in terms often used in oaths or

[45] T. L. Brensinger, "בָּחַן (bāḥan)," *NIDOTTE* on CD-ROM. Version 1.0.

[46] The Hb. בְּזֹאת, "by/in this," occurs nineteen times in the Hb. Bible and is always elliptical, never followed by a noun modified by "this." It sometimes means "on this [condition]" (Gen 34:15,22; 1 Sam 11:2), "in this [manner]" (Lev 16:3; Isa 27:9; Jer 9:24), "in spite of this" (Lev 26:27; Ps 27:3), and "because of this" (1 Chr 27:24; 2 Chr 19:2).

[47] Ahaz's pretended piety in disobediently refusing to "test the LORD" in Isa 7:12 resulted from his misapplication of Deut 6:16, which in term evidenced his spiritual blindness.

emphatic declarations. The words "and see" is not in the Hebrew, which is literally, "Test me in this . . . if I will not open for you . . ." The Hebrew words *ʾim lōʾ*, "if not," often introduce an oath where they may be translated "surely," as in Isa 14:24: "The LORD Almighty has sworn, *'Surely*, as I have planned, so it will be, and as I have purposed, so it will stand.' "[48] On the other hand, they may introduce an indirect question, as in Exod 22:8[7]: "But if the thief is not found, the owner of the house must appear before the judges *to determine whether* he has laid his hands on the other man's property." In this case, "to determine whether" translates *ʾim lōʾ* (similarly Exod 22:11[10]).[49] An even closer parallel to the construction in Mal 3:10 is found in Job 1:11, where Satan pleads with God, "But just stretch out your hand and touch all that he has, *and see if he will not* curse you to your face" (REB). Here as in Malachi is an imperative clause followed by an *ʾim lōʾ* clause with a future perspective. This is also in a context of testing, although the term is not used until later in the book (Job 7:18; 23:10; 34:36; 36:21). Because of the frequent use of indirect questions in the syntax of testing in the Hebrew Bible,[50] this is probably the correct understanding of Mal 3:10 and Job 1:11, although the NIV and most translations render the latter verse as an oath: "But stretch out your hand and strike everything he has, *and he will surely* curse you to your face."

The word translated "floodgates" occurs nine times in the Hebrew Bible and usually refers to an opening in the wall of a building, whether a window (Eccl 12:3) or a chimney (Hos 13:3). The phrase "floodgates of heaven" occurs elsewhere in Gen 7:11; 8:2 (where it is translated "floodgates of the heavens") as the source of the rain that flooded the earth. A similar phrase is used sarcastically by an unbelieving royal official in 2 Kgs 7:2. He claims that even a flood of divine provisions from (lit.) "windows in the heavens" could not remedy the severe famine caused by an Aramean siege of Samaria. This passage shows that the figure did not necessarily point to rain, since the problem was siege rather than drought, and the famine was ended by a miraculous divine provision of Aramean supplies. Such a miraculous provision was what the Lord promised to repeat in abundance for the Judean community of Malachi.

The promise to open the "floodgates of heaven" in response to Judah's obedience is amplified in two ways. The rest of v. 10 comprises the first amplification. The NIV "pour out so much blessing that you will not have room enough

---

[48] See *IBHS* §40.2.2b; *BHRG*, 310.

[49] See *BHRG*, 322.

[50] See Gen 42:16; Exod 16:4; 17:7; 22:11; Deut 8:2; 13:3; Judg 2:22; 3:4; Ezra 2:59. Cf. *GBH* §161*f*. In several of these sentences a verb of testing is followed by the interrogative particle הֲ, and then אִם לֹא occurs at the end of the sentence with a sense similar to English "or not." A verb of cognition such as רָאָה, "see," or יָדַע, "know," also often occurs (e.g., Gen 24:21; Num 11:23; Deut 8:2).

for it" is literally "and I will pour/empty out for you blessing until the cessation of sufficiency." The root of the Hebrew verb translated "pour out" refers to being empty (represented by the noun *rîq*, "emptiness," and the adjective *rêq*, "empty, vain"). The verb occurs only in the causative stem and means "empty out, pour out" (e.g., Eccl 11:3; Jer 48:12; Hab 1:17; Zech 4:12; it also is used in an idiom for "drawing a sword"). Here it refers emphatically to the flood of blessings[51] that would answer Israel's obedience of faith.

The final phrase of the verse may mean either "until there is no longer sufficient room for it" or "until there is no longer any need for it." The critical word *dāy* usually means "sufficiency" or "enough" (e.g., Exod 36:7, "For the material they had was *sufficient*" [NASB]; also Lev 25:26; Deut 15:8; Isa 40:16). But if that is the meaning here, the phrase would seem to indicate Judah would receive divine blessings until they no longer had enough. Most translations take this as referring to enough room to hold all the blessings (NASB, NET, NIV, NKJV, NLT, NRSV) or enough means to measure it (HCSB, NAB). An alternative interpretation is that God promised to empty out the heavenly blessings for them until his supply was depleted, which would be never. Although this view is possible, it would expect quite a lot from the listener or reader. If we are to understand, however, that in the world described by God divine sufficiency always matches human need, then the cessation of sufficiency would result from cessation of need. In Deut 25:2 the judge is to flog the guilty man (lit.) "according to the sufficiency of his wickedness in number." That is, the number of lashes should correspond to the amount of his wickedness. And in Prov 25:16 someone who finds honey should eat only (lit.) "a sufficiency for you," that is, enough to meet his need (also Prov 27:27). This solution may be better than introducing a concept such as "sufficient room."[52] Whenever the people had a need, the Lord's supply would be there waiting for them (like the lion in Nah 2:12).[53]

## *(2) Blessing from the Land (3:11)*

**[11]I will prevent pests from devouring your crops, and the vines in your fields will not cast their fruit," says the LORD Almighty.**

---

[51] A collective singular in Hb., בְּרָכָה, "blessing," as in the Tg. (Cathcart and Gordon, *Targum of the Minor Prophets,* 237). In 4QXII[a] it is preceded by the article plus the objective marker אֵת, hence "the blessing[s]" (Fuller, *DJD* XV, 227). The LXX has τὴν εὐλογίαν μου, "my blessing."

[52] Cf. *HALOT,* "until there is no more need." The interpretation preferred here, "until there is no more need," is favored by ESV and REB.

[53] The word occurs several times as the circumstantial particle מִדֵּי attached to the preposition מִן and carrying the meaning "whenever" (e.g. 1 Sam 1:7; 18:30; 1 Kgs 14:28). The Tg and Peshitta have "until you say, 'Enough!'" R. P. Gordon finds a similar Targumic paraphrase of the MT in Isa 66:24 (*Studies in the Targum to the Twelve Prophets: From Nahum to Malachi* [Leiden: Brill, 1994], 127).

This verse begins literally, "And I will rebuke for you the devourer." It contains the second amplification of the divine promise to "throw open the floodgates of heaven." Not only did that mean God would "pour out" abundant blessings (v. 10b); it also meant that he would "rebuke" the infestation of their crops. Here is the third of five uses of the Hebrew word *lākem*, "for you," in vv. 10–11 of this motivation section.[54] As he had been *against* them for their wickedness in the past (Lev 26:17–25; Deut 11:17; 28:20), so the Lord promised that he would be *for* them in opening the floodgates of heaven, in pouring out blessing, in rebuking whatever was destroying their crops, in protecting their produce from ruin and their vines from barrenness (cf. Joel 2:19,23–25; Zech 8:13–15; Mal 4:2).

The verb "rebuke" *(gʿr)* occurred earlier in Mal 2:3 in the warning to the priests, "I will rebuke your *[lākem]* descendants." Although the verb is one of speech rather than action, when God is the one speaking the two concepts are equivalent. As the divine creative word resulted in the physical universe, so the divine rebuke either restrains or destroys (see 2 Sam 22:16; Isa 50:2; 51:20). In 2:3 it referred to divine rejection and removal from blessing and service because of unfaithfulness and unbelief. Now he promised to "rebuke" Judah's enemies, putting a stop to the pests devouring their crops if they would repent. R. C. Stallman points out, "In contrast to reliance on magic to avert these disasters, the emphasis on moral repentance in the OT is unique in the ANE."[55]

Although "devourer" is a general term for something that eats, it is often found in idioms of destruction. It sometimes refers to fire (Hos 8:14) and sometimes to human armies (Jer 30:16). Joel uses both images to describe the locusts coming in judgment against Israel (Joel 1:4,19–20; 2:3,5,25). Stallman points out from Deut 28:38–52, "Ironically, the same locust plague that formed part of Yahweh's judgment on Egypt was also threatened by Moses on Israel, should God's people lapse into covenantal disloyalty. . . . In addition to this pest that would devour . . . the crop, Yahweh would bring a distant nation to 'swoop down' on Israel to devour . . . its livestock and land and then to besiege its cities."[56] He also notes the reappearance of the locust of divine judgment in Amos 4:9–10; 7:1–3.

---

[54] See the literal translation of these verses before the comments on v. 10b.

[55] R. C. Stallman, "אָרְבֶּה," *NIDOTTE* on CD-ROM. Version 1.0.

[56] Ibid. A strong tradition, including the Jewish interpreters Rashi, Ibn-Ezra, and Qimhi, exists that the אָכֵל in Malachi refers to the locust. Biblical evidence is lacking for such a specific identification, but V. A. Hurowitz has argued for "caterpillar" from Akk. evidence ("אכל in Malachi 3:11—Caterpillar," *JBL* 121 [2002]: 327–30). He notes that the term is "the exact morphological and etymological equivalent of the Akkadian noun *ākilu*," which usually appears with *mubattiru* and *mūnu*, words for "larva" or "caterpillar." The damage caused by such pests is more consistent, he says, with vines losing their fruit. See also H. Wolf, whose similar view is based on Deut 28:39 (*Haggai and Malachi: Rededication and Renewal*, EvBC [Chicago: Moody, 1976], 110).

Two results of God's rebuking the devourer are specified in two subsequent clauses, each introduced by the Hebrew *wĕlōʾ*, "and not." The NIV collapses the first result into the previous clause, but it is literally, "and [or "so that"[57]] it will not ruin for you the fruit of the ground." The second result is "and the vine in the field will not fail to bear for you." The expression "fruit of the ground" is used first of Cain's offering (Gen 4:3), then of the offering of "firstfruits" Israel was to bring to the sanctuary, bowing and declaring, "Now I bring the firstfruits of the soil that you, O LORD, have given me" (Deut 26:10). The words "cast their fruit" translate a Hebrew verb *(šākal)* that usually refers to losing one's children through miscarriage (Gen 31:38; Exod 23:26) or death (Lev 26:22; Deut 32:25). Its figurative application to vines losing their fruit is similar to its application to land being deprived of produce in 2 Kgs 2:19,21. Israel, who was compared to a vine that brought grief to its divine vinedresser by producing bad grapes (Isa 5:1–7; cf. Jer 2:21; Hos 10:1), had been punished by being picked clean, cut down, and burned up (Ps 80:8–16; also Jer 6:9). The prophets often associate God's judgment with the destruction of the vineyard. In Hos 2:12 he warned, "I will ruin her vines and her fig trees, which she said were her pay from her lovers; I will make them a thicket, and wild animals will devour them"; and Zeph 1:13 declares the fulfillment of the warning in Deut 28:19 that "you will plant a vineyard, but you will not even begin to enjoy its fruit" and 28:39 that "you will plant vineyards and cultivate them but you will not drink the wine or gather the grapes, because worms will eat them" (also Ps 78:47; Isa 16:8; Jer 5:10,17; 12:10; Amos 4:10).

Because Israel had refused to cling gratefully to their exclusive relationship with the Lord during the times of the Judges, he had disciplined them by bringing enemies against them "like swarms of locust" to ruin their crops (Judg 6:4–5; cf. Joel 1:4). Now after many punishments culminating in the affliction of exile (Jer 7:20), they had again refused to come to him in grateful obedience with the prescribed portions of their crops and other produce they would not have without his favor. Consequently, he had again ruined their crops, but again he was prepared to turn curse to blessing if they would repent, as passages such as Amos 9:14 had promised: "I will bring back my exiled people Israel; they will rebuild the ruined cities and live in them. They will plant vineyards and drink their wine; they will make gardens and eat their fruit" (also Deut 30:6–10; Jer 31:5).

### (3) Blessing from the Nations (3:12)

**12"Then all the nations will call you blessed, for yours will be a delightful land," says the LORD Almighty.**

---

[57] Cf. GKC §109g.

This final verse of the motivation section (vv. 10b–12) ends with the third divine quotation formula in this section, marking its conclusion and underlining its significance.[58] This verse contains the result of God's opening the "floodgates of heaven" in v. 10b. As the land of Edom became a symbol of God's judgment according to Mal 1:4, called "the Wicked Land" (*gĕbûl rišʿâ*, "territory of wickedness") and its people "a people always under the wrath of the LORD," so God promised a day when Israel would become a symbol of blessing, an object lesson in God's grace and favor. They would be called "blessed"[59] and "a delightful land" (*ʾereṣ ḥēpeṣ*, "land of delight"). The root *ḥpṣ*, "delight," has occurred three times in the book previously. The hypocrisy of Judah's "worship" had deprived the Lord of his delight in his people ("I am not *pleased* with you," 1:10); the people had wickedly claimed that God delighted in "all who do evil" (2:17); and the Lord delights in the coming divine "messenger of the covenant" (3:1). Here the Lord's blessing of his chosen and promised land would cause it to become a source of delight to its inhabitants but also to the God who had created, bestowed, and beautified it (Isa 4:2; 60:13; Jer 3:19).

Through the prophet Isaiah, God had described his future redemption as the creation of "new heavens and a new earth" and had declared: "I will create Jerusalem to be a delight and its people a joy. I will rejoice over Jerusalem and take delight in my people; the sound of weeping and of crying will be heard in it no more" (Isa 65:17–19; cf. 66:2). C. J. H. Wright explains that these verses

> introduce a wonderful section which portrays God's new world as a place which is joyful, life-fulfilling, with guaranteed work-satisfaction, and environmentally safe! It is a vision that puts most New Age dreams in the shade. This and related passages are the scriptural (Old Testament) foundation for the New Testament hope, which, far from rejecting or denying the earth as such or envisaging us floating off to some place else, looks forward likewise to a new, redeemed creation (Rom. 8:18ff.), in which righteousness will dwell after purging judgment (2 Pet. 3:10–13) because God himself will dwell there with his people (Rev. 21:1–4).[60]

---

[58] אָמַר יְהוָה צְבָאוֹת, "says Yahweh of hosts," also occurs three times in the final motivation section in 3:16–4:3[Hb. 3:21], the last occurrence concluding the section.

[59] "Call . . . blessed" renders the Hb. verb אָשַׁר, "be/consider someone fortunate/blessed" (cf. Ps 41:1[Hb. 2]; 72:17). It is related to the noun occurring forty-five times in the Hb. Bible rendered "blessed/happy is . . ." (cf. M. A. Grisanti, "אָשַׁר *ʾāšar II*," *NIDOTTE* on CD-ROM. Version 1.0).

[60] C. H. J. Wright, *Walking in the Ways of the Lord: The Ethical Authority of the Old Testament* (Downers Grove: InterVarsity, 1995), 195. See also R. L. Saucy, *The Case for Progressive Dispensationalism* (Grand Rapids: Zondervan, 1993), 50–57, who notes the significance of Paul's claim that Abraham and his seed would be "heir of the world" (Rom 4:13).

Jerusalem's destruction and degradation at the hands of the Babylonians had caused it to become the opposite of what is described here. According to Lam 2:15: "All who pass your way clap their hands at you; they scoff and shake their heads at the Daughter of Jerusalem: 'Is this the city that was called the perfection of beauty, the joy of the whole earth?'" But Malachi assures that repentance would restore their beauty and joy and would turn their shame to glory and the scorn of the nations to praise (cf. Isa 61:3; Ezek 36:15; cf. Ezek 36:26–27).[61] The heart of the Gentile nations will change because of the direct work of God's Spirit in cleansing them from sin and removing their blindness so that they may see the exalted Servant as he is (Isa 52:13–15; Luke 2:32). But another reason the nations "from the rising to the setting of the sun" will recognize the Lord's greatness and worship him as the great King (Mal 1:11,14) will be because of his mighty acts of redemption on behalf of Israel.[62]

The issue in Mal 3:7–12 is not tithing but apostasy. Judah is charged here with abandoning the God who had chosen and blessed them and turning away from the statutes he had given them to test their loyalty and to mark the path of life he would bless. By retaining for themselves the tithes and other offerings they owed to God, the people showed their idolatrous hearts in placing themselves before God, and they showed their callous hearts in leaving the Levites and landless poor to fend for themselves. These verses do not light the way to health and wealth and immediate prosperity. They point the way to a national repentance that will precede the earthly kingdom of Christ (Rom 11:26) and will be characterized by the Lord's protection, provision, prosperity, and his very presence (Joel 2:18–32).

### Excursus: Tithing in the Church?

How do these verses apply to the Christian today?[63] That the Old Testament law continues to instruct the church is indicated by the apostles' continued delight in it and use of it to reveal sin (Rom 7:7,22; 1 Tim 1:5–11; 2 Tim 3:16–17). A continuity between new covenant and old covenant instructions is shown both explicitly (Rom 13:8–10; Gal 5:14) and implicitly in citing old covenant law to confirm instructions under the new covenant (1 Cor 9:8–10; Eph 6:1–3; 1 Tim

---

[61] Note the continuing distinction here in the eschatological future between believing Israel and the believing Gentile nations (see also Amos 9:11–12).

[62] R. L. Saucy notes that according to Ezekiel (36:23,36; 37:28; 39:7) "the vindication of the name of God through the restoration of Israel under the new covenant would bring about Gentile recognition of Israel's God." He also cites Isa 42:6; 49:6; Jer 16:14–20 (*The Case for Progressive Dispensationalism* [Grand Rapids: Zondervan, 1993], 123). See also Deut 32:43; Ps 117:1–2; Rom 1:16; 11:11–12,15; 15:8–12.

[63] See the brief history of the issue of tithing in the church together with bibliography in D. K. McKim, "Tithing," in *Evangelical Dictionary of Theology*, 2d ed. (Grand Rapids: Baker, 2001), 1203.

5:18; 1 Pet 1:15–16). The New Testament writers taught, however, that the believer's relationship to the old covenant law is different since the coming of Christ. This is shown, for example, by the instruction Peter received from God to "kill and eat" and not to "call anything impure that God has made clean" (Acts 10:13–15) and by the apostolic church's rejection of the proposal that "the Gentiles must be circumcised and required to obey the law of Moses" (Acts 15:5). Furthermore, Paul asserted that the Christian is "not under law but under grace" (Rom 6:14; also Gal 5:18; 1 Cor 9:20), that he has "died to the law" and been "released from the law so that we serve in the new way of the Spirit, and not in the old way of the written code" (Rom 7:4,6; also Gal 2:19). He declared that the law was added to the promises "because of transgressions *until* the Seed to whom the promise referred had come" (Gal 3:19; also 1 Tim 1:9) and that

> before this faith [in Jesus Christ] came, we were confined under the law, imprisoned until the coming faith was revealed. The law, then, was our guardian *until Christ*, so that we could be justified by faith. But since that faith has come, we are *no longer under a guardian*, for you are all sons of God through faith in Christ Jesus. (Gal 3:23–26, HCSB)

He also declared that Christ has made peace and created "one new man" of Jew and Gentile by "destroy[ing] the barrier, the dividing wall of hostility, by abolishing in his flesh the law with its commandments and regulations" (Eph 2:14–16).

Furthermore, the church believed they were under a new covenant (1 Cor 11:25; 2 Cor 3:6–11) and worshiped on the first rather than the last day of the week (1 Cor 16:2). And finally, the author of Hebrews declared that Christ's death on the cross instituted a new priestly order and that "when there is a change of the priesthood, there must also be a change of the law" (Heb 7:12). He also described the new covenant as "superior to the old one" and pointed out from Jer 31:31–34 that "by calling this covenant 'new,' [God] has made the first one obsolete; and what is obsolete and aging will soon disappear" (Heb 8:6,13). More specifically, the "gifts and offerings" under the old covenant "are only a matter of food and drink and various ceremonial washings—external regulations applying until the time of the new order" (Heb 9:9–10). In this context we may understand Jesus' teaching (see Matthew 5) as "a new law that at once fulfills and surpasses the law of Moses,"[64] a law that Paul would call "the law of Christ" (1 Cor 9:21; Gal 6:2).

How to reconcile the New Testament teaching on the continuity and discontinuity between new covenant and old covenant instructions has been debated for centuries, and the literature is voluminous.[65] The evidence is clear enough, however, that one cannot simply apply directly to new covenant believers the laws, directives, warnings, and incentives given to Israel under the old covenant. D. Dorsey has argued, for example, that "the collection of 613 regulations com-

---

[64] G. Wenham, "Grace and Law in the Old Testament," in *Law, Morality, and the Bible* (Downers Grove: InterVarsity, 1978), 20.

[65] An effective introduction to the issues and literature is provided by F. Thielman, *Paul and the Law: A Contextual Approach* (Downers Grove: InterVarsity, 1994) and T. R. Schreiner, *The Law and Its Fulfillment: A Pauline Theology of Law* (Grand Rapids: Baker, 1993).

prising God's covenant with ancient Israel is not intended to legally govern the Church."

> The Sinaitic law code was very specifically designed by God to regulate the lives of the West Semitic inhabitants of the southern Levant. Nearly all the regulations of the corpus—over 95%—are so culturally specific, geographically limited, and so forth that they would be completely inapplicable, and in fact unfulfillable, to Christians living throughout the world today.[66]

The difficulty with trying to apply part of the Old Testament law to Christians is the lack of any biblical substantiation for such a division on the one hand and the biblical teaching regarding the unity of the law on the other hand.[67] Paul in Gal 5:3, for example, declares "to every man who lets himself be circumcised that he is obligated to obey the whole law" (also Jas 2:10–11). God's moral absolutes are eternal because they arise from his own character. But how those absolutes are manifest and administered in the different economies of old and new covenants will likely differ. An obvious example is that under the old covenant adultery was not only wrong but was punishable by execution (Lev 20:10). Under the new covenant the absolute prohibition remains, but the penalty apparently does not (Heb 13:4). What can be learned from the Old Testament prohibition is the seriousness and destructiveness of the sin.

On the positive side, the Old Testament included instruction to care for the landless poor, especially those whose responsibility was to minister in teaching the law and in maintaining the temple and its worship. This is matched by New Testament instructions regarding God's ownership of all we have (Matt 6:25–32; Acts 17:24–25; Col 1:16; Jas 1:17) and the Christian's responsibility for acts of mercy, kindness, care for the needy and for respect, love, and care for church leaders (1 Tim 5:17–18; 1 Thess 5:12). In response to the Spirit's warning of a coming famine, for example, "The disciples, each according to his ability, decided to provide help for the brothers living in Judea" (Acts 11:27–30; cf. 24:17). Paul speaks in Rom 15:26–27 of the obligation of Gentile Christians to meet the needs of the Jewish Christians in Jerusalem based on the principle that "they owe it to them. For if the Gentiles have shared in the Jews' spiritual blessings, they owe it to the Jews to share with them their material blessings." The basic principle of caring for the poor is repeatedly taught in the New Testament (Acts 4:34–35; Rom 12:13; Gal 2:10; Eph 4:28; Jas 2:16; 1 John 3:17). And similar to the Old Testament law of the tithe, one's gifts are to be in accordance with his financial resources. Paul's instruction to the Corinthians as well as others was that "each of you is to set something aside and save to the extent that he prospers" (1 Cor 16:1–2; also "according to your means" in 2 Cor 8:11–12).

---

[66] D. Dorsey, "The Law of Moses and the Christian: A Compromise," *JETS* 34 (1991): 325, 329.

[67] The popular division of the law into moral, civil, and ceremonial also fails to find clear and consistent criteria for making such distinctions. See also Dorsey, ibid., 329–31. He provides a cogent argument with examples of how the Mosaic law, though "no longer legally binding upon Christians," continues to be "profoundly binding upon Christians in a revelatory and pedagogical sense" and in its entirety, as 2 Tim 3:16 declares (p. 331). Cf. D. Moo, "The Law of Moses or the Law of Christ" in *Continuity and Discontinuity: Perspectives on the Relationship between the Old and New Testaments* (Westchester, Ill.: Crossway, 1988), 203–18.

Nevertheless, even though in Romans 15 Paul described these collections as spiritual obligations, he spoke of them in 1 Cor 16:3 as "gifts" (*charis*, rendered "act of grace" in 2 Cor 8:6 and "grace of giving" in 8:7), and in the major New Testament passage on giving, in 2 Cor 8:2, he described it in terms of "generosity" (*haplotēs*; also *eulogia*, "generous gift" in 2 Cor 9:5). He praised the Macedonians for giving "even beyond their ability" (8:3; see Mark 12:44). Paul offers a clue in 2 Cor 8:8 that giving under the new covenant follows different principles than under the old covenant when he says, "I am not commanding you, but I want to test the sincerity of your love by comparing it with the earnestness of others." Whereas the law of the tithe was an external obligation commanded of every member of the covenant community of Israel, giving under the new covenant is to be an expression of joy (2 Cor 8:2) and love (cf. 8:24; 9:7) produced by God's Spirit and giving evidence of the presence of the One "who works in you to will and to act according to his good purpose" (Phil 2:13; see Jer 31:33; Ezek 36:26–27; Rom 12:8). In 2 Cor 8:1 Paul had said that the Macedonians' giving was the result of the grace that God had given them (also 2 Cor 9:14–15). So the acceptability of one's offering was determined by it being proportional to one's means and the product of a willing and even "cheerful" heart (2 Cor 8:12; 9:7).

The question remains whether under the new covenant obedience to biblical principles of kindness and generosity carried motivations of material blessing (or deprivation) as under the old covenant.[68] One must recognize that the assurances of material blessing found in Mal 3:7–12 are based on the blessings and curses attached to the Mosaic covenant in Leviticus 26 and Deuteronomy 28. If the new covenant has replaced the Mosaic covenant in some sense, these blessings and curses are no longer in effect, at least not in a direct and literal sense. Yet one must ask if a similar motivation might be attached to New Testament guidelines for giving. At first glance 2 Cor 9:6–11 seems to echo Mal 3:7–12.

> Remember this: Whoever sows sparingly will also reap sparingly, and whoever sows generously will also reap generously. Each man should give what he has decided in his heart to give, not reluctantly or under compulsion, for God loves a cheerful giver. And God is able to make all grace abound to you, so that in all things at all times, having all that you need, you will abound in every good work. As it is written: "He has scattered abroad his gifts to the poor; his righteousness endures forever." Now he who supplies seed to the sower and bread for food will also supply and increase your store of seed and will enlarge the harvest of your righteousness. You will be made rich in every way so that you can be generous on every occasion, and through us your generosity will result in thanksgiving to God.

Closer examination, however, shows that the principles at work here are very different. Paul is not advocating giving that will result in blessing but rather blessing that will result in giving. The purpose of "having all that you need," he says (v. 8), is that you may "abound in every good work," not vice versa. The abundance of God's supply of seed and bread (quoting Isa 55:10) that makes "rich in every way" (v. 11) is for the *purpose* of being "generous on every occasion." What then is the harvest one reaps from the generosity that is sown, "the harvest of your

---

[68] See the comments and bibliography on prosperity in the OT in D. Howard, *Joshua,* NAC (Nashville: Broadman & Holman, 1998), 86–90.

righteousness"? It is not material blessings one may enjoy as the reward for righteousness and obedience. The harvest of generosity is rather "thanksgiving to God" (v. 11).[69] Paul elaborates in the next two verses:

> This service that you perform is not only supplying the needs of God's people but is also overflowing in *many expressions of thanks to God*. Because of the service by which you have proved yourselves, *men will praise God* for the obedience that accompanies your confession of the gospel of Christ, and for your generosity in sharing with them and with everyone else. (2 Cor 9:12–13)

The motivation of material blessing in the New Testament, therefore, has a different emphasis from that found in Malachi and the Old Testament. God blesses the Christian *for* giving not *because of* giving. Also different is the apparent lack of guidance about the amount to be given. Nowhere in the New Testament, even in these two chapters of 2 Corinthians dedicated to the issue, is the Christian instructed to give a "tithe" or "tenth." Since the giving requirement is no longer an external obligation required as "dues" from every member of the covenant community but rather is to be the expression of love from a regenerated and redeemed heart, the amount is also not specified. How much, then, should the Christian give? Since the New Testament lacks specific instruction on the amount one should give, though on the other hand continuing the principle of giving as one has prospered and according to one's means, and since the giving of a tenth is the pattern used in the Old Testament, even before the founding of the Mosaic covenant (Gen 14:20), the use of the tenth should be considered an initial guideline for New Testament giving.

## 3. Situation: Complacency toward Serving the Lord (3:13–15)

Although some indication of the situation to be addressed in this final division was necessarily introduced in the opening command section in 3:7–10a, more needed to be said. It can be inferred from the commands that the covenant community of Judah had still not returned to the Lord with all their heart (Deut 4:29–30) and that evidence of this could be provided by their failure to "bring the whole tithe" (Mal 3:10). What is not clear at this point is what sinful attitude was behind Israel's failure in this regard.[70]

This section consists mainly of the longest speech of Judah in the book, which adds vividness to the description of their sins. Unlike the postexilic confession of Neh 9:33—"In all that has happened to us, you have been just; you have acted faithfully, while we did wrong"—Malachi's audience has

---

[69] V. P. Furnish (*II Corinthians*, AB [New York: Doubleday, 1984], 446) finds the emphasis of 2 Cor 9:6–15 to be the importance of generous giving. Paul makes two fundamental points, he says: "God provides the means to be generous (9:6–10) and (therefore) generosity redounds to the glory of God (9:11–15)."

[70] Thus the view of S. L. McKenzie and H. N. Wallace that the book originally ended at 3:12 fails not only because of the book's structure, but also its logic ("Covenant Themes in Malachi," *CBQ* 45 [1983]: 560–63). They are mistaken that the issue of "Yahweh's fidelity and what good it does to serve him . . . has really been dealt with quite thoroughly" in 1:1–3:12.

responded to their difficulties by concluding that it is useless to serve God
since their so-called obedience has brought no "gain" or profit (3:14). The fortunate ones, they say, are those who have tested God's patience with wicked
lives and have escaped punishment (3:15). This section picks up themes from
the situation section in 2:17, helping to stitch the second and third divisions
together. In both places the Lord is displeased by what he hears the Judahites
saying about his treatment of the wicked. In 2:17 their words have "wearied"
him, and here their words against him are "harsh." In 2:17 the people's complaint is that God has not punished the wicked but is treating them as if they
were good. Here that complaint is extended and amplified. Not only is God
not punishing the wicked, but he is also not rewarding the righteous. Therefore, since in their minds life is about prosperity, it is better to be wicked than
righteous.[71] These verses add an antithesis to the previous verses of this division that give the initial command and motivation. *Although* the people of
Judah had developed such a warped, sinful attitude toward God and their own
lives (3:13–15), as signified by their selfishly hoarding their possessions (3:7–
10a), if they would repent and return to the Lord with faith and obedience, he
would flood them with permanent prosperity and peace (3:10b–12).[72] The
structure and logic of this opening section may be displayed by the following
chart using the author's translation. As in the case of similar previous charts,
the paragraph is portrayed in terms of multiple layers of embedding, indicated
by levels of indentation (see the introduction to 1:2–5).

God's statement: *Your words against me are harsh,*                                    *v. 13*
        <u>*says Yahweh.*</u>
The people's question: *And you say, "What have we spoken against you?"*
God answers by quoting the people:
    Thesis: *You say, "Serving God is useless,"*                              *v. 14*
    Amplification:
        Thesis: *and "What is the profit,*
            *for*[73] *we have kept his requirement*

---

[71] J. M. P. Smith calls this "a commercial type of piety" but supposes that "this prophet apparently accepts this standard of value for religion" ("Malachi," 76–77). On the contrary, Malachi is
about a faith in Yahweh that honors his name and obeys his moral precepts.

[72] Thus my objection to the common notion that 3:13 begins the final of six oracles or disputations (see the Introduction).

[73] The two occurrences of כִּי in this verse probably are causal. A similar construction occurs
in Exod 3:11, commonly rendered, "Who am I, that I should go to Pharaoh and bring the Israelites
out of Egypt?" Waltke and O'Connor explain similar interrogative sentences in Ps 8:5 and 2 Kgs
5:7 as כִּי clauses of result (*IBHS* §38.3b). The problem is that result is the opposite of cause, which
is the usual function of כִּי in this environment. A. Aejmelaeus argues that the interrogative followed by כִּי in such cases is equivalent of "why?" and is a subgroup of causal uses of כִּי. The idea
here is, "Why have we bothered to keep his requirements and walk mournfully?" ("Function and
Interpretation of כִּי in Biblical Hebrew," *JBL* 105 [1986]: 201–2).

*and we have walked mournfully before Yahweh of hosts?*
Result:
    Thesis: *So now we are calling fortunate the arrogant*       *v. 15*
    Reason:
        Thesis₁: *Not only have doers of wickedness prospered*
        Thesis₂:
            Antithesis: *They have also tested God*
            Thesis: *and they escaped."*

## *(1) Strong Words (3:13)*

### [13]"You have said harsh things against me," says the LORD.

**3:13** God's opening statement is marked as the most prominent of this paragraph by the quotation formula "says the LORD." It is literally, "Your words against me have been strong." The verb, which occurs almost four hundred times, means basically "to be/become strong." No close parallel to its use here with the preposition *ʿal,* "upon, against," and the noun *dābār,* "word," is found in the Hebrew Bible. This combination of terms occurs in 1 Chr 21:4//2 Sam 24:4, where the king's word and will is said to "prevail against" or "overrule"[74] the advice of his friend, Joab (cf. Judg 3:12; 2 Chr 27:5; Dan 11:5). This sense does not fit in Malachi, but it suggests the phrase here points to words that are insolent or combative.[75] Describing words as "harsh" in English usually refers to something spoken in a harsh *tone* and perhaps an arrogant or belligerent attitude. The Hebrew term usually describing such words is *qāšâ,* "be hard, difficult" (cf. Gen 42:7,30; 1 Sam 20:10; 2 Sam 19:43; 1 Kgs 12:13).

Judah's response to the charge uses a slightly different expression, which would have been synonymous (since we assume the prophet was paraphrasing the words of the opponents): "What have we *spoken against* you?" This was a common expression used in divine judgment speeches (1 Kgs 16:1; 2 Kgs 19:21; 22:19; Ezek 36:5; Amos 3:1), but it was also used to describe arrogant, slanderous, and insulting speech directed either against other people (Pss 31:18; 109:2) or against God. The emissaries of the Assyrian king Sennacherib "spoke . . . against the LORD God" and "wrote letters insulting the LORD, the God of Israel," accusing him of being unable to protect Jerusalem (2 Chr 32:16–17). The Edomites similarly "boasted against me and spoke against me without restraint" (Ezek 35:13). God had spoken concerning Israel through the prophet Hosea: "Woe to them, because they have strayed from me! Destruction to them, because they have rebelled against me! I long to redeem them [or "I

---

[74] F. Hesse, however, proposes that the king's word here is "harsh, almost unbearable" ("חָזַק *chāzaq," TDOT* 4:303). N. Waldman has suggested the sense, "Your words have been too much for me" ("Notes on Mal 3:6,13; Ps 42:11," *JBL* 93 [1974]: 545–48).

[75] *HALOT* explains the sense here in Malachi as the use of "insolent words."

redeemed them"] but they speak lies against me" (Hos 7:13). After observing the miracle of the furnace, Babylonian King Nebuchadnezzar took the role of advocate for Yahweh, decreeing that "the people of any nation or language who say anything against the God of Shadrach, Meshach and Abednego be cut into pieces and their houses be turned into piles of rubble" (Dan 3:29; also Dan 11:36). The Lord is quite capable, however, of dealing with those who speak against him. Jude 14–15 declares that "the Lord is coming with thousands upon thousands of his holy ones to judge everyone, and to convict all the ungodly of all the ungodly acts they have done in the ungodly way, and of all the harsh words ungodly sinners have spoken against him."

### (2) Worthless Worship (3:14)

**14"You have said, 'It is futile to serve God. What did we gain by carrying out his requirements and going about like mourners before the LORD Almighty?**

**3:14** The wicked attitude standing between these people (like many people today) and a satisfying relationship with God is expressed here in its essence: There is no profit in serving God. God's written "requirements"[76] were to them only a means toward personal gain—either guidelines of wisdom for success or a superficial way to please the supernatural gatekeeper of prosperity. The psalmist's love for God and for his instructions (Ps 119:36, "Turn my heart toward your statutes and not toward selfish gain") had no place in their hearts.

The people's rituals of mournful repentance were purely exhibitions intended to attract God's attention and win his favor. They had been "going about like mourners," which refers to behavior and appearance suitable to those either in mourning or repentance. The Hebrew verb *qādar* basically means to "be dark, to mourn." The connection between "dark" and "mourn" may have been the dark or gloomy facial appearance of mourners, or they may have dressed in dark clothing or just smeared ashes on themselves.[77] In a psalm of repentance David laments, "I am bowed down and brought very low; all day long I go about mourning" (Ps 38:6), and in Jer 14:2 the people are mourning because of a drought.[78]

---

[76] The term מִשְׁמֶרֶת is from the same root as "kept" in 3:7 referring to the keeping of God's "decrees." It refers to the obligations owed someone (*HALOT*), in this case God (Lev 8:35; 18:30; 1 Kgs 2:3 Ezek 44:8, etc.). On the Deuteronomic background of the term, cf. M. Weinfeld, *Deuteronomy and the Deuteronomic School* (Oxford: Clarendon, 1972), 335.

[77] J. Schwab, "קָדַר *qādar*," *TDOT* 12:518–20.

[78] Glazier-McDonald notes (*Malachi*, 213) that the LXX translator of Pss 35:14; 38:7; 42:10; 43:2 translated Hb. קדר with σκυθρωπάζειν, "to look angry or sullen, to be of a sad countenance" (J. Lust et al., *A Greek-English Lexicon of the Septuagint*, 2d ed. [Stuttgart: Deutsche Bibelgesellschaft, 2003]).

The Hebrew term translated "futile" can refer to something that is worthless, activity that is purposeless, pointless, or useless, and assurances that are deceitful or unreliable.[79] It can refer to elaborate preparations for something that never happens (Jer 4:30), procedures diligently and meticulously followed with no results (Ps 127:1; Jer 6:29; 46:11), a veneer of appealing promises and enticing words that hide corruption and disaster (Lam 2:14; Ezek 13:6; 22:28), or comforting dreams that promise prosperity but produce nothing but pain (Zech 10:2). Burning incense to idols is futile, and following prophets who speak on their own rather than from God is futile because worthless gods and worthless words can only lead to worthless lives (Jer 18:15; Ezek 21:29; Jonah 2:8). Depending on men or on the work of one's own hands rather than on God is futile (Pss 60:11; 127:1–2).

In fact, serving God as these people were doing—with external ritual carelessly and faithlessly followed while selfishly committing acts of treachery, sorcery, adultery, perjury, and neglect or exploitation of the defenseless and needy—was pointless, as Malachi had already said (1:10). These people were right; their "service" to God *was* futile (see Isa 1:13). So-called good works that do not arise from genuine faith and gratitude to God are simply "hot checks" drawn on an empty bank account. They may provide a temporary sense of self-satisfaction, but God recognizes their true value—zero, and he will eventually bring to justice anyone who tries to live on them. These people were not interested in righteousness or in a relationship with God, only in "gain," that is, profit, the bottom line, material prosperity. The Lord is speaking to those who consider material prosperity their right.

> For those who live in obedient relationship with God, increase of material goods is seen in the Old Testament as a blessing to be received as a gift and enjoyed responsibly; but never is it seen as a guaranteed 'reward,' and indeed some of God's most faithful servants remained materially poor. For those who live in alienation from God, however, growth in prosperity becomes an end in itself.[80]

The term *beṣāʿ*, "gain," was almost always used with negative connotations of greed, bribery, dishonest gain, or oppression. Although a few neutral uses occur (e.g., Gen 37:26), "there are no passages in the OT that use *betsaʿ* in the sense of a positive striving for gain."[81] For example, Isaiah describes Israel's "watchmen" as "these dogs" who "have fierce appetites; they never

---

[79] The basic meaning of שָׁוְא is usually said to be "worthless," but P. S. Johnston (*Shades of Sheol* [Downers Grove: InterVarsity, 2002], 82) agrees with J. F. A. Sawyer ("שָׁוְא *šawʾ*, deceit," *TLOT* on CD-ROM, Version 1.0) that its meaning is usually "deceit, evil, falsehood," with the meaning "worthless" found only nine times, as here.

[80] Wright, *An Eye for An Eye,* 72.

[81] D. Kellermann, "בֶּצַע *bṣʿ*," *TDOT* 2:207.

have enough. And they are shepherds who have no discernment; all of them turn to their own way, every last one for his own *gain*" (Isa 56:11; see also 33:15; 57:17; Jer 6:13; 22:17; Ezek 22:12–13). Malachi's audience was like their tragic ancestors who had liked to listen to Ezekiel's words, "but they do not put them into practice. With their mouths they express devotion, but their hearts are greedy for unjust gain" (Ezek 33:31).

### (3) Bitter Blessing (3:15)

**[15]But now we call the arrogant blessed. Certainly the evildoers prosper, and even those who challenge God escape.'"**

**3:15** In v. 14 an assertion of futility is expanded by a rhetorical question whose point is, "Our keeping God's requirements and performing rituals of repentance for him has gotten us nothing." Based on their analysis of the situation, they had reached a decision. From now on[82] they would call the arrogant fortunate, happy, or "blessed," which God said in v. 12 the nations would say of repentant Israel.[83] "The arrogant" refers to people with an "attitude or behavior that ignores or rejects the validity of God's authority," who have an "exaggerated opinion of their self-importance," or who "arrogantly mock those who follow God's instructions and attempt to take away the rights of the godly by violent acts" (e.g., Deut 1:43; Ps 86:14; 119:21; Prov 11:2).[84]

So those in Malachi's audience whom God had overheard did not just envy the prosperity of the wicked. The psalmist had "envied the arrogant," but he shared his personal intellectual and emotional wrestling over this issue after he had come through with his faith intact and matured (Psalm 73). He enveloped his account with affirmations that "God is good to Israel, to those are pure in heart" (v. 1) and with the recognition of faith (Ps 73:25–28):

> Whom have I in heaven but you? And earth has nothing I desire besides you. My flesh and my heart may fail, but God is the strength of my heart and my portion forever. Those who are far from you will perish; you destroy all who are unfaithful to you. But as for me, it is good to be near God. I have made the Sovereign LORD my refuge; I will tell of all your deeds.

Malachi's audience, on the other hand, had joined the company of those who

---

[82] The initial וְעַתָּה, "but now," which often serves as a clause level particle introducing a result, may be a temporal adverb here as in 2 Chr 13:8 (there it turns attention from past to present), where it is also followed by pronoun + participle. Hence P. A. Verhoef renders it "henceforth" (*Haggai and Malachi,* NICOT [Grand Rapids: Eerdmans, 1987], 317–18), "denoting what the people have determined to do from now on, and in the future."

[83] Note Isaiah's warning of "woe to those who call evil good and good evil, who put darkness for light and light for darkness, who put bitter for sweet and sweet for bitter" (Isa 5:20).

[84] G. V. Smith, "זִיד (*zîd*)," *NIDOTTE* on CD-ROM. Version 1.0. The LXX has ἀλλοτρίους, "stranger," and may have misread זֵדִים ("arrogant," NIV) as גֵרִים ("aliens").

were contemptuous of God and his laws. They gave two reasons for their supposed change of values. The first was that unlike their own case, "the evildoers prosper." These "evildoers" were literally "doers of wickedness," as Edom in 1:4 was called (lit.) "territory of wickedness." Edom there was determined to "rebuild" what God had destroyed, so here it looked like "the arrogant" had been built up (Jer 12:16; 31:4) or had "prospered." This is the passive stem of the same verb *bānâ*, "build," used in 1:4. There the Lord's assurance was "They may build, but I will demolish."[85] The second reason[86] Malachi's audience gave for their "switching sides" was that by their contemptuous disregard for God's requirements, the arrogant had "tested" (NIV "challenge")[87] God but had not been punished. They had "escaped." This verb for "escape" is the verb used of David's repeated escapes from King Saul (1 Sam 19:10), but it is also used of the Amalekite who had "escaped from the Israelite camp" (2 Sam 1:3) only to be executed by David because he claimed to have killed Saul, "the LORD's anointed" (vv. 14–15; see also 1 Kgs 19:17). God postpones answering his arrogant accusers in Malachi until 4:1. But elsewhere Scripture assures that "the wicked will not go unpunished, but the offspring of the righteous will escape" (Prov 11:21, HCSB; see also Matt 23:33; Heb 2:3; 12:25).

### 4. Motivation: The Coming Day (3:16–4:3[Hb. 3:16–21])

This section is marked as motivation especially by the use of future tense[88] (e.g., "they will be mine" and "I will spare them" in 3:17, and "you will again see" in 3:18) and by the *hinnê* plus participle clause beginning 4:1 (lit. "For behold, the day is coming burning like a furnace"). This motivation section begins in 3:16, however, like the first motivation section of the book (see 1:2), with a short embedded narrative introduced by the adverb *ʾāz*, "then, at that time."[89] It rhetorically conveys the fact that the Lord knows those who fear

---

[85] The LXX seems to makes this connection to Edom in 1:4 also, for it uses the same verb here (ἀνοικοδομέω, "build again," here pass. "be exalted") and adds πάντες: "and all doers of evil things are exalted" (καὶ ἀνοικοδομοῦνται πάντες ποιοῦντες ἄνομα).

[86] The Hb. particle גַּם used twice here, translated "certainly . . . even" is better rendered "not only . . . but also/even" (see HCSB, NRSV, *BHRG*, 316).

[87] The usual word for "test" in this sense of trying God's patience, provoking him, or daring him to punish is נָסָה. But בָּחַן is used here, partly because of its use in v. 10 (see comments there) and partly because of assonance with the verb in the previous גַּם clause: *nibnû . . . bāḥănû*.

[88] I.e., *waw* plus perfect or *wĕqāṭal*.

[89] Hill is incorrect, then, that "the insertion of this brief narrative is a unique feature among the prophet's six disputations" (*Malachi,* 337). What is unique about the verse is that it seems to be the only place Yahweh is not being quoted either directly or indirectly. See the Introduction: Literary Style. It is vitally linked to its context, however, contributing the antecedent to "they" in v. 17 and answering the objection in v. 14. S. D. Snyman argues for a twofold division of 3:13–4:3 but ends the first after 3:16 rather than 3:15. Although he supports this by certain formal features, like the appearance of "says the LORD Almighty" in 3:17, the grammatical structure as well as the semantic structure requires 3:16 to begin the second unit. I agree with his main argument, however, that 3:13–21 is a coherent unit ("A Structural Approach to Malachi 3:13–21," *OTE* 9 [1996]: 486–94).

him.[90] As God had heard the "harsh" words of the arrogant (v. 13), he also "listened and heard" the words of the faithful.[91] Here is the answer to the accusations that God does not distinguish and punish the wicked (2:17) and reward the righteous (3:13–15). The rest of the paragraph (3:17–4:3) comprises the predictive result of God's knowledge—a coming day when he will separate the righteous from the wicked and will bring joyful deliverance to his "treasured possession."

Whereas in the other two addresses the first motivation section is positive and the second negative, in this third division the second motivation section alternates between positive (3:16–17; 4:2) and negative (3:18–4:1) elements and finally combines them (4:3). Nevertheless, it is the negative part of the motivation that is marked as the most prominent by the *hinnê* clause in 4:1. Like the first motivation section in this address (3:10b–12), this one uses three divine quotation formulas, "says the LORD Almighty." The first is in the first future clause (3:17), "They will be mine"; the second underlines the negative motivation in 4:1, "that day that is coming will set them on fire"; and the third concludes the section at the end of the composite motivation in 4:3.

The structure and logic of this opening section may be displayed by the following chart using the author's translation. As in the case of similar previous charts, the paragraph is portrayed in terms of multiple layers of embedding, indicated by levels of indentation (see the introduction to 1:2–5). The most prominent element of a paragraph or subparagraph is typically marked as "Thesis." The overall paragraph comprises a thesis and a result. The thesis is an embedded narrative, and the result is actually a series of three sequential results. The third result is an embedded paragraph comprising a thesis and a reason, and in the reason are four additional layers of embedded paragraphs indicated by indentation.

Thesis: (Narrative)
  Background action:
      *Then those fearing Yahweh spoke together, each with his friend.*          *v. 16*
  Event₁: *Yahweh took notice and listened.*
  Event₂: *Then a book of remembrance was written before him*
      *for those fearing Yahweh and for those valuing his name.*
Result: *They will belong to me.*                                                *v. 17*

---

[90] On the concept of fearing God, see comments at 1:6.

[91] I reject the interpretation of Glazier-McDonald (*Malachi,* 207) and J. M. P. Smith ("Malachi," 76) that all of 3:13–21[4:3] is addressed to the "pious" who do not need to "return" to Yahweh but are the same as the "fearers of Yahweh" in 3:16. Smith emends אָז, "then," in that verse to זֹה/זֹאת, "this," referring back to vv. 13–15, on the basis of the LXX ταῦτα. Glazier-McDonald agrees that the Godfearers speak in vv. 13–15 (not out of "an exhausted piety" but "an anguished faith," pp. 210–11). But having disposed effectively of Smith's emendation, she retains אָז as indicating their change of heart (pp. 217–18). The introduction of a new term, however, יִרְאֵי יְהוָה, "fearers of Yahweh," indicates a new subject, not just a new characteristic of a previous one.

> *says Yahweh of hosts,*
> *on the day which I am preparing, a treasured possession.*
Result: *So I will have compassion on them,*
> *just as a man has compassion on his son who serves him.*
Result:
> Thesis: *So you will again see the difference*                           *v. 18*
> > *between the righteous and the wicked*
> > *between one who serves God and one who does not serve him.*
Reason:
> Thesis: *For behold, the day is coming, burning like a furnace.*        *4:1*
> Result:
> > Antithesis:
> > *All the arrogant and every evildoer will become stubble*
> > *Then the coming day will consume them,*
> > > *says Yahweh of hosts,*
> > > *so that it will not leave them root or branches.*
> Thesis:
> > Thesis: *Then for you who fear my name*                                 *4:2*
> > > *the sun of righteousness will rise with healing in its wings.*
> > Result: *And you will come out*
> > > *and paw the ground like fattened calves.*
> > Result: *And you will trample the wicked,*                             *4:3*
> > > *for they will be ashes under the soles of your feet*
> > > *on the day which I am preparing,*
> > > *says Yahweh of hosts.*

## *(1) A Book of Remembrance (3:16)*

**16Then those who feared the LORD talked with each other, and the LORD listened and heard. A scroll of remembrance was written in his presence concerning those who feared the LORD and honored his name.**

**3:16** "Then" (Hb. adverb *ʾāz*, "at that time" as opposed to "now"; cf. Gen 4:26; Josh 14:11) probably refers to the approximate time when the speakers of "harsh" words in 3:13–15 were speaking.[92] The population comprised more than just the arrogant and their admirers. A third group "who feared the LORD and honored his name" (see also 4:2) was also there.[93] Whether at least some of these are ones who have repented in response to Malachi's preaching, as some commentators have suggested, is

---

[92] Verhoef, on the other hand, considers that "the testimony of the faithful group is a direct reaction to and contradiction" of the previous words (*Haggai and Malachi,* 319).

[93] I agree, then, with J. L. Berquist's basic proposal of an "inner-group" of Godfearers (3:16–17), an "in-group" to whom Malachi primarily speaks (3:13–15,18), and an "out-group" of the arrogant evildoers in 3:15 ("The Social Setting of Malachi," *BTB* 19.4 [1989]: 123).

unclear from the text.[94] They may have been like the seven thousand whom God had "reserved" for himself "who have not bowed the knee to Baal," a "remnant chosen by grace" (Rom 11:4–5; 1 Kgs 19:18).[95] The speakers of "harsh" words spoke to "each other" (lit. "a man with[96] his neighbor") as well, and God took notice and listened, but only in the case of "those who feared the LORD" is God's attention made explicit.[97] On the other hand, whereas the content of the "harsh" words is specified in vv. 14–15, the speech of the Godfearers is not given;[98] no characterization or evaluation such as "harsh" is made of these words; nor are these people addressed directly as are those who spoke against God.[99] The content of their speech may have been words of repentance or spiritual encouragement to one another in view of the ruined crops (see Prov 27:17; Jer 31:34). Perhaps they were words of encouragement to do right, such as those of the leprous men in 2 Kgs 7:9—"Then they said to each other, 'We're not doing right. This is a day of good news and we are keeping it to ourselves. . . . Let's go at once and report this to the royal palace'" (see also Jer 36:16). Or perhaps

---

[94] Hill, *Malachi,* 337–38, who seems to base his view on the "logical force" of the temporal particle אָז, "then." The examples of such a use cited in *IBHS* §39.3.4f do not occur at the beginning of a paragraph as is the case here. The reason I consider אָז to indicate simultaneous rather than subsequent time is that it occurs with a *qatal* verb at the beginning of a narrative paragraph only loosely connected to the previous dialogue. That Malachi has not previously mentioned the presence of this group is insufficient evidence that 3:16–21 "clearly presumes a different audience and perspective" from those in 1:1–3:12 (McKenzie and Wallace, "Covenant Themes in Malachi," 560–61). Also Malachi's concern with three specific issues and three somewhat different (though overlapping) groups is the reason certain references earlier in the book (e.g., Judah, temple) are not found here. The reason no specific sins are mentioned in 3:16–21 is that these two final sections (3:16–21 and 3:22–24) deal with motivation and command.

[95] Verhoef, *Haggai and Malachi,* 313.

[96] Against the MT and the versions, 4QXII^a has עַל, "to," rather than אֵת, "with" (Fuller, *DJD* XV, 228–29). Whereas the Hb. phrase with אֵת occurs nine times in the Hb. Bible, it occurs with עַל with the meaning "against" twice (Exod 21:14; Deut 22:26) and meaning "to" only once (Jer 23:35 with אָמַר, "speak").

[97] Both here and in v. 13 the verb of speaking is *niphal,* indicating speaking to one another—a kind of gossip about God, devilish/hellish in the one case and godly/heavenly in the other.

[98] The LXX may have supplied the content, beginning v. 16 with ταῦτα κατελάλησαν: Those fearing the Lord "spoke ill of these things" (i.e. the harsh words). καταλαλέω is used in this way with an accusative in Polybius 18.45.1: κατελάλουν τὸ δόγμα, "they spoke ill of the decree" (I owe this reference to Peter Gentry). Petersen, on the other hand, interprets the LXX as having the Godfearers speaking the words of vv. 13–15 ("These things the fearers of the Lord spoke"; *Zechariah 9–14 and Malachi,* 220). *BHS* favors emending the Hb. אָז to זֹה, "this," following the LXX, but the LXX also renders אָז by a form of οὗτος in Gen 4:26 (which J. W. Wevers, *Notes on the Greek Text of Genesis* [Atlanta: Scholars, 1993], 66, judges to be a case of the LXX misreading). A few interpreters have considered the content of the Godfearers' speech to be "the LORD listened and heard." See Verhoef, *Haggai and Malachi,* 320.

[99] Contra Petersen, *Zechariah 9–14 and Malachi,* 220, the Godfearers are not addressed until 4:2–3.

they were simply "speak[ing] the truth to each other, and render[ing] true and sound judgment in [their] courts" (Zech 8:16).[100]

God's evaluation of such words is implied by his having them recorded in a "scroll/book of remembrance" (*sēper zikkārôn*). The Hebrew word *lipnê*, here rendered "in . . . presence" and often elsewhere "before," can also have the sense "by" (2 Sam 10:15, "The Arameans saw that they had been routed *by* Israel"; cf. Exod 32:32).[101] But here the picture is of the divine King surrounded by his heavenly servants instructing a scribe to record an event in the royal archives.[102] The term *zikkārôn* from the verb *zākar*, "remember," occurs twenty-four times in the Hebrew Bible and refers to a reminder, either a memorial day (Exod 12:14; Lev 23:24), a symbolic object (Exod 13:9; 28:12; Josh 4:7), or a record (Exod 17:14), as here. Records of decisions, actions, accomplishments, and various memorable events were kept by royal officials in the ancient world. The enemies of the Jews asked that the Persian king Artaxerxes search "the archives of your predecessors" for evidence of the Jews' past rebellions (Ezra 4:15), which he did (4:19). The term for "archives" here, *sĕpar dākĕranayyāʾ*, is the Aramaic equivalent of the Hebrew term in Malachi. Earlier during Darius's reign the regional governor had asked that a search be made in the "royal archives" (lit. "treasure house," Ezra 5:17) to verify Zerubbabel's claim that King Cyrus had authorized rebuilding the Jewish temple. Such a search produced the "memorandum" or record (Ezra 6:2, *dikrônâ*, almost identical to the term in 4:15) of Cyrus's decree, on the basis of which Darius issued a similar decree (Ezra 6:6–12). When Mordecai saved the king's life, a record was made of the event "in the book of the annals *[sēper dibrê hayyamîm]* in the presence of the king" (Esth 2:23). When the king later chose "the book of the chronicles *[sēper hazzikrōnôt]*, the record of his reign *[dibrê hayyamîm]*" as his bedtime reading, he discovered the memorandum and acted promptly to reward Mordecai.

H. Eising notes that the Hebrew verb *zākar*, "remember," "denotes an active cognitive occupation with a person or situation." It "often implies an action or appears in combination with verbs of action," and "some passages equate God's remembering with his mercy and forgiveness."[103] When God "remembers" a person, it almost always entails his action on their behalf (e.g., Gen 8:1; 30:22; Num 10:9; Judg 16:28; 1 Sam 1:19; Neh 13:14; Pss 25:7;

---

[100] Hill, *Malachi*, 337, believes the Godfearers are some from Malachi's audience who "took the speeches seriously and deliberated over their meaning and possible implication for postexilic Jerusalem."

[101] The LXX has ἔγραψεν, "he wrote [a book of remembrance]," reading *qal*, not *niphal*.

[102] Note the theme of God as King also in Mal 1:14. See D. C. Deuel, "Malachi 3:16: 'Book of Remembrance' or Royal Memorandum? An Exegetical Note," *TMSJ* 7 (1996): 107–11.

[103] H. Eising, "זָכַר *zākhar*," *TDOT* 4:66. See also W. Schottroff, "זכר *zkr* to remember," *TLOT* 1:385–86.

115:12; exceptions include Neh 6:14; 13:29), although God is also said to "remember" sin (Jer 14:10; Hos 7:2; 9:9). The point in Malachi is that God has instructed that a record be made of the righteous speech of "those who feared the LORD and honored *[ḥašab]* his name."[104] This memorandum will insure that on the future day described in the following verses they will be rewarded.[105]

The extent to which this is a figurative description is difficult to tell. It is *at least* a way of affirming that God not only knows but also remembers and acts to reward the past actions of those who fear and honor him. The fact that a heavenly record of some sort is also referred to several times elsewhere may suggest that this is more than just a metaphor (see Ps 56:8; Isa 65:6; Jer 22:30). The Bible, however, mentions several different kinds of heavenly records.[106] "The book of life" is mentioned in Exod 32:32; Ps 69:28; and Phil 4:3; Rev 3:5; 13:8; 17:8; 20:12,15; 21:27 (cf. "names . . . written in heaven" in Luke 10:20; Heb 12:23) and is called simply "the book" in Dan 12:1. It records the names of the righteous in a heavenly census (cf. Isa 4:3; Ezek 13:9), the purpose of which is to identify those entitled to the privileges and blessings of heavenly citizenship. According to Rev 13:8 and 17:8 the names are recorded "from the creation of the world."[107] Similar to this is "your book" in Ps 139:16, which contains God's decreed plan for the days of David's life, recorded before his birth. These "books" all have to do with one's destiny. On the other hand, "the books" in Dan 7:10 include a record of the sins of the "little horn" and those associated with him. "The scroll of the

---

[104] K. Seybold, "חָשַׁב *ḥašab*," *TDOT* 5:230, finds "two basic semantic elements" in the verb חָשַׁב. One involves calculation and includes the idea of value, and the other involves planning (Gen 50:20). Schottroff notes that the former involves "evaluative categorization of persons and things" ("חשׁב *ḥšb* to think," *TLOT* 2:480). It is found parallel to חָפֵץ (Isa 13:17) and רָצָה (Lev 7:18), "to be pleased with" and contrasted to בּוּז, "to denigrate, despise" (Isa 53:3), and מָאַס, "to reject" (Isa 33:8; Ps 36:5). The evaluative judgment is usually made explicit (Isa 5:4), but here as in Isa 13:17; 33:8; 53:3 it is used by itself to mean "to treasure, consider valuable, hold in high regard."

[105] Deuel, "Malachi 3:16," 111. J. Nogalski argues that the preposition לְ, "to, for" with לְיִרְאֵי יְהוָה means "for [not "concerning"] those fearing YHWH." Therefore the "scroll of remembrance" was not a record of names and deeds for God to read but a record of God's words for the Godfearers to read. It thus comprised, he says, either the Book of Malachi or more likely the entire book of the Twelve (*Redactional Processes in the Book of the Twelve,* BZAW 218 [Berlin: Walter de Gruyter, 1993], 206–10). But the preferable translation of the preposition לְ as "for" will hardly bear the weight of this interpretation, and the claim that context supports it fails as well. The context and the use of the terms elsewhere better support the common interpretation that the "scroll" was to be used by God for the benefit of the Godfearers. The view of Weyde (*Prophecy and Teaching,* 362) is preferable, that what was written in the scroll was the announcement of salvation contained in 3:17.

[106] E.g., L. Ryken, et al., eds., *Dictionary of Biblical Imagery* (Downers Grove: InterVarsity, 1998), 114.

[107] G. K. Beale, *The Book of Revelation,* NIGTC (Grand Rapids: Eerdmans, 1999), 279–80, 701–2.

LORD" in Isa 34:16 contains God's decreed judgments on a rebellious world.[108] In Rev 20:12, John saw a scene of universal judgment and alluded to both Dan 7:10 and 12:1–2 in his description:[109] "The dead, great and small, standing before the throne, and books were opened. Another book was opened, which is the book of life. The dead were judged according to what they had done as recorded in the books." God apparently keeps two sets of books. The book of divine decrees and the book of human deeds—divine sovereignty and human responsibility—meet in this verse. Both books establish the same verdict based on different data regarding individual lives, although the "algorithm" connecting them is a mystery (Rev 20:12–15). Malachi's "book of remembrance" is not a book of decrees because it is written after the event. On the other hand, it is a record of the deeds of the righteous rather than of the wicked. Not only will judgment be meted out to the wicked according to their deeds, but the deeds of the righteous will also be rewarded (cf. 2 Cor 5:10). Although God will not remember our sins (Isa 43:25), he will remember our righteous acts (including our speech) as well as our tears (Ps 56:8).

### (2) A Day of Distinction (3:17–18)

[17]"They will be mine," says the LORD Almighty, "in the day when I make up my treasured possession. I will spare them, just as in compassion a man spares his son who serves him. [18]And you will again see the distinction between the righteous and the wicked, between those who serve God and those who do not.

**3:17** Having expressed the thesis of this paragraph by means of the embedded narrative—God heard and recorded the godly speech of the righteous ones—3:17–4:3 comprises the result: God is preparing[110] an eschatological day on which he will redeem the righteous and judge the wicked. The prayer of the thief on the cross who asked Jesus to "remember" him "when you come into your kingdom" (Luke 23:42) will be answered.[111] The prophet thus returns to the eschatological theme of the final motivation section in the second address (3:1–6), which refers to "the day of his coming." Verses 17–18 contain a series of three results, each leading to the next.[112] The first result of

---

[108] J. N. Oswalt discusses the options and argues cogently that the scroll in Isa 34:16 is "the heavenly book of destiny" (*The Book of Isaiah Chapters 1–39,* NICOT [Grand Rapids: Eerdmans, 1986], 617–18).

[109] Beale, *The Book of Revelation,* 1032–33. See also his citing of extrabiblical references to the heavenly books.

[110] I consider סְגֻלָּה to be a *casus pendens* rather than the object of the participle עֹשֶׂה, thus, "Then they will become mine . . . on the day which I am making—a treasured possession."

[111] J. Oswalt, *Where Are You, God? Malachi's Perspectives on Injustice and Suffering* (Napance, Ind.: Evangel, 1982), 148.

[112] These three results are signaled by a series of three *wĕqātal* verbs.

God's memorandum, marked as the most prominent by the divine quotation formula, "says the LORD Almighty," is that on the coming day God will make these righteous ones his own personal treasure. The term *sĕgullâ*, "treasured possession," is found eight times in the Old Testament. The first is when Israel arrived at Mount Sinai and God instructed Moses to tell Israel:

> You yourselves have seen what I did to Egypt, and how I carried you on eagles' wings and brought you to myself. Now if you obey me fully and keep my covenant, then out of all nations you will be *my treasured possession*. Although the whole earth is mine, you will be for me a kingdom of priests and a holy nation. (Exod 19:4–6)[113]

As a king who owns everything in his kingdom would choose and treasure certain things above all else (1 Chr 29:3; Eccl 2:8), so God chose Israel out of all the peoples of the earth (Deut 7:6; 14:2). Psalm 135:4 is similar to the wording of Mal 3:17—"For the LORD has chosen Jacob *to be his own*, Israel to be his *treasured possession*." But the Exodus passage made clear from the start that this privileged position carried conditions of obedience and holiness. As the apostle Paul explained, "Not all who are descended from Israel are Israel" (Rom 9:6). So on this eschatological day it will be true Israel, the righteous remnant, who will be the Lord's own treasured possession.[114]

Like a shepherd coming to claim his lost sheep (Isa 40:11; Ezek 34:11–12; Mic 2:12–13; Luke 15:3–6; John 10:1–16; 1 Pet 5:4) and like a bridegroom coming for his bride (Isa 54:5–8; Hos 2:19–20; 2 Cor 11:2), God will come to claim his people who are prepared to meet him (Luke 1:17; Rev 19:7; 21:2). These verses describe the final fulfillment of the new covenant, when the law will be written on the hearts of God's people and "they will all know me, from the least to the greatest," and "I will be their God, and they will be my people" (Jer 31:33–34).

Just as Mordecai's honor was delayed until King Xerxes read the memorandum, so the full reward of the righteous is delayed until a future day that God has prepared. Mordecai's honor, ironically chosen by his enemy, was to wear a "royal robe" and to ride a royal horse through the city led by a royal servant crying, "This is what is done for the man the king delights to honor!" (Esth 6:6–9). But the glory that will belong to the righteous when the sons of God are revealed on the day the Lord is preparing is "an eternal glory that far

---

[113] Note the reference to this text as well as to Isa 43:20–21 and perhaps Mal 3:17 in 1 Pet 2:9. See W. E. Glenny, "The Israelite Imagery of 1 Peter 2," in *Dispensationalism, Israel and the Church* (Grand Rapids: Zondervan, 1992), 174.

[114] Hill, *Malachi,* 342. On the word's covenant connotations, see M. Weinfeld, "The Covenant of Grant in the Old Testament and the Ancient Near East," *JAOS* 90 (1979): 195. Hugenberger notes that "in Deut. 14:1–2 'special possession' is juxtaposed with an assertion of Israel's sonship, much as it is in Mal. 3:17" (*Marriage as a Covenant,* 50).

outweighs" all the afflictions that will precede it (2 Cor 4:17; Rom 8:18–19). This will be the day of "our adoption as sons, the redemption of our bodies," for which the righteous wait patiently (Rom 8:23–25), the day of "redemption of those who are God's possession—to the praise of his glory" (Eph 1:14).[115]

Arising from this glorious new relationship will be the second result, that when the Lord comes on that day to "set on fire" the "arrogant and every evil-doer" like "stubble," (4:1), he will "spare" the righteous "as a man spares his son who serves him." The verb *ḥāmal,* which occurs twice in this verse, is often said to mean "have compassion on, be sorry for."[116] This is what Pharaoh's daughter did for Moses when she found him in the basket (Exod 2:6). The word does not carry as much emotional freight, however, as other terms for compassion (*ḥûs, nāḥam, rāḥam*), as seen in Saul's "sparing" the best of the sheep for sacrifice (1 Sam 15:15) or the prophet Nathan's "rich man" being unwilling (NIV "refrained") to kill one of his own sheep for a traveler (2 Sam 12:4). The NIV "spare" probably is closer to the word's basic meaning (although the NIV adds "in compassion" to its second use here).[117] The word is usually used negatively of total, merciless, or indiscriminate slaughter (e.g. 1 Sam 15:3). The Lord does have compassion toward those who fear him, as a father toward his son (Ps 103:13, using *rāḥam*).[118] But the point in Malachi is that God's destructive judgment will not be total, merciless, or indiscriminate because he will spare those who fear him, thus making a distinction between the righteous and the wicked. On that day those who have placed their hope in him will not be put to shame (cf. 1 Pet 2:6).

The comparison to a father sparing his son "who serves him" is surprising. Nowhere else does the Old Testament explicitly refer to "sons" working for or "serving" their human father (but see Exod 4:23; 1 Chr 25:3,6), although sons being under their father's authority and working for him is indisputable. Jesus tells of a father who said to his son, "Son, go and work today in the vineyard" (Matt 21:28), and Paul said of Timothy, "As a son with his father he has served with me in the work of the gospel" (Phil 2:22; cf. John 5:36; 10:18,25). Verhoef considers the point of the description to be that this is a "diligent and

---

[115] Note article 37 of the Belgic Confession: "The faithful and elect shall be crowned with glory and honor; and the Son of God will confess their names before God his Father, and his elect angels; all tears shall be wiped from their eyes; and their cause which is now condemned by many judges and magistrates, as heretical and impious, will then be known to be the cause of the Son of God. And for a gracious reward, the Lord will cause them to possess such a glory, as never entered into the heart of man to conceive. Therefore we expect that great day with a most ardent desire to the end that we may fully enjoy the promises of God in Christ Jesus our Lord."

[116] M. Tsevat, "חָמַל, *chāmal*," *TDOT* 4:471.

[117] M. Butterworth, "חָמַל (*ḥāmal*)," *NIDOTTE* 2:174–75.

[118] On the father-son relationship between Yahweh and his people see comments on 1:6 and 2:10. See also Jer 31:9. Note the Westminster Confession of Faith (12.1) declaration that the justified are "pitied, protected, provided for, and chastened by Him as by a Father."

faithful son."[119] More important, it relates to the challenge of 3:14 regarding the futility of serving God and highlights the contrast made in v. 18 between those who serve God and those who do not.[120]

**3:18** The "you" in this verse takes us back to God's dialogue with the speakers of "harsh" words in vv. 13–15. Here God answers them directly. When they see how God treats those who are truly his servants (Esth 6:9), they will learn the difference between the righteous and the wicked. The third result of God's memorandum (v. 16) and more particularly of God's sparing those who belong to him on the coming day is that the righteous and the wicked will be distinguished.[121] As Jesus explained to his disciples the parable of the weeds in Matt 13:41–43:

> The Son of Man will send out his angels, and they will weed out of his kingdom everything that causes sin and all who do evil. They will throw them into the fiery furnace, where there will be weeping and gnashing of teeth. Then the righteous will shine like the sun in the kingdom of their Father. He who has ears, let him hear.

Jesus' parable suggests why God may say "you will *again* see the distinction."[122] When a garden is first planted, it is easy to see the difference between it and the surrounding countryside. The difficulty only arises after the onset of weeds. Likewise at the beginning of Israel's history the difference between God's people and the nations, especially Egypt, was clearly visible (1 Kgs 8:53). Beginning with the fourth plague, God would "make a distinction between my people and your people" (Exod 8:23), as was the case in all the remaining plagues (Exod 9:4,11,26; 10:6,23). Finally, the tenth plague against the firstborn would cause unimaginable anguish, "but among the Israelites not a dog will bark at any man or animal. Then you will know that the LORD makes a distinction between Egypt and Israel" (11:7). Afterwards the Sabbath would be a "sign" of Israel's distinction (Exod 31:13,17), as would the laws of the clean and unclean (Lev 10:10; 11:47; 20:25). But in spite of the object lesson at Mount Gerizim and Mount Ebal teaching Israel the conse-

---

[119] Verhoef, *Haggai and Malachi,* 323.

[120] Likewise Glazier-McDonald, *Malachi,* 227.

[121] The Hb. is literally "then you will return and see between the righteous and the wicked, between one serving God and one not his servant." "Return and see" is an idiom found also in 1:6. The use of the preposition לְ after בֵּין for "between X and Y" is not the most common but occurs elsewhere; e.g., Gen 1:6; Lev 27:33; Num 26:56; 30:16; 31:27; 2 Sam 19:36; 1 Kgs 3:9; Ezek 22:26; 34:17,22; 41:18; 42:20; 44:23; Jon 4:11.

[122] The Hb. idiom, as in 1:4, is וְשַׁבְתֶּם וּרְאִיתֶם, "then you will return and you will see." J. L. Berquist (*Judaism in Persia's Shadow: A Social and Historical Approach* [Minneapolis: Fortress, 1995], 103) argues for the conditional use ("If you return, you shall see . . ."). Though such a use occurs (GKC §112kk; Waltke-O'Connor, *IBHS* 32.2.3b), it is ruled out here by the preceding series of *wĕqāṭal* forms indicating future.

quences of obedience or disobedience (Deut 27:12–13; Josh 8:30–35), Israel soon lost their visible distinctiveness and became like all the nations (Deut 17:14; Ezek 20:32). Where God's repeated discipline had failed to restore his people, his coming to purify the priesthood (Mal 3:1–4) and destroy the wicked on that final day will succeed (3:5; 4:1,3). The situation of the prosperity of the wicked and the suffering of the righteous will no longer exist after the day of the Lord brings judgment and vindication.

Second Peter 3:10 declares that on the day of the Lord, "The heavens will disappear with a roar; the elements will be destroyed by fire, and the earth and everything in it will be *laid bare*."[123] The day of the Lord will lead to God's "discovery, naked and unprotected on the earth, of men and all their works."[124] Wright applies these texts to the situation of the righteous sufferer.

> In such cases in the OT, in the face of extreme injustice, the righteous person is sometimes seen 'committing his cause to the LORD,' in fervent hope of future vindication. He refuses to fight back, convinced that ultimately God will vindicate his cause and 'judge', i.e., in OT terms, put things right. Indeed, God has to do so to vindicate God's own name as a just God. This eschatological perspective is important, in that it releases the wronged sufferer from the need to achieve his own vengeance or to engage in desperate measures of self-vindication. The matter ultimately can be left confidently in God's hands.[125]

## (3) A Day of Burning (4:1–3)

**[1]"Surely the day is coming; it will burn like a furnace. All the arrogant and every evildoer will be stubble, and that day that is coming will set them on fire," says the LORD Almighty. "Not a root or a branch will be left to them. [2]But for you who revere my name, the sun of righteousness will rise with healing in its wings. And you will go out and leap like calves released from the stall. [3]Then you will trample down the wicked; they will be ashes under the soles of your feet on the day when I do these things," says the LORD Almighty.**

**4:1[Hb. 3:19]** Verses 1–3 explain the reason Malachi's harsh speaking listeners will "see the distinction between the righteous and the wicked." It is because of something God is going to do on a "day that is coming." Although that day is initially announced as (lit.) "burning like a furnace,"[126] it will actu-

---

[123] See the discussion of this verse in T. R. Schreiner, *1, 2 Peter, Jude,* NAC (Nashville: Broadman & Holman, 2003), 383–87; R. J. Bauckham, *Jude, 2 Peter,* WBC (Waco: Word, 1983), 314–22. As the Westminster Confession of Faith (33.2) asserts, "The end of God's appointing this day is for the manifestation of the glory of His mercy, in the eternal salvation of the elect; and of His justice, in the damnation of the reprobate."

[124] Bauckham, *Jude, 2 Peter,* 319.

[125] Wright, *Walking in the Ways of the Lord,* 284.

[126] The word for "furnace" here, תַּנּוּר, can also mean "oven" and is used as a divine image in Gen 15:17. Although the terms are different, the imagery also echoes the "refiner's fire" of Mal 3:2.

ally have two results.[127] The first will be the removal of all those arrogant and evildoers[128] referred to in 3:15. After the initial announcement of the coming day, this is the result described in v. 1. The second result concerns those who "revere my name" and is described in vv. 2–3.

Verse 1 begins this embedded paragraph with the introductory *kî hinnê* (lit. "for behold") followed by the participle clause "the day is coming." This construction, *hinnê* followed by a participle, is found in each of Malachi's three addresses in predictive paragraphs of negative motivation, that is, announcing judgment: 2:3 (lit.), "Behold me rebuking for you the seed," and 3:1 (lit.), "Behold me sending my messenger." It occurs once more, in 4:5[Hb. 3:23], echoing 3:1 (lit.) "Behold I am sending to you Elijah." The announcement found here of a coming day echoes one common to the earlier prophets. The word "day," however, is almost always plural and indefinite: "Behold days are coming." Nine of those are announcements of deliverance, almost all in Jeremiah,[129] but fifteen are of judgment.[130]

The day is initially described as "burning like a furnace," and the effect it will have on the wicked is figuratively but emphatically stated in two stages. First, God will make stubble *(qaš)* of them, chaff that is easily burned (Ps 83:13–15; Isa 5:24; 33:11). In Isa 40:24 it is what blows away after young immature plants are hit by a lethal hot wind that withers them. The term is often used of something worthless.[131] Then, as if that were not enough, the wicked will be "set on fire," the final result of which will be that not even a root or a branch will be left.[132]

The day announced here is also similar to the day of the Lord in Joel 2:1–3.

> Blow the trumpet in Zion; sound the alarm on my holy hill. Let all who live in the land tremble, for the day of the LORD is coming. It is close at hand—a day of darkness and gloom, a day of clouds and blackness. Like dawn spreading across the mountains a large and mighty army comes, such as never was of old nor ever will be in ages to come. Before them fire devours, behind them a flame blazes *[lāhaṭ]*. Before them the land is like the garden of Eden, behind them, a desert waste— nothing escapes them.

S. L. Cook notes that the verb translated "set on fire" in Mal 4:1 is the same

---

[127] After the participle clause expressing the thesis beginning 4:1[3:19], the remainder of the paragraph is tied together by six sequential *wĕqāṭal* forms marking future.

[128] Emendation of עֹשֵׂה to עֹשֵׂי so that "every evildoer" would become "all evildoers" with the versions, as commended by Elliger in *BHS,* is unnecessary. The versions and variant Hb. MSS were likely smoothing the text by matching the second subject with the first.

[129] Jer 16:14; 23:5,7; 30:3; 31:27,31,38; 33:14; Amos 9:13.

[130] 1 Sam 2:31; Isa 13:9 ("day of Yahweh"); 39:6//2 Kgs 20:17; Jer 7:32; 9:25; 19:6; 48:12; 49:2; 51:47,52; Ezek 7:10 ("the day"; cf. 7:5–6); Amos 4:2; 8:11; Zech 14:1 (sg.).

[131] M. D. Futato, "קַשׁ, *qaš*," *NIDOTTE* on CD-ROM. Version 1.0.

[132] The particle אֲשֶׁר here introduces a subordinate result clause (*IBHS* §38.3; *BHRG* §40.6).

one rendered "blazes" in Joel 2:3. Fire, "an important end-time element in Joel 2:3,5 and 3:3 (Eng. 2:30), often appears in apocalyptic descriptions."[133]

Blaising and Bock note that John the Baptist employed literary features from Mal 4:1 in Matt 3:11–12:[134]

> I baptize you with water for repentance. But after me will come one who is more powerful than I, whose sandals I am not fit to carry. He will baptize you with the Holy Spirit and with fire. His winnowing fork is in his hand, and he will clear his threshing floor, gathering his wheat into the barn and burning up the chaff with unquenchable fire.

**4:2[Hb. 3:20]**   The coming day, however, will not only remove the wicked; it will also heal the righteous.[135] Having figuratively described the end of the wicked by means of a sequence of destructive events, Malachi unfolds a series of events by which the righteous will be rewarded. The contrast expressed by the initial "but" is not marked grammatically[136] but by the contrastive nature of the events and the reintroduction of the Godfearers from v. 16.[137]

The initial sentence of v. 2 is literally, "Then the sun of righteousness will rise/shine *[zāraḥ]*[138] for you, fearers of my name, and healing in its wings." This confusing metaphor pictures the divine bearer of justice appearing like the dawn to those "living in the land of the shadow of death" (Isa 9:2; Matt 4:16) to vindicate his "treasured possession."[139] According to David, God revealed to him that "when one rules over men in righteousness, when he rules in the fear of God, he is like the light of morning at sunrise on a cloudless morning, like the brightness after rain that brings the grass from the

---

[133] S. L. Cook, *Prophecy and Apocalypticism: The Postexilic Social Setting* (Minneapolis: Fortress, 1995), 179. He identifies Joel as proto-apocalyptic literature. See also Ps 21:9; Isa 31:9. Cook also points out that the New England Puritans during King Philip's War between English settlers and Native Americans in 1675–76, called "the bloodiest conflict in seventeenth-century New England," interpreted that war as "the Dreadful Day" of Mal 4:1–3 (p. 64).

[134] C. A. Blaising and D. L. Bock, *Progressive Dispensationalism* (Wheaton: Bridgepoint, 1993), 234.

[135] On the theology of this section see B. K. Waltke, "A Canonical Process Approach to the Psalms," in *Tradition and Testament* (Chicago: Moody, 1981), 15.

[136] Despite Glazier-McDonald calling the initial *waw* a "*Waw* adversative" (*Malachi*, 234).

[137] Those referred to there as (lit.) "fearers of Yahweh" are here "fearers of my name" (despite the NIV's change from "fear" to "revere").

[138] H. Ringgren proposes that the basic meaning of זָרַח is "light up" or "shine forth" but that it is usually used of the sun's literal rising (e.g., Jonah 4:8; "זָרַח, *zārach*," *TDOT* 4:141).

[139] I agree with M. D. Carroll R. that in the immediate context "the meaning is probably that the righteousness of God will shine forth on that day of vindication" ("Malachi," in *Eerdmans Commentary on the Bible* [Grand Rapids: Eerdmans, 2003], 734). But in the broader canonical context this text is fulfilled in Jesus Christ. As Van Groningen explains, the sun points to "the Messiah as the One characterized by righteousness, one acting righteously and producing righteousness" (*Messianic Revelation in the Old Testament* [Grand Rapids: Baker, 1990], 933).

earth" (2 Sam 23:3–4). This passage suggests the emotional response the "sun of righteousness" will incite (cf. Jer 23:5–6). Psalm 84:11 declared that God is "a sun and shield," and according to Ps 104:1–3, God is "clothed with splendor and majesty," he "wraps himself in light as with a garment. . . . He makes the clouds his chariot and rides on the wings of the wind." The verb *zāraḥ* is used in the theophany of Deut 33:2, describing how "the LORD came from Sinai and *dawned* over them from Seir; he shone forth from Mount Paran. He came with myriads of holy ones from the south, from his mountain slopes." When God "put[s] on righteousness as his breastplate, and the helmet of salvation on his head" (Isa 59:17) to punish the wicked and vindicate his people, he "*rises* upon you and his glory appears over you," and all the nations will be attracted to the light (Isa 60:1–3). God will make his possession no longer "forsaken and hated" but "the everlasting pride and the joy of all generations" (Isa 60:15). Then

> the sun will no more be your light by day, nor will the brightness of the moon shine on you, for the LORD will be your everlasting light, and your God will be your glory. Your sun will never set again, and your moon will wane no more; the LORD will be your everlasting light, and your days of sorrow will end. Then will all your people be righteous and they will possess the land forever. They are the shoot I have planted, the work of my hands, for the display of my splendor (60:19–21).

At John the Baptist's circumcision, his previously mute father Zechariah praised God for "salvation from our enemies and from the hand of all who hate us" and acknowledged that his son would "go on before the Lord to prepare the way for him, to give his people the knowledge of salvation through the forgiveness of their sins, because of the tender mercy of our God, *by which the rising sun will come to us from heaven to shine on those living in darkness and in the shadow of death,* to guide our feet into the path of peace" (Luke 1:71,76–79, my italics). Although the light came into the world with Jesus Christ and shined on those who received him, the darkness will not be dispelled until he returns.[140] At that time he will "expose the motives of men's hearts," and "each will receive his praise from God" (1 Cor 4:5).

In the ancient Near East it was common to depict the sun's rays as the wings of a bird (Ps 139:9), and the connection with healing comes from the imagery of a bird's protective wings (Deut 32:11).[141] The healing announced

---

[140] Luke 22:53; John 1:4–9; 3:19; 8:12; 12:35,46; Acts 26:18; Rom 13:12; 2 Cor 4:6; 6:14; Eph 5:8,11; 6:12; Col 1:13; 1 Thess 5:4–5; 1 Pet 2:9; 1 John 2:8–9.

[141] Cf. J. H. Walton et al., *The IVP Bible Background Commentary: Old Testament* (Downers Grove: InterVarsity, 2000), 811. Merrill points out that "there is enough inner-biblical support for the winged sun of Malachi as an apt metaphor for blessing as not to require any cross-cultural borrowing" (*Haggai, Zechariah, Malachi*, 447).

here will be complete: physical, spiritual, and emotional. All that was signified by the curse of *ʿiṣṣābôn* on the man and the woman, "pain" and "painful
toil" (both translating the same word in Gen 3:16–17) will be removed, as
well as death itself (Zech 14:11; Rev 22:3). The Lord had assured Israel that if
they followed his Torah, he would protect them from such afflictions as the
Egyptians endured, for "I am the LORD, who heals you" (Exod 15:26). Even
after they sinned, if they would repent, "then will I hear from heaven and will
forgive their sin and will heal their land" (2 Chr 7:14; Isa 6:10; Isa 58:8; Hos
6:1). All true healing comes from God, for "I put to death and I bring to life, I
have wounded and I will heal" (Deut 32:39; Pss 103:3; 147:3). Although the
Lord is a God of justice, he "longs to be gracious to you; he rises to show you
compassion" (Isa 30:18) and promises a time when "the moon will shine like
the sun, and the sunlight will be seven times brighter, like the light of seven
full days, when the LORD binds up the bruises of his people and heals the
wounds he inflicted" (Isa 30:26; cf. 57:18–19; Jer 30:17; 33:6; Hos 14:4).
That healing will be total and permanent, for "he will swallow up death forever" and will "wipe away the tears from all faces; he will remove the disgrace of his people from all the earth" (Isa 25:8). The source of the healing
will be the substitutionary atonement of the suffering Servant: "by his wounds
we are healed" (Isa 53:5; cf. 61:1; Matt 4:23–24; Luke 7:22; 1 Pet 2:24).

The results of the healing work of the "sun of righteousness" on behalf of
those who fear the Lord will be twofold. First, they will "go out and leap like
calves released from the stall." It would be hard to find a more vivid image of
the excitement that will be felt by those who have just been delivered completely and forever from the darkness, pain, and grief of a world cursed by sin.

**4:3[Hb. 3:21]** The second result of the "sun's" healing work will follow
from the first. In the course of their "leaping" about, those who fear the Lord
will be "trampling" on the ashes of the wicked who were "set on fire" on the
day of burning (v. 1).

The NIV "on the day when I do these things" refers back to the almost
identical phrase (in Hebrew) in 3:17.[142] In both places it is better translated
"in/on the day which I am making/preparing." God is preparing a day when he
will come and identify the righteous who fear him as his treasured possession,
and they will trample the ashes of the wicked. The phrase, especially as it
occurs in both places (in reverse order) with "says the LORD Almighty,"
marks the beginning and end of the section describing the results of the Lord's
"book of remembrance." The Lord is taking notes and names, and at the
proper time he will "remember" those who are his.

---

[142] The only difference is the preposition: לְיוֹם in 3:17 and בַּיוֹם in 3:21[4:3]. Snyman shows
this to be a chiastic repetition, marking these inclusive verses as a unit ("A Structural Approach to
Malachi 3:13–21," 490).

## 5. Second Command: Remember the Law (4:4–6[Hb. 3:22–24])

⁴"Remember the law of my servant Moses, the decrees and laws I gave him at Horeb for all Israel.

⁵"See, I will send you the prophet Elijah before that great and dreadful day of the LORD comes. ⁶He will turn the hearts of the fathers to their children, and the hearts of the children to their fathers; or else I will come and strike the land with a curse."

The imperative "remember" that begins this final section of the address clearly marks it as expressing the command element of hortatory discourse. Nevertheless, like the first command section of this address in 3:7–10a, this one also includes a subordinate indication of motivation. Here it is the last two verses, introduced by the *hinnê* clause (see on 4:1; lit.), "Behold, I am sending you Elijah the prophet."

Because the Lord knows those who fear him and will distinguish and reward them on the coming day (3:16–4:3[Hb. 3:16–21]), he commands Judah through Malachi to "remember the Law of my servant Moses." This final paragraph relates to the previous one in 3:16–4:3 as the command for which the motivation has just been furnished.[143] In fact, it provides the "so what" or "therefore" the reader has been headed toward since the beginning of this final address in 3:7. The address began with the command to return to the Lord by repenting of false, disobedient, and arrogant attitudes and behavior regarding material possessions. Obedience to the Lord in that area meant obedience to the law of Moses, the "decrees" (3:7; same word as 4:4) from which Judah had turned and which they had forgotten. Therefore the command here to "remember the law of my servant Moses" simply fills out what is involved in returning to the Lord. As previously observed, God and his Word are inextricably bound together.

But this final paragraph of admonition also leads back to the book's beginning in 1:2. The issues of waning faith, disrespect or even contempt for God, empty religious ritual, self-seeking betrayal of marriage vows and of the rights and needs of others, greed, injustice, and materialism all have their solution in remembering the Lord's instruction to Israel through Moses. As the motivation provided in 1:2–5 extends beyond the first address to the whole book (see the introductory comments there), this concluding section provides the book's climactic command. As argued in the Introduction (Message and Purpose), Malachi begins by pointing to the past and ends by pointing to the future (4:5–6[Hb. 3:23–24]), thus appropriately grounding the ethical impact of the book in both redemption and eschatology. The eschatological dimen-

---

[143] I strongly disagree with P. L. Redditt's view that 4:4–6 does not "continue the thought of 3:13–4:3" (*Haggai, Zechariah, Malachi.* NCBC [Grand Rapids: Eerdmans, 1995], 185).

sion in view here assures us that God's work of redemption will be completed, establishing justice and peace. J. Barton points out that in these verses the English Old Testament ends with a passage in which eschatology and ethics "stand side by side in perfect harmony."[144]

Scholarly "orthodoxy" asserts that these verses were editorial additions to the book,[145] perhaps as early as the time of Ezra and Nehemiah.[146] They thus comprise one or two (4:4,5–6) "appendices," also termed "epilogue" or "colophon."[147] Some consider their purpose is to summarize the Book of Malachi, others consider them to conclude the postexilic prophets (Haggai–Malachi), the Book of the Twelve (the Minor Prophets), the latter Prophets (Isaiah–Malachi), the Former and Latter Prophets (Joshua–Malachi), the Torah (Pentateuch) and Prophets, or the Hebrew canon as a whole. Although I agree with Hill's opinion that "surely this appeal to Moses at the conclusion of Malachi has significance beyond the prophet's own message,"[148] I believe that the verses form an integral part of the original work penned by the prophet.[149] I also believe that focusing on the connection between these verses and the rest of Scripture can easily lose sight of their message, which involves a final appeal to the law of Moses in light of the fact that another Elijah is coming.

How much should be made of the position of this passage relative to the New Testament is difficult to tell. Although the Hebrew canon ends with Chronicles rather than Malachi, the conclusion to this last book of the prophets ties together Moses and the Torah, Elijah and the Prophets, and the New Testament, which often refers to the Old Testament as "the Law and the

---

[144] J. Barton, *Oracles of God: Perceptions of Ancient Prophecy in Israel after the Exile* (London: Darton, Longman and Todd, 1986), 16.

[145] A. Schart asserts, "Over the last decades a strong consensus has emerged that Mal 3:22–24 was added to the Book of the Twelve as a conclusion to the second part of the Hebrew canon, the 'Nebiim'" ("Reconstructing the Redaction History of the Twelve Prophets," in *Reading and Hearing the Book of the Twelve* [Atlanta: SBL, 2000], 45). D. L. Petersen, *Late Israelite Prophecy* (Missoula, Mont.: Scholars Press, 1977), 44, says the view that the last three verses were added later "is universally recognized."

[146] See the survey of views and their proponents in Hill, *Malachi,* 363–66.

[147] E.g., Petersen, *Zechariah 9–14 and Malachi,* 227, regards the verses as one appendix, whereas W. Rudolph, *Haggai-Sacharjah-Maleachi*, KAT (Gütersloher: Mohn, 1976), 291, considers them two unconnected appendices (likewise Redditt, *Haggai, Zechariah, Malachi,* 185, et al.).

[148] Hill, *Malachi,* 366. He says (p. 370), "the colophon serves primarily to append a later literary tradition (the Latter Prophets) to the earlier and already 'inscripturated' tradition of the 'Torah of Moses' (and the whole of the Primary History?)." Similarly R. Rendtorff, "How to Read the Book of the Twelve as a Theological Unity," in *Reading and Hearing the Book of the Twelve* (Atlanta: SBL, 2000), 86.

[149] Similarly, e.g., Glazier-McDonald, *Malachi,* 245–70. M. H. Floyd, *Minor Prophets: Part 2,* FOTL (Grand Rapids: Eerdmans, 2000), 568, argues that "the action narrated in 3:16 is explicated by a speech of Yahweh that extends from 3:17 through 3:24[Hb.]." Thus, "the claims of thematic discontinuity between [3:22–24 Hb.] and the preceding parts of the book have been greatly overstated."

Prophets" (Matt 5:17; 7:12; 11:13; 22:40; Luke 16:16; John 1:45; Acts 13:15; 24:14; 28:23; Rom 3:21). As argued in the comments on Mal 3:1, God's "messenger" there and Elijah here both find at least preliminary fulfillment in John the Baptist, who appears in the third chapter of Matthew. Elijah, in fact, is mentioned twenty-eight times in the New Testament.

**4:4[Hb. 3:22]** It does not surprise us that within the context of the Old Testament, Malachi should call Judah back to the law of Moses, but there are several unusual things about this verse. One is that nowhere else in the Old Testament is someone exhorted to remember God's law.[150] The majority of cases where someone is directed to "remember" is in prayers where God is to "remember" the supplicant (e.g., Exod 32:13; 2 Kgs 20:3; Jer 14:21; Ps 25:6; Neh 5:19).[151] The command to "remember" is given by God elsewhere, but not involving the law.[152] The idea of not *forgetting* the Lord (Deut 6:12; 8:11), his covenant (Deut 4:23; 2 Kgs 17:38), his works (Ps 78:7, "Then they would put their trust in God and would not forget his deeds but would keep his commands"), or his word (Ps 119:16, "I delight in your decrees; I will not neglect your word"; also vv. 83,93,109,141,153,176) does occur elsewhere. The term "remember" combines the ethical or behavioral with the cognitive (cf. Gen 40:14; Exod 20:8; Ps 115:12; Jer 14:10). W. Schottroff explains that "memory pertains to past events that the memory awakens to realization because of their present significance . . ., to places and objects to which the one remembering clings . . ., but also to present realities that have a formative character for existence . . . or demand observation as an obligation."[153] J. Pedersen explained that "when man remembers God, he lets his being and his actions be determined by him."[154] Judah is admonished to act in accord with what they know.

The expression "the law of my servant Moses" occurs nowhere else, but it almost certainly refers to the Pentateuch. The specific phrase "law of Moses" *(tôrat mōšeh)* is found thirteen times besides here,[155] and "the book of Moses" is found an additional four times (2 Chr 25:4; 35:12; Ezra 6:18; Neh 13:1). "The law" that God "commanded through Moses" is referred to in Neh 8:14 (similarly 9:14). The word for "law" is *tôrâ*, whose meaning usually is

---

[150] On the other hand, Joshua tells the Transjordan tribes to "remember the command that Moses the servant of the LORD gave you" about helping with the conquest (Josh 1:13), and Nehemiah asks God to "remember the instruction you gave your servant Moses" (Neh 1:8).

[151] The imperative of זְכֹר is found fifty-one times.

[152] 1 Chr 16:12; Neh 4:14; 13:31; Ps 105:5; Eccl 12:1; Isa 44:21; 46:8–9; Jer 51:50; Mic 6:5.

[153] W. Schottroff notes זָכַר, "remember," occurs opposite שָׁכַח, "forget" thirteen times and often occurs "parallel to verbs and expressions for acts of thought" ("זכר *zkr* to remember," *TLOT* on CD-ROM. Version 1.0).

[154] Cited by Hill, *Malachi*, 369.

[155] Cf. Josh 8:31–32; 23:6; 1 Kgs 2:3; 2 Kgs 14:6; 23:25; 2 Chr 23:18; 30:16; Ezra 3:2; 7:6; Neh 8:1; Dan 9:11,13.

the more general "instruction" since only occasionally is specifically legal material in view. The word occurs four times in Mal 2:6–9. There it refers to the process of instruction in God's truth (see comments at 2:6), whereas here it refers to the content of that truth,[156] the covenant document of Moses that the priests were supposed to teach (Deut 33:10) and by which Israel was condemned for disobeying.[157]

Whenever "the law/instruction" *(hattôrâ)* is mentioned, beginning with Deuteronomy,[158] it refers to God's written instruction to Israel through Moses (e.g., Neh 8:2; 13:3; Jer 2:8; Zech 7:12).[159] Reference is also made to "the book/scroll of the law" (Deut 28:61; 29:21; 30:10; 31:26; Josh 1:8; 8:34; 2 Kgs 22:8,11; 2 Chr 34:15; Neh 8:3), "the Book of the Law of Moses" (Josh 8:31; 23:6; 2 Kgs 14:6; Neh 8:1), and "the Book of the Law of God/the LORD" (Josh 24:26; 2 Chr 17:9; 34:14; Neh 8:8,18; 9:3).[160] The phrase "the decrees and laws," better rendered "the statutes and ordinances," also occurs in Exod 15:25; Deut 4:5,8,14; Josh 24:25; and Ezra 7:10. It refers to the specific regulations contained in "the law."[161]

Moses is referred to as the Lord's servant about forty times, almost half of which are in Joshua. This is the only place in the prophets, however, where it is found (except Dan 9:11). Its use here is followed in the Hebrew text by (lit.) "which I commanded him" or "whom I commanded," which emphasizes that the law of Moses was in fact the law of God. The point of this admonition, then, is that the Torah is still God's word to Israel after all that has happened to them.[162]

---

[156] It is usually plural (over two hundred times), occurring only forty-eight times in the singular as here. The singular is often found with a pronoun referring to instruction from God and often appears to refer to the Mosaic law.

[157] Cf. Neh 9:26,29,34; Pss 1:2; 78:10; 119:126; Jer 9:13; 26:4; 32:23; 44:10,23; Ezek 22:26; Dan 9:11; Hos 8:1,12. The plural תּוֹרֹת without a suffix is found only four times. Lev 26:46 and Neh 9:13 clearly refer to the written instructions given through Moses. The singular occurs 118 times, only 34 of which have the article.

[158] The five cases prior to Deuteronomy refer to individual regulations or legal decisions.

[159] It often occurs as "this law" (Deut 1:5; 4:8,44; 17:18; 27:3,8,26; 28:58,61; 30:10; 31:9,11,3,24,26; Josh 1:8; "all the law" in Josh 1:7; 8:34). That the singular *tôrâ* refers to all the Mosaic laws collectively is clear from such passages as 2 Kgs 17:37: "You must always be careful to keep the decrees and ordinances, the laws[sing.] and commands[sing.] he [Yahweh] wrote for you" (likewise 2 Chr 14:4). The reason may be that "the law" was understood at least originally to refer to the covenant's basic stipulation, as in Josh 22:5 ("the law that Moses the servant of the LORD gave you: to love the LORD your God . . .").

[160] Other passages clearly indicating the law of Moses was written: Exod 24:12; Deut 17:18; 27:3,8; 28:58; 29:20; 31:9,24; Josh 24:26; 1 Kgs 2:3; 2 Kgs 23:24; Jer 31:33; Hos 8:12; Dan 9:11,13; Ezra 3:2; Neh 10:35,37; 1 Chr 16:40; 2 Chr 23:18; 25:4; 31:3; 35:26.

[161] E. M. Meyers, "Priestly Language in the Book of Malachi," *HAR* 10 (1986): 230.

[162] Petersen, *Zechariah 9–14 and Malachi,* 229, but he exceeds the evidence when he adds that "no new covenant needs to be created, nor does an old one need to be renewed."

"Horeb" is referred to seventeen times in the Old Testament, twelve of which are in the Pentateuch (Exodus and Deuteronomy).[163] It was an alternate name for Sinai and had strong associations with the covenant God made with Israel (e.g., Deut 5:2). It was also the term used in Deut 4:8–10 (and again in v. 15). This is the only place where Horeb occurs together with the particular constellation of terms Malachi uses for the divine regulations ("law," "decrees," and "ordinances").[164]

> And what other nation is so great as to have such righteous *decrees* and *laws* as this body of *laws* I am setting before you today? Only be careful, and watch yourselves closely so that you *do not forget* the things your eyes have seen or let them slip from your heart as long as you live. Teach them to your children and to their children after them. *Remember* the day you stood before the LORD your God at *Horeb,* when he said to me, "Assemble the people before me to hear my words so that they may learn to revere [fear] me as long as they live in the land and may teach them to their children." (my italics)

If we add to that Josh 1:7,13, perhaps we have the primary passages Malachi was referring to:

> Be strong and very courageous. Be careful to obey all the *law my servant Moses* gave you; do not turn from it to the right or to the left, that you may be successful wherever you go . . . "*Remember* the command that *Moses the servant of the LORD* gave you: 'The LORD your God is giving you rest and has granted you this land.'" (my italics)

Remembering the book of the law was to cause Israel to fear God and honor his name, just as God's "book/scroll of remembrance" would cause him to act on behalf of those who feared him and "honored his name" (3:16). R. C. Ortlund observes that according to Num 15:38–40 Moses had instructed the people of Israel to wear "tassels" as constant reminders of the Lord's commandments. They were thus encouraged "to perceive all of life, throughout one's daily routine, with careful attention to the law of God."[165] Otherwise they would be enticed to "prostitute" themselves by "going [*tûr,* translated 'explore' in Num 13:2,16,17,21,25,32] after" their own "hearts and eyes" (v. 39). This striking, almost New Testament passage portrays the allurement of apostasy for Israel not as coming from the gods of the surrounding nations but from their own deceitful and wicked hearts (cf. Deut 4:9 quoted above;

---

[163] Exod 3:1; 17:6; 33:6; Deut 1:2,6,19; 4:10,15; 5:2; 9:8; 18:16; 29:1; 1 Kgs 8:9; 19:8; 2 Chr 5:10; Ps 106:19.

[164] The other places where "law(s)," "decrees/statutes," and "obligations/judgments" occur together are Lev 26:46; 1 Kgs 2:3; 2 Kgs 17:34,37; Ezek 44:24; Ezra 7:10; Neh 9:13; 10:30; 2 Chr 19:10; 33:8.

[165] R. C. Ortlund, Jr., *Whoredom: God's Unfaithful Wife in Biblical Theology* (Grand Rapids: Eerdmans, 1996), 39.

also Jer 17:9–10; Rom 7:21; Gal 5:17; Jas 4:1; 1 Pet 2:11). Israel's sinful tendencies were not unique but typical and paradigmatic of all human hearts, which constantly summon us like harlots to explore the regions of sin. As the Puritan J. Owen wrote, "This then is the dwelling place of sin—the human heart. Here dwells our enemy. Within this fort the tyrant sin maintains its rebellion against God all our days."[166] Owen urged that against such an enemy as the human heart we can only "commit the whole matter with all care and diligence to Him who searches the heart to the uttermost. He knows how to anticipate all its treacheries and deceit. Here is where our safety lies."[167]

Malachi was calling Judah to a lifestyle guided at all times not by human wisdom, ambition, or societal expectations but by the thoughtful application of God's Word. Only this divine lighthouse can guide God's people to avoid destruction on "that great and dreadful day." The summons in Malachi to "remember the law" is a message of hope for people in mortal danger, whose enemy has wormed its way into their very hearts, people "prone to wander." As Ortlund explains, "The law calls Israel both to deny what may seem right and expedient to oneself and to obey Yahweh even when the final outcome cannot be foreseen and assessed from a merely human perspective. Israel must trust Yahweh to be wiser than Israel in all the decrees of his law."[168]

**4:5[Hb. 3:23]** As Hill suggests, another reason Malachi mentions Horeb in 4:4 is because of its connection not only to Moses but also to Elijah, who "traveled forty days and forty nights until he reached Horeb, the mountain of God" (1 Kgs 19:8; cf. Exod 3:1).[169] Another connection between Moses and Elijah made by the reference to Horeb is that it was the location specified where Israel asked, "Let us not hear the voice of the LORD our God nor see this great fire anymore, or we will die" (Deut 18:16; cf. Deut 4:11–15). This request is the reason Moses gives why "God will raise up for you a prophet like me from among your own brothers" (Deut 18:15). Whether the "prophet" Moses pointed to was the Messiah as often argued, this passage in Malachi mentioning Horeb in connection with both Moses and Elijah would seem to confirm the view of many that it at least included the succession of prophetic

---

[166] J. Owen, "The Nature, Power, Deceit, and Prevalency of Indwelling Sin," in *Sin and Temptation: The Challenge of Personal Godliness* (Minneapolis: Bethany, 1996), 10. He also wrote with stark reality and biblical wisdom (p. 19): "The mind contends with its own darkness and vanity. The will wrestles with its own stubbornness, obstinacy, and perversity. Every affection deals with its own willfulness, sensuality, and aversion of God. Thus our knowledge is imperfect, our obedience is weak, our love is mixed in its virtues, our fear of the Lord is not pure, and our delight in God is not free and noble."

[167] Owen, "Indwelling Sin," 13.

[168] Ortlund, *Whoredom,* 39–40.

[169] Hill, *Malachi,* 368.

covenant mediators of which Elijah is considered the preeminent symbol.[170] Furthermore, as Petersen says, "this divine speech builds on the expectation that prophecy in some form will return before Yahweh acts decisively on his day."[171]

Following the command in 4:4 is a final motivating reference to the day God is preparing (see 3:17–4:3). But the motivation here does not point directly to that day itself but to an event that will precede the day. The case is similar to the motivation section of 3:1–6. There the motivation to "guard yourself in your spirit and do not break faith" (2:16) is specifically that the Lord is coming for judgment "like a refiner's fire" (3:2). Nevertheless, the initial announcement is of "my messenger, who will prepare the way before me" 3:1). In that passage, however, the messenger quickly recedes into the background, whereas in 4:5–6 he retains the focus, and the Lord appears only in the phrase "day of the LORD" and in the final (dependent[172]) clause "or else I will come and strike the land with a curse." The effect is to place more emphasis here on repentance and salvation.

Before (lit.) "the coming of the great and fearsome[173] day of Yahweh," which in 4:1 is called (lit.) "the day coming burning like a furnace," God will "send you the prophet Elijah." The Hebrew phrase more literally "I am sending" occurs seven other times in the Hebrew Bible,[174] once of the angel God was sending ahead of Israel "to guard you along the way and to

---

[170] See the stimulating article by D. I. Block, "My Servant David: Ancient Israel's Vision of the Messiah," in *Israel's Messiah in the Bible and the Dead Sea Scrolls* (Grand Rapids: Baker, 2003), esp. 26–32, and the responses by J. D. Hays, "If He Looks Like a Prophet and Talks Like a Prophet, Then He Must Be . .. " (57–69), and M. D. Carroll R., "New Lenses to Establish Messiah's Identity?" (71–81). D. G. Clark also argued that Elijah's similarity to Moses "especially in his meeting with Yahweh on Horeb and his power to perform miracles over nature" was the basis for the tradition that Elijah would be the eschatological prophet to fulfill Deut 18:15–19 ("Elijah as Eschatological High Priest: An Examination of the Elijah Tradition in Mal. 3:23–24" [Ph.D. diss., University of Notre Dame, 1975], 80 *et passim*.

[171] Petersen, *Zechariah 9–14 and Malachi*, 230; id., *Late Israelite Prophecy*, 38. On the intertestamental expectations of Elijah as a prophetic forerunner of the Messiah, see D. L. Bock, "Elijah and Elisha," *Dictionary of Jesus and the Gospels* (Downers Grove: InterVarsity, 1992), 203–5. He concludes, "So in Judaism the return of Elijah signals the arrival of the time of fulfilment, calls the people to reconciliation and brings judgment" (p. 203).

[172] Introduced by פֶּן, "lest, so that not." Cf. Waltke-O'Connor, *IBHS* §38.3c.

[173] The Hb. word rendered "dreadful" is the passive *(niphal)* participle of יָרֵא, "to fear," and can be rendered "feared, fearsome, dreaded, terrible, awesome," etc. Another interesting connection between Moses and Elijah provided by the Horeb reference is that when Moses led Israel from Horeb to Kadesh Barnea they passed through "the vast and dreadful" wilderness (Deut 1:19), which uses the same Hb. phrase הַגָּדוֹל וְהַנּוֹרָא used to describe the day of Yahweh in Mal 4:5.

[174] Cf. Exod 23:20; 1 Sam 21:3; Jer 25:15–16,27; 26:5. The slightly different phrase used in Mal 3:1 also occurs in Jer 16:16; 25:9; 43:10; Joel 2:19.

bring you to the place I have prepared" (Exod 23:20)[175] and once of "My servants the prophets I have been sending you time and time again" (Jer 26:5, HCSB). It is almost identical to the phrase in Mal 3:1 (where the Hebrew combines the words "behold" and "I"), to which it clearly refers (see the comments there and the relationship of "my messenger" and "Elijah" to John the Baptist in the NT). In view of the *mal'āk*, "messenger/angel," in 3:1, the reference to Exod 23:20 (and perhaps Jer 26:5) is surely intentional.[176] Elijah will be another *mal'āk* to help God's people reach the place prepared for them.[177]

Malachi places the day that is coming in the biblical context of the "day of the LORD," a term D. Garrett explains "refers to a decisive action of Yahweh to bring his plans for Israel to completion. This action may be an act of punishment or of salvation for Israel, but in either case it carries forward the purposes of God" (cf. Amos 5:18).[178] Although the phrase "day of the LORD" (*yôm yhwh*) occurs thirteen times in the Hebrew Bible,[179] it is described as "great and dreadful" elsewhere only in Joel 2:31.[180] Thus Malachi probably is alluding not only to that verse but to the whole theme of the day of the Lord in Joel.[181] There it combines elements of judgment against God's enemies and salvation and blessing for those who truly belong to him. The Book of Joel warns of an approaching divine judgment that could only be averted by a genuine national repentance.[182] If Israel would return to the Lord with all their

---

[175] Only in Mal 3:23[Eng. 4:5] and Exod 23:20 is the phrase שֹׁלֵחַ אָנֹכִי, "I am sending," preceded by הִנֵּה, "behold." This use of the participle signifies the imminence of the event.

[176] This may be the reason Malachi changes from his otherwise consistent use of אֲנִי (8x in Malachi, 23x in Haggai–Malachi, 50x in Hosea–Malachi, 881x in the HB), "I," to the alternate אָנֹכִי (only here in Malachi, 6x in Haggai–Malachi, 30x in Hosea–Malachi, 359x in the HB). Hill notes the connection to Exod 23:20 but does not relate it to his argument for 4:4–6 [3:22–24] as a later addition (*Malachi*, 375). In view of the many possible explanations for such a lexical change (climactic marking?), it is unwise to resort to textual splicing. Petersen sees the relationship between Exod 23:20 and Mal 3:1 as "too striking to be accidental" (*Late Israelite Prophecy*, 43).

[177] See the parallels between Elijah and Malachi drawn by B. S. Childs, *Introduction to the Old Testament as Scripture* (Philadelphia: Fortress, 1979), 495–96. The form of the name Elijah here is shortened to *'ēliyyâ* from the usual *'ēliyyahû*. It may be significant that the first time the shortened form is found is in 2 Kgs 1:3, "But the angel of the LORD said to Elijah the Tishbite."

[178] D. Garrett, *Hosea, Joel*, NAC (Nashville: Broadman & Holman, 1997), 306.

[179] Cf. Isa 13:6,9; Ezek 13:5; Joel 1:15; 2:1,11; 3:4; 4:14; Amos 5:18,20; Obad 1:15; Zeph 1:7,14.

[180] The Hb. phrase הַגָּדוֹל וְהַנּוֹרָא, "the great and dreadful/fearsome," occurs five times besides here and in Joel, describing the "vast and dreadful desert" (Deut 1:19; 8:15) and the "great and awesome God/Lord" (Dan 9:4; Neh 1:5; 4:14).

[181] Petersen (*Zechariah 9–14 and Malachi*, 231) also sees Joel 2:17–32 as "the conceptual backdrop for Mal. 3:22–24 [4:4–6]." Cf. id., *Late Israelite Prophecy*, 44.

[182] Note the literal rendering of Joel 2:11—"Yahweh gives his voice *before* his army, for very great is his camp, for mighty is one who does his word, for great the day of Yahweh and very fearsome, and who can endure it?" Could Malachi interpret Yahweh's voice coming *before* (same word as in Mal 4:5) the army of judgment, perhaps even the "one who does his word"?

heart, seeking his mercy in unity of faith, and if the priests would "weep between the temple porch and the altar," then he would deliver them from the approaching judgment and send them "grain, new wine and oil, enough to satisfy you fully" (Joel 2:12–19; cf. 2:24–27). Joel describes the physical and spiritual blessings associated with the coming day of the Lord (2:19–31) and then describes God's judgment of the nations and blessing of his people with abundance and security as well as his presence (3:1–31).[183]

**4:6[Hb. 3:24]**    Therefore reference to "that great and dreadful day of the LORD" in Mal 4:5 does not have only judgment in view. Elijah's ministry, besides being to "prepare the way before" the Lord (3:1), would be to "turn the hearts of the fathers to their children, and the hearts of the children to their fathers" (4:6). In fact, that would be how the Lord's way is prepared. Joel 2:28–31 declares that, like the coming of Elijah, the pouring out of God's Spirit "on all people" and the signs associated with it will occur "before" the day of the Lord. Elijah's coming before the day of the Lord will result in a great revival of faith in Israel, expressed here as fathers and their "children" (or sons, *bānîm*) "turning" (*šûb*, the same verb translated "return" in 3:7) their hearts toward each other (cf. *Sir* 48:10). The idiom of turning one's heart is similar to the idiom of placing upon the heart used in Mal 2:2 ("set your heart to honor my name"). Israel's future repentance after the Lord's discipline is referred to in Deut 30:1–2 as turning, restoring, or taking *(šûb)* God's instruction to one's heart: "When all these blessings and curses I have set before you come upon you and you *take them to heart* [lit., "you return to your heart"] wherever the LORD your God disperses you among the nations, and when you and your children *return* to the LORD your God and obey him with all your heart and with all your soul according to everything I command you today, . . ." (cf. Deut 4:39; 1 Kgs 8:47; 12:27; Isa 46:8; Lam 3:21). The expression in Mal 4:6 is literally "and he will return/restore the heart of fathers upon sons and the heart of sons upon their fathers." The point is that fathers and sons would no longer live self-serving lives, but fathers will take their sons to heart and sons will take to heart their fathers, considering the effects of their actions on one another in the course of their lives. Ezekiel had vividly portrayed a nation under the horrors of divine condemnation when he prophesied a sight of cannibalism during the siege of Jerusalem in the words, "Fathers will eat their children, and children will eat their fathers (Ezek 5:10; cf. Lev 26:29; Deut 28:53; 2 Kgs 6:28-29). Malachi's portrayal, on the other hand, was of a nation that had returned to the Lord and so had rediscovered the way of peace. Malachi's Israel was full of men committing acts of treachery and injustice against one another (2:10; 3:5), but Elijah's Israel would be

---

[183] See the summary of Joel in E. R. Clendenen, "Joel," in *Holman Concise Bible Commentary* (Nashville: Broadman & Holman, 1998), 349–52.

full of righteousness and peace; and his day would be one of revelation, repentance, and reconciliation.[184]

Hugenberger may be right that this verse alludes as well to the expression of the divine intention in 2:15 to produce "godly offspring."[185] Furthermore, the father-son relationships in view may be on several levels: the immediate family, the larger family of God's covenant people, and also between the contemporary children of the covenant and the men of faith at the nation's inception (Jacob in 1:2 and 3:6, Levi in 2:4–6 and 3:3, the "fathers" in 2:10, and worshipers of "days gone by" in 3:4). Verhoef understands Elijah's work especially in the latter sense of restoring the covenant of peace. He cites Isa 63:16, where the apostate children of Israel express a sense of disconnectedness from Abraham and Israel (Jacob) because of their sin.[186]

This multilevel interpretation fits that of the angel Gabriel, whose announcement to Zechariah was that his son John would "turn many of the sons of Israel to the Lord their God. And he will go before Him in the spirit and power of Elijah, to turn the hearts of fathers to their children, and the disobedient to the understanding of the righteous, to make ready for the Lord a prepared people" (Luke 1:16–17, HCSB). He has taken the "children" in the second half of Malachi's prophecy of Elijah to refer to "the disobedient" and "their fathers" as "the righteous." D. L. Bock observed that Luke sees John as "Elijah-like" but falls short of identifying John the Baptist as Elijah, leaving room for a further eschatological fulfillment of Malachi's prophecy.[187] The prophecy here was also fulfilled in part by John the Baptist (Matt 11:14; 17:10–13), but as U. Mondini explains, "As a result of Christ's rejection by Israel there is to be a yet future and final fulfillment of the predictions of Malachi and the day of the Lord."[188] But Jesus indicated that an additional fulfillment awaits the time of his return, perhaps as reflected in the prophecy of the two witnesses in Rev 11:3 (see Deut 19:15).

---

[184] See the discussion by W. C. Kaiser, Jr. of the rabbinic interpretation (*m. ʿEd.* 8.7) that Elijah would "establish legitimate Jewish descent, family harmony, and resolve differences of opinion and religious controversies" ("The Promise of the Arrival of Elijah in Malachi and the Gospels," *GTJ* 3 [1982]: 223). See further on the Jewish Elijah tradition in J. Jeremias, "Ἠλ(ε)ίας," *TDNT* 2:928–34.

[185] Hugenberger, *Marriage as a Covenant,* 140–41.

[186] Verhoef, *Haggai and Malachi,* 342–43.

[187] D. L. Bock, *Proclamation from Prophecy and Pattern: Lucan Old Testament Christology,* JSNTSup (Sheffield: Academic Press, 1987), 59–60, 295. For Luke the Lord's *way* is prepared by preparing for him a *people* whose hearts are right. Bock notes in *Sir* 48:10 Elijah was "destined to calm the wrath of God before it breaks out in fury, to turn the hearts of parents to their children, and to restore the tribes of Jacob."

[188] U. Mondini, *Prologomena to the Old Testament Prophets: The Minor Prophets* (New York/Rome: Pro Deo University Press, 2002), 252. He notes that final fulfillment must involve the restoration of all things (Matt 17:11; John 1:21; Acts 3:21).

Elijah appeared with Moses to testify to Jesus as the Messiah on the mountain of Jesus' transfiguration (Matt 17:3; Luke 9:29–31). Moses' presence perhaps signified that the foundational divine revelation in the Torah found its fulfillment in Christ and that Jesus was inaugurating a new covenant. Elijah's presence there perhaps signified that Jesus was the ultimate fulfillment of the prophetic office and the "messenger of the covenant" who had come to inaugurate the messianic kingdom and purify a people for the Lord.

Moses (4:4) was God's *prophetic servant* who was his agent of deliverance, who officiated at the marriage covenant of God and Israel when the original covenant was formed, and who brought Israel God's instruction that was to direct their relationship to him. Elijah was the quintessential prophet of repentance and would be God's *prophetic messenger* who would announce a new divine intervention and call people to repent. He would be another prophet like Moses, and God would hold accountable anyone who would not listen to the words he would speak in God's name (Deut 18:15–19).

The warning with which Malachi ends is not of the Lord's coming but of his curse. The issue would be how the people would be related to him when he comes. The final clause, "or else I will come and strike the land with a curse," uses the term for "curse" elsewhere associated with complete destruction (Deut 7:2; 13:16; Josh 11:11). The verse is rendered expansively in the Targum, "Lest I should reveal myself and find the whole land in its sins, and utterly wipe it out." Gordon comments that the Targum "spells it out that without the activity of Elijah *redivivus* the land would be unprepared for the divine visitation and therefore liable to destruction."[189] According to D. Stuart, "The curse of Mal 4:6 uses the term *ḥērem* in reference to the fate of the land if the future Elijah is not heeded, implying that those who reject the word of God will suffer the same fate as did those who violated the ban in Holy War, i.e., death."[190]

With J. Owen I pray on our behalf:

> May your soul never respond and say, "If I had attended more diligently and considered more wisely the vile nature of sin, and if I had not allowed my mind to be possessed by such vain hopes and delusions or allowed my mind to be filled with the things of the world to the neglect of my spiritual duties, then I would not now be so vile, weak, thriftless, wounded, decadent, and defiled. It was my careless and deceived mind that brought about the sin and transgression of my soul." Yet let such reflection lead to healing and restoration, which the performance of duties alone will never bring about (Ps 23:3).[191]

---

[189] Gordon and Cathcart, *The Targum of the Minor Prophets,* 238.

[190] D. Stuart, "Curse," in *ABD* 1.1218–19.

[191] Owen, "Indwelling Sin," 50–51.

# Selected Bibliography

## 1. Haggai and Malachi

Achtemeier, E. *Nahum—Malachi.* IBC. Atlanta: John Knox, 1986.

_____. *Preaching from the Minor Prophets.* Grand Rapids: Eerdmans, 1998.

Ackroyd, P. R. *Exile and Restoration: A Study of Hebrew Thought of the Sixth Century B.C.* OTL. Philadelphia: Westminster, 1968.

Baldwin, J. G. *Haggai, Zechariah, Malachi: An Introduction and Commentary.* TOTC. Downers Grove: InterVarsity Press, 1972.

Barthélemy, D. *Ézéchiel, Daniel et les 12 Prophètes.* Vol. 3 of *Critique textuelle de l'Ancien Testament.* OBO 50/3. Fribourg: Éditions Universitaires Fribourg; Göttingen: Vandenhoeck & Ruprecht, 1992.

Berquist, J. L. *Judaism in Persia's Shadow: A Social and Historical Approach.* Minneapolis: Fortress, 1995.

Brown, W. P. *Obadiah through Malachi.* Westminster Bible Companion. Louisville: Westminster John Knox, 1996.

Carter, C. E. *The Emergence of Yehud in the Persian Period: A Social and Demographic Study.* JSOTSup 294. Sheffield: Sheffield Academic Press, 1999.

Cathcart, K. J., and R. P. Gordon. *The Targum of the Minor Prophets: Translated, with a Critical Introduction, Apparatus, and Notes.* The Aramaic Bible 14. Wilmington: Michael Glazier, 1989.

Chisholm, R. B., Jr. *Interpreting the Minor Prophets.* Grand Rapids: Zondervan, 1990.

_____. "A Theology of the Minor Prophets." In *A Biblical Theology of the Old Testament.* Edited by R. B. Zuck. Chicago: Moody, 1991, 397–433.

Cody, A. "Haggai, Zechariah, Malachi." *NJBC.* Englewood Cliffs, N.J.: Prentice Hall, 1990, 349–61.

_____. *A History of the Old Testament Priesthood.* AnBib 35. Rome: Pontifical Biblical Institute, 1969.

Coggins, R. J. *Haggai, Zechariah, Malachi.* OTG. Sheffield: Sheffield Academic Press, 1987.

Craigie, P. C. *Twelve Prophets.* Vol. 2. DSB. Philadelphia: Westminster, 1985.

Davies, W. D., ed. *Second Temple Studies: 1. Persian Period.* JSOTSup 117. Sheffield: JSOT, 1991.

Davies, W. D. and L. Finkelstein, eds. *Introduction: The Persian Period.* Vol. 1 of *The Cambridge History of Judaism.* Cambridge: University Press, 1984.

Driver, G. R. "Linguistic and Textual Problems: Minor Prophets. III." *JTS* 39 (1938): 393–405.

Dumbrell, W. J. "Kingship and Temple in the Post-Exilic Period." *RTR* 37 (1978): 33–42.

Elliger, K. *Die Propheten Nahum, Habakuk, Zephanja, Haggai, Zacharja, Maleachi.* In *Das Buch der zwölf kleinen Propheten.* ATD 25. Göttingen: Vandenhoeck & Ruprecht, 1982.

Eskenazi, T. C. and K. H. Richards, eds. *Second Temple Studies: 2. Temple Community in the Persian Period.* JSOTSup 175. Sheffield: Academic Press, 1994.

Floyd, M. H. *Minor Prophets.* Part 2. FOTL 22. Grand Rapids: Eerdmans, 2000.

Fuller, R. "The Form and Formation of the Book of the Twelve: The Evidence from the

Judean Desert." In *Forming Prophetic Literature: Essays on Isaiah and the Twelve in Honor of John D. W. Watts.* JSOTSup 235. Sheffield: Sheffield Academic Press, 1996, 86–101.

_____. "The Text of the Twelve Minor Prophets." *CurBS* 7 (1999): 81–95.

_____. "Minor Prophets." In *Encyclopedia of the Dead Sea Scrolls.* Oxford: Oxford University Press, 2000, 1:554–57.

Fuller, R. E., ed. "[The Minor Prophets]." In *The Prophets.* Vol. 10 of *Qumran Cave 4.* DJD 15. Oxford: Clarendon, 1997

_____. "The Minor Prophets Manuscripts from Qumrân, Cave IV." Ph.D. diss., Harvard University, 1988.

Gelston, A. *Dodekapropheten—Daniel–Bel–Draco. Vetus Testamentum Syriace iuxta simplicem syrorum versionem, or The Old Testament in Syriac according to the Peshitta Version*, Part 3. Fascicle 4. Leiden: Brill, 1980.

_____. "The Foundations of the Second Temple." *VT* 16 (1966): 232–35.

_____. *The Peshitta of the Twelve Prophets.* Oxford: Clarendon, 1987.

_____. "The Twelve Prophets: Peshitta and Targum." In *Targum and Peshitta.* Targum Studies. South Florida Studies in the History of Judaism 165. Atlanta: Scholars Press, 1998, 2:119–39.

Gordon, R. P. *Studies in the Targum to the Twelve Prophets from Nahum to Malachi.* VTSup 51. Leiden: Brill, 1994.

Grabbe, L. L. Grabbe, *The Persian and Greek Periods.* Vol. 1 of *Judaism from Cyrus to Hadrian.* Minneapolis: Fortress, 1992.

Graffy, A. *A Prophet Confronts His People: The Disputation Speech in the Prophets.* AnBib 104. Rome: Biblical Institute Press, 1984.

Hanson, P. D. *The Dawn of Apocalyptic.* Philadelphia: Fortress, 1975.

Hoonacker, A. van *Les Douze Petits Prophètes.* Paris: Gabalda, 1908.

Horst, F. *Die zwölf kleinen Propheten: Nahum bis Maleachi.* 3d ed. HAT 14. Tübingen: Mohr (Siebeck), 1964.

Jones, B. A. "The Book of the Twelve as a Witness to Ancient Biblical Interpretation." In *Reading and Hearing the Book of the Twelve.* SBLSymS 15. Atlanta: Society of Biblical Literature, 2000, 65–74.

_____. *The Formation of the Book of the Twelve: A Study in Text and Canon.* SBLDS 149. Atlanta: Scholars Press, 1995.

Jones, D. R. *Haggai, Zechariah and Malachi: Introduction and Commentary.* TBC. London: SCM Press, 1962.

Kaiser, W. C., Jr. *Micah—Malachi.* Communicator's Commentary 21. Dallas: Word, 1992.

Keil, C. F. *Minor Prophets.* Commentary on the Old Testament. Grand Rapids: Eerdmans, 1982.

Kodell, J. *Lamentations, Haggai, Zechariah, Malachi, Obadiah, Joel, Second Zechariah, Baruch.* OTM 14. Wilmington: Michael Glazier, 1982.

Mackay, J. L. *Haggai, Zechariah, Malachi: God's Restored People.* Ross-shire, Scotland: Christian Focus Publications, 1994.

Mason, R. A. *The Books of Haggai, Zechariah and Malachi.* CBC. Cambridge: Cambridge University Press, 1977.

_____. "The Messiah in the Postexilic Old Testament Literature." In *King and Messiah in Israel and the Ancient Near East: Proceedings of the Oxford Old Testament Seminar.* JSOTSup 270. Sheffield: Sheffield Academic Press, 1998, 338–64.

_____. *Preaching the Tradition: Homily and Hermeneutics After the Exile.* Cambridge: Cambridge University Press, 1990.

_____. "The Prophets of the Restoration." In *Israel's Prophetic Tradition: Essays in Honour of Peter R. Ackroyd.* Cambridge: Cambridge University Press, 1982, 137–54.

McComiskey, T. E., ed. *The Minor Prophets: An Exegetical and Exegetical Commentary.* 3 vols. Grand Rapids: Baker, 1998.

McEvenue, S. E. "The Political Structure in Judah from Cyrus to Nehemiah." *CBQ* 43 (1981): 353–64.

Merrill, E. H. *An Exegetical Commentary: Haggai, Zechariah, Malachi.* Chicago: Moody, 1994.

_____. *Kingdom of Priests: A History of Old Testament Israel.* Grand Rapids: Baker, 1987.

Meyers, E. M. "The Persian Period and the Judean Restoration: From Zerubbabel to Nehemiah." In *Ancient Israelite Religion: Essays in Honor of Frank Moore Cross.* Philadelphia: Fortress, 1987, 509–21.

_____. "Second Temple Studies in the Light of Recent Archaeology: Part I: The Persian and Hellenistic Periods." *CurBS* 2 (1994): 25–42.

Moore, T. V. *The Prophets of the Restoration, or Haggai, Zechariah, and Malachi: A New Translation, with Notes.* New York: Robert Carter & Brothers, 1856.

Murray, D. F. "The Rhetoric of Disputation: Re-Examination of a Prophetic Genre." *JSOT* 38 (1987): 95–121.

Nogalski, J. *Literary Precursors to the Book of the Twelve.* BZAW, ed. O. Kaiser, no. 217a. Berlin: Walter de Gruyter, 1993.

_____. *Redactional Processes in the Book of the Twelve.* BZAW 218. Berlin: Walter de Gruyter, 1993.

_____. "Intertextuality and the Twelve." In *Forming Prophetic Literature: Essays on Isaiah and the Twelve in Honor of John D. W. Watts.* JSOTSup 235. Sheffield: Sheffield Academic Press, 1996, 102–24.

Nogalski, J. D. and M. A. Sweeney, ed., *Reading and Hearing the Book of the Twelve.* SBLSymS 15. Atlanta: Society of Biblical Literature, 2000.

Orelli, C.von. *The Twelve Minor Prophets.* Edinburgh: T&T Clark, 1893.

Perowne, T. T. *Haggai, Zechariah, and Malachi, with Notes and Introduction.* CBSC. Cambridge: University Press, 1886.

Petersen, D. L. *Late Israelite Prophecy: Studies in Deutero-Prophetic Literature and in Chronicles.* SBLMS 23. Missoula: Scholars Press, 1977.

_____. *The Roles of Israel's Prophets.* JSOTSup 17. Sheffield: JSOT Press, 1981.

Pierce, R. W. "Literary Connectors and a Haggai/Zechariah/Malachi Corpus." *JETS* 27 (1984): 272–89.

_____. "A Thematic Development of the Haggai/Zechariah/Malachi Corpus." *JETS* 27 (1984): 401–11.

Provan, I. et al., *A Biblical History of Israel.* Louisville: WJK, 2003.

Pusey, E. B. *The Minor Prophets: A Commentary, Explanatory and Practical.* 2 Vols. Grand Rapids: Baker, 1950.

Regt, L. J. de, et al, eds. *Literary Structure and Rhetorical Strategies in the Hebrew Bible.* Assen: Van Gorcum, 1996.

Redditt, P. L. *Haggai, Zechariah and Malachi.* NCB. Grand Rapids: Eerdmans, 1995.

_____. "Recent Research on the Book of the Twelve as One Book." *CRBS* 9 (2001): 47–80.

Redditt, P. L. and A. Schart, eds. *Thematic Threads in the Book of the Twelve.* BZAW 325. Berlin: Walter de Gruyter, 2003.

Reventlow, H. G. *Die Propheten Haggai, Sacharja und Maleachi.* ATD. Göttingen: Vandenhoeck & Ruprecht, 1993.

Rudolph, W. *Haggai—Sacharja 1–8—Sacharja 9–14—Maleachi, mit einer Zeittafel von Alfred Jepsen*. KAT 13/4. Gütersloh: Gütersloher Verlagshaus Gerd Mohn, 1976.

Schiffman, L. H. *From Text to Tradition: A History of Second Temple and Rabbinic Judaism*. Hoboken: Ktav, 1991.

Slavitt, David R., trans. *The Book of the Twelve Prophets*. Oxford: Oxford University Press, 2000.

Smith, G. A. *The Book of the Twelve Prophets Commonly Called the Minor*. Vol 2. 2d ed. EBC. London: Hodder & Stoughton, 1898.

Smith, R. L. *Micah—Malachi*. WBC. Waco: Word, 1984.

Stern, E. *The Assyrian, Babylonian, and Persian Periods: 732–332 BCE*. Vol. 2 of *Archaeology of the Land of the Bible*. ABRL. New York: Doubleday, 2001.

_____. *Material Culture of the Land of the Bible in the Persian Period 538–332 B.C.* Warminster, England: Aris & Phillips; Jerusalem: Israel Exploration Society, 1982.

Sweeney, M. A. *The Twelve Prophets*. Berit Olam: Studies in Hebrew Narrative and Poetry. Edited by D. W. Cotter. 2 vols. Collegeville: Liturgical, 2000.

Thomas, D. W. "The Sixth Century B.C.: A Creative Epoch in the History of Israel." *JSS* 6 (1991): 33–46.

Van Groningen, G. *Messianic Revelation in the Old Testament*. Grand Rapids: Baker, 1990.

Verhoef, P. A. *The Books of Haggai and Malachi*. NICOT. Grand Rapids: Eerdmans, 1987.

Walton, J. H. et al. *The IVP Bible Background Commentary: Old Testament*. Downers Grove: InterVarsity, 2000.

Watts, J. W. and P. R. House, eds. *Forming Prophetic Literature: Essays on Isaiah and the Twelve in Honor of John D. W. Watts*. JSOTSup 235. Sheffield: Academic Press, 1996.

Weinberg, J. *The Citizen–Temple Community*. JSOTSup 151. Sheffield: Sheffield Academic Press, 1992.

Widengren, G. "The Persian Period." In *Israelite and Judaean History*. Philadelphia: Westminster, 1977, 489–538.

Williamson, H. G. M. "Exile and After: Historical Study." In *The Face of Old Testament Studies: A Survey of Contemporary Approaches*. Grand Rapids: Baker, 1999, 236–65.

_____. "The Governors of Judah Under the Persians." *TynBul* 39 (1988): 59–82.

_____. "Judah and the Jews." In *Studies in Persian History: Essays in Memory of David M. Lewis*. Achaemenid History 11. Leiden: Nederlands Instituut voor het Nabije Oosten, 1998, 145–63.

Wolf, H. *Haggai, Malachi: Rededication and Renewal*. Chicago: Moody, 1976.

Woude, A. S. van der. *Haggai, Maleachi*. De Prediking van het Oude Testament. Nijkerk: Uitgeverij G. F. Callenbach, 1982.

Yamauchi, E. *Persia and the Bible*. Grand Rapids: Baker, 1990.

Ziegler, J., ed. *Duodecim prophetae*. 3d ed. Septuaginta, Vetus Testamentum graecum auctoritate academiae scientiarum gottingensis, vol. 13. Göttingen: Vandenhoeck & Ruprecht, 1984.

## 2. Haggai

Ackroyd, P. R. "The Book of Haggai and Zechariah I–VIII." *JJS* 3 (1952): 151–56.

_____. "Haggai." In *Harper's Bible Commentary*. New York: Harper & Row, 1988, 745–46.

_____. "Some Interpretative Glosses in the Book of Haggai." *JJS* 7 (1956): 163–67.

_____. "Studies in the Book of Haggai." *JJS* 2 (1951): 163–76; 3 (1952): 1–13.

Alden, R. L. "Haggai." In EBC. Grand Rapids: Zondervan, 1985, 7:569–91.

Amsler, S. "Aggée, Zacharie 1–8." In *Aggée, Zacharie 1–8, Zacharie 9–14, Malachie.* 2d ed. CAT 11c. Genève: Labor et Fides, 1988, 9–40.

André, T. *Le prophète Aggée: Introduction critique et commentaire.* Paris: Librairie Fischbacher, 1895.

Bedford, P. R. *Temple Restoration in Early Achaemenid Judah.* Supplements to the Journal for the Study of Judaism 65. Leiden: Brill, 2001.

Beuken, W. A. M. *Haggai—Sacharja 1–8: Studien zur Überlieferungsgeschichte der frühnachexilischen Prophetie.* SSN 10. Assen: Van Gorcum, 1967.

Boda, M. J. "Haggai: Master Rhetorician." *TynBul* 51 (2000): 295–304.

Bright, J. "Aggée: Un exercice en herméneutique." *ETR* 44 (1969): 3–25.

_____. "Haggai among the Prophets: Reflections on Preaching from the Old Testament." In *From Faith to Faith: Essays in Honor of Donald G. Miller on His Seventieth Birthday.* PTMS 31. Pittsburgh: Pickwick Press, 1979, 219–34.

Calvin, J. *Habakkuk, Zephaniah, Haggai.* Vol. 4. *Commentaries on the Twelve Minor Prophets.* Grand Rapids: Eerdmans, 1950.

Cashdan, E. "Haggai: Introduction and Commentary." In *The Twelve Prophets: Hebrew Text & English Translation, with Introductions and Commentary.* London: Soncino Press, 1994, 253–64.

Chary, T. "Le culte chez les prophètes Aggée et Zacharie." In *Les prophètes et le culte à partir de l'exil.* Vol. 3. Bibliothèque de théologie 3. Théologie biblique. Paris: Desclée, 1955, 118–59.

Clark, D. J. "Discourse Structure in Haggai." *JOTT* 5 (1992): 13–24.

Cody, A. "Haggai, Zechariah, Malachi." *NJBC.* Englewood Cliffs, N.J.: Prentice Hall, 1990, 349–61.

Collins, J. J. *Jerusalem and the Temple in Jewish Apocalyptic Literature of the Second Temple Period.* International Rennert Guest Lecture Series 1. Remat-Gan: Bar-Ilan University, 1998.

Curtis, B. G. "After the Exile: Haggai and History." In *Giving the Sense: Understanding and Using Old Testament Historical Texts.* Grand Rapids: Kregel, 2003, 300–320.

Feinberg, C. L. "Haggai." In *The Wycliffe Bible Commentary.* Chicago: Moody, 1962, 889–96.

Floyd, M. H. "The Nature of the Narrative and the Evidence of Redaction in Haggai." *VT* 45 (1995): 470–90.

Holbrook, D. J. "Narrowing Down Haggai: Examining Style in Light of Discourse and Content." *JOTT* 7 (1995): 1–12.

Japhet, S. "'History' and 'Literature' in the Persian Period: The Restoration of the Temple." In *"Ah, Assyria. . .": Studies in Assyrian History and Ancient Near Eastern Historiography Presented to Hayim Tadmor.* ScrHier 33. Jerusalem: Magnes, 1991, 174–88.

_____. "Sheshbazzar and Zerubbabel—Against the Background of the Historical and Religious Tendencies of Ezra–Nehemiah." *ZAW* 94 (1982): 66–98; 95 (1983): 218–29.

_____. "The Temple in the Restoration Period: Reality and Ideology." *USQR* 44 (1991): 195–251.

Kessler, J. *The Book of Haggai: Prophecy and Society in Early Persian Yehud.* VTSup 91. Leiden: Brill, 2002.

Lindsey, F. D. "Haggai." In *The Bible Knowledge Commentary.* n.p.: Victor Books, 1985, 1537–44.

Long, B. O. "Two Question and Answer Schemata in the Prophets." *JBL* 90 (1971): 129–39.

Luther, M. "Lectures on Haggai." In *Lectures on the Minor Prophets, I.* Luther's Works 18. St. Louis: Concordia, 1975, 365–87.

March, E. E. "The Book of Haggai: Introduction, Commentary, and Reflections." In *The New Interpreter's Bible*, 7:707–32. Nashville: Abingdon, 1996.

Mason, R. A. "The Purpose of the 'Editorial Framework' of the Book of Haggai." *VT* 27 (1977): 413–21. [Reprinted in D. E. Orton, ed., *Prophecy in the Hebrew Bible: Selected Studies from* Vetus Testamentum, Brill's Readers in Biblical Studies. (Leiden: Brill, 2000), 5:115–23.]

Matthews, I. G. "Haggai." In *Minor Prophets.* An American Commentary. Philadelphia: The American Baptist Publication Society, 1935, 2:5–18.

McEntire, M. "Haggai: Bringing God into the Picture." *RevExp* 97 (2000): 69–78.

Meyers, C. L., and E. M. Meyers. *Haggai, Zechariah 1–8: A New Translation with Introduction and Commentary.* AB. Vol. 25B. New York: Doubleday, 1987.

Miller, J. H. "Haggai—Zechariah: Prophets of the Now and Future." *CurTM* 6 (1979): 99–104.

Mitchell, H. G. *A Critical and Exegetical Commentary on Haggai and Zechariah.* ICC. Edinburgh: T&T Clark, 1912.

Morgan, F. C. *Haggai: A Prophet of Correction and Comfort.* London: Marshall, Morgan & Scott, 1935.

Napier, J. G. "The Historical and Biblical Significance of the Messianic Passages in Haggai." Th.D. diss., Dallas Theological Seminary, 1984.

North, F. S. "Critical Analysis of the Book of Haggai." *ZAW* 68 (1956): 25–46.

Peckham, B. *History and Prophecy: The Development of Late Judean Literary Traditions.* ABRL. New York: Doubleday, 1993.

Petersen, D. L. "Haggai." In *The Oxford Bible Commentary.* Oxford: Oxford University Press, 2001, 607–10.

_____. *Haggai and Zechariah 1–8: A Commentary.* OTL. Philadelphia: Westminster, 1984.

_____. "The Temple in Persian Period Prophetic Texts." *BTB* 21 (1991): 88–96.

_____. "Zerubbabel and Jerusalem Temple Reconstruction." *CBQ* 36 (1974): 366–72.

Pierce, R. W. "The Unresponsive Remnant: History, Structure and Theme in Haggai." Ph.D. diss., Fuller Theological Seminary, 1984.

Rooy, H. F. van. "Eschatology and Audience: The Eschatology of Haggai." *OTE* 1 (1988): 49–63.

Rothstein, J. W. *Juden und Samaritaner: die grundlegende Scheidung von Judentum und Heidentum: eine kritische Studie zum Buche Haggai und zur jüdischen Geschichte im ersten nachexilischen Jahrhundert.* BWA(N)T 3. Leipzig: Hinrichs, 1908.

Schottroff, W. "Zur Sozialgeschichte Israels en der Perserzeit." *VF* 27 (1982): 46–68.

Sim, R. S. "Notes on Haggai 2:10–21." *JOTT* 5 (1992): 25–36.

Stuhlmueller, C. *Rebuilding with Hope: A Commentary on the Books of Haggai and Zechariah.* ITC. Grand Rapids: Eerdmans; Edinburgh: Handsel Press, 1988.

Tadmor, H. "'The Appointed Time Has Not Yet Arrived': The Historical Background of Haggai 1:2." In *Ki Baruch Hu: Ancient Near Eastern, Biblical, and Judaic Studies in Honor of Baruch A. Levine.* Winona Lake: Eisenbrauns, 1999, 401–8.

Tetzner, L. *Die rabbinischen Kommentare zum Buche Haggai.* Munich: Dissertationsdruck, 1969.

Thomas, D. W., and W. L. Sperry. "The Book of Haggai." *IB.* New York: Abingdon,

1956, 6:1037–49.

Tollington, J. E. *Tradition and Innovation in Haggai and Zechariah 1–8.* JSOTSup150. Sheffield: JSOT Press, 1993.

Verhoef, P. A. "Notes on the Dates in the Book of Haggai." In *Text and Context: Old Testament and Semitic Studies for F. C. Fensham,* ed. W. Claassen, 259–67. Sheffield: JSOT Press, 1988.

Wendland, E. R. "Temple Site or Cemetery?—A Question of Perspective." *JOTT* 5 (1992): 37–85.

Wessels, W. J. "Haggai from a Historian's Point of View." *OTE* 1 (1988): 47–61.

Wiseman, D. J. "Haggai." In *The New Bible Commentary. Revised.* Grand Rapids: Eerdmans, 1970, 781–85.

Wolff, H. W. *Haggai: A Commentary.* Translated by M. Kohl. Minneapolis: Augsburg, 1988.

## 3. Malachi

Berquist, J. L. "The Social Setting of Malachi." *BTB* 19 (1989): 121–26.

Blake, R. D. "The Rhetoric of Malachi." Ph.D. diss., Union Theological Seminary, New York City, 1988.

Clendenen, E. R. "The Interpretation of Biblical Hebrew Hortatory Texts: A Textlinguistic Approach to the Book of Malachi." Ph.D. diss., The University of Texas at Arlington, 1989.

_____. "The Structure of Malachi: A Textlinguistic Study," *CTR* 2 (1987): 3–17.

_____. "Textlinguistics and Prophecy in the Book of the Twelve," *JETS* 46 (2003): 385–99.

Collins, J. J. "Marriage, Divorce, and Family in Second Temple Judaism," in *Families in Ancient Israel.* Louisville: WJKP, 1997.

Drinkard, J. F. "The Socio-Historical Setting of Malachi," *RevExp* 84 (1987): 383–90.

Dumbrell, W. J. "Malachi and the Ezra-Nehemiah Reforms," *RTR* 35 (1976): 42–52.

Fuller, R. "Text-Critical Problems in Malachi 2:10–16." *JBL* 110 (1991): 47–57.

Garrett, D. A. "Israel's Unfaithfulness: The Priests. Malachi 1:6–2:9" *Mid-America Journal* 11 (1987).

Glazier-McDonald, B. *Malachi: The Divine Messenger.* SBLDS 98. Atlanta: Scholars Press, 1987.

Hess, R. S. and M. D. Carroll R., eds. *Israel's Messiah in the Bible and the Dead Sea Scrolls.* Grand Rapids: Baker, 2003.

Hill, A. E. *Malachi,* AB 25D. New York: Doubleday, 1998.

Hugenberger, G. P. *Marriage as a Covenant: Biblical Law and Ethics as Developed from Malachi.* VTSup 52. Leiden: Brill, 1994. Pb. ed., Grand Rapids: Baker, 1998.

Instone-Brewer, D. *Divorce and Remarriage in the Bible: The Social and Literary Context.* Grand Rapids: Eerdmans, 2002.

Jones, D. C. "Malachi on Divorce." *Presb* 15 (1989): 16–22.

Kaiser, W. C., Jr. *Malachi: God's Unchanging Love.* Grand Rapids: Baker, 1984.

Kelly, J. C. *The Function of the Priest in the Old Testament.* Rome: Pontificum Athenaeum Antonianum, 1973.

Klein, G. L. "An Introduction to Malachi." *CTR* 2 (1987): 19–37.

Kruse-Blinkenberg, L. "The Peshitta of the Book of Malachi," *ST* 20 (1966): 95–119.

_____. "The Book of Malachi according to Codex Syro-Hexaplaris Ambrosianus," *ST* 21 (1967): 62–82.

Longacre, R. E. *Joseph: A Story of Divine Providence—A Text-theoretical and Textlin-*

*guistic Analysis of Genesis 37 and 39–48*. 2d ed. Winona Lake: Eisenbrauns, 2003.

McConville, J. G. "Ezra-Nehemiah and the Fulfillment of Prophecy," *VT* 36 (1986): 206–22.

_____. *Law and Theology in Deuteronomy*. JSOTSup 33. Sheffield: JSOT, 1984.

McKenzie, S. L. and H. N. Wallace. "Covenant Themes in Malachi." *CBQ* 45 (1983): 549–63.

Malone, G. H. *Furnace of Renewal: A Vision for the Church*. Downers Grove: Inter-Varsity, 1981.

Meyers, E. M. "Priestly Language in the Book of Malachi." *HAR* 10 (1986): 225–37.

Millar, J. G. *Now Choose Life: Theology and Ethics in Deuteronomy*. Grand Rapids: Eerdmans, 1998.

O'Brien, J. "Malachi in Recent Research." *CRBS* 3 (1995): 81–94.

_____. *Priest and Levite in Malachi*. SBLDS 121. Atlanta: Scholars Press, 1990.

Oswalt, J. *Where Are You, God? Malachi's Perspectives on Injustice and Suffering*. Napance, Ind.: Evangel, 1982.

Petersen, D. L. *Zechariah 9–14 and Malachi*. OTL. Louisville: Westminster, 1995.

Pfeiffer, E. "Die Disputationsworte im Buche Maleachi (Ein Beitrag zur formgeschichtlichen Struktur)." *EvT* 19 (1959): 546–68.

Redditt, P. L. "The Book of Malachi in Its Social Setting." *CBQ* 56 (1994): 240–55.

Schuller, E. M. "The Book of Malachi: Introduction, Commentary, and Reflections." In *The New Interpreter's Bible*, 7:842–77. Nashville: Abingdon, 1996.

Smith, J. M. P. *A Critical and Exegetical Commentary on the Book of Malachi*. ICC. Edinburgh: T&T Clark, 1912.

Snyman, S. D. "Antitheses in the Book of Malachi." *JNSL* 16 (1990): 173–78.

Sprinkle, J. M. "Old Testament Perspectives on Divorce and Remarriage," *JETS* 40 (1997): 529–33.

Tate, M. E. "Questions for Priests and People in Malachi 1:2–2:16." *RevExp* 84 (1987): 391–407.

Wendland, E. "Linear and Concentric Patterns in Malachi." *BT* 36 (1985): 108–21.

Weyde, K. W. *Prophecy and Teaching: Prophetic Authority, Form Problems, and the Use of Traditions in the Book of Malachi*. BZAW 288. Berlin: Walter de Gruyter, 2000.

Woude, A. S. van der. "Malachi's Struggle for a Pure Community: Reflections on Malachi 2:10–16," in *Tradition and Re-Interpretation in Jewish and Early Christian Literature*. Edited by J. W. van Henten et al. Leiden: Brill, 1986, 65–71.

Wright, C. J. H. *An Eye for an Eye: The Place of Old Testament Ethics Today*. Downers Grove: InterVarsity, 1983.

_____. *God's People in God's Land: Family, Land, and Property in the Old Testament*. Grand Rapids/Exeter: Eerdmans/Paternoster, 1990.

_____. *Walking in the Ways of the Lord: The Ethical Authority of the Old Testament*. Downers Grove: InterVarsity, 1995.

# Selected Subject Index

# Person Index

# Selected Scripture Index

485